A HISTORY OF JAPANESE TRADE AND INDUSTRY POLICY

A History of Japanese Trade and Industry Policy

Edited by

MIKIO SUMIYA

Editor and Part I author
Mikio Sumiya

Editor and author
Committee to Edit the *History of International Trade and Industry Policy*

Part II author
Ryoichi Miwa

Part III author
Haruhito Takeda

Part IV author
Yasuyuki Maeda

Part V author
Yoshimitsu Imuta

OXFORD

UNIVERSITY PRESS

OXFORD

UNIVERSITY PRESS

Great Clarendon Street, Oxford OX2 6DP

Oxford University Press is a department of the University of Oxford.
It furthers the University's objective of excellence in research, scholarship,
and education by publishing worldwide in

Oxford New York
Athens Auckland Bangkok Bogotá Buenos Aires Calcutta
Cape Town Chennai Dar es Salaam Delhi Florence Hong Kong Istanbul
Karachi Kuala Lumpur Madrid Melbourne Mexico City Mumbai
Nairobi Paris São Paulo Shanghai Singapore Taipei Tokyo Toronto Warsaw

and associated companies in Berlin Ibadan

Oxford is a registered trade mark of Oxford University Press
in the UK and certain other countries

Published in the United States
by Oxford University Press Inc., New York

Original Japanese edition © Committee to Edit the *History of International Trade
and Industry Policy*, and Mikio Sumiya, Ryoichi Miwa, Haruhito Takeda,
Yasuyuki Maeda, and Yoshimitsu Imuta, 1994

English translation © Foundation of International Trade and Industry
Research Institute, 2000

The moral rights of the author have been asserted
Database right Oxford University Press (maker)

First published in Japanese as *Tsusho Sangyo Seisakushi, Dai 1 Kan Souron*, 1994

This edition first published 2000

British Library Cataloguing in Publication Data

Data available

Library of Congress Cataloging in Publication Data
Tsusho sangyo seisakushi. 1, Soron. English.
History of Japanese trade and industry policy / edited by Mikio Sumiya.
p. cm.
English translation of vol. 1 of the projected 17-volume set entitled: Tsusho sangyo seisakushi.
Includes bibliographical references and index.
1. Japan—Commercial policy—History—20th century. 2. Industrial
policy—Japan—History—20th century. 3. Japan—Economic policy—1945–1989.
4. Japan—Foreign economic relations. 5. Japan—Economic conditions—1945–1989.
6. Japan. Tsūshō Sangyōshō. I. Sumiya, Mikio, 1916–
HF1601 .H53513 2000 338.952′009′045—dc21 00-035691

ISBN 0–19–829251–1

1 3 5 7 9 10 8 6 4 2

Typeset by Best-set Typesetter Ltd., Hong Kong
Printed in Great Britain
on acid-free paper by
Biddles Ltd.,
Guildford and King's Lynn

Preface

In the autumn of 1984, roughly a year before the fortieth anniversary of the end of the Second World War, the Ministry of International Trade and Industry (MITI) decided to compile a history of Japan's post-war economic rehabilitation, focusing mainly on policy in the areas of trade and industry. The history would relate Japan's recovery from the destruction of wartime defeat and the subsequent tremendous efforts made to place the Japanese economy in a foremost position in the global economy. The history, however, would not be written by government officials: objective researchers, such as university professors, would write the history after close analyses. To organize and promote the project, MITI organized the Committee to Edit the *History of International Trade and Industry Policy*.

The overall structure of this history of policy over the first thirty-five years of the post-war era, from 1945 to 1979, is divided into four periods: the post-war recovery period (1945–52); the period of establishing the economic foundations for getting Japan to stand on her own (1952–60); the period of high economic growth (1960–71); and the period of various developments relating to the growth of the global economy (1971–9). This history, together with the concluding remarks, a chronology, statistics, and other important appendix materials, comprises a tremendous literary work of seventeen volumes, on average 570 pages each. The Japanese economy confronted unique issues in each of the four periods, and because, like the world economy, it experienced vicissitudes and wide fluctuations, the selection and analysis of content was a severe challenge. Well-qualified persons were chosen to participate in this project who specialized in the necessary subject areas, and writing the text for each particular period, or some part of it, was assigned to more than seventy academics. The editors worked assiduously to give the voluminous writings a general consistency and to provide editorial supervision for each period and the work as a whole.

The overall history is a tremendous work of considerable and specific detail. There are three volumes each covering the first and second periods, and four volumes each covering the third and fourth periods, making the history complicated and an appreciation of the overall picture quite difficult. Accordingly, it was important to prepare a comprehensive introductory volume to provide a multi-faceted analysis and explanation of the structure of trade and industry policy and its role in the Japanese economy's development from the perspective of Japan's overall socio-economic situation. The introductory volume is Volume 1 of the *History of International Trade and Industry Policy*, and this is the English edition. Parts I–IV were written by the persons in charge of each of the four periods: period one is by Professor Ryoichi Miwa (Professor of Economics, Aoyama Gakuin University); period two is by Professor Haruhito Takeda (Professor of Economics, University of Tokyo); period three is by Professor Yasuyuki Maeda (Professor of Engineering, Hosei University); and period four is by Professor Yoshimitsu Imuta

(Professor of Business, Hosei University). Professor Mikio Sumiya (Professor Emeritus, University of Tokyo), who wrote Part I, was also chairman of the Committee and thus had overall responsibility for the editorial project. Part I, while avoiding redundancy with Parts II–V describing each period, analyses the cooperation and confrontation between MITI and the Japanese business community, a current that flowed at the very base of trade and industry policy throughout the four periods, while maintaining a perspective on the features and functions of the industrial structure that was the object of that policy.

When MITI originally planned the compilation of this history, emphasis was naturally placed at the initial stages on Japan's rapid recovery from war ruin, subsequent rapid economic growth, and eventual achievement of an economic status that gained global attention. The post-war experience of the Japanese economy, however, attracted considerable attention from the newly industrialized economies of East Asia that appeared in the early 1980s and that viewed Japan as a pioneer on the one hand, and as a model for the shift to a market economy on the other, especially as the dismantling of the communist economies progressed following the break-up of the Soviet Union in the late 1980s. At the same time, in international economic relations such as the Japan–US Structural Impediments Initiative, interest in the advantages and disadvantages of Japanese trade and industry policy attracted attention, and an effort was made to keep these developments in mind when compiling and writing this history.

One final comment I must make concerns the relationship between the observations in this work and MITI. As I mentioned above, the authors of this history are academics who made their analyses and observations from a scholarly point of view, even though the collection of material was assisted by, and viewpoints were discussed with, MITI officials. In that sense, this work is not the public history of the Ministry of International Trade and Industry but is basically the creation of academics, although it is recognized by MITI as the history of Japan's post-war trade and industry policy.

Finally, I would like to express my sincere appreciation to all the persons who worked so hard in writing and editing this work, as well as those who were involved in the English translation.

Mikio Sumiya
Chairman, Committee to Edit the *History of International Trade and Industry Policy*

Contents

PART I

Introduction

Introduction

After recovering rapidly from the ruins of war, Japan's economy began developing. In just three or four decades the country attained the status of an economic superpower second only to the USA. In per capita national income and in technological capabilities Japan caught up with the advanced Western countries, and even surpassed them in some respects. The country's remarkable growth generated diverse debate in the Western nations, and also attracted the attention of developing countries as a model for their own development efforts. In recent years, moreover, nations such as China and former communist countries, now undergoing transformation from planned to free-market economies, have shown a strong interest in the Japanese experience as a model of the successful transition from a controlled economy to a market economy.

This book is Volume 1 of seventeen volumes that comprise the *History of International Trade and Industry Policy of Japan*. The seventeen volumes chronicle and describe accurately and in great detail the evolution of Japan's international trade and industry policy over the years of remarkable growth from 1945 to about 1979, divided into four periods. Volume 1 has five parts, including this introductory part. Each of the other four parts summarizes the development of policy during one of the four periods and discusses distinguishing policy characteristics.

This introduction, without attempting to summarize a summary, considers the structure of the Japanese economy and its transformation under Allied occupation, and sums up the factors that made possible the development of the post-war Japanese economy. It also summarizes the role played by international trade and industry policy.

In writing this introduction, great effort was made to be as objective as possible, especially as this book is a history of policy prepared by a public agency, the Ministry of International Trade and Industry. In summarizing historical development, however, it is difficult to avoid using selective criteria in presenting facts. Or, more frankly, what is written is bound to reflect the author's view of history, whether the author is aware of it or not. At such times, the problem is not so much the fact that the writing reflects a historical view as how cogent that view is to the book's readers, including those who have been involved in formulating and implementing the policy discussed.

There has been ongoing and lively debate inside and outside Japan about the factors responsible for the remarkable post-war development of the Japanese economy. The various lines of arguments can be divided into three types. The first type analyses the Japanese economy from the perspective of historical development. This type of argument reviews the situation in which Japan after the war remedied the deficiencies in its capitalistic, free-market economy, sought to improve its productivity, and moved to catch up with and surpass the advanced industrial nations. Inasmuch as this book, a history of policy, is a recounting of history, it is natural for it to take at least in part the viewpoint of historical development in this line of argument.

The second type of argument, rather than taking a historical viewpoint, attaches great importance to the market principle, which has general applicability to the economies of the advanced Western nations. From that viewpoint, it seeks to analyse the behavioural patterns and consequences of Japan's post-war economic and related policies. This is the viewpoint of today's prevailing economic theory. It is a convincing argument insofar as it discusses the efficacy of economic policy at each level of development.

The third line of argument singles out the distinctive characteristics of Japanese culture or social organization, and emphasizes the role these characteristics have played in Japan's economic growth. Setting aside the issue of how much importance to attach to these characteristics, it is nonetheless necessary to consider them when we analyse the history of Japan's trade and industry policy.

The decision about which of these three lines of argument to emphasize the most is likely to depend greatly on the field of specialization, theoretical orientation, and values of the writer. And of primary importance is the extent to which the writer is aware of these differing orientations. In Part I, the writer has integrated the three lines of argument while heeding the views of the other persons involved in the project. As convincing a discourse as possible has been presented, which hopefully will measure up to the goal of this publication.

1

The Post-War Development of the Japanese Economy

1.1. Development of the Japanese Economy

Post-war chaos and Allied occupation policy

Japan is attracting worldwide attention today for its economic success: for an economy second in scale only to that of the USA, for the rapid growth that produced that economy, and for the vitality it has retained after reaching economic maturity. The nation completely reconstructed itself after the end of the Second World War from a condition best described as total collapse. The survey of the Japanese economy which follows begins by outlining how economic growth took place: its background, the policies applied, and the development processes.

In the first Economic White Paper issued in 1952, the Japanese government described the confused state of the economy in the immediate post-war period as follows:

The Japanese economy in the immediate post-war period was in a state of near paralysis. The nation had lost 44 per cent of its territories, and its population had increased by over 6 million persons during the two years following the cessation of hostilities (most being demobilized troops and repatriates from abroad). War damage not related to direct military activities amounted to 4.2 trillion yen (official prices prevailing at the end of 1948). Residential housing, industrial plants, transport facilities, levees, roads, and even forests were devastated. In addition, external trade was totally cut off. The Japanese economy was thus heavily encumbered with direct and indirect consequences of defeat in war.

Symbolic of the agonies of the post-war economy were the problems of price inflation and the food shortage. By the end of the war, accumulated monetary assets in the form of banknotes, bank deposits, and government bonds had reached several hundred billions of yen, despite the extensive depletion of corresponding tangible assets. This imbalance suggested an inevitable inflationary explosion. Adding fuel to this dangerous situation was the unrestrained disbursement of extraordinary military expenditures [and post-war payment of huge war indemnities—author]. Combined with large withdrawals of bank deposits, these disbursements brought about a phenomenal increase in currency in circulation, as well as sharp price increases. In February 1946, the government acted to deal with the situation by invoking the Emergency Financial Measures Order, under which it froze deposits in financial institutions and issued a new yen. In the autumn of the same year, moreover, the government implemented the Property Levy Law. Even such measures, however, succeeded in restraining economic disorder only briefly. Meanwhile, a disastrous

Table 1.1 Production indices of Japan and the USA,
1937–1950 (1953 = 100)

Year	Japan	USA
1937	92.7	44.1
1939	105.7	41.9
1941	114.3	61.7
1942	111.4	76.0
1943	112.6	90.3
1944	114.5	89.2
1945	50.3	77.1
1946	22.4	65.0
1947	27.9	71.6
1948	36.2	74.9
1949	46.6	70.5
1950	56.6	81.5

Source: Toyo Keizai Inc., *Showa Kokusei Soran Dai 3 Kan Kokusai
Hikaku Tokei Hen* (National Census of the Showa Period, iii: International Statistical Comparison).

rice crop in 1945 and black-market sales of rice by farmers disrupted the economic order.
Deliveries of rice to the government at the end of 1945 failed to reach even 30 per cent of
designated quotas, creating a serious deterioration of supplies of rice in the first half of
1946. At one point, the delay in rice deliveries in Tokyo exceeded twenty days. Social unrest
became a serious concern, culminating in the 'Food May Day' movement and the 'Give us
rice!' demonstrations of May 1946.[1]

The desperate state of the Japanese economy in the immediate post-war years
is clearly seen in Table 1.1, which shows production indexes for the years 1937
to 1950. The base year of these statistics is 1953, when industrial production
finally recovered to its pre-war (1934–6 average) level. The figures for the immediate post-war years of 1946 and 1947, however, were about a quarter of the
pre-war level, clearly showing the severe devastation of manufacturing and
mining activities. The situation worsened after the autumn of 1946 when an
unusual drought reduced electric power generation, creating a downward spiral
of production activities. The threat posed by the so-called 'March crisis of 1947'
was the cause of a great deal of anxiety in Japan.

At this point, the government introduced a 'priority production system' to
respond to this situation and to stimulate increased production. This programme
will be discussed in detail later. The even more significant development was the
Cold War that gradually emerged in clear shape from around 1947. The US
sought to bring Japan into the anti-Soviet line of defence in Asia, simultaneously
aiming to reduce the defence burden of US taxpayers. Accordingly, it gradually

Table 1.2   GNP growth rates at constant prices of selected OECD countries, 1954–1983 (unit: %)

Year	1954–58 average	1959–63 average	1964–68 average	1969–73 average	1974–78 average	1979–83 average
Japan	6.1	13.6	10.9	9.6	3.4	4.1
USA	1.7	4.3	5.1	3.5	2.8	1.3
UK	2.5	2.5	3.0	3.0	1.0	0.8
W. Germany	7.0	7.9	4.4	5.1	2.3	1.2
France	4.6	5.2	5.2	6.0	3.1	1.5

Source: Bank of Japan, *Kokusai Hikaku Tokei* (Comparative Economic and Financial Statistics, Japan and Other Major Countries).

abandoned the policy of constraining the Japanese economy—the centrepiece of its Occupation policy—and eased the policy of demilitarizing Japan.

Rapid growth of the Japanese economy

In the background of the foregoing changes, Japan's industrial production began an upturn from around 1948, and grew rapidly from the second half of 1950. Increases in total production after 1951 were 37 per cent during the four-year period between 1951 and 1955, 2.35-fold during the ten-year period between 1955 and 1965, and nearly 7.5-fold during the thirty-year period between 1955 and 1985.

Table 1.2 shows an international comparison of gross national product (GNP) growth rates at constant prices of selected countries from 1954 to 1983. During that thirty-year period, Japan's growth rate was always far ahead of that of the US, the UK, and France. As a result, although Japan's GNP in US dollar terms was lower than that of the US, the UK, France, and West Germany until 1965, by 1970 it had become the second highest among member countries of the Organization for Economic Cooperation and Development (OECD)—second only to that of the US and surpassing those of the UK, France, and West Germany (see Table 1.3). While Japan's GNP in dollar terms was only about 20 per cent of that of the US even in 1970, by 1980 it had not only reached 39 per cent of the US level but had widened its differences with the UK, France, and West Germany. Japan's GNP also exceeded that of Russia after the disintegration of the Soviet Union, securing for it the position of the world's second largest economic superpower.

Similar increases can be observed in per capita GNP. In 1960, Japan's per capita GNP of $477, as against $2,862 in the US, was conspicuously small, and would have ranked twentieth, at the bottom, if compared with OECD member nations at the time. From then on, it gradually climbed in ranking, reaching sixteenth

Table 1.3 Nominal GNP of selected OECD countries (unit: $m.)

Year	1960	1965	1970	1975	1980	1985
USA	517,053	707,489	1,016,471	1,601,458	2,736,059	4,008,199
Japan	44,439	91,036	203,301	498,569	1,066,963	1,367,696
France	61,218	99,894	143,467	343,037	667,506	520,252
W. Germany	72,143	114,550	184,617	418,455	816,942	626,461
UK	72,908	101,720	124,612	233,940	538,463	457,182

Source: OECD, *National Accounts*, 1991; figures for Japan are estimates by Dept. of National Accounts, Economic Planning Agency.

position in 1975—surpassing the per capita GNP of the UK and Italy that year and attaining 60 per cent of the US figure. In 1980, helped by the yen's appreciation against the US dollar, Japan's per capita GNP reached a level of about 70 per cent of that of West Germany, France, and the US. In 1988, Japan's per capita GNP was $18,850, surpassing the US figure of $15,839 and making it the third highest in the world after Switzerland and Luxembourg. Apart from considerations of the real purchasing power, this put Japan, at least nominally, among the richest countries in the world.

Upgrading of the industrial structure

The silk-reeling industry, which was self-sufficient in raw materials, led Japan's industrialization towards the end of the nineteenth century. However, the pivot of industrial activities shifted to the cotton-spinning industry, which used modern production technologies developed in Western countries. In the industrial structure which thus developed, exports of textiles earned the foreign currency to pay for imports of raw materials, machinery, and equipment.

The war economy drastically transformed this structure, and the impetus for change was tied to internal and external factors. To promote munitions industries, the government first of all provided strong support for the machinery industry, backward at the time in production technology. Support of the steel industry was later increased, and led to a generally unbalanced industrial structure, with unnaturally large heavy-machinery and chemical industries. The textile industry, meanwhile, lost its sources of raw material because of the war and was reduced to a tragically small size. Its production facilities were scrapped to provide material for munitions production. As mentioned earlier, moreover, those manufacturing plants were ravaged by heavy air raids during the closing months of the war.

In the foregoing context, efforts to reconstruct the Japanese economy after the war encountered great difficulties, especially since the remaining production plants in war-related industries had to be dismantled. There was no way for the nation to survive except by rebuilding the textile industry.

By 1946, the year after surrender, the textile industry made a dramatic come-back to play a central role among manufacturing industries, accounting for 23.9 per cent of manufacturing output. The country's subsequent industrial develop-ment, however, was led by the machinery industry, whose production capacity depended on the machinery and equipment remaining from wartime invest-ments. Naturally there were drastic shifts in the composition of manufactured products. Products whose 1958 output levels exceeded fifty times the level of 1951 production (=1) included washing machines (291.7), refrigerators (207.6), and television receivers (90.2, with 1953 level as 1). Production of small four-wheel cars (14.8) and small four-wheel trucks (10.8) also recorded sizeable increases,[2] as the automobile industry started on the road to recovery in the second half of the 1950s. In contrast, the shipbuilding industry, which had expanded its production base during the war years, led the world in production as early as 1960. Japan subsequently surpassed the US in television-set produc-tion too. Various of Japan's other industries grew rapidly thereafter, with many—including automobiles and newly developed industries—becoming world leaders (see Table 1.4).

The emergence of trade friction

The development of Japanese industry led to the emergence of trade friction with the US, the world's foremost manufacturing nation. In the mid-1950s, for example, Japanese exports of textile products generated a controversy in the form of the 'one-dollar blouse' issue. At this stage, Japan's low wage rates were blamed for the problem, and Japanese goods suffered from their pre-war image of being cheap and shoddy. By the beginning of the 1970s, however, the situation had changed drastically. As Japan's national income rose sharply, wage rates of workers came to surpass those of the UK and France and approached those of the US. Criticism of Japan's low wages disappeared with these changes and instead Japanese technology and Japan's industrial organization came to attract atten-tion from the mid-1970s onwards. Japan's steel industry, for example, which did not catch up with its British counterpart until around 1960, began rapidly expanding its output thereafter with modernized production facilities. In 1980, it surpassed its US counterpart and assumed second place in the world after the USSR (Table 1.4). In 1975, moreover, Japan had thirteen blast furnaces, each with a capacity exceeding 3,000 cu.m., far more than the three such furnaces in operation in the USSR, which ranked second in the world in number of large blast furnaces. The production technology of Japan's steel industry reached the world's highest level, and the pressure of Japanese steel exports dealt a crushing blow to the US steel industry. Japanese-made tape recorders, stereo receivers, motorcycles, and even zippers overwhelmed world markets, and Japanese products drove Swiss watches and German cameras and lenses from their positions of world domi-nance. In the 1980s, Japan's car production came to surpass that of the US auto-mobile industry, the indisputable world leader until then, and there was also a

Table 1.4 International comparison of production volume of selected manufactured products

	1960 Country	Production volume	1970 Country	Production volume	1980 Country	Production volume	1985 Country	Production volume
Steel tons ('000s)	World	346,600	World	593,900	World	699,389	World	685,741
	Japan	22,138	Japan	93,322	Japan	111,395	Japan	105,276
	USA	90,067	USA	119,309	USSR	147,941	USSR	155,004
	USSR	65,294	USSR	115,889	US	101,456	USA	79,248
	W. Germany	34,100	W. Germany	45,040	W. Germany	43,838	China	46,716
	UK	24,695	UK	28,316	China	37,120	W. Germany	40,500
	China (PRC)	18,450	France	23,773	Italy	26,501	Italy	23,892
	France	17,281	China	18,000	France	23,176	Brazil	20,364
	Italy	8,229	Italy	17,277	Poland	18,648	France	19,008
Passenger cars units ('000s)	World	12,810	World	22,640	World	29,079	World	31,937
	Japan	165	Japan	3,179	Japan	7,038	Japan	7,647
	USA	6,675	USA	6,642	USA	6,376	US	8,002
	W. Germany	1,817	W. Germany	3,528	W. Germany	3,530	W. Germany	4,165
	UK	1,353	France	2,458	France	3,488	France	2,631
	France	1,136	Italy	1,720	Italy	1,445	Italy	1,384
	Italy	596	UK	1,641	USSR	1,327	USSR	1,332
	Canada	326	Canada	923	Spain	1,048	Spain	1,217
	Australia	151	Belgium	734	UK	924	Canada	1,075
Television receivers units ('000s)	World	—	World	13,782	World	71,544	World	96,365
	Japan	3,578	Japan	13,782	Japan	15,205	Japan	17,727
	USA	5,611	USA	8,298	USA	10,320	China	16,677
	W. Germany	2,164	USSR	6,682	USSR	7,528	USA	13,716
	UK	2,141	W. Germany	2,936	S. Korea	6,819	USSR	9,371
	USSR	1,726	UK	2,214	W. Germany	4,425	S. Korea	7,803
	France	655	Italy	2,030	Brazil	3,254	W. Germany	3,738
	Australia	435	France	1,511	China	2,492	UK	2,972
	E. Germany	416	Brazil	726	UK	2,364	Brazil	2,190

Source: Toyo Keizai Inc., *Kokusai Hikaku Tokei* (International Comparative Statistics).

rapid increase in the share of the US market held by Japanese car manufacturers (Table 1.4). Much of this success was attributed to production technology that produced cars with high fuel economy and low breakdown rates. The source of the competitive strength of these products was technological innovation; it was no longer related to low wages. Modern manufacturing facilities and high productivity became the primary driving forces of the Japanese economy's development.

The rapid growth of Japanese industry, especially from 1965, was led by the machinery industry, with the steel industry providing the materials needed for machinery production. From around 1975, the electronics industry also grew rapidly, centred on computers. Although Japan's electronics industry trailed its US counterpart in technological development, it nevertheless grew rapidly on the strength of the so-called Japanese-style production system, and threatened to surpass the US. As result, Japanese industry, led by the broadly defined electric and electronics industries, succeeded in securing a leading position in the world, although pressures from rapidly growing developing countries brought about serious stagnation in Japan's textile and other industries (Table 1.5).

1.2. The Direction of Industrial Development in Post-War Japan

Reconstruction policies

Given the situation in which Japan found itself under Allied occupation, Japan's policymakers were uncertain about the direction in which post-war Japanese industry should develop. There were two main opinions. The first said that for resource-poor Japan, import of raw materials was the primary consideration and therefore there was no alternative but to develop industries having international trade as their main objective, as was done in pre-war years. Against this position, which may be called the 'trade first' doctrine, was the alternative prescription of emphasizing the development of domestic resources and markets. This policy prescription, which may be called the 'development first' doctrine, attributed pre-war Japan's military ambitions in Asia to a 'trade first' obsession for securing raw materials, which in turn was attributed to the small size of the domestic market, a result of poverty. Those who advocated the 'development first' approach, therefore, argued that Japan's first order of business should be to develop domestic resources and markets.[3]

It cannot be denied that Japan's orientation towards trade had much to do with the speed with which Japan, an industrial latecomer, developed into an industrial power in the Meiji period and afterwards. Using terminology from post-war economic development theory, Japan's pre-war economic policy may be characterized as import-substituting industrialization centred on cotton goods and steel products, with fast-growing exports providing the foreign currency needed to import raw materials to produce these exports. Those who embraced the 'trade first' doctrine argued, therefore, that the only way open to Japan—which had

Table 1.5   Indices of value added in industrial production (1985 = 100)

Year	Mining and manufacturing	Manufacturing	Iron and steel	Machinery and equipment	General machinery	Electrical machinery	Transportation equipment	Chemicals	Textiles	Mining
Weight[a]	10,000.0	9,950.0	607.2	4,393.2	1,291.7	1,793.9	1,142.6	912.3	673.4	50.0
1960	15.8	15.4	17.7	6.8	11.4	3.5	9.1	12.9	45.3	134.7
1965	27.4	27.0	32.3	13.5	19.7	6.5	23.0	23.1	65.6	145.5
1970	56.4	56.1	74.6	36.1	54.1	21.0	51.8	50.1	99.5	149.8
1975	61.0	60.8	79.2	41.1	51.5	24.1	70.7	57.7	94.5	107.6
1980	84.4	84.3	99.1	68.4	81.3	48.9	91.9	82.3	102.5	105.8
1985	100.0	100.0	100.0	100.0	100.0	100.0	100.0	100.0	100.0	100.0
1988	113.0	113.1	105.0	118.2	110.3	132.3	105.5	120.4	94.5	85.9

[a] Weights of Manufacturing do not total 9,950.0 because 'the other industries' are omitted.

Source: Kokogyo Shisu Soran (Long-Term Data Book of Standard Indices of Industrial Production), 1988.

fallen behind technologically in the cocoon-like wartime system and suffered from a shortage of capital—was to adopt the pre-war-type 'trade first' strategy. Advocates of the 'development first' doctrine argued against this position by pointing out that nearly all the world's markets were closed to Japan, the prospects for a change in this area were poor, and therefore Japan could not count on rapid economic growth through trade. Instead, they said, Japan should aim for steady and sound development of its domestic resources, and act to achieve gradually expanding economic activities based on these resources.

As matters evolved, both prescriptions were incorporated into actual policies in *ad hoc* response to changing circumstances. The so-called priority production plan, for example, used as a measure for expanding the production of coal, was more or less a 'development first' policy. On the other hand, the eventual change in the name of the Ministry of Commerce and Industry to the Ministry of International Trade and Industry (MITI), and the fact that the names of most of its bureau contain the words 'international trade', are a reflection of the 'trade first' doctrine. In other words, the two philosophies have closely interacted in shaping actual policies.

Both policy prescriptions, by the way, assumed a capital shortage and a labour surplus. Accordingly, the industries which played important roles in economic reconstruction, i.e. the textile and machinery industries, were characterized by labour-intensive operations. Reconstruction along this line, however, soon reached its limits. The focus of further developmental efforts had to be shifted to 'industrial rationalization' supported by the transfer of advanced technology from abroad.

At a meeting in autumn 1949, the Cabinet approved the resolution on 'Matters Regarding Industrial Rationalization' which proposed to clarify the future direction in which each industry should develop along a path of rationalization. The resolution energetically promoted the import of advanced technology, with the principal objective of closing the gap between domestic and world prices, while keeping international markets in mind. Actually, industrial rationalization was a means to rebuild the world economy, and was introduced from the advanced Western countries in the early years of the Showa period (the late 1920s) as a form of industrial policy. Because its application in Japan happened to coincide with a recession and was tied to wholesale dismissal of workers, the working class disliked it. This time, however, given the dire circumstances of the post-war Japanese economy, its application was considered unavoidable. The newly established Industry Rationalization Council concluded that the rationalization and modernization of industrial machinery and equipment were objectives of the highest priority. The Council maintained that industry should aim for bold modernization of its production facilities through the formation of industrial capital. To that end, the Council recommended that the government invest public funds aggressively into the programme and promote rationalization by adopting tax-preference measures and fostering the securities market. The basic posture of Japan's industrial policy throughout the post-war years can be characterized as the nurturing of industry with an emphasis on technological innovation and rationalization.

The tasks of international trade and industry policy

The industrial policy described above was formulated naturally and inevitably by the Japanese government, particularly within MITI. MITI interprets development of that policy in the following manner.

Since the end of the Second World War, Japan has been operating within the framework of a liberal economic order. Individual corporations, therefore, are held responsible for the consequences of their actions. Nonetheless, there were at least three areas in which the government had to accept a measure of responsibility. Its first assignment was the promotion of faster economic growth. Though economic growth is a most important task for any society, it was especially important for post-war Japan, whose economy was so devastated. Japan had to grow faster than other countries in order quickly to catch up with the industrially advanced countries.

The second government assignment related to the minimizing of social conflict. According to nineteenth-century liberal thinking, what is rational will prosper and what is irrational will perish. Also, private corporations are responsible for their own fortunes and misfortunes. Although MITI was able to accept such propositions, it was nevertheless convinced that it was incumbent on the government to minimize the level of social conflict even in terms of the nation's liberal economic order. A typical policy reflecting this type of thinking was seen in the measures MITI took towards declining industries.

The third area was one where MITI questioned the strict applicability of the principle of liberal economic order to the Japanese economy at its level of development at the time, particularly given the unique situation of Japanese society. In MITI's view, valuing the principle of free competition as a means was one thing, but regarding it as an end in itself quite another. In other words, the principle must not be elevated to the level of a divine canon. MITI sought to introduce the perspectives of stability and balance into the process of economic development. MITI considered these arguments as a justification for the industrial policy it should pursue, regardless of the specific forms that policy might assume.[4]

In Japan, a latecomer among the industrial nations, it was taken for granted that the State would play a positive role in nurturing industry and minimizing social conflict involving industries. Since the Meiji era, therefore, the Ministry of Agriculture and Commerce, and later the Ministry of Commerce and Industry were established, and pursued policies considered necessary for each period, as well as policies designed to meet future expectations of industrial development. Countries such as the US and the UK, however, regard such a role as state intervention in the free conduct of private enterprises and, as such, view it as undesirable in a free and competitive society. This issue will be examined more carefully later; at this point, it should be simply identified as a fundamental argument in examining and discussing the history of Japan's industrial policy.

1.3. International Trade and the Domestic Market

The trend of international trade in post-war years

Trends in Japan's merchandise exports and imports, the international friction generated in the trade area, and the policy measures implemented to cope with them are examined in this final part of the survey section on the post-war development of the Japanese economy.

Because exports relate closely to changes in the structure of domestic production, it is important to examine the composition of Japan's exports by commodity. The share of textile products in Japan's exports, for example, which was close to 50 per cent of total exports in 1950, fell to 30 per cent in 1960, and to below 10 per cent in 1975. Textile exports thus gradually came to account for a negligible portion of Japan's exports. As expected, machinery and equipment came to replace textiles; their share of total exports, which had stood at barely 10 per cent in 1950, exceeded 30 per cent in 1965, 50 per cent in 1975, and 70 per cent in 1985, and they came to form a mainstay among exports (Table 1.6). In contrast, the share of crude oil in imports rose sharply year after year, approaching 50 per cent of total import value in 1980, which was in part due to the sharp rise in oil prices. The shares of all other products declined gradually, partly because of the rising share of crude oil imports.

Concerning the total values of exports and imports, in 1955 Japan's exports accounted for only 2.4 per cent and imports only 2.8 per cent of total global trade values. These figures rose gradually thereafter, and in 1980 they reached 7.0 per cent of world exports and 7.5 per cent of world imports, thus coming to exert a considerable influence on world trade (Table 1.7). Moreover, Japan's trade balance, which up to 1980 had fluctuated between surplus and deficit from year to year, showed an overwhelming export surplus from 1981, turning Japan into a huge trade-surplus country. The imbalance was particularly pronounced in trade with the US, giving rise to serious trade problems. Japan's trade surplus, however, exists not only in trade with the US but with virtually all countries except the oil-producing nations. Problems thus exist with countries other than the US. Because Japan's exports are price competitive in overseas markets even after incurring considerable transportation costs, the sources of that competitiveness have become controversial issues.

Economic development and the market structure

One matter to note at this point is that Japan's industrial structure, which has produced such a great stir in world markets, is by no means a simple export-led structure. In fact, the sum of Japan's exports and imports as a percentage of its

Table 1.6 Export percentage by selected product

	Grand total ($000)	(%)	Foodstuffs (%)	Textiles and textile products (%)	Chemicals (%)	Machinery and equipment (%)	Metals and metal products (%)
1947	28,189	100.0	26.6	—	—	—	—
1950	827,836	100.0	6.3	48.2	1.9	9.9	18.3
1955	2,010,600	100.0	6.3	37.3	4.7	12.3	16.7
1960	4,054,537	100.0	6.6	30.2	4.2	22.9	13.9
1965	8,451,742	100.0	4.1	18.7	6.5	31.3	20.3
1970	19,317,687	100.0	3.4	12.5	6.4	46.3	19.7
1975	55,752,805	100.0	1.4	6.7	7.0	53.8	22.4
1980	129,807,025	100.0	1.2	4.9	5.2	62.8	16.4
1985	175,637,772	100.0	0.8	3.6	4.4	71.8	10.5
1988	264,916,803	100.0	0.6	2.6	5.3	74.3	8.2

Source: Ministry of Finance, *Gaikoku Boeki Gaikyo* (Summary Report on Trade of Japan).

Table 1.7 Japan's imports and exports as percentages of world exports and imports

	1955			1960			1965		
	World (A)	Japan (B)	B/A	World (A)	Japan (B)	B/A	World (A)	Japan (B)	B/A
Gross domestic product (market-economy countries; in $100m.)	9,000	288	3.2	12,548	634	5.1	16,194	946	5.8
Trade (market-economy countries; in $100m.)									
Value of exports (FOB)	843	20	2.4	1,130	41	3.6	1,648	85	5.1
Value of imports (CIF)	892	25	2.8	1,194	45	3.8	1,748	82	4.7

	1970			1975			1980		
	World (A)	Japan (B)	B/A	World (A)	Japan (B)	B/A	World (A)	Japan (B)	B/A
Gross domestic product (market-economy countries; in $100m.)	24.732	1,969	8.0	49,450	4,913	9.9	97,081	10,362	10.7
Trade (market-economy countries; in $100m.)									
Value of exports (FOB)	2,802	193	6.9	7,882	558	7.4	18,441	1,298	7.0
Value of imports (CIF)	2,941	189	6.4	8,017	579	7.2	18,855	1,405	7.5

Source: Bank of Japan, Statistics Department, *Nihon Keizai wo Chushin to Suru Kokusai Hikaku Tokei* (Comparative Economic and Financial Statistics, Japan and Other Major Countries).

GNP stood at only 15.6 per cent in 1955, was still less than 20 per cent in 1965, finally rose to 23.1 per cent in 1975, and was 26.1 per cent in 1980. Although these percentages are higher than their equivalents for the US, they are considerably lower than those of countries in Europe. Comparable figures for countries like South Korea and Taiwan, whose growth has been led by exports, approached 100 per cent, suggesting significant differences in their economic structure from that of Japan (Table 1.7).

Offsetting Japan's low trade percentage is the large size of Japan's domestic market. As stated earlier, Japan's post-war industrial policy was predicated upon the need to import large quantities of industrial raw materials and technology, as well as the machinery and equipment that embodied that technology. To pay for imports, it was felt that Japan had to establish viable export industries. In other words, international trade was regarded as a crucially important factor for the viability of Japanese industry. This awareness did not wane in the subsequent course of economic growth, and the promotion of trade remained one of the important tasks of industrial policy. In retrospect, however, it is realized that the relative importance of international trade as a percentage of GNP was never very great even from the beginning.

Rising domestic purchasing power

Why was international trade relatively less important for Japan? In a nutshell, the answer lies in the huge purchasing power of the domestic Japanese economy. Two developments fuelled the rise in purchasing power: one was the expansion of the market for consumer durables; the other was the expansion of the market for producer goods.

One of the pillars of post-war economic reform was liberalization of the labour movement. As the unionization rate rose rapidly, the pattern of how wage rates were determined changed drastically from pre-war practices. Wages and salaries came to be determined through collective bargaining, and they rose steadily each year. Using 1970 as the base year (100), the average wage rate of 24.4 in 1955 doubled to 47.9 in 1965 and just five years later rose to 100. The index rose further to 238.1 in 1975. During the five years between 1975 and 1980 wages and salaries rose another 50 per cent, with the index reaching 355.2.

Consumer price increases must also be considered. A look at the twenty-five years from 1955 to 1980 shows that real wages nearly tripled, from 51 in 1955 to 150 in 1980. At the same time, due mainly to land reforms, farmers were freed from the dire poverty of pre-war days, and the price of rice rose nearly in proportion to consumer price increases. As the economy developed, farming household members, including many heads of households, became employed workers, and the primary source of farming household income shifted to wage income. As a result, farming household income rose along with the rise in income of industrial workers. These income increases translated into huge domestic purchasing power, particularly for consumer durables. This purchasing power was responsible for the increased production, mentioned earlier, of washing machines, refrigerators, television sets, and eventually of cars, whose sales picked up rapidly from around the mid-1950s.

The relatively low distribution rate of domestic production going to labour in Japan, as compared with Western countries, has been a target of international criticism. This low rate is offset by the larger share going to capital, which is devoted to gross domestic capital formation, or, to put it in concrete terms, to gross fixed capital formation. The ratio of gross fixed capital formation to gross domestic product, which was les than 20 per cent in 1955, rose to 30 per cent in 1965 and exceeded 35 per cent in 1975. Moreover, the greater part of the fixed capital goods was supplied by the domestic machinery, steel, and other industries, generating huge purchasing power. The expression 'investment breeds investment' in the process of high economic growth is a reference to this industrial mechanism.

Industrial policy contributed to the remarkable post-war economic growth of Japan, growth that has attracted worldwide attention despite being burdened with a variety of problems and causing friction on occasion. The following chapters examine the various economic factors and circumstances which were both the immediate and background causes of this economic development, including those that took place prior to and during the war.

NOTES

1. Economic Deliberation Board, *Nenji Keizai Hokoku* (Economic Survey of Japan), 1952.
2. MITI, Minister's Secretariat, Research and Statistics Dept., *Nihon Keizai no Genjo* (Current Condition of the Japanese Economy), 1959.
3. Toshihiko Tsuruta, *Sengo Keizai no Sangyo Seisaku* (Industrial Policy in the Post-war Economy), Nihon Keizai Shimbun, Inc., 1982, see introduction.
4. Yoshihiko Morozumi, *Sangyo Seisaku no Riron* (Theory of Industrial Policy), Nihon Keizai Shimbun, Inc., 1966. When Morozumi wrote this book he was Director-General of the Enterprise Bureau. His book is a compilation of discussions held by members of an industrial policy study group he organized, with participation from junior officials in his bureau. Although the volume—as Morozumi notes in his preface—'does not represent MITI's views', it is nonetheless an important work that sums up the opinions of MITI officials.

2

The Transformation of the Economic Structure during Occupation

2.1. The Dismantling of the Pre-War and Wartime Structure, and Democratization

The breakdown of the wartime controlled economy

As a means to overcome the Depression of the 1930s, the Key Industry Control Law (April 1931) was promulgated to establish cartel policy, leading also to more complete control of Japan's industrial policy. After that, industrial policy took on a strong control colouring, and following the outbreak of the Sino-Japanese War in 1937 industrial policy came to control the entire economy. The 'three wartime control laws', including the Temporary Funds Adjustment Law, were enacted in September 1937, followed in April 1938 by the National General Mobilization Law, which was to govern the nation's wartime economy. Article 1 of the latter defined 'national general mobilization' as 'controlling and deploying manpower and material resources for the optimum and most efficient development of the nation's total capacity for defence in time of war.' Material resources included not only military-related material but all 'materials needed for mobilization'. More important from the economic standpoint, however, was the Materials Mobilization Plan, initiated at the beginning of 1938. The purpose of state control of the economy was to steer the operations of private-sector enterprises in certain directions through the exercise of administrative authority. But there was a limit to how far the private sector was willing to cooperate with the State's planning at the expense of private interests, and often there were discrepancies between the goals of a state plan and the realities of the economy, making it difficult for economic controllers to achieve their objectives. In fact, the Materials Mobilization Plan foundered less than six months after it was introduced. Related to that, the government declared:

Although we have made great strides in our war efforts in China, we still have far to go before accomplishing our objectives. . . . Our balance of payments shows a large deficit owing to decreases in exports and for other reasons, making it extremely difficult to meet the targets of the Materials Mobilization Plan formulated in 1938. . . . the government, therefore, has decided to introduce resolute steps to overcome various obstacles, mobilize various facilities to accomplish the war objectives, issue a declaration to awaken public officials and citizens to the seriousness of the situation, urge the entire nation to resolve firmly to cope with the situation, and enforce the following measures considered urgent for the survival of the State.[1]

The government then introduced sterner measures to control prices and ration materials in order to ensure an adequate supply of military material, promote exports, and maintain the living standards of the people. As the country plunged into the Second World War, state control of the economy was intensified. Although the production of military material was increased, it was done at the expense of the material well-being of the people. That this policy soon reached its limits was evident from the following document prepared by the military towards the end of the war.

Since the outbreak of the Greater East Asia War, the material resources of our country, notwithstanding the optimistic outlook at the start of the war . . . have been gradually depleted each year as supply sources have been cut. We have met the rising demand for military material by sacrificing production of civilian goods, especially the basic material needs of the general population. Although we have managed to ensure the minimum production of staple foods, all other industries have been forced to curtail or suspend production. It cannot be denied that even production of the highest-priority military goods has declined since reaching a peak in early 1944. It is becoming increasingly difficult, moreover, to maintain the current living standard of the people. In short, by the end of 1944, the fourth year of the war, the resilience of the national economy will have largely been lost.[2]

At an Imperial Conference held in early June 1945, a report was presented on the collapse of industrial production, including military material, and the straitened living conditions of the people. The report even stated that 'Economic disorder has become pronounced as prices have risen sharply, black marketing is rampant, and economic morals have become corrupted. Depending on how matters evolve, a threat of inflation is not without foundation.'[3]

The Japanese economy collapsed despite the government's control efforts, and the war came to an end two months after that Imperial Conference. What became obvious was that the expansion of the production of military material had been at the expense of the people's living standards, and that a controlled economy, including efforts to promote munitions production, could not function—as a free-market economy does—without cooperation from not only private-sector business but also the entire population.

The zaibatsu and their dissolution

The US Initial Post-Surrender Policy for Japan, which the US government formulated after Japan's surrender on the basis of the Potsdam Declaration, stated that Japan itself was to initiate steps to rebuild its economy and thoroughly reform the patterns of its economic behaviour and economic structure. The objectives of the Occupation, other than the demilitarization of Japan, may be summarized in the following three measures: (1) dissolution of the zaibatsu financial cliques, which served as mainstays of Japan's production of military material and supported its military structure; (2) dissolution of the feudalistic tenant-farming system of landownership which provided a social base for Japan's military expansion; and (3) liberalization of Japan's labour movement in order for it to become a driving force in Japan's democratization.

Concerning dissolution of the zaibatsu, it is seen that in the process of developing itself economically after entering the twentieth century, Japan experienced the growth of considerable industrial and banking capital, much of which foundered and vanished under the weight of frequent depressions. Some accumulations of capital, however, grew steadily and attained immense proportions. These conglomerates were called zaibatsu, the largest being the Mitsui, Mitsubishi, and Sumitomo zaibatsu. Only these large combines were capable of responding to rapid changes in the wartime economy and promoting development. In the early stages of the war, the military was openly critical and disdainful of the zaibatsu, but as the war economy progressed the military had no choice but to seek their cooperation. Table 2.1 shows the relative importance of the three largest zaibatsu in the Japanese economy at the end of the war, measured in terms of equity percentage or paid-in capital. It is particularly noteworthy that 74.8 per cent of the holdings of these three zaibatsu was in heavy industry, which accounted for 31.7 per cent of the national total of paid-in capital in heavy industries. Also, these large figures were the result of rapid growth during the war years, which accounted for the harsh post-war attitude of the Occupation Forces towards the zaibatsu.

The vertical relationship of control that existed between the parent company, subsidiaries, and sub-subsidiaries in a zaibatsu group was made possible by intercorporate control through stock ownership and by appointment of officers of higher-level companies as directors of lower-level companies. The stocks of the holding companies were owned by members of the Mitsui, Iwasaki, and Sumitomo families. The zaibatsu, therefore, were also called 'family concerns'. In the process of expanding military production, however, the zaibatsu could not cope with a situation that required huge sums of capital. Also, they felt a need to blunt the wartime criticism levelled at them. For these reasons, they decided during the war years to offer shares for public subscription, thereby modifying their closed character. In the first half of the 1930s, however, only the zaibatsu more or less resisted the gunbatsu (military clique), and for that reason they became a target of attacks by the militarists. Nonetheless, the zaibatsu were regarded by the Occupation Forces as the business groups that realized the greatest increases in profits and enlarged scales of operation during the war. That was why they were made the primary target in the programme of dismantling the militaristic economy as carried out under Occupation policy. Zaibatsu assets were frozen in November 1945, the holding companies and zaibatsu families were forced to transfer their stocks in April 1946, and the use of zaibatsu trade names and logos was banned in January 1950. In name and in fact, the zaibatsu were thus dissolved. In that way, the zaibatsu, the main force in large capital formation in pre-war and wartime Japan, disappeared from the scene.

Table 2.1 Relative importance of three largest zaibatsu in Japan's economy in terms of equity percentage or paid-in capital (unit: %)

Industry	Mitsui			Mitsubishi			Sumitomo			Totals		
	No. of companies	% of company total	% of national total	No. of companies	% of company total	% of national total	No. of companies	% of company total	% of national total	No. of companies	% of company total	% of national total
Financial	(1) 4	4.9	13.9	4	5.1	13.1	4	3.4	5.4	(1) 12	4.6	32.4
Heavy industry	(26) 115	72.0	12.7*	(23) 85	68.8	10.7	(15) 84	89.7	8.4	(64) 284	74.8	31.7
Light industry	(19) 46	10.7	6.0	(11) 24	3.7	1.6	(1) 14	1.6	0.7	(28) 84	6.1	8.2
Others	(15) 47	12.4	4.5	(18) 44	22.4	6.7	17	5.3	1.1	(33) 108	14.4	12.2
Company total	(61) 212	100.0	9.5	(52) 157	100.0	8.3	(16) 119	100.0	5.1	(129) 488	100.0	23.0

Notes: Figures in parentheses under 'No. of companies' are number of companies located outside Japan proper; '% of company total' refers to the amount of paid-in capital in the industry inside and outside Japan proper compared to all the companies of that zaibatsu inside and outside Japan proper; '% of national total' refers to the amount of paid-in capital in that industry inside Japan proper compared to all the companies of that zaibatsu inside Japan proper: asterisk means the original table shows this figure as 72.4; subsidiaries are companies in which the parent company's equity ownership (or paid-in capital) was 10% or more at the time the parent company was designated as a zaibatsu (September 1946).

Source: Compiled from Holding Company Liquidation Commission, *Nihon Zaibatsu to Sono Kaitai* (Japan's zaibatsu and their dissolution), Text Volume, 95, 113, and 122; and Data Volume, 426, 428, and 468.

The landlord system and land reform

To understand the nature of the landlord–tenant system, the second target of the dismantling progamme, it is necessary first to understand its earlier history. Because of the small size of the land they farmed and high land rents, Japan's tenant farmers had been driven to extreme poverty. Bitter tenancy disputes had been common since the 1920s, and the policy of establishing a system of owner-farmers had become a national issue. As the economy took on a deeper war colouring the government exhorted farmers to increase food production, but the farming population decreased as farmers were drafted into the military or conscripted to work in munitions plants. As a background to the crisis the agricultural system thus came to face, land rents were lowered and the amount of land cultivated by owner-cultivators increased. The landowner class, which wielded significant political influence in pre-war Japan, rapidly lost that influence, and many people began to regard the landlord system itself as fetters of the wartime structure.

In view of this situation, agricultural officials were already considering a plan soon after the war to reform the landowner–tenant system when SCAP, in December 1945, issued a memorandum for agrarian reform directing the Japanese government to 'provide cultivating farmers more equal opportunity in order to destroy the economic bondage which had enslaved the Japanese farmer to centuries of feudal oppression.' Subsequent land reform programmes in February and June 1946 eliminated Japan's pre-modern tenant-farming system. Specifically, the reform programmes required that: (1) all the land owned by absentee landlords and tenant-cultivated land in excess of an average of 1 cho (about 1 hectare or 2.45 acres) in Honshu, Kyushu, and Shikoku, and 4 cho in Hokkaido, owned by non-cultivating resident landlords was to be purchased by the government and sold to the tenants; and (2) for the remaining tenant land, the traditional system of collecting rent in kind was to be abolished and replaced by low money rents. As a result of these measures, of the 2.37 million cho (about 5.81 million acres) of tenant land which constituted 45.9 per cent of the nation's total cultivated area in November 1945, 1.9 million cho (about 4.66 million acres) were freed, lowering the percentage of tenant land to 9.9 per cent. Moreover, ensuing inflation meant that the former tenant-farmers ended up paying almost nothing for their land.

Noteworthy here is the fact that the dismantling of the landowner system, one of the pillars of Japan's social system since the Meiji era, was accomplished with virtually no resistance. This was indeed an unprecedented event in the history of the world.[4] In the subsequent process of economic growth, as will be discussed later, liberation of the farmers came to provide Japanese industry with large consumer-durable and producer-goods markets.

Industrial relations and the labour unions

The other institution to be discussed in the post-war socio-economic transformation towards democracy is the labour union movement. After the First World War, the labour movement in Japan made some progress, growing by the early 1930s to the point where 8 per cent of all workers, about 400,000 persons, were unionized. Because of the government's harsh oppression, the unions turned radical, however, which led to intensified oppression that forestalled further unionization. In 1940, the year before Japan plunged into the Second World War, the labour movement was virtually outlawed, and labour unions were disbanded, including the relatively moderate Japan Federation of Labour (Sodomei).

SCAP believed that one reason why Japan had rushed into war with little internal resistance lay in the fact that oppression had eliminated internal organization of resistance. Thus, SCAP freed imprisoned communists and promoted the organizing of labour unions. Prompted by SCAP's actions, the Japanese government in December 1945 enacted and promulgated a democratic Labour Union Law. Records show that in June 1946, less than one year after the end of the war, there were 12,000 labour unions and 3.68 million union members, and that the rate of unionization was 40 per cent. Japanese workers found a way out of the post-war chaos and inflation in their union movement. Those who assumed leadership roles were, as described earlier, male skilled workers trained before and during the war. The apprenticeship system had been practised widely in Japan since before the Meiji era, and was brought into modern industrial plants. Once into the twentieth century, when encouraging the growth of modern skilled industrial workers became an important task, the education and training facilities of large corporations assumed that responsibility. Corporations also developed wage structures and benefit systems designed to encourage trained workers not to move to other companies. The mobility of workers was close to 100 per cent until the early years of the twentieth century but fell rapidly after the 1920s. The average longevity of workers, particularly skilled workers, grew every year. In the second half of the 1920s, most of the labour unions in large corporations were already employees' unions organized at the enterprise level, or 'enterprise unions' in post-war language. During the war, this enterprise-level union organization and the Industrial Patriotic Associations organized at the plant level together constituted the nucleus of wartime labour organization.

Post-war labour unions organized primarily by workers at large corporations were also enterprise unions. Japanese workers, following the democratization trend and prompted by SCAP's urging, organized their unions along the lines of labour union movements in Western countries. What emerged, however, was an enterprise union inseparable from Japan's indigenous labour–management relations. Also, post-war Japanese unions embraced both blue- and white-collar employees in their organizations. In representing the interests of all employees in a company, they sought a doubling or tripling of wages in the inflationary climate of the times and demanded the democratization of management. These unions, having emerged from the historical development described above, and working within the constraints of being enterprise-based unions, demanded wages sufficient to support daily life, advocated corporate democratization, and energetically worked towards the goal of achieving a socialist order. The relationship of the labour unions with Japanese society thus changed dramatically.

2.2. The Road to Economic Reconstruction

Economic control under Occupation

Almost as soon as the war was over, the Ministry of Commerce and Industry (MCI), which had been merged into the Ministry of Munitions during the war, was revived. Three weeks after the end of the war, it was decided to abolish twenty-one wartime laws and ordinances, including the Key Industries Association Control Ordinance, followed by the repeal in December 1945 of the National General Mobilization Law. The post-war economy, however, was in total chaos. MCI was thrown into confusion, with influential officials arguing that it was impossible to carry out measures of economic control under an Occupation whose aim was to democratize Japan. If left to take its own course, however, the economic situation could very well generate serious social disorder. In the circumstances, the most effective policy was not *laissez-faire* but a method of economic control in which the government had gained considerable experience during the wartime years of destitution, or, more specifically, the method of the Materials Mobilization Plan. As early as the autumn of 1945, shortages of daily necessities worsened to the point of requiring immediate attention, leading to formulation of a materials supply and demand plan in the third quarter of 1945. Although SCAP's primary aim was to democratize the economy, it was basically positive towards this emergency control measure. SCAP Directive No. 3 (Economic Control) stated the following:

A. The Imperial Japanese government shall be responsible for developing and maintaining firm control of wages and the prices of daily necessities.
B. The Imperial Japanese government shall be responsible for developing and maintaining a strict allocation plan for daily necessities in short supply to ensure their equitable distribution.

What SCAP demanded of the Japanese government was not a conversion of the economic order to a free-market system but the establishment of strict control and planning. In the end, the government responded by enacting and putting into effect, during the autumn 1946 economic crisis, the Law on Temporary Measures for Commodity Supply and Demand Control of October 1946, which essentially contained the same control measures used in the wartime Materials Mobilization Plan. During the wartime years, control associations (*toseikai*) were created at the industry level for smoother cooperation in allocating materials. SCAP considered these associations as collaborators with the military and disbanded them one by one between the end of 1945 and the summer of 1946. Such measures, however, did not signify SCAP's rejection of economic control as such, and the authority to control the economy, as described above, could readily be granted to the government if necessary. In that sense, it might even be possible to argue that the potential for state control of the economy became greater after the war.[5]

Economic control for economic reconstruction

SCAP's two primary objectives were the demilitarization and democratization of Japan, which was interpreted to mean that its policy was to eliminate economic control tied to military-related production while aggressively promoting liberalization of the economic system. Dissolution of the zaibatsu, for example, was certainly aimed at dismantling the mechanism by which huge business combines monopolistically controlled the entire economy, and this measure was followed by the Law on Exclusive Measures for the Excessive Concentration of Economic Power (Deconcentration Law) and the Law Relating to Prohibition of Private Monopolization and Methods of Preserving Fair Trade (Anti-Monopoly Law). Liberalizing the labour movement and promoting the organization of labour unions were also regarded as measures directed at economic democratization. Although the Occupation Forces were governing the country only indirectly, the Japanese government thought it necessary to internalize the policy of the Occupation and naturally aimed for a freer economic system. Its basic approach was to thoroughly re-evaluate all methods of economic control developed during the war, and to transform the entire system into a free-market economy to the maximum extent possible. The Liberal Party, which held political power for many years after the war, was composed, more or less, of persons who were oppressed by the military clique (*gunbatsu*) during the war and who considered themselves liberals. Many of these politicians had as their political bases the owners of small businesses and ordinary citizens, neither of which were direct targets of SCAP's programme of purging wartime collaborators. The Liberal Party adopted a positive attitude towards eliminating wartime control measures, and expected that SCAP would naturally support liberalization of the economy and order its implementation. Disbanding the control associations was understood as a move in this direction.

Contrary to expectations, however, SCAP directed the Japanese government to curb economic liberalization and strengthen its control measures. Thereupon the government established a number of *kodan* (public corporations) as external agencies. In April 1947, the Coal Distribution Kodan, Petroleum Distribution Kodan, Industrial Reconstruction Kodan, and Fertilizer Distribution Kodan were established. Subsequently, five other distribution *kodan* were created: Staple Food, Grocery, Fodder, Oil and Fat, and Liquor Distribution Kodan, raising the number of distribution *kodan* to eight.

During the post-war years, trade was strictly controlled, and there was no move to open it to private capital. The Foreign Trade Public Corporation Law was promulgated in April 1947 and four trade *kodan*—Mining and Industrial Products, Textiles, Food, and Raw Materials Trading Kodan—were established in May 1948. Unlike the control associations, established in each industry during the war as organizations for coordinating and controlling private-sector companies, and which were disbanded after the war, these kodan were placed under direct control of the government as external agencies.[6]

SCAP had two considerations for choosing this method. First, it held a critical view of those managing business in Japan, which was expressed in its policy of dissolving the zaibatsu. SCAP had misgivings about, or, more specifically, was distrustful of, voluntary control of the supply of materials by private corporations, fearing it might lead to monopolization. If controls were needed in an economic crisis, SCAP reasoned, it would be more fitting for the promotion of democracy if the government, which was responsible for surveillance of monopolistic practices, were directly involved.

The second of SCAP's considerations was its concern about social disorder caused by economic disruption and the possibility that this could lead to communist domination. Because private companies were in a state of chaos—and therefore had little capacity to overcome the economic disruption and work towards building a stable economy—there was no alternative, it was felt, but to let the government deal directly with the situation.

Paradoxically, therefore, although SCAP's primary aim was dismantling Japan's war structure and democratizing the nation, it was supportive of economic control and promoted a policy of direct governmental control of the economy rather than self-control by private business. The Japanese business community believed that a freer economy was the proper direction and resisted this policy of SCAP, but the Japanese government complied with SCAP's wishes despite not being totally convinced of the policy's aptness.

Adoption of a priority production plan

The problem of distributing materials discussed above had two major dimensions. The first was that of distributing daily living necessities, i.e. the question of how to allocate scarce daily necessities equitably to households. The second was that of allocating production materials, i.e. the question of the pattern of the economy's reconstruction. The basis of SCAP's policies towards Japan was stated as follows: 'The plight of Japan is the direct outcome of its own conduct, and the Allies will not undertake the burden of repairing the damage.' SCAP took some measures for easing food shortages and removing obstacles to execution of Occupation policy, but the Japanese government could not expect cooperation from SCAP in matters pertaining to economic reconstruction. Supplies remaining from the war were used up by the autumn of 1946, and the economy faced a production crisis as inventories of production materials were nearly depleted. This crisis, however, could be overcome only by Japan's own efforts. To deal with the situation, the government developed and implemented a 'priority production plan'.

The two most strategic materials for economic recovery were coal—the key energy source for Japan, since it has no petroleum resources—and steel, a key manufacturing material. A strategy was formulated based on the theory that an increased supply of these two products would pave the way for other industries to develop. The government quickly adopted the system of priority production, and incorporated it, starting in the fourth quarter of fiscal year 1946, into the materials supply-and-demand plan formulated according to the Law on Temporary Measures for Commodity Supply and Demand Control mentioned earlier. By and large, this industrial plan could accomplish its objectives. As noted in the preceding chapter, the Japanese economy began from 1947 gradually to extricate itself from its destitute circumstances.

As matters evolved, the priority production plan did not develop along the lines of the initially conceived pattern of circular development focused only on coal and steel. Coal, a key material for industrial development, has by nature a wide range of uses. Particularly important among its many uses were railway transport and electric power generation. With that fact in mind, the initial plan gave highest allocation priority to the steel industry (Table 2.2). Actually, however, other industries were added to the priority list during implementation of the system, including electric power generation, railway transport, chemical fertilizers, and others. Electric power generation was added after the severe drought of 1947 and the ensuing serious shortage of power, which related to the fact that the electric power industry depended more heavily on hydroelectric power sources than on thermal power generation. Increased allocation of coal to railways, meanwhile, was prompted by the disruption of markets caused by the lack of rail transport facilities. And the reason for more coal being allocated to support the production of chemical fertilizers was because of the demand for increased food production. Overall, MITI carried out its 'priority production plan' of materials allocation flexibly, while watching developments in the economy as a whole.

Table 2.2 Coal distribution plan and actual distribution in fiscal year 1947

	Firdscal year 1946 3rd quarter (tons)[a]	Fiscal year 1946 4th quarter (tons)[a]	Fiscal year 1947 (1,000 tons)[b]
For Occupation Forces	284,700	317,500	1,466
Coal for exports	186,800	188,500	3,294
Japanese National Railways	1,770,000	1,815,000	6,863
Electric power industries	444,000	784,000	2,348
Steel industries	325,700	522,400	2,270
Chemical industries	494,100	489,400	2,649
Others	2,553,100	2,541,600	10,215
Total	6,058,400	6,658,400	29,105

[a] planned figures.
[b] actual figures.

Source: Economic Stabilization Board, Statistics Section, *Sengo no Sekitan Sangyo Tokei-shu* (Post-War Coal Industry Statistics).

Reconstruction financing

In implementing the priority production plan, the post-war Japanese industrial system faced a particularly serious problem: a critical shortage of funds. The zaibatsu had been important sources of funds in pre-war days, but they were dissolved; there were unpaid balances of wartime indemnities owed by the government to former producers of material for the military, but they were suspended; inflation rendered government bonds held by the nation valueless; and the destitution of the general populace meant they could not save any part of their income. For resuming and expanding production, however, industry required huge amounts of capital. It was the government that responded to this need by developing a financing plan to supply funds. It began providing reconstruction financing in the summer of 1946 with special financing by the Bank of Japan (BOJ). In October 1946, the Reconstruction Finance Bank Law was enacted for supplying industrial funds needed for the resumption of manufacturing, and in January 1947 the Reconstruction Finance Bank (RFB) began business. The RFB's loan funds, except for the capital paid in by the government, were supplied mostly by BOJ purchases of its securities or loans. The size of special financing, which was only 6 billion yen at the end of fiscal year 1946, quickly increased tenfold to reach 59.5 billion yen at the end of fiscal year 1947. Most funds were allocated to industries designated in the priority production plan. Initially, priority financing took the form of loans for operating funds, partly because private financial institutions were short of loanable funds. In 1948, however, financing for investment in plant and equipment became predominant. For example, of 132 billion yen in loans outstanding at the end of fiscal year 1948, 94.3 billion yen was for capital investment. Among those totals, lending to the coal, chemical fertilizer, and electric power generation industries increased sharply, but lending to the steel industry, which had excess capacity, was not very substantial. At any rate, economic reconstruction progressed, helped by government planning and control in financing.

One point about financing that is worth careful examination is the system of subsidies for offsetting the cost–price disparity. A system of paying a subsidy to cover the difference between the cost of production and the official price was used during the war to promote production of coal, steel, chemical fertilizers, and food. This system was continued essentially unchanged after the war to maintain price stability. It was applied to the priority production plan on an enlarged scale to provide powerful support from the price side. Specifically, general-use products were given official prices determined by calculating post-war costs, assuming that general prices were sixty-five times and wages were twenty-eight times their respective pre-war levels. In contrast, the official prices of basic materials, such as steel, coal, fertilizers, electric power, gas, and others were fixed at below-cost levels, as calculated by the above formula, and the government covered the difference between official price and cost as a cost–price differential subsidy, thereby seeking to hold down the general level of prices. Despite these measures, prices kept rising and the government had to revise the price structure in June 1948. At any rate, the purpose of the price system with subsidies was to control prices and wages while promoting healthy increases in production. This viewpoint of social coordination may well be considered the guiding principle of the Japanese government's control of the process of post-war economic reconstruction.

Reorganization of financial institutions

In the midst of the post-war economic devastation and inflation, the most urgent need was for capital, as described above. Although there was considerable war damage to most industrial equipment and facilities, some industries, including steel and shipbuilding, were able to resume production relatively early and begin expanding their operations because their facilities had survived the war largely intact. As well, workers were more than abundantly available, and necessary raw materials could somehow be imported. In the circumstances, it was the shortage of capital to provide a foundation for business operations that was felt most keenly. For that reason, SCAP could only provide a minimum of support. As noted earlier, priority financing was implemented to support the priority production plan, using a variety of subsidies and taking advantage of the large increase in the note issue by the Bank of Japan.

Industrial funds and the financing that supports them can be characterized as the basis of all economic activities. A very curious fact in this context, therefore, was that SCAP—which had the landlord system dismantled, enforced the dissolution of the zaibatsu, and, by means of the Deconcentration Law, sought to curb the monopolistic market behaviour of large corporations—did virtually nothing that affected Japanese banks negatively, although the banks had been important components of the zaibatsu system. The Japanese side, however, had long felt that reorganization of financial institutions was inevitable. In the revised edition of *Basic Problems in Reconstruction of the Japanese Economy* (September 1946), compiled by a Special Study Committee of the Ministry of Foreign Affairs, the Japanese financial system is analysed as follows:

The financial business of our country has reached a very high level of concentration, with a small number of large banks controlling the entire national financial market. Regional banks are subjugated to these large banks; they absorb regional funds and supply them to the large banks. Moreover, most of the large banks are owned and operated by the zaibatsu, providing an important base for their concentration of power in industry. In short, the combination of financial capital and industrial capital in the zaibatsu is a significant fact of Japanese economic life. . . . The funds amassed by the zaibatsu were spent for expanding military-related industries and purchasing government bonds, with little returned to benefit the general public.[7]

The publication further states that 'The financial system of our country requires immediate and drastic reconstruction. Financial institutions are burdened with enormous amounts of watered-down assets and are about to rupture. . . . Economic democratization should begin with the democratization of finance.'

It then adds that 'thoroughgoing reform is necessary', with emphasis on 'greater autonomy and the public responsibility of financial institutions'.[8]

SCAP did not try to dismantle the 'monopolistic' zaibatsu banks, and actually only ended up supporting their reconstruction and further development. When wartime indemnity payments were cancelled, for instance, measures were taken to minimize the damage to financial institutions. Their accounts were divided into old and new accounts, and the old accounts were frozen. Also, the Financial Institutions Reconstruction and Readjustment Law, enacted in October 1946, provided measures for rescuing financial institutions, including an effective way to handle their losses related to cancelled war indemnity payments.

Furthermore, the Emergency Financial Measures Ordinance issued in February 1946 froze all existing deposits and debts, thereby providing *de facto* relief to banks and other financial institutions at the public's expense. Financial institutions were also exempted from application of the Law on Exclusive Measures for the Excessive Concentration of Economic Power (Deconcentration Law), thus saving them from sure disaster. The Deconcentration Law was applied not only to industrial concerns but also to trading companies, including Mitsui & Co. and Mitsubishi Corporation, which were each broken into over 100 smaller trading companies. Only banks escaped application of the law unscathed, except that they were prohibited from using their former zaibatsu names. If anything, their survival was protected and even guaranteed. Why was this so?

The continued existence of former zaibatsu banks, and occupation policy

The only conceivable reason why SCAP would allow the zaibatsu banks to continue in business was that it feared uncontrollable chaos in economic activities which might lead to the collapse of the Japanese economy. Although the primary objective of the Occupation was Japan's complete demilitarization, SCAP could not ignore the requirement of 'promoting the reconstruction of the Japanese economy, which will permit reasonable peacetime requirements of the population to be met.'[9] It may be concluded that SCAP condoned the continued existence of the private-sector financial structure as a minimal safeguard for meeting this requirement.

There was another consideration as well. Japan's financial institutions were not so much organizations deeply rooted in the livelihood of the people as they were entities closely tied to the national economy's functioning. If the national economy faced chaos, therefore, it would be difficult to consider dismantling or reorganizing financial institutions. At such times, in fact, their reinforcement would be called for. The publication quoted above describes the unique characteristics of Japanese financial institutions as follows:

Japanese financial institutions are linked closely to the government. They are highly dependent on the State, and the State enjoys enormous power of influence over them. We can cite as concrete manifestations of this relationship the existence of many special banks, including the Hypothec Bank of Japan and the Industrial Bank of Japan, the use by banks of large issues of government bonds as collateral to obtain funds from the Bank of Japan, wide-ranging payment guarantees by the government to cover various obligations of financial institutions, and so on.[10]

From SCAP's perspective, the stronger the government regulatory authority over banks, the less likely it would be for powerful financial combines to monopolize the market, no matter how great their market control. Thus, another reason why SCAP allowed the large banks to continue in business might have been that it felt the problem of bank dominance would basically be solved if the government's control of the banks was assured.

A unique characteristic of Japanese financial markets that could not be ignored was the powerful market control of the Bank of Japan. Compared to the Federal Reserve Bank of the US, whose shares are held by member banks and whose Board of Governors actively seeks the cooperation of member banks, the Bank of Japan has been directly tied to the government. SCAP had sought to change the BOJ's structure radically by reorganizing it in the image of the US system, but after agonizing discussions it was decided to increase the autonomy nf the BOJ under a newly established Policy Board with members from business and other circles. In the end, the reform resulted essentially in strengthening the system centred on the Governor of the Bank of Japan.[11] This development is noteworthy in that it accounted for the subsequent predominance of the BOJ in Japan's financial and industrial activities.

When the Japanese economy began to grow in the 1950s, the rising relative importance of heavy industry and the increasing introduction and development of new technology led to a need for large amounts of capital. Procurement of funds had to rely heavily on private-sector financial institutions, which had survived Occupation reforms in the way mentioned above. One important source of the funds those financial institutions used for making loans was the government's Fiscal Investment and Loan Programme (FILP), in which the financial institutions participated by relying on credit created by the Bank of Japan through an 'overloan' mechanism.

Through these activities, large banks—primarily former zaibatsu banks—gradually improved their capital positions and developed to become the core of business groups that will be discussed later, at the same time developing closer relationships with large former zaibatsu industrial concerns. The large banks, which therefore escaped dissolution, came to play an important role in Japan's post-war economic rehabilitation and reconstruction. They restored the former zaibatsu names of Mitsui, Mitsubishi, Sumitomo, and so on, after the Peace Treaty and independence. One aspect of Japan's economic reconstruction is seen in those developments.

2.3. Inflation and the Road to Liberalization

Inflation and overcoming it

Inflation complicated the chaotic post-war economic situation and impeded economic recovery. Inflation had already begun during the war years, manifesting itself particularly in the form of black-market prices because of the imbalance between the supply of and demand for consumer goods, but it flared up after the war as the government lost its ability to control the economy. Banks held an enormous amount of uncollectable loan claims against manufacturers of military material whose prospects for resuming production were far from certain, and had to continue accommodating their requests for bridging finance. They also had to make repayments to impoverished depositors for savings deposits they had been forced to make during the war years. Unless measures were taken, it was virtually certain that banks would be forced into bankruptcy. To cope with the situation, the government introduced drastic measures in the form of freezing bank deposits and issuing a new yen. This was accomplished in February 1946 with the Emergency Financial Measures Ordinance, through which the government issued the new yen and suppressed excessive purchasing power by requiring households to deposit their currency holdings and then freezing all deposits except for 300 yen for the head of a household and 100 yen for each member of the household, and limiting monthly withdrawals of the new currency to 100 yen per month per household member.

As a result of these tough measures, the volume of BOJ notes in circulation—the main source of inflation—was reduced briefly, but soon began to increase rapidly. This failure to curb the rising volume of currency in circulation was attributed to the failure to find ways to initiate a beneficial production cycle, limit government expenditures, and restrain credit expansion caused by RFB and other bank loans and withdrawals of bank deposits. As Figure 2.1 shows, the amount of BOJ note issues and price levels surged towards the end of 1949. This high rate of inflation was unprecedented in Japanese economic history.

Workers struggled against inflation by fighting for higher wages, but wage increases they won were quickly surpassed by worse inflation. In July–September 1948, the index of household expenses was 12,700 (1934–6 = 100) whereas the consumer price index was 27,400, resulting in an index of household expenses in real terms of 46; this means that the living standard of the populace had fallen to less than half the pre-war level.

Once into 1949, however, the situation began to improve little by little. The low production level and the attendant supply–demand imbalance—the most important causes of inflation—were gradually eliminated. Coal production reached 29.33 million tons in 1947, just under the 30-million-ton goal of the priority production plan, and rose further to 34.79 million tons in 1948. Steel production in 1949 reached 3.11 million tons, returning it to its pre-war (1933) level. Production of fertilizers, essential to agricultural production, also improved, as indicated by the output of ammonium sulphate reaching 1.18 million tons in 1949, an amount sufficient to meet demand. Overall production also gradually recovered, with the growth rate of the economy reaching 13.0 per cent in real terms in 1948 and the index of industrial production rising by 31.9 per cent. As production increased and the excess of demand over supply was reduced, the rate of inflation declined. The annual rate of increase in wholesale prices, which was

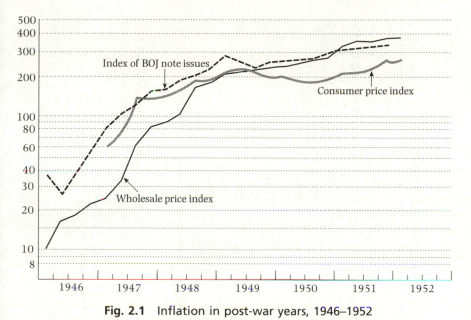

Fig. 2.1   Inflation in post-war years, 1946–1952

Note: Wholesale price index based on BOJ's Wholesale Price Index for Tokyo; consumer price index based on Consumer Price Index (Tokyo) prepared by the Statistics Bureau, Prime Minister's Office.

Source: Economic Planning Agency, *Keizai Hakusho* (Economic Survey of Japan), 1952.

164.4 per cent in 1948, dropped to 62.8 per cent in 1949 and further to 18.1 per cent in 1950. Increases in consumer prices were 82.7 per cent in 1948, 32.0 per cent in 1949, and minus 6.9 per cent in 1950. Table 2.3 shows changes in prices during this period in greater detail. It shows that once into 1949, black-market prices began to fall. Partly because of that, the effective price of consumer goods began to fall after April, while that of producer goods continued to rise somewhat. Although the priority production plan was partly to be credited for the increase in production and the winding down of inflation, the 'Dodge Line' of deflationary policy to be discussed later played a decisive role in slowing down price increases after 1949.

Economic consequences of inflation

What were the economic consequences of post-war inflation? A look at financial institutions shows they did not suffer a net loss because the decrease in the value of bonds they held was offset by the decrease in the value of their deposit liabilities. At any rate, they escaped a bankruptcy crisis because of the provisions of the Emergency Financial Measures Ordinance and the Financial Institutions

Table 2.3 Price level indices in post-war years: January 1947–May 1950 (1934–6 = 1)

	1934–6	1947	1948	1949	1949				1950		
					Jan.–Mar.	Apr.–June.	July–Sep.	Oct.–Dec.	Jan.–Mar.	April	May
Effective prices											
Producer goods	1	59	123	188	176	186	190	203	210	210	221
Consumer goods	1	96	167	209	208	219	206	202	202	190	198
Official prices (wholesale)											
Average	1	48	128	204	192	202	207	213	223	221	221
Producer goods	1	45	111	167	157	164	170	178	197	195	198
Consumer goods	1	50	144	242	229	243	248	250	247	243	240
Black-market prices											
Producer goods		100	158	146	164	156	139	125	118	108	106
Consumer goods		100	173	184	190	196	185	165	141	119	117

Notes:

1. 'Effective prices, Producer goods' are for entire country, based on BOJ figures.

2. 'Effective prices, Consumer goods' are calculated by linking Consumer Price Index (Tokyo) (1948 = 1) prepared by Statistics Bureau, Prime Minister's Office, with earlier index calculated by Economic Stabilization Board (1934–6 = 1; 1948 = 156); since index value of 167 for 1948 is obtained by finding simple arithmetic average of monthly figures, it does not agree with linking index value of 156; index value for 1949 would be 196, rather than 209, if direct linking index value of 1948 = 156 were used rather than using indirect linking value of 1948 = 167 (obtained by averaging monthly figures).

3. 'Official prices' (wholesale) are for Tokyo, based on BOJ figures; officially fixed prices are used if available; if not, free prices are used.

4. 'Black-market prices' are for Tokyo, based on BOJ figures.

Source: Economic Planning Agency, *Economic White Paper*: Fiscal year 1950.

Reconstruction and Readjustment Law. Manufacturers lost huge amounts of assets in the war and went heavily into debt afterwards to stay in business. But these loans were virtually cancelled out by inflation. Those companies gradually rebuilt their production capabilities, aided mainly by loans from the Reconstruction Finance Bank, and managed to increase employment opportunities for workers. Although inflation and measures to curb it gave the manufacturing industry breathing space, they had no net gains worthy of mention. It was the government that benefited the most from inflation. It had issued huge quantities of war bonds for the war and for meeting termination-of-war expenses and post-war economic reconstruction needs, but inflation drastically reduced its liabilities in real terms. Government debt, which was a burden for tax-paying companies and citizens, diminished in value as a result of inflation. This line of logic leads to the conclusion that, in the final analysis, those who lost the most from inflation were ordinary citizens who held government bonds and other instruments of debt. However, although inflation in the post-war period caused much social distress and economic confusion, it ended without producing a major breakdown in the economy.

The Cold War and the easing of economic controls

As noted repeatedly above, the basic objectives of Occupation policy were the demilitarization and democratization of Japan. There were also Allied policy planners who believed it was not proper to allow Japan to regain an economic position superior to that of the nations of Asia which had long endured the torment of Japanese colonialism and directly suffered the severe damages of war. They felt that the target of Japan's economic recovery should be set at a level prevailing during a relatively recessive pre-war period, specifically the level of the 1930–2 period, in the midst of the Great Depression. Thus, the initial US stance towards Japan's reconstruction was rather stern. From around the second half of 1947, however, this stance gradually softened in the changing climate of international relations. The most important cause of the change was the emergence of the Cold War. As for the Far East situation, the confrontation in China between Nationalists and Communists intensified, and the tide of the civil war shifted in favour of the Communists. The Korean Peninsula, meanwhile, was divided into two regimes along the 38th parallel, and North Korea adopted a communist system of government under Soviet influence. Communist pressures were thus mounting in the Far East, and the US had no alternative but to pay serious attention to Japan as a link in the chain of anti-Soviet defence. In this regard, Japan's industrial potential could not be ignored. The thinking of US policy planners thus gradually shifted towards allowing Japan a degree of economic expansion under US control, thereby seeking to ease social conflicts in Japan and improve Japan–US relations.

Once into 1948, SCAP began to allow a considerable degree of autonomy to the Japanese government, which was under the rule of indirect sovereignty by

SCAP. To proceed further with this new policy, SCAP thought it was necessary to change drastically the way the post-war Japanese economy was being managed. The task of giving substance to this measure fell on Joseph M. Dodge, who came to Japan in February 1949 as financial adviser to SCAP. He was directed to develop a plan for a self-supporting Japanese economy. Dodge concluded that Japan should first be freed from dependency on US aid, to which it had become accustomed. He also proposed that Japan rid itself of the government subsidies to which its industries were habituated, and of the attendant deficit financing, and that it create a self-supporting economy by improving its export capabilities. He characterized the Japanese economy as walking on 'stilts' of US aid and government subsidies, and argued that disposing of those stilts should be the first step towards economic self-support. The implementation of the Dodge Plan resulted in a drastic reduction of government subsidies and discontinuance of lending by the Reconstruction Finance Bank in fiscal year 1948, leading to reduced government spending. Inflation, which had been fuelled by deficit financing, cooled off quickly, and some deflationary conditions even emerged. Contributions to Japan under the US programmes of Government and Relief in Occupied Areas (GARIOA) and the Economic Rehabilitation in Occupied Areas (EROA) were separated from Japan's budget proper, and limitations on the use of related funds were introduced with creation of the US Aid Counterpart Fund Special Account.

The basic objective of the Dodge Plan was to change the Japanese economic system drastically by freeing it from subsidies and control and integrating it into the free-market system. Rationing and price controls were drastically curtailed in 1949, and some kodan engaged in these activities were abolished (Table 2.4). Exporting was freed in principle from December 1949, and importing by private traders was permitted from January 1950 within the framework of the foreign-exchange budget.

Table 2.4   Trends in number of kodan and controlled items

	Most numerous period	April 1949	August	December	April 1950
Materials designated for controlled production	252 (February 1946)	233	179	76	48
Materials designated for rationing	64 (February 1947)	57	36	31	15
Kodan	15 (March 1948)	12	11	10	7
Items with controlled prices		2,128	1,772	1,299	531

Source: Economic Planning Agency, *Economic White Paper*: Fiscal year 1950.

Development and dismantling of the military machinery industries

One Occupation policy was the dismantling of the munitions industries that provided the production base for Japan's military set-up. Japan's pre-war machinery industry was underdeveloped, and only military-operated factories developed technology, built warships, and produced munitions, artillery, and other weapons. After the war, therefore, the former facilities of the Imperial Army and Navy became immediate targets for dismantling. As the war progressed, however, the military-operated factories became unable to satisfy all the requirements for manufacturing capacity and technology, and Japan's machinery industry had to cooperate with the military and rapidly expand their production capacity. Because of that cooperation, the Occupation Forces included machinery and equipment in the list of facilities designated for reparations removal. This machinery and equipment, of course, was no longer productive when military demand ended with the war's conclusion. Using 1955—when the machinery industry was still not fully recovered—as 100, the machinery production index for 1936 was only 39.9, a very low level of development. The index rose during the war years, however, as the industry expanded rapidly. It was 101.2 in 1941, exceeding the 1955 level, and 135.6 in 1944, when military production reached its peak. It overshadowed all other industries. From late 1945, however, the industry shrank rapidly in size due to the circumstances described above (Table 2.5).

The machinery industry's position changed considerably after the war. In 1950, the production index based on 1955 was 44.7 for the overall

Table 2.5   Production indices of major manufacturing industries (1955 = 100)

Year	Mining and manufacturing	Manufacturing		
			Iron and steel	Machinery and equipment
Weight	10,000.0	9,227.5	967.1	1,835.3
1936	71.6	68.9	50.0	39.9
1941	103.4	100.2	76.2	101.2
1944	103.5	101.2	84.2	135.6
1946	18.0	16.1	9.9	17.4
1950	47.4	44.7	52.2	41.6
1955	100.0	100.0	100.0	100.0
1960	227.9	236.3	220.8	442.4

Source: *Kokogyo Shisu Soran* (Long-Term Data Book of Standard Indices of Industrial Production), 1961.

manufacturing industry and only 41.6 for the machinery industry. In 1960, however, those figures were 236.3 and 442.4, respectively, showing that the machinery industry led post-war growth in industrial production.

To revive the stagnant machinery industry after the war, the Ministry of Commerce and Industry at first encouraged it to start producing machinery and utensils for civilian use, such as radios, sewing machines, bicycles, and hotplates, and other home electric appliances, for which production was restrained during the war. Also gradually increased was the production of machinery and equipment for the production of consumer goods, such as spinning and weaving machinery, parts for textile machinery, agricultural machinery, food-processing machinery, machinery and equipment for producing fertilizers, and mining machinery. Large loans from the Reconstruction Finance Bank for capital investment made possible plant and equipment investment in major industries, which generated a large demand for products from the machinery industry. The machinery industry, therefore, destined to lead the economic reconstruction activities in earnest in the early 1950s, was the first industry to expand production sharply. Its growth was based on its legacy from the wartime economy, although there was a considerable difference in the nature of its growth in the post-war period.

The steel industry can be viewed as having played the same role, and showed the same pattern of growth as the machinery industry. The steel industry was important to the industries producing war materials, as well as to the machinery industry after the war, because steel is a key material product. The industry therefore grew into a major industry in the wartime economy, and was rebuilt early in the post-war period. Before long, it also faced the task of rationalizing its operations in the context of global competition, just as the machinery industry did. Efforts to rebuild and develop the Japanese economy were thus started by somehow converting facilities previously used for producing military material to meet peacetime demands, and making use of the legacies of their wartime production capacity.

The Korean War and special procurements

The liberalization of economic control was a private aspiration of industry and government leaders, who thought the nation had made a good start in economic growth under the Occupation, and they were prepared for Dodge's exhortation of economic self-help. His prescription for eliminating the 'stilts' of the Japanese economy, however, was much more drastic, and was implemented much more rapidly than they had expected. The economy promptly rid itself of inflationary pressures and slid into a deflationary condition. Government subsidies were cut and companies were exposed to competition and forced to curtail production under the heavy burden of mounting inventories of unsold goods. Liquidation and bankruptcies of smaller firms mushroomed, unemployment increased, and the government, faced with a crisis, lost its sense of direction and struggled to find a way out of a difficult situation.

An event suddenly occurred, however, that changed everything: the Korean War broke out. As US troops in Japan were deployed to the Korean Peninsula, a demand for 'special procurements' suddenly developed from the UN forces in Korea. Japan became a sort of 'rear base', and orders to Japanese industry covered heavy-industry products and repair services. Special procurements comprised a 'rear demand' for the war and stretched across a broad range of products, including trucks, locomotives, railway sleepers and lines, barbed wire, drums, military rations, clothing, and pharmaceutical products. The demand for repair services, including those for trucks, was also significant. Thanks to this special-procurement demand, accumulated inventories said to be in the order of 100 billion yen were promptly sold, and Japanese industry regained its vitality. Foreign-exchange earnings related to special-procurement purchases amounted to $150 million in 1950, $590 million in 1951, and $820 million in 1952. These earnings constituted a large percentage of Japan's total foreign-exchange earnings, reaching 26.4 per cent in 1951 and 36.8 per cent in 1952, and played an important role in revitalizing Japan's economy.

The Korean War may be regarded as a war by proxy fought in the context of the Cold War. It was something the US could not have anticipated, and it became an unexpected blessing for the Japanese economy. It gave Japan's economy the opportunity to be given a toehold in the process of growth in the free-market economic system.

The demand for special procurements from the UN forces in Korea not only generated a tremendous demand for products from the Japanese machinery industry, such as trucks, but also brought about a marked change in the industry's production structure and increased its exports.

Concerning the composition of the machinery industry by product, the share of rolling stock increased because of replacement demand. Relative shares of products such as trucks and automotive parts, which were not significant in pre-war years, also increased, changing the product make-up of the machinery industry markedly compared to pre-war years.

The post-Korean War recession and measures for dealing with it

Because much of the demand for special procurements was for urgent wartime use, requisitions of materials did not pass through the usual competitive market. Therefore, after the war passed its peak and demand fell, needless to say, the Japanese machinery industry—which was not internationally competitive—could not compete with foreign producers in export markets or even with foreign imports in the home market. It thus faced a crisis.

Attention turned to industrial rationalization as a means to overcome the crisis situation. This will be discussed later. Another solution was made-to-order production of labour-intensive products. A typical example of this type of production was that of hydroelectric-power-generating equipment in the heavy electric equipment industry. Another example was shipbuilding. The Japanese shipbuilding industry had docks it had used to build warships and it had basic technology in shipbuilding. By introducing newer technology from abroad, the industry could acquire the capability to compete on an equal footing with overseas shipbuilders.

There was another direction as well: the production of arms. The special procurements during the Korean War had included military goods whose production was previously prohibited, ranging from ammunition to firearms, and the trend was towards expansion. In the context of the Cold War becoming a reality, the US became interested in recruiting Japan into its line of defence, and sentiments in Japanese industry were to respond positively to the US overture because of the potential that Japanese industry had for producing military goods.

This consideration, however, was suppressed by concern for the 'peace' provision of the new Constitution and objections to rearming Japan. The strengthening of the defence system was restricted, and prohibition on the export of military goods effectively forestalled the further development of Japan's military industry. Although Japan's military posture underwent a few minor changes afterwards, this basic line was essentially maintained. As a result, Japan has continuously had the lowest ratio of military expenditure to GNP in the world.[12] Defence production with government financial support often leads to technological progress, but Japan not only caught up with the advanced nations in non-military fields, but by limiting its expenditure on non-productive military production and devoting all available resources to the growth and development of its economy, it eventually surpassed the advanced nations. In this sense, the dismantling of militaristic Japan had provided one of the basic conditions favouring the rapid post-war growth of the Japanese economy.

2.4. International Economic Relations and Trade Policy

Post-war changes in international relations

After the war ended, Japan experienced fundamental changes in its international relations in three areas. First, it goes without saying, Japan was under the Occupation of the Allied Powers. Specifically, it was under the control of SCAP, not only administratively but in economic activities as well. Unlike in Germany, however, the Allied Powers did not divide Japan for Occupation purposes, and SCAP exercised authority indirectly through the existing form of government in Japan. The second change was the liberation of Japan's former colonies. As a result of the Sino-Japanese War (1894–5), China had ceded Taiwan to Japan. And at the end of the Russo-Japanese War (1904–5), Russia had ceded the southern half of Sakhalin to Japan, the right of lease Russia exercised over the Liaotung Peninsula at the southern tip of Manchuria (now China's north-east area), and some of its interests in Manchuria, including the South Manchuria Railway. In addition, Japan annexed Korea in 1910. At the beginning of the twentieth century, therefore, Japan was a major imperialist colonizing power, though a latecomer. International conflicts generated by its subsequent economic expansion plunged it into the Pacific War. As a result of defeat, Japan lost all that territory. Taiwan and the Liaotung Peninsula were returned to China, and Korea became independent, divided by the USA and USSR between south and north under different rule. The Sakhalin and Kuril Islands (except, from Japan's viewpoint, for the four northern islands of Habomai, Shikotan, Kunashiri, and Etorofu) became Soviet territories. Through these changes, Japan lost 45 per cent of its pre-war territory. Modern colonial rule has often generated problems between colonies and colonizing powers. In the process of colonies gaining independence after the Second World War, some former colonizing powers like Great Britain managed to maintain Commonwealth relationships with their former colonies. For Japan, however, relationships with former colonies were suspended for a rather lengthy period because there generally were harsh backlashes related to former Japanese rule and because Japan was under Allied Occupation. Moreover, Japanese citizens who had resided in the former colonies were repatriated to Japan within about a year after the war ended, leaving everything they owned behind.

The third change was related to the areas Japan had occupied in what it termed 'The Greater East Asia Co-Prosperity Sphere'. The Philippines gained independence from the US, the Dutch East Indies gained independence from the Netherlands and became Indonesia, and French Indo-China became independent Vietnam, Cambodia, and Laos. Malaysia became independent from Britain, and Singapore soon afterwards left Malaysia and declared its independence. Post-war anti-Japanese feelings were particularly ugly in countries like the Philippines, where local resistance to Japanese rule had been strong. There was little contact between these countries and Japan, not only during the Occupation but also for a long period afterwards. Post-war Japan, therefore, was internationally isolated, with virtually all of its relationships with the countries of Asia suspended, countries with which Japan had had significant economic relationships before the war.

Changes in the reparations issue

The first post-war international economic issue for Japan, which was quite natural, was the question of reparations. The 'US Initial Post-Surrender Policy for Japan' stated under the section on reparations and restitution that reparations shall be made:

(a) Through the transfer—as may be determined by the appropriate Allied authorities— of Japanese property located outside of the territories to be retained by Japan.

(b) Through the transfer of such goods or existing capital equipment and facilities as are not necessary for a peaceful Japanese economy or the supplying of the occupying forces. . . . No form of reparation shall be exacted which will interfere with or prejudice the program for Japan's demilitarization.

In this sense, unlike the requirement for reparations from Germany after the First World War, the Allied Powers after the Second World War made efforts to establish peaceful future economic relations with their former enemies. Moreover, the stern reparations requirements established immediately after the war were relaxed somewhat after 1947. Reparation removals of purely military facilities went on as planned, but the removal requirements for industrial facilities were relaxed, and decisions were made against exacting reparations in the form of products. It was decided that 30 per cent of the Interim Reparations Programme was to be carried out, and the equipment removed was transferred to the Republic of China (Taiwan), the Philippines, Indonesia, Burma, and other countries. After these removals, there were no further reparations in kind. This easing of the reparations programme was motivated by SCAP's concern that the reduced industrial level of Japan would inevitably necessitate an increase in US aid to Japan and ultimately an increase in the burden on US taxpayers. Furthermore, in the climate of the intensifying Cold War, the US wanted to maintain and utilize Japan's industrial capacity. The so-called Draper Report issued by SCAP in the spring of 1949 was officially titled, 'Report on the Economic Position and Prospects of Japan and Korea and the Measures Required to Improve Them', and its content leaned more heavily towards the rehabilitation policy of Asian economies than towards the reparations issue. Many of the Allied Powers were critical of the new softer line of the US on the Japanese reparations issue, but the US pushed through with its policy.

The Board of Trade and government trading

In terms of international trade relations, SCAP allowed Japan to import with its approval only raw materials to satisfy peacetime needs, and to export products approved beforehand by SCAP to pay for imports. Under SCAP's directive to create an agency to conduct foreign trade, the Japanese government established, as early as the end of 1945, the Board of Trade as an external bureau of MCI. SCAP did not approve of Japan's plan to set up the Board as an agency to regulate private trading, and directed that the Board handle trading directly. For this reason, the start of the Board's operation was delayed until April 1946. The Board of Trade operated directly under SCAP in what may be called 'government trading'. To handle the practical side of the business, four government corporations (*kodan*)— Mining and Manufactured Goods Trading Kodan, Textiles Trading Kodan, Foodstuffs Trading Kodan, and Raw Materials Trading Kodan—were created in April 1947. All operating funds of these kodan were paid from a special account of the government. The kodan method of organization described above was used for these organizations because SCAP was distrustful of private Japanese corporations. Until the end of 1946, imports were heavily weighted in favour of foodstuffs because of food shortages. Food imports of $170 million accounted for 55.7 per cent of total imports, and imports of raw cotton and other materials—needed for producing exports of textile products ($60 million, or 60.1 per cent of exports) which were in part to pay for food imports—amounted to $100 million or 34.7 per cent of imports. In 1947, food imports of $300 million continued to account for a large portion (56.1 per cent) of imports, and textile exports of $130 million accounted for 75.5 per cent of total exports. The Board of Trade, however, was not permitted to be involved in the overseas business of these trading activities, over which SCAP exercised complete control. It was not until August 1947 that SCAP permitted overseas traders to visit Japan and negotiate directly with Japanese importers and exporters. Japan's international trade was liberalized gradually thereafter.

Japan's economy, however, remained essentially closed to the outside world. What little human and economic intercourse there was with foreign countries took place through the Occupation Forces. In the circumstances, no single exchange rate existed that could be called a yen exchange rate. At first that was not a problem, because flows of goods took place only in the form of aid or barter exchange. When foreign trade began to develop, however, it became necessary to determine an exchange rate. As a preliminary step, exchange rates were set for different product categories as an expedient in October 1948. A unified rate of 360 yen to $1 was finally established in April 1949. The Japanese business community had hoped for as low as possible an exchange rate to help Japan's export efforts, but the rate was set at a higher level than was expected. This 360-yen rate eventually became an important factor which made it necessary for Japanese industry to rationalize itself to improve its international competitiveness. Setting a fixed exchange rate was the first step in internationalizing the Japanese economy. The 360-yen rate remained unchanged for more than twenty years.

The development of the post-war economy and international trade

As described above, Japan under Occupation was totally isolated from the rest of the world in trade relations. SCAP exercised total control over exports and imports, including the import of foodstuffs needed to maintain the livelihood of the populace. The 'Initial Post-Surrender Policy for Japan' stated as follows:

Although Japan will eventually be allowed to engage in normal commercial relations with other nations, during the Occupation it will only be permitted, under appropriate control, to import materials and other products for peacetime needs and to export products to pay for approved imports.

As mentioned above, imports during the immediate post-war period consisted mainly of foodstuffs. To pay for these imports, and to meet pressing domestic needs, the import of raw cotton was essential. This basic structure of the import trade changed little for the first five years after the war. In fiscal year 1950 as well, while foodstuffs accounted for 33.5 per cent of total imports, natural fibre imports were as high as 38.2 per cent.

When self-sustenance and the growth of the Japanese economy came to be discussed towards the end of the Occupation, a debate started concerning the optimum direction of economic development. This debate was introduced earlier as the 'development first or trade first' controversy. The advocates of the 'development first' approach were fully aware that trade was indispensable to Japan, but argued, in part reflecting on the developmental pattern of pre-war Japan, that the principal growth strategy should be to develop the nation's latent domestic resources and technology. Those who advocated the 'trade first' approach, however, maintained that a strategy for fast growth should give highest priority to trade; this was considering the course of the economy's development in the past and the reality of its poor natural resource endowments. Emphasis on trade would also be a means to absorb the excess supply of labour. Despite the relative merits of these two arguments for the optimum direction of development, the main point is that trade was an immediate and pressing problem for Japan.

Even though demilitarization of the economic structure was the primary task of the Occupation, returning Japan to an agrarian society was impossible in the context of the sharply increased population size and the reduction in land area. SCAP also realized that industrialization was the only viable path for Japan.

To promote industrialization, three major obstacles had to be overcome. The first was the question of importing raw materials. The need for food imports had gradually lost some of its urgency, in part because of the success of land reforms. On the other hand, increased imports of the raw materials for textiles and of iron ore and coal for producing steel, key to industrial development, were needed. The second obstacle had to do with exports to pay for these imports. Textile products—one of Japan's key exports since before the war—were about to be replaced by chemical and synthetic fibres on the one hand, and, as described earlier, by machinery and apparatus—an unexpected legacy of wartime military-related production—on the other. These exports, however, were affected negatively by the decline in the demand for special procurements tied to the Korean War and the falling demand in overseas markets. These developments led to the third obstacle, that of international competitiveness. In order to gain a firm foothold in overseas markets, Japanese industry—the machinery industry in particular—had to develop a viable market competitiveness.

To that end, however, the import of advanced technology was urgently required. Japan had fallen seriously behind other industrial nations in terms of technology because of the interruption of international relations during the war and post-war years. At the same time, industrial rationalization was also necessary so that imported technology could be appropriately applied to production processes. The increased import of machinery and equipment was thus also called for.

Another noteworthy point was Japan's difficulty in restoring to pre-war levels its trade with former colonies and with countries it occupied and ruled in the name of the 'Greater East Asia War'. The difficulty was mainly because of the hostile feelings those countries harboured towards Japan. And while that task was difficult enough, it was also difficult for Japan to expand its exports to areas other than Asia, with the exception of the US. Exports to Asia via Hong Kong and other routes continually accounted for roughly 40 per cent of Japan's total exports. Also, Japan's trade relations with the US drew much closer than in pre-war days, partly because the US played the dominant role during Japan's Occupation and Japan was under its protection, and partly because the US economy was the world's strongest in the post-war era. Concerning imports, in particular, Japan was dependent on the US for raw materials and advanced machinery and equipment.

Establishment of MITI

One absolute requirement for developing Japanese industry was the establishment of a solid foundation for the nation's trade structure. It was in this context that the reorganization of the Ministry of Commerce and Industry into the Ministry of International Trade and Industry took place.

During the Occupation, the Board of Trade, created as an external bureau of MCI, was responsible for trade administration. In the tradition of the pre-war government organization, the Ministry of Foreign Affairs generally handled trade-related matters abroad and MCI handled matters relating to exports from and imports into Japan. Some variations in this format existed during the war concerning trade with areas under Japanese control. After the war, as described above, there were no administrative duties overseas related to trade. The Board of Trade supervised domestic trade, and its staff included officials from the Ministry of Foreign Affairs. When MITI was created in May 1949, Japan still did not have formal diplomatic relations with other countries because of the Occupation. But the Ministry of Foreign Affairs gradually increased the number of its overseas resident officers to prepare for the normalization of diplomatic relations. Together with MITI's establishment, however, Prime Minister Shigeru Yoshida, though himself a former diplomat, centralized the administration of trade matters in this reorganized ministry and named it the Ministry of International Trade and Industry, taking into close consideration the future of the country's trade relations. Also, the prefix 'international trade' (*tsusho*) was placed in front of the name of each of MITI's bureaux, as in International Trade Enterprise Bureau and International Trade Machinery Bureau.

International trade policy and bureaucratic structure

As supporters of the wartime system, the military, of course, as well as the zaibatsu and the landowner class were dissolved. The political and economic systems were then reorganized with a view to democratizing them. However, in this process, another group allowed to remain largely intact, along with private banks as described above, was Japan's bureaucracy. The Allied Powers were well aware of the important role played by the bureaucracy in the wartime system. It was the Ministry of Home Affairs and the police structure tied to it that became the main targets of SCAP's denunciation. As a link in its programme to reform the old bureaucratic system, therefore, SCAP abolished the Home Affairs Ministry and established a system of local autonomy. As a concrete measure in this reform, it dismantled the centralized police system, created a new police system focusing primarily on municipal police forces, and set up Public Safety Commissions for local police control.

SCAP naturally sought fundamental reform, not only of the Ministry of Home Affairs and the police system but also of the bureaucratic system itself. The new Constitution, proclaimed with the inherent problem of the bureaucracy in mind, contains the following statement in Article 15 on public service: (1) the people have the inalienable right to choose their public officials and to dismiss them, and (2) all public officials are servants of the whole community and not of any group thereof.

The National Public Service Law, promulgated in 1947, aimed to replace traditional officialdom with a new system that would administer civil servants based on position classifications. The law provided for creation of the National Personnel Authority as a comprehensive agency for administering civil service employment and revamping the institutions in the old bureaucratic structure. It cannot be denied that these reforms served in their way the intended purpose of transforming the pre-war bureaucratic system, characterized by the *kanson-minpi* (officialdom revered, people disdained) mentality. The personnel administration of the independent National Personnel Authority definitely played a role in this transformation.

As matters evolved, in the post-war circumstances this new civil service system fulfilled quite different functions from those intended initially. One basic reason was the system of indirect governance. The Occupation policies of the Allied Powers were implemented by a cadre of Japanese bureaucrats who were held responsible for the results. It was plausible for the Occupation Forces to use the bureaucracy, and, in the process, to induce changes in it. Because the bureaucracy was capable, however, SCAP gradually became dependent on it, and ended up accepting the continued existence of its essential character. Another reason was that the bureaucratic machine had a monopoly on specialized knowledge, or, more precisely, on functional expertise, which it had accumulated through years of experience. When the centralized style of government was reformed to place greater emphasis on local autonomy, therefore, it was former central and local government bureaucrats, not local citizens, who assumed positions of responsibility in the reformed local governments. As a comparison, whereas most bills submitted to the US Congress are prepared by lawmakers, bills in post-war Japan were still mostly prepared by bureaucrats. At any rate, Japan's bureaucratic system was thus reformed superficially, and its essential character remained unchanged.

In the chaotic post-war economy, moreover, SCAP seldom intervened in the affairs of the economic bureaucracy, particularly those of the Ministry of Finance or Ministry of Commerce and Industry. As described earlier, the former Ministry of Commerce and Industry, which had been part of the Ministry of Munitions, was separated from the latter and emerged as a new MCI immediately after the war. When the Economic Planning Board was created—at the suggestion of SCAP—to formulate policy for post-war economic stabilization and rehabilitation, MCI transferred a group of key bureaucrats to the new agency.

In general, the economic bureaucracy managed to preserve its machine because SCAP believed that it was necessary to maintain economic stability in the post-war chaos. To do so, it was expedient to utilize the functional expertise and administrative skills of existing officials. More specifically, in the post-war system of indirect governance discussed above, SCAP rejected the notion of letting the private sector exercise self-control to ensure economic stability, and opted instead for economic control by government agencies. This was a system of bureaucratic control, and only experienced bureaucrats could carry it out. In this manner, the economic bureaucracy preserved its essential characteristics after the war, and became a key player in the development of Japan's post-war economic system.

NOTES

1. Yoshio Ando (ed.), 'Kokka Sodoinjo Kinkyu wo Yosuru Shoseisaku no Tettei Kyoka ni Kansuru Ken' (Concerning All-Out Reinforcement of Urgently Needed Policies for General National Mobilization), *Kindai Nippon Keizaishi Yoran* (Outline of the Economic History of Modern Japan), University of Tokyo Press, 1975: 130.
2. Ministry of Munitions, 10 Aug. 1944, 'Kaisen Iko Butteki Kokuryoku no Suii Narabi Kongo ni Okeru Mitoshi Setsumei Shiryo' (Changes in Japan's Material Resources since the Outbreak of the War and Prospects for the Future: Explanatory Materials), in *Haisen no Kiroku* (Record of the Defeat), Hara Shobo, 1967: 59.
3. Imperial Conference, 8 June 1945, 'Kokuryoku no Genjo' (The Actual Situation Regarding National Resources), *Haisen no Kiroku*: 270.
4. To our knowledge, land reforms are seldom successful in other Asian countries, primarily because the landowner class is so powerful. The only exception is Taiwan. On this point, see Mikio Sumiya *et al.*, *Taiwan no Keizai* (The Economy of Taiwan), University of Tokyo Press, 1991.
5. Chalmers Johnson, who analysed the accomplishments of the Ministry of Commerce and Industry and MITI throughout the pre-war and post-war periods, wrote as follows concerning the important role played by this law: 'To this day, the MITI Press Club refers to the Occupation as MCI's "golden era", the period in which it exercised total control of the economy. The government's assumption of all functions previously shared with the private sector, its recreation of the economic general staff and the materials mobilization plans under new names but in much stronger forms, and its enactment of legislation that made the National General Mobilization Law pale by comparison led to an enormous growth of the bureaucracy.' Chalmers Johnson, *MITI and the Japanese Miracle*, Stanford University Press, 1982: 176 (trans. as *Tsusansho to Nippon no Kiseki* Under the supervision of Toshihiko Yano, TBS Britannica, 1982: 192–3).
6. An Economic Stabilization Board publication describes the nature of a 'kodan' as follows: 'A kodan is a public corporation fully owned by the government. Although it is regarded as a legal entity separate from the government proper, it has strong characteristics of a government organization in that its personnel are public officials and other types of public employees whose salaries are paid from the national treasury and its offices and other facilities are acquired by the government for use by the kodan. The only advantage of having it assume the form of a juridical person is that its financial activities are not subject to the provisions of the Finance Law or the Public Accounts Law. In that sense, although a kodan is an agency of the Japanese government, it is regarded as having a temporary existence. The format was selected out of necessity as a means to exercise public control, as a compromise between the necessity for economic control and the prohibition of private monopoly.' The publication concluded: 'The kodan must strictly serve the purpose of returning the Japanese economy to a free-market system.' Summary of Economic Stabilization Board, 'Kodan ni Tsuite' (Concerning Kodan), Sept. 1947.
7. 'Shiryo: Sengo Nihon no Keizai Seisaku Koso' (Materials: Formulae for Economic Policy for Post-War Japan), *Nihon Keizai Saiken no Kihon Mondai* (Basic Problems of Reconstructing the Japanese Economy), i, University of Tokyo Press: 166.
8. Ibid. 210.

9. 'The United States Initial Post-Surrender Policy for Japan', Sept. 1945.
10. *Nihon Keizai Saiken no Kihon Mondai*, i. 166. SCAP's policy towards the special banks was rather stringent. The Yokohama Specie Bank, a special bank dealing with foreign exchange, acquired strong military colouring during the war, serving as an organ to mobilize munitions in the Japanese-occupied areas in the south. It was ordered closed in December 1946, but its new accounts were taken over by the newly established Bank of Tokyo. Although the Occupation Forces had intended to close all the special banks, the Japanese government held repeated negotiations with SCAP and succeeded in obtaining its approval to allow the continued existence of the Industrial Bank of Japan as a financial institution for long-term credit raising funds by floating debentures, and to allow the conversion of the Nippon Kangyo Bank and Hokkaido Takushoku Bank to ordinary banks. In other words, SCAP relaxed its stringent stance towards the financial system.
11. The 'democratization' of the Bank of Japan through the establishment of the Policy Board was criticized as 'mere window dressing'.
12. Even after 1955, Japan's defence expenditures were kept low. The Miki government in 1974 established the policy of keeping defence expenditures within 1 per cent of the GNP. This limit has been observed since, although actual figures at times slightly exceeded the 1 per cent level.

3

The Formation of the Post-War Industrial System

3.1. The Move towards Liberalization of the Economy and the Self-Support System

Even at the end of 1950, when the path to a peace treaty became clearly visible, the Japanese economy was still being kept afloat with US aid of several hundred million dollars each year. The primary task in those days, therefore, was the earliest possible return of the economy to being self-supporting. The Self-Supporting Economic Council (formerly the Economic Reconstruction Planning Council) settled on a three-year Economic Self-Supporting Plan in January 1951. As expected, the Council identified the steel industry as the core investment-goods industry and the mainstay of the Japanese industrial order. It also characterized the textile industry as the key exporting industry, one that was extremely important for the improvement of Japanese living standards. The plan specified the chemical fertilizer industry as important for increased production of food and for exports. Noteworthy was that the plan contained no mention of the machinery industry, a reflection of the fact that policy planners in those days paid no attention to the machinery industry. It should be mentioned that given the turbulent conditions of the times this self-support plan was not adopted as an operational plan.

Easing of economic control

The economic order, however, had already been changing gradually. The most noteworthy of the changes was the greater freedom of economic activities as various control measures were relaxed. As described earlier, the industrial policy under the Occupation could be summarized in one word—'control'. From the beginning of fiscal year 1949, however, as a result of the following sequence of events, controls were eased rapidly, one after the other. Manufacturing activities were restored to some extent, but the purchasing power of the people decreased. Inventories of unsold goods mounted and signs of overproduction were apparent everywhere. In this situation, the 'Dodge Line', which aimed at liberalization of economic activities, produced much greater effects than had been expected. From the second half of 1949, the rationing of materials was abolished rapidly. Although MITI did not relax the controls on strategic materials and imported goods, it decontrolled materials designated for production so that the number of such materials fell from over 100 in April 1949 to only twenty-five in March

1951. The relaxation of controls began with non-ferrous metals and proceeded to textiles, chemicals, and then to metals.

The number of materials designated for rationing, which stood at fifty-seven in April 1949, fell to eight items two years later. Most food items other than staple foods were decontrolled. Daily necessities such as tissue paper and light bulbs, as well as household fuels and dairy products, were also decontrolled. In line with these steps, price controls were also lifted. Controlled prices of major commodity categories that numbered 2,128 in April 1949 were steadily abolished, except for goods still in short supply and goods involved in cost–price disparity subsidies. In March 1951, only 263 prices remained controlled.

Concurrently, government agencies in charge of administering controls were reduced in scale, and the public corporations, which had regulated supply and demand through the purchase and sale of controlled goods, were abolished in steps. In April 1949, the Raw Materials Trading Kodan and the Foodstuffs Trading Kodan were disbanded, followed by dissolution of the Coal, Liquor, Grocery, and Fodder Distribution Kodan. All of the remaining distribution *kodan*, including Foodstuffs and Fertilizers, were dissolved by April 1951. The kodan-type public corporations, which characterized the post-war economic controls exercised by the Japanese government, thus became history.

In line with these changes, cost–price disparity subsidies were radically reduced. In the budget for fiscal year 1949, 102.3 billion yen were budgeted as subsidies for such materials as steel and fertilizers, and an additional 73.1 billion yen were appropriated as subsidies for foodstuff imports. In fiscal year 1950, a total of 94.4 billion yen, or 13.7 per cent of total expenditure, were initially budgeted. During that year, however, subsidies were suspended or reduced, so that actual subsidies in the settled accounts were slimmed down to 64.0 billion yen, or 9.6 per cent of total expenditure. In fiscal year 1951, further cuts were made, leaving only food import subsidies of 22.5 billion yen, or 3.4 per cent of total expenditure.

Path to liberalization

Against the political background of the imminent Peace Treaty and restored independence, the main framework of economic control established during the Occupation was removed, and Japanese production and consumption activities became free in principle. The Japanese government had great interest in, and expectations regarding, how the post-independence economy could become self-supporting and develop within the framework of US–Japanese cooperation. Of the various projections it made, one that attracted considerable attention was the Five-Year Plan for Economic Self-Support announced in 1955 by the Hatoyama Administration. The plan called for bolstering the economic base by developing the electric power and the textile industries, and by improving transport by developing the Japanese National Railways (JNR). Further, it envisaged a scale and structure of international trade that would be in harmony with the economy's high dependence on imports. The Five-Year Plan aimed to expand the scale of the

Table 3.1 Production indices in Five-Year Plan for
Economic Self-Support

	1954	1960
(1) Primary industries	100.0	120.5
(2) Secondary industries	100.0	153.7
Mining	100.0	125.2
Food processing	100.0	142.0
Spinning	100.0	132.0
Printing and bookbinding	100.0	135.7
Chemicals	100.0	183.0
Rubber and leather	100.0	140.5
Lumbering	100.0	144.5
Ceramics	100.0	155.3
Metals	100.0	159.0
Machinery	100.0	160.0
(3) Tertiary industries	100.0	128.7

Source: Economic Planning Agency, *Sengo Keizai-shi* (Post-War
History of Japan's Economy).

economy by implementing these programmes, thereby expanding employment
opportunities. Based on that plan, the estimated indexes of production for 1960,
with 1954 as 100, are shown in Table 3.1. These targets implied an annual industrial growth rate of about 7 per cent. Because of the importance of fertilizer production, the plan projected the highest growth rate for the chemical industry. It
also anticipated a high growth rate for the machinery industry, which suggested
that, unlike the proposed Plan for Economic Self-Support mentioned above, this
plan was formulated with high expectations regarding changes in the real condition of the economy.

The Japanese economy was about to start down the self-supporting path. To
realize that goal, however, it was necessary first for it to be weaned from the protection provided by the US, and to acquire economic capabilities which would
enable it to participate in international competition without US help. To build a
basis for such capabilities, Japan had to press ahead first with rationalization of
its industries in order to close the technological gap between itself and other countries that had developed during the wartime and post-war years.

3.2. The Path to Industrial Rationalization

The Enterprise Rationalization Promotion Law
Because of the ten-year vacuum during the wartime and post-war periods, the
level of technology of Japanese industry lagged conspicuously behind that of the
advanced Western countries. Production facilities were old and run-down, and

industry could not hope to compete effectively in world markets. The first task of Japan's industrial policy, therefore, was to improve the technological capabilities of Japanese industry and enhance the productivity made possible by it. In the priority production plan mentioned earlier, the fundamental policy measure of postwar economic reconstruction, the price of coal produced in ill-maintained mines, particularly the price of coke for use in making pig-iron, was quite high relative to prices in world markets. Also, the productivity of open-hearth furnaces and rolling mills used in steelmaking was inordinately low by world standards. Burdened by such high prices and low productivity, it was almost impossible for Japanese industry to participate effectively in world markets. Surmounting these difficulties required, first and foremost, industrial rationalization, or technological innovation.

Starting as early as 1948 and 1949, when the Japanese economy was taking its first steps towards sustained growth, industrial rationalization was already a serious concern. The implementation of the Dodge Line put both government and industry under heavy pressure to rationalize industry. Enacted under these circumstances, the Ministry of International Trade and Industry Establishment Law placed rationalization at the top of the list of corporate-related service functions of the International Trade Enterprises Bureau of the newly established ministry. That bureau was placed in charge of matters related to the rationalization of business operations under MITI's jurisdiction. In order to make this policy definite, MITI in December 1949 established the Industrial Rationalization Council. The first task taken up by this new council was rationalization of the steel and coal-mining industries. The aim was to promote rationalization in all aspects of the operation of these two industries, expected to form the foundation of a self-supporting industrial system. To this end, the government pledged all-out cooperation by securing funds for rationalization programmes and facilitating the import of machinery. Also, in order to press ahead vigorously with its programme of promoting rationalization, MITI, in cooperation with the Ministry of Finance, established and put into effect in March 1952 the Enterprise Rationalization Promotion Law. The law's objectives were 'to promote the rationalization of companies by encouraging the development of technology and swift modernization of the facilities of important industries, and by promoting, through guidance, the improvement of the product unit cost of raw materials and energy resources, thereby contributing to the self-supporting capabilities of the economy.' To that end, tax-reduction measures were introduced which subsequently played a major role in accelerating the modernization of production facilities.

The impact of the Korean War on rationalization efforts

The sudden emergence of the Korean War boom, however, worked to thwart positive efforts to achieve rationalization. Enterprises discovered that there was little need to proceed with rationalization by investing scarce financial resources in it to reduce costs. Ample demand existed without making such efforts, against a background of worldwide inflation where pressures of foreign competition receded. Although investments to expand manufacturing capacity increased, they did not necessarily have the effect of rationalizing operations. Vigorous investments were made in the textile, paper and pulp, and chemical industries, chiefly for coping with increased demand resulting from the rising purchasing power of consumers. Investment was particularly sluggish in the basic industries, attributed in part to their low capacity-utilization rate. The most important reason for sluggish investment, however, was the shortage of funds needed for long-term investment. In the US, long-term capital was raised primarily in the equities market, and the functions of banks were limited to providing short-term operating funds. SCAP regulated the Japanese financial market from that perspective, but the Japanese equities market was weak and rationalization did not progress as much as hoped.

Anticipating that the Korean War boom would eventually come to an end, and intent on creating a sound system of long-term financing, the Japanese government in March 1951 established the Japan Development Bank (JDB) to succeed the defunct Reconstruction Finance Bank with a view to 'promoting the reconstruction of the economy and the development of industry'. Table 3.2 shows the sources of funds for industrial equipment after independence. It is noteworthy that private financial institutions were responsible for more than half of the funds supplied.

As mentioned earlier, financial institutions were not subjected to the reform programmes carried out by SCAP. Ignoring the designs of SCAP, Japanese financial institutions played a central role in providing resources for equipment investment, supplemented by governmental funds, in the post-war process of restoring economic self-support. The distribution of funds, by industry, is shown in Table 3.3. The first point that attracts attention is the fact that the chemical industry consistently received the largest percentage of investment funds. As noted earlier, the government, in order to alleviate the food shortage, made efforts to restore the chemical fertilizer industry, and succeeded in swiftly restoring its output to pre-war levels. After the Korean War ended, however, and as low-priced ammonium sulphate from Western countries made inroads into Asian markets, the Japanese government in June 1954 enacted the Law Concerning Extraordinary Measures for Rationalization of the Ammonium Sulphate Industry and Ammonium Sulphate Export Adjustment, and implemented it with a view to reducing fertilizer prices through rationalization and obtaining foreign exchange by increasing fertilizer exports. Once into the 1960s, moreover, investment in the petrochemical industry began.

The second noteworthy point had to do with the steel industry. Although that industry's facilities expanded during the war, and although the industry was supported by measures such as subsidies to offset the cost–price disparity after the war, it failed to regain its relative position qualitatively, that is, in terms of technological excellence. In the First Rationalization Plan, which started in 1951, emphasis was placed on rolling mills. The industry received assistance in the form

Table 3.2 New sources of industrial equipment funds, fiscal years 1952–9 (unit: 100m. yen)

	1952	1953	1954	1955	1956	1957	1958	1959
Securities markets	1,028	1,137	458	398	1,880	1,777	1,561	2,900
	22.2%	20.4%	10.3%	8.0%	20.8%	17.3%	13.4%	19.4%
Private financial institutions	2,503	2,875	2,531	3,056	5,300	5,910	7,154	8,940
	54.1%	51.7%	56.8%	60.9%	58.8%	57.7%	61.2%	59.7%
Public funds	1,048	1,481	1,303	1,364	1,595	2,131	2,313	2,606
	22.7%	26.6%	29.2%	27.2%	17.7%	20.8%	19.8%	17.4%
of which JDB	460	871	575	494	455	637	596	687
	10.0%	15.7%	12.9%	9.9%	5.0%	6.2%	5.1%	4.6%
Foreign sources	46	68	165	197	240	430	654	524
	1.0%	1.3%	3.7%	3.9%	2.7%	4.2%	5.6%	3.5%
Total	4,625	5,561	4,457	5,015	9,015	10,248	11,682	14,970
	100.0%	100.0%	100.0%	100.0%	100.0%	100.0%	100.0%	100.0%

Notes: JDB loans do not include loans made in foreign currencies (1.4 bn. yen in fiscal year 1953, 5.7 bn. yen in fiscal year 1954, 6.4 bn. yen in fiscal year 1955, 4.0 bn. yen in fiscal year 1956, 8.5 bn. yen in fiscal year 1957, 26.7 bn. yen in fiscal year 1958, and 27.4 bn. yen in fiscal year 1959). The amounts of JDB loans of fiscal year 1952–3 do not include those financed by counterpart fund of US aid, and other (12.3 bn. yen for fiscal year 1952 and 1.5 bn. yen for fiscal year 1953).

Source: Japan Development Bank, *Kaigin Gyomu Geppo* (Monthly Report on Operations), no. 23.

Table 3.3 Net increases in industrial equipment investments, 1952–6 and 1957–60 (unit: 100 m. yen)

		1952–6	1957–60
Textiles	Industrial equipment investment	2,431	3,055
	Special depreciation	429	120
	Percentage	17.6%	3.9%
Chemicals	Industrial equipment investment	3,421	8,924
	Special depreciation	294	155
	Percentage	8.6%	1.7%
Iron and steel[a]	Industrial equipment investment	2,563	8,668
	Special depreciation	515	1,165
	Percentage	20.1%	13.4%
Machinery[b]	Industrial equipment investment	2,205	7,890
	Special depreciation	264	580
	Percentage	12.0%	7.4%
Mining	Industrial equipment investment	1,606	2,317
	Special depreciation	174	139
	Percentage	10.8%	6.0%
Total	Industrial equipment investment	12,226	30,854
	Special depreciation	1,676	2,159
	Percentage	13.7%	7.0%
Cars[c]	Industrial equipment investment	232	1,057
	Special depreciation	47	207
	Percentage	20.3%	19.6%

[a] Iron and steel includes non-ferrous metals.
[b] Machinery includes cars, electronics, etc.
[c] Information on cars not in the original table as included under machinery.

Sources: Industrial equipment investment figures are from *Nippon Kaihatsu Ginko 25-nen Shi* (25-Year History of the Japan Development Bank); special depreciation figures are from *Sangyo Gorika Hakusho* (White Paper on Industrial Rationalization).

of special depreciation and exemptions from import duties, but it did not invest such a large amount in blast furnaces. In the Second Rationalization Plan period that began in 1956, however, the demand for steel increased as the nation's industrial structure became increasingly more sophisticated. Against this background, and stimulated by newly developed technology, the construction of integrated iron and steel manufacturing plants was planned, which led to a sharply increased demand for investment funds.

The third point worthy of note was the rationalization of the machinery industry. During the pre-war years, the demand for machinery in Japan was satisfied almost exclusively by imports, and home-made products were regarded as low-grade products. During the wartime autarky, machinery production increased in quantitative terms, but there was little progress qualitatively and almost all superior machinery was imported. As discussed earlier, in the first half of the 1950s there was considerable recovery in some industries classified as part of the 'machinery' industry. Their primary products, however, consisted of consumer products such as bicycles, sewing machines, cameras, binoculars, and some processing machinery. It was considered that true rationalizaton and development of the machinery industries should provide a driving force in industrial development. To that end, the Law on Temporary Measures for the Promotion of Machinery Industries (Machinery Industries Law) was enacted in 1956. Aggressive equipment investments were made in the machinery industry, and their magnitude approached that of investments made in the chemical and steel industries.

Another related development was the promotion of small and medium enterprises. Deterioration of facilities and poor productivity were particularly pronounced in these enterprises. The post-war development of the machinery industry was restrained because it was inherently based on these enterprises, which by nature suffered from limitations related to their backwardness. Rationalization and productivity enhancement of smaller companies, therefore, was the most important task for industrial development. That, precisely, was one of the objectives of the Machinery Industries Law. This point will be discussed in more detail later.

In any event, technological innovation moved forward within the framework of the Second Rationalization Plan, and the words 'technological innovation' and 'automation' came to be widely used.

3.3. Formation of the Oligopolistic Competition Structure, and Enterprise Groups

The zaibatsu were dissolved after the war because they were regarded by some as monopolies. Some large corporations were also broken up by applying the Deconcentration Law, and cartels and trusts were strictly outlawed by applying the Anti-Monopoly Law, which some viewed as overly harsh. Subsequently, in the process of economic reconstruction and growth, excessive competition and business recession caused many companies to fail, delivering severe blows to the economy. This development resulted in exempting certain cartels, depending on the case, from the Anti-Monopoly Law. The business community, however, demanded relaxation of the exacting Anti-Monopoly Law in the interest of smoother economic development. As a result, the September 1953 amendment of the Anti-Monopoly Law was realized first after restoration of independence. The amendment permitted cooperative activities between companies to avert a recession or for rationalization, and the holding of shares between companies when the results did not limit competition.

By the end of the 1945–54 decade, the industrial structure of Japan had acquired a character markedly different from the competitive market structure envisaged by SCAP. In a word, the new order was oligopolistic, and the market behaviour therein could best be described as oligopolistically competitive. Specifically, each of the pre-war monopolies in the paper, steel, and shipbuilding industries was broken up into two or three companies, whose market power was considerably weakened. Furthermore, in the steel industry, Kawasaki Steel, Sumitomo Metal Industries, and others which had been ordinary steelmakers before the war joined the ranks of integrated steelmakers, further adding to the competitive pressure in the industry. Although new entrants intensified the competition, the number of companies in key industries ranged from two or three to ten at most, which fits the description of an oligopolistic market. As the centre of gravity of industrial activities shifted to heavy industry, requiring huge sums of money for equipment investment, the number of companies able to enter the market naturally became limited. Moreover, each company in an industry did not necessarily use the same set of technologies, and in some industries product designs varied considerably between companies. Because of the difficulty in raising investment funds as well as the nature of the products, a relatively small number of companies came to dominate each market, and fierce competition developed among these oligopolies. Even though the Anti-Monopoly Law was relaxed somewhat, cartelization among oligopolies was not allowed. As technology advanced rapidly, oligopolies engaged in fierce rivalry in importing new technologies. The basic order of the Japanese economy from the decade of 1955-64 and after could thus be best described as one of oligopolistic competition. This order generated the driving force for expanding industrial capacity.

On the one hand, the oligopolistic market structure was in danger of turning into monopoly, as witnessed in the beer industry. On the other hand, as was observed in the steel industry, steps were taken to lessen competition among the oligopolies. Thus, while the business community demanded further relaxation of the Anti-Monopoly Law, some industry observers advocated making the Anti-Monopoly Law tougher. Another distinctive characteristic to be noted with regard to oligopolistic competition was that oligopolistic companies competed not so much for larger profits as for gaining larger shares of the market. Table 3.4, for instance, uses market share as an indication of market concentration. In other words, the objective of business activities was securing and increasing market shares, although, of course, the results of these activities were measured by the size of profits. Dividends paid by Japanese oligopolies, however, did not accurately reflect the changed size of profits, which remained relatively stable over time. The greater portion of profits, including their variations, was retained internally for further investment in plant and equipment. Through this investment, companies introduced new technologies into their production systems, withstood competition, and managed to maintain and at times expand their market shares.

Enterprise groups and cross-shareholding

While an oligopolistic market structure was being formed, a corporate structure was in the making, which gave substance to the self-supporting industrial order of Japan. This new structure was generally called 'enterprise grouping'. An

Table 3.4 Share of output of major industries by leading manufacturers, 1955–1965 (unit: %)

		1955	1960	1965
Beer	Kirin Brewery	36.9	44.7	47.6
	Sapporo Breweries	31.4	26.1	25.2
	Asahi Breweries	31.7	27.2	23.1
	Suntory Ltd.	—	—	2.2
	Takara Shuzo	—	2.1	1.9
Nylon	Toray Industries	78.0	53.7	46.8
	Unitika	22.0	28.2	24.9
	Teijin	—	6.3	9.4
	Kanebo	—	7.4	8.9
	Toyobo	—	2.9	4.9
	Asahi Chemical Industry	—	1.2	4.6
Pig-iron	Yawata Steel	34.3	28.0	25.0
	Fuji Steel	31.5	31.0	24.0
	Nippon Kokan	17.8	14.1	13.9
	Kawasaki Steel	6.3	8.4	13.2
	Sumitomo Metal Industries	2.8	5.2	11.7
	Kobe Steel	2.9	8.1	6.6
Small cars	Toyota Motor	35.0	33.3	39.7
	Nissan Motor	35.8	41.9 ⎫	35.8
	Prince Motor	5.8	8.4 ⎭	
	Mazda Motor	—	—	6.6
	Mitsubishi Motors	—	4.8	5.5
	Isuzu Motors	9.1	5.9	4.8
	Hino Motors	14.2	5.2	4.2
Paper and Pulp	Oji Paper	8.4	13.0	16.0
	Jujo Paper	19.1	15.5	14.6
	Daishowa Paper Mfg.	7.4	8.0	10.3
	Kokusaku Pulp Industry	2.6	2.6	5.4
	Tohoku Pulp	2.9	3.7	4.4
	Honshu Paper	8.5	6.1	3.7
	Kanzaki Paper Mfg.	3.5	4.7	3.1
	Others	6.1	3.9	7.3
Ammonium sulphate	Ube Industries	12.0	8.5	12.7
	Toyo Koatsu Industries	17.9	16.1	12.1
	Toagosei Chemical Industry	3.6	7.0	10.7
	Nissan Chemical Industries	6.3	6.3	7.9
	Sumitomo Chemical	8.3	7.9	7.1
	Seitetsu Kagaku	6.5	6.0	6.3
	Showa Denko	13.0	9.9	6.2
	Nitto Chemical Industry	11.6	10.8	6.1
	Mitsubishi Kasei	6.2	6.6	5.7
	Nippon Suiso Kogyo	5.0	7.2	5.6

Note: Fuji Heavy Industries (0.4%) also produced small cars in 1960, as did Daihatsu Motor (2.0%) and Honda Motor (1.2%) in 1965.

Sources: *Toyo Keizai Tokei Geppo* (Toyo Keizai Monthly Statistics), June 1964, June 1967, and Aug. 1974.

enterprise group was formed around a former zaibatsu bank by a group of former zaibatsu corporations. Coordination among member companies in a group was attained through periodic meetings of their presidents. Representative clubs were the Kin'yokai (Friday Club) of the Mitsubishi group, Itsukakai (Fifth-of-the-Month Club, renamed the Nimokukai, or Second-Thursday-of-the-Month Club in 1965) of the Mitsui group, and the Hakusuikai (White Water Club) of the Sumitomo group. The activities of these clubs consisted of 'coordinating corporate policies within each group, formulating joint projects of the group, and deciding whether the use by a company of the former zaibatsu name be allowed, among others.'[1] The companies in the Mitsubishi, Mitsui, and Sumitomo groups, though they varied somewhat over time, were as follows.

Mitsubishi Kin'yokai Group (26 companies)
Mitsubishi Bank, Mitsubishi Trust & Banking, Mitsubishi Corporation, Mitsubishi Heavy Industries, Mitsubishi Mining, Mitsubishi Metal, Mitsubishi Electric, Mitsubishi Kasei, Asahi Glass, Mitsubishi Rayon, Mitsubishi Steel Mfg., Mitsubishi Oil, Nippon Yusen, Mitsubishi Paper Mills, Mitsubishi Cement, Mitsubishi Petrochemical, Mitsubishi Warehouse & Transportation, Mitsubishi Estate, Mitsubishi Kakoki, Mitsubishi Monsanto Chemical, Mitsubishi Edogawa Chemical, Mitsubishi Plastic Industries, Tokio Marine & Fire Insurance, Nippon Kogaku, Kirin Brewery, and Meiji Mutual Life Insurance

Mitsui Nimokukai Group (17 companies)
Mitsui Bank, Mitsui Trust & Banking, Taisho Marine & Fire Insurance, Mitsui Mutual Life Insurance, Mitsui & Co., Mitsui Mining, Mitsui Toatsu Chemicals, Toray Industries, Mitsui Petrochemical Industries, Mitsui Engineering & Shipbuilding, Mitsui OSK Lines, Mitsui Mining & Smelting, Mitsui Warehouse, Mitsui Real Estate Development, Sanki Engineering, Hokkaido Colliery & Steamship, and the Japan Steel Works

Sumitomo Hakusuikai Group (16 companies)
Sumitomo Bank, Sumitomo Trust & Banking, Sumitomo Life Insurance, Sumitomo Marine & Fire Insurance, Sumitomo Corporation, Sumitomo Metal Industries, Sumitomo Coal-Mining, Sumitomo Metal-Mining, Sumitomo Electric Industries, NEC, Sumitomo Chemical, Nippon Sheet Glass, Sumitomo Heavy Industries, Sumitomo Cement, Sumitomo Warehouse, and Sumitomo Realty & Development

As these lists clearly show, former zaibatsu-group companies were all represented. And, as mentioned, banks and other financial institutions formed the nuclei of these groups. As discussed earlier, these financial institutions survived the post-war reforms intact, and lent a helping hand to the member companies of the group when they needed large sums of long-term capital in the process of post-war rehabilitation and reconstruction, as well as after the formation of the groups. Another noteworthy point regarding the financial relationships among member companies of a group was the fact that they held each other's shares.

Although not all member companies held shares in all other members, financial institutions and trading companies, because of the nature of their businesses, generally established close relationships with member companies through this mechanism. It was safe to conclude, therefore, that the relationships of mutual dependency and cooperation among companies within these enterprise groups were rather significant. Herein lies one of the distinguishing characteristics of the Japanese industrial structure.

3.4. Dual Structure and Its Transformation

Small and medium enterprises, and the subcontracting system

Despite the decades of Japanese modernization since the turn of the century, small and medium enterprises were far more numerous in Japan than in the US and other Western nations. That their management and technology retained a great deal of pre-modern features was noted as early as in 1930. It was pointed out that this sector worked as an effective repository of surplus labour. Conversely, the argument went, this repository served as an ample source of cheap labour, working as a lever for the inroads of Japanese products into South-East Asia. Later, from the end of the 1930s, attention came to be focused on the subordinate relationships of smaller companies, in which companies were compelled to work under wretched conditions as subcontractors for parent manufacturers or wholesalers. During the post-war period of economic disruption, these subcontracting relationships broke down, allowing smaller companies to engage in unrestrained activities for a while. As reconstruction of the economy made headway, an increasing number of smaller companies again began working as subcontractors of parent manufacturing companies or wholesalers. To be successful in the fierce competition in their own markets, parent manufacturers pressured smaller subcontractors making parts for them to lower their unit prices. Smaller companies, under this cost pressure, could only provide extremely poor working conditions for their workers. Their financial health also being very shaky, many of them bankrupted in the mildest of recessions.

From around 1947, the government began to pay attention to this problem. In 1948, the Small and Medium Enterprise Agency was established as an external agency of the Ministry of Industry and Commerce. The purpose of the agency was to conduct comprehensive studies of the problems of smaller business companies, explore possible solutions, and formulate and implement policy measures for their solution. Recognizing that the most significant cause of bankruptcy of smaller companies was the shortage of funds, the government sought to improve their financial basis by establishing the People's Finance Corporation in June 1949 and the Small Business Finance Corporation in 1953.

The dual structure thesis

Once into the 1955–64 decade, the oligopolistic market structure discussed above was firmly established, and the economic growth of the country began to get under way spearheaded by large corporations. Once again, the problem of smaller companies began to attract serious attention in Japanese society. The impetus for this attention was provided by the 'dual structure thesis' propounded by the Economic White Paper for fiscal year 1957, which stated as follows.

Wage-rate differentials by size of company were substantial in Japan. The ratio of average wages of large corporations to that of small companies employing between ten and thirty employees was about 100:50, as compared to 100:90 or 100:80 in the US and other Western nations. In order to compete effectively in world markets, large Japanese corporations adopted advanced technology, enjoyed high labour productivity, and paid wages determined by collective bargaining. Workers who were left out of this modern sector, however, could find employment only in the small-business sector, where both productivity and wages were low. 'It is as though a dual structure consisting of an advanced nation and a developing nation existed side by side in one nation. The statement that Japan is an intermediately developed country should be understood in this sense.'[2]

How could the dual structure problem be solved? Protective measures were a possibility, but they would not be a viable solution inasmuch as they would impact adversely on the national economy. The only viable alternative was a policy of nurturing more strongly, organizing, and modernizing small and medium enterprises. Such was the conclusion reached by the policymakers of the times. The specific manifestation of that conclusion was found in such legislation as the Machinery Industries Law. According to a study made by the Fair Trade Commission (FTC) at the time, the subcontracting dependency percentages of representative manufacturing industries were 50 per cent for sewing machines, 40 per cent for textile goods, and between 20 per cent and 30 per cent for ships and machinery. 'The success of the shipbuilding industry in leading the world, as well as the remarkable growth in Japanese automobiles, owe much to the technological progress of their subcontractors.' The fiscal year 1957 Economic White Paper then concluded that 'the fact that large corporations are vying with each other to organize their subcontractors into vertical keiretsu groupings suggests that modernization of large corporations is no longer possible unless the parts subcontracting industry is fostered and strengthened.'[3]

From subcontracting to keiretsu

It appears that the White Paper of fiscal year 1957 was not particularly mindful of the difference between a subcontracting relationship and a vertical keiretsu relationship. The subcontracting relationship that existed in the pre-war and immediate post-war periods was a subordinate relationship of low-price subcontracting for manufacturing parts and processing products. If small subcontractors went bankrupt, the large manufacturer could simply find other subcontractors. As the industrial structure became increasingly more sophisticated and competition among major manufacturers became keener, however, not only prices but also product quality became important, and product standards became more rigid. Such developments required that the manufacturing processes of small subcontractors themselves be mechanized and rationalized. Parent manufacturers, therefore, found it necessary to provide technical and financial assistance to their subcontractors. They thus developed close working relationships, which came to be referred to as (vertical) *keiretsu* groupings and which were to produce marked changes in the traditional subcontracting relationships. Through these new relationships, modernization gained headway in the Japanese small-business sector. The products of smaller companies, as component parts of the products of large manufacturing corporations, came to acquire world-class competitiveness.

In the second half of the 1950s, MITI sought to develop small and medium enterprises as one of its policy objectives. In the early 1960s, moreover, the ministry took another step forward and began working towards the modernization or qualitative improvement of smaller companies. As a formal expression of this new policy stance, the ministry in 1963 established the Small and Medium Enterprise Basic Law. A look at the situation regarding the supply of industrial funds as an indication of their being a factor related to the policy of promoting small and medium enterprises, shows that the Japan Development Bank made loans to large corporations, the Small Business Finance Corporation tended to provide loans to medium-sized companies, and the People's Finance Corporation mainly financed the needs of small companies. As for the source of the funds provided by the Fiscal Investment and Loan Programme (FILP), in 1955 the Japan Development Bank received 30.5 billion yen while the two public loan and finance corporations for smaller businesses, between them, received 19.0 billion yen. In 1960, the comparable figures were 43.0 billion yen for the JDB and 60.5 billion yen—a sharply increased amount—for the two public loan and finance corporations for smaller businesses. This trend continued afterwards.

Characteristics of the dual structure

Lastly, two facts on the characteristics of the Japanese dual structure will be noted. The first has to do with profitability. It is generally believed that small and medium enterprises working as subcontractors for a large manufacturing firm, or being integrated into its keiretsu order, had to work with low contract prices imposed by the manufacturer, and therefore accept a low rate of profit. It is true that their ratio of profit to net sales tends to be low; ordinarily it is about one-half, on average, of that of larger companies. But regarding the rate of returns on total capital, differentials are not as great. This is because small and medium enterprises have a more favourable capital turnover rate which is about 1.5 times as high as that of larger companies. Thus, while it is true that smaller companies tend to be more susceptible to the adverse effects of business fluctuations and are

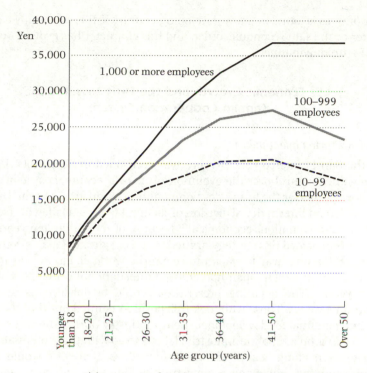

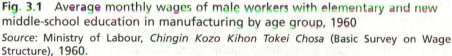

Fig. 3.1   Average monthly wages of male workers with elementary and new middle-school education in manufacturing by age group, 1960
Source: Ministry of Labour, *Chingin Kozo Kihon Tokei Chosa* (Basic Survey on Wage Structure), 1960.

more prone to bankruptcy during recessions, their profit rates are not as low as generally believed. The second point to be noted about smaller companies is the question of wage differentials. Smaller companies have the ability to maintain their tenacious existence by taking advantage of their low wages, said to be 50 or 60 per cent of those paid by larger companies. Upon closer examination, however, as Figure 3.1 shows, wage differentials for workers under 30 years of age are not so pronounced, in part because of the competition for younger workers in the labour market. Differentials widen only for workers 30 years or older. In the Japanese wage system, the length of service of employees is an important determinant of their wages. It so happens that the average length of service is greater in large companies than in smaller companies because the labour turnover is higher in smaller companies for various reasons. The reason for the widening wage differentials between large and small companies lies in this difference in the average length of service.

To be sure, the Japanese industrial structure has been, and still is, characterized by dualism. It is not, however, a coexistence of two dissimilar systems within an economy, as is found in many developing countries. It is essentially a dualistic character of the same economic order, and this character has evolved over many years in a unique manner.

3.5. Economic Growth and the Drift towards the Kanmin Cooperation System

Policy of nurturing infant industries

When the San Francisco Peace Treaty was concluded in September 1951 and Japan regained control over the evolution of its own economic system, it found two major options for the future development of its industrial system. One was a path based on an international division of labour. Japan had fallen far behind the advanced Western nations economically because of more than ten years of war. Those who advocated this strategy argued that, considering Japan's comparative advantages, the only way for Japan to rejoin the world economy was to rely on light industries in which Japan had enjoyed international competitiveness from pre-war years.[4] The opposing prescription could be labelled as an import-substitution strategy. Those who took this position pointed out that the country had built a potential for developing its heavy industry during the war years, and that it had an ample supply of industrial labour to go with that potential. A policy of development along heavy industrialization lines, therefore, would not only provide expanding employment opportunities but also induce a demand for products of related industries. Although this was an aggressive strategy that would temporarily require protective tariffs, it would bring the benefit of accelerating industrialization, increasing domestic demand, and nurturing the ability of domestic companies to compete effectively in the market place. This approach was also the position taken by MITI, whose policy objective was to foster domestic industry.[5]

From the above-mentioned perspective, MITI devoted its efforts to foster infant industries and emerging industries that were non-competitive but were considered important for the future development of the nation's industrial order. The targets for this policy were the motor-car, petrochemical, and synthetic fibre and other industries. Concerning the motor-car industry, after independence imports of cars were freed subject to the ceiling imposed by the foreign-exchange budget. With this change as a stimulus, a large number of foreign cars made inroads into Japan, facing little competition from domestic products. MITI considered nurturing the industry as a typical case of import-substitution policy, but automobile users such as taxi operators objected to the idea and favoured an import-promotion policy from the viewpoint of relatively high quality and low prices. In the end, however, the government decided on a policy of fostering the development of domestically made cars, and energetically encouraged the licensing of technology from foreign companies. Japanese car manufacturers vied with each other in forming technical tie-ups with small-car manufacturers in countries like the UK and France and sought to import design and manufacturing technologies.

A question arose as to how foreign direct investment in Japan by overseas companies should be handled. Some industrial leaders argued that Japan, which was suffering from a shortage of capital and low levels of technology, should aggressively seek foreign investment in Japan. Fearing the control of the management of Japanese companies by foreign capital, however, MITI decided to limit equity acquisition by foreign companies to 49 per cent of a company's capital. Furthermore, in consideration of the negative effects of foreign-exchange repatriation of income on the balance of payments, the cases of foreign direct investment approved through the decade of 1955–64 took the form of so-called 'yen-based investment', for which approval was granted on condition that no foreign-exchange repatriation of profits would be allowed. Under these conditions, Japanese industry pressed forward with its rationalization, imported foreign technology, and achieved rapid growth once into the 1955–64 decade, albeit with alternate periods of growth and stagnation. The Japanese government, and MITI in particular, played a leading role in this process.

Hunger for autonomous coordination

As noted earlier, a condition of oligopolistic competition developed from 1955, and enterprise groups began acquiring a greater voice in the formulation of economic policy. Leaders of Japanese industry became increasingly vocal in arguing that they should resist the encroachment of MITI's trade and industrial policy and be allowed to coordinate their actions autonomously. This trend was seen typically in the steel industry which was controlled by mammoth corporations. Being granted an exemption from duties on imported equipment, liberalized methods of calculating depreciation, and loans from the JDB, the steel industry had been the most favoured of all industries in MITI's trade and industrial policy. These favours were carried over to the Second Rationalization Plan formulated in 1955. In the meantime, however, the voice of the steel industry became noticeably stronger. A manifestation of this was found in the role played by the industry in the Open Sales System. Under this system, steelmakers reported to MITI their monthly production plans by product category along with their expected prices, and output was sold at published prices. Although production quantities and prices were determined in advance through informal consultations between steel industry executives and MITI officials, MITI had to attach considerable weight to the wishes of the industry. The voice of industrial circles grew steadily stronger, and at times it became critical of the MITI policies.

The industry, however, often faced situations where it required intervention by MITI. Autonomous coordination among large oligopolistic companies was often difficult in the environment of oligopolistic competition. In Japanese industry as elsewhere, the competitive theory of the survival of the fittest was at work in the long run. In the short run, however, various forms of coordination and adjustment took place. This coordinating function was provided by MITI during and immediately after the Occupation. Once into the 1955–64 decade, autonomous coordination among companies came to replace the coordinating function of MITI. The move that began in the early 1950s to relax the Anti-Monopoly Law was part of this trend. Autonomous coordination among companies, however, was difficult to achieve for decisions that might decisively affect their success or failure in their struggle for market share, e.g. decisions involving large investments in new equipment or importation of new technology. Representative cases in point were the construction of petrochemical plants and capital investment in the steel industry. The representatives of steel manufacturers discussed matters at meetings of the Japan Iron & Steel Federation. When mutual accommodations could not be worked out, the companies expected mediation by MITI, which often broke the impasse.[6]

Formation of the kanmin cooperation system

Out of frequent deadlocks in autonomous coordination and resulting requests for governmental mediation, a new relationship of cooperation between government and industry gradually emerged. In Japanese industry around 1960, even the largest of the oligopolistic companies could not compete effectively in international markets. It was thought, therefore, that engaging in fierce competition at home was not necessarily a desirable state for the healthy development of the national economy. MITI felt that coordination of some kind would be in order. Some industry leaders, fearing that voluntary coordination among companies might lead to a breach of the Anti-Monopoly Law, looked to MITI to provide necessary coordination. The kanmin cooperation system between government and business was born under these circumstances. In concrete terms, the system worked primarily through two channels. In the first channel, MITI expressed its preferences directly when it provided, through public loan and finance institutions such as the Japan Development Bank, funds to industry for consolidating manufacturing capabilities or developing new domestic technology. Using such funds as basic loans, MITI also obtained the cooperation of private financial institutions in providing participation loans to manufacturing companies. Using these loans as levers, MITI sought to give substance to the kanmin system of industrial cooperation.

The second channel of the kanmin cooperation system was the advisory council system. The various roles played by the Industrial Rationalization Council were discussed earlier. Until about 1955, the government posed a problem to an appropriate advisory council, provided the council with background material necessary for deliberation and with an outline of its proposed policy measures, and requested a report on the problem. It was customary of a council to submit a report containing recommendations. This type of reporting remained predominant in subsequent years. On some questions for which there was no broad agreement in a particular industry, however, the 'inquiry' became less specific, and the report of the advisory council or its recommendations often became quite important in shaping MITI's subsequent policy. An advisory council usually consists of representatives of the relevant industry and 'persons of learning and experience' (academics, journalists, former bureaucrats, etc.). It is supported by an appropriate bureau or section of the ministry which serves as its secretariat. MITI provides relevant materials to the council and indicates its proposed policy. The industry representatives state their views on the proposed policy, the 'persons of learning and experience' reconcile the differences, and the ministry officials make the final arrangement. This process is generally used for deliberations in all advisory councils. The largest and most influential council attached to MITI is the Industrial Structure Council, created in 1964 by merging the Industrial Structure Advisory Committee and the Industrial Rationalization Council. Within the council, committees are established as needed. Advisory councils and their committees have worked to build consensus within an industry and between industry and government, functioning as an effective institution for government–industry cooperation and coordination.

NOTES

1. Yoshikazu Miyazaki, *Sengo Nihon no Kigyo Shudan* (Enterprise Grouping in Post-War Japan), Nihon Keizai Shimbun, Inc., 1976: 61.
2. Economic Planning Agency (ed.), *Keizai Hakusho* (Economic Survey of Japan), 1957, Printing Bureau, Ministry of Finance (MOF). Some economic development theorists in those days interpreted the phenomenon of underdevelopment as essentially constituting a dual structure consisting of a modern sector and a traditional, pre-modern sector. The Economic Survey of Japan based its argument on this theory, which was in error. Whereas a wide gap existed between the two sectors in developing countries, the small-business sector in Japan—although not without some remnants of pre-modernity—constituted an integral part of the modern economy.
3. Ibid.
4. The most influential of the advocates of this position was Naoto Ichimada, then governor of the Bank of Japan. Concerning the car industry, Ichimada argued from the perspective of exporting that 'Japan should follow the principle of international division of labour; it is meaningless for it to foster the development of a car industry.' When Kawasaki Steel sought financing from the World Bank to build its Chiba Plant, Ichimada opposed it saying 'The plant will be dilapidated, with nothing but weeds on the site.'
5. This so-called infant-industry argument was not without controversy among Japanese economists. See Takashi Negishi, *Boeki Rieki to Kokusai Shushi* (The Gains from Trade and the International Balance of Payments), Sobunsha, 1971.
6. Teizo Horikoshi, secretary-general of Federation of Economic Organizations (Keizai Dantai Rengokai; Keidanren), wrote as follows: 'It is an unfortunate fact that quite a few industries are incapable of working out autonomous accommodation. It appears that mediation by a third party is a necessity, especially in problems involving plant and equipment investment', *Nihon Keizai to Shin Sangyo Taisei* (The Japanese Economy and the New Industrial Order), Toyo Keizai Inc., 1962.

4

Economic Growth and the Industrial Order

4.1. Economic Growth and the Economic Plan

The tide of economic growth

From the end of 1958, business recovery forged ahead in Japan. This new phase of expansion, called the Iwato Boom, lasted for three and a half years, until the first half of 1962.[1] The growth rate of the economy, which was at a relatively moderate level of 9.2 per cent in 1959, exceeded 10 per cent thereafter, recording 13.1 per cent in 1960 and 11.6 per cent in 1961. Business activities subsequently fell off in 1962, and the growth rate dropped to 8.7 per cent in 1962 and 8.4 per cent in 1963. Business picked up again in 1964, and once again the growth rate exceeded 10 per cent. Business expansion in 1964, however, was referred to as 'prosperity without the feeling of a boom', because it was not as robust as the Iwato Boom. In 1965, the growth rate fell to 5.8 per cent, prompting many observers to argue that the structure of the Japanese economy's high-level growth had reached its limits and the economy had entered a phase of 'structural depression', or economic anaemia of a systemic nature. Once into 1966, however, business recovered. In fact, the new period of prosperity lasted nearly five years. The growth rate of the economy was 10.4 per cent in 1966, 11.0 per cent in 1967, 12.2 per cent in 1968, and 12.1 per cent in 1969. Because the scale of this boom exceeded that of the Iwato Boom, it was called the Izanagi Boom, or the greatest economic boom 'since the era of Izanagi'. It was a reference to the legend of Izanagi in Japanese mythology, which is even more ancient than the Iwato legend. Inasmuch as the economy expanded rapidly during almost the entire 1960s, the decade was called the 'era of high growth'. In 1965 prices, gross national per capita expenditure in real terms rose from 211,000 yen in 1960 to 326,000 yen in 1965 and further to 545,000 yen in 1970, a 2.6-fold increase in ten years. As will be discussed later, the actual rate of growth exceeded the target growth rate of the National Income Doubling Plan which the government had announced in 1960.

The government economic plan

Before examining the factors that were responsible for the remarkable growth of the 1960s, it is good to review briefly the role played by the government economic plan mentioned above. One major characteristic of the economic policy of the

Japanese government is that it formulates an economic plan—often for a five-year period—on which it then bases the conduct of its economic policy. The first of such plans was the Five-Year Plan for Economic Self-Support formulated in December 1955. This plan, however, was revised after only two years, into the New Long-Term Economic Plan. The following review refers to the latter and the three subsequent plans. These four plans were all implemented during the era of high growth (Table 4.1).

The New Long-Term Economic Plan drawn up towards the end of 1957 was a five-year plan covering the period 1958–62. Although the plan aimed for 'maximizing growth', its target growth rate was set at 6.5 per cent, partly because the economy was in the early stage of the lingering recession of 1957–8 known as the recession shaped like the 'bottom of a frying pan'. As it turned out, the economy grew an average of 10 per cent annually during the plan period. Full employment, one of the objectives of the plan, was also achieved, with the rate of wholly unemployed workers remaining at a low 1.3 per cent. When Prime Minister Hayato Ikeda formed his new government in July 1960, the economy was in the midst of the Iwato Boom. The Japanese political scene, however, was in the midst of turmoil created by the controversy over the revision of the US–Japan Security Treaty. In that situation, the new Ikeda Cabinet launched a National Income-Doubling Plan covering the ten-year period from 1961 to 1970, with its primary aim being social stability. The plan called for doubling gross national product in ten years—a rather ambitious target in those days—which required an annual growth rate of 7.8 per cent. Actual performance, however, was over 10 per cent, exceeding the target rate by a wide margin. The Medium-Term Economic Plan drawn up in 1964 by the new government of Prime Minister Eisaku Sato aimed at 'correcting distortions', especially because of widespread talk about 'structural depression' and the end of the period of high-level growth. Although business turned downward, however, it soon picked up again, and economic growth resumed at rates exceeding 10 per cent. A revision of the medium-term economic plan became necessary, and an Economic and Social Development Plan was put into effect from fiscal year 1967. Actual growth, which averaged over 10 per cent per year, consistently surpassed planned rates.

Not everything, however, proceeded smoothly, partly because actual growth was faster than planned and consumer prices rose more quickly than projected, although wholesale prices remained stable. The Medium-Term Economic Plan projected consumer price increases at an annual average rate of about 2.5 per cent; the actual rate of 5.0 per cent was much higher than planned. A similar rate of inflation was recorded during the period of the Economic and Social Development Plan, which started in 1967.

The actual work of formulating plans was done by the Economic Council. The membership of the council, which varied somewhat from period to period, was large and comprehensive. Authorities from universities, business, and research institutions participated as regular members, joined by directors-general and directors of research divisions of various ministries and agencies who served as

Table 4.1 Government economic plans

	New Long-Term Economic Plan	National Income-Doubling Plan	Medium-Term Economic Plan	Economic and Social Development Plan
Date drawn up	December 1957 (Aug.–Nov. 1957)	December 1960 (Nov. 1959–Nov. 1960)	January 1965 (Jan.–Nov. 1964)	March 1967 (May 1966–Feb. 1967)
Prime Minister	Kishi	Ikeda	Sato	Sato
Plan period (fiscal years)	1958–62 (5 years)	1961–70 (10 years)	1964–8 (5 years)	1967–71 (5 years)
Plan objectives	Maximizing growth Improving quality of national life Full employment	Same as in preceding plan	Correcting distortions	Attaining balanced, enriched economy and society
Real GNP growth rate				
Planned	6.5%	7.8%	8.1%	8.2%
Actual	10.0%	10.3%	10.4%	10.0%
Unemployment rate				
Planned	—	—	—	—
Actual	1.3%	1.2%	1.1%	1.3%

Increase rate in consumer prices				
Planned	—	—	Average annual rate of about 2.5% during period	About 3% by end of period
Actual	3.4%	5.7%	5.0%	5.7%
Current-account balance at end of period				
Planned	$150 m.	$180 m.	$0 m.	$1.45 bn.
Actual	–$20 m.	$2.35 bn.	$1.47 bn.	$6.32 bn.

Notes:

1. Actual GNP growth rates are based on new SNA (System of National Account of United Nations; calendar year 1980 = 100).

2. Rates of increase in consumer prices are in terms of a comprehensive index exclusive of prices for one's own home.

3. Because each new Cabinet formulated a new economic plan, plan periods diverged considerably from actual periods.

4. Months in parentheses shown after 'date drawn up' indicate periods of work on plan formulation.

Source: Economic Planning Agency, *Keizai Yoran* (Handbook of Economic Statistics).

specialist members and committee staff. The responsible ministries and agencies submitted material for discussion to the council, and discussions took place in the committees and subcommittees. Reports drafted by the staff and others were studied and revised by the parties concerned before submission to specialized committees of the council. They were then revised further before submission to the Coordination Committee of the council, which in turn submitted them to the plenary meeting of the council for formal adoption. The process took nearly a year.

The role of economic plans

There are differences of opinion concerning the importance of the role economic planning played in the actual process of economic growth in Japan. As the above shows, plans were gradually formulated by seeking the counsel of many people, but actual performance often diverged markedly from plan targets. The least charitable view is that plans were simply window-dressing for government policy, intended primarily for foreign nations. More commonly, however, planning is regarded highly as having indicated to corporations and other economic entities the direction of development by demonstrating to the industries the overall framework of economic growth. In fact, during the 1960s many large corporations regarded national economic plans as the basis for their own investment plans, and carried out investment programmes exceeding the pace of national plans in order to gain the advantage over competitors. These efforts produced actual growth that surpassed plan projections.

At any rate, corporations invested vigorously because they knew that their investments were required when enhanced productivity was essential for competing in domestic and overseas markets in the era of increasingly vocal demands internationally for Japan's foreign-trade liberalization. Also, markets expanded with the increased production generated by these investment activities. Of course, the market expansion was attributable in part to the increased demand for producer goods generated by the intensified investment activities, but the positive effect of the increase in the purchasing power of consumers should not be overlooked. These points are examined below.

Unfolding of high growth

Inconsistent with the economic plans, the Japanese economy began to grow rapidly from 1959. Buttressed by the National Income Doubling Plan of 1960, the economy raced forward at a high pace through 1970, with only 1964 and 1965 showing any slowdown. As Tables 1.2 and 1.3 show, the Japanese economy grew at an annual average rate in excess of 10 per cent during the period 1959 until 1968, and in 1970 Japan's GNP became the second highest in the free world next to that of the US.

What factors made such rapid growth possible? To answer this question, three factors must be examined: productivity, or technology; the capital to make the use of technology possible; and the sales of the products produced. Regarding technology, as was pointed out earlier, a rationalization policy was implemented from about 1955, when advanced facilities such as transfer machinery were installed and put into operation. In 1956, the Machinery Industry Promotion Law—which focused on small and medium enterprises—was enacted, and the machinery industry, which lagged in development, began to make strides. Moreover, in approving the licensing of foreign technology, the major source of high technology, MITI was guided by the principle of equal opportunity to all companies. A typical example of this equal treatment was in the importation of computer technology. MITI negotiated with IBM Corporation, for instance, to have them grant a patent licence to every Japanese firm that wanted to enter the industry.

The fact that new technology was introduced to Japan without preferential treatment helped intensify interfirm rivalry, and made the securing of funds for fixed capital investment that much more urgent. Companies, however, did not have adequate funds. Funds were supplied largely by so-called main banks, although the role of over-loans cannot be ignored. Companies sought funds from city banks for their ambitious investment programmes. City banks, in turn, relied heavily on credit created by the Bank of Japan through an 'over-loan' mechanism, as well as on-call loans from regional banks, to cover their chronic shortage of funds. It is safe to say that the role of the over-loan mechanism is unique to the Japanese financial system. In any event, corporations raised much of their investment funds indirectly, i.e. through loans from banks rather than through capital markets. In 1965, external liabilities accounted for 55.7 per cent of funds raised by corporations; in other words, corporations operated on borrowed money. In a way, however, external funding was more advantageous than internal funding because interest paid on borrowed funds was a deductible expense for corporate tax purposes. Corporations achieved their rapid growth by raising funds for capital investment in this manner.

Concerning markets, the home electric appliances and automobile industries were representative industries that showed remarkable growth during the high-growth era. Wages rose in the course of high growth, and a rising trend in the prices of agricultural products raised farming household income. As a result, domestic purchasing power increased rapidly, leading to a demand for home electric appliances and cars. Production rose rapidly, however, and domestic purchasing power was not able to provide sufficient demand to absorb the increased supply. From 1965 in particular, the excess supply was directed at overseas markets, and exports rose sharply (Table 4.2). The drive for the increase in exports was the enhanced productivity made possible by new technology, as mentioned above, and the improved international competitiveness brought about by that productivity.

The next question is the relationship between high growth and international trade and industrial policy. There are three alternative views on this question: (1) policy played an important role, making high growth possible; (2) competition in the market place was the primary factor; policy intervention, if anything, had an

Table 4.2 Trends in Japan's balance of payments: 1953–1970 (units: $1 m.; annual ave.)

	Period of attaining self-support 1953–7	Period of high growth and transition to open economy 1958–64	Period of high growth 1965–70
Trade balance	−360	151	2,588
(Exports)	(2,041)	(4,480)	(12,601)
(Imports)	(2,401)	(4,329)	(10,013)
Services	211	−304	−1,239
Unrequited transfers	12	−64	−160
Current balance	−137	−217	1,189
Long-term capital	23	116	−670
Basic balance	−114	−101	519
Short-term capital, errors and omissions	33	85	303
Overall balance	−81	−16	822

Source: Bank of Japan, *Kokusai Shushi Tokei Geppo* (Balance of Payments Monthly). Figures for years before 1961 are estimates by the Domestic Research Division of the Economic Planning Agency.

adverse effect on growth (this view emphasizes successful development of the competitive system); and (3) high growth resulted from optimum interaction between policy and market competition. Judging from available information regarding the circumstances at the time, it seems appropriate to accept the third position, which leans somewhat towards the first.

4.2. Workers and Economic Growth

From labour surplus to labour shortage

Japan had been plagued with the problem of a labour surplus since before the war. A large population on a limited land area was the primary source of the problem, and in fact was the main factor leading to pre-war Japan's political and military expansion into East Asia. After the war, when Japan lost its former colonies and there was an influx of repatriates from East Asia and elsewhere, the surplus of labour became a more serious problem. But overpopulation and attendant low wages and low income, along with the paucity of natural resources, were accepted as Japan's fate. The agriculture and small-business sectors became repositories of excess population, and workers in these sectors were even regarded as underemployed. In part because of the post-war chaos, the size of the working population was roughly balanced between the agriculture and forestry sectors and the rest of the economy until about 1950. From the pre-war years until immediately after the war, the number of farming households remained unchanged at about 4.5 million. The great majority of these households had very small farms, averaging 1 hectare. The general pattern was that the eldest son took over the farm, and younger sons left farming and moved to the cities to find work.

Economic growth, however, rapidly changed this pattern. First, as industrialization progressed in the course of restoring economic self-sufficiency, the demand for young workers increased, inducing an outflow from rural areas of not only younger sons but also eldest sons. From the beginning of the 1960s, eldest sons and even their fathers began seeking work in the cities. Agriculture became increasingly mechanized, and farming acquired the characteristics of what was called '3-chan farming', or farming by *jiichan*, *baachan*, and *kaachan* (grandpa, grandma, and mama).

Table 4.3 shows population changes and changes in the labour force from 1955 to 1970. During those fifteen years, Japan's population increased by about 15 million and the labour force increased by 10 million. Workers in agriculture and forestry, however, decreased by more than 6 million (43 per cent), whereas workers in non-agricultural industries increased by more than 16 million. Moreover, post-war land reform succeeded in raising farming income, one result of which was that rural areas no longer served as reservoirs of surplus labour. Also, as will be seen below, the standard of living of non-agricultural workers rose sharply. Although there were still remnants of underemployment in villages and in the small-business sector around 1955, those traces completely disappeared after Japan entered the high-growth period from 1960. With an index of 100 for 1960, real wages of workers rose to 120 in 1965 and to 180 in 1970. And as labour shortages developed, the disparity in wages between large (1,000 or more

Table 4.3 Labour force: 1955–1970 (unit: 10,000 persons)

	1955	1960	1965	1970
Total population	8,906	9,326	9,803	10,357
Population 15 years old and over	5,925	6,520	7,287	7,885
Labour force	4,194	4,511	4,787	5,153
Unemployed	105	75	57	59
Agriculture and forestry	1,478	1,273	1,046	842
Self-employed workers	491	456	394	363
Family workers	913	723	593	451
Employees	74	94	59	29
Non agricultural industries	2,612	3,164	3,684	4,251
Self-employed workers	537	550	545	614
Family workers	371	338	322	354
Employees	1,704	2,276	2,817	3,277
Ratio of unemployed in labour force	2.5	1.7	1.2	1.1

Source: Statistics Bureau, Prime Minister's Office, *Rodoryoku Chosa Hokoku* (Labour Force Survey).

employees) and small companies (30–99 employees), measured as the ratio of wages paid by small companies to those paid by large companies, increased from lows of 49 in 1955 and 52 in 1960 to 64 in 1965.

Labour–management relations in Japan

The principal factor behind the rise in wages in post-war Japan was the labour movement. Labour unions began practising *Shunto* ('spring labour offensive') wage negotiations from 1955.[2] Although the rate of annual wage increases won in agreements during shunto negotiations differed according to the business situation in each particular year, it was as high as 13.8 per cent in 1961 during the Iwato Boom and climbed to 18.5 per cent in 1970 during the Izanagi Boom.

The labour–management relations at the base of the Japanese industrial system have two distinct characteristics not found in Western countries. First, the class distinction between labour and management lost most of its relevance after the war. The post-war dissolution of the zaibatsu, the imposition of the Capital Levy Tax, and other changes in the tax system had the effect of nearly destroying Japan's capitalist class. Today, the power of control in large Japanese corporations resides not with stockholders but with senior executives who have risen from the ranks of ordinary employees. Second, in post-war Japan the status distinction between white-collar and blue-collar employees virtually disappeared. Labour unions in Japan are organizations for all employees, and white-collar employees hold union membership until they assume managerial positions of section manager rank (*kacho*) or above. Since senior executives rise through the ranks, both labour and management essentially constitute a continuum in a Japanese corporation. The Japanese class system was virtually dissolved when the Meiji Restoration of 1868 destroyed feudalism, and people in the lower strata of society were encouraged to make the effort to improve their status, with education playing a major role in providing the channel for upward mobility. Japanese society was democratized after the war, and viewed from international standards Japan today can be called an egalitarian society with little class distinction.

In post-war Japan, an increasing number of young people continued in school beyond the nine years of compulsory education. In 1965, for instance, 95 per cent of junior-high-school graduates advanced to senior high school (grades 10, 11, and 12). Around the same time, the jobs of industrial workers were coming to require so much technical skill that those workers came to be referred to as 'grey-collar' workers. Today, the introduction of new technology meets virtually no resistance from these workers. Moreover, since long-term employment relationships are common in Japanese companies, as suggested by the term 'lifetime employment', workers are not laid off when new technology is introduced, as is frequently done in the US and other Western countries. Instead, workers are usually retrained in their techniques, and if it is impossible to use them there, they are transferred to other sections within the same company, with dismissals being avoided as far as possible. The legendary hard work of Japanese employees and

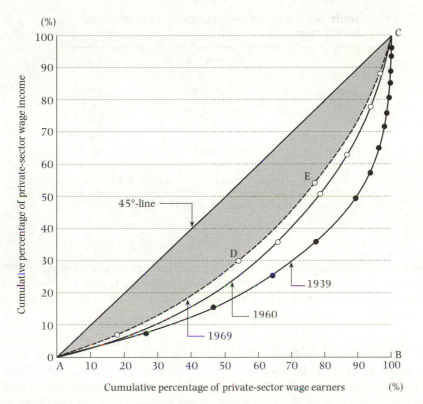

Fig. 4.1 Lorenz curves showing equalization of private-sector wage income, 1939–1969

Notes:
1. Prepared from Ministry of Finance, *Zaisei Kin'yu Tokei Geppo* (Monthly Statistics of Government Finances and Banking) and National Tax Administration Agency, *Minkan Kyuyo Jittai Chosa* (Study on Private-Sector Wages).
2. Figures for 1939 were for income of taxpayers, including proprietors' income and public-sector wages.
3. Gini coefficients are represented by ratio of area ADEC and area ABC.

their loyalty to their employers are related closely to these employment practices and human relations in the workplace.

Another important characteristic of labour–management relations in Japan today is the small disparity in wage income between the lowest and highest levels of employees. This reflects the nature of the relationships among employees as described above. Figure 4.1 shows the change in the Lorenz curves for private-sector wage income from before the war to 1969. Since 1939, the Lorenz curve has come closer to the 45-degree line, which indicates perfect equality. The attendant decline in the Gini coefficient signifies that the distribution of income

Table 4.4 International comparison of personal saving rates

	1952–60	1961–70
Japan	15.5%	19.2%
USA	7.3	6.7
UK	4.6	7.9
W. Germany	12.4	14.5
France	6.0	10.4

Source: Bank of Japan, Statistics Department, *Nihon Keizai wo Chushin to Suru Kokusai Hikaku Tokei* (Comparative Economic and Financial Statistics, Japan and Other Major Countries), 1965, 1971, and 1972.

has become more equal. Around 1970, Japan had one of the most equal distributions of income in the world. Partly for that reason, surveys at the time reported that 70 per cent of Japanese considered themselves members of the middle class. Japan became an extremely stable society.

The high rate of personal savings and its economic functions

Another aspect of the Japanese economy is the high rate of personal savings. As Table 4.4 shows, the personal savings rate in Japan is extremely high, reaching the 15–20 per cent level. According to many studies, the most frequently mentioned reason for the high savings rate is the desire to be prepared for unforeseen expenses related to sickness or disaster. The other reasons are for buying a house, preparing for education or marriage of children, and for old age. Regardless of the reason for saving, the most convenient means of saving for the Japanese is postal savings. In fact, deposits by ordinary citizens in postal savings are the main sources of funds for the Fiscal Investment and Loan Programme (FILP) of the Ministry of Finance. FILP funds are channelled to strategic public and private investment projects. Besides the post office, private-sector financial institutions, unlike in pre-war years, also invite savings from ordinary people. And in the high-growth process, ordinary citizens came to show much interest in equity markets. Personal savings thus increased steadily with these functions.

4.3. From Trade Liberalization to Capital Liberalization

Progress in trade liberalization

The world economic system after the Second World War was basically oriented towards liberalization of international trade. In 1955, when Japan joined the General Agreement on Tariffs and Trade (GATT), a representative agreement embodying that orientation, the liberalization ratio of its imports was only 16 per cent. With abundant and low-cost labour, Japan inevitably specialized in labour-intensive products, and its exports after the war in fact consisted largely of textile products and sundry goods. Those products, however, had a low income elasticity of demand. Therefore, if Japan were to follow the principle of comparative advantage, it would be locked into specialization in light-industry products whose future prospects were dim. When Japan made efforts to upgrade its industrial structure in the post-war period by leaning increasingly towards the chemical and heavy industries, international trade liberalization became a crucial question for its economy. As discussed earlier, MITI adopted a policy of protecting infant Japanese industries in the process of re-establishing the nation's economic self-sufficiency, protected the automobile and many other industries, and nurtured high-tech industries. From MITI's viewpoint, the infant industries were characterized by small-scale operations which could not compete effectively in world markets. Industries such as textiles, on the other hand, which were more or less competitive, were engaged in 'excessive competition' in world markets. One group needed protection, therefore, and the other needed regulation. MITI felt that transition to a system of free trade was premature and would harm the economy.

Once past the mid-1950s, however, Japan began to experience surpluses in its international balance of payments, and external pressures demanding Japan's trade liberalization grew stronger, especially from the US. The Japanese government launched its trade liberalization programme in June 1960, when Japan's liberalization percentage was roughly 40 per cent, by adopting the Outline of the Liberalization Plan for Foreign Trade and Foreign Exchange. This was adopted because it became increasingly necessary to take advantage of less expensive overseas resources through trade liberalization. Also, MITI became keenly aware of the need to open Japan's closed economic system, which was suppressing the increase in efficiency in economic activities. It wanted to contain the proliferation of very small companies, end the preservation of inefficient marginal firms, and rationalize business operations. The government thus launched a programme for raising the liberalization percentage to 90 per cent in three years. The programme progressed steadily, and liberalization reached 89 per cent in 1963. Next, in April 1964, Japan accepted the obligation of Article 8 of the International Monetary Fund. By becoming a member of the Organization for Economic Cooperation and Development (OECD), Japan formally became a member of the international economic community, and its economy became more open. The trend continued, and in 1965 the import of cars was liberalized.[3] The progress came to a stop at that point, however, and liberalization of remaining products stagnated. Liberalization of agricultural products, in particular, made virtually no progress, and became a source of trade friction between Japan and the US.

The question of capital liberalization

Membership of the OECD required a commitment to liberalize capital flows. MITI, however, saw a problem on this point relating to implementation of its policies.

That was the question of whether Japanese companies, with their scale of operation and capital size, could compete internationally under conditions of free capital flows. In that context, the ministry submitted the Draft Law on Provisional Measures for the Promotion of Specified Industries (Specified Promotion Bill) to the Diet. The proposed law was to designate cars, petrochemicals, special steels, and others as specified industries. With requests from their respective trade associations for designation as important industries whose competitiveness needed strengthening, MITI would then implement measures for mergers and other rationalization programmes, and support the industries with tax exemptions and special financing, thereby improving the ability of companies in these industries to compete with foreign firms. The proposal, however, met with severe criticism from industrial leaders—particularly in the banking community—who favoured deregulation, as an attempt to reconstruct the kanmin kyocho system (see below) of close public–private cooperation. In the end, the bill never came to a vote. This episode suggests that the business community was gaining confidence in its ability to deal, by its own devices, with trade liberalization and eventually even the liberalization of capital flows.

Nonetheless, it was not without reason that MITI was concerned with capital liberalization. In the 1960s, US capital dominated world markets. Concerning the motor-vehicle industry, for example, in the mid-1960s three US companies or their subsidiaries—Ford Motor, Vauxhall (General Motors), and Rootes Motors (Chrysler)—controlled over half the car production in the UK. In West Germany, Opel (General Motors) and Ford Motor produced one-third of all motor vehicles, and their share continued rising afterwards. In the computer industry, General Electric acquired Machines Bull of France and the computer division of Italy's Olivetti in 1964, and IBM totally dominated the West German market. The only indigenous West European company manufacturing computers was ICL of Britain. MITI could not view the situation lightly, because it sought at the time to nurture the car and computer industries as the leading industries of Japan.

Liberalization of capital flows

According to the Law Concerning Foreign Capital (Foreign Capital Law) of 1950, foreign investment was recognized only if it did not interfere with the autonomy of management in Japanese companies and contributed to the introduction of technology to Japan. That represented the extent of approval possible by the Bank of Japan. If the Minister of Finance granted approval, however, applications for acquiring 15 per cent or more of a company's equity stock acquisitions were allowed. In practice, however, there was not a single case of such validation, and there were no joint ventures with foreign capital holding 50 per cent or more of the equity of a company. So the regulation of capital inflows was severe. This situation applied to investment in foreign currencies. In terms of yen-based investments, however, IBM established IBM Japan and Coca-Cola established Coca-Cola (Japan). Fuji Xerox, Caterpillar-Mitsubishi, and other joint ventures were 50 per cent owned by foreign capital, but many more foreign investors had holdings of 49 per cent or less in companies they invested in. The first round in the programme of liberalizing foreign investment was initiated in 1967, and the system of automatic validation of direct investment was introduced. Further, the second and third rounds of the liberalization programme were announced in 1969 and 1970. Perhaps because the 'liberalized' industries were not attractive to foreign investors, investments in them did not cause much unrest in Japanese industrial circles. The automobile industry was liberalized in 1971, but because the domestic industry had already been well established there was not much room for foreign investors to make serious inroads into the market. In the fourth round of liberalization announced in 1971, 100 per cent investment became free as a rule, and the liberalization of capital flows became nearly total (Table 4.5). Since the liberalization of foreign investment was implemented according to a clearly stated schedule as described above, Japanese companies had ample time to modernize their facilities to meet competition with foreign investors and strengthen their competitiveness. In part because of this, and in part because foreign investors were not familiar with Japanese-style management, the share of foreign-affiliated firms in the Japanese economy remained small. At the beginning of 1970, their share in terms of sales was less than 2 per cent. In this sense, although the liberalization of foreign investment acted as a catalyst for modernizing Japanese industry, it did not have as much impact on the Japanese economy as trade liberalization. It might be said that Japanese industry had become strong enough to withstand the inroads of foreign capital.

4.4. The Development of Domestic and International Distribution Systems

Once into the 1960s, Japanese industry continued to grow at a fast pace. As for international affairs, trade liberalization was followed by liberalization of capital flows, and the standard of living of the people became correspondingly higher. How did the system of distribution that linked the productive machine with consumers respond to the changing conditions? Since the matter of the distribution process has seldom been mentioned above, this Section will examine in some detail the characteristics of the Japanese domestic distribution system—small and very small retailers and wholesalers—and the general trading companies, which play an important role in international trade.[4]

Retailers as key players in domestic trade

Commerce which takes charge of domestic distribution in Japan is handled overwhelmingly by small or very small establishments. Retailing, in particular, is the realm of very small stores. As Table 4.6 shows, 71 per cent of retailers in 1960 had one or two persons, and 19 per cent had three or four persons; in other words, 90 per cent of retailers were very small business establishments. Subsequently,

Table 4.5　Capital liberalization programmes in terms of number of liberalized industries

	Establishing new company			Acquiring shares in existing company		
	Non-liberalized industries	Industries with acquisitions limited to 50% equity	Industries with acquisitions up to 100% equity permitted	By one foreign investor	By all foreign investors	
					Non-resricted industries	Restricted industries
Prior to first round	All			5% or less	15% or less	10% or less
First round (July 1967)		33	17	7% or less	20% or less	15% or less
Second round (March 1969)		160	44	ditto	ditto	ditto
Third round (September 1970)		447	77	ditto	less than 25%	ditto
Cars (April 1971)		453	77	ditto	ditto	ditto
Fourth round (August 1971)	7	Free as rule/2	228	less than 10%	ditto	ditto

Notes:
1. 19 industries including banking and electric power.
2. Starting in this round, foreign investment in new companies with up to 50% equity became free as a rule, and the method was changed to listing the exceptional cases of non-liberalized industries which required case-by-case review.

Source: Compiled from MITI, *Tsusho Hakusho 1973* (White Paper on Japan's International Trade, 1973), 122.

1,000 persons)

No. of persons		Wholesale			Retail		
		1960	1964	1968	1960	1964	1968
No. of establishments	1–2	62.2	56.7	54.7	914.6	916.8	942.7
	3–4	52.0	49.2	52.1	247.7	250.9	305.0
	5–9	62.1	62.4	65.7	97.3	98.3	131.2
	10–19	31.9	35.8	38.3	20.5	26.3	36.6
	20–49	13.8	18.5	21.0	6.5	9.9	13.3
	1–49	222.0	222.6	231.8	1,286.6	1,302.2	1,428.8
	50 or more	3.6	6.7	7.7	1.3	2.3	3.6
	Total	225.6	229.3	239.5	1,287.9	1,304.5	1,432.4
No. of persons	1–2	98.5	92.0	90.5	1,405.8	1,412.4	1,482.5
		(5.1)	(3.6)	(3.4)	(40.3)	(37.0)	(31.9)
	3–4	180.1	170.3	180.7	824.3	835.1	1,019.1
		(9.3)	(6.8)	(6.7)	(23.6)	(21.9)	(22.0)
	5–9	406.3	411.4	432.4	595.9	609.5	818.5
		(20.8)	(16.3)	(16.0)	(17.1)	(16.0)	(17.6)
	10–19	421.9	475.9	511.1	263.5	340.0	474.8
		(21.9)	(18.9)	(19.0)	(7.6)	(8.9)	(10.2)
	20–49	402.8	537.6	618.8	185.7	284.1	381.9
		(20.8)	(21.0)	(22.9)	(5.3)	(7.5)	(8.2)
	1–49	1,509.6	1,687.2	1,833.5	3,275.2	3,481.1	4,176.8
		(77.9)	(66.9)	(68.0)	(93.9)	(91.3)	(89.9)
	50 or more	418.3	836.6	863.7	213.9	329.7	469.4
		(22.1)	(33.1)	(32.0)	(6.1)	(8.7)	(10.1)
	Total	1,927.9	2,523.0	2,697.2	3,489.1	3,810.8	4,646.2
		(100.0)	(100.0)	(100.0)	(100.0)	(100.0)	(100.0)

Notes:
1. Figures in parentheses are percentage of total.
2. Figures for 1968 were compiled according to new Japan Standard Industrial Classification (JSIC), and continuity from figures up to 1966 is lost.

Source: MITI, *Shogyo Tokeihyo* (Census of Commerce).

Table 4.7   International comparison of scale of retail establishments

		Japan (1964)	UK (1961)	USA (1958)
Statistics	Annual sales per establishment (1,000 yen)	6,410	16,650	48,500
	No. of persons per establishment	2.9	4.4	5.7
	Annual sales per person (1,000 yen)	2,200	3,790	8,530
Indices	Annual sales per establishment	100	260	757
	No. of persons per establishment	100	152	197
	Annual sales per person	100	172	388

Source: *Chusho Kigyo Hakusho Showa 41 Nendo* (White Paper on Small and Medium Enterprises in Japan, Fiscal year 1966)
References: Japan: MITI, *Shogyo Tokeihyo* (Census of Commerce); UK: *Report on the Census of Distribution*; USA: *Census of Business*

very small retailers increased absolutely but gradually decreased in relative terms, falling to 87 per cent of the total in 1968. In terms of the number of retail stores per 10,000 persons, Japan had 140 (1964) stores as compared to 110 (1961) in the UK and 60 (1959) in the US. Although these differences can be explained in part by the differences in the purchasing power—or income levels—of the people in those days, the more important reason was the differences in the market structure. Table 4.7, which compares the size of retail stores in these three countries, shows that very small stores that managed to earn a family's livelihood were predominant in the consumer market in Japan. This type of establishment characterizes the market for daily necessities in Japan, although there were some changes in those days because of the emergence of supermarkets and other types of large stores. As was discussed earlier, the percentage of small and medium enterprises in manufacturing industries is also very high in Japan. In commerce, the proportion is naturally even more pronounced. In 1969, there were 733,000 small and medium-size establishments (with fewer than 300 employees) in manufacturing, in contrast to 2,281,000 (with fewer than fifty employees), or three times as many, in retailing and wholesaling.

Wholesalers linking producers and retailers

Next, concerning wholesalers, the smaller the scale of retailers, the greater the number of wholesalers needed between them and the producer to accomplish the necessary functions of providing variety in products and geographic distribution. In the Japanese distribution system, the wholesale business, too, is crowded with a large number of very small companies. However, owing in part to the response to the development of mass production and mass consumption in the process of high-level growth, the number of very small establishments decreased rapidly, and the average scale enlarged markedly. The larger scale was an essential condition for providing modern distribution functions such as larger stores, extensive financing, and market development. Wholesalers could respond to mass production in one of two opposing directions: specialization or integration. In general, smaller wholesalers became specialized in specific products, whereas larger ones tended towards mass sales of mass-produced goods. Smaller wholesalers aimed at increasing the efficiency of their operation through specialization, and larger ones increased their scale of operation with a view to benefiting from economies of scale.

The channels of distribution from producer to consumer are complex. One typical channel is the vertical (*keiretsu*) integration of sales outlets by a large manufacturer. In industries such as electrical machinery, cars, and pharmaceuticals, where the mass-production system is well established and the industry is oligopolistically organized, manufacturers made efforts to develop a keiretsu alignment in order to secure sufficient sales outlets. In this case, wholesalers lost some of their characteristic functions as they were reduced to becoming mere distributors of products. In contrast, wholesalers of diverse products manufactured in small volumes, such as textiles and sundry goods, strengthened their economic base as many of them provided financial services besides such basic functions as collection, distribution, and inventory control.

General trading companies as key players in international trade

The key players in Japan's foreign trade are totally different from those in the domestic market. On the international scene, huge trading companies, of a size unheard of in Western countries, emerged in Japan in the 1960s.[5] Trading companies had already existed in Japan before the war, representative of which were Mitsui & Co. and Mitsubishi Co. As discussed earlier, however, these companies were eliminated in the post-war programme of zaibatsu dissolution. As of 1953 (Table 4.8), their names had not yet reappeared in Japanese business. In April 1954, some of the smaller companies into which Mitsubishi had been divided, including Fuji Shoji, Tokyo Boeki, and Tozai Koeki, merged to form the new Mitsubishi Corporation. This merger was followed by a similar movement in 1959 by Daiichi Bussan, Daiichi Tsusho, and other dissolved Mitsui-group companies, which reformed the present Mitsui & Co. In 1960, these two mammoth trading companies occupied the first and second positions on the list of top Japanese trading companies. Prior to that year, textile traders C. Itoh & Co. and the Marubeni Corporation had held dominant positions reflecting the post-war structure of Japan's foreign trade. They remained as major trading companies even after the comeback of Mitsubishi and Mitsui. Whereas C. Itoh and other textile based companies were called 'yarn traders', Iwai & Co., the Nissho Company,

Table 4.8 Leading Japanese trading companies ranked by sales (unit: 100 m. yen)

Second half fiscal year 1953		Fiscal year 1960		Fiscal year 1965		Fiscal year 1970	
Company	Sales	Company	Sales	Company	Sales	Company	Sales
C. Itoh & Co. Ltd.	715	Mitsubishi Shoji Kaisha	6,444	Mitsui & Co. Ltd.	15,264	Mitsubishi Shoji Kaisha	40,699
Marubeni Corp.	620	Mitsui & Co. Ltd.	6,395	Mitsubishi Shoji Kaisha	14,646	Mitsui & Co. Ltd.	37,505
Daiichi Bussan	564	Marubeni-Iida Co. Ltd.	6,127	Marubeni-Iida Co. Ltd.	11,669	Marubeni-Iida Co. Ltd.	27,022
Nichimen Co. Ltd.	523	C. Itoh & Co. Ltd.	5,446	C. Itoh & Co. Ltd.	11,352	C. Itoh & Co. Ltd.	25,520
Daiichi Tsusho	437	Nichimen Co. Ltd.	3,056	Toyo Menka Kaisha Ltd.	6,404	Nissho-Iwai Co. Ltd.	18,614
Toyo Menka Kaisha Ltd.	415	Toyo Menka Kaisha Ltd.	2,778	Nichimen Co. Ltd.	5,819	Sumitomo Shoji Kaisha Ltd.	17,041
The Gosho Co. Ltd.	406	The Nissho Co. Ltd.	2,117	Sumitomo Shoji Kaisha Ltd.	4,988	Tomen Corp.	13,807
Fuji Shoji	403	Sumitomo Shoji Kaisha Ltd.	1,966	The Nissho Co. Ltd.	4,884	Nichimen Co. Ltd.	8,791
Kanematsu & Co. Ltd.	363	Kanematsu & Co. Ltd.	1,529	Iwai & Co. Ltd.	3,247	Kanematsu-Gosho Ltd.	8,436
Tokyo Boeki	305	Ataka & Co. Ltd.	1,447	Kanematsu & Co. Ltd.	3,120	Ataka & Co. Ltd.	8,427
Tozai Koeki	291	The Gosho Co. Ltd.	1,413	Ataka & Co. Ltd.	3,022		
The Nissho Co. Ltd.	261	Iwai & Co. Ltd.	1,219	The Gosho Co. Ltd.	2,165		
Sumitomo Shoji Kaisha Ltd.	249						
Iwai & Co. Ltd.	244						
Ataka & Co. Ltd.	236						

Note: Figures for 1953 are for second half of fiscal year.

Source: Hidemasa Morikawa, *Sengo Keieishi Nyumon* (Introduction to Post-War Business History).

References: Kosei Torihiki Iinkai Jimukyoku (Fair Trade Commission Secretariat); *Saihensei Katei ni Aru Boeki Gaisha no Kihon Doko* (Basic Trend of Trading Companies in the Process of Reorganization); Toyo Keizai Inc., *Shukan Toyo Keizai* (Weekly Toyo Keizai), various issues; Toyo Keizai Inc., *Kaisha Shikiho* (Quarterly Report of Corporations), various issues.

Ataka & Co., and others—trading companies handling products of the steel industry, Japan's top industry in the 1950s—were popularly referred to as 'metal traders'. These companies began to change into general trading companies and expanded their scale of operation as the volume of Japan's international trade increased rapidly in the 1960s.

The functions of trading companies consist of two sets: (1) general distribtion functions such as marketing research, coordination of supply and demand of products, collection, after-sales service, and advertising; and (2) international trading functions such as specialized knowledge regarding foreign trade, market information, information networks, and fund-raising capabilities. Beside these functions, the success or failure of a trading company is decisively affected by facilities of short-term financing related to transactions, long-term trade credits, supplying funds to finance production, as well as the ability to organize—multilaterally and swiftly—the information, technology, related firms, personnel, and funds needed to carry out specific projects. Gigantic trading companies having these diverse functions were not found anywhere in the world except in Japan. These companies helped to create a worldwide network of project-organizing functions which served as the backbone of the post-war expansion of Japan's foreign trade.

The functions of general trading companies were not limited to those relating to international trade, but, using those functions as a launching pad, trading companies expanded the scope of their business to include activities in domestic markets. For instance, in importing foodstuffs such as wheat, soya beans, and sugar, it is important for trading companies to develop wharves equipped with cargo-handling facilities for joint use, unload cargo and store it, and jointly use domestic sales channels and facilities for transporting merchandise—besides providing the other vital services listed above. Responding to these requirements, trading companies established subsidiaries which share commonly owned wharves, silos, and warehouses in coastal industrial zones, and developed industrial complexes in joint ventures with related manufacturing companies. The scope of operation of Japanese general trading companies, however, was not limited to these projects; they also became active in many other fields in domestic markets.

Each of the six general trading companies, down to Sumitomo Shoji Kaisha (renamed Sumitomo Corporation in July 1978), in the 1970 list of trading companies in Table 4.8, was a key member of the enterprise groups discussed earlier. Mitsubishi, Mitsui, and Sumitomo belonged to groups bearing their names. Marubeni Corporation, meanwhile, was a member of the Fuyo group, C. Itoh & Co. belonged to the Dai-Ichi Kangyo Bank (DKB) group, and Nissho-Iwai Co. was a member of the Sanwa group. Each of these trading companies, along with the key bank in each group, played a leading role in its group. In fact, a general trading company often plays the role of the organizer of various projects and overseas undertakings which member companies in an enterprise group formulate jointly.[6]

4.5. The Formation of the Japanese Industrial Order

Controversy over draft law on temporary measures for promotion of
specified industries

In the process of high-speed growth described above, Japanese industry gradually acquired economic autonomy, and intensified its stance of rejecting government intervention in its activities. The classic illustration of this changed attitude was the controversy over the Special Industries Bill and its outcome, which became a major issue in 1963 and 1964. In 1963, the Industrial Organization Committee of the Industrial Structure Research Committee argued—in part internalizing the view of MITI—as follows in its report. Technical innovation, it said, was advancing as the economy moved towards an open economy with a focus on trade liberalization. For effectively responding to such a change in the business environment, Japanese corporations were still too small by world standards, and they tended to engage in wasteful cut-throat competition among themselves. Meanwhile, foreign capital was about to make inroads into Japanese markets. The Japanese economy was unable to respond effectively to these changes and develop in appropriate directions. Since it was necessary to move swiftly to overcome these difficulties, wasting time on ineffective policy measures was to be avoided as far as possible. Therefore—the committee report concluded—the only viable strategy was the '*kyocho hoshiki*', the system of close cooperation by the private sector with government in coordinating resource allocation. In those days, there were rising sentiments in the business community, and particularly among large corporations, in favour of minimizing government regulations and liberalizing private business initiatives. Therefore, MITI's policy stance met with nearly total opposition. MITI submitted the Special Industries Bill to the Diet in January 1964 but was compelled to make a series of compromising revisions to it. In the end, because of the fear of renewed bureaucratic control and criticism that the bill would strengthen the oligopolistic system and harm the interest of consumers, it was abandoned without coming to a vote. This episode could be viewed as symbolic of the demise of the system of bureaucratic control of industry.

Government–business relationships in post-war Japan

Defeat of the Specified Industries Bill, however, did not signify a decisive retreat of MITI's involvement with industry. Rather, it served as a catalyst for creating a new relationship between government and business.

Before examining the new relationship, it is necessary to touch on one important characteristic of the system of government–business cooperation in post-war Japan. Many have pointed out that the Japanese government intervenes intensively with private business affairs, so much so that '*kanmin kyocho*' (cooperation by business with public authorities)—the kanmin cooperation system—is part of the Japanese industrial system. It must be admitted that there is an element of truth in this view. It must also be remembered, however, that there are no nationalized industries in Japan, with the exception of industries of high public-utility content, such as transport and communications. Certainly none of the ordinary industries over which MITI has competence is nationalized. In France and the UK, on the other hand, waves of nationalization engulfed the steel, shipbuilding, car, aircraft, and coal-mining industries; all of these industries are privately operated in Japan. Japanese industry is more deeply rooted in the market place than industries in advanced Western nations, which are regarded as essentially market-oriented. To be sure, nationalization of the coal-mining industry was once debated in Japan, but in the end it turned out that the industry was subjected to state control for only a few years. The synthetic rubber industry, which began as a state undertaking, was transferred to private ownership when earnings were stabilized a few years after its inception.

The question remains, then, of why it was that in Japan—where public authorities enjoyed ample power to control the affairs of private business—nationalization of industries did not make headway. Why did bureaucrats advocate the kanmin cooperation system—while convinced it was necessary to retain the power of control—yet were negative, if anything, towards nationalization? To answer these questions, it is important first of all to consider the political philosophy of the members of the liberally oriented political parties that governed post-war Japan. Being critical of the wartime controlled economy, these politicians ardently espoused a liberal economic philosophy. State bureaucrats who served under these party politicians, while being held responsible for controlling the economy under the directives of SCAP, were likely to be convinced that the economy should be deregulated once the national economy regained its vitality. Although the socialist parties and the labour unions under their influence agreed that nationalization was the proper path for Japan, industrial leaders, it goes without saying, conservative politicians, and the bureaucrats who actually managed economic policies were critical of nationalization. This was the fundamental character of the post-war Japanese political economy.

The second, and in practice more important, reason for the passive attitude towards nationalization is found in the belief of the bureaucrats that administration of the economy would be more flexible and efficient if the conduct of business were left to the workings of the market place, rather than nationalizing problematic industries and directly controlling them. If government had to, it should interfere only to move industry in the desired direction. Most of MITI's industrial policies can be understood from this perspective.

For the third reason, it is necessary to consider the relationship between the administrative authorities and businesses. When the economic foundation of business firms was weak, they relied heavily on assistance from the government. And yet they were adamant in their opposition to nationalization. In the process of economic growth, business corporations gradually acquired economic strength and began to travel their own paths. At this point, political and bureaucratic interference with the conduct of their business affairs became irksome.[7]

Business, however, cooperated with government when it was considered necessary, and at times even asked for government intervention. It can be said that the rejection by business of the Specified Industries Bill, which MITI officials drafted in the belief that the restoration of state control in the market place was necessary, was made against such a background.

Nature of the kanmin cooperation system

At this point, industrial leaders criticized the traditional posture of Japanese business managers, as follows:

It is well known that each enterprise, which should be guided by the principle of self-responsibility, finds it difficult to rid itself of the inclination to rely on government help. Top managers keep a close eye on the baton the government uses in conducting the industrial orchestra, and when they make their moves following it, they often move much more than the conductor, the government, actually wants. This is the unfortunate but true picture of Japanese industry up to this point.

The comment continues on what the relationship between government and industry should be:

As far as economic matters are concerned, it is natural for government to respect the views of the business community and listen attentively. The relationship between government and business should not be one between the controller and the controlled; it must always be one of complementary cooperation based on mutual understanding and trust.[8]

Subsequently, however, MITI continued to practise administrative guidance, vigorously at times. The classic example was the implementation of the Petroleum Industry Law enacted in 1962. The law was intended to nurture and strengthen domestic petroleum producers; it gave MITI authority to control the industry through output coordination and price decisions. Such coordination became a habit, and was later ruled 'a mistake of illegality' by the Tokyo High Court. The trade association was found innocent of the charges filed against it on the grounds that it was not aware it was violating the Anti-Monopoly Law. The 'absence of awareness' was suggestive of the relationship between government and industry.

In Japan, consultations are held within an industry, and between the industry and MITI, on matters pertaining to international trade and industrial policy, and agreements reached in these consultations are called kanmin cooperation. The problem, however, is that agreements are not always reached in formal consultation sessions. More likely they are arrived at in 'nemawashi' (informal spadework) activities taking place prior to formal consultations. In these activities, leaders of trade associations or appropriate officials of MITI hold conversations individually with relevant parties in an effort to create an overall consensus. This process could be described as the manifestation of Japanese-style democracy based on community relationships or awareness, which have long existed at the very foundation of Japanese society.[9] It could also be argued that this relationship began to attract attention because of the increased importance of the interests of corporations, and especially because of the stronger voice of business leaders who articulated those interests.

Administrative guidance and its functions

Manifestation of the guidance aspect of government intervention is found in the '*kankoku sohtan*' (advice to curtail operations) of the 1950s. At that time, however, the control aspect was more pronounced than the cooperative aspect. As the influence of the business community increased once into the 1960s, it became difficult as well as inappropriate for MITI to continue relying on the methods of control of the 1950s in implementing its policy. The general method which MITI adopted to replace the former methods was 'administrative guidance'. This method proved highly effective in adjusting and coordinating the various prob-lems which arose in industries in the process of high-speed growth. Business conditions kept changing rapidly, generating a variety of problems, to which administrative guidance was applied in a very flexible manner. Administrative guidance did not have the legal force of compulsion, of course. But it was utilized effectively. When an industry required some sort of adjustment or coordination, it consulted with MITI and had the issue resolved through 'administrative guidance'.[10]

Of course there were cases where leading corporations acted independently in defiance of MITI's advice concerning industrial adjustments. The Idemitsu Kosan Co. case of 1963 involving the quantity of petroleum production, and the Sum-itomo Metal Industries case of 1965 involving investment in equipment in the steel industry were examples of corporate defiance towards MITI's administrative guidance. Subsequently, in 1969 in the car industry—which had developed with a background of protection from foreign capital, and where joint ventures with foreign car manufacturers were not permitted—Mitsubishi Heavy Industries completed capital ties with Chrysler in disregard of MITI's policy, which eventu-ally led to the creation of Mitsubishi Motors.

These cases, however, were exceptions to the rule of MITI–industry relations. In general, administrative guidance until the 1980s was an important method of implementing international trade and industrial policy. In that sense, both the Japanese government and industry—which have in principle espoused the free-market system—acknowledge the validity of not only the 'invisible hand' of the market place but also the 'visible hand' of government.

It is a mistake to conclude that international trade and industrial policy in Japan has evolved around the 'invisible hand'. MITI's policy is based on numer-ous statutes, Cabinet orders, and ministerial ordinances. Examples are the Foreign Exchange and Foreign Trade Control Law in the international trade area, and the Law on Temporary Measures for the Promotion of Specified Machinery and Information Industries in the field of industrial policy. In this sense, Japan is a country governed by law. It has been shown above how the voice of industry has been reflected in legislation and how flexibly the laws have been enforced.

NOTES

1. Japanese mythology has Jimmu as the first emperor of Japan. The first post-war period of prosperity from 1955 to the end of 1957 was dubbed the 'Jimmu Boom' because it was the most remarkable period of prosperity in Japan's history, or more specifically the biggest boom in modern Japanese economic history since the Meiji era. Because the scale of the boom that began in 1958 exceeded that of the 'Jimmu Boom' it was called the 'Iwato Boom', referring to a legend which was even more ancient than the Jimmu legend.
2. Because post-war labour unions were enterprise unions, enterprise-wide wage negotiations would be harmful to the competitive position of individual enterprises in an industry. Therefore, a system of industry-wide wage negotiations developed in which enterprise unions within an industry coordinated their wage demands and cooperated to negotiate with their employers. These industry-wide struggles were further expanded horizontally to form a nation-wide organization of collective bargaining. During the spring months, wage negotiations are conducted throughout Japanese industry, spearheaded by unions in prosperous industries or in industries which are not adversely affected by recession. This system of scheduled wage negotiations was dubbed the 'Shunto' the 'Spring wage offensive'.
3. Subsequently, high-end electronic desk calculators, electronic accounting machines, and integrated circuits were liberalized in Apr. 1973, followed in Dec. 1975 by the liberalization of electronic computers and related peripheral equipment. These changes left eighty-two products on the list of restricted imports.
4. In discussions of Japanese industry, the term 'industry' generally refers to the manufacturing industry, with commerce seldom being examined. The *Chusho Kigyo Hakusho* (White Paper on Small and Medium Enterprises in Japan), however, makes cursory reference to commerce. This is because, as will be discussed later, commerce in Japan is conducted predominantly by a host of small and very small firms. Their relative importance in number makes it difficult for the Small and Medium Enterprise Agency to ignore them.
5. Notwithstanding the important roles played by trading companies, the number of studies that analyse them is small. The first government-level study of trading companies was a report made in Aug. 1972 by the Distribution Study Committee established by the Economic Council in 1971. This was followed by the *Sogo Shosha ni Kansuru Chosa Hokokusho* (Report on the Survey of General Trading Companies), released in January 1974 by the Fair Trade Commission.
6. A brief survey of trading companies appears each year in the annual *Tsusho Hakusho* (White Paper on International Trade). In 1972, a study by the Fair Trade Commission of the business conditions of the six largest trading companies revealed that in fiscal year 1972 trading companies were responsible for 3,700 billion yen worth of exports and 3,800 billion yen worth of imports, which accounted for 40% and 50%, respectively, of total Japanese exports and imports. Their combined net worth was 330 billion yen, total liabilities were 4,600 billion yen, and combined loans and accounts receivable amounted to 7,400 billion yen. This financing by trading companies was the catalyst for organizing their customers into keiretsu, groups of affiliated companies. These six trading companies were the leading stockholders of 1,057 companies, which served as their *de facto* keiretsu companies. See Fair Trade Commission, *Showa 48-nendo Nenji Hokoku* (Annual Report for Fiscal Year 1973). In some industries, manufacturers as well as trading companies conduct large proportions of exporting and importing activities. Regarding exports, manufacturers accounted for 60.5% of petroleum products and 45.3% of cars and other machinery and equipment; regarding imports, manufacturers were responsible for 50.4% of coal and petroleum, and 23.2% of raw materials for chemical products. See MITI, *Tsusho Hakusho*, 1971.
7. An interesting case in this respect was the process of formation of the nine electric power companies. On this point, see MITI, Committee to Edit History of International Trade and Industry

Policy, *Tsusho Sangyo Seisakushi* (History of International Trade and Industry Policy), iii, ch. 4, Tsusho Sangyo Chosakai (Research Institute of International Trade and Industry), 1992.

8. Moriatsu Minato, ' "Sangyo Chosei Kaigi" no Koso' (The Concept of the 'Industrial Adjustment Forum'), in *Nihon Keizai to Shin Sangyo Taisei*.

9. The community relationships model attracted the interest of a number of American scholars studying the singularity of Japanese industry. Their representative works include: Ezra F. Vogel, *Japan as Number One*, 1979 (trans. by Atsuo Ueda, TBS Britannica, 1979); and Daniel I. Okimoto, *Between MITI and the Market*, Stanford University Press, 1989 (trans. as *Tsusansho to Haiteku Sangyo* by Satoshi Watanabe, Simul Press, Inc., 1991).

10. By the mid-1960s, some in the business community began to find administrative guidance irksome. The first (1964) report of the Provisional Commission for Administrative Affairs examined the proposed legislation of an Administrative Procedures Law, which failed to produce a draft bill. Subsequently, the issue was repeatedly discussed in the commission. As noted earlier, the Tokyo High Court in 1972 found the trade association innocent of the charges of forming a petroleum cartel. The judgment, however, restrained administrative guidance by stating that MITI's 'exercising guidance on a trade association to enforce production cutbacks on its members is not permissible under the provisions of the Anti-Monopoly Law.'

5

The Emergence of Japan as an Economic Superpower in the Changing Global Economy

5.1. End of US Dominance over the World Economy

Decline of the US economy and the Nixon 'shock'

On 15 August 1971, President Nixon of the US announced a new economic policy which included suspension of gold convertibility of the US dollar—the key currency *par excellence* of the post-war era—and imposition of a 10 per cent surcharge on imports to the US. These measures sent massive shock waves around the world, but they were a particularly severe blow to the Japanese economy which had relied heavily on the US economy. The move by President Nixon symbolized a loss of prestige of the US economy which had dominated the global economic order since the Second World War.

Following the cessation of hostilities in 1945, the world's major industrialized nations, including the UK and France, to say nothing of defeated Germany and Japan, were in economically precarious positions. Only the US, far and away the mightiest economic power, enjoyed stability. The US operated the Marshall Plan without placing much of a burden on its economy, and returned the economies of Western Europe on a growth path. Even with imports accounting for only a few percentage points of its GNP, the US economy served as a huge market, which was fully open to the rest of the world. Technologically the US economy was by far the most advanced in the world, producing high-technology goods which had no equals anywhere. Moreover, the US was richly endowed with petroleum resources, a resource not found in West European countries. The US economy grew steadily. Once into the 1950s, West European countries succeeded in launching themselves on a path of fast economic growth with their growth rates significantly surpassing that of the US. In terms of GNP size, however, no country's GNP was close to that of the US.

The launching of Sputnik 1, the first artificial earth satellite, by the Soviet Union ahead of the US in 1957 came as a rude awakening that the US no longer had a monopoly on high technology. Further, US involvement in the war in Vietnam that began in 1960 turned into a full-scale war with US bombing of North Vietnam in 1965. In part impaired by the mounting war expenditures, the US economy gradually lost its vigour. In February 1961 President Kennedy announced a bill for measures to defend the dollar. Once into the second half of the 1960s, Vietnam war expenditures rose sharply. While social unrest was growing, deficits in the federal government budget became chronic. Meanwhile, the international competitiveness of US industries began to decline. As the US balance of trade, which in the past had recorded overwhelming surpluses, deteriorated year after year, a drift towards protectionism became increasingly evident. The decline in the relative position of the US in the world economy steadily lowered the confidence of foreign creditors in the US dollar. In 1968, a rush on gold centred on Europe spread throughout the world, triggering an international currency crisis. That same year, the US recorded the first post-war deficit in its balance of payments. Therefore, the announcement by President Nixon in August 1971 of a series of economic measures, including the suspension of gold convertibility of the dollar, was essentially something that eventually could have been expected, rather than being a shock or a surprise.

The transformation of the world economy

In the 1960s, the world economy underwent a great transformation. As Table 1.3 shows, in the 1960s the US had by far the largest GNP, and even that of the UK or West Germany did not come within 15 per cent of the US figure, with the GNP of Japan being less than 10 per cent of the US level. As late as 1965, the situation was not very different, except that Japan's GNP became relatively larger, approaching 13 per cent of the US GNP. During the next five years, however, Japan made remarkable advances, surpassing West Germany, France, and the UK to become the second largest economy in the world. In 1970, Japan's GNP was at 20 per cent of the US level, followed by that of West Germany which was 18 per cent. The growth of the Japanese economy accelerated subsequently, and its GNP reached 30 per cent of the US level in 1975.

These changes in the relative size of GNP naturally resulted from the differences in annual growth rates. As Table 1.2 shows, Japan's annual growth rate from the second half of the 1950s exceeded 10 per cent, while that of the US was below 5 per cent on average. The UK was left out of the world growth league, whereas the rise of the West German and French economies was worth noting.

These differences in growth rates were attributable to the international differences in technological advances and equipment investment in the 1960s, and the attendant rise in productivity. Take, for example, the steel industry in which the US industry led by US Steel Corporation had held a dominant position in the world until the beginning of the 1960s. The Japanese steel industry rapidly raised its productivity and production by installing larger blast furnaces and converters, and adopting continuous casting and computer-controlled production. The US steel industry, in contrast, was slow to invest in new technology, partly because of complications involving objections raised by labour unions. Once into the

1970s, it was surpassed by its counterparts in the Soviet Union and Japan (Table 1.4). A similar situation developed a little later in the automobile industry in which the US had enjoyed indisputable pre-eminence. Until the beginning of the 1970s, the automobile industry was the glamour industry of the US; it lorded it over the world, with no other firm being able to equal General Motors. Once into the 1970s, however, partly because of the oil crisis, which will be discussed later, US-made cars came to be jostled out of the US market by Japanese products. In 1980, Japan became the world's leading car-producing nation. German-made cars also made remarkable advances. Thus, during the 1970s, the premier position of the US in the automobile industry foundered. The same situation developed in the television industry, but in a more pronounced manner. The leading position held by the US in the industry in the 1960s was replaced by Japan in the 1970s. US television-set manufacturers closed their production facilities in the US, and moved them to South-East Asia and Latin America. Ironically, television production in the US even came to be conducted by Japanese-affiliated makers.

The post-war world economy led by the US thus underwent a profound transformation from the second half of the 1960s into the 1970s, with the rapid advance of Japanese industry playing a key role in the process.

Stagflation in leading industrial nations

Another noteworthy development in the pivotal transformation of the world economy from the end of the 1960s to the beginning of the 1970s was the economic problem known as stagflation.

During this period, prices continued to rise throughout the world despite the fact that the US economy was in a recession, the economy of the UK was stagnant, and business suffered a cave-in of the market of the European Community (EC). This was a type of situation that the free-market economies had never experienced. Once into the 1970s, production increases were sluggish, equipment investment was weak, and business was at a standstill in the US and West European countries. Unemployment rates rose and business earnings deteriorated in all countries.

During this period, however, prices continued to rise despite the sluggish business conditions. This new phenomenon led to the coining of a new word, 'stagflation', which combined 'stagnation' and 'inflation', and widespread debate as to its causes ensued. Generally speaking, price increases are caused by demand pull, where demand exceeds available supply, or cost push, where production costs rise mainly because of higher wages. During this period, however, cost push became a serious problem even though demand-pull pressure was not strong, owing to sluggish equipment investment and other reasons mentioned above. This cost push was attributable to the fact that labour disputes became acute, leading to frequent strikes in many countries, resulting in sharp wage increases, including cases of wage drifts where wage increases exceeded those set in previously negotiated wage agreements. To cope with this situation and contain inflation, governments everywhere from around 1970 began implementing so-called income policies designed to contain aggregate demand while freezing wages and other prices. However, income policies which engendered a transformation of the post-war system of economic growth centring on the US economy could not produce anything more than temporary relief wherever they were introduced, marking a turning point in the global economic situation. In Japan, prices and wages rose sharply following the Nixon shock, but productivity also improved markedly, thereby absorbing wage increases. Japan was thus able to weather the critical situation without resorting to an incomes policy.

5.2. Arab Oil-Producing Countries and the First Oil Crisis

The first oil crisis and the world economy

There arose another issue that shook the world economy. When the fourth Middle East War broke out in October 1973, the Organization of Arab Petroleum Exporting Countries (OPEC) adopted the strategy of using oil as a weapon, including cutbacks in oil production and oil embargoes. The five Persian Gulf states belonging to OPEC unilaterally raised the price of crude oil to $5.12 per barrel, a 70 per cent increase, and decided to cease or reduce exports of petroleum to countries supporting Israel. These steps sent a massive shock wave through the global economy, which had come to rely heavily on Persian Gulf oil.

The reality of the matter, however—apart from the 70 per cent increase in the price of crude oil—was that the oil situation in the Middle East had been changing dramatically since the beginning of the 1960s. Because of the devaluation of the dollar associated with the Nixon shock, the real price of oil expressed in US dollar terms had been declining, and OPEC in January 1972 had raised the official price of crude oil by 8.2 per cent. The changes in the situation in the Arab oil-producing countries, however, could be attributed to other factors as well. Since the 1950s, nationalism had been on the rise in every part of the developing world. Oil extraction in the Persian Gulf countries had been virtually under the control of the large international oil companies, the 'majors'. The Gulf nations demanded that the majors raise their shares of the profits and stepped up their demands to management participation and even to nationalization, and they formed OPEC in the 1960s. With the success of OPEC, the oil-producing countries came to regard their petroleum resources as a strategic weapon, and moved to increase their say in decisions on oil production and prices.

Once into the 1970s, Algeria succeeded in participating in the management of oil-extracting operations of the Anglo-American and French majors, followed by similar participation by the Libyan government in British Petroleum and the Iraqi government in Iraq Petroleum Company (IPC). In 1972, Saudi Arabia gained partial ownership of Arabian American Oil Company (Aramco), with Iraq and Kuwait following suit. In 1973, oil operations were nationalized in Iran in March

Table 5.1   Price increase rates in selected industrial countries, 1969–1974 (unit: %)

	Japan		USA	
	Wholesale prices	Consumer prices	Wholesale prices	Consumer prices
1969–72 average	1.4	6.0	3.8	4.7
1973	15.9	11.7	13.8	6.2
1974	31.3	24.5	18.8	11.0

Source: OECD, *Main Economic Indicators*.

and in Libya in June. Thus, the oil situation in the Middle East was changing rapidly. In Japan, meanwhile, dependence on petroleum as a source of raw material and fuel sharply increased during the period of high-level growth in the 1960s; in the 1970s, Japan became overwhelmingly dependent on overseas energy sources, with 90 per cent of its crude oil being imported from OPEC countries. For this reason, MITI watched the situation in the Middle East closely, and in May 1973 MITI Minister Nakasone visited the Middle Eastern countries to affirm Japan's friendly relations with them.

Then the fourth Middle Eastern War broke out in October 1973. The Arab nations utilized petroleum as a strategic commodity, curtailing exports by member nations to pro-Israel countries, and unilaterally doubling its prices, as described above. Although higher prices had been anticipated as a general trend, no one could have predicted such drastic changes taking place so suddenly. Massive shock waves engulfed the entire world. The impact was especially great in Japan, which relied heavily on Middle Eastern oil, striking not only industrial circles, but also the consumers, who made frantic efforts to hoard goods.

In January 1974, the six OPEC nations further raised the official price of crude oil to $11.65 per barrel, over double the existing prices. Meanwhile, it soon became clear that Japan was not included in the list of countries the Arab nations regarded as 'friendly'. This realization prompted the Japanese government to tackle programmes in earnest for securing dependable supplies of oil and reducing oil consumption. At the same time, however, it was compelled to reassess the policy it had promoted since the 1960s of switching its source of energy to petroleum. Essentially, the first oil crisis turned out to be more than merely sharp increases in oil prices; it symbolized a counter-offensive by developing countries against the post-war world economic order dominated by the advanced industrial nations. Therefore, it became clear that Japan could no longer be expected to continue its economic growth by merely introducing an energy-saving programme.

UK		W. Germany		France	
Wholesale prices	Consumer prices	Wholesale prices	Consumer prices	Wholesale prices	Consumer prices
6.2	7.1	4.0	4.0	6.2	5.8
7.3	9.2	6.7	6.8	14.7	7.3
23.4	16.1	13.2	7.0	29.2	13.6

First oil crisis and Japanese economy

It is probably safe to say that the Japanese economy received the greatest negative impact from the first oil crisis. As Table 5.1 shows, prices in Japan rose in 1974 at rates unparalleled elsewhere, with consumer prices rising by 24.5 per cent and wholesale prices by 31.3 per cent. Although a large part of the increases related to the first oil crisis, they were also amplified appreciably by the effects of the earlier Nixon shock and the subsequent response of Japan's economic policy.

For a while after the announcement of President Nixon's 'new economic policy', Japan alone among the industrially advanced nations adhered to the fixed-exchange-rate system by maintaining the old rate of 360 yen per dollar through foreign-market operations. Within two weeks, however, it became clear that this rate could not be maintained, and Japan, too, adopted a floating-exchange-rate system. In the Smithsonian Agreement of December 1971, the yen was revalued upwards to 308 yen to the dollar, by far the sharpest revaluation among all the currencies affected. Foreign-exchange markets, however, remained unstable, and the US in February 1973 devalued the dollar for the second time by 10 per cent. This move compelled Japan to return once again to a floating-exchange-rate system, and the Smithsonian system of managed floating collapsed. Although the US still had significant influence in world currency markets, it lost its position of leadership. The yen subsequently appreciated to the level of 245 per dollar, and remained roughly at that level, supported by intervention in the foreign-exchange market by the Bank of Japan.

Meanwhile, business conditions in Japan began to recover from the end of 1972. Government expenditures increased to fund public works projects stimulated by the 'Japanese archipelago remodelling scheme' that was popular at the time. On the other hand, manufacturing industries were in a state of confusion owing to the effect of the higher yen rates, producing supply shortages in many sectors of the economy. Once into 1973, the tight supply–demand situation began to accelerate price increases.

It was at this time that the first oil crisis occurred. As Table 5.1 shows, the rates of increase in wholesale and retail prices in Japan in 1973 were already higher than those in other industrial countries. Once into 1974, however, the differences widened further, with the rate of increase in consumer prices in Japan being higher by 10 percentage points or more compared to the rates in other countries. Although one reason for the sharp increase was the Japanese economy's total dependence on petroleum imports, particularly those from OPEC countries, the increase was also affected in no small measure by the concern of consumers over the inflation trend that had set in earlier. Immediately after the start of the oil crisis, therefore, Japanese consumers made frantic efforts to hoard everything from tissue paper to paraffin oil.

The first oil crisis had a serious impact on the Japanese economy. In 1974, Japan's GNP in real terms (1960 as standard) amounted to 207.2 trillion yen, a decline of 0.6 per cent from the 208.5 trillion yen recorded in 1973. This was the first time in the post-war period that Japan's GNP fell in real terms from one year to another.

The high yen rate caused by the Nixon shock and the high prices of crude oil which resulted from the oil crisis combined to have a serious adverse effect on the Japanese economy. Although the high yen rate somewhat mollified the inflationary impact of higher oil prices, it was not significant enough to neutralize it. The petrochemical industry, which had developed using crude oil as its raw material, was severely affected, and the steel industry, which used petroleum as a primary source of energy, also received a harsh blow. The Japanese economy as a whole was thus forced to make serious efforts to transform its industrial structure. Meanwhile, industries which were not adversely affected by the oil crisis—including car and TV-set manufacturing—managed to increase their exports despite the higher yen rate. They ran up sizeable export surpluses in dollar terms, although increases in their export volumes were not so great, thereby adding fuel to trade friction with the United States.

5.3. The Concept of Knowledge-Intensification of Industry

MITI's vision of 'International trade and industry policy for the 1970s'

The growth of Japanese industry in the 1960s centred on the so-called 'heavy-thick-long-and-large' industries, a reference to industries such as steel and chemicals. The primary task of developmental efforts was to enlarge the scale of operations of those industries for increased international competitiveness. This objective was achieved in large part by the end of the 1960s, although not without complications. From the end of the 1960s, MITI initiated a study of a new direction of development for the Japanese economy in the 1970s. The ministry's basic idea was presented to the Industrial Structure Council for deliberation, and in May 1971 the council presented an interim report entitled

'International Trade and Industry Policy for the 1970s'[1] ('Vision of MITI Policies in the 1970s'). The report stated: 'Never has Japan experienced in the course of its history a situation like the current one, where its economy has grown immensely and is closely entwined with the global economy' and submitted that 'the accomplishments attributed to the assiduous efforts of an era, and the accumulation of conflicts they generated, combine to engender a new era.' Arguing that 'the single-minded pursuit of large-scale operations is an anachronism,' the report called for a fundamental reassessment of the policy of promoting ever-greater competitiveness in international trade, and proposed a new formula for industrial structure policy. This proposal came to be known as the 'concept of the knowledge-intensification of industry'.

Immediately thereafter, however, the Nixon shock occurred, and the traditional policy line came to an impasse as a result of the yen's appreciation and accelerating inflation. It appears that this 'Vision of MITI Policies in the 1970s' report had foreseen these changes in the world economy. As stated earlier, the US dollar had for some time been plagued with instability. The vision statement, therefore, may be viewed as an attempt to look ahead to the decade of the 1970s anticipating these new developments, while taking into due consideration the limits of the MITI policy of the 1960s.

Another point worthy of note concerning the 'Vision of MITI Policies in the 1970s' report is its urging that market mechanisms should be allowed to play a wider role in the overall management of the economy. To that end, it argued that the Japanese economy should 'set high store in private initiatives and rely heavily on the creativity and vitality which competition engenders.' One of the distortions created by the high growth rate of the 1960s had to do with the so-called debt-laden structure of Japanese corporations. Many companies were excessively indebted to banks for equity financing, and for many large corporations the owned equity capital percentage was between 10 and 20 per cent. This situation arose from the race to invest in equipment in order to achieve enhanced international competitiveness. Although this race produced sharp increases in Japanese exports and made possible the high-level growth of the economy, there was little doubt that it also led to a weakening of the financial make-up of Japanese corporations. Correcting this situation and restoring normalcy was an important task in terms of corporate management and MITI's industrial policy. In fact, throughout the 1970s the average debt ratio of Japanese companies declined, as corporations enjoying favourable business conditions, such as Toyota Motor Company and Matsushita Electrical Industries, rapidly built up their own equity capital. This trend, however, had the effect of lessening the need for industrial financing by the government, which in the past had worked to prime the pump of industrial development and provided a driving force for it, while allowing greater autonomy to private corporations and accelerating liberalization of the financial market. It was in recognition of these developments that the 'International Trade and Industry Policy for the 1970s' report advocated that 'greater respect should be given to the autonomy of private companies'. As the economy grew, autonomy in the industrial sector increased and a change in the role of international trade and industrial policy became inevitable. What was called for now was a broadened perspective in search of a new approach for such a policy.

Development of concept of knowledge-intensification of industry

MITI's 'International Trade and Industry Policy for the 1970s' envisioned a new industrial structure centred on knowledge-intensive industries, those which were relatively intensive in the use of intellectual activities. Worded differently, knowledge-intensive industries were viewed as the converse of labour-intensive industries. The vision statement argued that because labour-intensive activities in Japan were destined to be supplanted in the 1970s and onwards by advances made in the developing economies, Japanese industry had to expand into knowledge-intensive areas as soon as feasible. This is an example of MITI policy playing a key role in determining the future direction of the Japanese economy, because Japanese industry in the 1970s essentially followed this path of development.

Some of the examples of knowledge-intensive products mentioned were computers, industrial robots, integrated circuits, fine chemicals, aircraft, and battery-powered (electric) cars. Among these, MITI placed particular emphasis on computers. MITI began to pay attention to computers from the mid-1950s, and in 1957 enacted the Law on Extraordinary Measures for the Promotion of the Electronics Industry with the aim of promoting the development of consumer electronic products such as black-and-white television sets, but also keeping computers in mind.

At that time, IBM was the unchallenged world leader in computers. After lengthy negotiations, the government granted IBM permission to manufacture computers in Japan on the condition that it would license basic patents to all interested Japanese manufacturers. IBM concluded technology licensing agreements with Japanese companies. In the following three years, Japanese computer manufacturers entered into further technical assistance agreements with such US manufacturers as RCA, Honeywell, and General Electric. IBM, however, remained the largest computer manufacturer and exporter in Japan.

To support domestic computer manufacturers in their development efforts, MITI, in consultation with them, sponsored the establishment of the Japan Electronic Computer Company (JECC), a computer-leasing organization aimed at facilitating the marketing of hardware produced by domestic manufacturers. Appropriate measures were taken to provide much of the working capital of the company through the facilities of the Japan Development Bank. When an extension of the Electronics Industry Promotion Law expired in March 1971, MITI recognized the need for even stronger supportive legislation. It therefore combined the expiring law with a companion law also expiring at the same time—

the Machinery Industry Promotion Law—and enacted in March 1971 the Law on Temporary Measures for the Promotion of Specified Electronics Industries and Specified Machinery Industries. The new law authorized MITI to take measures, towards industries designated by MITI, to secure funds, exempt from provisions of the Anti-Monopoly Law, and to provide special taxation measures. Because IBM was developing third-and-a-half-generation computers, the System/370 series, at the time, MITI, as a measure to prepare for the imminent liberalization programme of the computer industry, moved to divide six computer manufacturers into three groups to which it would provide direct support for developing new domestic computer models. Specifically, MITI created in its budget a new item for computer industry promotion, and allocated to it the unprecedented amounts of 5.2 billion yen for fiscal year 1972, 12.0 billion yen for fiscal year 1973, and 20.0 billion yen for fiscal year 1974.

It was around this time that the first oil crisis occurred, making the concept of the knowledge-intensification of industry ever more urgent. The intention of the government to tackle the development of computers with greater diligence was attested to by the large size of the promotional budget mentioned above. Meanwhile, domestic computer manufacturers tackled their R&D activities with heightened enthusiasm while competing vigorously with each other. Those that participated in the computer development project were major corporations in the electrical machinery industry, such as Hitachi and Toshiba. They had developed during the period of rapid economic growth in the 1960s, and had ample funds to spend on R&D, accumulated through earnings and the issue of stocks and bonds. Government subsidies for developing the computer industry, therefore, decreased rapidly until the late 1970s when the industry began to develop Very Large-Scale Integration (VLSI) semiconductors.

Throughout the 1970s, the Japanese electronics industry grew rapidly in such knowledge-intensive industries as computers, facsimile machines, and office automation equipment. In many product areas, such as 16K RAMs, it caught up and surpassed its counterpart in the US. One thing worth noting at this point was the fact that the electronics industry in the US received huge government support for R&D activities, primarily for military goods, and its market was supported largely by military demand. In contrast, the Japanese electronics industry developed initially by catering to industrial needs, and later grew rapidly by producing consumer products as well. Automation made headway in every sector of Japanese industry, and Japanese manufacturers of automated machine tools and industrial robots gradually became world leaders. In the field of consumer electronics, too, Japanese industry built a system of volume production based on advanced technology, and expanded its markets throughout the world.

Japanese industry encountered serious hardships ranging from the Nixon shock to the oil crisis, but once provided with the direction of knowledge-intensification of industry promoted as MITI policy it overcame these difficulties and was able to continue to grow.

5.4. Emergence as an Economic Superpower and Responsibility in the Community of Nations

Japan as an economic superpower

The Japanese economy suffered a series of hardships as it navigated the rough straits of the Nixon shock and the oil crises. Although it could no longer sustain the high-level growth it once did, its growth rate from 1975 onwards, albeit slower, was considerably higher than that of the Western countries (Table 5.2). As a consequence, Japan became the world's second largest economic power next to the US, as noted above. Supporting this rise was the stronger international competitiveness of Japanese industry resulting from increased productivity (Table 1.2). Even after the oil crises, Japan's labour productivity in the precision instruments, electric and electronics machinery and equipment, car, steel, and other industries exceeded that of West Germany, to say nothing of the US. Although productivity declined in relative terms in such traditional industries as textiles and wood products and in tertiary industries such as services and commerce, it continued to improve in leading-edge manufacturing fields. Not being able to come near the US level in the 1960s, it caught up with it in the 1970s, and surpassed the US productivity level in the 1980s even in the automobile industry, where the US had long held the leading position.

Economic growth centred on high technology, and trade friction

Two factors accounted for Japanese industry's increased productivity. One factor was the recession that followed the first oil crisis. The government could not stimulate domestic demand through an expansionary economic policy partly because the recession generated huge budgetary deficits and partly because of the after-effects of rampant inflation in 1974 and 1975. Because domestic demand remained sluggish, industry had to develop overseas markets. This familiar pattern of exports increasing during a recession and leading the Japanese economy to recovery was known as the 'export drive effect'. As a result of this drive in the mid-1970s the balance of trade showed surpluses of $10 billion in 1976 and $17 billion in 1977. What made this export drive possible—notwithstanding the criticism that it was accelerated by dumping and other means—was the increased productivity of Japanese industry and the attendant improvement in its international competitiveness.

Another point that merits attention was the change in the types of products that headed the export drive. Cars and other high-technology products replaced the leading exports of the past, such as textiles and steel products. The percentage of gross domestic product (GDP) accounted for by plant and equipment investment in the 1970s exceeded 30 per cent in Japan while the comparable figure for the Western countries was around 20 per cent, suggesting that capital investment in Japan was oriented towards developing new industries, which generally tended to be high-tech industries. The expansion of Japan's exports centred

Table 5.2 Economic growth rates of selected countries (per cent increase *vs.* year before)

	Japan		USA		UK		W. Germany		France	
	Nominal	Real	Nominal	Real	Nominal	Real	Nominal	Real	Nominal	Real
1971	10.1	4.3	8.6	2.8	12.3	2.8	11.3	3.0	11.4	4.8
1972	14.7	8.5	10.0	5.0	10.7	2.5	9.7	4.2	11.7	4.4
1973	21.8	7.9	12.1	5.2	15.2	7.7	11.4	4.7	14.4	5.4
1974	19.1	1.4	8.3	0.5	13.9	0.9	7.3	0.2	15.3	3.1
1975	10.6	2.7	8.5	1.3	26.4	0.7	4.4	1.4	12.8	0.3
1976	12.3	4.8	11.5	4.9	19.1	3.6	9.4	5.6	15.7	4.2
1977	11.5	5.3	11.7	4.7	15.2	1.1	6.5	2.7	12.8	3.2
1978	10.2	5.2	13.0	5.3	15.4	3.6	7.7	3.3	13.8	3.3
1979	8.5	5.3	11.5	2.5	17.0	2.3	8.1	4.0	13.7	3.2
1980	8.2	4.3	8.9	0.2	17.2	1.9	6.4	1.5	13.2	1.6

Source: Toyo Keizai Inc., *Showa Kokusei Soran* (National Census of the Showa Period, iii: International Statistical Comparison): 574.

Table 5.3 High-technology export shares of selected countries, 1970–1985[a]
(unit: %)

	1970–3	1973–6	1976–9	1979–82	1982–5
OECD	95.57	93.93	91.52	88.79	86.80
USA	29.54	27.36	24.37	25.07	25.24
Canada	4.25	3.05	2.45	2.03	2.47
Japan	7.07	7.54	9.21	10.06	12.93
EC 9 countries[b]	46.38	47.50	47.48	44.14	39.26
W. Germany	16.59	17.07	16.52	14.66	12.98
France	7.22	8.06	8.78	8.10	7.26
UK	10.12	9.47	9.70	9.87	8.45
Italy	4.41	4.15	4.10	3.92	3.72
Others	8.04	8.74	8.38	7.59	6.84
Greece, Portugal, Spain	0.50	0.65	0.71	0.85	0.91
EFTA[c]	7.56	7.53	7.06	6.11	5.53
Non-OECD countries	3.99	5.64	7.61	9.29	12.03
Asian NICS	1.3	2.28	3.18	4.06	6.05

Notes:

1. NICS, or newly industrializing countries, in Asia include Hong Kong, South Korea, Singapore, and Taiwan.

2. [a] Figures are averages of high-technology exports of each country/bloc as percentages of world high-technology exports, as defined by Guerrieri and Milana.

   [b] The nine countries of the European Community before Greece, Portugal, and Spain were admitted; includes, besides the four countries listed in the table, Belgium, Denmark, Ireland, Luxembourg, and the Netherlands.

   [c] EFTA (European Free Trade Association) includes Austria, Iceland, Norway, Sweden, Switzerland, and Finland (associate member).

Sources: SIE-World Trade Data Base: Paolo Guerrieri and Carlo Milana, 'Technological and Trade Competition in High-Tech Products,' BRIE Working Papers 54 (Berkeley: University of California, Berkeley), Oct. 1991; Laura D. Tyson, trans. under supervision of Heizo Takenaka, *Dare ga Dare wo Tataite Irunoka?* (Who's Bashing Whom?), Diamond Inc., 1993.

on industrial products, particularly high-technology products. Table 5.3 shows that Japan's share of world high-tech exports stood at 7.07 per cent during the period 1970 to 1973 but gradually increased thereafter and rose to 10.06 per cent in the 1979–82 period. Only the newly industrializing countries in Asia (NICS, renamed NIES—newly industrializing economies—in 1988) experienced similar increases in their shares of world high-technology exports, with the Western countries all showing decreases in their shares. Because Japan's exports were centred on high-technology products, this rapid increase in Japan's share of world high-technology exports intensified competition in these product areas.

US–Japanese trade friction started in the 1950s with negotiations about the textile industry. In 1976, friction related to Japanese steel exports prompted the US government to introduce a trigger price mechanism. And early in the 1980s an agreement was reached to limit Japanese car exports to the US 'voluntarily' to 1.68 million units per year. Trade friction with Japan spread from the US to the EC and the UK.

Trade friction naturally brought to the surface various criticisms of Japanese trade practices. Although not all of these criticisms were necessarily valid, Japan made efforts to reduce and eliminate factors contributing to friction in the interest of the long-term development of free trade. On the occasion of the Tokyo Round of GATT negotiations that began in 1979, for instance, Japan reduced its tariff rates extensively prior to agreed-upon target dates. As a result, Japan's average tariff rates became the lowest in the world. Although Japan still maintained import quotas mainly on beef and agricultural products, the number of items with quotas was smaller than the number with quotas set by European countries. European countries also had more numerous non-tariff trade barriers than Japan did. On the other hand, Japan's imports of manufactured goods, both in per capita terms and as a percentage of total imports, remained smaller than those of the US and other Western nations. What became an issue here was the structural idiosyncrasies of the Japanese economic system, or, more specifically, the difficulty foreign companies experienced in accessing and making inroads into Japanese markets. The US criticism of Japanese practices came to be focused on the issue of barriers to entrance into Japan. The US argued that it was difficult for its products and capital to gain access to Japanese markets whereas Japanese products and capital could enter US markets freely, often in the form of dumping.

Capital exports and Japan's responsibility

The world came to face a second oil crisis in 1979. The price of crude oil was raised to $24 per barrel in November 1979, to $30 in August 1980, and to $34 in October 1981. Although the absolute size of the increase was much greater than that of the first oil crisis, the disruption of the Japanese economy was smaller. The government, relying on experience gained during the first crisis, tightened credit and suppressed price increases. Japan's response to the second crisis was actually better managed than that of the Western countries, except for West Germany. But because wages in Japan had risen to the levels in the US and other Western countries and trade friction with those countries had intensified, Japanese companies searched for favourable overseas investment countries and began siting operations in overseas locations (Table 5.4). The wave of Japanese foreign direct investment can be divided into a first phase up to the mid-1970s when destinations were primarily in the developing countries, and a second phase when investment efforts centred in North America and Europe. In

Table 5.4   Japan's foreign direct investments by region (unit: $m.)

	Total	Asia and Middle East	Europe	North America	South America	Oceania	Africa
1970	904	194	335	192	46	123	14
1975	3,280	1,296	333	905	372	182	192
1980	4,693	1,344	578	1,596	588	448	139
1985	12,217	1,479	1,930	5,495	2,616	525	172

Note: From 1981, investments do not include acquisition of real estate.

Source: Ministry of Finance

1975 and earlier, the largest percentage of Japan's overseas investment was directed towards Asian countries, as Japanese companies searched for lower wages. From 1980 onwards, however, the US and Canada became the largest recipients of Japan's foreign direct investment. Japanese companies moved their operations to North America in order to circumvent trade issues such as import restrictions and dumping charges. This trend became even more pronounced in the mid-1980s; investment in North America became conspicuously large, while that in Asia stagnated and was even surpassed by investments in Europe.

As the magnitude of Japanese capital increased in the global market, Tokyo became an important international financial centre. The outstanding balance of total issues of yen-denominated bonds, known as samurai bonds, reached 19 per cent of the total outstanding balance of foreign bonds in the world in 1979. Yen-based exports increased and accounted for over 30 per cent of total exports from Japan in 1982. Together with London and New York, Tokyo became one of the world's three largest capital markets.

5.5. Overcoming the Negative Effects of Industrial Development

Worsening pollution problems

Industrial growth raised Japan's GNP and its national per capita income, which was 40 per cent of that of the US and about two-thirds of that of West Germany in 1970, rose to about three-quarters of the US, German, and French levels, and about the same level as that of the UK in 1980 (Table 5.5). The great disparity that existed in the 1960s between Japan and the industrially advanced countries in the West nearly disappeared in the 1970s. This change was brought about by technical innovations and the increased productivity discussed earlier, as well as by the international expansion made possible by industrial development which gave a concrete form to those improvements.

Table 5.5   Per capita GNP of selected countries,
1965–1980 (unit: $)

	1965	1970	1975	1980
USA	3,641	4,957	7,415	12,013
Japan	930	1,963	4,471	9,137
UK	1,872	2,240	4,162	9,562
France	2,048	2,826	6,509	12,389
W. Germany	1,954	3,044	6,768	13,269
Italy	1,292	2,012	3,819	8,040

Source: OECD, *National Accounts*.

These developments in Japan, however, had negative aspects. As the Japanese economy grew, industrial pollution and environmental disruption surfaced as serious issues, provoking the public to demand socially responsible behaviour on the part of industry. One reason for this heightened public awareness was that the Japanese began to expand the focus of their attention to the quality of life as their standard of living rose. It was also prompted by the fact that while industrial activities became increasingly more extensive, concentrated, and sophisticated technologically, technological assessment lagged and industrial pollution became widespread and intense.

Pollution problems were already a social issue by the beginning of the 1960s. The initial concern was emissions of toxic industrial waste into water and the air, and the attendant harm done to the health and lives of people. Representative cases of water pollution were the Minamata and Itai-Itai (painful-painful) diseases caused by waste industrial water, whereas representative cases of air pollution were Yokkaichi asthma discovered around a petrochemical complex in Yokkaichi city, and, more generally, the photochemical smog detected in large cities. Once into the 1970s, pollution problems became increasingly widespread and intense. Because similar problems were common to all industrially advanced—and also developing—countries, in June 1972 the United Nations held a meeting of the UN Environment Programme (UNEP) in Stockholm, Sweden, and issued the following declaration: 'We have reached a turning point in history. Now, everywhere in the world, we must regulate our economic activities by paying much closer attention to their impact on the environment.'[2]

Industrial pollution was considered a consequence of waste industrial water released from specific plants, whereas air pollution was attributed to a wide range of causes, including chimney gases causing wide-area air pollution and engine emissions from cars that polluted urban air. The causes of pollution, therefore, were regarded as being rooted in the very structure of contemporary society, and came to be called environmental disruption. To cope with pollution problems, the Japanese government in 1967 enacted and enforced the Basic Law for Environmental Pollution Control. That law was widely revised during the 'pollution Diet', the 64th Diet session in 1970, accompanied by enactment of the Law Concerning the Settlement of Environmental Pollution Disputes and the Water Pollution Control Law. With the enactment of these anti-pollution laws, the government adopted a policy of giving the highest priority to preservation of the environment.[3] In July 1970, MITI unified its anti-pollution control by changing the name of its Mine Safety Bureau to the Environmental Protection and Safety Bureau. It renamed it again in July 1973 as the Industrial Location and Environmental Protection Bureau and began to tackle pollution problems in earnest. Moreover, following the example of the Muskie Act in the US, enacted to set federal engine emission standards with a view to preserving the environment and protecting people's health, in 1972 the Central Council for Environmental Pollution Control released the Interim Report on Controlling Automotive Emissions. In 1974, the Environment Agency established the maximum permissible limits on automotive emissions (1975 standards).[4]

As pollution problems became a serious social issue in Japan, a related problem arose in Japan's relationship with developing countries. From the mid-1960s, Japanese companies began siting their operations overseas. Initially, the main reason for this action was the search for low-cost labour. As government control concerning pollution became more stringent, however, an increasing number of Japanese companies began relocating their operations in developing countries that had no anti-pollution regulations and welcomed the Japanese plants. But the 'export of pollution' by Japanese companies later became an increasingly serious problem in those countries.

Criticism of growth-first policy

For many years in post-war Japan, consumer orientation tended to be overshadowed by other considerations in MITI's policy scheme. In the process of high-level growth, the expression 'consumer is king' was often used, but that was merely another way of expressing the market orientation of producers, their interest in customers who purchased their products. Whereas public economic policy tended to be oriented towards consumers in the UK and the US, the focus of Japanese industrial policy was on producers.

Criticism of the producer orientation of industrial policy was inherent in the pollution debate in Japan. It shed light on the dark side of economic growth. The critical view of the growth-first philosophy, which originated and was gaining popularity in other industrially advanced countries, began to spread among the Japanese people, who were increasingly tired of high-level growth. It even took the form of a 'Damn the GNP!' movement.[5] As a by-product of rapid economic growth in Japan, prices were increasing at a significant rate, substantially offsetting the benefits of wage increases in excess of 10 per cent won through spring labour offensives. Thus, the Nixon shock and the oil crisis were serious 'shocks' not only to Japanese companies but to the common people as well.

Popular criticism concerning economic policy did not surface as long as the economy grew quickly, the standard of living rose, and people enjoyed its benefits. But as pollution threatened the livelihood of the people and as inflation generated price confusion in their living conditions, popular criticism of economic policy surfaced and intensified. MITI policy up to that point had generally been formulated and introduced through relationships of conflict and agreement between MITI and industrial circles, with the voice of the people seldom heard in the process. It was during the period of serious inflation in the early 1970s that MITI began paying close attention to the livelihood of the common people. In 1973, MITI established the Industrial Policy Bureau, and created in it a Price Policy Division in addition to a Consumer Affairs Division. That the government was reflecting on its neglect of the livelihood of the people in its economic growth policy manifested itself in the way it changed its objective from the 'pursuit of economic growth' to the 'utilization of economic growth' revealed in the 'Vision of MITI Policies in the 1970s' discussed earlier. That the government was moving to give serious consideration to the welfare of the people was also expressed in economic policy when 1972 was designated as the 'First Year of Social Welfare', the goal being the provision of substantial security to society. Although this policy evaporated in the subsequent fight against inflation, the government nonetheless was compelled later to follow a policy of balanced and stable growth rather than high-level growth, and the economic growth rate in the second half of the 1970s fell to about 5 per cent per year. The industrial organization of the Japanese economy changed dramatically, both domestically and internationally, as compared with the period of high-level growth in the 1960s.

NOTES

1. Industrial Structure Council, *70-nendai no Tsusho Sangyo Seisaku* (Vision of MITI Policies in the 1970s), 1971.
2. Environmental Science Research Institute, *Ningen Kankyo Sengen* (A Human Environment Manifesto), Nippon Sogo Shuppan Kiko, 1972: 12.
3. The Basic Law for Environmental Pollution Control enacted in 1967 internalizing MITI's views, contained the phrase 'in harmony with wholesome development of the economy' in Art. 1, 'Objectives'. Against the background of the worsening pollution problem, these words were deleted when the law was amended in 1970.
4. A 1975 report of the OECD stated that 'Japan has lowered pollution levels in a number of areas. In particular, it has made remarkable progress in controlling air pollution and harmful chemical effluences.'
5. 'Down with the GNP!' was the slogan used by the Asahi Shimbun in May 1970 in a campaign to mobilize public opinion.

6

Post-War International Trade and Industry Policy and Economic Growth

6.1. Evolution of Post-War Policy for International Trade and Industry

Development of international trade and industrial policy

The preceding five chapters reviewed problems Japanese industry faced after the war and how MITI policy tackled them, with close attention paid to the distinctive characteristics of each period. This chapter presents the overall picture of MITI policy by re-examining various policy measures in their totality.

What were the key policy objectives of post-war MITI policy? Up to now, the key policies were not examined in depth, but an answer to that question may be found in the list of 'Priority Objectives of International Trade and Industry Policy' MITI published each year. This list corresponds to the list of priority items in MITI's budget. From around March of each year, each MITI bureau prepared draft proposals which were then consolidated and coordinated by the Minister's secretariat and studied by the Coordination Committee of the Industrial Structure Council. Having been approved towards the end of August as a skeleton budget, the draft proposals formed the basis of MITI's budget requests and the foundation on which it entered into budget negotiations with the Ministry of Finance. Table 6.1 summarizes the priority items for each year from 1949—when MITI was established—to 1981. The priority policy objectives are closely related to what is discussed in this volume; the list shows how MITI policy evolved over time. As this table shows, there were two main categories of priority objectives. One consisted of MITI objectives that were consistently given priority throughout the entire period. The other was a group of important objectives defined for each of the newly emerging problems of international trade and industry, and were kept at the forefront until they were disposed of one way or another.

In the former category, two types of objectives can be identified. The first is promoting foreign trade with emphasis on export promotion. For ten years, from fiscal year 1949 to 1958, this objective occupied the top position on each year's list. Although it was placed second on the list for fiscal years 1959–61, 'promoting liberalization of foreign exchange' was directly related to, or was one aspect of, the international trade issue itself. From fiscal year 1962, 'overseas economic cooperation' was added to export promotion, and the combined objective again took first position in the period 1964–6. In fiscal year 1970, the scope further widened to 'internationalization of the economy', which was placed first on the list in fiscal years 1970 and 1972. From 1973, this objective fell somewhat in rank listing, and the theme of internationally oriented policy goals changed to achieving harmonious coexistence with the global economy, contributing positively to the world economy, and forming harmonious foreign economic ties, symbolizing the changing role of Japan in the world economy. This change clearly demonstrated the primary objectives of MITI policy and how the growth of the Japanese economy changed them.

The second type of key objectives relates to policy towards small and medium enterprises, which emerged as an important policy for the first time in fiscal year 1950. Having ranked between third and fifth during the first ten years, this policy rose to the first spot in fiscal year 1962 and 1963 as the modernization of small and medium enterprises—their backwardness had become a bottleneck in the process of economic growth—became a serious policy issue. During the period fiscal years 1965–8, this policy objective consistently held second position on the list. As measures were given priority to deal with the problems of small and medium enterprises, and because some stability was realized, the ranking of those problems from 1968 trended downward. From around 1980, the policy for small and medium enterprises became more forward-looking, e.g. fostering dynamic small and medium enterprises, and developing a policy that met the needs of the new age in response to changes in the overall structure of industry.

Economic development and changing priority in MITI policy

As seen above, the major policies MITI pursued throughout the post-war period changed their emphases and goals in response to changing economic conditions. Besides these consistent policies, various other key policy objectives were pursued in response to specific problems that arose from time to time. For instance, 'industrial rationalization'—which will be examined in Part II in conjunction with the discussion on economic self-support—had been an important policy objective since the establishment of MITI. During the period fiscal years 1952–4, it occupied second place on the list of key objectives. From around that time, the objective of industrial rationalization was at times combined with that of promoting industrial technology. During the fiscal years 1959–61 period, the objective resurfaced as 'enhancing international competitiveness through industrial rationalization.' At this stage, however, the objective of industrial rationalization was tentatively achieved. It disappeared from the list in subsequent years, being subsumed under such other objectives as the promotion of mining and industrial technology.

Then the energy problem emerged in place of the industrial rationalization issue. During fiscal years 1959–61, the energy problem appeared in the form of 'promoting measures to deal with structural depression of the coal-mining

Table 6.1   Changing priorities in MITI policy

Fiscal year	First	Second	Third	Fourth
1949	Promoting foreign trade	Promoting industrial rationalization		
1950–1	Promoting foreign trade	Increasing productive power	Promoting industrial rationalization	Promoting small and medium enterprises
1952–4	Promoting exports	Enhancing international competitiveness of products through enterprise rationalization	Improving economic self-support and curbing imports	Promoting comprehensive energy policy
1955–8	Promoting foreign trade	Reinforcing industrial base	Promoting small and medium enterprises	Promoting industrial technology
1959–61	Promoting liberalization of foreign exchange	Promoting exports	Enhancing international competitiveness through industrial rationalization	Improving industrial infrastructure
1962	Promoting small and medium enterprises	Reinforcing and expanding measures to deal with liberalization	Promoting exports and increasing overseas economic cooperation	Promoting mining and manufacturing technology
1963	Modernizing small and medium enterprises and enacting Small and Medium Enterprise Basic Law	Improving and establishing economic order adapted to international economy	Promoting exports and overseas economic cooperation	Promoting mining and manufacturing technology
1964	Promoting exports and overseas economic cooperation	Improving quality of industry	Promoting measures to deal with distribution and consumption	
1965	Promoting exports and expanding LDC policies	Drastic expansion of small and medium enterprises policies	Improving quality of industry for reinforcing international competitiveness	Securing industrial safety and preventing industrial pollution
1966	Promoting exports and overseas economic cooperation	Expanding and ensuring permeation of small and medium enterprises policies	Promoting technology development	Enhancing international competitiveness of industry
1967	Promoting structural reform of industry	Radically expanding and reinforcing policies for small and medium enterprises	Nurturing technology development capabilities and promoting high-technology industries	Promoting foreign trade and increasing economic cooperation with developing countries
1968	Reinforcing enterprise structure and promoting structural reform of industry	Expanding and reinforcing small and medium enterprises policies	Nurturing technology development capabilities and promoting high-technology industries	Promoting foreign trade and increasing economic cooperation with developing countries
1969	Promoting foreign trade and increasing overseas economic cooperation	Promoting structural reform of industry and reinforcing enterprise structure	Expanding small and medium enterprises policies	Nurturing technology development capabilities and fostering high-technology industries
1970	Stepping up internationalization of economy	Improving quality of people's living conditions	Securing basic requirements for economic growth	Promoting modernization of small and medium entrprises and distribution sectors

Fifth	Sixth	Seventh	Eighth
Promoting industrial technology			
Promoting small and medium enterprises	Promoting industrial technology		
Promoting small and medium enterprises	Promoting measures to deal with structural depression of coal mining industry	Promoting industrial technology	Improving measures to deal with distribution and consumption
Optimizing industrial location and reinforcing industrial base	Pursuing comprehensive energy policy	Preventing industrial pollution and promoting consumer administration	
Optimizing industrial location and reinforcing industrial base	Pursuing comprehensive energy policy and reinforcing measures to deal with coal problems	Harmonizing industrial activities and people's living conditions	Enhancing administrative capability and improving quality of public service
Expanding consumer administration			
Pursuing comprehensive energy policy	Adjusting optimum industrial location environment	Expanding distribution and consumer administration	
Optimizing industrial location and improving industrial location conditions	Pursuing comprehensive energy policy	Expanding distribution and consumer administration	
Optimizing industrial location and bolstering measures to control industrial pollution	Pursuing comprehensive energy policy and promoting natural resources development	Expanding and reinforcing distribution and consumer administration	Preparing for 1970 Japan World Exposition
Pursuing comprehensive energy policy and promoting natural resources development	Pursuing measures to control industrial pollution and optimizing industrial location	Reinforcing consumer protection and modernizing distribution sector	Preparing for 1970 Japan World Exposition
Aiming for creative economic growth	Others (hosting of Japan World Exposition, etc.)		

Table 6.1 *Continued*

Fiscal year	First	Second	Third	Fourth
1971	Improving quality of people's living conditions	Stepping up internationalization of economy	Securing basic requirements for economic growth	Modernizing small and medium exterprises and distribution sectors
1972	Stepping up internationalization of economy	Promoting knowledge-intensive development of industrial structure	Optimizing industrial location and promoting environmental preservation	Promoting comprehensive development of natural resources and energy policies
1973	Building pollution-free society	Improving consumer living conditions	Rebuilding Japanese Archipelago	Developing small and medium enterprises capable of meeting internationalization
1974	Stabilizing prices and improving consumer living conditions	Building pollution-free society and promoting environmental preservation	Developing all-out policy to promote welfare-oriented small and medium enterprises	Securing reliable supplies of natural resources and energy
1975	Stabilizing prices and improving consumer living conditions	Securing reliable supplies of natural resources and energy	Securing industrial safety and improving measures to control industrial pollution	Further development of small and medium enterprises policy
1976	Promoting industrial policy for realizing recovery and sustained growth of Japanese economy	Positively promoting small and medium enterprises policies for period of adjustment of internal and external economies	Promoting comprehensive policy for securing reliable supplies of natural resources and energy	Pursuing external economic policy aimed at stable development of international economy
1977	Furthering industrial policy under conditions of stable economic growth	Pursuing external economic policy designed to contribute to stable development of international economy	Improving small and medium enterprises policies	Securing reliable supplies of natural resources and energy
1978	Stimulating business and pursuing new industrial policy	Overcoming energy constraints and securing stable supplies of natural resources	Positively contributing to international economy	Reinforcing small and medium enterprises policies
1979	Formulating 'International Trade and Industry Policy for the 1980s' ('Vision of MITI Policy for the 1980s')	Forming harmonious foreign economic ties and contributing positively to world economy	Steady economic recovery and developing new industrial policy	Improving small and medium enterprises policies
1980	Securing assured supplies of energy resources	Forming harmonious foreign economic ties and contributing positively to world economy	Pursuing future-oriented industrial policy and promoting technology development	Fostering dynamic small and medium enterprises
1981	Securing assured supplies of energy resources and preparing for post-petroleum society	Founding nation through intensive application of industrial technology	Developing external economic policy for era of mutual dependency	Developing industrial policy that makes best use of creativity

Fifth	Sixth	Seventh	Eighth
Aiming for creative economic growth			
Expanding small and medium enterprises policy	Promoting consumer benefits and modernizing distribution sector	Promoting technology development	Promoting development of economy of Okinawa
Achieving harmonious coexistence with global economy	Advancing toward society of future	Securing reliable supplies of natural resources and energy	
Studying industrial activities toward improved national welfare	Creating advanced society of future	Contributing to world economy through international cooperation	
Creating industrial structure that meets people's needs	Promoting technology and systems development towards realization of welfare society	Energetically pursuing international economic policy	
Promoting policies for stable and improved living conditions	Securing industrial safety and improving measures to preserve environment	Promoting technology development for creative economic growth	
Promoting technology development	Normalizing and improving people's living conditions	Harmonizing industrial activities and people's living conditions	
Promoting technology development and fostering next-generation leading industries	Promoting measures for stable and improved consumption conditions and promoting industrial location and environmental policies		
Aggressively pursuing comprehensive energy policy	Fostering next-generation leading industries and improving industrial technology policy	Promoting industrial location and environment policies and promoting measures for stable and improved consumption conditions	
Promoting balanced development of national land and realizing improved living conditions			
Developing small and medium enterprises policies that make best use of vitality and knowledge	Creating attractive regional economic societies and improving quality of people's living conditions		

industry', which from fiscal year 1962 turned into 'pursuing comprehensive energy policy', and came to a pause in fiscal year 1969. With the outbreak of the first oil crisis in 1973, however, 'natural resources and energy policy' became an important task from 1974. The efforts to overcome the difficulties imposed by the second oil crisis of 1979 turned 'securing assured supplies of energy resources' and 'preparing for post-petroleum society' into the leading policy objectives of fiscal years 1980–81.

Two other types of objectives which had been more or less hidden behind these major objectives gradually gained relative importance. One was matters related to distribution and consumption. In fiscal year 1959, 'improving measures to deal with distribution and consumption' appeared for the first time as item no. 8 on the list of important objectives, and remained on the list thereafter. Once into the 1970s, a new situation emerged. As the Japanese economy reached a high level of development and its trade balance showed continuous surpluses, the objective of attaining stable and improved living conditions for the Japanese people came to be viewed as equally important to that of promoting economic growth. In fiscal year 1971, 'improving the quality of people's living conditions' was placed first on the list of key objectives. In fiscal year 1973, 'improving consumer living conditions' occupied second position, and in fiscal years 1974 and 1975 'stabilizing prices and improving consumer living conditions' again became the leading objective, with an added new dimension of the need to control inflation. The objective remained on the list thereafter, although it declined in ranking.

Besides those mentioned above, other objectives—including some not on the list—were clearly stated in some years, such as 'furthering industrial policy' and 'The Vision of MITI Policies in the 1980s', the intent of which could not be understood by their wording alone. The intent was readily understood, however, if viewed in the context of the contemporary situation. At any rate, the trail of varied important objectives decided on after discussions inside MITI, often lasting more than six months, provides a synopsis of the post-war history of MITI policy.

Composition and scale of the MITI budget

The policy objectives thus formulated closely correspond to the composition of MITI's budget. After the Second World War, Japan's military expenditures were thoroughly limited by the Constitution, promulgated in 1947. In their place, public expenditure for economic policies gained in relative importance, although the budget appropriations for MITI programmes were relatively meagre. Approximately 10 per cent of the general account budget was claimed by the Ministry of Agriculture, Forestry and Fisheries, much of it being spent on its rice price support programme. The Construction Ministry's budget, spent primarily on road and highway projects and forest and river conservation programmes, exceeded 10 per cent of the general account budget. MITI's budget, in contrast, amounted to about one-tenth of the budget of each of these ministries, or roughly 1 per cent of the general account budget (Table 6.2). Nonetheless, fitting sums were spent

Table 6.2 Expenditures settlement of general account, by ministry, fiscal years 1950–1980 (unit: million yen)

	Total	MITI	Finance	Agriculture, Forestry, and Fisheries	Transport	Construction	Health and Welfare	Others
1950	633,295	4,917	95,870	48,548	18,900	60,770	34,276	370,016
	(100.0)	(0.8)	(15.1)	(7.7)	(3.0)	(9.6)	(5.4)	(58.4)
1955	1,018,169	7,211	124,004	96,230	27,188	110,143	88,037	565,356
	(100.0)	(0.7)	(12.2)	(9.5)	(2.7)	(10.8)	(8.6)	(55.5)
1960	1,743,148	17,654	147,914	163,441	45,414	201,583	176,532	990,611
	(100.0)	(1.0)	(8.5)	(9.4)	(2.6)	(11.6)	(10.1)	(56.8)
1965	3,723,017	56,024	156,238	396,777	96,529	489,922	512,851	2,014,675
	(100.0)	(1.5)	(4.2)	(10.7)	(2.6)	(13.2)	(13.8)	(54.1)
1970	8,187,697	97,215	624,249	1,043,674	188,498	922,596	1,120,240	4,191,225
	(100.0)	(1.2)	(7.6)	(12.7)	(2.3)	(11.3)	(13.7)	(51.2)
1975	20,860,879	296,217	1,675,539	2,262,073	721,562	2,240,335	4,030,641	9,634,512
	(100.0)	(1.4)	(8.0)	(10.8)	(3.5)	(10.7)	(19.3)	(46.2)
1980	43,405,026	651,351	6,281,031	3,820,170	1,381,443	4,354,162	8,204,196	18,712,674
	(100.0)	(1.5)	(14.5)	(8.8)	(3.2)	(10.0)	(18.9)	(43.1)

Source: Ministry of Finance, Zaisei Tokei (Budget Statistics), various years.

by MITI on industrial adjustment programmes, such as coal-mining measures, and on energy measures, policies for small and medium enterprises, and technology development programmes. Still, if MITI's policy exerted a significant influence on the patterns of development of Japan's international trade and industry, it was not because it directly guided or controlled industries under its jurisdiction by spending, as some other ministries did, large sums of government funds. The subsidies and other forms of assistance given by MITI accounted for a surprisingly small percentage of the national budget.

This point can be confirmed by examining the changing make-up of MITI's budget (Table 6.3). From fiscal year 1965, programmes for small and medium enterprises consistently accounted for the largest part of MITI's budget. Nonetheless, these programmes, regardless of their necessity, played more or less secondary roles among MITI's policies. In fiscal year 1960, when the high-level growth of the economy began, MITI's appropriations amounted to only about 1 per cent of the total general account budget. Expenditures on programmes to promote mining and manufacturing technologies, which accounted for a relatively large portion of MITI's budget, were spent primarily on research support at experimental research institutions. As such, the expenditures did not reflect specifically identifiable policies. The greater portion of appropriations for natural resources and energy programmes, which headed the list in fiscal year 1965, was almost totally for supporting the declining coal-mining industry up to the second half of the fiscal year. Appropriations increased in 1965 because the coal-mining issue became a serious problem. As a result, the support programme was transferred to the Special Account for Coal Mining Measures from fiscal year 1967.

After the first oil crisis, a need to bolster energy policy was keenly felt, and a petroleum tax was established after 1975. From fiscal year 1978 the revenue from this tax was transferred from the general account to the expanded Special Account for Coal, Petroleum, and Petroleum Substitution Energy. With these steps, MITI sought to thoroughly reinforce the petroleum stockpiling and development programmes, and to develop alternative energy sources.

Increased appropriations from fiscal year 1970 for programmes to promote mining and manufacturing technology reflected the beginning of large-scale research projects in nuclear power generation, computers, and other programmes. Prior to this period, budget appropriations in this category had been primarily for such items as patent administration expenses. Once into fiscal year 1975, the target shifted to nurturing and reinforcing leading industries, aiming to develop knowledge-intensive industries.

This table also reveals that the programmes for industrial water—although this industrial policy history does not deal with the subject extensively—were an important budget item, suggesting that high-level growth was accompanied by serious water problems. In fiscal year 1975, moreover, expenditures for industrial structure programmes included in the 'others' category increased sharply, attributable mainly to the 1975 Okinawa International Ocean Exposition.

Table 6.3 MITI general account appropriations by programme categories, fiscal years 1955–80 (unit: million yen)

	1955	1960	1965	1970	1975	1980
For promoting mining and manufacturing technology	1,299 (16.0)	4.657 (26.5)	9,803 (15.9)	21,924 (22.5)	59,214 (20.5)	83,226 (11.6)
For small and medium enterprises	543 (6.7)	2.394 (13.6)	14,989 (24.3)	37,096 (38.1)	102.226 (35.3)	181,351 (25.2)
For problems of natural resources and energy	57 (0.7)	2.899 (16.5)	15,592[a] (25.3)	3,225 (3.3)	9,823 (3.4)	262.246[b] (36.5)
For promoting foreign trade and overseas economic cooperation	929 (11.5)	2.768 (15.8)	6,000 (9.7)	8,015 (8.2)	11,810 (4.1)	11,702 (1.6)
Overseas economic cooperation				2,230 (2.3)	4.977 (1.7)	11,981 (1.7)
Pollution control and industrial safety		61 (0.3)	158 (0.3)	650 (0.7)	5,250 (1.8)	6,394 (0.9)
Industrial water (water resources)		1.271 (7.2)	8,268 (13.4)	9,301 (9.6)	16,207 (5.6)	15,574 (2.2)
Others	5,282 (65.1)	3.514 (20.0)	6,810 (11.1)	14,586 (15.0)	79.785 (27.6)	146,864 (20.4)
Total	8,110 (100.0)	17,564 (100.0)	61,620 (100.0)	97,260 (100.0)	289,292 (100.0)	719,338 (100.0)

Notes:

[a] Of which 14.689 m. yen was for coal-mining measures. The budget for this programme was transferred to the special account for Coal Mining Measures created in 1967.

[b] The special account for Coal and Petroleum Measures was created in 1972. From fiscal year 1978, the appropriation was first recorded in the MITI account and then transferred to the special account. Of the fiscal year 1980 amount, 252,000 m. yen was transferred to the special account.

Source: Tsusho Sangyo-sho Nenpo (MITI Annual Report), various years.

Although this table does not show it, almost the same amount was expended in 1973 on the Japan World Exposition.

These changing budget outlays paralleled the changing priorities in MITI policy discussed earlier. Although they indicate changes in MITI policy, they do not necessarily give the entire picture of MITI policy, and the relative size of budget expenditures should not be regarded as reflecting the importance of the policy measures. Since the total budget of MITI was relatively small as a percentage of the national budget, figures such as 20 or 30 per cent of the total MITI budget did not have a decisive impact on the importance of particular policies. Nor did the relatively small size of the total MITI budget suggest a relative unimportance of MITI policies in overall Japanese economic policies. Although the expenditures were indeed made when needed, such as for small and medium enterprises programmes, the basic MITI policies, it should be said, were put into effect in non-financial measures. One characteristic of MITI's budget was that it did not have financial resources provided by its own budget, as other ministries and agencies did, to carry out its own projects or to provide financial assistance to private projects. To that extent, MITI had no direct control over the private sector. On the other hand, such a stance was one factor that made political intervention in MITI policy from outside relatively insignificant.

MITI-related FILP outlays

In discussing the finances of the economic policies of the Japanese government, it is necessary to mention the Fiscal Investment and Loan Programme (FILP), the so-called second budget. The total annual FILP outlay, although varying from year to year, is generally about 40 per cent of the general account budget. The surplus funds of postal savings and the welfare pensions and national pensions are channelled into the FILP, and those funds are then invested in, or provided as loans to, private-sector investment projects which further the government's policy objectives. In MITI-related areas, FILP funds are made available for programmes related to small and medium enterprises, basic industries, and international trade and overseas economic cooperation. As Table 6.4 shows, the composition of FILP outlays resembles that of the general account. The share of programmes for small and medium enterprises was large in 1955 and increased afterwards. In contrast, the share of basic industry programmes, which stood at 15.8 per cent in 1955 and 13.3 per cent in 1960, decreased sharply from 1965, and fell to only 3.0 per cent in 1975 and to 2.8 per cent in 1979. This trend reflected the improved self-sufficiency in the funds of Japanese industry. It also revealed the changing pattern of MITI policy, as was seen also in the changing composition of the general account budget.

Worth noting here is the large absolute size of FILP outlays for MITI programmes. Of total FILP outlays in fiscal year 1953 of 322.8 billion yen, 101.0 billion yen—or one-third—were MITI-related. In fiscal year 1975, 2,709.5 billion yen—or about 30 per cent of total FILP outlays of 9,310.0 billion yen—was

Table 6.4 Financial investment and loan programme by use of funds, 1955–79 (unit: 100 m. yen; per cent)

	Small and medium enterprises		Living standards related, total		Regional development related, total		Basic industries		Trade and economic cooperation		Total	
1955	262	8.1	1,455	45.1	1,033	32.1	506	15.8	225	7.0	3,219	100.0
1960	774	12.7	2,863	47.2	1,900	31.3	827	13.3	479	7.9	6,069	100.0
1965	2,045	12.6	8,561	52.8	5,164	31.9	1,262	7.8	1,219	7.5	16,206	100.0
1970	5,523	15.4	20,179	56.3	9,792	27.4	2,028	5.4	3,800	10.6	35,799	100.0
1975	14,505	15.6	59,724	64.2	23,452	25.2	2,764	3.0	7,160	7.7	93,100	100.0
1979	29,073	17.3	119,143	70.8	33,955	20.2	4,728	2.8	10,501	6.2	168,327	100.0

Note: 'Use of funds' categories are based on the Trust Fund Bureau Funds Law, as amended. 'Small and medium enterprises' is included in 'living standards related, total'. Total, therefore, is the sum of 'living standards related, total' and the next three categories.

Source: Tsusho Sangyo-sho 30-nen shi (30-Year History of MITI).

allocated to MITI-related projects. These FILP funds were channelled through public policy financing institutions in the shape of loans to private-sector projects which were in keeping with specific MITI policy objectives.

A look at the programme for small and medium enterprises illustrates MITI's use of FILP funds. In fiscal year 1965—and the pattern was not much different in other years—FILP outlays on MITI's small and medium enterprises programmes were 204.5 billion yen, just under fourteen times MITI's general account budget expenditures of about 15 billion yen for those programmes. Those FILP outlays were 3.3 times the size of MITI's total budget that year of 61.6 billion yen. The FILP funds were channelled as loans to small and medium enterprises and others through the Japan Finance Corporation for Small Business, the People's Finance Corporation, and the Shoko Chukin Bank (Central Bank for Commercial and Industrial Cooperatives). MITI controlled the flow of these funds for such projects as converting lines of business, anti-pollution, and modernizing the distribution system, in keeping with the key policy objectives of each period. FILP outlays thus played an important role in MITI policy.

In this context, FILP loans for promoting basic industries and international trade and economic cooperation programmes are worth noting, particularly for the 1955–64 period. These investments and loans were carried out through the Japan Development Bank, the Export-Import Bank of Japan, and the Overseas Economic Cooperation Fund. Policy directives of MITI had a major impact on the flow of these funds as far as their use for international trade and industrial policy matters was concerned.

Thus viewed, it may be concluded that MITI's direct and indirect financial support for its projects was quite substantial. Such financial assistance, however, was not large enough to enable the ministry to exercise direct control over the economy, with the exception of coal-mining industry measures, to be examined below. MITI policy can be characterized as having been development oriented, and Japanese industry certainly developed rapidly. The financial outlays connected with this development, however, were not as large as supposed.

The basic characteristics of MITI policy

In view of the foregoing discussion, it would be a mistake to conclude that MITI's direct financial assistance was the primary instrument of MITI policy. Generally speaking, MITI formulated policy measures to promote industry, enacted laws as needed, and provided financial incentives to private-sector projects that were in conformity with its plans and policies. Additionally, it had FILP support, as described above, as well as special tax incentives, as effective instruments for providing guidance.

In terms of tax measures, MITI arranged special tax provisions for corporation tax and income tax, created special local tax measures, and utilized them effectively as instruments for guiding private activities towards realizing specific policy objectives, such as export promotion, pollution control, energy saving, and the greater sophistication of industry. These special tax measures were formulated by the Ministry of Finance at MITI's request and were ultimately approved by the Diet according to the provisions of relevant laws.

One aspect of MITI policy which should not be overlooked was the preparation and proclamation of policy 'visions'. Because these visions attracted much public attention, MITI policy was dubbed, with a measure of sarcasm, as 'mouth and paper' policy. 'Paper' here referred to the fact that MITI suggested that industrial circles develop their investment and other plans in accordance with the government's own economic plans, such as medium-term and other plans, as expressed on 'paper'. Of particular importance in this regard were the 'Vision of MITI Policies in the 1970s' announced at the beginning of the 1970s and the 'Vision of MITI Policies in the 1980s' announced at the beginning of the 1980s. 'Mouth' referred to explaining these ideas via journalism and trying to persuade industrial circles to go along with them. With the exception of structural problems which were dealt with by policies such as those for small and medium enterprises and the coal-mining industry, the weight of 'soft' elements—the percentage of those that did not require extensive use of financial resources, such as ideas, coordination, and mediation—was high in MITI policy. MITI used a multitude of diverse policy instruments in its arsenal, by themselves or in combination, according to the nature of each case. In this sense, MITI can be characterized more appropriately as a policymaking rather than an adminstrative agency.

Japanese industrial development and research expenditure

With regard to the above discussion, some consideration should be given to R&D expenditure, which served as a prime mover of Japanese industrial development. Whether in the car industry, the electrical machinery industry, or the steel industry, Japanese manufacturers developed themselves by financing almost all their experimental research with their own funds. The small subsidies they received from the government for R&D, however, often produced positive results for their technological development programmes that far exceeded the monetary value of the subsidies. Before the Second World War, investment in research was carried out primarily by the government at national experimental research institutions and universities. From fiscal year 1955, however, as the private sector gradually acquired ample funds, the initiative in research investments came to be taken by the private sector. In fiscal year 1967, total R&D investments of 60 billion yen accounted for 1.8 per cent of national income, 32 per cent of which was accounted for by the government, including assistance to the private sector.

As the internationalization of the economy made headway, however, it became necessary for Japanese industry to develop its own technology in order to catch up with other industrial nations and compete with overseas companies that had plentiful supplies of capital and excellent R&D capabilities. Embracing the proposal forwarded by the Industrial Technology Committee of the Industrial Structure Council for promoting large-scale research projects, MITI in fiscal year 1966 instituted 'the system of development for large-scale R&D in industrial technology.' Funds appropriated for related projects were 1 billion yen in the first year, 2.7 billion yen in the second year, 3.8 billion yen in the third year, and 11.8 billion yen in 1975. In 1971, MITI launched an electronic computer promotion programme in order to cope with the dominance of the worldwide market by the US computer industry. The budget for the programme, which stood at 5.2 billion yen in fiscal year 1972, was increased to 11.9 billion yen in 1973.

These sums, however, were small compared to total R&D expenditure of the electronics industry. But the contribution which government investment made to private research activities could not be gauged solely by its monetary value. Subsidies by MITI to the computer and microchip industries make this clear. Using those subsidies as a lever, for example, MITI urged Japan's computer manufacturers to work jointly on R&D in Large-Scale Integration (LSI) circuitry. LSI research was beyond the capability of any single manufacturer. At the same time, it was almost impossible for computer manufacturers voluntarily to form a joint research project because of the fierce rivalry among them. But MITI provided subsidies to form the basic funds for a research consortium and persuaded the companies concerned to form a joint-research arrangement, which eventually produced positive results.

6.2. The Roles of MITI

The basic stance of MITI policy

As noted above, the financial underpinning of MITI policy was not substantial. Nonetheless, in formulating polices MITI gave special attention to, and at times did not spare financial assistance for, the task known as 'structural adjustment', or programmes to deal with the industrial structure as it changed in the process of economic growth. MITI implemented its structural adjustment policy in two general areas, at times appropriating certain amounts of financial support. One area is exemplified by the support to the joint LSI research project mentioned above, where MITI identified new industries vital for the future of Japanese industry and moved forward aggressively with programmes to nurture them. The other area covered instances where MITI formulated remedial measures for declining industries on which the Japanese economy had relied heavily in the past. The former may be likened to the nursing care of infant industries, whereas the latter may be likened to terminal or geriatric care for industries in their declining or terminal stages.[1]

Rapid changes in the industrial structure throughout the world in the 1970s gave rise to an interest in formulating policies for declining industries. As a measure of responding to depressed industries or to industrial decline caused by rapid changes in the industrial structure, the OECD Ministerial Council in June 1978 adopted the 'General Policy Guidelines towards Positive Adjustment Policies (PAP)'. The PAP guidelines said that industrial adjustments should fundamentally be left to free-market forces, but also recognized the necessity of public support measures and of incurring social costs for that purpose. This same approach, however, had already been practised in Japan under the rubric of industrial adjustment policy, which was essentially based on the same philosophy that emerged in PAP. Whereas PAP more or less stressed measures to aid declining industries in response to the conditions prevailing at the time, industrial adjustment policy had an extra dimension of fostering new industries. In that sense, as mentioned, it had aspects of nursing care for infant industries and declining or terminal industries.

One view of MITI policy history, in an attempt to give theoretical content to these discussions, argued that 'MITI's intervention tends to follow the trajectory of a product life cycle.'[2] In this view, MITI intervenes aggressively in an industry's early phase of development, reduces intervention as the industry matures, and again intervenes actively as the industry loses its comparative advantage and faces problems related to excess capacity. Certainly this theory may account for events in certain industries, but generalizing from such cases may not be entirely appropriate.

The computer industry as typical case of infant-industry care

A representative case of the policy of providing nursing care for an infant industry was the computer industry. Facing imminent US dominance of the world computer industry spearheaded by IBM Corporation, MITI formulated and put into effect a programme of creating and nurturing the Japanese computer industry, taking into consideration the future prospects of the industry in Japan. It is worthwhile examining the process in detail.

One method devised in Japan for providing nursing care for an infant industry was the system of technology research associations. This system was provided according to the Research Association for Mining and Manufacturing Technology Law of 1961. Its aim was to promote the creation of research associations for joint research efforts among private enterprises in order to develop efficiently new technologies and keep Japan from falling behind overseas advances. Soon after the law was put into effect, the Polymeric Materials Technology Research and Development Association was formed, followed within a year by the formation of five other associations. Further, in September 1962, a number of companies in related industries formed the Electronic Computer Research and Development Association to develop a mainframe computer using domestic technology.

From the time when an experimental vacuum-tube computer was developed at the University of Tokyo ten years earlier, computer design had progressed rapidly through the period of transistors and into the era of semiconductor integrated circuits. Around 1960, however, as many as 70 per cent of digital computers used in Japan were still imported. For the domestic manufacture of computers, the introduction of advanced technology from IBM, the company that dominated the world market with its technology, was indispensable. In 1960, concerted efforts by government and business circles made it possible for IBM patents to be used by Japanese manufacturers, leading to full-scale domestic production of computers. In 1961, NEC, Hitachi, Toshiba, and other companies designed and manufactured computers of their own. After production began, however, a problem arose regarding sales. IBM used a rental system, considering that computers were so expensive that many users could not afford to buy them. Also, frequent model changes were necessary to keep up with technological advances. But for Japanese manufacturers, without such large financial resources as IBM, the rental system was not a feasible alternative. Under MITI's guidance, therefore, Japanese computer manufacturers jointly established the Japan Electronic Computer Company (JECC), a computer rental corporation. To give the company a financial lift, MITI in 1961 provided a low-interest loan of 400 million yen by way of the Japan Development Bank, followed by additional loans of close to a billion yen a year afterwards. This arrangement made it possible for Japanese computer users to avail themselves of high-performance computers produced by fledgling Japanese computer manufacturers. It also helped Japan to nurture domestic computer manufacturers who could more or less compete with US companies. In 1962, subsidies were given to a newly established computer research association which was formed in order to develop domestic technology. By 1966, government subsidies totalling 350 million yen—an unprecedented sum in those days—had been provided, launching the domestic computer industry on the path of producing mainframes. Against this background, the installation of mainframes in Japan gained headway. Along with West Germany, Japan in 1965 had the second largest number of mainframes installed next to the US. From 1966, under MITI guidance, the industry was divided into three groups of producers. Fujitsu and Hitachi, NEC and Toshiba, and Oki Univac and Mitsubishi Electric. Each group pursued its own programme of developing high-performance computers, and achieved a measure of success by 1970.[3] With this success, the Japanese computer technology made further progress, and the disparity between the US and Japanese levels was substantially reduced. Development was accelerated not only of semiconductor technology, such as that relating to LSIs and ICs, but also of the overall electronics industry. Success in those areas also contributed in no small measure to software development, an area in which Japan lagged behind other industrial nations.

Although the focus was somewhat different, the positive involvement of MITI policy in fostering small and medium enterprises can also be regarded as essentially of the same nature as that in promoting the computer industry. Although small and medium enterprises were not an industrial sector where substantial growth could be generated by means of promotional policy, it was, nonetheless, a sector which eventually would have to be nurtured by the government. A great number of small companies constituted the foundation of the Japanese industrial structure. Accordingly, those companies could not be left to decline and fail either naturally or accidentally, receiving no help from society. For such reasons, MITI had provided, as described above, considerable financial aid to this sector out of its limited budget, although small companies were expected to make efforts to help themselves. The Electronics Industry Promotion Law and the Machinery Industry Promotion Law were typical examples of how small companies were helped. Of course, the Japanese government has to consider the health and well-being of overall industry, but because industry has an innate vitality, it tends to grow by itself without much governmental help. And once it reaches a certain level of development it tends to view government intervention as onerous and wishes to reject it. In that sense, there are not so many industries that need nurturing by the government, and such nurturing need not be provided for a long period of time.

The coal industry as a typical case of the terminal care of industry

As compared to the infant care of industry, terminal care—or home geriatric care for less serious cases—entails many difficulties. Typical cases of home geriatric care in Japan were the cotton and silk textile industries; a typical case of terminal care was the coal mining industry. The former were Japan's leading industries and principal exporters before and directly following the war, whereas the latter was the core industry during the post-war period of economic reconstruction. MITI had high hopes for their healthy growth, and gave them as much support as it could. When they became victims of the changing industrial structure and turned into declining industries, MITI found it necessary to attend to their difficulties in view of the sheer magnitude of their impact on the national economy.

Concerning the coal mining industry, first, from around 1955 low-cost petroleum became available in large quantities, precipitating the so-called energy revolution. In order to overcome a resultant slump in the coal industry, there were strong demands to reduce coal prices through all-out rationalization of the industry. With that as a momentum, improvements could then be expected in the basic conditions of the industry, which would lead to its stabilization. As a response to the strong demands, the Law on the Promotion of the Rationalization of the Coal Mining Industry was amended substantially in 1960. Coal miner unions—the most militant of post-war unions—staged 'policy conversion struggles' to combat such action, but to no avail. It was difficult to restore the economic benefits of coal, and the conclusion that it could no longer compete with heavy oil was all but inevitable.

Regarding the situation as extremely serious, the Japanese government in 1962 requested that a Mission for Coal Survey be organized to investigate countermeasures. A subsequent report recommended large-scale closing of low-efficiency mines, including small and medium mines, relief measures to deal with the large-scale unemployment that would necessarily follow after mines were closed, and measures to provide aid to impoverished coal mining regions. The Cabinet thereupon adopted the 'Guidelines for Coal Measures', and moved in an all-out effort to tackle the problem. Initially, the new measures yielded satisfactory results as the business climate had turned favourable, but the situation took a sudden turn for the worse as the economy entered the recession of 1965. In response, the government adopted a radical programme for stabilizing the coal mining industry in fiscal year 1966. The programme consisted of: (1) reducing coal production targets, (2) taking over 100 billion yen in debt in order to improve the financial well-being of coal mining companies, (3) giving 'stabilization subsidies' to small and medium coal mines, and (4) establishing the 'Special Account for Coal Measures' with revenue from import duties on crude and heavy oil. Despite these measures, the deterioration in the situation of the coal mines continued unabated. In a sense, the condition of the patient continued to worsen. In this period, the coal mining problem was discussed at a Cabinet Members Conference on Coal Measures, including not only MITI but other relevant ministers, because the problems concerned not just an industry under MITI's jurisdiction but also unemployed coal miners and the coal mining regions. MITI's Coal Bureau, reorganized in 1952 with the aim of rationalizing the coal-mining industry and increasing its production, was in the early 1960s busily occupied in the defensive position of securing demand for coal through the industry's rationalization. In fiscal year 1963, coal subsidies and related expenditures exceeded 10 billion yen, accounting for more than one-quarter of MITI's budget. In order to deal with the increasingly heavier burden of coal-programme expenditures, the government in fiscal year 1967 transferred them, as mentioned earlier, from the general account to a special account. In fiscal year 1968, those expenditures reached 60 billion yen, an amount equal to about 70 per cent of MITI's general account budget of 85 billion yen. In fiscal year 1970, they further rose to 97 billion yen, roughly equivalent to MITI's entire general account budget. These expenditures were clearly not for promoting and fostering the coal mining industry; they were actually expenses for terminal care.

Nurturing of the textile industry and home geriatric care

The conditions of the textile industry and MITI's responses to them were somewhat different from those of the coal mining industry. As the leading post-war export industry, the cotton textile industry recovered quickly under a reconstruction programme initiated by the Ministry of Commerce and Industry. The industry also expanded its production capacity, riding on the crest of the wave of the unprecedented business boom during the Korean War period. From the mid-1950s, however, the earlier expansion boomeranged on the industry, thrusting it into a situation where it was overproducing. To cope with its adversities, the industry repeatedly introduced production cutbacks and sent inexpensive products to overseas markets. A major factor contributing to the industry's hardships was, as was true with the coal industry, the emergence of an industry which produced a highly competitive product. For the textile industry that product was synthetic fibres. The first appearance of synthetic fibres in the Japanese market was after the war, led by nylon developed and marketed by Dupont of the US. In order to achieve an equilibrium in the nation's balance of payments, the Ministry of Commerce and Industry limited the increasing import of raw cotton, which was raw material for cotton textiles, and moved to create and nurture the synthetic fibre industry. For instance, it provided assistance for construction of Toyo Rayon's 'Amiran' (a synthetic fibre much like nylon) plant and Kurashiki Rayon's 'Vinylon' plant. One after another, large companies in the cotton-spinning and chemical fibre industries initiated R&D on new synthetic fibres. In 1953, MITI adopted the 'Five-Year Plan for Developing the Synthetic Fibre Industry', and provided research subsidies, financial assistance, and tax incentives. As a result, the development of the industry gained headway from the mid-1960s. This led quite naturally to the problem of competition between this new industry and the traditional textile industry which was suffering from overproduction.

An analysis of the textile industry requires a review of its industrial structure. The industry consisted of large cotton-spinners and medium-size spinners called 'new spinners' and 'new new spinners' established during the boom period. The fibres produced by the spinners were woven into fabrics by weaving companies. Following them were the manufacturers of garments and other textile products. In general, textile manufacturers covered spinning and weaving activities. Among the manufacturers of apparel and other textile products, medium-size and larger firms were usually manufacturers and wholesalers. They manufactured key products by themselves, but subcontracted work on other goods to small sewing firms and further to microcosmic proprietors subordinated to them. For the manufacturing industry, MITI classifies firms having 301 or more employees as large-scale enterprises and firms of all sizes having no more than 300 employees as 'small and medium enterprises'. Of these, those having no more than twenty-one workers are classified as 'small firms', assumed to be operated as family businesses. As an industry well established in Japanese society from before the war, the textile industry was well represented by firms of all sizes with deep roots in the Japanese social structure. In 1966, these firms numbered more than 100,000 (Table 6.5).

As mentioned above, policy towards the textile industry after the Korean War boom ended had two dimensions: fostering the synthetic fibre industry, and providing home geriatric care to the cotton-spinning industry. From the mid-1950s, MITI engineered production cutbacks in the cotton textile industry to deal with

Table 6.5 Size of the 103,987 companies in textile industry

No. of employees	1–3	4–9	10–19	20–49	50–99	100–199	200–299	300–499	500–999	1,000 or more
No. of companies	45,247	31,323	7,780	6,503	1,868	749	216	165	109	67

Source: *Dai 3-kai Chusho Kigyo Sogo Kihon Chosa Hokokusho* (Report on Third Comprehensive Basic Study of Small and Medium Enterprises), 1966.

the twin problems of excess capacity and the high foreign-exchange cost of raw cotton imports. Countries in South-East Asia, meanwhile, began imposing restrictions on imports of cotton textiles from Japan. Many trading firms specializing in textile exports went bankrupt, and low-price imports of 'one-dollar blouses' from Japan became a controversial issue in the US and elsewhere. In response to this situation, the Japanese government in 1956 promulgated the Law on Temporary Measures for Textile Industry Equipment. Under the provisions of this law, the government placed restrictions on the use of surplus spinning machines of large spinners and required them to be mothballed. It also engaged in a purchase-and-scrap programme for eliminating surplus looms of very small operators. In this sense, the history of MITI policy towards the traditional textile industry from the early 1950s can be regarded as a history of production cutbacks. The focus of policy was how best to ensure the stable and viable existence of the industry. The situation, however, continued to worsen. The industry faced a crisis situation in the early 1960s, owing partly to the fact that the developing countries were catching up and partly to labour shortage and attendant higher labour costs. From the mid-1960s, industry-wide scrapping of spinning machines was mandated. In total, 800,000 spindles were purchased and scrapped by the government, including those voluntarily scrapped by owners. From the early 1970s, although the traditional textile industry waned rapidly, many firms retained a measure of viability by adopting new technology and improving their product quality; at that point, few segments of the industry had reached the terminal stage. Also, conversion to other lines of business was relatively easy for small and medium enterprises in areas such as fabric weaving. They found a way out of their difficulties, partly because of considerations made by MITI, and managed to continue in business.

The economy and society in MITI policy

Although MITI exerted itself for both infant nursing care and terminal care for industries, if anything it took greater interest in the nursing care of infant industries. It engaged in terminal-care activities, it should be said, not because of the economic importance of the relevant industries but rather because of their social importance. In many cases, those industries that required terminal care in Japan consisted largely of small and medium enterprises. The industries were also likely to be local industries dispersed widely throughout the country. A classic example was the cotton textile industry mentioned above. When a company in this industry lost in market competition and withdrew from it, it could often continue its existence—thanks to the growing economy—by becoming a subcontractor for its competitors. In cases of very small family-run firms, the successor to the owner, who retired because of advancing age, often converted to a new business because of the uncertain prospects of the business. Consequently, the terminal care provided for industries, with a few exceptions—such as the coal-mining industry—did not last long and its financial burden on society was not excessive.

When an industry did not have such a significant social base as the industries noted above, the government did not provide such care. The aluminium industry was a good example. Attracted by a strong demand for aluminium after the Second World War, large companies expanded into aluminium-refining, and from the mid-1950s the industry made considerable progress, producing 1 million tons per year by around 1975. The industry, however, was a heavy user of electric power. When the first oil crisis led to sharp increases in electric power rates, therefore, the cost of aluminium-refining rose sharply. Unable to bear the increased production costs, many companies left the industry one after another in the early 1980s, and the industry vanished from the scene in the second half of the 1980s. Partly because the companies themselves were capable of handling the financial aspects of withdrawal, and partly because the social impact of the withdrawal process was minimal, the terminal care MITI provided for this industry was for a relatively brief period.

As seen, then, MITI introduced appropriate measures in the form of nursing care for infant industries and terminal care for declining industries by providing subsidies and other assistance measures such as FILP funds, tax incentives, and special financing. It should be clear from this description, however, that MITI was even more deeply involved with industrial activities that provided the motive power for Japan's economic growth. These measures attracted the attention of foreign media and scholars, and the nature of 'Japan, Inc.' came to be widely discussed. The following is a review of MITI policy as observed from the outside.

6.3. The Japan, Inc. Model and Government–Business Cooperation

The Japan, Inc. model

The viewpoint of comparing the structure of Japanese industry with that of a corporation—equating MITI to the corporate headquarters and large Japanese corporations to branches or divisions taking orders from headquarters—seemed to gain in popularity from around 1970, when the development of Japanese industry began to attract worldwide attention and its 'uniqueness' began to be debated.[4] The gist of this view was summarized in the following manner:

With respect to the relationships between business and government in Japan, we find that the government in many ways is involved with business activities far more deeply than in the United States. MITI wields much power. It develops strategic plans for Japanese industry in the world market; it also determines which industries are to be developed, and directs the Bank of Japan and every parent bank to provide the industry sufficient financing to facilitate its growth. It is said that this set-up may be described as 'Japan, Inc.'[5]

A view like this could certainly apply to some aspects of the pre-war Japanese economy. After the war, however, and especially after the end of the Allied Occupation, business gained a stronger voice with the government, and this version of the 'Japan, Inc.' model, which equated the government to a corporate head-quarters, met with criticism and lost its appeal, even in the US.

A somewhat different view of Japan, Inc. was represented by the report on Japan the US Department of Commerce published in 1972 entitled 'Japan: The Government–Business Relationship'.[6] That report's main points are worth examining. First, the report argued that although it was not appropriate to over-emphasize government initiatives, 'Japan, Inc.' was nonetheless an undeniable economic fact. It attributed the dramatic growth of the Japanese economy to the successful implementation of the programmes of fostering and aiding priority sectors through close collaboration between government and business. It acknowledged that close working relationships between government and business existed even in the US, as in the case of the military-industrial complex, but it nonetheless argued that the relationship between the Japanese government and industrial circles had a singular style and dimension. 'A qualitative difference, a style peculiar to the Japanese, derives from Japan's history and culture with its emphasis on the consensual approach, a tradition of government leadership in industrial development, and a generally shared desire to advance the interests of the Japanese nation.'[7]

The view of the Commerce Department was that the Japanese system was not a monolithic one, as was often described, in which the business community blindly followed government initiatives, but rather was a relationship based on a consensus built between government and business. It reasoned that as a means to build this consensus the Japanese government made ingenious use of 'financing, special taxation measures, subsidies, technical assistance, and other incentives'.

The Commerce Department study explored the matter yet further. It identified another factor that contributed to the close working relationship between government and business in Japan: administrative guidance. It said that ' "administrative guidance" is the expression most typically used to describe the varying degrees of persuasion that MITI employs with industry to encourage implementation of the nation's economic priorities.'[8] Notwithstanding the use of the word 'guidance', the wide latitude of initiatives and autonomy which the government allowed the business community to have, argued the report, produced the energy for industrial development. Two factors were at work in this respect:

(1) a reluctance on the part of both business and government to unilaterally adopt policies or undertake major moves in the high priority sectors of the economy without consulting each other; and (2) a propensity, which all Japanese share, for a consensual approach to harmonizing differences that may exist within as well as between each group.[9]

Of course the government was prepared to provide subsidies, financing, taxation measures, and other incentives as noted earlier, and business also expected and required them, but these, argued the report, were the security deposit or earnest money which the government paid, and the cost of implementing policy measures was borne by business.

Consensus formation

It is not an easy matter to discover the process of forming a consensus. Since the age of high-level economic growth, the most commonly used method was the advisory councils discussed earlier. The Commerce Department recognized this point in its report. Having noted that the Industrial Structure Council was the most representative of the advisory councils, the report gave the following account of the Electronics Industry Council.

The Electronics Industry Deliberation Council, which the Diet directed be established within MITI, is a fine example of this kind of consensus-making apparatus. Although said to be dominated by its secretariat, the Electronics Industry Section of the MITI Bureau of Heavy Industry, the Electronics Industry Deliberation Council is still widely representative of the industrial interests involved. Outside experts, economists, physicists, and engineers are also included in this policymaking body. Problems, research topics, and ultimately policy proposals are brought before this 40-member group by MITI's Electronic Industry Section. The Council's position is announced after consensus is achieved, all differences being first harmonized within the group. The Council's position then represents a formal guideline to MITI policy.[10]

The report was correct in noting that although not all policy proposals were deliberated by advisory councils, the government and industrial circles nonetheless 'seldom took important steps without consulting each other first.'

Another point to which the report of the Commerce Department called attention was the clashes that developed between MITI and other agencies when MITI tried to implement measures it believed were appropriate. Clashes with the Ministry of Finance are cases in point. When MITI moved to strengthen the international competitiveness of Japanese industry by shifting to an open economy and giving massive aid to programmes to increase production capacity, the Ministry of Finance—which holds the purse strings to the State's coffers—kept a tight rein on MITI for fear that increased investments might create inflationary pressures. In another more controversial case, MITI was pitted against another government agency, the Fair Trade Commission (FTC), in a direct conflict. Whereas MITI, if anything, approved of cartelization or tried to promote mergers, the FTC objected to these policies on the principle of the Anti-Monopoly Law, and took issue with MITI. On the question of possible breach of the Anti-Monopoly Law, MITI at various times persisted in its position or withdrew, depending on the particular economic and social conditions.

The limits of the Japan, Inc. model

The report of the US Commerce Department was rather cautious about defining Japan as a 'corporation'. In particular, it was extremely critical of regarding the relationship between government and business like that between a corporation's headquarters and branches, or that between an organization that formulates policy and directs its execution with financial backing and organizations that receive the directives and execute them. To that extent, the views expressed in this report were fair. The report was based on a fairly minute study; as can be seen from the above quotes, specific cases were discussed on the basis of an accurate understanding of the subject matter.

The report, however, had two limitations, as pointed out by some critics in the US. One had to do with the fact that MITI policy varied considerably from industry to industry. As discussed above, the infant-industry nursing case and the terminal-care case differed greatly by their nature. There was also a vast difference between MITI policy applied to the steel and automobile industries, whose primary players were large corporations, and policy implemented for the textile industry, which was made up of a large number of small and medium enterprises. An attempt to apply a single view, such as the Japan, Inc. model, to this complex reality naturally has serious limitations.

The other limitation related to the failure to fully account for changes occurring in the course of economic development. As this volume clearly shows, MITI policy changed its content markedly in the process of development, not only during the Occupation but also in response to changing growth patterns during the period of high-level growth. Subsequently, after Japan acquired the status of 'economic superpower', MITI policy changed greatly in response to changes in international relations and the domestic economic structure. Although the report of the Commerce Department did not totally ignore these changes, it appeared to have sought to find a common thread of Japan, Inc. throughout these changes. The limitation seems to lie in the attempt to interpret MITI and its policy by using, as a model, the behavioural patterns and achievements of a private economic organization, a corporation.[11]

It must be admitted, however, that the fact that external criticisms of the Japanese system often contain elements of the Japan, Inc. model has some significance in itself. In the US and similar societies, much importance is attached to the market system. Economic activities are driven by the profit motive, and it is an anomaly for industrial policy to assist the development of those activities. Instead, it is believed that the government is responsible for regulating the activities of business firms when it is necessary to prevent them from impairing the welfare of the consuming public. In contrast, the focus of policy in Japan is, if anything, on protecting and assisting producers, rather than on protecting consumers. It appears that foreign critics feel uneasy about this difference, and try to find in it the peculiarity of Japanese industrial policy.

The role of laws concerning international trade and industry policy

There is yet another point missing from the Japan, Inc. model, and from the criticisms of Japanese industrial policy in general. It is the series of laws that define the nature of MITI policy.[12] The report by the US Commerce Department discussed above, as well as critiques of the report, barely touch upon the existence and functions of MITI-related statutes, Cabinet orders, and ministerial ordinances.

On the other hand, in this introductory Part, as well as elsewhere in this volume describing the development of MITI policies in each respective period, there is frequent reference to the process of formulating relevant laws and ordinances that specify the nature of those policies. For instance, it is safe to say that a considerable part of MITI's deliberations on energy policy was devoted to formulation of relevant laws and ordinances. Furthermore, specific work MITI carried out consisted of guiding industries in specified directions, supervising their behaviour, and in some cases disposing of complaints according to these laws, as well as according to Cabinet orders and ministerial ordinances that enforced the laws. In the process of formulating and implementing legislation, MITI listened to the views of industrial leaders, attempted to reconcile its views with those of political parties, and, as needed, also listened to the views of consumers. In formulating particularly important laws, MITI consulted with the relevant advisory council for drafting legislation and prepared final bills on the basis of the report of the council, as described earlier.

It is impossible to describe here in detail all the individual laws and ordinances, but the following is a brief listing as of 1975. First, in the area of international trade, there were: the Foreign Exchange and Foreign Trade Control Law (1949, Law 228) which defined the basic framework; and its enforcement orders, the Export Trade Control Ordinance (1949, Ordinance 378) and the Import Trade and External Payments Control Order (1949, Cabinet Order 414); as well as the Export and Import Transaction Law (1952, Law 299), the Export Inspection Law (1957, Law 97), the Export Credit Insurance Law (1950, Law 67), the Law Concerning Japan External Trade Organization (1958, Law 95), and others. Laws, Cabinet orders, and ordinances promulgated by various ministries based on the above laws, as well as rules and notifications to enforce them, including laws and ordinances concerning matters under the jurisdiction of other ministries and agencies, totalled 124 in number.

In the areas of the Anti-Monopoly Law and fair trade, there were twenty-nine laws and regulations, including the basic law—Law Concerning the Prohibition of Private Monopoly and the Preservation of Fair Trade (1947, Law 54)—and those based on it, including Specified Unfair Trade Practices in the Soy Brewing Industry (1953, FTC Notification 13) and the Unfair Competition Prevention Law, which was enacted before the war. Concerning the machinery and information industries, there were sixty-six laws and regulations, including the Measurement Law (1951, Law 207), the Law of Temporary Measures to Promote the Export of Plants, etc. (1959, Law 58), and the Law on Temporary Measures for the Promotion of Specified Electronics Industries and Specified Machinery Industries (1971, Law 17), which appears frequently in Part IV as the 'Electronics and Machinery Industries Promotion Law'.

A similar situation existed for other industries. Also, in the area of small and medium industries, which MITI aimed to nurture and protect as the foundation of Japan's industrial structure, there were as many as 145 laws and regulations, including the Small and Medium Enterprise Basic Law (1963, Law 154), which defined the guiding principles of small and medium enterprises policy, as well as the Law Concerning the Organization of Small and Medium Enterprises Organizations (1957, Law 185), the Law on Financial and Other Measures for

Aiding Small and Medium Enterprises (1956, Law 115), the Small and Medium Enterprise Modernization Promotion Law (1963, Law 64), the Law on the Promotion of Subcontracting Small and Medium Enterprises (1970, Law 145), the Law on the Promotion of Small and Medium Retail Business (1973, Law 101), as well as the Circular Knit Socks Adjustment Regulation (1961, MITI Ordinance 12), and the Scarf Exports Adjustment Regulation (1962, MITI Ordinance 45).

These laws and regulations may be considered as an aspect of the fundamental character of Japan as a nation governed by law. They were revised as conditions changed, and the mode of their application was altered within their objectives. Also, systems of laws and regulations were created for new industries in response to the new conditions. This well-developed system of laws and regulations covers every aspect of the Japanese industrial system, prompting industrial circles to demand deregulation. It is also one cause of criticisms by the US and other countries, which argued that it contributes to the closed nature of Japanese markets to foreign capital and generates trade friction.[13]

In this volume on the history of MITI policy, 'government–business cooperation' and 'administrative guidance', among other subjects, are discussed and are characterized as distinctive features of MITI policy. It goes without saying, however, that the principle of 'Japan as a country governed by law' lies at the foundation of this characterization, and that MITI policy is in keeping with this principle. The reasons why government–business cooperation is considered a distinctive feature of MITI policy were that in part it is compared with practices in countries such as the US and the UK, and that in part MITI's approach, as compared to that of other Japanese ministries and agencies, is flexible, even though it is based on as large and complex a system of laws and regulations as that of other agencies. In order to respond appropriately to rapid changes in domestic and worldwide industrial conditions, MITI could not help but be cooperative and flexible in its relationships with industry. It may be understood that this was the primary reason why MITI policy contributed so successfully to the Japanese economy's post-war development.

Evaluation of MITI policy

The pattern of post-war trade and industrial policy in Japan certainly was not consistent. As will be analysed in the remainder of this volume, the dismantling of the wartime order and its conversion into a democratic system during the Occupation was enforced by orders from SCAP; the Ministry of Commerce and Industry did not take the initiative in this conversion. After the Occupation ended, the ministry which was reorganized into MITI made efforts, in cooperation with industrial circles, to create a self-supporting economy. At this stage, MITI exercised a considerable degree of leadership. As Japanese industry, riding on the crest of the wave of high-level growth, improved its productivity and gained in competitiveness, it became less hard-pressed for investment funds from around 1960.

In some instances, however, it came to regard MITI's guidance and intervention as onerous. MITI, too, began more often to seek the promotion of industrial development and transformation through cooperation with the business community. It may be safe to assert that the prototype of the Japan, Inc. model was developed during this period, when the Japanese economy was beginning to attract worldwide attention. In this process, little conflict arose in formulating MITI policy because domestic and international information concerning industry was communicated fairly freely between the public and private sectors. Meanwhile, however, the global economy underwent gradual changes. The Nixon shock and the two oil crises dealt severe blows to Japan's heavy and chemical industries, and the conversion to a so-called 'light-thin-short-and-small' industrial structure—in other words, to a knowledge-intensive structure—became an urgent task. In this process, MITI played a key role by suggesting the new direction in which to head, enacting the Law on Temporary Measures for Stabilization of Specified Depressed Industries, and guiding the conversion to a knowledge-intensive industrial structure while fostering the structural reform of the 'heavy-thick-long-and-large' industries.

There is little doubt that the Japanese economy is based on the free-market principle. There are many social factors, however, that make it inadvisable to leave all economic decisions to the workings of the free market, as is patently the case with the small and medium enterprises sector. The Japanese economy began to develop later than other industrial economies, and it later made a renewed start from the wartime and post-war confusion. As such, it could not be left totally to the workings of a free-market system, a system that essentially exists only in pure theory. Therein lay the proper role of MITI policy, which as a whole could be said to have effected a relatively smooth development of the economy. It was for that reason that the Japanese industrial system attracted attention, or criticism, as having formed Japan, Inc. It would not be an exaggeration to say that of the policies put into effect by all OECD countries, the trade and industrial policies which MITI implemented were by and large the most effective way of bringing about economic development. This conclusion is attested to by the fact that the NIES and many other developing countries, and recently the former Communist-bloc nations seeking to find a way out of their present difficulties, are showing an unusually strong interest in Japan's trade and industrial policy and its applicability to their economies. These points will be returned to later in this chapter.

6.4. International Perspective on Japanese-Style Trade and Industry Policy

The model of development-oriented policy

The foregoing overview of the post-war trade and industrial policy of Japan gives rise to a distinctive characterization. It is a system of development-oriented policy based on industrial nurturing and aimed at increasing the efficiency of industry, strengthening its international competitiveness, and catching up with, and surpassing, the economic levels of the other industrially advanced countries. The viewpoint that focuses attention on this aspect of trade and industry policy, and defines it as a development-oriented model, came to be embraced fairly widely in the 1980s.[14] This development orientation was shared by all the developing countries in the post-war period, and for that reason the Japanese model came to attract attention as the policy which helped to build the Japanese economy.

In the background of this positive approach to economic policy is the nagging question of whether today's developing countries, by relying on free-market competition, can achieve a sufficiently efficient allocation of resources to reach the stages of economic growth attained by more advanced countries. Many believe that, instead, developing countries should take a hard look at their market imperfections and turn to development-oriented policy as a means to overcome them. Certainly an examination of the pattern of economic development of post-war Japan reveals that the role played by trade and industrial policy cannot be ignored.

On the other hand, however, it must be remembered that for the development-oriented policy to work effectively, there must be an industrial structure or corporate characteristics compatible with such policy. In general, industrial policy tends to be discussed within a framework of orthodox economic theory based on individualism. But because Japan's economic system—or that of Germany—has a philosophical foundation essentially different from individualism, perhaps the question of policy for optimal development should be discussed with this difference clearly in mind. More specifically, this view suggests that perhaps there exists a paradigmatic difference between the individualistic capitalism of the Anglo-American world and the more group-oriented capitalism of Japan and Germany. The difference between the two basic orientations became clear in the process of the global economy's development from the post-war ruin. It can be said that the rivalry between the two orientations has intensified since the 1980s.[15]

Japanese vs. Anglo-American corporations

The Japan, Inc. view of the structure of industrial development in Japan has already been discussed. The following examines the structural characteristics of corporations themselves, with reference to the above discussion about industrial structure and enterprise characteristics. Japanese corporations differ in their structure and mode of operation from Anglo-American corporations. Economics textbooks tell us that the 'members' of a corporation are its stockholders, who own the corporation. In a Japanese corporation, however, the 'members' are its employees.[16] Although major stockholders of Japanese corporations at times exercise their decision-making authority, they ordinarily remain in the background. Also, in Anglo-American corporations, the primary responsibilities of the officers (president and directors) are to maximize profits and dividends. Stockholders readily replace officers who fail to fulfil these responsibilities. And if stockholders do not believe that replacing the officers will improve the situation, they will sell their shareholdings and invest in more attractive corporations. At times, too, corporations take over other companies. All such practices are regarded as in keeping with the rules of a free market. The post-war Japanese corporation, however, differs considerably from the Anglo-American corporation. Most senior officers in a Japanese corporation, for instance, are selected from among out-standing employees who served many years in the company, and there is a much closer relationship in the Japanese corporation between management and employees. Corporate officers are more interested in their company's health than in short-term profits, and they aim to maximize long-term profits. The company's major stockholders share the same view, and short-term changes in dividends do not affect their decisions to sell or buy shares of the company. Some shares of listed companies are traded on stock exchanges, of course, but to ensure stable management most of the outstanding shares of large corporations are held through mutual consent by the company's main banks and customers, who serve as 'stable' stockholders.

Table 6.6 compares studies made by British and Japanese stock exchanges on the structure of share ownership. In Britain, pension funds, investment trusts, and other financial institutions, which are interested in high dividends, hold relatively large percentages of shares. In Japan, in contrast, banks (the corpora-tion's main banks) and affiliated corporations are relatively large stockholders. Moreover, these corporations often mutually hold each other's shares. Corpora-tions are thus seldom sold or taken over in Japan, although these are frequent practices in the UK and the US. Concerning the relationship between labour and management, meanwhile, economic theory says that labour is sold and bought in the labour market, and even in Japan that is how the phenomenon is explained in abstract terms. Actually, however, Japanese workers do not feel that they are

Table 6.6   Structure of stock ownership

	(1981) UK	(1983) Japan
Individuals	28	27
Securities companies	—	2
Pension funds	27	0
Insurance companies	21	17
Banks	0	18
Investment trusts and other financial institutions	10	3
Commerce and industry corporations	5	26
Central and local governments	3	0
Foreign investors	4	6
Charitable organizations	2	—
Total	100	100

Source: R. Dore, *Taking Japan Seriously*, 112.

selling their labour in a market but that they are employed as workers. Corporations, too, are more aware of the social dimensions of the employer–employee relationship than they are of the economic aspects of buying labour. Japanese-style employment practices and wage systems developed in such an environment.

Stability and longevity of corporate management

The idea of a stable relationship holds true not only for the corporate organization but is seen in business transactions as well. In the US, the basic rule of the market place is to buy materials and parts at as low a price as possible, and to sell products at as high a price as possible. In Japan, however, the relationship between a corporation and its suppliers and customers is much less fluid. Although the parties will negotiate lower prices and other terms of transactions, the outcome does not affect their stable relationship. This stability forms the foundation of the subcontracting relationship.

From the standpoint of the free-market principle in the US and other countries, however, the stable relationships in Japan seem to be manifestations of the closed nature of Japanese markets, and are therefore difficult to accept. They comprise barriers to market entry and are factors giving rise to trade friction. According to the Anglo-American view, in other words, the stable relationships in Japan are nothing less than obstacles to healthy economic development. But in Japan the stability in financial and product markets contributes to the relationship of trust in business transactions, which in turn makes possible the government's industrial policy and the long-term investment of Japanese corporations. In specific cases, of course, there may be refusals, negotiations, and adjustments, but in general the Japanese business community does not reject cooperation with MITI, welcomes MITI's suggesting the direction of economic development while listening to the views of industrial leaders, and expects MITI to function as a mediator when necessary and to find solutions to certain problems.

Another noteworthy point concerning Japanese corporations is that the focal point of corporate management is on retaining internally a considerable portion of earnings rather than paying them out as dividends, and channelling the retained earnings to investment. In that sense, Japanese corporations can be said to be managing their affairs and investing their resources with a long-term perspective. This practice provides a motive power for development of the Japanese economy, and ensures the long-term growth of corporations. The long-term stability of corporate management serves as a foundation that enables MITI to plan the direction in which the Japanese economy will develop and to implement its plan by collaborating with the business community. As seen, therefore, the behavioural patterns of Japanese corporations are radically different from those of their Anglo-American counterparts.

Similarities and differences between the Japanese and German industrial systems

West Germany, along with Japan, attracted worldwide attention by achieving remarkable economic growth after the Second World War. An examination of the industrial structure of West Germany reveals that it was similar in many ways to that of Japan, rather than to that of the UK, to say nothing of the US. In post-war West Germany, the antipathy of the Allied Powers and of the German labour unions towards the wartime collaboration of German business managers with the Nazis produced an economic philosophy holding that business corporations should be regarded as quasi-public organizations. Accordingly, employees were represented in the management organs of a corporation, such as the board of auditors, and workplaces had works councils that were much more powerful than their counterparts in Japan. Labour unions, although eager to improve working conditions, attached greater importance to the stability of employment. German workers were thus in a position to be called members of the corporation, and enjoyed considerable say in corporate management. The Works Constitution Act of 1952 established the legal basis for that arrangement. It stipulates, although limiting its applicability to collective agreement, that 'both the employer and the works council shall cooperate in good faith for the benefit of the enterprise and its employees in due consideration of their mutual prosperity.'

West Germany regarded its economy more as a socially minded market economy than as a free-market economy. Accordingly, the government owned considerable portions of the shares of corporations in such key industries as car manufacture, steel, electric power, and transportation, and extensively intervened in these markets when required to do so from a social viewpoint.

The industrial structure of West Germany is reviewed here because the characteristics of a 'corporation'—characteristics often regarded as unique to the Japanese industrial structure—appear more patently manifested in West Germany than in Japan. It should be pointed out, moreover, that a danger exists in overemphasizing the particularistic aspects of Japan, either in order to criticize Japan or because of the inclination to analyse the Japanese industrial structure only from an American viewpoint. Actually, in terms of government intervention in private-sector business affairs, the UK government is highly active, and the French government is even more so.

NIES and Japanese industrial policy

After the Second World War, the foremost national objective of developing countries was economic development. As a model for their development, they looked to Japan. With a social framework somewhat different from that of the advanced Western countries, Japan was a latecomer that began rapidly developing economically from the end of the nineteenth century and caught up with the advanced capitalist countries. Since the economy of developing countries everywhere is based on underdeveloped agriculture, the development theories in these countries were oriented towards industry, which implied a need for higher productivity than in agriculture. Excessive imports of such consumer goods as cotton products constituted a serious problem for these countries, and developing import-substituting industries became the primary goal of their industrialization drives. Some Latin American nations certainly achieved high-level growth in the

1960s using this type of industrial policy. But while import-substituting industries in those countries won domestic markets, they were not necessarily successful in exporting. This industrialization strategy soon reached its limits, therefore, and fell into disfavour.

As stated earlier, Japan's development pattern quickly shifted into one of export-led growth relying on technological development and low wages. South Korea, Taiwan, Hong Kong, and other countries in East Asia followed Japan in this respect. Once into the 1970s, these Asian NIES (newly industrializing economies) came to be called the Little Dragons (or Tigers), following the footsteps of the Big Dragon, Japan. Any inquiry into the nature of Japanese-style industrial policy, however, must answer the question of what the structure of Japan's export-led growth is. In Japan today, the government's leading role, based on the legal authority of the State, is on the wane, and the initiatives are shifting to collaboration among companies or between the government and companies. This collaboration, however, is not a characteristic of the Asian NIES. To that extent, one cannot say that therefore Japan has served as their model.

Characteristics of Japan's dual structure

Another aspect of Japanese-style economic development and industrial policy has to do with the 'two-sectors model'.[17] Agriculture and industry differ in their patterns of production. Whereas industry is highly modernized, agriculture tends to be extremely traditional. Furthermore, the Japanese industrial sector itself has a dual structure consisting of large corporations, on the one hand, and small and medium enterprises, on the other. It has been argued that the Japanese dual structure is a unique industrial structure not found in the advanced Western countries, and Japan has succeeded in industrialization by making the best use of low wages in the low-productivity sector. The so-called two-sectors model which is frequently discussed in the theory of underdevelopment, however, differs in nature from the dual structure in the Japanese economy. In Japan, the two sectors vary in the degree of development within the same framework of the overall level of development of the national economy, and there is continuity between the two sectors. Accordingly, products manufactured in the small and medium enterprises sector are used as parts and components by large manufacturers. When Japanese cars containing large quantities of these parts were exported to the US in the 1970s, their quality came to be highly regarded. In contrast, the two sectors in developing countries vary considerably in their levels of development, so much so that the traditional sector in many cases is incapable of producing parts to be used in modern manufacturing industry. In the Asian NIES, very small firms can be utilized for processing consumer goods such as textile products, but it is questionable to what extent they can be used for the production of parts for sophisticated manufactured products. In this sense, the dual-structure model of the Japanese economy has limited usefulness as a model of development for today's developing countries.[18]

The model of transition from planned economy to market economy

Socialist economic planning provided another model for developing countries aspiring to develop their economies. During colonial days, little capital was accumulated in the colonized countries. And when the developing countries first began their economic development programmes, they rejected the option of turning to advanced capitalist nations for investment funds because of the resentment they felt towards their colonial past. Relying on their own means, however, meant they had to rely on state coffers. This reliance would naturally lead to the formation of industrialization programmes under state leadership. Both Indonesia and India characterized their economic systems as being 'socialistic', although there were differences in the degree of 'socialism'. The People's Republic of China and the People's Democratic Republic of Korea moved to develop themselves centred on communist economic planning. The former Soviet Union, meanwhile, began introducing free-market mechanisms when its system collapsed. Around that time, there emerged a renewed interest in the development process of the Japanese economy. As noted earlier, Japan adopted a system of a controlled economy during the war and immediately afterwards. The system differed in principle from socialist planning but nonetheless it was characterized by a degree of planning in managing the national economy. Examples were implementation of the materials mobilization plan and introduction of a system of rationing goods. After the Peace Treaty became effective, Japan made fairly rapid progress towards deregulating its economic controls. Programmes for liberalizing domestic economic activities, foreign trade, and capital flows, for instance, gained headway at a relatively steady pace, although not without considerable struggle and hardships. In the process, the government repeatedly announced 'five-year' and other types of 'economic plans', even though they were not mandatory. In the process of the recent collapse of the communist economic order or the development of former communist economies in new environments, it has become necessary for corporations, primarily because of their need for funds, to establish close working relationships with the government. It has also become necessary for the concerned governments to exercise control over markets in certain situations. At such times Japan's industrial policy from late in the Occupation period through the period when the nation achieved economic self-support might serve as a useful model. Theoretical research on this point has only recently got under way.[19] This volume on the history of MITI policy may provide reference materials on a wide range of these topics.

It might also be mentioned that the free-market economies of Europe and the US have encountered various difficulties, and today the pros and cons of these systems are being extensively debated. Although the merits and demerits of Japanese trade and industrial policy have been debated from various perspectives in recent years as noted above, it is a widely acknowledged fact that after the end of the Second World War Japan grew faster than the free-market economies of the Western countries and succeeded in achieving the economic status it has today. Japan should thus serve as a valuable model of development for former communist economies.

6.5. Concluding Remarks

This volume on the history of MITI policy is an attempt to describe, with as much detail as possible, the evolution of the post-war Japanese economy and its international trade and industrial policy up to about 1980. This introductory Part provides an overview of the evolutionary process.

As with any historical account, the contents of Japan's international trade and industrial policy, the subject matter of this volume, are the socio-economic phenomena of a period in the past which is now history. Extending those phenomena into the future, therefore, and passing verdicts upon similar policies in subsequent periods may lead to mistaken conclusions. It is also possible that in the evolution of trade and industrial policy after 1980, new problems not considered as important in this volume might have arisen. After due consideration, Part I will be finished with brief remarks on the transformation of MITI policy in the 1980s, which immediately followed the period covered in this volume.

As will be noted in Part V, MITI, in ushering in the 1980s, asked the Industrial Structure Council to formulate a report on a 'Vision of MITI Policies in the 1980s'. The council filed a report in March 1980, advocating the following policy direction. Building on ideas that had emerged towards the end of the 1970s, the report said it was incumbent upon Japan—an economic superpower whose activities account for one-tenth of world output—to clearly establish national objectives worthy of its newly acquired status, and to ensure that its trade and industrial policy is in harmony with these objectives. As national objectives, the report identified the following three, and proposed specific policy measures for each:

1. Contributing to the world community in ways commensurate with the nation's economic superpower status.
2. Overcoming the limitations imposed by the paucity of the nation's natural resources.
3. Achieving a balance between economic vitality and relaxed and comfortable living conditions.

The 'sense of the times' of the council which engendered these suggestions was that the 1980s would be a period during which knowledge would be actively utilized creatively with farsightedness, so that economic security could be achieved and the nation's growth could be further advanced through intensive application of technology. This perspective signified a departure from the development-oriented, catching-up pattern of modernization that prevailed over the 100 years of Japanese history up to and including the 1970s. It served as an overture to a period of transition to a new trade and industrial policy based on the theme of a keen awareness of the global role expected of Japan.

As mentioned at the beginning of chapter 6, MITI annually publishes the key objectives of its policy ranked by priority. It is worth noting that since the late 1970s policy objectives attaching great importance to Japan's international role have risen to the top rank. Although it is not possible to report in this volume how these objectives were eventually met, the ranking reveals the evolution of MITI policy to a pattern adapted to a period in which international farsightedness is the order of the day. It is also worth noting that when the Industrial Structure Council's 'Vision of MITI Policies in the 1980s' report stressed a balance between vitality and comfort, it was raising the issue of the quality of life in a new Japan.

NOTES

1. A special issue of the British magazine *The Economist* entitled 'Japan, 1983', discussed this point by stating that 'The main job of MITI is to serve as a midwife and an undertaker to major industries.' Tetsuya Koseki, trans., *Nippon wo Hadaka ni Suru* (Baring Japan), Futami Shobo, 1984: 97.
2. Daniel I. Okimoto: 50 (trans.: 73).
3. R&D subsidies for VLSI started at 3.5 billion yen in 1976, increased to 10 billion yen in 1978, and fell to 7 billion yen in 1979. In other words, the length of the infancy nursing period became shorter.
4. In as early as June 1970, Yoshihisa Ohjimi touched on this point in a speech delivered at a meeting of the OECD's Industry Committee: 'Basic Philosophy and Objectives of Japanese Industrial Policy', June 1970. Ohjimi was the Administrative Vice-Minister of MITI.
5. John C. Lobb, 'Japan Inc.—The Total Conglomerate', *Columbia Journal of World Business*, Mar.–Apr. 1971: 41–2. Incidentally, the term 'Japan, Inc.' was coined by an American, not a Japanese.
6. Eugene J. Kaplan, 'Japan: The Government-Business Relationship', 1972. This report, subtitled 'A Guide for US Businessmen', was the result of a study conducted by the Far East Division of the Bureau of Commerce of the US Department of Commerce. Kaplan was head of the division.
7. Ibid. 69; Susumu Ohara and Toyoaki Yoshida, trans., *Kabushikigaisha Nippon* (Japan, Inc.), Simul Press, Inc., 1972: 125.
8. Ibid. 30; trans., 55.
9. Ibid. 10; trans., 19.
10. Ibid. 43–4; trans., 81.
11. Daniel I. Okimoto wrote a foreword to the Japanese translation of the Commerce Department report in n. 6 above. In the foreword, 'The Fallacy of the "Japan, Inc." Model', the crux of Okimoto's argument, as he himself noted, was 'trying to examine MITI in a broader context of the entirety of the complex system in which MITI functions, rather than focusing on MITI itself.'
12. MITI-related laws and ordinances are listed in each year's *Tsusho Sangyo-sho Nenpo* (MITI Annual Report).
13. From the standpoint of industrial circles, this complex system of laws and regulations translates into a large number of approvals and licences that must be obtained from the government in starting and maintaining a business. Because of the large areas of industry under the jurisdiction of MITI, the number of approvals and licences totalled 1,870 items in 1985, the largest number among all ministries except the Ministry of Transport. In providing support, for instance, MITI requested businesses to submit project plans in order to ensure the proper use of public funds. Moreover, for establishing and operating MITI-related organizations such as chambers of commerce and industry and cooperative associations of small and medium enterprises, MITI's regulation entails approval of establishing an organization and the requirement of submitting financial statements and reports on their business condition. As a specific example, the regulation of the energy industry for the purpose of stabilizing energy supplies is summarized as follows: *Synopsis*: Stable supplies of petroleum products (55). Requires approvals and licences for business activities in petroleum refining and petroleum distribution in order to secure stable supplies of

petroleum and petroleum products. *Laws*: Petroleum Industry Law (19), Petroleum Supply and Demand Optimization Law (3), Petroleum Reserve Law (15), Petrol Retail Business Law (15), Provisional Measures Law on the Importation of Specific Petroleum-Refined Products (3). (Note: Figures in parentheses following the law names indicate the number of regulated business activities. Although these regulations may benefit the regulated industries, they are often irksome, giving rise to demands for deregulation. *Specific Examples*: Petroleum Industry Law. Approval required for establishing petroleum-refining industry and building new facilities. Notifications required for establishing petroleum-importing business and petroleum products distribution business.

14. A representative view is found in Chalmers Johnson, *MITI and the Japanese Miracle*, mentioned above.

15. See, e.g. Lester Thurow, *Head to Head: The Coming Economic Battle among Japan, Europe, and America*, Morrow, 1992: 32 (trans. as *Daisessen* by Naohiko Tsuchiya, Kodansha, 1992: 49).

16. Before the war, only white-collar workers were regarded as 'members'; blue-collar workers were treated as 'employees' (hired hands). As a result of the post-war 'democratization struggle' mounted by labour unions, blue-collar workers came to be included among corporate 'members'. Their basic wage structure was changed to that of monthly salaries, and their semi-annual bonuses were paid according to the same criteria as those of white-collar members.

17. The representative work on the two-sector model was J. C. H. Fei and Gustav Ranis, *The Development of the Labor Surplus Economy*, Irwin, 1964.

18. As a study that analysed the development of the Japanese economy in its relationship to developing countries, and therefore with a focus on the theories of economic development, see Penelope Francks, *Japanese Economic Development: Theory and Practice*.

19. See e.g. Fusae Ohta, Hiroya Tanikawa and Tasuke Ohtani, 'Russian Economic Reform and Japan's Industrial Policy', *MITI Research Review*, 1, Printing Bureau, MoF, 1993.

PART II

The Reorganization of the Japanese Economy

7

The Formulation and Reversal of the Japanese Occupation Policy

7.1. Dismantling of the Wartime Industrial Structure

The Imperial Rescript on Surrender issued by Emperor Hirohito on 15 August 1945 brought an end to the long Pacific War. Unlike Germany, however, which was administered directly by the Allied military government, Japan had accepted the terms of the Potsdam Declaration of July 1945 and was administered indirectly, with the Supreme Commander for the Allied Powers (SCAP) in overall command but with the Japanese government managing the Japanese economy, although the direction in which the post-war Japanese economy moved was naturally defined largely by the Occupation policies of the Allied Powers. The Potsdam Declaration enumerated the Occupation policies as agreed to by the heads of the Allied Powers. Paragraph 11 stated that 'Japan shall be permitted to maintain such industries as will sustain her economy and permit the exaction of just reparations in kind, but not those which would enable her to rearm for war.' The Declaration also stated that Japan would eventually be permitted to participate again in world trade relations. In fact, however, the terms of the Potsdam Declaration were more severe than they appeared.

Soon after the outbreak of the Pacific War, the United States began to formulate a Japanese Occupation policy and to study measures for regulating post-war Japanese industry.[1] For instance, a paper titled 'An Economic Study on Post-war Japan' prepared in July 1943 by the Division of Economic Studies of the US Department of State examined, as methods for demilitarizing the post-war Japanese economy, the pros and cons of the following three alternatives: (1) dismantling Japan's modern industrial facilities and isolating Japan from world trade; (2) permitting light industries and allowing resumption of foreign trade, but dismantling heavy industries and banning the shipping industry; and (3) dismantling the defence industries, and prohibiting the aircraft manufacturing and shipbuilding industries. The paper concluded that the third alternative was most appropriate.

In the subsequent process of deliberating policies on Japan, a variety of hard-line and less harsh policies were proposed. The policy paper titled 'US Foreign Economic Policy toward Japan' prepared by the Foreign Economic Administration in January 1945 visualized, as the possible character of a post-war Japanese economy, the following three types: (1) an economy primarily oriented towards producing heavy-industry producer goods; (2) an economy primarily oriented towards producing consumer goods for export; and (3) an economy primarily oriented towards producing consumer goods for domestic consumption. Having judged that the third alternative would be the most desirable in that it would minimize the chance of a resurgence of Japan's military adventurism, the report recommended restricting the output of basic heavy industries such as steel, aluminium, and copper; placing limitations on the shipbuilding, machinery, and chemical industries; and regulating the level of electric-power generation and the quantities of raw material imports.

This policy paper further proposed the 'abolition or diminution of the tenant-farming system in order to provide adequate income for farmers', 'protection of fundamental rights of workers to raise their income', and 'dismantling of the zaibatsu, which prevented the development of domestic markets, suppressed the growth of democratic elements, and served as tools for aggression and war.' These proposals were based on the belief that in order to prevent the resurgence of Japanese militarism it was not enough to destroy armaments production or heavy-industry capabilities that could potentially lead to militarism; rather, it was necessary to reform the very economic structure that engendered the impulse for expansionism. The objective of the Occupation of Japan as set forth in the Potsdam Declaration was to destroy Japan's 'war-making power'—the wording used in Paragraph 7. The Occupation policy to implement this objective, therefore, was likely to be rather harsh.

When the Potsdam Declaration was issued, basic US policy on the Occupation of Japan was still incomplete. After Japan's surrender, therefore, the US hastened to complete a post-surrender policy. On 29 August 1945, the State-War-Navy Coordinating Committee (SWINCC) developed the 'United States Initial Post-Surrender Policy for Japan' ('Initial Policy for Japan'), approved by President Truman on 6 September. Subsequently, a policy document enumerating more specific measures was prepared and delivered to General MacArthur on 3 November as the 'Basic Initial Post-Surrender Directive to Supreme Commander for the Allied Powers for the Occupation and Control of Japan' ('Basic Initial Directive'). These two documents came to constitute the basic documents for Japanese Occupation policy.

The policy of the Occupation Forces on controlling the Japanese economy was implemented in two main areas. One was economic demilitarization; the other was economic viability. The former related to the fundamental objective of the Occupation; there, drastic measures were implemented in a short period of time. The Basic Initial Directive, meanwhile, clearly stated that SCAP 'will not assume any responsibility for the economic rehabilitation of Japan or the strengthening of the Japanese economy', establishing the principle that the maintenance of economic viability was the responsibility of the Japanese people and their government. Nonetheless, in the course of implementing Occupation policy, the Occupation Forces could not help but become involved in various economic policies.

The policy of demilitarizing the economy as a means of realizing the Occupation's basic objective of demilitarizing Japan was implemented in two directions.[2]

The first was the policy of fostering democracy, which would eliminate war-making potential from the Japanese economy and prevent Japan's rearmament. The second was the policy of eliminating from the Japanese economy the source of aggressive aspirations and militaristic behaviour. As a policy of the first type, dismantling defence industries and reducing war-supporting capabilities were planned. As a policy of the second type, dissolution of the zaibatsu, land reform, and labour reform were implemented.

With regard to dismantling the defence industry, the first task was the physical destruction of facilities used specifically for the production of arms. Munitions plants, aircraft manufacturing plants, and specialized machine tools of private-sector plants were scrapped, and machinery and equipment convertible to civilian use was designated to be removed for reparations. The issue of reparations removal went through a series of complex and convoluted processes, and starting in the autumn of 1947 three rounds of removal were carried out, following the policy of 30 per cent advance delivery as specified by the Advance Transfer Programme approved by the Far Eastern Commission (FEC). Approximately 30 per cent of the principal machinery and equipment of munitions plants—the primary bases for munitions production—was removed and transferred abroad.

The policy of destroying the war-supporting potential of Japanese industry was initially planned to be carried out by reparations removal and the subsequent regulation of Japanese industry. Edwin W. Pauley, who formulated the first proposal for exacting reparations from Japan, wrote in his preliminary statement on the Report on Japanese Reparations that the significance of the reparations programme lay in demilitarizing Japan and depriving it of the power of economic control over other nations by allocating its industrial equipment to East Asian countries. An interim report from the Pauley Mission issued in December 1945 was predicated on a plan of leaving in Japan just enough productive capacity to maintain a standard of living equivalent to that of the 1926–30 period (a period of economic recession in Japan), and removing as war reparations the production capacity exceeding that level.

Specifically, the interim report proposed a plan, as the first stage of the reparations programme, for removal of: (1) one-half of the country's production capacity of machine tools; (2) all army and navy munitions plants, aircraft manufacturing plants, and ball-bearing plants; (3) all facilities of twenty shipyards; (4) steel-production capacity in excess of 2.5 million tons per year; (5) one-half of all thermoelectric power plants; (6) all the contact-process sulphuric acid plants, the most modern plant among the four largest Solvay-process soda ash plants, and twenty of the forty-one largest caustic soda plants; and (7) all the magnesium-aluminium alloy manufacturing plants. Pauley submitted his final report to the Department of State in April 1946, in which he recommended increasing the removal quantities of the manufacturing facilities for steel, machine tools, soda ash, and ships listed in the interim report. He also added, as objects of reparations removals, merchant vessels and a wide range of industrial equipment related to iron-ore refining, nickel, copper, edged tools, industrial tools, heavy electric equipment, rolling stock, communications equipment, spinning machinery, gunpowder, nitric acid, celluloid, tar, petroleum refining, petroleum storage, synthetic oil, alcohol, and synthetic rubber.

The US submitted to the FEC its plan for reparations removals based on the Pauley Mission's interim report. The FEC voted on various aspects of the report in a piecemeal manner, and by December 1946 approved a programme of interim reparations which was essentially the US plan with some moderation. Notwithstanding the moderating revisions, the FEC's interim reparations programme was rather harsh, since it was in line with the key provisions of the Pauley Mission's report.

Meanwhile, the State-War-Navy Coordinating Committee began deliberations on a policy paper titled 'Reducing the War-Making Potential of Japanese Industry'. The paper proposed that: (1) all specialized machinery and equipment in Japan used for producing armaments be destroyed; (2) all machinery and equipment of factories in the primary defence industries (industries producing armaments, civil aviation, and merchant vessels exceeding 5,000 gross tons) and of that portion of war-supportive industries (metals, machinery, chemicals, etc.) which exceeded peacetime needs be removed for reparations; and (3) during the Occupation, the rebuilding of the primary defence industries be prohibited, and the production capacity of designated war-supportive industries (seven industries, including steel and shipbuilding) be limited to specified levels. The third of these proposals is worth special note, inasmuch as it proposed limiting the rebuilding of productive capacity after facilities were removed for reparations. In other words, it advocated the extension of the policy of eliminating the physical capacity to make war from one-time scrapping and reparations removal to a prolonged measure of regulating the economy's industrial capacity. The US submitted this policy paper as well to the FEC.

If the policy of eliminating Japan's physical war-making potential, including the three measures of scrapping, reparations removal, and regulation of rebuilding, had been implemented, Japan's economy would have suffered a tremendous setback. This policy, however, was not implemented. As will be seen, the US eventually reversed its policy towards Japan in the changing international climate of the post-war era.

7.2. The Dissolution of Zaibatsu and the Prohibition of Private Monopoly

The second aspect of the policy of demilitarizing the Japanese economy, i.e. eliminating the source of militarism, was implemented within a short span of time in the form of three major economic reforms: dissolution of the zaibatsu, land reform, and labour reform.

The US was determined to dissolve not only the gumbatsu (the military clique) but also the zaibatsu as the driving forces of Japan's war of aggression. The Initial Policy for Japan called for 'the dissolution of the large industrial and banking combinations which have exercised control of a great part of Japan's trade and industry.' Besides these large combinations, moreover, the Basic Initial Directive specified 'other large concentrations of private business control' as targets for dissolution. The dissolution of the zaibatsu and large business enterprises was to be carried out according to these directives.[3]

SCAP's Economic and Scientific Section (ESS), in charge of zaibatsu dissolution, requested first of all that the four major zaibatsu combines submit dissolution plans. The Yasuda zaibatsu responded first. On 12 October 1945, President Hajime Yasuda of Yasuda Hozensha paid a visit to Col. Robert Kramer, head of the ESS, and informed him of the plan to dissolve the holding company of the Yasuda zaibatsu. On the following day, Yasuda announced to the press the voluntary dissolution plan of Yasuda Hozensha. The Sumitomo zaibatsu, too, expressed its intention to dissolve itself. The Mitsui zaibatsu expressed a strong desire to retain its 'Honsha' as a holding company, and the Mitsubishi zaibatsu refused voluntary dissolution until the very end.

The dissolution plan which emerged from the negotiations between SCAP and Yasuda was called the Yasuda Plan. The gist of the plan was that all members of the Yasuda family would resign from their business positions; Yasuda Hozensha would cease to function; all zaibatsu-appointed directors would retire; all securities owned by the family members, the holding company, and related banks would be transferred to the Holding Company Liquidation Commission (HCLC); and the Yasuda trade name would be abolished. The Yasuda Plan was sent to the US, but the State Department expressed dissatisfaction over the method of voluntary dissolution of the zaibatsu, and suggested that the measure for dissolving the zaibatsu should be developed with a broader perspective. The State Department agreed to approve the Yasuda Plan, but only as a preliminary step in the zaibatsu dissolution programme, and indicated that it would dispatch a team of antitrust experts to Japan to allow formulation of a broader policy.

SCAP requested the Japanese government to submit a proposal on dissolving the zaibatsu, which it did with a memorandum titled 'Dissolution of Holding Companies' (dated 4 November 1945). On 6 November, SCAP issued a memorandum ordering the Japanese government to implement, as a preliminary step in democratizing the economic order, four of the proposals contained in the memorandum, which were: transfer of securities owned by the zaibatsu holding companies to the HCLC; cessation of the exercise of direction or control by the holding companies; resignation of holding company directors; and resignation of zaibatsu family members. SCAP also directed the Japanese government to submit three additional plans: (1) a plan for dissolving combines other than the big four zaibatsu; (2) a programme for abrogating all legislative or administrative measures which tend to strengthen private monopoly; and (3) a programme to enact laws for eliminating and preventing private monopoly, undesirable interlocking directorates, undesirable intercorporate security ownership, and segregation of banking from commerce, industry, and agriculture.

Following the SCAP memorandum, the Japanese government took steps to execute the zaibatsu dissolution programme by issuing the Ordinance Concerning Restrictions on the Dissolution of Companies, the Holding Company Liquidation Commission Ordinance, and the Restriction of Corporate Security Ownership Ordinance. After the big four zaibatsu were dissolved, the holding companies of such lesser zaibatsu as Asano, Shibusawa, and Okura were also dissolved. The securities owned by the holding companies were transferred to the HCLC and subsequently sold to the general public through the Securities Coordinating Liquidation Commission. Securities owned by zaibatsu subsidiaries that were holding, operating companies were also disposed of similarly, thereby dissolving the relationship of intercorporate control through ownership of securities. Furthermore, fifty-six persons of ten zaibatsu families were prohibited from assuming corporate directorship positions, and the assumption of interlocking directorships was also prohibited. The purge of wartime leaders from public positions was expanded to include business leaders. Corporate control through interpersonal relations was thus also eliminated.

Meanwhile, a mission to study the Japanese zaibatsu, led by Corwin Edwards, a consultant on cartels to the State Department, arrived in Japan in January 1946. Having gathered information and deliberated on policy matters, the Edwards Mission submitted a report in March to the Department of State and the War Department. Taking into consideration the new trend in antitrust regulation in the US, the Edwards Report made detailed recommendations on the policy of dissolving the Japanese zaibatsu. The State Department placed this report before SWINCC, which then formulated its 'Statement of US Policy with Respect to Excessive Concentrations of Economic Power in Japan'. In May 1946, this statement was submitted to the FEC for discussion and adoption as Allied policy. The statement of policy, designated 'FEC 230', advocated the dissolution of large operating concerns which were considered as excessive concentrations of economic power in terms of asset value, size of working force, fields of operation, or market share. It also called for wide-ranging anti-monopoly measures, including the elimination of financial support for excessive concentrations; creation of an antitrust law; and changes in the patent, corporate, and tax laws. The policy of dissolving economic combines with the aim of disbanding large zaibatsu thus developed into a policy of dissolving economic concentrations aimed at all large business corporations in Japan.

Earlier, soon after MacArthur's 'Statement to the Japanese Government Concerning Required Reforms', dated 11 October 1945, the Ministry of Commerce and Industry (MCI) had begun preparations for preparing antitrust legislation. The ministry was studying the prospective framework of a post-war economic control mechanism to supplant the about-to-be dismantled wartime economic control system rooted in the National General Mobilization Law. By the end of October, MCI developed a plan for a basic law for industry which would outlaw armaments industries and prohibit private monopoly. Responding to the SCAP directive on antitrust legislation, the ministry in charge prepared in December the 'First Draft of the Plan Directed by Paragraph 6 of the SCAP Memorandum Dated

6 November 1945 on Dissolution of Stock-Holding Companies'.[4] Antitrust law conceptualized in this draft was in the tradition of the Unfair Competition Prevention Law and the Important Industries Control Law, a law promoting cartelization but which also had the character of a law regulating cartelization through government intervention in the public interest. Further, the ministry prepared the 'Outline of the Bill on Orderly Industry (Third Draft)' in January 1946. Meanwhile, the ministry also worked on an ordinance prohibiting participation in private international cartels. This was promulgated, with SCAP approval, as the 'Ordinance on the Prohibition of International Agreements or International Contracts' on 23 January 1946.

In the summer of 1946, when SCAP presented the Japanese government with the outline of an antitrust bill called the 'Kime Plan', developed on the basis of the Edwards Report, MCI was compelled to revise its 'Bill on Orderly Industry' drastically. The Economic Stabilization Board prepared the 'Summary of Anti-Monopoly Policy System (Draft)' based on the alterations worked out by MCI, which the government submitted to SCAP in December.

SCAP was highly critical of the Japanese government's proposal, and directed it to fully incorporate into the bill the content of the Edwards Report and the Kime Plan. Days of long negotiations between SCAP and the Japanese government eventually produced a bill which revised the Japanese draft considerably and strengthened its antitrust effects. The bill was submitted to the 92nd Imperial Diet in March 1947. The Law Concerning the Prohibition of Private Monopoly and the Preservation of Fair Trade, which provided for stern anti-monopoly measures unprecedented in the history of antitrust legislation in any country, was passed by the Diet, and was promulgated on 14 April.

With the arrival of Edward Welsh as chief of its Antitrust and Cartel Division, SCAP began to devote its energy to measures to eliminate excessive concentrations of economic power. Although the Japanese government had earlier been advised of SCAP's intention of incorporating the principle of breaking up very large corporations into the enterprise reconstruction programme based on the Enterprise Reconstruction and Reorganization Law, the particulars of SCAP's aim had not been made clear. Welsh developed a 'Standards of Enterprise Reorganization' based on FEC 230 then being studied by the FEC, and presented it to the Japanese government and business leaders. The Antitrust and Cartel Division began work on enacting this standard, and after conducting negotiations with MCI and the Economic Stabilization Board presented the draft bill for an Economic Reconstruction and Reorganization Standard Law in July 1947 to the Japanese government.

In that same month, meanwhile, SCAP issued a directive ordering a thorough dismantling of the two general trading companies, Mitsui & Co. and Mitsubishi Shoji, companies of immense size unheard of in Western countries. This measure was taken to prevent the resurgence of monopoly by the mammoth trading companies in the context of foreign trade in the private sector being scheduled for resumption on 15 August. Mitsui & Co. was divided into about 170 and

Mitsubishi Shoji into about 120 companies. It seems that SCAP ordered the thorough dismantling of the two large trading companies, keeping the image of the American-style free market in mind, in order to demonstrate its firm stand on the policy of eliminating excessive concentrations of economic power.

The Japanese government feared that the content of the draft bill for an Economic Reconstruction and Reorganization Standard Law would have an adverse impact on the reconstruction of the Japanese economy. Accordingly, it advocated that the law should be applied only to large companies with capital of 10 million yen or more, and should not include public utilities and financial institutions. In September, Prime Minister Tetsu Katayama sent a personal letter to General MacArthur to convey the wishes of the Japanese government. Meeting with MacArthur's flat rejection of the appeal, however, the Japanese government had no alternative but to comply with the wishes of SCAP. It approved a bill similar to the draft bill at an extraordinary Cabinet meeting in September, and submitted it to the Diet in October.

As will be seen below, this was a period of transition in US policy on the Japanese Occupation. Coordination between SCAP and the US government was delayed because the latter reacted negatively to the proposed measures for eliminating economic concentration in Japan. For that reason, deliberations in the Japanese Diet on the Bill for the Elimination of Excessive Concentration of Economic Power were made in an abnormal situation where deliberations were interrupted twice by SCAP directives to suspend them. In the end, the first Diet passed the Bill just before the end of the session, but only after the ruse ordered by SCAP of stopping the clock on the floor of the Diet, an event unheard of in the chronicle of Japanese legislation. Although the Law for the Elimination of Excessive Concentration of Economic Power had severe provisions, full play was never given to them because of a reversal in US policy towards Japan, as will be discussed later.

7.3. Land and Labour Reforms

Initiatives for land reform came at first from the Japanese side.[5] Although the landowner system had been weakened during the wartime economy, it was considered desirable to move further to modernize the farmland system in order to stabilize post-war Japanese society. The US government recognized the need for land reform but was fearful of disrupting Japan's agricultural production and creating a food crisis. Because of this fear, it chose not to specify land reform in the Initial Policy for Japan and other documents.

Since the Taisho Period (1912–26), the Ministry of Agriculture and Forestry had worked on improving the relationship between landlords and tenants through policies such as creating owner-cultivators and legislation on tenant farmers. The ministry developed its own draft plan for land reform which would limit landownership of resident landlords to an average of 5 cho (about 5 hectares, or 12.3 acres), sell the ownership in excess of that size and all absentee-landlord land to tenant farmers, and require rents on the remaining

tenant land to be paid in money. At the time, the economic control of landowners had been weakened by wartime legislation, including the Farmland Adjustment Law (Law 67, 2 April 1938; effective 1 August 1938) and the Farm Tenancy
Rent Control Ordinance (Imperial Ordinance 823, 6 December 1939), and by the
system of state control of rice. It was also necessary to take steps in the context
of the intensified class struggle between landlords and tenant farmers in the post-
war period. Because of these considerations, the Japanese government proposed
a land reform plan.

The Bill to Amend the Agricultural Land Adjustment Law, submitted to the Diet
in December 1945, met strong opposition, which argued that such legislation
would violate the right to hold private property. By this time, SCAP had finally
decided to introduce reforms into Japan's farmland system, which it regarded as
pre-modern. But it had not yet developed specific measures. Accordingly, for the
time being it sent a memorandum on rural land reform to the Japanese government dated 9 December 1945, directing it to submit a programme on rural land
reform. Under the aegis of this SCAP memorandum, the Diet passed the Bill to
Amend the Agricultural Land Adjustment Law, and the first stage of land reform
legislation entered the phase of preparing for implementation.

The first version of the Land Reform Bill was epoch-making in the history of
Japan's agricultural policy, but it was criticized inside and outside Japan as a luke-
warm measure that in effect would preserve the semi-feudalistic landowner
system. SCAP rejected the reform plan, having judged that even more thoroughgoing reform was needed in order to achieve democracy in Japan. The first land
reform programme thus could not be carried out. The question of land reform
was studied further by SCAP, primarily in its Natural Resources Section. However,
when the Soviet member of the Allied Council for Japan proposed in April 1946
to put the question of land reform on the agenda of the Council's meetings, the
centre of deliberations on land reform policy shifted to the Council. Discussions
on a land reform plan were held in its sessions in May and June 1946, and SCAP
developed an outline for a second Land Reform Bill based on these discussions.
The Allied Council became a forum for arguments between the US and the USSR,
and often had little impact on substantive aspects of Occupation policy. The active
role it played in land reform, therefore, was a notable anomaly.

The Allied Council for Japan studied plans presented by the British Commonwealth and the Soviet Union. Both plans advocated much more thorough reform
than the first Land Reform Bill. The Soviet plan, however, called for lowering the
purchase price for land exceeding a certain size, and confiscating very large land
holdings without compensation. Objections were raised to both ideas in the Soviet
plan as violations of the Potsdam Declaration, and the Soviet Union at one
point appeared willing to accept a compromise. In the end, however, the members
could not agree on a joint recommendation by the Council concerning the Soviet
plan. In contrast, the Council members generally agreed with the British Commonwealth plan in terms of the scope of tenant land purchase, the methods
of purchase, and the implementation period. It is noteworthy that the British

Commonwealth plan contained a provision that ownership of land would be limited to an average of 3 cho on the main islands other than Hokkaido. If landownership of cultivating farmers were to be limited, land reform would now serve a second objective, that of redistributing property, besides the primary objective of liberating tenant farmers.

By means of a memorandum, SCAP unofficially conveyed to the Japanese government a draft reform plan along the lines discussed by the Allied Council for Japan. After negotiations, a second-stage Land Reform Bill was drafted. Its main features were as follows: (1) absentee landlords must sell all their land, and non-cultivating landlords resident in villages must sell tenant land in excess of an average of 1 cho (2.45 acres) in Honshu, Shikoku, and Kyushu, and 4 cho in Hokkaido; (2) direct land negotiations between landlords and tenants would not be allowed, and the government would purchase land from the landlords and sell it at average rates to the tenant farmers; and (3) the reform programme was to be accomplished in two years. SCAP was quite aggressive in supporting the idea of limiting landownership by owner-cultivators, but the Japanese side was opposed to it. In the end, a limit was placed only on land owned by persons judged unsuitable for cultivating it. Moreover, as a measure to deal with instances where landlords dispossessed their tenants of land after the war, it was decided that compulsory sale of land would be retroactive to the ownership relations in effect on 23 November 1945, the date the first land reform outline was announced.

The amended Agricultural Land Adjustment Law (Law 42, 21 October 1946; effective 22 November 1946) and the Owner-Farmer Establishment and Special Measures Law (Law 43, 21 October 1946; effective 29 December 1946) were enacted on 21 October 1946, and the second land reform programme was implemented. Land purchases were conducted on the basis of land purchase orders issued by prefectural governors according to plans prepared and announced by local land commissions and approved by prefectural land commissions. Most purchases were completed between the first round of purchases in March 1947 and the tenth round in December 1948. By the sixteenth round conducted in July 1950, a total of 1,741,955 cho (about 4,268,000 acres) of farmland had been purchased, of which 1,704,934 cho (about 4,177,000 acres) were tenant land, 25,959 cho (about 63,600 acres) were owner-cultivated land, and the remaining 11,062 cho (about 27,102 acres) were largely uncultivated land. Of the owner-cultivated land, only 1,603 cho (about 3,927 acres) were owned by persons judged unsuitable for cultivating it; the remainder was mostly sold voluntarily by landowners.

Besides land that was purchased, a total of 1,933,009 cho (about 4,736,000 acres) of land, including farmland turned in as in-kind payments of property taxes, national land such as that formerly used by the military, and some property of the Imperial Family, were sold to former tenants and small farmers. As a result, about 80 per cent of the tenant land, which had constituted 45.9 per cent of total farmland as of November 1945, was freed, and the percentage of tenant land fell to 9.9 per cent in August 1950. The landowner system characterizing pre-war Japanese villages was almost completely abolished by this land reform programme.

Concerning labour reform, the initiatives taken by the Japanese side were even more pronounced than in land reform.[6] In October 1945, General MacArthur issued a statement to Prime Minister Shidehara directing him to institute five major reforms for securing the rights of individuals, including the encouragement of the unionization of labour. Prompted by this statement, the Japanese government worked swiftly to prepare labour union legislation. The government of Prince Higashikuni had earlier secured Cabinet agreement on creating a deliberation council for studying formulation of a trade union law as a post-war measure. Having inherited this agreement, the Shidehara government established a Labour Legislation Study Committee, whose membership included representatives of labour, management, academia, the civil service, and the Diet. Within a month of its first plenary meeting held on 27 October 1945, the Committee submitted, on 24 November, a draft Trade Union Bill to the government.

The Labour Legislation Study Committee recommended a Labour Union Law that would guarantee three rights to workers: the right to organize, the right to bargain collectively, and the right to strike. In the process of the Committee's deliberations, a memorandum from SCAP on the substantive content of the proposed legislation was limited to insertion of a clause on protection and promotion of the right of collective bargaining. The recommendations to the government, therefore, were essentially as developed by the Committee. The US had not developed specific labour legislation for Japan, although it had for some time studied a Japanese labour policy and regarded labour reform as one of the primary objectives of Occupation policy. Led mainly by labour law scholar Professor Izutaro Suehiro, and reflecting the views of the members representing labour, including Komakichi Matsuoka, the Committee drafted its proposal in a very short period of time. In doing so, it took advantage of the historical experience in working toward labour legislation since the Taisho period. SCAP commended the Japanese draft plan as appropriate for 'democratizing labour'.

The government developed its own plan by revising a portion of the Committee's recommendation, but SCAP directed the government to restore the plan to the lines of the Committee's recommendation. In the end, a bill paralleling the Committee's recommendation was submitted to the Diet in December 1945, was passed without modification, and was promulgated on 22 December. The Trade Union Law identified as its objectives, 'improvement in the lot of workers' as well as 'contributing to economic prosperity', suggesting that the development of a harmonious working relationship between labour and management was expected. The enactment of the law accelerated the organizing of labour unions, and helped uplift the labour movement which had been suppressed since pre-war years.

The Trade Union Law was soon followed by the enactment of the Labour Relations Adjustment Law (Law 25, 27 September 1946; effective 13 October 1946) in September 1946 and the Labour Standards Law in April 1947, completing the three basic labour laws. This chapter of labour reform history came to an end with enactment of other labour-related laws during 1947, including the Workmen's Compensation Insurance Law (Law 50, 7 April 1947; effective 1 September 1947), the Employment Security Law (Law 141, 30 November 1947; effective 1 December 1947), and the Unemployment Allowance Law (Law 146, effective 1 December 1947).

The economy's democratization, which SCAP identified as an important means for realizing the objective of demilitarizing Japan, took place with 'the force of a storm' during the early years of the Occupation, with the more or less positive cooperation of the Japanese government, thereby bringing about a radical transformation in Japan's socio-economic system. In the changing climate of international relations, however, this 'period of demilitarization and democratization' made a transition into a new 'period of economic reconstruction'.

7.4. Development of the Cold War

The British wartime prime minister Winston Churchill predicted the approaching conflict between the East and West in his 'Iron Curtain' speech of March 1946. A year later, in March 1947, President Truman requested Congress for an appropriation of $400 million for emergency aid to Greece and Turkey. The 'Truman Doctrine' clearly expressed the US determination to confront communism, stated that it was the duty of the US to provide aid to free peoples resisting totalitarian aggression, and thus raised the curtain of the Cold War era.

Dean Acheson, the US Under-Secretary of State, in a speech given at Cleveland, Ohio, in May 1947, said the Truman Doctrine was the basic premiss of US foreign-aid policy. He emphasized that the economic reconstruction of Germany and Japan, the two major industrial nations in Europe and Asia, should be accelerated. Acheson described worldwide conditions of food crisis and material shortages, which contrasted sharply with the affluence of the US, and suggested the need for US aid. He said that because the US could not supply the needs of the entire world, its aid should be focused on regions which would contribute most to promoting freedom and democracy, and therefore the economic rehabilitation of Japan and Germany was essential. Although Acheson's speech primarily stressed the need to rebuild the European economy, it attracted attention as the first speech by a high-ranking US official mentioning reconstruction of the Japanese economy.

In June 1947, US Secretary of State George Marshall announced a US plan—later called the Marshall Plan—to provide aid to Europe. The plan offered to provide aid to a programme for conquering hunger and poverty developed jointly by the European countries, regardless of their political ideology. Initially, the door was open for the Soviet Union and other East European countries to participate. At a meeting of the British, French, and Soviet foreign ministers held in Paris in July, however, the Soviet foreign minister refused to participate in the Marshall

Plan, attacking it as nothing but a scheme for applying the Truman Doctrine to all of Europe.

Meanwhile, George Kennan, director of the State Department's policy planning staff, elucidated a strategy of 'containment' to oppose Soviet expansionism in an article signed 'X' and published in *Foreign Affairs* in July 1947. In September, the Soviet Union permitted the Comintern to come out into the open in the greatly enlarged Communist Information Bureau (Cominform). The East–West conflict now emerged in clear form.

Inasmuch as the Marshall Plan anticipated the economic revival of West Germany (British, US, and French zones of occupation), a reassessment of German Occupation policy by the Western Allies became inevitable. In July 1947, the US replaced the German Occupation policy document JCS 1067, which had outlined a hard-line demilitarization and denazification policy, by a new policy document JCS 1779 that focused on economic reconstruction. The reversal of US Occupation policy thus began in Germany in response to changing conditions in Europe.

Subsequently, in the process of implementing the new German Occupation policy, arguments over currency reforms led the Soviet Union to begin a blockade in April 1948 of all land transportation between Berlin and the West. As a countermeasure, the US organized a massive airlift of vital food and fuel supplies. The Berlin blockade and the subsequent airlift thus developed into a confrontation between the US and the USSR. With the founding of the Federal Republic of Germany (West Germany) in May 1949 and of the German Democratic Republic (East Germany) in October, the Cold War order in Europe became institutionalized.

In the Far East, peace negotiations between the Chinese Nationalist and Communist parties broke down in November 1946, leading to a resumption of civil war in China. Although the US had provided aid at random to the Nationalist government, it did not have a clearly established policy on China. The fluid civil war situation soon changed in favour of the Communists. In the autumn of 1947, the People's Liberation Army began a major offensive against the Nationalists, and by 1948 the tide had clearly shifted in favour of the Communists. In the spring of 1949, the capital city of Nanjing fell to the Liberation Army, forcing the National government to evacuate to Taiwan. In October, establishment of the People's Republic of China was proclaimed. In July and August of 1948, meanwhile, the Republic of Korea and the People's Democratic Republic of Korea were established, firmly dividing the Korean peninsula into north and south, with the 38th parallel forming a border between them. The intensification of the Cold War in Asia became a direct catalyst leading to reversal of US Occupation policy on Japan.

Because Japan still possessed the greatest industrial potential in Asia, the intensification of the East–West conflict compelled the US to reassess its existing Occupation policy. Its strategy began to shift towards placing Japan under the control of the Western powers and utilizing it as the first line of defence against communism in the Far East.

7.5. Reversal of Policy towards Japan

The US War Department pressed the button signalling the reversal of US policy towards Japan.[7] In part, the reversal was in quick response to the emerging Cold War situation. More directly, however, it was in response to requests made by SCAP, which was administering the Occupation. Having launched major reform measures, SCAP began to show a strong interest in the stabilization of the Japanese economy. Concluding that the absence of a clear solution to the reparations problem was the greatest impediment to the resumption of normal industrial production, SCAP requested the US government in December 1946 to resolve the reparations problem by regarding the FEC's programme of interim reparations as constituting the final phase of the programme.

In Japan at that time, the management and maintenance of machinery and equipment designated for reparations removal was certainly a major problem. The Ministry of Commerce and Industry, responsible for administering reparation matters related to plants in the private sector designated for reparations removal (excluding shipyards), was directed by means of a SCAP memorandum to keep the designated machinery and equipment in 'like new' condition. The designated companies had to spend time and effort for maintenance operation, inspection, and lubrication of machinery and equipment to prepare them for inspections SCAP conducted almost weekly. The financial and human resources required for maintenance were a considerable burden on the companies. Designated machinery and equipment had been removed from production and remained idle, restraining the recovery of production activities. Furthermore, the threat of removal for reparations was a factor delaying formulation of the enterprise reconstruction and reorganization plan. All in all, an early resolution of the reparations problem was earnestly sought.

The War Department dispatched a mission of executives headed by Clifford Strike to Japan, and began reassessing the reparations problem. Strike presented his first report (the First Strike Report) to the War Department in February 1947, recommending an easing of the reparations programme, and based on that report the War Department recommended that a new reparations programme be developed. The US government ordered implementation of the FEC's programme of interim reparations requiring advance removals of 30 per cent, and also submitted a proposal to the FEC about regarding the reparations programme as completed when the interim reparations were finalized. Reversal of the policy towards Japan thus started with the reparations issue.

The War Department aimed at a policy reversal from another angle as well. It proposed to SWINCC a substitute plan for softening the effects of the programme for 'Reduction of Japanese Industrial War Potential' which the FEC was studying. Discussions in SWINCC resulted in the programme's modification by setting a time limit to be determined jointly by the secretaries of State, War, and Navy on the proposed programme of regulating the industrial capacity of the Japanese economy. There were strong feelings of objection in the FEC against the revised proposal, but eventually an agreement was reached on terminating the limitations placed on Japanese industry as of October 1949 but saying the policy would be re-evaluated if the Occupation should continue beyond that point. The setting of a time limit took the bite out of the Occupation policy of limiting Japan's industrial capacity, which appeared quite harsh on paper.

Meanwhile, the policy of eliminating excessive concentration of economic power was beginning to take concrete shape at about this same time, which means it was moving in the opposite direction to the easing of policies on reparations and industry-capacity regulation. That there existed two diametrically opposed policy directions suggests that this was the beginning of the period of reversal in US policy on the Japanese Occupation. The Second Strike Commission, sent to Japan by the Army Department, submitted the Second Strike Report in February 1948, recommending a sizeable reduction in the scale of the reparations programme. It may be noted parenthetically that a report prepared privately by a member of the Commission, James Lee Kauffman, created a stir among US business leaders and high-level government officials. In his report, Kauffman attacked the policy of eliminating excessive concentration of economic power and other Occupation policies of SCAP. He argued that a gigantic economic experiment was being conducted in Japan which would impose an un-American economic order on Japan at the expense of US taxpayers, and advocated a reversal of US policy.

SCAP criticized Kauffman as having distorted the facts, but William Draper, Under-Secretary of the Army, who happened to be visiting Japan, conveyed the message to his government that in his opinion Kauffman's report accurately identified the problem. When the Army Department suggested to General MacArthur that enactment of the Law for the Elimination of Excessive Concentration (the Deconcentration Law) should be postponed, MacArthur responded by sending a radio message strongly objecting to the growing criticism of policy in Japan, arguing that enactment of the Deconcentration Law would complete the policies already in place. The heated discussion between the Army Department and SCAP caused two interruptions in Diet deliberations, as mentioned earlier. In the end, a compromise was struck. The law would be passed, but its implementation would be subject to the advice of a Deconcentration Review Board to be dispatched from the US.

On 6 January 1948, Secretary of the Army Kenneth Royal frankly acknowledged in a speech in San Francisco that the original concept of demilitarizing Japan was no longer compatible with the new objective of building a self-supporting nation. He declared that the policy of the US was to solve this dilemma by placing emphasis on creating a sound and self-supporting economy in Japan. This speech was followed by a statement by General Frank McCoy, the US delegate to the FEC, saying the focus of US Occupation policy in Japan should be placed on stabilizing the Japanese economy.

Meanwhile, the State Department found a champion of policy reversal in George Kennan, director of the newly established Policy-Making Staff. Kennan visited Japan in February 1948, met with MacArthur, and briefed the general on the reversal of policy. After returning to Washington, Kennan submitted a report recommending that the main priority in Occupation policy be shifted to economic reconstruction and that efforts for further reforms be suspended. In March, Army Under-Secretary Draper returned to Japan accompanied by the Johnston Committee. The Committee later submitted a report recommending that the reparations programme be scaled down below the level recommended by the Second Strike Report, that deconcentration be carried out at the minimum level necessary to ensure reasonable competition, and that priority be placed on balancing the budget.

The State Department drafted a new policy document by integrating the views contained in the Draper–Johnston Report into Kennan's recommendations, and submitted it to the National Security Council (NSC). In October 1948, the NSC adopted the Recommendations of US Policy on Japan (NSC 13/2), thereby officially establishing the reversal of US policy towards Japan.

Meanwhile, the Deconcentration Review Board that had visited Japan in May 1948 suggested a new principle whereby the Deconcentration Law be applied only to clear-cut cases of unreasonable restraint of trade, and began examination of 325 companies designated under the law. This principle was derived from the traditional, old theory of monopoly in the history of US antitrust policy. It met strong opposition from the Antitrust and Cartel Division of SCAP, staffed heavily with those who embraced the new monopoly theory of the New Deal school. In the end, only eighteen companies were ordered to be reorganized.[8]

Concerning reparations, the conversion of plants originally designated for reparations removal to civilian production moved forward quickly after May 1948. The reparations policy was studied on the basis of the recommendations of the Johnston Committee, but SCAP strongly argued for terminating the programme because it was about to issue a nine-point stabilization programme, which will be discussed later. In May 1949, General McCoy, US Representative on the FEC, announced the policy, approved by the NSC, of terminating reparations removal after the advance delivery of interim reparations was completed. Concerning the policy of 'Reduction of Japanese Industrial War Potential', the FEC had formulated no new policy for the period after October 1949, the end of the effective period of its existing policy.

Thus, the reversal of US Occupation policy greatly relaxed the restrictions placed on the Japanese economy, and the reconstruction of the economy now emerged as the foremost task.

NOTES

1. MITI, Committee to Edit History of International Trade and Industry Policy, *Tsusho Sangyo Seisakushi* (History of International Trade and Industry Policy), ii, ch. 1, Tsusho Sangyo Chosakai (Research Institute of International Trade and Industry), 1991.

2. Ibid.
3. Ministry of Finance, Historical Studies Office, 'Dokusen Kinshi' (Anti-Monopoly), *Showa Zaiseishi—Shusen kara Kowa made* (History of Fiscal and Monetary Policies in Japan: The Allied Occupation Period, 1945–52), ii, Toyo Keizai Inc., 1982.
4. Ibid.
5. Concerning land reform, see Keiki Owada, *Hishi—Nippon no Nochi Kaikaku* (A Secret History of Land Reform in Japan), Nihon Keizai Shimbun, Inc., 1981.
6. Mitsutsugu Endo, *Nippon Senryo to Roshi Kankei Seisaku no Seiritsu* (The Occupation of Japan and the Formulation of Labour Relations Policy), University of Tokyo Press, 1989.
7. *Tsusho Sangyo Seisakushi*, ii, ch. 1, sect. 2.
8. Ibid. iii, ch. 3, sect. 1.

8

Continuity and Change: Pre-War and Post-War Years

8.1. War Destruction

War and the Japanese economy

As discussed, the Occupation of Japan, unlike that of Germany, was administered indirectly. SCAP set basic Occupation policy and the Japanese government carried it out. In matters relating to industrial policy, Ministry of Commerce and Industry officials who understood the Japanese situation explained it to SCAP authorities, and at times argued against SCAP policies. This chapter examines the pre-war and wartime situation in the Japanese economy, war damages, Japanese responses to measures taken by the Occupation authorities, and those elements of the wartime economy that were instrumental in Japan's war effort but nonetheless survived the Occupation unscathed.

As noted earlier, Japan accepted the terms of the Potsdam Declaration on 14 August 1945, putting an end to a period of war that had lasted over fifteen years from the Manchurian Incident in September 1931, and a few months short of four years from the outbreak of the Pacific War in December 1941. During this period, Japanese society and the Japanese economy underwent extensive transformation.

During the period between 1930—in the midst of the Showa Depression—and 1941, when Japan plunged into the Second World War, Japan's real income increased by more than 80 per cent and real per capita income rose by nearly 60 per cent (Table 8.1). These growth rates were rather remarkable when compared to those of other areas in Asia at the time, or even those of the industrialized nations of the West. The nature of the growth, however, was not completely normal. Following the Manchurian Incident the Japanese economy gradually adopted a strong war footing as war material production was expanded. And after the Sino-Japanese War began in July 1937, the economy rapidly became militarized and war-related industries became the leading growth sector. The percentage of capital formation, especially fixed capital formation, in national income rose, with an attendant decline in the relative size of personal consumption expenditures. It can be said that economic growth at that time took place at the expense of the living standards of the populace.

These developments accelerated in 1941, when Japan–US relations became strained. The war-material industry, as well as the steel and machinery industries which served as the base for armament production, grew rapidly.

In contrast, the share of the output of the spinning and weaving industries—such as the silk and cotton industries—which had been the nucleus of the Japanese economy since the late 1860s, declined rapidly. It dropped from 35.4 per cent to 8.8 per cent in the twelve years from 1930. The silk industry, cut off from the US market by the war, receded into the background because its products were regarded as non-essential luxuries, although it supplied the military with silk for parachutes. The cotton industry, whose market was limited to Asia, was forced to reduce its production when the import of raw cotton became difficult. The industry was eventually placed in the unfortunate position of having to convert its facilities to war production and scrap its spinning machinery to provide metals needed for war production. Naturally, the quality of clothes available to consumers deteriorated. Under the system of clothes rationing, even with ration coupons people could obtain only poor-quality rayon products, and only in limited quantities.

The output of the food industry also fell as a percentage of total output, accompanied by deteriorating quality of the food available to consumers. Sugar was rationed in very small amounts, and the production of such 'table luxuries' as rice wine (sake) and sweets was restricted. The supply of wheat products, called 'rice substitutes', decreased owing to the limited importation of wheat. A more serious problem was the decline in agricultural production indices. The production of rice, the staple food of the Japanese, fell from 66.88 million koku (10.03 million tons) in 1930 to a low level of 58.56 million koku (8.78 million tons) in 1944. Although this decline was in part attributable to the rich harvest of 1930, it is worth noting that the decline was also seen in decreased rice acreage—from 3.239 million hectares in 1930 to 2.979 million hectares in 1944. This reduction in acreage under cultivation was brought about by the shortage of farm labour caused by wartime mobilization. Japanese agriculture had maintained its productivity for years through the use of labour- and fertilizer-intensive methods and it therefore lost its production capabilities as both labour and fertilizers became scarce during the war. Rice rations continued, but they were scanty, and the Japanese people were hard-pressed to obtain even enough staple food for their diet.

The war stopped imports from Great Britain and the US, which meant the supply of essential goods (crude oil, scrap iron, machine tools, etc.) was halted, creating hardships in production activities. It was almost impossible to find alternative sources for these goods in Asia. Although the so-called 'southern resources' (crude oil, tin, raw rubber, etc.) were available in the 'Greater East Asia Co-Prosperity Sphere', they soon were beyond Japan's reach as an unexpectedly large number of ships became casualties of the war and Japan rapidly lost the ability to ship these resources to the Japanese mainland.

The shortage of so many goods should have resulted in rising prices. According to government figures, however, wholesale and retail prices for the fourteen-year period from 1930 to 1944 rose by only about twofold. This relative stability was due to strict wartime control measures, with the twin systems of officially

Table 8.1 Comparison of changes in real national income: 1930–46

	National income (million yen)	Price level index (1930–4 = 100)	Real national income (million yen)	Real national per capita income (yen)	Index of real national per capita income (1930–4 = 100)
1930	10,636	106.3	10,005	155	93.9
1934	13,082	104.0	12,578	184	111.5
1935	14,532	108.2	13,430	193	117.0
1937	19,414	137.0	14,370	201	121.8
1939	28,358	161.6	17,145	235	142.4
1941	39,448	215.7	18,288	246	149.1
1942	47,771	276.3	17,289	230	139.4
1943	53,025	315.6	16,801	219	132.7
1944	58,963	397.8	14,822	201	121.8
1945	90,000	1,012.0	8,892	123	74.5
1946	300,000	4,781.6	6,274	85	51.5

Sources: National income: Figures for 1930–9 are estimates by Statistics Bureau, Prime Minister's Office; figures for 1941–6 are estimates by Ministry of Finance. Price level index: Bank of Japan, Overall Wholesale Price Indices.

Table 8.2 Trends in wartime mining and manufacturing production (indices)

	1938	1939	1940	1941	1942	1943	1944	1945
General mining and manufacturing	131.3	164.0	161.9	169.4	142.7	113.5	86.1	28.5
Army and Navy armament	352	486	729	1,240	1,355	1,805	2,316	566

Note: 'General mining and manufacturing' indices use the weighted average of 1935–7 as 100. 'Armaments' includes warships, warplanes, munitions, and other material. The base year is 1925 (100); for reference, the index value for 1937 was 190.

Source: Yoshio Ando (ed.), *Kindai Nippon Keizaishi Yoran* (Outline of the Economic History of Modern Japan), University of Tokyo Press. 1975.

fixed prices and commodity rationing maintaining superficial price stability. But while the quantity of goods available at officially fixed prices was very much limited, black markets flourished, evading control authorities. Black-market prices naturally were much higher than official prices. According to the Bank of Japan's Overall Wholesale Price Indices (Table 8.1), the average price index was 215.7 in 1941 and rose to 397.8 in 1944.

The Japanese economy, overstrained in trying to satisfy wartime demands, reached its limitations for producing military material in 1944, let alone providing daily necessities for the populace. As Table 8.2 shows, general mining and manufacturing peaked in 1941 and declined thereafter, falling below the 1935–7 level in 1944 and reaching a pitifully low level in 1945. The production of armaments for the army and navy, on the other hand, rose at a considerably rapid rate until 1944; but that production, too, recorded a devastating decline in 1945. Even if this figure represented production from 1 April (start of the fiscal year) to 15 August (end of the war), it would have been only 1,509 on an annual basis. Once into 1945, Japan had lost the ability to continue the war.

War devastation

Japan caused a great deal of damage in many countries in Asia and elsewhere during the war, and the Japanese people also suffered considerably. During the Pacific War alone, the estimated number of Japanese military deaths was 2.4 million, and the estimated number of civilian deaths or those missing was 320,000. The population of Japan proper in 1941 was about 72.22 million, which means that thirty-eight out of every 1,000 Japanese died during the war.

Table 8.3 lists Japanese government estimates of damage to the national wealth during the Pacific War. According to these estimates, 25.4 per cent of the entire national wealth was lost, and the total value at the end of the war was not very different from the total value in 1935. This table does not list the value of warships and warplanes, but for reference the figure would have been 40,382 million yen if there had been no damage. Since the actual damage rate was 83.8 per cent, the value at war's end was 6,526 million yen. All remaining armaments were destroyed after the war, however, which meant that nearly all the results of production activities from 1935 to 1945 were lost because of the war.

Damage to shipping was particularly severe. According to estimates provided by another study, total merchant marine tonnage at the end of the war, including ships built or captured during the war, would have been approximately 10.12 million gross tons. Of this total, about 85 per cent was lost, and only about 1.5 million gross tons of ships remained at the end of the war. Of these remaining, only about 1 million gross tons were serviceable, approximately the same as the size of Japanese merchant marine at the time of the Russo-Japanese War (1904–5). In other words, the war set back the shipping industry by about forty years.

Table 8.3 Damages to national wealth during the Pacific War (unit: million yen)

Type of asset	Total value of damage (a)	Value of direct damage	Value of wealth at end of war (b)	Assumed value of wealth at end of war if no damage (c) = (a) + (b)	Damage rate (d) = (a)/(c) (%)	Wealth in 1935 (e)
Buildings and structures	22,220	17,016	68,215	90,435	24.6	76,275
Industrial machinery and equipment	7,994	4,684	15,352	23,346	34.2	8,501
Railroads	884	104	11,618	12,502	7.1	10,903
Rolling stock	639	364	2,274	2,913	21.9	2,461
Vessels	7,359	6,564	1,766	9,125	80.6	3,111
Electricity, gas	1,618	898	13,313	14,931	10.8	8,987
Telephone, telegraph, broadcasting	293	243	1,683	1,976	14.8	1,531
Waterworks	366	271	1,814	2,180	16.8	1,698
Products	7,864	7,864	25,089	32,953	23.9	23,541
Furniture and household effects	9,558	9,558	36,869	46,427	20.6	39,354
Others	5,483	1,083	10,859	16,342	33.6	10,389
Total	64,278	48,649	188,852	253,130	25.4	186,751

Notes:
1. 'Others' include port facilities, canals, bridges, coins, jewellery, etc., but do not include roads, trees, cultural assets, etc., nor military armaments.
2. 'Total value of damage' is the sum of direct damage and indirect damage (damage suffered from scrapping, evacuation, poor repairs, etc.).
3. 'Direct damage' is damage caused by aerial and naval bombardment; value is included in total damage.
4. 'Wealth in 1935' is in terms of prices at end of war.

Source: Economic Stabilization Board, Director-General's Secretariat, Policy Planning Department Research Division, *Taiheiyo Senso ni Yoru Waga Kuni no Higai Sogo Hokokusho* (Comprehensive report on damage to Japan in Pacific War), 1949: 135.

The rate of damage to buildings and structures was estimated to be about 24.6 per cent, which meant that their value at the end of the war was below the 1935 level. This damage included the loss of about 2.18 million homes. Considering there were 14.22 million households in 1940, at least 15 per cent of all households lost their homes. The wartime loss of homes, furniture, and household effects exacerbated the housing shortage in the immediate post-war period.

Damage to public facilities such as railways, and to utilities such as the electric, gas, and water systems, was relatively light. The rate of damage to rolling stock was 21.9 per cent, and the value of the remaining rolling stock fell below the 1935 figure. Much of the damage was related to wartime appropriation for military use, as well as to damage due to inadequate maintenance and repair.

Although military material production was practically halted, the production facilities themselves suffered relatively light damage. Major military production plants were heavily damaged by naval and aerial bombardments, especially in 1945, but there had been considerable expansion of production facilities during the war, and thus many facilities remained when the war ended. As Table 8.3 shows, 1.8 times the amount of industrial machinery that existed in 1935 was available at the end of the war, even though the rate of damage was as high as 34.2 per cent. This point deserves closer examination.

Industrial capacity at the end of the war, as compared to that of 1937, was 5.6 million tons of pig-iron, a 1.87-fold increase; 7.7 million tons of rolled steel, a 1.18-fold increase; 129 thousand tons of aluminium, a 7.59-fold increase; and a 2.45-fold increase of machine tools. Thus, the capacity for producing metals and machinery at the end of the war was fairly high, although it was somewhat lower than the wartime peak level. In contrast, the production capacity of the textile industry had declined substantially. Selected production capacity indexes, with 1937 as 1, were: 0.19 for cotton spinning, 0.16 for rayon yarn, 0.41 for staple fibres, 0.31 for cotton weaving, and 0.38 for silk and rayon weaving. In the chemical industry, meanwhile, caustic soda and soda ash retained high production capacities at the end of the war, but capacities fell noticeably for ammonium sulphate and superphosphate of lime, needed for producing chemical fertilizers (Table 8.4).

During the war, the heavy and chemical industries specialized in production of military material and armaments. This was done at the expense of light industry. Although the production facilities of the heavy and chemical industries suffered heavy damage from air raids, a considerable portion was still serviceable at the end of the war. Many facilities that survived the war, however, had been over-worked during the war and were badly in need of repair. In fact, many were technically obsolescent because Japan had been isolated from the technical progress that took place in the Western countries.

In the energy industry, power-generation capacity at the end of fiscal year 1945 was 10.385 million kW, comprised of 6.435 million kW of hydroelectric power and 3.95 million kW of thermoelectric power. Although this capacity was

Table 8.4 Production capacity for selected products

Product	Production capacity at end of war (a)	Capacity in 1937 (b)	Comparison (c) = (a)/(b)	Peak wartime capacity	Fiscal year of peak wartime capacity
Pig-iron (1,000 tons)	5,600	3,000	1.87	6,600	1944
Rolled steel (1,000 tons)	7,700	6,500	1.18	8,700	1944
Copper (1,000 tons)	105	120	0.88	144	1943
Aluminium (1,000 tons)	129	17	7.59	127	1944
Caustic soda (1,000 tons)	661	380	1.74	723	1941
Soda ash (1,000 tons)	835	600	1.39	889	1941
Ammonium sulphate (1,000 tons)	1,243	1,460	0.85	1,243	1941
Superphosphate of lime (1,000 tons)	1,721	2,980	0.58	2,846	1941
Cement (1,000 tons)	6,109	12,894	0.47	9,621	1941
Cotton spinning (1,000 spindles)	2,367	12,165	0.19	13,796	1941
Rayon yarn (10,000 pounds)	886	5,700	0.16	5,700	1937
Staple fibre (10,000 pounds)	18,400	45,100	0.41	81,300	1941
Carded wool (cards)	373	684	0.55	733	1940
Cotton looms (units)	13,752	362,604	0.31	393,291	1941
Silk and rayon looms (units)	135,582	356,119	0.38	343,845	1942
Machine tools (units)	54,000	22,000	2.45	60,134	1940

Source: Kokumin Keizai Research Institute, *Nippon Keizai no Genjo* (Current Condition of Japanese Economy), Taihei Shobo, 1947: 18–19.

approximately 1.49 times that of fiscal year 1937, the actual amount of power generated in fiscal year 1945 was only 21.9 billion kWh, or 72 per cent of the 30.25 billion kWh generated in fiscal year 1937. This underutilization of capacity was largely due to the shortage of coal needed for thermal generation, although the decreased demand for power related to the reduced industrial production during the chaotic post-war period was also a factor.

The coal mining industry managed to maintain an annual production level of about 50 million tons until 1944, but it did so through the inhumane method of forcing Chinese and Korean labourers to work in coal-mines in order to cover the shortage of Japanese labour. As soon as these workers were freed from their forced labour after Japan's defeat, coal production fell drastically and a serious coal shortage developed. Also, mining conditions had deteriorated terribly because of unreasonable production demands during the war which exploited promising coalfields without paying proper attention to the maintenance of tunnels and the repair of mine tracks.

As can be seen from the foregoing, the extent of the damage to Japanese industry varied from sector to sector. For the overall economy, however, it can be said that a highly unbalanced industrial structure was passed on to post-war Japan, with considerable war production capacity and a drastically reduced capacity to produce civilian goods. The first task for the post-war Japanese economy, therefore, was to revive non-military production capacity by converting war-production facilities to civilian-goods production. The task, however, had to be tackled within the strong constraints of the reparations issue and trends regarding the demilitarization of Japan, the foremost goal of Allied Occupation policy. In addition, the difficult matter of post-war inflation had to be coped with.

SCAP initially emphasized a policy of restricting the rehabilitation of Japanese heavy industry as part of its demilitarization programme, but it eventually reversed its position in the context of the emerging global Cold War. A new path to Japan's post-war economic development opened as the reparations issue receded into the background and SCAP adopted a new policy of promoting the reconstruction of Japan's economy, including its heavy and chemical industries.

8.2. Continuity and Change

Democratic currents

As described in the preceding chapter, Japanese society underwent great structural changes amidst post-war reform programmes undertaken according to Allied Occupation policies. Politically, the organizing principle of the country was altered from what was embodied in the Constitution of the Empire of Japan (the Meiji Constitution) to what is set out in the new Constitution of Japan.

The Constitution of Japan was promulgated in November 1946 under the direction and moral support of SCAP. It pronounced that sovereignty resides with the people, guaranteed fundamental human rights—both freedoms and social rights—as eternal and inviolable, and established the principle of the separation of the three powers based on a system of parliamentary government. The emperor system, which the wartime leaders had desperately tried to safeguard, was preserved by the declaration that the emperor is 'the symbol of the unity of the people', made in part as a concession to US views. This Constitution was also the first in the world to renounce the right to wage war.

A comparison of the pre-war and post-war Constitutions reveals a 'revolutionary' change between them.[1] Historical facts, however, do not agree with the view that divine sovereignty existed under the Meiji Constitution and had been preserved until the end of the war, when it was suddenly transformed into popular sovereignty. Even during the period under the Meiji Constitution, there was an unmistakable undercurrent of democratization.

Popular criticism of the bureaucratic oligarchy of the Meiji period (1868–1912), dominated by a few powerful feudal clans, escalated into a political current known as Taisho democracy. In the Taisho period (1912–26), political party shadow Cabinets became well established. Popular involvement in politics was expanded as universal adult suffrage without a property qualification was introduced, although it was not granted to women. The mainstream interpretation of the Constitution viewed the emperor as an organ, arguing that sovereignty resided in the State and that the emperor was merely an organ of the State. Unfortunately, this move towards democracy was interrupted by the rise of militarist fascism from around 1935, thrusting the nation into a dark wartime period of suffocating oppression.

The independence of the emperor's supreme command, a fatal flaw in the Meiji Constitution, carried the Japanese people down an unfortunate historical path to fifteen years of war during an age of intensifying conflict among the world's major powers, and resulted in Japan causing much damage and hardship to many other nations. Japanese reflection on their past behaviour, and their aspiration to revive the interrupted current towards democracy, became the foundation of the promulgation of the post-war Constitution of Japan, and made it possible for them for half a century afterwards to preserve what came to be called the 'Peace Constitution'.

Still, it is not possible to ignore the continuity of Japanese society maintained through preservation of the position of the emperor, albeit as a 'symbol of the unity of the people'. Although SCAP undertook drastic reform measures in other areas, it chose to preserve the emperor system because it recognized in it the basic unifying principle of Japanese society, and moved to ensure social stability by taking advantage of it. In that sense, to the extent that the emperor system survived the post-war period of reforms, one can see in it the continuity of Japanese society.

In the Constitution of Japan, a decisive change from pre-war days is seen in the principle of peace through renunciation of the right to wage war or bear arms. As described earlier, Japan followed a path of military expansion, beginning with the Manchurian Incident and ending with the Pacific War, in order to gain a foothold in Asia in competition with the advanced imperialist powers. As noted, the basic goal of the Allied Occupation was to dismantle Japan's capacity to wage war. This goal was gradually achieved in the context of Occupation policies, based on Japanese reflection on their past. All the reform measures of the Occupation—dissolution of the zaibatsu, land reform, labour reform, and the new Constitution—were undertaken with that basic goal of Occupation policy in mind. The Occupation's disarmament policy had a major impact on the subsequent development patterns of the Japanese economy, although it was partially relaxed in the emerging Cold War climate. As will be discussed later, the Japanese industrial structure was to develop around its heavy and chemical industries. But it was not to be focused on military production as before but rather was to be driven primarily by consumer demand. War-related production is by nature wasteful, and contributes little to the circular flow of output and income. As shown, after 1941 the Japanese economy followed a downward spiral in production. In this sense, the peaceful nature of Japan's post-war economy can be regarded as one of the key factors contributing to its high-level growth.

Sophistication of the industrial structure

With respect to continuity and change in the post-war Japanese economy, the second point to consider is the increased sophistication of its industrial structure. During wartime, emphasis was placed on the heavy and chemical industries in order to meet military production needs. The primary goal of the Occupation, however, was to dismantle this wartime industrial structure. The Allied Powers thus sought to dismantle military production plants by carrying out a severe reparations programme and removing much machinery and equipment. The condition of those plants at the war's end has already been discussed. From around 1947, however, SCAP's industrial policy towards Japan began to change gradually under the influence of the Cold War, resulting in a decision to allow Japan to keep most of the remaining facilities. What was the significance of this decision for Japan's post-war economy?

After the First World War, the heavy and chemical industries in Japan began to expand steadily even as traditional light industries continued to grow. By the mid-1930s the economy was thus capable of meeting the domestic needs for both consumer and producer goods. Nonetheless, Japan's heavy and chemical industries were still weak in many areas as compared to the same industries in the advanced Western nations. For instance, motorization was in progress, with the US at the forefront, but Japan's car industry could not produce passenger cars in volumes large enough to compete with the knock-down production in Japan of Ford and General Motors, although the industry was somewhat more successful in manufacturing trucks and buses. In the electric machinery industry, Japanese companies were far from developing markets for consumer durables for home use (vacuum cleaners, washing machines, refrigerators), although such markets were already well developed in the Western countries. Concerning machine tools,

Japanese companies could not produce high-precision machine tools, e.g. those for making gears and bearings, and depended on imports for their supply.

After the Sino-Japanese War broke out in 1937, the heavy and chemical industries shifted their priority towards military production, and by the eve of the Pacific War, as noted earlier, an extremely distorted industrial structure had emerged with pronounced specialization in armament production. Nonetheless, the basic metals and machinery industries acquired a degree of advanced production capability in response to meeting the demand for producing sophisticated military goods. The magnitude of production and quality-orientation of the metals and machinery industries were thus inherited by the post-war economy as legacies from the wartime economy and became important factors contributing to the growth of the post-war economy.

Another factor that made the post-war growth pattern possible was the pool of skilled male workers in the labour force. In pre-war Japan, the growth of Japanese industry was led by textiles, and young female workers constituted the core of the labour force. This fact has been often quoted and it is verified by labour-force statistics. During the war years, however, when the emphasis turned to developing the heavy and chemical industries, especially for military production, male workers, particularly skilled workers who received training in factories, became the backbone of the industrial labour force. Some of these workers became unemployed after the war, when plants devoted to military production were dismantled. As post-war economic reconstruction got slowly under way, however, and steel mills and machine shops resumed operations, these skilled workers immediately began functioning in the new production system. This was another of the unexpected legacies of the wartime economy.

Structural changes in the domestic market

Another change to mention concerning industrial workers is the labour union movement. In pre-war years, the labour union movement made some progress despite official hostility, and in 1931 there were 400,000 union members, a unionization rate of 8 per cent. The government suppressed the movement during the war years, and in 1940 disbanded all unions. After the war the Occupation authorities moved quickly to reform industrial relations in Japan, especially because they regarded the labour union movement as an important factor in democracy.

As matters evolved, the skilled industrial workers described above became the nucleus of the labour union movement. In this regard, it is noteworthy that most workers had developed their skills through long years of service in one company. Since the late Meiji period, large Japanese corporations had established education and training programmes in their factories for developing skilled workers they hoped would remain with them for many years. Moreover, it was the Industrial Patriotic Associations organized in factories during the war years that responded most energetically to the urgings of SCAP to organize labour unions, and the leaders in these associations were no other than the skilled workers and staff members who had had many years of service in their respective companies. The labour unions that resulted, therefore, were 'enterprise unions' organized in each company. Because most workers after the war feared unemployment and hoped for years of continuous service in the same company, this type of labour-union organization was accepted by them without resistance. Actually, most pre-war labour unions were also enterprise unions. And although post-war unions were widely organized and engaged in radical activities—the two features that made the post-war labour movement totally different from its pre-war counterpart—both pre-war and post-war unions were organized at the enterprise level by workers with long years of service. In this sense there was continuity, which made their rapid growth possible.

The post-war labour unions fought hard for higher wages, amidst inflation, and made one demand unheard of before the war. They demanded elimination of the status difference between blue-collar workers and white-collar workers. From the Meiji period (1868–1912) onwards, a sharp status distinction had always existed between these two categories of employees in Japan. In fact, the same distinction existed in Western countries. Apart from blue-collar workers in Japan being paid daily wages while white-collar workers were paid monthly salaries, white-collar workers were paid biannual bonuses while blue-collar workers were paid only small additional allowances at the o-bon season in July and at the end of the year. The conditions for using company housing also heavily favoured white-collar workers. But membership of post-war unions, unlike pre-war unions, generally included both blue-collar and white-collar workers in the same union, and the post-war labour union movement thus demanded elimination of discriminatory treatment. So while pre-war and post-war unions were identical in the sense of being enterprise unions, in the new situation management eliminated the status distinction between the two types of workers and all workers came to be called simply 'shain' ('company members', i.e. 'employees') and came to be treated equally in terms of pay increases and bonuses. This feature of post-war industrial relations in Japan is markedly different from pre-war days.

The elimination of the status difference also had a major impact on the wage structure. In post-war Japan, the difference between the wages of blue-collar workers and the salaries of white-collar workers essentially disappeared. Both came to be called wages, and the difference between the highest and the lowest wages inside a company's wage structure became extremely small. The wage structure from the Taisho period (1912–26) onwards had been based on the seniority system, but with elimination of the status difference, wage-rate differentials between blue-collar and white-collar workers due to seniority differences narrowed markedly. As a consequence, income distribution in Japan became far more equitable than before. This is attested to by the fact that an international comparison of Gini coefficients shows highly equal distribution in Japan. As Japanese income levels rose with economic growth, a more equitable distribution of income served to increase the size of the domestic market and played an active role in expanding the consumer-durables market as the industrial structure of Japan became increasingly more sophisticated from the second half of the 1950s.

Land reform played an equally important role in equalizing income distribution and expanding the consumer-durables market. Tenant farmers, formerly regarded as constituting the bottom rung of the most destitute Japanese, became owner-farmers as a result of post-war land reform. The income of farmers also rose because the price of rice was stabilized under the food control system. The pre-war distinction between landlords and tenant farmers disappeared, and the distribution of farming income became much more equitable. Farming villages became large markets for industrial products, particularly consumer durables.

The more equitable distribution of income brought about an expansion in the domestic market. It was originally thought that as economic growth accelerated, Japan's dependency on imports would rise above the pre-war level and the import of raw materials and fuels would become a serious problem. But largely because of structural changes in the size of the home market, this fear proved unfounded in the actual growth process.

Ownership and control in corporate management

The next topic to be discussed is continuity and change brought about by dissolution of the zaibatsu. As seen in the preceding chapter, the Allied Occupation Forces aggressively sought to dissolve the zaibatsu, blaming them for having worked closely with the military and providing economic support to the military's activities. As shown in Table 8.5, during the war years the zaibatsu clearly accumulated capital, expanded their fields of production activities, and by the end of the war came to occupy very important positions in major industrial fields. The overnight dissolution of the zaibatsu brought about monumental changes between ownership and management relations in the Japanese economy.

In reflecting here on Japanese corporate management, it should be remembered that Japan was an industrial latecomer compared to the advanced Western nations. Although the scale of business operations expanded together with advances in technology, and the need for operating capital increased, the accumulation of private capital lagged, driving Japanese companies—even before the war—to adopt the corporate, particularly the joint-stock corporate, form of business. Of all corporations in Japan in 1945, 48.1 per cent were joint-stock corporations. This situation remained essentially unchanged after the war, with the percentage of joint-stock corporations rising to 64.8 per cent in 1950 against a background of an increasing number of corporations seeking the advantages of the Corporate Income Tax Law.[2] Nonetheless, major shareholders generally had a powerful voice in these corporations because the stock market was not fully developed. During the war, zaibatsu corporations, in which zaibatsu families monopolized stocks, began offering their stocks for public subscription in order to

Industry		Four major zaibatsu				Total by industry	% vs. national total
		Mitsui	Mitsubishi	Sumitomo	Yasuda		
Finance	Banking	148,125	87,675	53,675	193,361	482,836	48.0
	Trust	15,000	7,500	5,000	7,500	35,000	85.4
	Insurance	6,250	64,700	6,750	8,550	86,250	51.2
	Subtotal	169,375	159,875	65,425	209,411	604,086	49.7
Heavy industry	Mining	481,300	274,275	111,150	1,000	864,725	28.2
	Metal manufacturing	270,005	185,000	530,200	4,150	989,355	25.8
	Machinery and tools	838,567	1,207,655	638,660	95,183	2,702,265	44.9
	Shipbuilding	58,125	11,647	1,600	10,000	81,372	5.0
	Chemicals	566,169	187,455	167,850	9,080	918,804	31.0
	Subtotal	2,214,166	1,866,032	1,449,460	119,413	5,556,521	31.7
Light industry	Paper	4,131	10,980	—	9,000	24,111	4.5
	Ceramics	63,496	14,750	11,230	—	89,476	28.4
	Textiles	125,273	10,900	2,000	85,946	224,119	17.4
	Agriculture, forestry, fisheries, food	24,113	6,800	1,322	—	31,635	2.7
	Miscellaneous	56,685	29,600	14,760	22,017	115,382	9.1
	Subtotal	273,698	73,030	29,312	116,963	484,723	10.6
Others	Electric power, gas	—	—	20,000	—	20,000	0.5
	Land transportation	18,682	13,254	1,075	12,600	45,461	4.9
	Marine transportation	179,127	399,922	6,525	17,500	598,074	60.3
	Real estate, construction	48,937	40,000	16,680	30,647	136,264	22.7
	Warehousing						
	Commerce and trade	157,145	151,400	58,205	3,000	349,590	12.8
	Subtotal	403,891	604,576	102,485	63,747	1,149,389	12.7
Total		3,061,130	2,703,513	1,646,682	509,534	7,794,719	24.1
% of national total		9.5	8.3	5.1	1.6	24.1	

Note: Figures represent paid-up capital of zaibatsu-affiliated companies. 'Percentage versus national total' represents percentage of total paid-up capital of the zaibatsu versus that of all companies located in Japan proper.

Source: Showa Zaisei-shi: Shusen kara Kowa made (History of Fiscal and Monetary Policies in Japan: The Allied Occupation Period, 1945–52), ii: Dokusen Kinshi (Anti-Monopoly) compiled by Historical Studies Office, Ministry of Finance. Toyo Keizai Inc. 1982: 23.

raise funds needed for financing their rapidly expanding operations. Even with those corporations, however, the control of the corporations was in the hands of zaibatsu families. At any rate, capital ownership and corporate control were closely related, and corporations were managed from a long-range perspective. As typified by the results of the zaibatsu dissolution programme, however, ownership and management came to be separated.

The zaibatsu families themselves, which represented capital ownership, had in pre-war years already receded into the background, and actual management was often in the hands of professional managers called '*banto*'. In the post-war post-zaibatsu period, the position of zaibatsu families became even weaker. Much capital was raised in the stock market by public subscription, but even then stockholders were seldom involved directly in managing the companies they invested in. As the proportion of external funds, such as bank loans, increased in the capital structure of corporations, senior executives came to exercise control over the companies they worked for. This development, known as the separation of ownership and management, was regarded as a means to achieve economic democracy. This was another major change that took place after the war in the form of the joint-stock corporation, whose legal form remained unchanged.

Also, the proportion of corporate investors holding shares increased gradually. The percentage of shares owned by individuals, which stood at 69.1 per cent in 1949, fell to 53.1 per cent in 1955, accompanied by corresponding increases in the percentages of shares owned by financial institutions and other business corporations. Mutual shareholding among corporations also became widespread. This development became a factor in accelerating economic growth in that it stabilized corporate management and enabled corporations to make investments from a long-range viewpoint.

Post-war economic growth

The foregoing examined continuity and change in the Japanese industrial structure between the pre-war and war years on the one hand, and the post-war period on the other. The changes were essentially brought about by the implementation of SCAP policies for demilitarizing and democratizing the Japanese economic system. In the transition towards the Cold War system, these changes, if anything, worked to accelerate subsequent economic growth. By looking more carefully, however, at the background of the post-war changes having a positive effect on the economy it is actually possible to see a continuity of economic factors. Post-war reforms were compatible with the post-war economy precisely because they were heading in the same direction as the trends that had developed in the Japanese economy from pre-war days—establishment of owner-farmers, the labour union movement, and separation of ownership and control. Moreover, post-war reforms were able to function as positive growth factors only because there had been continuous development from pre-war days of the heavy and chemical industries and formation of a class of skilled industrial workers.

The Japanese economy recovered from post-war chaos and difficulties at a fairly rapid rate, and was soon well on its way down a path towards high-level growth.

Japan experienced a quite substantial decline in its industrial production towards the end of the war, and the situation worsened during the chaotic post-war period. Once into the 1950s, however, it achieved rapid recovery and continuous growth. It is interesting to observe that West Germany, another defeated nation, experienced a pattern of recovery and growth closely resembling that of Japan. In contrast, the US economy underwent extremely rapid industrialization during the war, stagnated for four or five years after the war as it reoriented itself to peacetime conditions, and grew moderately afterwards. At any rate, the growth of the Japanese economy in the 1950s was extremely rapid, which was a result of the relatively successful linking of continuity and change that occurred in various dimensions of the economy between the pre-war and post-war years. The subsequent growth of the economy based on this linking will be examined in the chapters that follow.

NOTES

1. Toshiyoshi Miyazawa, 'Hachigatsu Kakumei no Kenposhi-teki Imi' (Constitutional Significance of the August Revolution), *Sekai Bunka*, May 1946.
2. Management and Coordination Agency, *Nihon Choki Tokei Soran* (Historical Statistics of Japan) 4, Nihon Tokei Kyokai (Japan Statistical Association), 1988: 162.

9

Economic Rehabilitation and Industrial Policy

9.1. Combating Inflation

The post-war Japanese economy faced a threat of serious inflation. The inflation that had begun towards the end of the war accelerated in the immediate post-war chaos. The index of black-market prices in Tokyo in February 1946 was nearly double that in September 1945 (see Table 9.1). This inflation was attributed to an imbalance between supply and demand, marked by a shortage of goods due to a sharp decline in production and to the rapid increase in currency in circulation brought about by payment of contingent military and other expenses which began immediately after the war.

The government attacked the inflation on three fronts: (1) suppressing purchasing power by using fiscal and financial measures, (2) controlling prices by using a revised system of wartime price controls, and (3) closing the inflationary gap by increasing the supply of goods. On 26 August 1945, the Ministry of Munitions and the Ministry of Agriculture and Commerce were abolished and were replaced by the revived Ministry of Commerce and Industry (MCI) and the Ministry of Agriculture and Forestry. At MCI, the General Affairs, Commercial Affairs, Industrial Affairs, Mining, Fuel, and Electric Power Bureaux were charged with the responsibility of combating inflation through control of the supply of materials. Their first tasks were to dismantle the wartime system of control that had been established to channel materials towards munitions production, and to convert munitions industries to civilian-goods industries. In dismantling the wartime control system, one major question was how to control the supply and demand of daily necessities. Because the system of official prices had come to exist in name only, discussions proceeded with a view to abolishing it. Although SCAP worked towards creating a free-market system, it was nonetheless reluctant to permit total abrogation of the price-control system for fear of causing disruptions in the economy. In October 1945, MCI established an emergency headquarters for promoting increased production of daily necessities, and drafted a proposal to remove controls on the sale of goods whose production was expected to increase once it was freed. With regard to controlled goods, production was to be planned with an assured supply of needed raw materials, and rationing was to be maintained. Controlled goods included kitchen utensils such as metal pots and kettles, textile products, china and porcelain, shoes, umbrellas, electric appliances, bicycles, soap, matches, stationery, and toilet paper. When controls were lifted on

Table 9.1 Inflation as revealed by trends in black-market and free prices, 1945–1950

	Prices of consumer goods		Prices of producer goods	
	Indices	Multiples of official prices	Indices	Multiples of official prices
1945 October	92	28.7		
December	128	29.7		
1946 February	200	39.8		
April	187	21.3		
June	201	20.6		
August	186	13.5		
October	180	8.8	107	5.9
December	222	8.3	134	7.2
1947 February	275	9.9	185	9.3
April	348	11.2	231	11.1
June	419	13.1	292	12.7
August	452	8.3	362	9.3
October	508	6.6	401	9.8
December	558	5.1	418	5.3
1948 February	617	5.5	456	5.8
April	674	6.0	479	6.0
June	760	7.3	479	5.9
August	744	4.6	486	3.0
October	746	3.1	490	2.8
December	769	2.9	501	2.9
1949 Average	758	1.8	444	1.7
1950 Average	543	1.3	371	1.2

Note: Prices were Tokyo black-market and free prices. Base periods were Sept. 1945 for consumer goods and Aug. 1946 for producer goods.

Source: Compiled by Okura-sho Zaisei-shi Shitsu (Ministry of Finance, Historical Studies Office), *Showa Zaisei-shi: Shusen kara Kowa made* (History of Fiscal and Monetary Policies in Japan: The Allied Occupation Period, 1945–52), xix: Statistics, Toyo Keizai Inc., 1978: 57 and 64.

perishable foods other than staple foods in November 1945, their prices rose sharply even though their supply also increased. Observing this development, SCAP opposed the plan of removing controls on certain daily necessities. Accordingly, controls on such items were maintained for the interim. Meanwhile, price-support subsidies on basic materials—coal and metals—were abolished in principle, and their prices were raised substantially.[1]

As for the conversion of munitions industries, SCAP announced a policy of allowing arsenals to manufacture civilian goods by using their existing facilities on a case-by-case approval basis. MCI proceeded with programmes of conversion to civilian use—while negotiating with SCAP to obtain approval on a case-by-case basis—of soda for textiles and ammonium sulphate, speciality steels and small generators for farm machines and implements, and raw cotton for consumer-goods production. Once into 1946, approval was granted to convert wartime heavy-industry plants to the production of farm, transport, chemical, mining, and food-processing machinery and equipment. The capacity/utilization ratio in the converted plants, however, remained low owing to serious shortages of materials, including fuels. Moreover, conversion of facilities to civilian use was limited by the reparations problem (designation of equipment and machinery for reparations removals). These problems were serious obstacles to restoration of peacetime production activities.

Effective measures were not taken during the chaos of the immediate post-war period, and inflation accelerated. From the end of 1945, the government began taking steps to develop a comprehensive policy of controlling inflation. As part of the programme, in February 1946 it introduced a series of emergency financial measures. By invoking the Emergency Financial Measures Ordinance and the Bank of Japan Notes Deposit Ordinance, the government implemented the following measures: (1) existing Bank of Japan notes would cease to be legal tender as of 2 March 1946; (2) financial institutions were to accept deposits of old notes until 7 March, and limit subsequent withdrawals to 300 yen per month for the head of a household and 100 yen for a family member, as well as limiting wage payments by enterprises to an employee to 500 yen per month; and (3) old yen notes would be exchanged for new notes (including old notes with certificate stamps attached), with a limit of 100 yen per person, between 25 February and 7 March. By these measures, currency in circulation decreased from 61.8 billion yen on 18 February to 15.2 billion yen on 11 March, and for the time being the inflationary pressure from the swollen money supply decreased.

In March 1946, the government abrogated the Price Control Ordinance, which had been the principal ordinance for wartime price controls, and put into effect the Price Control Order, which had the effect of reorganizing wartime controls into a comprehensive new system of controlling production, distribution, and pricing of a wide range of goods, including perishable food items. An official price system (the '3.3 Price System') was developed. In this system, wages were calculated from the price of rice, which formed the basis of official coal prices, and then the official prices of other goods were determined. The cost of living for an average household was estimated to be 500 yen per month. Price-support subsidies were to be paid to producers of staple foods, coal, perishable food items, and other goods in cases where production costs exceeded official prices.

In August 1946, the post-war price control system was further enhanced with establishment of the Economic Stabilization Board (ESB) for planning emergency measures for economic stabilization and establishment of the Price Agency for implementing price controls. The ESB was a powerful interministerial agency headed by the prime minister and having a state minister as its director-general.

A large number of capable officials were sent to this agency from MCI and participated in formulating and implementing various policy measures.

Regarding the control of materials supply which was to underpin the price control system, the Japanese government contemplated a system of indirect control by private organizations to be formed by reorganizing the wartime control associations along democratic lines. In August 1946, however, SCAP ordered the dissolution of the wartime control associations and establishment of a system of materials control by a public agency. Responding to the expiration of the Materials Control Ordinance based on the National General Mobilization Law, from May 1946 onwards MCI began a study of a law for temporary measures for post-war industry. In July, it drafted the bill for Temporary Materials Supply and Demand Control Law. The bill was submitted to the Diet in July, and was enacted in October 1946 after major changes were made. It came to serve as the basic law for post-war control of materials supply. For methods of control, the government sought to use a combination of direct control by the government and autonomous control by private organizations. SCAP, however, feared that control by private organizations might tend towards monopolization and therefore strongly advocated governmental control, suggesting creation of a public corporation wholly funded by the government. The Japanese government, being fully aware of the problems encountered in the wartime system of materials control, sought to develop freer markets regulated by private initiative. In contrast, SCAP wanted to promote governmental control because it doubted, in view of the seriousness of the price problem, that a market system based on control and led by the initiatives of private enterprise could adequately address the problem. Following the wishes of SCAP, the government established, from April 1947, eight distribution *kodan*—Coal, Petroleum, Fertilizer, Staple Food, Grocery, Fodder, Oil and Fats, and Liquor, four trade *kodan*—Mining and Manufactured Goods, Textiles, Foodstuffs, and Raw Materials, and the Price Adjustment *kodan*, among others.

The wartime Materials Mobilization Plan was carried into the post-war period in the form of the Fiscal 1945 Third Quarter Basic Materials Supply and Demand Plan, formulated in October 1945. From fiscal year 1946, a Materials Supply and Demand Plan, a Daily Necessities Supply and Demand Plan, a Freight Transport Plan, and an Industrial Fund Supply and Demand Plan were developed, with the aim of adjusting the balance between supply and demand each quarter, based on the Temporary Materials Supply and Demand Control Law.

9.2. Cancellation of War Indemnity Payments and the Rehabilitation of Enterprises

After emergency financial measures were implemented, the currency in circulation bottomed on 12 March and then began to increase gradually. On the other hand, immediately before the conversion of old to new yen people used their old yen to acquire goods, and prices rose sharply. They then remained relatively stable until about the autumn of 1946 (Table 9.1). In the meantime, however, SCAP issued a directive to implement the cancellation of war indemnity payments, a policy that had a seriously adverse effect on Japanese companies.

Immediately after the war, the government wasted little time making wartime indemnity payments to private companies. With commencement of the Occupation, however, payments were suspended, leaving a considerable sum of claims unsettled. According to one estimate, the government indebtedness for wartime indemnities amounted to 56.5 billion yen, including 32.9 billion yen for war-risk insurance (government guarantees on payments by insurance companies), 10.5 billion yen for loss indemnities (compensation for losses related to production or facilities expansion ordered by government authorities), and 10.0 billion yen in accounts payable (payments for semi-finished goods and goods in process when contracts were cancelled). Outstanding indebtedness to private companies, after subtracting payments made during and immediately after the war, amounted to roughly 30.2 billion yen.[2]

Because general account expenditures in the original 1945 budget were approximately 21.5 billion yen, the war indemnity indebtedness was certain to be a heavy burden on post-war public finances. Considering that large government expenditures made during a short period immediately after the war had sharply increased the money supply and had triggered post-war inflation, it was suggested that war indemnity payments be cancelled as a means of curbing inflation. This viewpoint was supported in a radio address in October 1945 by the public finance scholar Hyoe Ouchi, in which he urged Finance Minister Keizo Shibusawa to be recklessly daring in cancelling war indemnity payments. In November 1945, SCAP issued a memorandum ordering the imposition of a war profits tax and a property tax, as well as a freeze on public debt repayments. The memorandum identified the objective of the policy as 'making all Japanese become fully aware that war does not pay'. The government responded to these directives by proposing personal and corporate property taxes while honouring war indemnity obligations. SCAP rejected this proposal, and in May 1946 directed the Japanese government to suspend war indemnity payments and establish an individual property tax.

For the personal property tax, the government sought to set the tax exemption point at 20,000 yen and to apply progressive rates of 10 per cent to 70 per cent on the assessed value of property above that point. Its aim was to absorb a maximum amount of purchasing power, as a means of curbing inflation, by extending the application of the property tax down to households of relatively limited means. SCAP reacted negatively to this proposal, maintaining that the objective of the personal property tax was a redistribution of national wealth. To that end, it insisted that the purchasing power of households of limited means should be left untouched and inflation should be fought by cancelling war indemnity payments and other means.

Finance Minister Tanzan Ishibashi of the first Yoshida Cabinet was seriously concerned about the great potential damage to corporations that cancellation of war indemnity payments might cause, and the subsequent negative effect on economic rehabilitation. He therefore proposed to SCAP that the government make *de facto* indemnity payments up to the excess of the external debt of companies over the market value of their existing assets. The government, however, faced rough going in negotiations on this point because SCAP firmly insisted on cancelling war indemnity payments. Finally, Prime Minister Shigeru Yoshida sent a personal letter to General MacArthur, beseeching him for favourable consideration of the matter as the decision would have a serious impact on the future of the Japanese economy. The reply from MacArthur, however, said that payments to enterprises would not be allowed, but the Japanese government would be authorized to pay up to 50,000 yen of war-risk insurance per private individual. In the end, the government found no alternative but to impose a 100 per cent war indemnity special tax on war indemnity claims, thereby effectively cancelling war indemnity payments. On 18 October 1946, the War Indemnity Special Measures Law was put into effect, and personal property was taxed at progressive rates of 25 per cent to 90 per cent and an exemption limit was set at 100,000 yen.

The war indemnity special tax was levied on all indemnity claims as well as payments made during and after the war, and was collected in instalments over several years starting in 1946. Tax collections amounted to 57.5 billion yen, of which 49.1 billion yen was collected from companies. Although enterprises were allowed a deduction of 10,000 yen per case, for all practical purposes war indemnity payments were cancelled in their entirety.

Companies which had suffered war damage in the form of a loss of facilities from bombing and confiscation of overseas assets were counting on war indemnity payments as a source of funds for their post-war reconstruction efforts. Cancellation of these payments, therefore, dealt them a severe blow. It was apparent that not only currently operating companies but also financial institutions which had made loans to them would be severely impacted. If left alone, many companies would possibly go bankrupt. The government, therefore, implemented special measures to rescue companies concurrently with its decision to levy the special tax on war indemnity payments. First, in August 1946, it enacted the Law Concerning Emergency Measures for the Accounts of Companies and the Law Concerning Emergency Measures for the Accounts of Financial Institutions, under which it designated 'special accounting companies'. Those companies that were thus designated were to settle their accounts as of 12 a.m. on 11 August 1946, divide their assets and liabilities into those necessary for the continuation of their business ('new accounts') and those unnecessary for this purpose ('old accounts'), and to continue their operations with the new accounts.

In October 1946, the Enterprise Reconstruction and Reorganization Law and the Financial Institutions Reconstruction and Readjustment Law were promulgated. These laws allowed the 'special accounting companies' to draw up plans to dispose of their 'special losses'—or plans for their financial reorganization—to the Finance Minister for approval, and to resume their business operations with new sets of accounts. In other words, the 'special accounting companies' were to offset their special losses—losses arising from cancellation of war indemnity payments, loss of overseas assets, loss of claims, and loss of assets—by profits, reserves, and profits that accrued from assets revaluation, as of August. Any remaining special losses were to be covered by capital reduction and old claims. Their financial reorganization plans were to declare whether they expected to continue conducting their business carrying both old and new accounts, or establish second companies leaving the old accounts untouched. Plans were to be submitted to the appropriate minister and the Finance Minister.

Thus, the rehabilitation and reconstruction of companies was to be effected by disposing of their post-war losses arising from cancellation of war indemnity payments and others. SCAP, however, said it intended to utilize the enterprise rehabilitation programmes as a means to eliminate excessive concentrations of economic power. In the process of formulating the Enterprise Rehabilitation and Reconstruction Law, SCAP suggested that the Holding Company Liquidation Commission participate in the process of approving rehabilitation plans. The participation of this commission, which was responsible for dissolving the zaibatsu, meant that the rehabilitation programme would acquire an additional dimension. Although this suggestion was not incorporated into the law in the end, companies found it necessary to add perspectives of zaibatsu dissolution and deconcentration to their rehabilitation plans because SCAP had *de facto* power to approve or reject those plans.

Large corporations were informally instructed by SCAP to incorporate into their enterprise rehabilitation plans the aims of its antitrust policy, later to be legislated as the Anti-Monopoly Law and the Deconcentration Law. Many companies went through periods of uncertainty formulating their rehabilitation plans, which included proposals to break up the company into smaller units or split divisions into separate companies. They then sounded out the opinion of SCAP and afterwards reformulated the plans. As discussed earlier, however, once into 1947 the policy of eliminating concentrations of economic power petered out as the US Occupation policy towards Japan was reversed. In the end, only eighteen corporations were designated for reorganization under the Deconcentration Law. Nonetheless, some companies put reorganization plans into effect even though they had been released from designation. It may be concluded, therefore, that the rehabilitation and reconstruction measures had significant effects on Japanese enterprises.

Enterprise rehabilitation and reconstruction were implemented with considerable delay beyond the initial plan because of the intrusion of the deconcentration policy, which was alien to the initial objective of the programme, and because of the delay in handling the reparations problem. In the end, it took until about 1948 for the rehabilitation programmes for financial institutions to be completed and until about 1949 for those for non-financial companies. These delays in effecting enterprise rehabilitation and reconstruction were one of the factors that impeded swift post-war restoration of production activities.

9.3. The Priority-Production System and State Control of Coal Industry

Once into 1946, production activities that had fallen to rock bottom in the disruption immediately after the war began somehow to improve. This recovery was made possible by depleting inventories of raw materials acquired during the war years, and a sharp decline in production was predicted as the stock of materials became depleted. Relying on a suggestion that General MacArthur made when he ordered the cancellation of war indemnity payments—that SCAP might approve emergency imports of materials—the Japanese government requested importation of twenty items, including raw cotton, pig-iron, and heavy oil. Negotiations on these imports took time, however, and production began to sag after reaching a peak in September 1946. From November prices began to rise sharply. The primary reason for the slowdown in production activities was the shortage of fuel; therefore, increased production of domestic coal was sought as a means of boosting industrial production.

Restoration of coal production had earlier been regarded as the highest-priority task. In October 1945, the Cabinet decided to implement emergency measures for coal production, and made priority allocation of funds, materials, food, and labour to coal production. In December, the Coal Agency was established as an external agency of MCI; with it, a system was thus in place for efficiently administering coal policy. These measures produced some positive results; coal production which fell in November 1945 to 550,000 tons (6.6 million tons per year)—or less than one-fifth of the pre-war level—increased to 1.64 million tons in March 1946 and to an annual rate of 20 million tons in the first half of fiscal year 1946. Coal production, however, remained insufficient. The estimated production of 23 million tons for fiscal year 1946 would leave only 9 million tons for general industrial use after the needs for electricity generation, transport, heating, and allocation to the Occupation Forces were subtracted from the total. With only this much coal available to industry, a downward spiral in production was considered all but inescapable. Increased coal production required repair of wartime ravages caused by reckless over-mining, which required increased allocation of steel products to coal mines. Steel production, however, was low—despite adequate production capacity—because of the shortage of coal. In other words, there existed a vicious cycle of coal shortages and steel shortages, one working as a constraint on the other.

The priority-production plan was developed to eliminate this bottleneck in production recovery.[3] In the Planning Office created towards the end of October 1945 in the General Affairs Section of the MCI Secretariat, some young officials and scholars began examining Japan's fundamental commercial and industrial policies. Around the autumn of 1946, the Planning Office study group discussed the idea of focusing on a policy of expanding production of coal and steel as a means of preventing a downward spiral in production. This idea was conceived by Professor Hiromi Arisawa of the University of Tokyo, bearing in mind Karl Marx's reproduction models and Wassily Leontief's interindustry input–output analysis. Arisawa was a member of a luncheon discussion group sponsored by Prime Minister Yoshida. His idea was taken up at one of the meetings of the group, and it led to the creation in November 1946 of the 'Coal Committee' as a personal brain trust of the prime minister. Headed by Arisawa, the Coal Committee worked energetically to concretize the priority-production idea.

At that time, the Coal Agency had planned coal production of 27 million tons for fiscal year 1947. The Coal Committee, however, estimated that 30 million tons of coal were needed annually for successful economic reconstruction. If 30 million tons could be produced, about 16 million tons could be allocated for industrial use. That would increase industrial production by about 70 per cent over the level of fiscal year 1946, enabling the economy to break out of its downward spiral. Many believed, however, that 30 million tons was next to impossible in the situation where even production of 27 million tons was considered difficult.

Just at this time, the request that had been made to SCAP on the importation of heavy oil was approved. SCAP was at first reluctant to approve the request for emergency importation of basic raw materials, fearing that heavy oil imports would deter efforts to increase production of domestic coal. Thereupon the Board of Trade, an external agency of MCI, advocated emergency importation of iron and steel products, such as rails and cast-iron pipes, and heavy oil for gas generators to be used for increased production of steel materials. SCAP was inclined to approve this request. Further, in December 1946, Prime Minister Yoshida, following the advice of the luncheon group members, wrote a letter to General MacArthur stressing the importance of emergency imports of heavy oil, cast-iron pipes, and rails in order to solve the coal crisis. On 7 December, SCAP responded to this letter stating that it would take immediate steps to allow imports of heavy oil for steelmaking, although imports of steel products would be difficult to obtain because of the worldwide shortage. This move opened the door for putting into effect the priority-production plan, whereby imported heavy oil would be allocated to steel production, increased output of steel materials would then be allocated primarily to coal mines, and increased output of coal would in turn be allocated primarily to the steel industry. By repeating this process, the system was expected to achieve coal production of 30 million tons and a comparable increase in steel production, leading to sustained economic recovery.

On 27 December 1946, the Cabinet decided to adopt the Formulation and Implementation Guidelines for the Fiscal 1946 Fourth Quarter Basic Materials Supply and Demand Plan. And in January 1947, the Economic Stabilization Board developed the Formulation Guidelines for the Fiscal 1946 Fourth Quarter Coal Supply and Demand Plan. From January 1947, the priority-production plan was put into operation, involving priority allocation of coal and steel to strategic industries, special allocation of materials and foodstuffs to coal mines, and priority financing by the Reconstruction Finance Bank, which started operations in

January 1947. Although the system did not operate as smoothly as planned owing to a delay in the imports of heavy oil and other problems, coal production was restored to the level of 30 million tons per year in the second half of fiscal year 1947. The priority-production plan thus played an important role as a motive power for restarting Japan's production machine.

Along with the priority-production plan, state control of the coal industry as a means of increasing coal production became a controversial issue.[4] At the fourteenth meeting of the Far Eastern Commission held in September 1946, the US representative raised the question of the Japanese coal industry, which led to a proposal by the representatives of the UK, China, and the Soviet Union to nationalize the industry. Although the Far Eastern Commission failed to reach a conclusion on the issue, the debate raised an important question for the Japanese. The Liberal Party and the Progress Party—the parties then in power—objected to nationalization from the standpoint of preserving a free-market economy. Among the non-governmental parties, the National Cooperative Party and the Democratic Party lukewarmly supported the idea in view of the urgent need for reviving industrial production, whereas the Socialist Party was positively in favour as it was a socialist policy. The communists opposed it as meaningless under the existing regime. Thus, the idea found ayes and noes divided in a complex pattern. In the general election held in April 1947, the Socialist Party emerged as the leading party, which led to the formation of a new Cabinet headed by Tetsu Katayama, in coalition with the Democratic Party and National Cooperative Party. Prior to forming the Katayama Cabinet, a meeting of the heads of the three coalition parties and the Liberal Party produced a policy agreement among them, with the Socialist Party withdrawing its demand for nationalization of the coal industry in favour of state control.

The Ministry of Commerce and Industry in June 1947 proposed the basic formula for state control of the coal industry by formulating the 'Draft Outline of Emergency Measures for Increased Coal Production'. MCI ironed out differences with the Economic Stabilization Board, and developed the key points of a government bill. The resulting Draft Outline of State Control of the Coal Industry, however, met with criticism in both the conservative and radical camps, and generated sharply divided opinions among the parties in power. After many twists and turns, the Emergency Coal Industry Control Bill was submitted to the Diet in September 1947. Debate concerning the bill was thrown into confusion, and only after many disruptions—and even fist fights—the bill was finally promulgated in December and went into effect on 1 April 1948.

Under the Emergency Coal Industry Control Law, coal-mine owners appointed a controller at each coal mine designated by an All-Japan Coal-Mine Control Committee. Each of those mines was managed by a Production Council, whose members were the controller and representatives of management and labour. Four regional Coal Bureaux were established for examining and approving operation plans submitted by coal mines in their region, and to secure funds and materials necessary to carry out approved operation plans. Fifty-nine large mines around the country were thus designated, and state control of the coal industry was now in place. As the priority-production plan produced its intended results and coal production increased, however, the need for these emergency measures became less keenly felt. Also, as the government changed from the Katayama Cabinet to the Ashida Cabinet, and further to the second Yoshida Cabinet, it became less eager to maintain control over the coal industry. Overall, the policy of state control of the coal industry did not play an important role, although it had an effect of heightening management-participation awareness of workers through the production councils—organizations similar in nature to joint management councils—and thus helped to increase coal production to some extent. The Emergency Coal Industry Control Law was abrogated prematurely in May 1950, prior to the end of its legislation period of three years.

9.4. Economic Controls and Economic Planning

While efforts were being made to expand production capacity by means of the priority-production plan, ways were also sought for strengthening economic controls for curbing inflation, the tempo of which was quickening again. The Katayama Cabinet formed in June 1947 announced emergency economic measures developed by the Economic Stabilization Board. These comprehensive measures consisted of eight points, including a secure supply of foodstuffs, firm establishment of a materials distribution system, wholesale revision of the wage and price systems, healthy development of fiscal and financial systems, promotion of exports, and state control of private companies that were performing poorly. The proposal of state control of companies was characteristic of a socialist regime, which, as discussed earlier, led to state control of the coal industry. SCAP, which had been advocating the efficacy of economic control as a means to combat inflation, welcomed the arrival of the Socialist government. It reacted positively to the Socialist government's espousal of economic planning and socialization, in contrast to the Liberal Party's hostility towards economic controls, and urged the government to tighten economic controls.

MCI studied the Katayama Cabinet's emergency economic measures, and formulated its own policies of reinforcing the rationing system, improving the price-control system, tightening controls over black-market activities, increasing production of basic producer goods, and strengthening the management of financing. Turning to the price-control system first, the government in July 1947 implemented a thorough revision of the official price system. In the new system, the prices of basic materials were set at sixty-five times the 1934–6 level (the stability range). Price-support subsidies were paid to producers to offset the difference between production cost and the official prices. Official prices were to be maintained on the basis of fixed prices of selected materials in the stability range (coal, steel, non-ferrous metals, chemical fertilizers, and soda). Price-support subsidies previously limited to coal and foodstuffs, thus found an expanded use as an important means of price control.

The July 1947 price revision raised official prices two- or three-fold in a single step, narrowing the disparity between official and market prices. The wage income of an average household was estimated to be 1,800 yen per month. To secure a reasonable standard of living for the people, however, a system for providing daily necessities at official prices had to be developed. Steps were thus taken to reinforce the control of materials distribution. Efforts were made to improve the distribution *kodan* system and the ration coupon system, to wipe out black-market activities, and to secure deliveries of food by farmers to government agencies. Although SCAP also contemplated wage controls at this time, it was not practical to expect a Socialist government, whose political base was the working class, to impose wage controls against a background of a growing labour movement.

In May 1947, an organizational reform was implemented to strengthen the Economic Stabilization Board. Planning functions of all the economic ministries and agencies were transferred to the ESB. Economic inspectors responsible for strict enforcement of economic control were appointed and regional economic stabilization bureaux were established in each administrative district. These were the measures taken by the Yoshida Cabinet following the March 1947 letter from General MacArthur. The ESB, reinforced as the agency responsible for formulating economic policy, was most active during the period of the Socialist government. Hiroo Wada, former Minister of Agriculture and Forestry in the Yoshida Cabinet, and having the reputation of being a reformist bureaucrat, served as the director-general of the ESB. Capable and influential persons from the private sector were appointed to key positions. For instance, Shigeto Tsuru, Shigeo Nagano, and Teizo Horikoshi were appointed deputy directors-general and Hidezo Inaba became vice-director-general. Other ministries also sent able directors, deputy directors, and section chiefs to this agency, whose organization was nick-named the 'Wada ESB', because Wada handpicked so many members. Among the economic ministries, MCI supplied the largest number of staff members to the ESB—including Takayuki Yamamoto appointed as director-general—many of whom played key roles in formulating policies.

Having formulated the emergency economic measures mentioned above, the ESB published in July 1947 Japan's first Economic White Paper, the Report on Economic Realities, aimed at explaining the importance of implementing the emergency measures. From July, it worked to formulate a long-term economic plan. The exercise was in part a manifestation of the desire of the government led by the Socialist Party, which espoused a planned economy, to develop a unique programme of its own, but the realities of the times also demanded long-term planning.

After the war, many blueprints were drawn up for post-war reconstruction of the Japanese economy. A Special Study Committee, commissioned by the Research Bureau of the Ministry of Foreign Affairs—whose key members included Hiromi Arisawa, Koichi Aki, and Hidezo Inaba—completed in March 1946 a report titled 'Basic Problems of the Reconstruction of the Japanese

Economy'. In November 1946 it also announced a plan titled 'The Standard of Living and the Japanese Economy', which can be regarded as the first post-war long-term economic plan. The exercise involved assessment of the conditions required for restoring, by the year 1950, the standard of living that prevailed in 1930. MCI also conducted a similar study, using 1950 as the target year, by making detailed estimates on the basis of the method used for formulating the Materials Mobilization Plan. At about the same time, the Ministry of Home Affairs and the Industrial Rehabilitation Council also announced draft plans of their own. These economic plans, however, were nothing but depictions of fantasies as long as the Allied Occupation policy focused on a rigid demilitarization of Japan, as revealed in the Pauley Plan on reparations.

The situation, however, began to change subtly once into 1947, when Occupation policy began showing signs of reversal. A study was initiated inside SCAP on a plan to rebuild the Japanese economy, and the move was detected by the Japanese side. The situation was now such that not only implementing short-term measures to control inflation but also formulating medium- and long-term policy measures to rebuild the economy were both necessary and feasible. A long-term planning working group was established in the ESB, and work to develop a long-term plan with fiscal year 1952 as the target year was initiated under the leadership of Vice-Director-General Hidezo Inaba.[5] The first draft of the plan was completed in January 1948, and a committee consisting of members representing various circles in industry and government was formed to evaluate it. The Katayama Cabinet, however, resigned *en bloc* amid the parliamentary confrontation concerning the special livelihood allowance issue. In March 1948, a new Cabinet headed by Hitoshi Ashida, president of the Democratic Party, was formed in coalition with the Socialist and National Cooperative Parties.

The Ashida Cabinet sought to promote economic rehabilitation relying on foreign aid and, more importantly, foreign investment. As a prerequisite to foreign investment in Japan, it was thought that a clearly articulated economic rehabilitation plan should be developed first. In May 1948, the Economic Reconstruction Planning Committee (the prime minister serving as chairman, and the director-general of the ESB serving as vice-chairman) was established, which began deliberating on the first draft of an Economic Reconstruction Plan. The First Draft Plan was a five-year plan aimed at restoring by 1952 the living standards of 1930–4. Its tenet was nation-building through trade and heavy industrialization. To revive heavy industries and raise the percentage of heavy industrial goods in total exports, the modernization of production facilities was considered essential. To that end, imports of foreign capital were regarded as crucial.

A major premiss of the Economic Reconstruction Plan was that inflation had to be halted. The plan as initially formulated, however, did not contain measures to control inflation. To deal with inflation, which maintained a brisk tempo, a second currency measure was discussed with utmost secrecy during the Katayama period. The contemplated measure would bring inflation under control at a stroke by means of a freeze on bank deposits accompanied by a currency denomination. Because the government changed, however, the plan never surfaced. The new Ashida Cabinet opted for an 'intermediate stabilization method', one that would work to control inflation gradually, piecemeal so to speak, without resorting to currency-related measures. In June 1948, the ESB developed the Draft Plan for Intermediate Economic Stabilization. Being based on the premiss of increased foreign aid to Japan, this plan envisaged a comprehensive programme covering materials supply, labour, funds, and public finance, with the aim of creating a state of 'intermediate stabilization' (a state of controlled inflation). Intermediate stabilization would eventually lead to permanent stabilization. Basic policies of the Economic Rehabilitation Plan were formulated on the premiss of incorporating this intermediate stabilization programme into the first half of the plan period.

The Ashida Cabinet, however, resigned in the wake of the Showa Denko scandal, and in October 1948 the second Yoshida Cabinet was formed. The Economic Reconstruction Planning Committee continued its work, and in May 1949 completed the Economic Reconstruction Plan (a five-year plan targeted for 1953). Prime Minister Yoshida, however, refused to accept it. Although he was reported to have criticized it as being 'based on the idea of autarky, and lacking in international sense', his true motive was not clear. As will be discussed later, it was the period in which SCAP had issued the Nine Principles for Economic Stabilization to promote powerful deflationary programmes along the Dodge Line. Thus, many of the conditions on which the Economic Reconstruction Plan was based had been drastically changed. The first full-scale, long-term economic plan, developed over a period of nearly two years with the cooperation of a large number of persons outside the government, was never put into effect.

9.5. Signs of Recovery

The efforts of the Japanese people to recover from the chaotic immediate post-war years began to bear fruit, albeit very gradually. Industrial production, which continued its decline and fell by 59.5 per cent in 1946 over 1945, rose by 25.6 per cent in 1947, and continued expanding by 31.9 per cent in 1948 (Table 9.2). The wholesale price index, meanwhile, which increased 400 per cent in 1946, was down to 195 per cent in 1947 and further to 164.4 per cent in 1948. The increase in consumer prices, too, moderated from 115 per cent in 1947 to 82.7 per cent in 1948. In other words, inflation showed signs of slowing down as production recovered. Although the absolute level of gross national product was still very low, its rate of increase in real terms rose fairly rapidly, from 8.4 per cent in 1947 to 13 per cent in 1948.

Table 9.3 shows the production volume of major mining and manufacturing products. Owing to adoption of the priority-production plan, coal production in 1948 exceeded the target volume of 30 million tons, reaching the level of the early years of the Showa period.

Table 9.2   Indices of economic recovery (unit: %)

	Real growth rate	Rate of increase in industrial production	Rate of increase in wholesale prices	Rate of increase in consumer prices
1946	—	−59.5	400.0	—
1947	8.4	25.6	195.0	115.0
1948	13.0	31.9	164.4	82.7
1949	2.2	29.9	62.8	32.0
1950	10.9	22.5	18.1	−6.9
1951	13.0	38.2	38.7	16.4
1952	11.7	7.2	2.2	4.9

Note: Rate of increase in consumer prices was calculated by using indices of consumer prices (all cities, 1960 = 100) compiled by Statistics Bureau, Prime Minister's Office. The rate of increase in 1947 represents the percentage of the average of 1947 prices over the average of prices for the period August–December, 1946.

Source: *Tsusho Sangyo Seisakushi* (History of International Trade and Industry Policy), xvi: 88–9.

Table 9.3   Production volume of major mining and manufacturing products, 1945–1952 (unit: 10,000 tons)

Year	Coal	Pig-iron	Crude steel	Cotton yarn	Raw silk	Ammonium sulphate	Cement	Paper pulp
1945	2,234	97.7	196.3	2.3	0.5	24.3	117.6	22.8
1946	2,252	20.3	55.7	5.8	0.6	47.0	92.9	19.5
1947	2,934	34.7	95.2	12.2	0.7	72.1	123.7	25.8
1948	3,479	80.8	171.5	12.4	0.9	91.7	185.9	37.6
1949	3,730	154.9	311.1	15.7	1.1	118.2	327.8	49.5
1950	3,933	223.2	483.9	23.8	1.1	150.2	446.2	64.8
1951	4,649	312.7	650.2	33.7	1.3	159.4	654.8	91.1
1952	4,375	347.4	698.8	35.3	1.5	186.0	711.8	105.4

Sources: *Tsusho Sangyo Seisakushi* (History of International Trade and Industry Policy), xvi: 130, 142, 154, 158, 160, and 164. For raw silk: *Norinsho Ruinen Tokei-hyo* (85-Year Statistics of Agriculture and Forestry), 1955: 78.

Steel production recovered quickly as allocations of coal to the steel industry increased under the priority-production plan, and was further aided by allocations of imported coal and heavy oil.[6] In 1948, iron ore importation from Hainan Island was resumed. The rates of price-support subsidies that were provided from 1947 rose to high levels of 73 per cent of the production cost for pig-iron and 53 per cent for steel materials, providing an incentive for manufacturers that wished to increase production. The related office in MCI—which had earlier been reduced to the Iron and Steel Section of the Mining Bureau—was revived in July 1948 as the Iron and Steel Bureau. Further, the Headquarters for the Promotion of Production Increase of Steel and the Committee for Production Increase of Steel were established, and a framework was thus formed for close cooperation between government and business.

The capacity-utilization rate of blast furnaces rose from 2.5 per cent in 1946 to 24.7 per cent in 1949, and that of open-hearth furnaces and converters rose from 2.3 per cent to 33.4 per cent during the same period. Pig-iron production reached approximately 1.55 million tons, and that of crude steel reached 3.11 million tons, roughly returning to pre-war (1993) levels.

In the chemical industry, renewed production of chemical fertilizers was sought as part of the programme for resolving the food shortage. The jurisdiction over chemical fertilizers, which had been a joint responsibility of the Ministry of Commerce and Industry and the Ministry of Agriculture and Forestry, was moved to MCI in May 1947. At that time it was decided that MCI would exclusively administer the chemical fertilizer industry, and a Chemical Fertilizer Department was created in MCI's Chemical Bureau. MCI made priority allocation of raw materials, equipment, and funds to the chemical fertilizer industry to promote fertilizer production. The production volume of ammonium sulphate, which had declined to about 20 per cent of the pre-war peak level of 1.24 million tons (1941), was restored to 1.18 million tons in 1949, almost at the pre-war peak level. The production volume of superphosphate of lime was restored to the pre-war (1935) level in 1949.

The bottleneck in the supply of fuels delayed the recovery of cement production, but in 1949 production nearly returned to the pre-war (1930) level. Paper pulp production, meanwhile, was restored to approximately 500,000 tons in 1949. Production of textiles will be discussed in the following chapter on export industries. The remainder of this chapter addresses reorganization of business operations in the electric power industry.

The electric power industry recovered relatively early because, as mentioned in Chapter 7, power-generating plants suffered relatively little damage during the war. Although thermoelectric power plants on the outskirts of large cities suffered considerable damage, hydroelectric plants lost little of their power-generation capacity. Consequently, in the 'water first, fire second' scheme, the power-generation capacity of the industry as a whole remained large. Nonetheless, the supply of electric power in the immediate post-war years was limited for several reasons. First, the capacity utilization rate and operating efficiency of thermoelectric plants were low owing to the shortage of coal and the poor quality of the available coal. Second, inadequate maintenance and repair during the war years led to a high incidence of accidents and malfunctions at power plants. Third, wartime bombing caused a deterioration of power-distribution facilities, leading to a high loss ratio. Finally, the designation of thermoelectric power plants for reparations removal delayed the start of restoration work. All these negative factors combined to reduce electric power generation to 21.9 billion kWh in

1945, or about 58 per cent of the 37.7 billion kWh generated in the record year of 1943. As facilities were repaired and coal supplies increased, however, power generation recovered, and reached 37.8 billion kWh in 1948, surpassing the peak wartime level.

Before the war, electric power administration was the responsibility of the Ministry of Communications. This jurisdiction was moved to MCI (MITI from May 1949) after the war, and MCI made reconstruction of the electric power industry one of its primary policy tasks. As part of the wartime economic order, the electric power industry had been organized into a system called 'state control of electric power', consisting of the Japan Electric Power Generating and Transmission Company and nine power-distribution companies. After the war, demands for the reorganization of the electric power industry arose throughout the economy.[7]

Local governments mounted a campaign to bring power distribution under public management, and labour unions in the electric power industry demanded that state control of the industry be abolished and that the power-generation, transmission, and distribution businesses be unified. SCAP suggested that, first, the Electric Power Bureau of MCI be abolished and replaced by an Electric Power Industry Management Commission patterned after US regulatory commissions. As a form of managing the electric power industry, it then recommended the creation of unified management of power generation, transmission, and distribution in each region. Furthermore, once the Deconcentration Law was put into effect, SCAP ordered that the law be applied to the electric power industry as well. MCI, in cooperation with the ESB, began to study reorganization of business operations in the electric power industry, and drafted several plans involving alterations of power generation, transmission, and distribution systems while keeping intact the system consisting of the Japan Electric Power-Generating and Transmission Company and the nine power-distribution companies.

The Ashida Cabinet established the Electric Utilities Industry Democratization Committee, and asked it to study reorganization plans. In October 1948, the committee submitted a report along the lines suggested by MCI's study. Because the government changed, however, the report never saw the light of day. Meanwhile, SCAP studied the five-bloc plan and others as alternative reorganization plans for creating a region-based system of unified management of power generation, transmission, and distribution. In 1949, it unofficially suggested to the Japanese government a seven-bloc plan, and further indicated that it would accept a nine-bloc plan.

In response to the strong interest in reorganization shown by SCAP, the Yoshida Cabinet established the Electric Utilities Industry Reorganization Council and worked towards formulating concrete plans. In the first meeting of the Council held in November 1949, Yasuzaemon Matsunaga, who had consistently opposed state control of electric power and advocated private management, was elected chairman of the Council. Matsunaga proposed a nine-bloc plan which he had developed, but the proposal met with objections from Council members. Meanwhile, SCAP newly suggested a ten-bloc plan that separated the Shin'etsu region, complicating the Council's deliberations. The report of the Council submitted in January 1950 proposed reorganization based on the establishment of an Electric Power Accommodation Corporation, which would inherit part of the power-generation capacity of the Japan Electric Power Generating and Transmission Company but would serve merely as a wholesaler of electric power, and establishment of nine companies engaged in power generation, transmission, and distribution. The nine-bloc plan of Matsunaga was appended to the report as reference material.

SCAP, however, took strong exception to this proposal, and directed Heitaro Inagaki, Minister of International Trade and Industry, to submit an alternative plan to the Seventh Diet then in session. MITI hurriedly considered how best to deal with the situation, quickly developed a plan based on Matsunaga's nine-bloc plan, and negotiated with SCAP. Although SCAP approved the nine-bloc plan, it did not approve continuance of an Electric Power Bureau in the Agency of Natural Resources, and demanded that an independent Public Utilities Commission be established. MITI preferred to have such a commission established as an advisory council reporting to the Minister of International Trade and Industry; in the end, SCAP granted approval to make the commission an external agency of the Office of the Prime Minister. The Yoshida Cabinet submitted the Electric Utilities Industry Reorganization Bill and the Public Utilities Industry Bill to the Seventh Diet of April 1950. Deliberation experienced rough going, with numerous objections even from within the Liberal Party, the party in power. In the end, the two bills were tabled, and were dropped when the Diet session ended.

Displeased with the situation, SCAP took a hard-line attitude towards the Japanese government, informing it that it would suspend accommodations to electric power-generation projects out of the counterpart funds (US Aid Counterpart Fund Special Account, created in fiscal year 1949 as part of the Dodge Line of deflationary policy), and would not approve any new equipment investment and capital increases for the Japan Electric Power-Generating and Transmission Company or the nine power-distribution companies. The Yoshida Cabinet made efforts to revise the bills, but found itself in a difficult situation when it could not obtain the approval of SCAP on the nature of the revisions. In November 1950, General MacArthur sent a letter to Prime Minister Yoshida demanding early implementation of a reorganization programme developed along the lines suggested in the government bills which had been submitted to the Seventh Diet. In response to this directive, Prime Minister Yoshida finally decided to carry out reorganization of the electric power industry by invoking Potsdam ordinances which did not require parliamentary approval.

Under the Electric Utilities Reorganization Ordinance and the Public Utilities Industry Ordinance promulgated in November 1950, the electric power industry was reorganized into a system of unified management of power generation, transmission, and distribution by nine privately owned regional power companies. With regard to electric power administration, the Electric Power Bureau of the

Agency of Natural Resources was abolished, and a Public Utilities Commission was established. After this complicated series of events, the post-war system of nine electric power companies made a start in May 1951.

NOTES

1. Concerning systems of economic control, see *Tsusho Sangyo Seisakushi*, iii. ch. 3, sect. 3.
2. Ministry of Finance, Historical Studies Office, 'Seifu Saimu' (Public Debt), *Showa Zaiseishi*, xi (1938): 35–7.
3. Concerning the priority production system, see *Tsusho Sangyo Seisakushi*, iii, ch. 3, sect. 2 and ch. 4, sect. 2.
4. Ibid. iii, ch. 3, sect. 2, for a discussion of state control of coal mines.
5. Concerning the Economic Reconstruction Plan, see *Tsusho Sangyo Seisakushi*, ii, ch. 2, sect. 4. For materials on the formulae for rehabilitation, see 'Nihon Keizai Saiken no Kihon Mondai' (Basic Problems of Reconstructing the Japanese Economy), *Shiryo—Sengo Nippon no Keizai Seisaku Koso* (Materials: Formulae for Economic Policy for Post-War Japan), i, University of Tokyo Press, 1990.
6. Concerning steel, see *Tsusho Sangyo Seisakushi*, iii, ch. 4, sect. 2.
7. Ibid. iii, ch. 4, sect. 1, for a discussion of reorganization of the electric power utilities industry.

10

The Reopening of Foreign Trade and the Establishment of MITI

10.1. The Reopening of Private Foreign Trade

From 1947, production activities in Japan began to show clear signs of recovery. In order to maintain the sustained development and growth of the economy, however, a full return to world trade was essential. Strenuous efforts were made, therefore, towards reopening and expanding international trade, despite the difficult conditions under the Allied Occupation.

The Potsdam Declaration stated in part: 'Eventual Japanese participation in world trade relations shall be permitted.' During the initial period after the Occupation began, however, foreign trade was under SCAP's strict control. Imports were permitted only in cases where they were judged indispensable for sustaining the Japanese economy, and exports would be allowed only to the extent necessary to pay for such imports. Resumption of foreign trade was an urgent task for Japan because the economy obviously could not be sustained if isolated from world trade. There was also a pressing need to import foodstuffs because the disastrous rice crop of 1945 threatened to cause a food crisis. From around October 1945, exports of coal to Korea and wooden posts for coal mines to China began in the form of military material, and salt was imported from these countries. Recognizing the need for a planned resumption of foreign trade for Japan, SCAP directed the Japanese government to submit its import and export plans. The Ministry of Commerce and Industry led the Japanese effort to work on the plans, and in November 1945 submitted lists of planned imports and exports to SCAP. The list of urgently needed imports contained foodstuffs, fertilizers, salt, petroleum, and coal. Proposed exports included textile products (raw silk, silk fabrics, and cotton fabrics), ceramics, rubber products, celluloid products, bicycles, radios, canned foods, and tea.

In considering post-war plans for imports and exports with a view to reconstruction and long-term development of the economy, the pressing task obviously was the importation of raw materials for key industries. Economic rehabilitation and reconstruction were unthinkable without adequate supplies of raw cotton, iron ore, and petroleum. Another important problem was how to develop export industries in order to pay for these imports. In any event, an obvious conclusion was that Japan had to rely heavily on international trade for its future development.

In anticipation of the reopening of foreign trade, SCAP ordered the development of a system of controlling trade flows. The Japanese government responded to this directive by creating the Board of Trade as a centralized trade organization. Opinions were split concerning the appropriate affiliation of the organization; proposed ideas included placing it directly under the Cabinet or attaching it to the Ministry of Foreign Affairs. In the end, the argument of the Ministry of Commerce and Industry—that administration of foreign trade and that of production should be handled by MCI—prevailed. In December 1945, accordingly, the Board of Trade was established as an external bureau of MCI.[1] Tadaharu Mukai was invited from Mitsui & Co. to assume the position of the first director-general of the new agency. An official from MCI was appointed director of the General Affairs Bureau, an official from the Ministry of Agriculture and Forestry was appointed director of the Import Bureau, and the director-general served concurrently as director of the Export Bureau.

The Board of Trade was a government agency working under SCAP's direct supervision, and exercising authority on all aspects of business relating to international trade. In June 1946, the Temporary Regulations for Foreign Trade, etc. was issued, followed by the promulgation in November of the Special Account for Foreign Trade Fund Law, thus putting into order the legislation for foreign trade in the immediate post-war era. In the earlier phase of the programme, the domestic end of trade business dealing with purchasing, delivery, and storage of goods was handled by trade associations that acted as export and import agents for each product category (forty exporting associations and thirty-nine importing associations as of the end of 1946). In May 1947, based on the Foreign Trade Public Corporation Law promulgated in March, four governmental corporations (*kodan*)—the Mining and Manufactured Goods Trading Kodan, Textiles Trading Kodan, Foodstuffs Trading Kodan, and Raw Materials Trading Kodan—were established with total equity provided by the government to handle specific trading.[2]

The system of foreign trade around the spring of 1947 was as seen in Figure 10.1.

As for Japanese imports, goods purchased by the US War Department from overseas private traders were delivered to the Board of Trade by way of SCAP. They were then sold to domestic private traders by trading corporations. Japanese exports were acquired by trading corporations from domestic private traders and delivered to SCAP via the Board of Trade. SCAP then consigned them to USCC for sale to overseas private traders.

SCAP used its own account to handle US dollars and foreign currencies for settlement of payments for imports and exports, and domestic yen transactions were handled through the Special Account for Foreign Trade Fund. In this anomalous payments system, there was no logical connection between the two. Because imports purchased at world market prices were sold in Japan at official domestic prices, and because exports purchased at domestic prices in Japan were sold at world prices abroad, the rate of exchange for domestic and world prices varied from product to product. In short, there was a *de facto* system of multiple exchange rates.

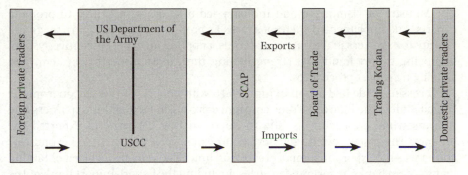

Fig. 10.1 System of foreign trade in early phase of allied occupation

Note: United States Commercial Company (USCC) was an agency of the US government which existed until the end of 1947. USCC's business was later taken over by SCAP's New York office.

The early phase of post-war foreign trade was pure state trading conducted by the Board of Trade; contact between domestic and foreign private traders was prohibited by SCAP. In March 1947, the US government announced a policy of relaxing trade restrictions on Japan and Germany. Responding to this announcement, SCAP developed a plan to permit limited private foreign trade in Japan, which was approved by the US government, and private export reopened on 15 August 1947. In this system, foreign trade representatives visiting Japan conducted negotiations with Japanese exporters on the basis of samples exhibited at fairs held in six cities. When price and other terms were agreed on, the foreign buyer submitted a purchase and sales agreement, and the Japanese exporter filed an application to the Board of Trade for concluding a formal agreement. That application was then forwarded to SCAP for its approval. Although it was called private foreign trade, the party to the export agreement on the Japanese side was the Board of Trade, which issued a pick-up order to a trading corporation. The trading corporation concluded purchase and sale agreements with domestic firms, accepted delivery of goods from them, and consigned the handling of shipping and other export procedures to exporters.

In the early phase of reopened private trade, raw silk and cotton fabrics were not included in the list of products eligible for export. Also, the frequency of visits and the length of stays by foreign buyers were restricted. In early 1948, however, these exceptions and restrictions were removed to encourage private trade, although these steps did not necessarily lead to a steady growth of exports. There was a serious dollar shortage in Asian countries—particularly in pound sterling areas—which were the primary destinations of Japanese exports. Therefore, the ability of those countries to import Japanese goods was limited. Domestically, rampaging inflation raised the prices of Japanese exports, and shortages of raw materials, other materials, and fuels hindered production of exportable goods.

The Ministry of Commerce and Industry led a study of measures to promote exports, and implemented such measures as promoting processing trade, giving priority to exporters in allocating materials, adopting an export incentive system, improving export financing, strengthening the export inspection system, and simplifying export procedures.

Processing trade had begun in June 1946 with imports of raw cotton from the United States. The Board of Trade consigned processing to domestic spinners and weavers while preserving its title to imported raw cotton, and exported the product. The system eventually devised to extend processing trade beyond raw cotton was the export and import revolving fund. The scheme involved obtaining loans—from banks in various countries, including the Export-Import Bank of the United States—to finance the import of raw materials using as security convertible precious metals such as gold and silver, and jewellery, which were in SCAP's custody. The loans were to be repaid with the proceeds from exports of processed goods. In August 1947, SCAP established the Occupied Japan Export-Import Revolving Fund (OJEIRF). The Japanese side established a special committee for this programme, and began work on export and import plans. This revolving fund, however, did not work as well as initially expected because the loan conditions of overseas banks were very stringent.

The variants of processing trade other than the revolving fund scheme included compensatory trade in which imported wool was processed into woollen fabrics and exported, and payment for the processing was made in wool. In another form of processing trade, imports of coke and iron ore were linked to exports of steel materials.

The export incentive system was created in response to a memorandum SCAP issued in March 1948. When an exporter succeeded in concluding an export agreement at a price above the minimum dollar price of a designated product, the exporter was paid the difference between the yen equivalent of the transaction price and the official domestic price (the price at which the Board of Trade purchased the product from the exporter). This system began with exports of miniature electric bulbs, vitamin pills, cameras, and electric fans; it was later extended to chemicals, agricultural and fishery products, machinery and metal products, and sundry goods.

Table 10.1 shows the changing values of exports and imports in the immediate post-war years. Exports, which were approximately $1.08 million in 1945, rose to $471.79 million in 1949. Imports increased from $2.66 million in 1945 to $790.15 million in 1949.

Exports in the early post-war years consisted mainly of raw silk and metal products which survived the war, foodstuffs such as tea and processed marine products, and coal. From around 1947, cotton fabrics, which had been major exports before the war, became the major exports again. It is noteworthy that iron and steel and vessels, which had been key ingredients of the wartime economy, also became significant export products. As for imports, foodstuffs were most important, followed by raw cotton imports, which were related to cotton fabric exports.

Table 10.1 Japan's exports and imports by major product category, 1945–1952

Exports (unit: $1,000)

	Total	Foodstuffs	Iron and steel	Vessels	Cotton yarn and thread	Cotton fabrics	Chinaware
1945	1,078	208	17	6	0	36	6
1946	6,278	586	3	—	86	11	3
1947	28,189	7,503	11	14	742	7,975	1,225
1948	144,506	7,747	1,908	1,250	1,869	30,822	6,917
1949	471,786	21,778	32,025	4,247	13,322	134,947	16,914
1950	827,836	51,853	72,089	26,175	17,564	205,836	18,142
1951	1,357,714	69,800	205,519	16,278	32,636	309,806	33,297
1952	1,272,897	98,789	263,133	10,936	28,408	180,389	29,142

Imports (unit: $1,000)

	Total	Foodstuffs	Raw cotton	Iron ore	Coal	Crude oil
1945	2,658	642	333	6	61	36
1946	11,302	4,608	5,311	—	—	450
1947	56,292	29,669	6,586	—	69	8,944
1948	167,464	80,250	13,128	2,297	9,356	25,808
1949	790,153	340,827	123,431	19,281	34,606	644
1950	967,211	323,897	274,608	14,114	10,608	24,961
1951	2,047,892	566,283	495,336	58,106	48,908	66,647
1952	2,028,756	651,561	430,261	92,503	83,647	101,742

Source: Tsusho Sangyo Seisakushi (History of International Trade and Industry Policy), xvi: 238, 240, 242, and 244–47.

Table 10.2   Geographic distribution of Japan's international trade, 1945–1952

Exports (unit: %)

	Asia	Europe	North America	South America	Africa	Oceania
1945	100.0	—	—	—	—	—
1946	33.1	1.2	65.1	—	—	0.6
1947	67.2	8.5	18.4	0.0	3.3	2.6
1948	47.3	10.5	34.0	0.7	5.2	2.3
1949	49.8	13.4	20.2	0.6	11.7	4.4
1950	46.3	12.0	25.4	3.8	8.9	3.6
1951	51.5	10.8	15.7	5.9	8.3	7.9
1952	51.5	14.1	21.0	2.9	7.4	3.1

Imports (unit: %)

	Asia	Europe	North America	South America	Africa	Oceania
1945	95.0	0.3	2.3	2.2	0.1	0.0
1946	8.8	1.2	86.4	—	2.9	0.7
1947	8.3	0.8	87.9	0.1	2.1	0.8
1948	16.1	2.7	74.9	1.7	2.9	1.7
1949	21.4	6.8	63.4	0.7	4.3	3.4
1950	32.6	4.0	47.9	4.1	2.7	8.7
1951	28.9	7.8	46.2	5.4	3.9	7.8
1952	31.2	6.9	49.6	2.2	2.6	7.6

Source: *Tsusho Sangyo Seisakushi* (History of International Trade and Industry Policy), xvi: 250–3.

The geographic distribution of Japan's trading partners, although varying considerably from year to year, was characterized by the relative importance of Asia in exports and North America in imports (Table 10.2). In Japan's trade with pound sterling areas, the shortage of US dollars for payment was a serious problem. SCAP sought to increase Japan's trade with these areas by concluding a payment agreement with the UK mission in Japan.

10.2. The Recovery of Export Industries

In the early post-war period, silk-reeling materials became the key earner of the foreign exchange Japan needed to pay for imports of essential materials, the same role that industry played during the Meiji (1868–1912) and Taisho (1912–26) periods. In September 1945, SCAP issued directives to the Japanese government instructing it to freeze the existing stock of raw silk and silk goods in Japan and to begin preparing to export raw silk, an item in which it was self-sufficient. In March 1946, the first post-war shipment of raw silk left Yokohama for the USA. The raw silk jumped off to a good sales start, commanding a high average price of $9.70 per pound at the first public sale conducted by United States Commercial Company (USCC) in July 1946. The price began to slip, however, from the second sale onwards, and reached a low of $4.57 per pound at the seventh sale held in February 1947. Sales volumes were also disappointing. Shipments to the US of 84,475 bales in 1946 fell sharply to 4,094 bales in 1947.[3]

The sluggishness of raw silk exports was attributed in part to the slow recovery of the US silk industry, which had been reduced in size during the war, and in part to the poor quality of the exported products. A fundamental reason, however, was the fact that synthetic fibres such as nylon began to make inroads into the raw silk market. From the standpoint of relative price competitiveness, there was small chance of raw silk recovering its earlier position of dominance. Although raw silk as a product category occupied a top position among Japanese exports in the immediate post-war years, therefore, and although the silk-reeling industry gradually increased its production volume as seen in Table 9.3, the industry was no longer capable of providing a means of economic recovery as a key export industry.

Cotton textiles was Japan's other representative export industry. As long as adequate supplies of raw cotton could be secured, in fact, it was the most promising industry during the period when Occupation policy was aimed at containing Japan's heavy industries. As well, there was a worldwide shortage of textile products and this boded well for the cotton textile industry's recovery. The Textile Mission to Japan (Taylor Mission) that visited Japan in January 1946 submitted a report in March to the State and War Departments recommending that Japan's cotton textile industry be rebuilt as the country's key export industry.

In the cotton textile industry, the wartime programme of industrial reorganization reduced the number of cotton-spinners to ten large companies. Because many spinning machines were scrapped during the war, the ten spinning companies had only about 2.19 million installed spindles immediately after the war. Counting yet-to-be-installed and reparable spindles the number was 3.49 million. This figure was equivalent to only about 25 per cent of the 13.8 million spindles in operation in 1941.[4] The interim Pauley Report recommended that Japan be allowed to maintain 3 million spindles. In July 1946, the Japan Textiles Association applied for recovery financing by setting the recovery target at 3,665,366 spindles. In October 1946, the Three-Year Plan for Reconstruction of the Textile Industry developed by the Textile Industry Reconstruction Committee—organized by industrial leaders and scholars under the leadership of MCI—was submitted to SCAP. The plan suggested 4.37 million spindles as the target for rebuilding.

In February 1947, SCAP issued a Memorandum on Cotton Textile Capacity, announcing that the tentative target for rebuilding the cotton-spinning capacity was set at 4 million spindles. To deter existing firms from monopolizing the market, SCAP ordered the government to assign about 340,000 spindles, the difference between 4 million and the number held by the ten spinners, to newly created spinning companies. Thereupon MCI spelled out the procedures for establishing new spinning companies by means of the ministerial Policy on the Restoration of the Cotton Spinning Industry issued in September 1947. To implement this policy, MCI established the Committee of Examination of Restoration of Facilities of Cotton-Spinning Industry headed by the director-general of the Textiles Bureau. The committee selected twenty-five companies from among 100 or so applicants, and the ministry gave permission to them to install new spindles. Each of these so-called 'new spinners', having been allotted a number of spindles ranging from 5,000 to 55,000 began operations in 1948 or 1949.

Although the rebuilding of the spinning industry made strides as described above, the bottleneck encountered in production recovery in the early post-war years was found more in the shortage of workers, materials, and power than in inadequate facilities. The extremely poor food conditions induced many female workers in cotton-spinning mills to return to their home villages, and reduced the work efficiency of the remaining workers. The situation deteriorated so much that the Cabinet was prompted to pass, in August 1946, a resolution entitled 'Policy for Promoting Full Production in the Textile Industry', which provided measures for making special allocations of rice to about 300 major cotton-textile mills, and ensuring for them adequate supplies of other food items and seasonings, fuels, and materials.

In October 1946, MCI mounted a nationwide mass-education drive stressing the importance of the textile industry, and continued strenuous efforts to secure for it adequate supplies of labour, materials, electric power, and funds.

The available stock of raw cotton when the war ended was only 44,500 bales, which called for an early resumption of raw cotton imports. SCAP responded swiftly to this need. In February 1946, an agreement to supply raw cotton to Japan was concluded among appropriate organizations in the US, a major producer of raw cotton. Under this agreement, raw cotton held by the Commodity Credit Corporation (CCC) was to be shipped to Japan. In the background of this arrangement was the fact that the CCC had surplus stocks of raw cotton, and the US government was anxious to unload them. As described earlier, the processing trade method was used whereby imported raw cotton was paid for by exports of cotton goods.

The rebuilding of the cotton industry, however, was slow, as the statistics on changes in cotton yarn production in Table 9.3 suggest. Whereas the shortages of labour, materials, and fuel gradually eased, the shortage of raw cotton remained the most serious bottleneck. In processing trade, increased exports of cotton goods would allow corresponding increases in raw cotton imports. In the worldwide situation of a shortage of dollars, however, exports of Japanese cotton goods did not grow as much as expected, resulting in insufficient imports of raw cotton. Because of the shortage of raw cotton and the sluggish demand for cotton goods, the first production cutbacks after the war were carried out as early as July up to October of 1947, followed by further cutbacks from July to September of 1948.

As a means of raising funds to pay for raw cotton imports, Army Under-Secretary William Draper led the initiative in concluding a $60-million raw cotton loan agreement between a US banking consortium and SCAP in May 1948. This loan, secured by the OJEIRF mentioned earlier, made possible the import of approximately 600,000 bales of raw cotton. Further, initiatives taken by the so-called cotton senators in the US Congress led to the creation in June 1948 of the Occupied Areas Natural Resources Procurement Revolving Fund and subsequent imports by Japan of about 2.2 million bales of raw cotton in 1949 and 1950.

Despite many bottlenecks, the Japanese cotton textile industry thus started down the road to recovery. However, the production of cotton yarn in 1949 was only 157,000 tons, about 24 per cent of the average production of 644,000 tons of the 1934–6 period.

During the period when exports of textile products were not growing as fast as expected, the steel and shipbuilding industries became new foreign-exchange earners. Although early Occupation policy was predicated upon the strategy of severely restricting the rebuilding of heavy industries in Japan, SCAP—realizing that what Japan could successfully export was limited—gradually showed a willingness to approve the export of heavy industrial goods. Steel was exported to earn foreign currency even before domestic demand was fully satisfied. And the export of ships became very important to the shipbuilding industry, burdened as it was with huge idle facilities while the prospect for recovery of the merchant marine industry was uncertain.

The shipbuilding industry began building new ships under a planned programme inaugurated in 1947. Because the size of the ships to be built was initially limited to 5,000 gross tons and the number of ships the industry was allowed to build was also restricted, the industry had a large unused production capacity. The effort to cultivate overseas markets led to orders from Norway in 1948 for two whalers of 490 gross tons each. In 1949, the industry succeeded in obtaining orders for five whalers and one tanker (18,000 deadweight tons) from Norway; one freighter (3,500 gross tons) and one tanker (17,000 deadweight tons) from Denmark; and 3 freighters (7,500 gross tons each) from the Philippines.

Receipt of orders for ship exports not only improved the business condition of the shipbuilding industry by improving the capacity utilization rate in its shipyards, but also brought about advances in its technology. In building ships for export, Japanese shipbuilding engineers had opportunities to visit shipyards in the US and other Western countries. There, they were exposed to the latest shipbuilding technologies developed during the war years—modern welding techniques, the 'block' building system, and photomarking techniques—and brought the new knowledge back with them to Japan. That knowledge was conveyed to every shipyard in Japan through the horizontal network of the technology study committee organized by the Japan Shipbuilders' Association. These efforts to acquire, absorb, and develop new shipbuilding technology subsequently enabled the industry to lead the world in shipbuilding tonnage. Efforts to export ships very early in the post-war period were thus highly significant for the shipbuilding industry.[5]

10.3. US Aid to Japan and Nine Principles for Economic Stabilization

As the rehabilitation of the Japanese economy got under way and its foreign trade recovered, US aid to Japan emerged as a major issue. As Table 10.1 clearly shows, Japan's post-war trade balance showed large deficits, primarily in the foodstuffs account but also in others. Such large import deficits were possible because the US provided Japan with aid goods, mainly foodstuffs, out of its Government and Relief in Occupied Areas (GARIOA) funds. The GARIOA aid to Japan was enormous, amounting to $92.63 million in US fiscal year 1946 (July 1945 to June 1946), $287.33 million in fiscal year 1947, and $351.40 million in fiscal year 1948.[6]

Since GARIOA aid was aimed at preventing hunger and social unrest in US occupied areas, a new type of aid programme was called for once the chaotic early post-war years passed, and securing raw materials and fuels for economic reconstruction became an urgent task. The Marshall Plan for Europe was aid for economic rehabilitation that replaced relief aid, and it was felt desirable to budget for a Marshall type of aid programme for Japan as well. As the Occupation policy towards Japan was reversed in the Cold War era, the US Army Department made a request to the US government for the creation of an aid programme for economic reconstruction of Japan and Korea, besides the existing GARIOA fund, for fiscal year 1949.[7]

As a prerequisite for such an aid programme, the National Advisory Council on International Monetary and Financial Problems (NAC) that studied the proposal demanded first of all that Japan's economy be stabilized. Although Congress did not approve the aid programme proposed by the Army Department, it approved instead the spending of funds from the GARIOA budget in the Economic Rehabilitation in Occupied Areas (EROA) programme for importing industrial raw materials needed for economic reconstruction. Congress also urged the early adoption of economic policies that would help Japan's economy support itself and enable termination of the US aid programme at the earliest possible date. In short, although Congress recognized the need for economic rehabilitation aid, it also demanded implementation of an economic policy that would make the aid effective so that the burden on US taxpayers would be lightened as soon as possible.

The principal economic problem Japan faced was the need to stabilize its economy by curbing inflation. The Johnston Committee Report of April 1948 set out in overall terms US policy for reconstruction of the Japanese economy for the first time and recommended—besides reducing the scale of reparations and relaxing the deconcentration policy—strong economic stability measures for achieving a balanced budget, reducing subsidies, strengthening the tax collection programme, imposing wage controls, and establishing a fixed yen–dollar exchange rate.

On the Japanese side, however, the Ashida Cabinet had opted for the path of an intermediate (middle-of-the-road) stabilization programme whereby inflation was to be controlled step-by-step, and had no intention of trying to achieve economic stability quickly by adopting 'stabilization-at-a-single-stroke' tactics. Neither was SCAP considering introducing a stabilization-at-a-single-stroke policy by means of severe fiscal tightening, concluding that it would be possible to combat the already decelerating inflation by curbing wages. Thus, a difference in outlook had arisen between the Japanese government and SCAP on the one hand, and the US government on the other, regarding the kind of economic policy that was appropriate for Japan. Whereas the former was trying to control inflation by using US aid to Japan as leverage, the US government regarded controlling inflation as a prerequisite for economic aid to Japan. This difference in policy outlook engendered a conflict between the US government and SCAP in the second half of 1948, which led to the dispatch of Joseph Dodge to Japan.

The confrontation which surfaced revolved at first around the Young Mission Report of June 1948. On the occasion of General MacArthur's request for revision of the yen–dollar exchange rate for military transactions, a mission headed by Ralph Young, deputy director of research and statistics, Board of Governors of the Federal Reserve System, was dispatched to Japan to study the yen–dollar exchange rate question. The Young Mission concluded that a uniform rate was essential for economic reconstruction, particularly for restoring a stable currency, and recommended establishing by 1 October 1948 a single rate covering both commercial and military transactions.

As discussed earlier, Japan's post-war foreign trade was conducted for a while under a multiple exchange rate system. This system had an effect similar to that of a system of trade subsidies. In it, the domestic prices of exports were maintained at levels that guaranteed a profit to producers, and *de facto* export subsidies were paid to exporters. Import prices, on the other hand, were set below domestic prices, and importers were paid *de facto* import subsidies. The exchange rates for exports in the multiple exchange system were by necessity set at levels that undervalued the yen and had the effect of weakening the desire of exporters to improve their productivity, thereby working contrary to government efforts to curb inflation. Also, the apparent deficit in the trade balance did not immediately lead to a demand for deflationary policies to conserve foreign exchange, because foreign exchange was controlled by SCAP. Moreover, the Foreign Trade Fund Special Account became short of funds owing to expenditure on importation and storage expenses and mounting inventories (congestion of imported raw materials and export goods), requiring borrowing from the Bank of Japan. Despite the deficit in the trade balance, therefore, the Foreign Trade Fund Special Account became a net supplier of liquidity to the economy, thereby contributing to the inflationary pressure.

The system of managed trade and multiple exchange rates thus isolated the Japanese economy from the world economy, generating inflationary pressures of its own. Recognizing this fact, the Young Mission recommended that a single exchange rate be established as soon as feasible. The report of the mission recommended, as measures supplementing the creation of a single rate, a wide range of policy measures, including limiting credit extension to public and private financial institutions, raising the official discount rate, reducing budget expenditures by 20 per cent, prohibiting the Foreign Trade Fund from borrowing funds from the Bank of Japan, revising the tax system, improving the system of allocating material to producers, and controlling wages. These suggestions amounted to recommending the stabilization-at-a-single stroke policy using the exchange rate as a lever, i.e. a policy focused on the external—not domestic—dimensions of Japan's currency.

SCAP vehemently opposed the Young Mission's recommendations. MacArthur argued that immediate adoption of a single rate would cause economic and social collapse because prices would rise, production would fall, and unemployment would increase. He therefore insisted that the exchange rate be set only after implementing powerful stabilization measures to restore foreign trade indices to the levels of production indices.

Having studied both the Young Mission's report and General MacArthur's views, NAC recommended that the Young Mission's recommendations be implemented as early as feasible, except that the timing for setting the exchange rate be proposed by the Army Department after having consulted with General MacArthur.

Even though SCAP was aware of the views of NAC, it did not alter its determination that a single rate should be established only after economic stability was achieved. As for the other aspects of the Young Mission's recommendations, SCAP directed the Japanese government in July 1948 to put into effect the Ten Principles of Economic Stabilization, which contained: (1) increasing production, (2) strengthening the allocation and rationing system, (3) improving the efficiency of the food collection system, (4) strictly enforcing official prices, (5) implementing wage-stabilization measures, (6) strengthening the tax collection system, (7) raising taxes and equalizing the tax burden, (8) reducing the deficits in special accounts, (9) improving the operation of foreign-trade controls and transferring foreign-exchange controls to Japanese agencies, and (10) strengthening controls on credit extension. The Ashida government, however, could not tackle the ten principles in earnest because it was preoccupied with the National Public Service Law revision issue, which arose out of a letter General MacArthur sent immediately after the directive concerning the ten principles saying that a strike by public employees 'is unthinkable and intolerable'. The second Yoshida Cabinet, formed in October 1948, was negative towards the ten principles, in part because the Democratic Liberal Party had committed itself publicly to substantial economic deregulation and in part because Prime Minister Yoshida had declared that his new Cabinet was merely a caretaker government.

In the United States, meanwhile, Resolution NSC 13/2 of the US National Security Council—which formalized the major shift in the basic policy of the US towards Japan—had been adopted, as was discussed in an earlier section of Part II, and concrete measures for reconstructing and stabilizing the Japanese economy were being studied. The Army Department submitted to NAC a budget proposal for economic aid to Japan for the forthcoming fiscal year. NAC, however, was highly critical of the aid proposal, being convinced that the effect of aid would be dubious unless appropriate steps were first taken to stabilize the economy. At the plenary meeting of the council held on 3 December 1948, Secretary of the Army Kenneth Royall managed to obtain support for the EROA appropriation request after stating that the Army Department would issue directives concerning economic stabilization measures to General MacArthur, dispatch an appropriate person to Japan to oversee the implementation of the measures, and study a clear timetable for setting the exchange rate.

The Army Department drafted its directives to General MacArthur, had them studied by the NSC and approved by President Truman, and transmitted them to the general on 11 December as a formal 'interim directive'. It instructed General MacArthur to direct the Japanese government to put into effect the so-called Nine Principles for Economic Stabilization, which consisted of: (1) balancing the consolidated budget, (2) strengthening the programme of tax collection, (3) limiting credit extension, (4) establishing a programme for wage stability, (5) strengthening price-control programmes, (6) improving the operation of foreign trade and foreign-exchange controls for delegation to Japanese agencies, (7) improving the allocation and rationing system in order to maximize exports, (8) increasing the production of raw materials and manufactures, and (9) improving the food-collection programme. Furthermore, the interim directive instructed SCAP to establish a single general exchange rate not later than three months after the initiation of the economic stabilization programme.

The conflict between the US government and SCAP revolving around the Young Mission Report thus ended, and, in order to obtain economic assistance for Japan, the establishment of a single exchange rate and implementation of a severe deflationary policy became all but inevitable.

10.4. The Dodge Line of Deflationary Programmes

The Nine Principles of Economic Stabilization were imposed on the Japanese government by means of General MacArthur's letter to the Japanese prime minister dated 19 December 1948. Although Prime Minister Yoshida stated in his reply to the general's letter that 'my government determines to respond to your faith in the ability of the Japanese people in the achievement of these objectives', the Draft of Guidelines for Comprehensive Measures which the Economic Stabilization Board drafted on 23 December retained much of the characteristics of the 'intermediate' stabilization programme. The third Yoshida Cabinet formed after the elections of January 1949 adopted in February the outline of a draft budget bill for fiscal year 1949. The outline planned for a tighter budget but not one that would halt inflation at a single sweep. For instance, it contained expenditures for trade subsidies using the surplus in the Foreign Trade Fund Special Account, as well as investments in public works and basic industries through the flotation of construction bonds and debentures of the Reconstruction Finance Bank. One reason for the optimistic response of the government was that some in SCAP were opposed to the interim directive, and failed to show clearly to the Japanese side the basic differences between the nine principles and the ten principles. For instance, General MacArthur's December letter did not specify the time limit for establishing the single exchange rate as 'not later than three months', but instead used the more general expression 'as rapidly as possible'.

After the Young Mission returned to the US, the Japanese government began studying the exchange rate issue. One proposal was to set the rate at 620 yen to one US dollar, which would allow 83 per cent of exports to be profitable. Another proposal was to set the rate at 300 yen to one dollar, assuming that trade subsidies would be retained. After receipt of the nine principles, a Council for Introduction of a Single Fixed Foreign Exchange Rate was established at the behest of SCAP. In unofficial discussions after the first meeting of the council held on 30 December 1948, SCAP representatives revealed to the Japanese side, as 'top secret' information, that the time limit for establishing the exchange rate was 'not later than three months'. Thereupon MCI and other economic agencies began moving quickly with their exercise of calculating the proposed rate, and submitted the results of their work to the council. In January 1949, MCI formulated a plan to set the rate between 350 yen and 400 yen to one dollar, with export subsidies continuing for six months to one year.[8]

While the government was attempting to respond to the nine principles outlined in the letter from General MacArthur, Joseph Dodge arrived in Japan in February 1949 with the rank of minister to serve as financial adviser to SCAP. It was Army Under-Secretary Draper who selected Dodge, a Detroit banker, for the top position of implementing the economic stabilization programme. Draper was familiar with Dodge's capabilities from the days when they were colleagues in Occupied Germany. Dodge served there as assistant financial adviser to General Clay, military governor of the US zone in Germany. Dodge had participated in formulating the currency reform programme for West Germany, following which a single exchange rate was established in April 1948. A new currency was issued in June and bank deposits of the old currency were redenominated downwards. These measures showed remarkable results in curbing inflation and restoring production. One day after the 'interim directive' was issued to MacArthur, President Truman—who had just been re-elected—requested Dodge to visit Japan, which he accepted. Dodge and a staff of six persons, including Ralph Young, arrived in Japan escorted by Secretary of the Army General Royall, and immediately began their work.

Dodge did not submit a systematic report enumerating his recommendations. Instead, he provided concrete guidance to the process of formulating policy measures and putting into effect a series of programmes which came to be known as the Dodge Line of economic policy. The fundamental scheme of the Dodge Line for achieving reconstruction, stabilization, and self-support for the Japanese economy stood on three pillars: (1) maximizing exports by containment of domestic demand to reduce excess purchasing power, (2) restoring the market mechanism and promoting economic rationalization by establishing a single exchange rate and abolishing subsidies, and (3) supplying funds for private capital investment through government savings and US aid to Japan, thereby expanding production.

The policy of restraining aggregate demand—the first pillar of the Dodge plan—was not carried out with a currency reform, as in West Germany, but by a shift in fiscal policy. The budget for fiscal year 1949 prepared under the guidance of Dodge showed a surplus of 156.7 billion yen in the consolidated balance—the combined sum of the general accounts, special accounts, and accounts of government-affiliated agencies—minus duplications. This figure was a dramatic swing in the budget from a deficit of 141.9 billion yen in fiscal year 1948 (the deficit in fiscal year 1947 was 103.9 billion yen). The size of the budget increased substantially because of natural increases caused by inflation and explicit recognition of the previously hidden trade subsidies. Efforts were made, however, to bolster tax collections and raise public service rates (train fares, postage rates, etc.) on the revenue side. On the expenditure side, spending was reduced for public works and unemployment relief programmes, as were operating expenses for the national railways and telecommunications. The result of these steps was an 'overbalanced' budget, which, combined with the ban on issuing Reconstruction Finance Bank debentures, eliminated the sources of inflationary pressures on the financial side and brought about stability. Concerning the real side of the economy, reduced government expenditures also contributed to a reduction in domestic purchasing power, which was expected to increase the volition of manufacturers to increase their export efforts.

The second pillar of the Dodge plan—restoring the market mechanism—was implemented from the international and domestic sides. On the international side, policy measures consisted of establishing, in April 1949, the exchange rate of 360 yen to one dollar; abolishing export subsidies; and gradually reducing import subsidies. On the domestic side, policy measures consisted of gradually decreasing price-support subsidies and reducing the overall scope of economic control. The third pillar—providing funds for private capital formation—was effected by using the surplus in the consolidated budget for redeeming government bonds, beginning with RFC debentures. Also, proceeds from the sale of relief goods were paid into the Counterpart Fund Special Account. The surplus in this special account was then used to redeem government bonds or as investment funds for the private sector.

The Japanese government was still inclined to opt for the intermediate stabilization path of gradually curbing inflation utilizing US aid, even though it was compelled by the requirements of the nine principles to modify its policy somewhat. The Dodge Line, therefore, was a much more restrictive policy than it had anticipated. SCAP, meanwhile, still believed that an intermediate stabilization programme and wage controls were sufficient to contain inflation, and could not bring itself to wholeheartedly embrace Dodge's stabilization-at-a-stroke policy. Despite the stubborn opposition of SCAP and the Japanese government, however, Dodge did not compromise his stern position, and held fast to his convictions.[9]

Regarding the exchange rate, Dodge suggested 330 yen to one dollar as a rate which would allow 80 per cent of exports to remain competitive without subsidies. He accepted the recommendations of the National Advisory Council on International Monetary and Financial Problems (NAC) in its report, which is said to have anticipated the pound sterling crisis, and acceded to the 360 yen rate, although at the time that rate was felt to be a substantial undervaluation of the yen.

The effects of the Dodge Line of deflationary policy were immediate. Prices began to decline appreciably starting around the spring of 1949. The black-market prices of producer goods fell by 35 per cent between January 1949 and May 1950, and their levels as multiples of official prices fell 2.8-fold to 1.2-fold during the same period. Consumer prices fell by 38 per cent, with the multiples declining 2.7-fold to 1.3-fold. Although a downward trend in prices had already been observed in the second half of 1948, the Dodge Line measures had the effect of pushing them down decisively.

The deflationary policy caused a shortage of loanable funds, and the tight money situation became widespread. The government, with the concurrence of SCAP, put into effect measures to neutralize that situation starting around June 1949. The measures included purchases by the Bank of Japan of government bonds through open market operations, easing of the penalty interest rate system, and expanding the loan accommodation service of the Bank of Japan. When the fiscal policy designed to slow down inflation began to have a deflationary effect on the economy, the monetary policy worked in the direction of moderating that policy's deflationary impact.

The increased exports that the restraints on aggregate demand were expected to produce materialized to a certain extent in the spring of 1949. In June 1949, however, exports turned sluggish and the slowdown became more pronounced from around August. This occurred at the time of the first business downturn in the post-war era experienced by the world's capitalist nations, which started with a recession in the US that was triggered by a sharp decline in agricultural prices from February 1949. In September 1949, the UK was forced to devalue the pound. These changes in the international economic environment darkened the prospects for the success of the Dodge Line.

While the Japanese economy's rehabilitation and stabilization made continued progress, there were signs that business conditions were worsening. For instance, inventories were accumulating, money was becoming tighter, and unemployment was growing. Dodge, however, directed the Japanese government to prepare another 'overbalanced' budget for fiscal year 1950. Because Dodge was energetically lobbying the US government to continue its aid to Japan in its 1950 budget, continuation of the stabilization policy in Japan was imperative. Consolidated Japanese budget expenditures (net budget) for fiscal year 1950 was 15.2 per cent smaller than that for the previous year, with a budget surplus of 41.5 billion yen. The smaller budget was due on the expenditures side to substantial decreases in termination-of-war expenses and price-adjustment compensation, as well as decreases in transfers of general-account funds to special accounts and accounts of government-affiliated agencies to make up for shortfalls. On the revenues side, there was a loss in tax revenue accompanying tax system reforms recommended earlier by the Shoup Mission. In the end, the 1950 budget retained a strong disinflationary character, although it included increases in public works and unemployment relief expenditures, and investment of surplus funds in the Counterpart Fund in railways, telecommunications, electric power generation, and sea transport.

From around March 1950, SCAP began to admonish the government about the 'overloan' condition resulting from the anti-deflationary application of monetary policy, compelling the government and the Bank of Japan to shift their monetary policy towards restraint. The Dodge Line was in its second year, and its deflationary character was becoming stronger. Japan's stock exchanges reopened in May 1949, and stock prices fell by roughly 50 per cent in one year. Private companies tried to tide over their financial difficulties through workforce reductions, and state-owned enterprises dismissed a large number of employees as they were transformed into public corporations and put on a business accountability basis. Owing to the workforce streamlining programmes of large corporations and the bankruptcies of smaller firms, the number of unemployed workers rose to 430,000 in June 1950, up from 260,000 at the end of 1948. This unemployment statistic was likely to have understated the actual unemployment situation. Bitter labour disputes erupted around this time in large corporations. And a series of controversial incidents with undiscovered causes occurred, including the Shimoyama incident involving the mysterious death of the president of the Japan National Railways, the Mitaka incident in which an unmanned train ran out of control, and the Matsukawa incident in which a train of the Japan National Railways was sabotaged and overturned. Social unrest intensified, and the prospects for the Japanese economy turned gloomier. There was a dramatic turn of events in June 1950, however, with the outbreak of the Korean War.

10.5. Establishment of the Ministry of International Trade and Industry

While the Dodge Line of deflationary policy was under way, on 25 May 1949 the Ministry of Commerce and Industry was reorganized into the Ministry of International Trade and Industry (MITI). MCI had made a restart on 26 August 1945 immediately after the close of hostilities when the Ministry of Munitions and other wartime organizations were disbanded. After repeated reorganization, MCI as of August 1948 had eleven internal bureaux, including the Minister's Secretariat and ten other bureaux (General Affairs, Machinery, Electronics Machinery and Communications Equipment, Chemicals, Textiles, Mines, Iron and Steel,

Electric Power, Daily Commodities, and Research and Statistics). It also had five external agencies (Small and Medium Enterprise Agency, Coal Agency, Board of Trade, Agency of Industrial Science and Technology, and Patent Office) and eight regional Commerce and Industry Bureaux. On the eve of the Pacific War in 1941, MCI had eight internal bureaux and four external bureaux. The Ministry's organization in 1948 compared to 1941 was characterized by establishment of four new internal bureaux—Electronics Machinery and Communications Equipment, Electric Power, Daily Commodities, and Research and Statistics—and two external bureaux—the Small and Medium Enterprise Agency and the Agency of Industrial Science and Technology. The Electronics Machinery and Communications Equipment Bureau was split off from the Machinery Bureau in response to the demand of SCAP for improved production of communications machinery and equipment. Administration of the electric power industry was under the jurisdiction of the Ministry of Communications before the war, but it was transferred to MCI's newly created Electric Power Bureau when the Ministry of Munitions was dissolved. The Daily Commodities Bureau had jurisdiction over such consumer-related commodities as daily necessities, paper and wooden products, and building materials, reflecting the wartime control functions of the ministry's predecessor. The creation of the Research and Statistics Bureau reflected the need for a bureau to carry out control measures as well as a demand from SCAP. The Small and Medium Enterprise Agency was established in August 1948 on the conviction that the promotion of small and medium enterprises—which accounted for a large portion of industry—was indispensable for the reconstruction of the economy. The Agency of Industrial Science and Technology was established also in August 1948, patterned after the US National Bureau of Standards. It was responsible for promoting improvements in production technology through research and experiments as well as technical exchange.

In October 1948, the Showa Denko scandal forced the Ashida Cabinet to resign *en bloc*, and led to formation of the second Yoshida Cabinet. The public demand for uprooting corruption from officialdom and the platform of the ruling Democratic Liberal Party—which was a return to a market economy and readjustment and reduction of economic controls—combined to turn administrative reform into a major issue. As for matters pertaining to MCI, the idea of separating the Board of Trade from MCI and placing it directly under the Cabinet was discussed.

When the government was directed by SCAP to put the nine principles into practice, administrative readjustment (retrenchment) as a means to attain a balanced budget became an issue. In January 1949, the Administrative Reform Council was established. The February report of the council proposed a programme of streamlining ministerial organization, which involved staff reductions of approximately 30 per cent. At the same time, for the administration of economic matters the report pointed out the need to 'shift the focus to the promotion of international trade in response to the new situation.'[10]

The final report of the Administrative Reform Council did not specify concrete reorganization programmes for each ministry and agency. Instead, a basic policy of organizational reform was appended to the report as reference material. With respect to MCI, the proposal suggested that (1) the ministry absorb the Board of Trade and be reorganized as a ministry of industry and trade, (2) its control functions be thoroughly reviewed and the control-related organization be drastically reduced in size, and (3) the Agency of Industrial Science and Technology and the Small and Medium Enterprise Agency be disbanded. In other words, the council suggested the reorganization of the Ministry of Commerce and Industry into a ministry of international trade and industry. MCI strongly objected to the suggestion that the two newly established agencies be disbanded, however urgent the need for administrative streamlining might be.

Prime Minister Yoshida was convinced that the post-war economy had to be focused on international trade. Accordingly, his basic formula for reorganizing MCI consisted of switching the focus of commercial and industrial policy to the promotion of international trade, placing an International Trade Bureau as the centrepiece of the new ministry, and promoting personnel exchanges between it and the Foreign Affairs Ministry. In pre-war days, the overseas business of Japan's foreign trade was handled by the Ministry of Foreign Affairs, and MCI had jurisdiction over export business conducted in Japan. Yoshida's idea was to combine the two functions while Japan was still not permitted to handle its overseas export business. Meanwhile, MCI in February 1949 prepared its own draft outline of a Plan for Establishment of a Ministry of International Trade and Industry. According to this plan, the ministry was to be renamed the Ministry of International Trade and Industry, and was to consist of the Minister's Secretariat and ten bureaux (International Trade, Promotion, International Trade Accounting, International Trade Textiles, International Trade General Merchandise, International Trade Machinery, International Trade Chemicals, International Trade Iron and Steel, Enterprises, and Research and Statistics), and four external bureaux (Resources Agency, Agency of Industrial Science and Technology, Patent Office, and Small and Medium Enterprise Agency).

The Third Yoshida Cabinet formally adopted an administrative reorganization programme involving a 30 per cent personnel retrenchment of all ministries and agencies, and established the Administrative Reform Headquarters headed by the director-general of the Administrative Management Agency (AMA). Negotiations between the AMA and MCI resulted in a new reorganization plan of MCI which outlined eight internal and four external bureaux.

Bills for the establishment of various new ministries were successively submitted to the Fifth Diet of 1949. The MITI Establishment Bill submitted in April was passed into law with minor revisions, and was promulgated on 24 May and implemented the following day. The new organization of the ministry consisted of the Minister's secretariat and eight bureaux (International Trade, International Trade Promotion, International Trade Enterprises, International Trade Textiles, International Trade General Merchandise, International Trade Machinery, International Trade Chemicals, and International Trade Iron and Steel), four external bureaux (Resources Agency, Small and Medium Enterprise Agency, Agency of Industrial Science and Technology, and Patent Office), eight regional bureaux of International Trade and Industry, and four regional Coal Mining bureaux. The final organization differed from that contained in the draft outline in that the proposed Research and Statistics Bureau was changed to the Research and Statistics Department in the Minister's secretariat, and the International Trade Accounting Bureau was placed in the International Trade Promotion Bureau as the Accounting Division.

The key elements of this organizational reform were (1) bringing the Board of Trade, an external MCI bureau, inside the ministry and dividing its functions between the new International Trade Bureau and the International Trade Promotion Bureau, (2) beginning the names of the bureaux having jurisdiction over different industries with the words 'International Trade' and giving them responsibility to handle export business, (3) creating the Resources Agency by combining the Coal Agency and two internal bureaux—the Mining Bureau and the Electric Power Bureau, (4) abolishing the internal General Affairs Bureau and apportioning its functions to the secretariat, the International Trade Bureau, and others, and (5) creating a new International Trade Enterprise Bureau to prepare the ministry for forthcoming enterprise rationalization programmes. Furthermore, the interchange of personnel with the Ministry of Foreign Affairs, which Prime Minister Yoshida promoted, was accomplished by importing a large number of officials from the Foreign Ministry to key positions in MITI dealing with international trade policy, including the newly established positions of senior officer for international trade affairs and director-general of the International Trade Bureau. There were some who had misgivings about the ability of the former MCI and Foreign Affairs Ministry officials to work together harmoniously. According to recollections by Tokio Nagayama, first head of the MITI secretariat, 'The merger of the two groups took place much more harmoniously than expected. The new ministry enjoyed a smooth start, and its subsequent operation was generally as successful as expected.'

10.6. Readjustment of Economic Control

In July 1949, the newly reorganized MITI adopted a basic policy plan titled 'Outline of International Trade and Industry Policy'.[11] The essential elements of MITI policy revealed in this outline were: (1) promoting exports (establishing the principle of 'exports first', nurturing export industries, and seeking greater freedom for conducting trade activities abroad), (2) promoting the realization of economic self-support (seeking to raise efficiency and increase production in such basic industries as electric power, coal-mining, iron and steel, and chemicals, because it was necessary to rationalize development of domestic resources and strengthen the industrial base), (3) securing industrial investment funds (in order to avoid a breakdown of the industrial base by the Dodge Line of deflationary policy, it was necessary to provide adequate supplies of needed capital investment and operating funds and to promote importation of foreign capital), and (4) promoting economic rationality (seeking maximum freedom of economic activities and rationalization of enterprise operation by simplifying economic controls).

The key policy of the plan was consistent with the three pillars of the Dodge Line—namely, maximizing exports, promoting economic rationalization, and expanding production. It was thought that, in order to return to the world economy using the single rate of 360 yen to one dollar and maintaining the sustained growth of the economy, it was essential to maximize exports on the basis of the export-first principle. To that end, it was indispensable for the efficient development of domestic resources and the rationalization of enterprises to reduce the production costs of export industries.

Nonetheless, the Outline also contained elements of a policy for countervailing the effects of the Dodge Line. In other words, it was a policy designed to eliminate, as much as possible, the adverse effects of the Dodge Line of deflationary policy on industries. It called for measures to counter the tight-money situation caused by Dodge Line measures by proposing specific new financial measures, including: (1) requiring city banks to set aside a portion of their loanable funds for meeting corporate demands for funds for capital investment and rationalization programmes, (2) setting up a system for compensating losses suffered in this special-category lending, (3) charging low interest rates on US Aid Counterpart Fund loans to basic industries, and (4) raising the ceiling on corporate bond issues by means of revaluation of assets and expanding the scope of assets acceptable by the Bank of Japan as collateral. The aims of these measures were met to a certain extent by implementation of the easy-money policy that started around June 1949, as described earlier.

For restoring the market mechanism the Dodge Line plan pursued as a means to rebuild the economy, a gradual reduction in price-support subsidies was essential. Even more important, however, was reducing economic controls.[12] In February 1949, MCI had already adopted at a ministerial meeting a plan for reducing the scope of controls. The plan included reducing controls on materials designated for controlled production, promoting competition in the sale of products through a system of allocations to sales companies, and reducing the scope of commodities handled by trading corporations (*kodan*) and simplifying their organization.

As of April 1949, 233 products were designated as materials for controlled production. They were decontrolled one by one, and in April 1950 the number declined to forty-eight (see Table 2.4). Decontrolling continued afterwards, leaving in May 1951 only sixteen products still controlled, including crude oil, industrial salt, nickel, phosphate rock, sulphite ore, pig-iron, soda ash, caustic soda, raw cotton, and paper for textbooks.

As for materials designated for rationing, chiefly consumer goods, controls were lifted on most perishable foods between October 1947, when fruit was de-designated, and April 1949. As of June 1949, fifty-five products, including fish, textiles, and daily necessities, were still being rationed. Subsequently, controls were lifted on silk products in June 1949; tissue paper, umbrellas, light bulbs, canned and bottled foods in July; home fuels (except charcoal) in August; and hemp products and fish in September. In December 1949, the number of designated products fell to thirty-one items. At the end of May 1951, products still being rationed were rice, barley, and their products; sugar; petroleum products; pharmaceuticals; materials for the fishing industry; and sake for industrial workers.

The abolition of price controls made steady progress along with readjustments and reductions in price-support subsidies. The number of product categories in which prices were controlled stood at 2,129 in March 1949. The number fell to 1,299 in December 1949, 355 in December 1950, and further to 263 in March 1951. Of these 263 categories, 120 were public service rates, such as electric and gas rates and train fares, and only 143 were goods.

The public corporations (*kodan*), which were created as key organizations for economic activities at the behest of SCAP, were abolished as their objectives were met. Beginning with the Petroleum Distribution Kodan in March 1949, by March 1950 the Foodstuffs Trade Kodan, Raw Materials Trade Kodan, Liquor Distribution Kodan, Coal Distribution Kodan, Grocery Distribution Kodan, Fodder Distribution Kodan, and Shipbuilding Kodan were all disbanded. The remaining seven *kodan* (Fertilizer Distribution; Mining and Manufactured Goods Trade; Textiles Trade; Staple Food Distribution; Oil Stuff and Sugar Distribution; Industrial Recovery; and Price Adjustment) were also disbanded prior to April 1951.

Thus, as Japan's economic rehabilitation got under way, and controls were steadily lifted, goods came to be sold and bought in free markets. With this development, the reopening of commodity exchanges was sought. Although the Commodity Exchange Law of 1893 was still in effect, it required thorough revision. MITI undertook a study of the law and a new Commodity Exchange Law was promulgated in August 1950. Exchanges dealing with such commodities as textiles and related products, rubber, marine products, and beans were established throughout the country.

NOTES

1. *Tsusho Sangyo Seisakushi*, iv, ch. 6, sect. 1.
2. Ibid. iv, ch. 5, sect. 2.
3. Kanagawa Prefecture, *Kanagawa Kenshi* (History of Kanagawa Prefecture), Overview 7, 1982: 831.
4. Concerning the cotton textile industry, see *Tsusho Sangyo Seisakushi*, iii, ch. 4, sect. 3.
5. Keiichiro Nakagawa, *Sengo Nippon no Kaiun to Zosen* (Merchant Shipping and Shipbuilding in Post-War Japan), Nihon Keizai Hyoron-sha, 1992: 54.
6. *Tsusho Sangyo Seisakushi*, iv. 183.
7. Ibid. ii, ch. 1, sect. 3, for remainder of this section.
8. Ibid. iv, ch. 4, sect. 3.
9. Ibid. iii, ch. 2, sect. 5, for a discussion of the realities of the Dodge Line.
10. Ibid. iv, ch. 6, sect. 3, regarding the establishment of MITI.
11. Ibid. ii, ch. 2, sect. 5.
12. Ibid. iii, ch. 3, sect. 3, regarding the relaxation of economic controls.

11

The Korean War and Special Procurements

11.1. The Emergence of Special Procurements

The Korean War broke out on 25 June 1950. It was around the same time that the results of the Dodge Line of deflationary policies began to produce serious adverse effects on the Japanese economy. On 27 June, the UN Security Council, acting during a Soviet boycott, passed a US resolution calling for action by UN member nations to aid South Korea. On 30 June, US ground forces were ordered to Korea, and on 8 July General MacArthur was appointed to assume the unified UN command. MacArthur ordered the UN forces, comprised of troops from sixteen UN member nations, to counter-attack North Korean forces. The UN forces recaptured Seoul in September and advanced into North Korea, crossing the 38th parallel and entering Pyongyang, the North Korean capital, in October. On 25 October, however, the Chinese People's Voluntary Army crossed the Yalu River and joined in the war. The combined Chinese and North Korean forces recaptured Pyongyang in December, and in January 1951 swept further south, crossing the 38th parallel and reoccupying Seoul.

General MacArthur advocated a hard-line strategy, including bombing the Chinese mainland, deployment of National Chinese troops in Korea, and use of nuclear weapons. President Truman, however, decided to keep the Korean War as a limited war with conventional weapons, reflecting the wishes of the sixteen UN member nations with troops in Korea. Because MacArthur publicly resisted official policy, on 11 April 1951 Truman relieved him of all his commands as Supreme Commander in the Far East, Supreme Commander for Allied Powers, and Supreme Commander for UN Forces. Lieut.-Gen. Ridgway, commander of the US Eighth Army, was appointed to replace MacArthur. Thus, General MacArthur, the first Supreme Commander of the Allied Powers during the Occupation in Japan, left Japan before the Occupation ended.

A UN counter-offensive subsequently began, but the frontlines were stabilized along the 38th parallel. A cease-fire proposal made in June 1951 by Jacob Malik, the Russian delegate to the United Nations, led to the start of cease-fire negotiations on 10 July. The truce talks dragged on, interrupted by outbreaks of fighting, and the war became a stalemate, with both sides fighting a holding action. In the end, a truce agreement was reached on 27 July 1953, and the war ended.

With the outbreak of the war in Korea, the US sharply increased its defence appropriations. It initiated a reassessment of its Asian policy, and in May 1951 approved the National Security Commission's 'United States Objectives, Policies and Courses of Action in Asia' (NSC 48/4) spelling out its new Asian policy. NSC 48/4 envisaged a line of defence forming an arc linking Japan, the Ryukyu Islands, the Philippines, Australia, and New Zealand, and clearly established the policy of defending South Korea, Taiwan, and Indo-China. With respect to Japan, the document explicitly stated the policy of providing aid so that Japan could become a friendly nation capable of defending itself against external aggression and contributing to peace and stability in the Far East. NSC 48/4 thus formally defined the rearmament of Japan as US policy.

US policy towards Japan, which had shifted from demilitarization to economic reconstruction when the Cold War started, changed once again, at the outbreak of the Korean War, to Japan's rearmament. It thus completed a 180-degree turn from its initial policy.[1]

On 8 July 1950, thirteen days after the opening of hostilities in Korea, General MacArthur sent a letter to Prime Minister Yoshida informing him that Japan was now authorized to establish a National Police Reserve of 75,000 men and to increase the size of the Maritime Safety Patrol by 8,000 persons. Although MacArthur had previously opposed Japan's rearmament, he could no longer adhere to the basic policy of demilitarizing Japan now that US ground forces in Japan were deployed in Korea and the Cold War was turning into a 'hot' war.

The Korean War resulted in drastic external changes that affected the Japanese economy. First of all, the world economy, which had been suffering from the first recession since the end of the Second World War, suddenly became activated. The value of world trade (total exports of all countries except those in the Socialist bloc), which had stood at $54.8 billion in 1949, increased to $56.7 billion in 1950, and rose sharply to $76.6 billion in 1951. Between 1950 and 1951, the unit price of exports rose by about 22 per cent, and the volume of exports increased by about 12 per cent. Although the Korean War boom cooled off after Malik's cease-fire proposal, and although the value of world exports fell to $73.9 billion in 1952, the world economy entered an era of high growth against the background of US-led programmes to increase armaments.

In effect, the Korean War was fought in Japan's back yard, and Japan benefited not only from the worldwide economic prosperity but also from the emergence of war-related purchases that came to be called 'special procurements'. This demand helped Japan to break the yoke of the Dodge Line recession and enter a favourable business period. The US forces, which formed the main portion of the UN forces in Korea, procured from Japan such goods as munitions materials, coal, jute bags (for sandbags), automotive parts, cotton cloth, steel materials for construction, barbed wire, iron posts, drum cans, military rations, and cement, as well as such services for military consumption as building construction, automotive repair, transportation, communications, and machinery repair. These goods and services were either shipped from Japan to Korea or utilized to reinforce US military bases in Japan. The contents and the size of special procurements varied with developments in the war. Between June and December 1950, special procurement contracts totalled $191.36 million, of which $127.33 million were for goods and $64.03 million for services. In 1951, special procurement contracts totalled $353.64 million, of which $254.51 million were for goods and $99.13 million for services.

Because Japan's GNP in fiscal year 1949 was estimated at 3,375.2 billion yen, the special-procurement contracts in 1950 of approximately 68.9 billion yen amounted to about 2 per cent of GNP, and the 1951 contracts of approximately 127.3 billion yen amounted to about 3.8 per cent of GNP. Thus, special procurements were not truly significant in terms of their absolute monetary value. For the Japanese economy, however, struggling under the burden of the Dodge deflation measures, that extra demand was manna from heaven. Besides, it was highly significant that, in principle, special procurements were settled in US dollars. In 1949, Japan's exports amounted to $509.7 million and imports amounted to $904.85 million, with a trade deficit of $395.15 million. Since in those days the shortage of foreign exchange limited the import of much needed materials and worked as a bottleneck in economic reconstruction, the economic effect of special procurements producing earnings of a few hundred million dollars was dramatic indeed.

Against the background of the Korean War boom, real GNP grew at an annual rate of 10.9 per cent in 1950 and 13.0 per cent in 1951. The annual growth rate of industrial production in 1950 was somewhat low at 22.5 per cent, but rose to a high level of 38.2 per cent in 1951 (Table 9.2). In 1951, Japan's industrial production, real GNP, and personal consumption expenditures in real terms all surpassed their respective pre-war (1934–6 average) levels. Business earnings that had suffered from the recession improved dramatically, and the profit rate of total liabilities and net worth in the manufacturing sector rose sharply from 3.16 per cent in the second half of fiscal year 1949 to 12.15 per cent in the same period a year later. Despite the tight budget situation, the increases in exports and special procurements led to a huge injection of liquidity into the private sector as dollar earnings were converted into yen deposits through the Foreign Exchange Funds Special Account. Bank of Japan notes outstanding reached 425.4 billion yen at the end of 1950, an increase of 67.5 billion yen over the end of 1949. They rose further to 510.3 billion yen at the end of 1951. Consumer prices that fell by 6.9 per cent in 1950 over the preceding year as a result of Dodge Line deflation rose by 16.4 per cent in 1951.

Concerned about the possibility that the Korean War boom might rekindle inflation, the government adopted a policy of curbing price increases by controlling key prices individually and easing the tightness in supply through imports, while maintaining a policy of generally relaxed control.[2] In August 1950, a policy measure known as the 'Guidelines for Controlling Profiteering' was established to control business that was conducted at prices exceeding the officially decreed standard prices, as well as pernicious hoarding and cornering. A Profiteering Control Headquarters was established in Osaka. Because prices of textiles rose sharply during the so-called textile boom that resulted from increased consumption, standard prices were established for rayon yarn, staple fibre, worsted goods, raw silk, and other textiles. To promote imports, meanwhile, from August 1950 the Automatic Approval (AA) System was adopted. Under this system, foreign-exchange budget allocations were made for each large geographic zone representing import sources—which contrasted with the previous system of allocating funds by product category and place of purchase—and applications for imports were validated automatically until the total allocation for a particular zone was exhausted. The AA System covered forty-eight products at first and in February 1951 was expanded to 170 products. In addition, the Bank of Japan established an import usance system. Under the Dodge Line of deflationary policy, MITI gave highest priority to the expansion of exports and emphasized the promotion of industrial rationalization programmes aimed at reducing costs. With the changes in the external situation, however, MITI considered shifting the direction of its policy towards paying attention also to import promotion and increased production of key materials.

11.2. US–Japan Economic Cooperation Scheme

In July 1950, the month after war broke out in Korea, the Economic Reconstruction Planning Committee changed its name to the Economic Self-Support Council and began formulating a new long-term economic plan. In January 1951, the Council submitted to the government a report entitled 'Three-Year Plan for Economic Self-Support'. The objective of the plan for the target year 1953 was to raise industrial production 30 per cent above the pre-war level (1932–6 average) and the standard of living of the people to 89 per cent of the pre-war level (1934–6 average), while attaining equilibrium in the balance of payments without external aid. As for concrete policy measures for achieving these goals, the plan stressed three points: securing imports, raising the self-sufficiency level, and accumulating capital. It was characteristic of this plan that securing imports was listed first among the priorities, since it was a plan formulated during the Korean War boom. As for exports, it merely expressed a wish for a Marshall Plan in Asia.

In January 1951, John Foster Dulles, adviser to the US secretary of state, visited Japan for the second time to negotiate with Prime Minister Shigeru Yoshida the terms of the impending peace treaty with Japan. Requested by Dulles to consider rearming Japan, Yoshida expressed a view opposing it, maintaining that rearmament would be a heavy burden on the economy just as it was moving to achieve self-sufficiency and might contribute to reviving militarism in Japan. General MacArthur supported Prime Minister Yoshida's position, stating that 'What the free world seeks in Japan should not be military strength. Japan has the capacity to produce armaments, and has manpower. The free world should strengthen itself by supplying materials to Japan, taking full advantage of her productive capacity, and utilizing the resultant products.' This comment by General

MacArthur no doubt reflected the majority view of high-level SCAP officials. While coping with the war in Korea, SCAP from around the autumn of 1950 had been studying the possibility of mobilizing Japan's industrial capacity for war purposes.

In February 1951, the Economic and Scientific Section (ESS) of SCAP prepared a report on the potential industrial capacity of Japan. The report concluded that although Japan's Second World War military production capabilities had been destroyed, Japan still possessed considerable production capabilities and a high-quality labour force which could be effectively utilized for manufacture of armaments. The report further stated that although it would be destabilizing to the economy to ask Japan to develop a comprehensive military defence set-up, it would be desirable to have Japan contribute to worldwide armaments build-up through maximum utilization of its excess production capacity.

Thus, against the background of the war in Korea, the US showed a keen interest in mobilizing Japan's industrial potential for war purposes. Meanwhile, Japan had high hopes for securing stable export markets and receiving the infusion of foreign capital needed to put the economy—which had recovered rapidly on the strength of special procurements—on the path to stable growth and to achieve its long-cherished wish for self-support. This interest of the US and the expectations of Japan combined to produce the US–Japan economic cooperation scheme.[3]

In February 1951, by means of a letter, General MacArthur directed Prime Minister Yoshida to study ways for establishing a US–Japan economic cooperation set-up. Subsequently, General Marquat, head of the ESS, instructed the director-general of the Economic Stabilization Board (ESB) to modify the production plan of Japanese industry so that it could swiftly respond to US demands for expanded armaments production. In March, the ESB submitted to SCAP the results of what was called a top-level study on Japan's industrial capacity and a document tentatively titled 'Emergency Economic Policy for Economic Cooperation'. This document stressed that in order for Japan to take full advantage of its excess production capacity and increase its export capabilities for the US–Japan cooperation programme, it was essential that importation of badly needed raw materials be increased and the number of Japanese ships be increased. The document then requested US economic aid, induction of US capital, and extension of credit.

General Marquat returned to Washington for consultation with his government. Upon returning to Japan in May 1951, General Marquat made an announcement concerning the US–Japan economic cooperation programme. He said that although the US would announce no comprehensive programme for procuring goods and services from Japan over a long period, Japan could participate in the emergency procurement programmes of the US on a short-term, commercial contract basis. He also stated that Japan would be permitted to export consumer goods to the US, supply special procurement exports to international markets, and export producer and consumer goods—which West

European countries, devoting themselves to armament production, could not supply—to South-East Asia and other areas. Marquat further said that in order to strengthen its abilities to supply these goods Japan would be permitted to import basic and strategic materials, would be given access to credit facilities of international organizations, the US government, and private sources, and would be given opportunities to receive technological assistance and specialized machine tools from US companies on a commercial basis. Marquat pointed out, however, that for Japan to be able to participate in this economic cooperation programme, it would be necessary for it to make efforts to curb inflation, maintain a balanced budget, rectify high domestic prices as compared with those in other countries, and develop domestic resources. Marquat also asked the Japanese government to establish a fundamental, long-term economic plan and make it public.

Responding to General Marquat's statement, the Japanese government in June 1951 announced major economic policies. The basic policies were the curbing of inflation, maintaining a fixed exchange rate, promoting economic cooperation with the US and other democratic nations, expanding the scale of production and foreign trade, and raising the standard of living of the people. Specific measures were then identified along these basic lines.

These statements by the US and Japanese governments clarified the basic direction of the US–Japanese economic cooperation programme, and preparations were made to give concrete form to it. The situation changed drastically, however, when the Malik proposal in June 1951 led to the start of cease-fire talks in Korea in July. The Korean War boom ended, and the prices of stocks and commodities fell sharply. Fearing that decreases in exports and special procurements might adversely affect the Japanese economy which had just begun to grow steadily, Japan pinned even greater hopes on the US–Japanese economic cooperation programme for ensuring the continuation of special procurements.

In December 1951, the US–Japan Economic Cooperation Committee was established in the Economic Stabilization Board. Its membership consisted of representatives from concerned ministries, agencies, and organizations. In February 1952, the Economic Cooperation Supreme Conference was created as a higher-level organization of this liaison council.

Also in February 1952, Director-General Hideo Shuto of the ESB sent a memorandum titled 'Realization of Economic Self-Support and Promotion of Economic Cooperation' to General Marquat, in which he spelled out the following set of policies. First, aided by technical and financial assistance from the US, Japan would rebuild its defence industries, contribute to the rearmament programme of the US, and secure stable dollar earnings. Second, Japan would cooperate with South-East Asian countries in their development efforts, and increase imports of products and raw materials from them. And third, with financial assistance from the US, Japan would rapidly increase its capacity to generate electric power, shortages of which in the past had created serious bottlenecks.

In response to Shuto's memorandum, General Marquat in March 1952 issued conditional permission to manufacture aircraft and armaments. Next, in April, a joint ministerial ordinance concerning the limitations placed on the manufacture of armaments was revised, making it possible for Japanese manufacturers to produce armaments and aircraft with the approval of SCAP. This was the period just prior to effectuation of the Treaty of Peace with Japan (San Francisco Peace Treaty), and SCAP's lifting of the ban on armaments manufacture was tantamount to a declaration of the end of regulation of Japanese industry as Occupation policy. At the same time, the action suggested the nature of a possible relationship between the two countries after restoration of Japanese sovereignty.

As the Korean War special procurements abated, the US began placing so-called 'new special procurement' orders for defence-related materials and services. Although it is difficult to distinguish statistically between new special procurements and Korean War special procurements, Table 11.1 shows the changing values and reveals that special procurements in a narrow sense were $457 million in 1952—an increase from the preceding year—and were $595 million in 1953. The percentage of special-procurement receipts in Japan's foreign-exchange earnings was 20.4 per cent in 1952, and rose to a high level of 28.1 per cent in 1953, indicating that special procurements even after the cessation of hostilities in Korea continued to play an important role for Japan when it was suffering from shortages of foreign exchange.[4]

The US–Japanese economic cooperation scheme produced results in the form of new special procurements. Nonetheless, a review of its history from the Dulles–Yoshida meeting of 1951 reveals a shift in the focus of the scheme.

Table 11.1 Special procurement receipts, 1950–1954 (unit: $1m.)

	Special procurements in broad sense, A	Special procurements in narrow sense, B	B as a percentage of total exports (%)	B as a percentage of foreign-exchange earnings (%)
1950	149	91	11.8	9.0
1951	592	342	26.4	15.3
1952	824	457	35.5	20.4
1953	810	595	51.5	28.1
1954	596	454	29.6	19.7

Notes:
1. These figures are on a disbursement basis; they do not necessarily agree with the figures in the text, which are on a contract basis.
2. Special procurements in a broad sense include consumption expenditures by US military and civilian personnel in Japan and their dependants.

Source: Takafusa Nakamura, *Nichibei 'Keizai Kyoryoku' Kankei no Keisei* (Formation of US–Japan 'Economic Cooperation Ties'), *Nenpo Kindai Nippon Kenkyu 4, Taiheiyo Senso* (Journal of Modern Japanese Studies, iv: Pacific War), Yamakawa Shuppan-sha, 1982: 284.

Initially, the utilization of Japan's armaments production potential was an overriding factor in the scheme. There occurred a change in the US stance, however, as the prospects of a cease-fire in Korea became certain. Earlier, in the tense situation where the eruption of a third world war was not inconceivable, the US showed a keen interest in Japan's potential armaments-manufacturing capacity. As the 'hot war' ended and the Cold War resumed, the US adopted a policy of arming West European and Asian countries with its own armaments production capabilities, while gradually reducing offshore armaments procurements. As the US interest in Japan's armaments-manufacturing capacity waned, the focus of the US–Japanese economic cooperation scheme shifted to its other pillar—improving conditions for Japan's economic self-support. In the post-war Japanese economy, the period in which the military aspect appeared to gain in significance turned out to be brief; Japan resumed its economic growth path focusing on peacetime industries.

NOTES

1. *Tsusho Sangyo Seisakushi*, ii, ch. 1, sect. 3–2.
2. Ibid. ii, ch. 2, sect. 6.
3. Ibid. ii, ch. 1 and ch. 2, sect. 3–2.
4. Takafusa Nakamura, 'Nichibei Keizai Kyoryoku Kankei no Keisei' (Formation of US–Japanese Economic Relations), *Nenpo: Kindai Nippon Kenkyu 4-Taiheiyo Senso* (Annual: Study on Modern Japan—Pacific War), Yamakawa Shuppan-sha, 1982.

12

Building the Foundation for a Self-Supporting Economy, and MITI Policy

12.1. Conclusion of Peace Treaty

When the San Francisco Peace Treaty went into effect on 28 April 1952, Japan was freed from the Allied Occupation that had lasted over eight years and regained its sovereignty. The following is a review of the convoluted sequence of events that led to this outcome.[1]

The initial discussion of a peace treaty with Japan dates to October 1946 when the Office of Far Eastern Affairs of the US Department of State began the study of a draft treaty. In March 1947, General MacArthur urged the quick conclusion of a peace treaty with Japan, and the US began preparations for a peace conference. In August 1947, the British Commonwealth countries exchanged their views on this issue at a meeting in Canberra, Australia. Against the background of the intensifying Cold War, however, a treaty with Japan was considered premature in the US, and the movement towards an early peace treaty did not gain headway.

The first draft treaty prepared by the State Department's Office of Far Eastern Affairs, as well as the formula worked out at the Canberra conference, prohibited Japan's rearming and munitions manufacturing in order to keep Japan demilitarized, and proposed continuing Allied control and surveillance over Japan's industry and foreign trade. But the plan to incorporate into the peace treaty a provision for demilitarizing Japan—the guiding principle of the early phase of the Occupation—became patently inappropriate in the climate of the Cold War. The US reversed its policy towards Japan from demilitarization to economic reconstruction. Also, the US military showed a strong interest in maintaining military bases in Japan after the peace treaty went into effect, as well as having Japan acquire defence capabilities. The US plan for the peace treaty, in other words, underwent a major reversal.

John Foster Dulles, appointed foreign policy adviser to the US secretary of state in April 1950, exercised the leadership in bringing about a peace treaty with Japan based on the new thinking. In June 1950, by coincidence just before the Korean War broke out, Dulles visited Japan and exchanged views with General MacArthur and Japanese government leaders. Although the Korean War prompted the resurgence of the view within the US military that a peace treaty with Japan was premature, the State Department pressed ahead with its study of a draft treaty, convinced that the need for friendly relations with Japan was even more urgent because of the Korean War. In September 1950, the US National Security Council adopted a basic policy on the peace treaty with Japan (policy document NSC 60/1), which advocated that Japan would not be prevented from rearming itself, US forces would remain in Japan, and the US would maintain its control over the Ryukyu Islands, which included Okinawa. President Truman approved this policy.

Dulles, who besides being adviser to the US secretary of state was a special envoy of the president, circulated a memorandum to the concerned countries listing seven principles regarding a peace treaty with Japan. He then began negotiating with them. The Japanese, who had taken every opportunity to appeal to the US for favourable terms, found the seven principles rather satisfactory since they neither called for limiting economic activities—which had been feared—nor allowed for the right to demand reparations. By the same token, many of the concerned countries expressed dissatisfaction with the seven principles, requiring Dulles to grapple with the task of reconciling the different positions.

The first source of dissatisfaction by the concerned countries related to the reparations issue. Australia, Indonesia, New Zealand, the Philippines, and Vietnam objected to the US proposal of surrendering the right to demand reparations for war damages. The Nationalist Chinese government acceded to the proposal, on the condition the other countries did likewise. India and the UK agreed to the proposal but in reverse proposed that the gold bullion, precious metals, and jewellery the Japanese government possessed, as well as overseas Japanese assets, be exacted as reparations. The Soviet Union asserted that Japan was responsible for paying reparations.

Dulles made special efforts to reach accommodations with the UK, and in June 1951 prepared a revised version of the joint US–UK draft treaty. Its essential elements were: (1) Japan would agree to pay reparations in principle, but the Allied Powers would recognize that it lacked the ability to pay, (2) Japan would negotiate with the countries concerned for paying reparations for war damages by providing such services as the manufacture of goods and salvage of sunken vessels, and (3) Japanese overseas assets would be at the disposal of the countries where they were located. Although the principle of no reparations was abandoned and Japan's obligation to pay reparations was affirmed, it was also recognized that Japan, which was yet to achieve a self-supporting economy, was not capable of paying reparations. Japan was thus relieved, *de facto*, of its obligation to pay reparations. The door was left open, however, for those countries which insisted on their right to demand reparations to enter into bilateral negotiations with Japan for reparations in the form of services. As for the proposal for exacting precious metals and other assets of the Japanese government as reparations, the US government objected to the proposal, arguing that such assets were essential for Japan's economic rehabilitation, and the UK withdrew its demand.

The San Francisco Peace Treaty adopted its final form on the basis of this revised joint US–UK draft. Burma (which did not participate in the peace conference), Cambodia, Indonesia, Laos, the Philippines, and Vietnam expressed their intention to seek reparations, but in the end Cambodia and Laos surrendered their right and only four countries concluded reparations agreements with Japan after the signing of the treaty.

The reparations agreements with those four countries called for payments of $550 million to the Philippines (over twenty years), $223.08 million to Indonesia (over twelve years), $200 million to Burma (over ten years), and $39 million to Vietnam (over five years). Additionally, the agreements called for economic development loans of $250 million, $400 million, $50 million, and $16.6 million, respectively. Subsequently, the China–Japan Joint Communiqué of 1972 declared that the People's Republic of China surrendered its right to seek reparations, thus nearly ending the reparations problem.

The second source of dissatisfaction by the concerned countries was the Japanese rearmament issue. Countries such as the Soviet Union and the People's Republic of China expressed misgivings about Japan's rearmament, and felt that the demand to restrict Japanese munitions manufacturing was only natural. Even the British Commonwealth countries insisted on maintaining control over specific industries.

In meetings held in Canberra from August 1947, the British Commonwealth countries adopted a policy of prohibiting, at the peace conference, Japan's rearmament and rebuilding of munitions industries, and limiting its production capacity of ships, steel, and aluminium. Subsequently, at the Colombo conference held in January 1950, Australia and New Zealand advocated continuation of the policy adopted at the Canberra meeting, but no agreement was reached. At the meeting of the Commonwealth Working Party on the peace treaty with Japan in May 1950, regulation of Japanese economic activities after the treaty went into effect was discussed from a variety of standpoints. New Zealand persisted in its demand for strong control, but other countries wanted to limit regulation only to shipbuilding.

Building on the results of the study of the Commonwealth Working Party, the UK in December 1950 developed a plan containing the following proposals: (1) in terms of long-term control over the Japanese economy, an international system would be developed to exercise surveillance over Japanese imports of strategic materials indispensable for munitions industries (crude oil, rubber, bauxite, etc.), although this provision would not be incorporated in the peace treaty itself; and (2) owing to the fact that Japan's shipbuilding capacity, which had been developed for wartime needs, was excessive relative to peacetime demand, and that shipbuilding industries around the world were suffering from excess capacity, Japan's excess shipbuilding capacity would be reduced. The British military held the view that, from the standpoint of military strategy, there was no need to forbid Japan to maintain and build its merchant marine. It was reasonable to assume, therefore, that the British government's proposal for limiting Japan's shipbuilding capacity was made in the interest of the British shipbuilding industry.

The British government submitted this proposal to a Commonwealth prime ministers' meeting held in London in January 1951. Because Australia and New Zealand objected at the meeting to Japan's rearmament and insisted on limiting Japan's manufacturing capabilities, the meeting ended without reaching a general agreement.

In the United States, too, there were expressions of concern over the resurgence of the Japanese merchant marine. In response to a report that Japan wished to rebuild a merchant marine with four million gross tons, the National Federation of American Shipping announced, as early as February 1949, that two million gross tons of ships were adequate for Japan. In February 1951, that organization and eight others involved in ocean shipping forwarded a letter to President Truman opposing expansion of the Japanese shipping industry to a size far out of proportion to the volume of Japan's foreign trade. Also, the Pacific American Steamship Association in May 1951 announced six principles regarding the peace treaty, demanding that the loading percentage of trade cargo be set at 50 per cent, and that triangular shipping be prohibited.[2]

As seen from the above discussion, there were rather strong demands for incorporating into the peace treaty provisions for controlling Japan's rearmament and limiting its economic activities. In February 1951, Dulles visited Canberra and exchanged views with the governments of Australia and New Zealand in an effort to soften their stance on the content of the peace treaty with Japan. Although these two countries were extremely wary of Japan, Dulles succeeded in bringing them along to a certain extent, using as a trump card their keen interest in concluding the mutual security treaty (the ANZUS Pact) with the United States.

In June 1951, Dulles visited London to continue negotiations. He pressed ahead with efforts to find an accommodation with the British, while strongly urging them to accede to the US plan. In the end, the UK agreed to abandon the proposal to limit Japan's shipbuilding capacity. In return, the US agreed to the British demand regarding the shipping issue. Concerning national treatment in shipping, the US plan had contained a proviso that coastal and inland water navigation rights were to be excluded. The US acceded to the British demand to delete this proviso. The UK demanded this deletion on the grounds that the text of the Britain–Japan Trade and Navigation Treaty of 1911 did not contain a provision excluding British vessels from Japan's coastal and inland waters. Although this revision had little practical significance, it had an effect of saving British face.

It was in these circumstances that the restrictions on economic activities which the British Commonwealth countries advocated were not incorporated into the peace treaty. Post-independence Japan was thus permitted to engage in unrestricted economic activities.

The San Francisco Peace Treaty Conference convened on 4 September 1951. Of the fifty-three countries invited to the conference, Burma, India, and

Yugoslavia declined the invitation, leaving fifty-two countries, including Japan and the US, the host country, as participants in the conference. As regards the participation of China, negotiations faced rough going and failed to produce an agreement between the UK, which had recognized the People's Republic of China and strongly supported its participation, and the USA, which sought the participation of the Chinese Nationalist government. The dispute between the USA and the UK was settled by an agreement to invite neither the Communists nor the Nationalists to the conference and to have Japan deal with the problem of a peace treaty with China separately, after it regained sovereignty.

After completing eight plenary sessions, the signing of the San Francisco Peace Treaty was held on 8 September 1951 with representatives from forty-nine nations in attendance. Czechoslovakia, Poland, and the Soviet Union attended the conference but did not sign the treaty. The Soviet Union declined to become a signatory, protesting the non-participation of the People's Republic of China and the absence of a provision in the treaty to prevent the re-emergence of Japanese militarism.

Starting at 5.00 p.m. on 8 September 1951, a ceremony to sign the United States–Japan Security Treaty was held by the representatives of the two governments. Two treaties were thus signed in San Francisco, which went into effect on 28 April 1952.

12.2. Initiation of the Industrial Rationalization Policy

Achieving a self-supporting status for its economy was the major task for post-independence Japan. Additional economic burdens that arose with independence included: (1) expenditures associated with war reparations, redemption of pre-war foreign-currency bonds, indemnities for property of the Allied nations, and debt to the United States; (2) sharing defence expenditures with the US; and (3) expenses associated with a gradual increase in defence capabilities. Efforts to build the foundation of a self-supporting economy had already begun with a view to upgrading the industrial structure centred on chemicals, metals, and machinery, and bolstering export industries. These efforts started from about the time when the Allied Occupation policy towards Japan was reversed and prospects improved for relaxing restrictions on Japan's industrial structure based on the policy of demilitarization. In this process, the government placed priorities on industrial rationalization designed to improve international competitiveness.[3]

Adoption in December 1948 of the Draft Outline of Comprehensive Measures clearly set forth industrial rationalization as post-war government policy. In order to improve the production and other facilities and the technical capabilities of important industries—many of which were export industries—and promote their rationalization, the Outline proposed such measures as providing funds, special depreciation allowances, and priority allocation of materials for renovating and mechanizing facilities and importing technologies. Subsequently, as the Dodge Line of anti-inflation programmes were implemented and MITI was established, its International Trade Enterprises Bureau began operating as a bureau specializing in industrial rationalization. The bureau in July 1949 referred to a ministerial meeting a proposal entitled 'Matter Concerning the Establishment of Enterprise Rationalization Measures'. In September, the Cabinet formally adopted an Industrial Rationalization Resolution.

Listed in that resolution as basic policies for industrial rationalization were: (1) firmly establishing policy for guiding each industry from the standpoint of the nation's future industrial structure; (2) swiftly reducing the disparity between domestic and world prices; (3) nurturing an appropriate environment for promoting rationalization; and (4) promoting improved efficiency and the adoption of outstanding technologies. The Resolution also called for MITI to examine rationalization plans submitted by basic and other industries and to provide advice concerning them. Specifically, it advocated providing guidance on the improvement of efficiency, promoting experimental research, securing funds for rationalization programmes, promoting the induction of foreign capital, initiating an industrial rationalization movement, and removing obstacles to rationalization. Specific measures suggested for removing obstacles to rationalization included drastically relaxing controls on materials allocations, abolishing price controls, implementing a revaluation of assets, lowering corporate tax rates, and improving communications and transportation. The Resolution also called for the establishment of the Industrial Rationalization Council as an advisory organ to the Minister of International Trade and Industry for studying and deliberating on matters required for implementing rationalization programmes.

The first plenary meeting of the Industrial Rationalization Council was held in December 1949. MITI Minister Heitaro Inagaki posed the question 'What measures should be adopted with regard to industrial rationalization?' to the Council. The Industrial Rationalization Council membership included industrialists, financiers, academics, and senior staff members from related government agencies such as MITI. Its deliberations took place in the coordination committee and thirty industry-specific committees. The committee's deliberations became protracted after conditions changed with the outbreak of the Korean War. In February 1951, the first report of the Industrial Rationalization Council was submitted to the MITI minister.

In its first report, the Council recommended that the focus of the rationalization programme be placed on modernizing machinery and equipment which during the wartime and post-war years had become grossly obsolete compared to that in the Western countries. It then suggested adoption of such measures as improving communications and transport facilities; lowering the prices of materials, fuels, and electric power; importing foreign technologies; securing adequate funds for rationalization programmes; amending the Anti-Monopoly Law to enable companies to achieve industrial rationalization by organizing joint action with other companies; and promoting the creation of small business and other types of cooperative associations. Having emphasized that expanding and reinforcing electric power generation and shipbuilding—as well as rationalizing the shipbuilding, coal mining, and steel industries—would provide the foundation for the rationalization of all other industries, the report urged MITI for the interim to give highest priority to these areas.

The coal mining and steel industries, which the Industrial Rationalization Council emphasized in its report, were of course the same industries MITI had attached great importance on ever since adopting the priority-production system. Prior to the Industrial Rationalization Council's report, the coordination committee of MITI's Industrial Structure Council had released a report entitled 'On Rationalization of the Steel and Coal Mining Industries'. Based on that report, MITI had prepared a report entitled 'Outline of Measures for Rationalization of the Steel and Coal Mining Industries', which the Cabinet decided on in August. The Outline presented a formula for placing the steel industry on a solid footing, which included the following elements. Rationalization of the steel industry would be stepped up so that production costs per ton of steel materials be reduced from 25,230 yen to 24,300 yen ($67.50) on the basis of annual production of 3.7 million tons of ordinary (unfinished) steel materials in fiscal year 1953. Since the export price of steel to realize an acceptable profit level was estimated to be $60 per ton, the average shipping price of coal (ex-coal mines)—which accounted for a large percentage of the total production cost of steel—was to be reduced from 2,960 yen to 2,440 yen per ton through efforts to rationalize coal production. The Outline then suggested that realization of this formula would require implementing such measures as securing funds for rationalization, special measures for the import of machinery and technology, securing imports of coke and increasing the allocation of electric power.

Electric power generation, meanwhile, another industry to which the Industrial Rationalization Council attached great importance along with the coal-mining and steel industries, had been suffering from chronic output shortages, giving rise for some time to demands for radical remedial measures. The response to these demands, however, was delayed by complications owing to reorganization of the electric power industry. Reconstruction Finance Bank loans had been channelled into the electric power industry on a priority basis, and they were used gradually to increase power-generating capacity. The source of funds, however, was switched from the Reconstruction Finance Bank to the US Aid Counterpart Fund. Then, in July 1950, SCAP ordered suspension of the Counterpart Fund financing to the power industry. Delays in reorganizing the industry was the cause of this action, which dealt a severe blow to the power development programme. As discussed earlier, a full-scale move towards electric power development became feasible only after the Electric Utilities Industry Reorganization Ordinance was promulgated in November 1950 and the system of nine electric power companies made a start in May 1951. The aims of the Industrial Rationalization Council report were finally realized with promulgation in July 1952 of the Electric Power Development Promotion Law and the establishment in September 1952 of Electric Power Development Co. under the provisions of that law.

Another important policy task of the post-war period was reconstruction of the shipping industry, which had been dealt a crushing blow by the war. From 1947, a planned shipbuilding programme was carried out with financing by the Reconstruction Finance Bank. From the Fifth Shipbuilding Plan of 1949, the building of large oceangoing vessels was permitted as a result of the reversal of the Allied Occupation policy towards Japan, and the reconstruction of Japan's merchant marine began. In April 1950, shipping was privatized. Until then, ships had been operated by the Civil Merchant Marine Committee which chartered the ships from their owners. With the return of operation of ships to private shipping companies, Japan's shipping industry returned to its normal state from the anomaly of the wartime state control. Although a sharp increase in the number of ships was urgently called for, the shipping companies had been weakened financially by cancellation of war indemnity payments and they had to rely heavily on the planned shipbuilding programme. It was in these circumstances that the Industrial Rationalization Council proposed to give policy priority to the shipping and shipbuilding industries. The Shipbuilding Industry Rationalization Council (subsequently renamed Shipping and Shipbuilding Rationalization Council), established in August 1950 in the Ministry of Transport—which had jurisdiction over those two industries—was to deliberate separately on the programme of rationalizing the shipping and shipbuilding industries.[4]

Of the proposals contained in the Industrial Rationalization Council report, the greatest importance was attached to the task of securing funds for rationalization programmes. After the Reconstruction Finance Bank—which had provided long-term funds needed for post-war reconstruction programmes—ceased operation as a result of the Dodge Line of anti-inflation policy, the US Aid Counterpart Fund, established in April 1949, came to provide long-term financing. However, 27 billion yen out of Counterpart Fund loans of 51.6 billion yen in fiscal year 1949 were channelled to telecommunications and Japan National Railways projects. Of the loans made available to the private sector, 18.4 billion yen were allocated to electric power generation and shipping, leaving relatively little for other industries. In fiscal year 1950, 38.1 billion yen out of a total of 71.9 billion yen were channelled to public enterprises. The Counterpart Fund was thus inadequate as a source of funds for financing the long-term investment needs of private enterprises, giving rise to what was called the 'blank period in long-term financing'. The situation was serious enough to prompt MITI to discuss, towards the end of 1950, the scheme for creating a Special Account for Modernization of Industrial Machinery Facilities to provide funds for rationalization programmes.

The government sought to reconstruct an industrial financing system, and in December 1950, with the concurrence of Joseph M. Dodge, who was in Japan at the time, resumed the subscription of bank debentures by the Deposits Bureau of the Ministry of Finance. In April 1951 the Deposits Bureau was reorganized into the Trust Fund Bureau, and funds in that bureau were then made available to private enterprises for long-term investment. Also in April 1951, the Japan

Development Bank was established, thus completing a system whereby 10 billion yen (initially 2.5 billion yen) were to be made available from the Counterpart Fund to private enterprises for industrial investment purposes. After independence, the Japan Development Bank Law was amended to enable the Japan Development Bank to avail itself of government funds (primarily Trust Bureau funds). A stable supply of funds for rationalization programmes was thus ensured as funds were channelled to private enterprises through the Japan Development Bank and the Industrial Bank of Japan.

MITI also promoted promulgation of the Enterprise Rationalization Promotion Law, which was enacted in March 1952. Besides special depreciation allowances (50 per cent extra depreciation over three years) permitted by the March 1951 revision of the Special Taxation Measures Law, the law institutionalized the system of special short-term depreciation (50 per cent depreciation in the first year) of machines and equipment for modernization in important industries, and the special short-term depreciation (straight-line depreciation over three years) of machines and equipment for experimental research. The law also provided for giving subsidies for experimental research, reduction of or exemption from property tax on machines and equipment subject to special depreciation, promoting the improvement of unit productivity of raw materials and energy resources, and enterprise consulting for small and medium enterprises. The system of subsidies for experimental research was already in effect in fiscal year 1949; in fiscal year 1951 a total of 450 million yen was given to 334 research projects.

The various programmes for promoting industrial rationalization were thus put into place, and their positive results would soon produce the high-level growth of the Japanese economy.

12.3. Import of Foreign Capital

Although the import of advanced foreign technology for rationalizing industry was much in demand, many in Japan also hoped, from around the time of the Ashida Cabinet, that foreign capital could be imported to provide funds for Japan's economic reconstruction.[5] In post-war Japan, funds were in short supply for industrial reconstruction, particularly for the import of advanced technology. SCAP, however, maintained a rather stringent attitude towards the import of capital. In early 1949, it established within its organization a Foreign Capital Council, and introduced a policy whereby it permitted investment by foreign enterprises to resume their pre-war operations in Japan but limited new investment in Japan to only those undertakings which would produce foreign-exchange earnings or positively contribute to Japan's economic recovery. Investment in existing enterprises, moreover, was limited to cases that would lead to an increase in the assets of those enterprises. Meanwhile, the Japanese government in March 1949 promulgated the Ordinance on Ownership of Assets by Foreigners, and established the Foreign Capital Council as an administrative board attached to the Economic Stabilization Board for performing duties related to approval of investments. The June 1949 revision of the Anti-Monopoly Law included measures to simplify the procedures for importing foreign capital, including requiring only notification after the fact, rather than prior approval, for entering into international agreements or contracts.

Foreign capital imports during the early post-war period centred on the petroleum industry.[6] SCAP had from the beginning provided the petroleum industry with positive assistance with regard to production of domestic crude oil, including induction of new technologies related to oil-prospecting and drilling. Although production of domestic crude oil reached 2.06 million barrels in 1950, there were few oilfields in Japan proper or in its coastal waters. Oil refineries on the Japan Sea coast used for refining domestic crude oil suffered from low productivity. Therefore, hopes were pinned on resuming the import of crude oil and using the refineries on the Pacific coast, whose operation had been halted as part of the policy to demilitarize Japan. After the reversal of Occupation policy, SCAP reviewed its internal policy towards permitting the importation of crude oil and reopening of the Pacific coast refineries. In June 1949, it issued a memorandum permitting the resumption of operations.

In order to resume the refining of imported crude oil, it was necessary for Japanese refiners to tie up with foreign oil companies, not only to secure stable supplies of crude oil but also to improve and expand facilities and to introduce new technology in areas where Japan lagged behind because of the wartime vacuum. Anglo-American oil companies showed a keen interest in cooperating with Japanese companies because of the increased production of oil in the Middle East and introduction of the system of refining oil in the country of consumption. Negotiations for cooperative arrangements with foreign oil companies had begun from around the end of 1946, and in anticipation of SCAP approval participation agreements were concluded successively from February 1949. The agreements included capital participation, consigned refining of crude oil, and technical licensing. In capital participation, Toa Nenryo Kogyo accepted 51 per cent participation by Standard Vacuum and Nippon Sekiyu Seisei, Mitsubishi Oil, Showa Oil, and Koa Oil all had 50 per cent foreign participation. These companies made strenuous efforts to restore and improve their facilities. Nine refineries along the Pacific coast—with a combined daily crude-oil-processing capacity of 53,400 barrels—began operation between January and August of 1950.

Initially, induction of foreign capital—with the exception of the petroleum industry—did not progress as smoothly as anticipated because there was no guarantee of foreign-currency repatriation of investment income, and there were strict rules concerning the Anti-Monopoly Law and the tax system. In that situation, the government in May 1950 promulgated the Law Concerning Foreign Capital, established approval criteria for foreign-capital importation, and guaranteed foreign-currency repatriation of dividends, interest, payments for technical assistance, and amortization of principal. Amendment of the Foreign Capital Law in April 1951 further relaxed regulations. For stock acquisitions which did not involve repatriation of dividends, for example, application for approval was no longer required and instead only notification would suffice.

After the Foreign Capital Law was put into effect, and especially from fiscal year 1951, the induction of foreign capital increased sharply. The combined total of portfolio investments for fiscal years 1949 and 1950, which was only $3.15 million, increased to $13.33 million in fiscal year 1951. The number of cases of Type I technology licensing agreements increased from twenty-seven in fiscal years 1949 and 1950 to 101 in fiscal year 1951. Most technology licensing agreements were concluded with US partners. The number was seventy-four out of 101 cases in fiscal year 1951. Other agreements included sixteen with Swiss and six with Swedish companies.[7] Of those 101 agreements, fifty were in the machinery industry, twenty-three in the chemical industry, nine in the metal and metal products manufacturing industry, and six in the rubber-manufacturing industry.

Because Japan fell so far behind other nations technologically in many fields of industry during the war, the induction of foreign capital involving technology licensing continued to increase from fiscal year 1952, providing a powerful driving force for industrial rationalization. Although Japanese companies had difficulties securing funds and therefore sought them in imports of foreign capital, Japanese industry—with the exception of the petroleum industry—did not come under foreign domination because the scale of the economy had already become substantial.

12.4. Building a New Economic Structure

Japan devoted all its energy to the war effort during the Second World War, resulting in an economy that placed disproportionate emphasis on munitions manufacturing. When the post-war economy made its new start the level of production was so extremely low it could scarcely provide the subsistence the Japanese people needed. During fewer than seven years after the war ended, however, up to the restoration of independence, Japan succeeded in rehabilitating its economy to the point where a foundation was in place for achieving a self-supporting status. In this process, policy measures for reconstruction, including the priority-production system, gradually produced their intended effects, although they were constrained by the Allied Occupation policy. In 1951, during the Korean War boom, Japan's real GNP and industrial production surpassed the pre-war level (1934–6 average). A little later, in 1953, per capita GNP and consumption expenditures reached their pre-war levels.

As long as the primary objective of the Occupation policy was the demilitarization of Japan, the only option open to Japan in the process of converting from a wartime to a peacetime economy was an economic path centred on light industries. After the reversal of Occupation policy, however, a new direction of economic development was established with a focus on the heavy and chemical industries, while reorganizing the legacies of the wartime industrial system. Land and labour reforms brightened the prospects for enlarged markets for consumer goods, and the rebuilding of the heavy and chemical industries—which gained headway in the competitive market conditions brought about by dissolution of the zaibatsu—expanded the markets for producer goods. The post-war Japanese economy, therefore, moved down a path of growth that relied primarily on domestic markets, although it had to depend heavily on imports, primarily of raw materials and fuels. Dependency on the international economy was even more indispensable to the Japanese economy than it was before the war.

It was no easy task to rebuild peacetime industry based on heavy industries, resume membership in the international economic community, and raise the standard of living of Japanese citizens while maintaining equilibrium in the balance of payments. Part II has traced the history of the efforts made by the Japanese people to attain these objectives, from the perspectives of commercial, industrial, and trade policies. Before venturing into examining the second phase (1952–60) of the post-war period, a review of the Japanese economy prior to restoration of independence (1952) will be useful. The standard of living of the Japanese people, which had fallen to the subsistence level at the end of the war, recovered considerably by around 1951. According to average statistics, the per capita daily calorie intake of the Japanese people, which fell to 1,448 kcal. in 1946, rose to 1,858 kcal. in 1951, reaching approximately 90 per cent of the per-war (1931–5 average) level of 2,058 kcal. Per capita annual consumption of sugar increased from 0.2 kg. in 1946 to 6.31 kg. in 1951, reaching approximately 45 per cent of the pre-war (1934–6) level of 13.94 kg. Per capita annual consumption of cotton fibre, meanwhile, increased from 0.79 kg. in 1946 to 2.17 kg. in 1951. Without considering quality, cotton fibre consumption was thus restored in 1951 to 59 per cent of the pre-war (1934–6) level of 3.65 kg. Based on these figures, it may be concluded that by 1951 the Japanese people had managed to escape from the grip of dire shortages of food and clothing, though what was available was by no means plentiful.

Although overall industrial production reached the pre-war level in 1951, the standard of living failed to do likewise. One reason for the lag was the fact that the population of mainland Japan had increased by 22.1 per cent owing to the repatriation of overseas Japanese and the post-war baby boom. The other reason was that the recovery of industrial production first occurred in producer goods; the recovery of consumer goods production came later. As Table 9.3 shows, the 46.49 million tons of coal produced in fiscal year 1951 exceeded pre-war (1934–6 average) output by approximately 20 per cent. Similarly, production of pig-iron and crude steel was about 66 and 42 per cent, respectively, both above the pre-war levels. In contrast, production of cotton yarn was only about 52 per cent of the pre-war level, although cotton yarn may not be the best example for explaining the delay in the recovery of consumer goods production since a large portion of cotton yarn output in pre-war days was exported as raw material or processed goods. The production index (1960 = 100) of processed foods stood at 42.8 in 1951, or about 74 per cent of the pre-war level of 57.9.

In short, a distinctive characteristic of the post-war reconstruction period was that the recovery of producer goods production preceded that of consumer goods. Reflected in this pattern was the nature of the commercial, industrial, and trade policies of the period, best expressed by the priority-production system. The policy choice of achieving post-war economic reconstruction by placing a burden on the daily lives of the people and making best use of recovery in the producer goods sector may be rated highly successful in view of its results. The results spilled over to consumer goods production in the second phase of the post-war period, significantly raising the Japanese people's living standard.

Production recovery that emphasized producer goods manifested itself in the increasing relative importance of heavy industries in selected indices for manufacturing industries. Table 12.1 shows indices for number of employees, value of

Table 12.1   Selected indices for manufacturing industries, 1951 (unit: %)

	No. of employees	Value of shipments	Value added
1. Iron and steel	6.7	12.0	9.6
2. Non-ferrous metals	1.9	5.0	4.6
3. Metal products	3.6	2.7	3.0
Subtotal 1–3	12.2	19.7	17.2
4. General machinery	8.2	5.1	6.7
5. Electrical machinery and equipment	4.1	3.1	4.4
6. Transport machinery and equipment	6.7	5.3	5.2
7. Precision machinery and equipment	1.3	0.7	0.9
Subtotal 4–7	20.3	14.2	17.2
8. Chemicals	8.0	11.8	13.8
9. Petroleum and coal products	0.7	1.7	1.8
10. Rubber products	1.6	1.9	1.5
11. Pulp and paper	3.3	4.7	6.1
Subtotal 8–11	13.6	20.1	23.2
Subtotal 1–11	46.1	54.0	57.6
12. Non-metallic mineral manufactures	5.4	3.5	5.0
13. Textiles	21.4	21.2	18.1
14. Textile products	2.5	1.5	1.3
15. Wood and wood products	7.1	3.5	3.5
16. Furniture and fixtures	1.7	0.6	0.8
17. Food products	9.1	11.3	7.8
18. Publishing and printing	3.4	2.5	4.1
19. Leather and leather products	0.5	0.7	0.5
20. Others	2.8	1.2	1.3
Subtotal 12–20	53.9	46.0	42.4
Total	100.0	100.0	100.0

Source: Census of Manufacturers.

shipments, and value added for selected industries in 1951 as reported in the Census of Manufactures. Heavy industries (metals, machinery, chemicals, etc.) accounted for 46.1 per cent of manufacturing employment, 54 per cent of the value of shipments (including income from processing and repair work), and 57.6 per cent of value added in production. Considering that heavy industries accounted for approximately 44 per cent of manufacturing output in 1935 and about 56 per cent in 1940, the 'weight of heavy industry' in 1951 can be said to have been roughly equal to that in the second half of the 1930s. Having lost its munitions industries, the post-war Japanese economy was on its way towards building a new structure centred on heavy industries. In other words, the post-war industrial structure underwent a transformation from the pre-war structure based on light industries to one centred on heavy industries.

Can it be concluded that the rising 'weight of heavy industry' enabled Japan to realize self-supporting status for its economy? As of 1951 or 1952, that conclusion would have been premature. The balance of trade recorded deficits of $291.7 million in 1951 and $407.3 million in 1952, with the current account balance barely kept in the black by special-procurements earnings. It is worthwhile reviewing the source of these deficits in the balance of trade through statistics on the commodity make-up of trade. As Table 12.2 shows, textile materials accounted for 37.3 per cent of imports in 1951, followed by another significant category, foodstuffs, which accounted for 27.5 per cent. In contrast, textiles and textile products accounted for 45.9 per cent of total exports, and heavy industry products (metals and metal products, machinery, and chemicals) accounted for only 37.2 per cent. In other words, notwithstanding the high 'weight of heavy industry' in manufacturing, the composition of trade was primarily centred on light industry products. The weakness of heavy industry products as foreign-exchange earners turned out to be the primary cause of the balance-of-trade deficits.

Table 12.2   Composition of Japanese exports and imports, 1951 (unit: %)

Exports		Imports	
Foodstuffs	5.1	Foodstuffs	27.5
Textiles and textile products	45.9	Textile materials	37.3
Chemicals	2.7	Metal ores and scrap	4.6
Non-metallic mineral manufactures	4.4	Mineral fuels	7.8
Metals and metal products	22.1	Chemicals	1.8
Machinery and equipment	8.0	Machinery and equipment	2.8
Others	11.8	Others	18.2
Total	100.0	Total	100.0

Source: *Tsusho Sangyo Seisakushi* (History of International Trade and Industry Policy), xvi: 238–41. Import percentages are revised partially.

For the Japanese economy to achieve a self-supporting status, it was necessary for its heavy industries to acquire competitiveness in world markets. During the Occupation period, the economy was converted from a wartime structure to a peacetime structure while preserving the legacies of the wartime structure. Having this new structure plant its roots deeply into Japanese soil was the principal task of MITI policy in the subsequent period.

NOTES

1. *Tsusho Sangyo Seisakushi*, ii, ch. 1, sect. 3.
2. Ryoichi Miwa, *Senryoki no Nihon Kaiun* (Japanese Merchant Shipping During the Occupation Period), ch. 4, Nihon Keizai Hyoron-sha, 1992.
3. Concerning industrial rationalization, see MITI, *Shoko Seisakushi* (History of Commercial and Industrial Policy), x, Shoko Seisakushi Kankokai, 1972; and *Tsusho Sangyo Seisakushi*, ii, ch. 3, sects. 4 and 5.
4. Although the shipbuilding industry, as a comprehensive industry, is an important manufacturing industry and has occupied an extremely important position in overall Japanese industry, it has been under the jurisdiction of the Ministry of Transport because of its relationship with the shipping industry. As such, it has not been a subject of direct study in this *History of International Trade and Industry Policy*, except where necessary.
5. *Tsusho Sangyo Seisakushi*, iii, ch. 3, sect. 4–1, for a discussion of the import of foreign capital.
6. Ibid. iii, ch. 4, sects. 1–2, for a discussion of the petroleum industry.
7. Ibid. iii, ch. 3, sect. 5–2, for a discussion of the import of foreign technology.

PART III

Attainment of Economic Self-Support

13

The Reorganization of the Political and Economic Order

13.1. Changes in the Institutional Framework

Japan's independence

Japan regained its independence on 28 April 1952 as the San Francisco Peace Treaty signed in September 1951 came into effect.[1] The Allied Occupation, that had lasted nearly seven years, finally came to an end. Even with the restoration of independence, however, Japan still faced a number of problems before it could achieve a complete return to the international community in the greatly changing climate of the post-war period, particularly the intensifying East–West conflict. Japan's tasks included resumption of normal relations with the Eastern-bloc countries and reparations negotiations. Accordingly, the first order of business for newly independent Japan was to build a framework of post-war international relations, including resumption of diplomatic relations with the USSR, membership of the United Nations, and reparation negotiations with the countries of South-East Asia.

The restoration of independence was also a catalyst for producing major changes in the existing political and economic framework. During the Occupation, SCAP was of decisive importance in every aspect of Japan's political and economic life. Independence meant that the government no longer faced the severe restriction of having to coordinate its policymaking processes with the Occupation Forces. Of course, Japan's internal and external policies did not begin to develop in autonomous directions totally unrelated to past practices; that would not have been possible, because the Japanese government at the time attached great importance to relations with the US in the international climate of the Cold War. Independence, however, marked a significant turning point for Japan as it began to play its own role in the international community exercising its own responsibility, and to devote its creativity and energy to rebuilding and sustaining its economy.

With sovereignty restored, Japan began to reassess the various policies implemented during the Occupation and seek new policy measures that would meet the objective of achieving a self-supporting economy. As will be discussed below, a reassessment of Occupation policies had already begun towards the end of the Occupation, as directed by SCAP. The new circumstances, however, created new problems. Of particular importance was the fact that political conflicts now became constraints in formulating and implementing necessary policies. During this period, various political views emerged over the question of the direction in which an independent Japan should develop. Being deprived of an arbitrator with absolute authority—the Occupation Forces—the nation followed a tortuous, confused path in formulating its policies. A number of diverse political forces emerged as a result of successful democratization of political life. They advocated their particular views, constantly changing their alignment and preventing the formation of stable political groups in the Diet. This transient chaos of political realignment emerged as soon as the Occupation ended and independence was regained.

A chaotic political situation

Even before independence, various political parties and factions were quick to express their criticism of the political stance of the Yoshida Cabinet, which championed the San Francisco Peace Treaty. There was strong opposition from leftist groups, who branded the treaty as being one-sided. The conservative camp was also showing signs of division. The depurging of political and business leaders carried out before independence allowed Ichiro Hatoyama, Taketora Ogata, Nobusuke Kishi, and others to return to the central political arena and to begin making moves towards political realignment.

These moves threw post-independence politics into confusion, creating a backlog of badly needed legislation. This is exemplified by the failure of the Diet to pass the budget for fiscal year 1953 on time, which forced the government to resort to a temporary budget for the first four months of the fiscal year. The political instability drew criticism from all corners of society. On 21 April 1953, for example, the four major business organization—Keidanren (the Japan Federation of Economic Organizations), Nissho (the Japan Chamber of Commerce and Industry), Nikkeiren (the Japan Federation of Employers' Association), and Keizai Doyukai (the Japan Committee for Economic Development)—jointly urged political leaders to form a stable government. This action reflected their dissatisfaction over the competition for leadership within the conservative camp, which was wasting valuable time needed for thoroughgoing debate on comprehensive policy from a long-term perspective that aimed at economic independence. As a remedy, some business leaders proposed reorganization of the conservative political parties. There was also a move within the fragmented reformist camp, centred on Sohyo (the General Council of Trade Unions of Japan), to seek unification of the disjointed Socialist Party.

Until the 1955 merger of the conservative forces, therefore, various power groups in both political camps sought ways to reunite within themselves, jockeying for leadership, and they inched their way towards a new political order. This was a long process towards a new political framework suitable for the new environment created by independence. The development of events leading to the conservative merger will be discussed later. At this point, the focus of this analysis returns to the period immediately prior to independence in order to identify important changes about to take place, as they related to trade and industrial policy.

13.2. Reassessment of Occupation Policy

The Ridgway announcement

The impending end of the Occupation prompted an overall revision of economic policy.[2] That is not to say, of course, that all the measures for economic democratization adopted and implemented by the Occupation Forces were questioned and re-examined. Revision was made only to those portions of measures considered unfitting to Japanese institutions or needing modification in view of the realities of Japan's political and economic situation. Many in the business community, in particular, were convinced that the democratization measures were depriving Japan's economy, industry, and corporations of their vitality, and strongly voiced their demand for change. Their wish for such a policy reversal was the background to their criticism of the political situation.

The reassessment effort was triggered by a statement issued by General Ridgway on 1 May 1951. Ridgway announced that SCAP was prepared to relax its Occupation policies in view of the impending conclusion of the peace treaty, and, as a link in the process, it was authorizing the Japanese government to re-examine existing laws and ordinances promulgated to carry out SCAP directives.

Being granted authority to reassess Occupation policies and make necessary revisions in them prior to restoration of sovereignty, the Japanese government commenced a full-scale re-examination of policies at each ministry, covering a wide range of economic democratization and demilitarization measures adopted earlier. These measures included ordinances and orders issued, *pro forma*, in connection with Japan's acceptance of the terms of the Potsdam Declaration. Measures such as these, institutionalized without due legislative process, had to be reviewed and presented anew as needed, as part of overall reorganization of laws and ordinances.

Repeal of laws and ordinances

Of the democratization measures subject to reassessment, the laws and ordinances relating to the dissolution of the zaibatsu had by and large fulfilled their purposes during the Occupation, as described in Part I. They included, for instance: the Holding Company Liquidation Commission Ordinance, the Law for the Termination of Zaibatsu Family Control, the Elimination of Intercorporate Security Ownership Ordinance, and the Ordinance Concerning the Restriction of Employment of Former Directors and Officers of Mitsui and Company and Mitsubishi Corporation (Ordinance 340, 21 Nov. 1950).

Not all the laws and regulations considered for abrogation were repealed immediately. For instance, the Law for the Elimination of Excessive Concentration of Economic Power and the Enterprise Reconstruction and Reorganization Law were not immediately repealed. Although the basic objectives of both laws had been met, the approval and implementation processes of corporate division and reconstruction plans had not been completed. The Deconcentration Law was finally repealed in 1955, but only after it was clear that surveillance of de-designated corporations and elimination of the abuses of monopoly as stipulated by the law were to be dealt with by applying the Anti-Monopoly Law. The Reconstruction Law remained in force, after it was amended in April 1954 to expedite final disposition of wartime accounts.

Other repealed laws and ordinances included ordinances relating to reparations and laws relating to post-war control of the supply of commodities. As was discussed in Part II, a variety of ordinances regulating the maintenance and management of facilities designated for reparations removals were promulgated in the stern post-war climate of all-out disarmament and exaction of reparations in kind. With the reversal of Occupation policy, however, these ordinances lost their significance. Other laws for dealing with the confused post-war economic conditions required revision or repeal after controls were lifted. Measures were introduced as needed for these laws. For example, the Temporary Commodity Supply and Demand Control Law was retained, but its purpose was limited to regulating the distribution and consumption of commodities in short supply worldwide.

Disbanding of the Public Utilities Commission

Another controversial issue was the continued existence of the system of administrative agencies introduced as a new system of administrative organization during the Occupation among other democratization measures.[3] There were strong sentiments favouring revision of the system to make it more fitting to the conditions of Japanese society. Agencies that were independent from the executive, judicial, and legislative bodies, and not bound by Cabinet decisions, caused problems because they made it difficult to maintain uniformity of administration conducted by ministries and other executive agencies. Of the various agencies relating to trade and industry administration, except for the Fair Trade Commission, the main targets of reassessment and wholesale revamping were the Public Utilities Commission and the Foreign Exchange Control Commission.

The Public Utilities Commission, established in December 1950, was responsible for regulating the electric power industry, which was reorganized in November. As a result of the reorganization, nine private electric power companies were established and the Commission replaced the Agency of Natural Resources as the agency responsible for regulating them. However, subsequent actions by the Commission—including actions related to electric power rates and the question of who would take the initiative in promoting the development of electric power—led to serious conflicts with the Economic Stabilization Board, MITI and other ministries, and the Liberal Democratic Party then in power. For those and other reasons, the Public Utilities Commission was abolished in August 1952, and MITI's Public Utilities Bureau became the new agency for electric power administration.

From the start, however, the administration of the Public Utilities Bureau faced a serious inadequacy of legal provisions for administering the electric utilities industry. For example, although the Public Utilities Ordinance and others proclaimed under the authority of the Potsdam Ordinance were due to expire 180 days after the peace treaty went into effect, no legal provisions had been made to replace them. Worse yet, the bill for the Law for Temporary Measures on Electricity and Gas Utilities, submitted to the Diet for a *de facto* extension of the existing provisions, failed to pass the 13th and 14th sessions of the Diet. It was finally passed by the 15th Diet, convened in December 1952. Although what was needed first was a basic re-evaluation of laws related to the electric power industry, as well as action to put into order permanent legislation for promoting a system of electric power administration suitable for industrial rationalization policy, administrative reorganization was carried out before such action was taken. Early in 1953, therefore, MITI established a council to study revision of the electricity and gas utilities law, and the council eventually provided MITI with a report on permanent legislation. In discussions about the bill for the new Electric Utilities Industry Law, opinions were sharply divided between MITI and the electric power industry. In relation to the monopolistic supply of power in designated areas, MITI also wanted to allow the supply of power to specific non-designated areas, but the industry opposed that idea. The legislation was further postponed because MITI and the Ministry of Construction held differing opinions concerning the validation of water rights. Finally, after many twists and turns, the new Electric Utilities Industry Law was enacted in July 1964; over the many years until that law was enacted, the unusual situation of a temporary measures law governing the administration of electric utilities continued.

Disbanding of the Foreign Exchange Control Commission

Two other administrative agencies that became targets of reorganization were the Foreign Exchange Control Commission and the Foreign Capital Commission, both established to control foreign-currency transactions.[4] The Ministry of Finance initiated the examination of the agencies, focusing on the relationships between the ministry, the Bank of Japan, and the Foreign Exchange Control Commission. For its part, MITI took the position of studying from its own perspective ways to rationalize the foreign-exchange control system as part of the overall administrative system related to international trade. In particular, MITI wanted to study specific measures for handling the control of international trade and foreign exchange as an integral whole.

In those days, actual management of the foreign-exchange budget was highly fragmented. MITI handled those aspects of the budget relating to imports and exports, and payments and receipts of foreign currency relating to trade; the Foreign Capital Commission handled those relating to foreign investment; and the Ministry of Finance handled the rest. With regard to international claims, MITI handled those relating to international trade; the Foreign Exchange Control Commission handled settlements of short-term commercial transactions; the Foreign Capital Commission dealt with those relating to foreign investment; and the Ministry of Finance handled the rest. Coordination among these organizations was a major problem.

MITI expressed several basic criticisms concerning the system of foreign-exchange control. The basic policy relating to foreign exchange, for example, which served as the foundation of the foreign-exchange budget, was formulated from the diverse standpoints of agencies such as the Foreign Exchange Control Commission, in charge of managing foreign currencies, and the Ministry of Finance, responsible for coordinating international finance. It was extremely unclear where the responsibility was located for integrating and coordinating differing opinions. Foreign-exchange control and the management of foreign currencies were completely separate activities, and international trade policy was subordinated to the nation's foreign-currency position. Furthermore, duplication in the areas of responsibility of the various agencies in the overall organization for controlling foreign exchange wasted time and expense. As a result, banks dealing in foreign-exchange transactions and companies engaged in international trade had to overcome a number of bureaucratic barriers, and thus could not act quickly.

In order to resolve these problems, MITI studied measures with the basic aims of clarifying the jurisdiction of foreign-exchange control, achieving overall coordination of foreign-exchange administration, and simplifying and normalizing foreign-exchange control. Negotiations with the Ministry of Finance and other concerned agencies led in the spring of 1952 to a government decision to disband the Foreign Exchange Control Commission and Foreign Capital Commission, and a new system of foreign-exchange control was put into place.

Under the new system, a Cabinet council was established and made responsible for formulating the foreign-exchange budget. Headed by the Prime Minister, the council members included the Ministers of Finance, Agriculture and Forestry, International Trade and Industry, and Transport, as well as the Director-General of the Economic Deliberations Agency. The Finance Ministry became responsible for managing foreign currency and the foreign-exchange funds special account. MITI, in charge of controlling international trade and foreign-exchange transactions relating to trade—under the principle of unified control of international trade and foreign exchange—became responsible for formulating the foreign-exchange budget as it related to international trade. As a consequence, MITI acquired, as discussed below, a powerful policy tool for fostering and promoting high-priority industries through the use of approvals and validations related to foreign-exchange control.

Resumption and promotion of arms and aircraft industries

With Japan's disarmament in mind, the prohibition of ordnance industries was an aspect of Occupation policy designed to prevent a resurgence of militarism. To that end, many of the machines and much of the equipment of the war industries were earmarked for reparations removal. As related earlier, however, this stern disarmament policy was gradually relaxed as the international environment changed. With US cooperation, Japan began looking for ways to rearm itself and resume production of arms and aircraft, against the background of the Korean War and establishment of the National Police Reserve.[5]

The reversal of Occupation policy became evident in March 1952 when SCAP approved arms manufacturing. The fact that such a policy reversal was made on the eve of Japan's independence suggested that the US had an urgent need for the repair and production of arms as the Korean War intensified.

Concerning the resumption of arms manufacturing, MITI's basic policy is said to have vacillated between defining the arms and aircraft industries as special-procurement industries or as ordnance industries with a prospect of rearmament. Although the nature of the demand for special procurements gradually shifted from mere repair of arms to their manufacture, the government found it difficult to adopt a policy of fostering ordnance industries when its policy towards rearmament was still indeterminate. In that situation, the government in the summer of 1952 adopted a policy of protecting the arms and aircraft industries as special-procurement industries. Pursuing this policy, the government fostered and protected the arms industry through such programmes as transferring former Imperial Army and Navy arsenals to private ownership and curtailing competition for orders. One problem that arose in this process, as noted earlier, was that expiration of the Potsdam Ordinance in October 1952 invalidated the legal basis for permitting arms manufacturing based on SCAP directives. Accordingly, MITI formulated the Ordnance Manufacturing Law, coordinated arms-manufacturing activities, and required prior approval for arms manufacture to prevent overproduction.

US special procurements were key to the development of mass-production systems by the arms-manufacturing industry. But the rapid decline in special procurements following the cessation of hostilities in Korea in 1953 meant that the arms industry could no longer be called a special-procurements industry. In June 1954, the US–Japan Mutual Defence Assistance Agreement was signed under the provisions of the Mutual Security Act of the United States. The Defence Agency was established, and the Self-Defence Forces were also inaugurated at that time. Accordingly, it became necessary to maintain the arms-manufacturing industry. A new policy was thus adopted, maintaining and fostering the arms industry as a defence industry under the assumption that the special-procurements demand from the US military would end. In fiscal year 1956, subsidies for maintaining defence-industry facilities were granted to the arms industry, over half of whose productive facilities were idle. The subsidies were granted from the standpoint of preserving the nation's defence base to meet the demand for increased defence capabilities under the US–Japan Security Treaty.

The Aircraft Manufacturing Law, meanwhile, was enacted in haste in July 1952 in response to the problem—as with the arms industry—of resuming aircraft manufacturing after expiration of the Potsdam Imperial Ordinance. As with arms manufacturing, the immediate purpose of resuming aircraft manufacturing was to meet the demand for repairing US warplanes. MITI, however, characterized this industry as an integrated machinery industry requiring highly advanced technology, one whose development should be promoted from the standpoint of greater technological sophistication of the nation's overall industrial structure. It considered aggressively providing assistance to the industry to ease problems such as insufficient demand, difficulty in procuring funds, technological backwardness, inadequacy of the industries supplying key materials to it, and underdeveloped corporate organizations. In November 1952, therefore, the Minister of International Trade and Industry requested the Aircraft Manufacturing Council to study and report on measures for promoting rehabilitation of the Japanese aircraft industry. The report of the Council submitted to the minister in June 1953 concluded that a long-term plan had to be formulated for rebuilding the aircraft industry. It suggested, as positive support measures, acceleration of capital accumulation through tax reductions under preferential tax measures; priority foreign-exchange allocations for imports; mediation with the Japan Development Bank for procuring funds; and priority allocation of testing and research subsidies and industrialization subsidies. The conceptual framework for these measures had much in common with the policy scheme embodied in the Machinery Industry Promotion Temporary Measures Law and the Electronics Industry Promotion Temporary Measures Law that were to follow. The Council's report pointed out that in the aircraft industry—as in the arms industry—legislation of an 'industry law' requiring government approval for opening a business in the industry was essential.

Following the policy just described, the Aircraft Manufacturing Industry Law was enacted in June 1954, and the promotion of the aircraft industry began in earnest. A series of measures were subsequently implemented, including a programme for promoting domestic production of jet aircraft following the increase in defence demand; the commencement of the YS-11 airplane development programme for the domestic manufacture of medium-size commercial airplanes; the promulgation in 1958 of the Aircraft Industry Promotion Law; and the establishment of Nihon Aeroplane Manufacturing Co. Ltd.

13.3. Merger of Conservative Parties and the Reorganization of Business Organizations

The Hatoyama Cabinet's reassessment of Occupation policy

Prime Minister Shigeru Yoshida held power during the Occupation and into the post-independence period. He faced a rising popular distrust of politics, however, propagated by the Hozen Keizaikai scandal—which became a political issue in January 1954—and the 'shipbuilding scandal'. His Cabinet resigned *en bloc* in December, putting an end to his seven-year-long regime.

A new Cabinet led by Ichiro Hatoyama of the Japan Democratic Party was formed on 10 December to succeed the Yoshida Cabinet. The main policies of the new government were the promotion of 'peace diplomacy' centring on Soviet–Japanese negotiations, and preparations for constitutional amendment. This policy orientation had the following background. The peace that was won by the Yoshida Cabinet was criticized as being one-sided in favour of maintaining harmonious relations with the US. Hatoyama wanted to correct the imbalance by restoring diplomatic relations with the USSR, thereby completing Japan's return to the international community. Furthermore, the chaotic political situation after the peace treaty was based on a sharp ideological confrontation, as symbolized by the expression 'reverse course', concerning the defence issue and interpretation of the Constitution. A radical dissolution of this confrontation, Hatoyama believed, required a constitutional amendment. Thus, the Hatoyama Cabinet's tasks were, in a broad sense, a reassessment of and an adjustment to Occupation policy.

Chances for a constitutional amendment became remote, however, when the conservative camp failed to secure two-thirds of the seats in the House of Representatives. Meanwhile, the negotiations with the USSR did not proceed smoothly, because of territory issues, and were frequently suspended. As early fulfilment of its campaign pledges became difficult, the Hatoyama Cabinet experienced difficult times in the Diet. For example, the regime had earlier announced its intention to study new economic policy measures by first formulating a long-term economic plan based on the six-year plan for economic self-support being developed by the Economic Deliberations board, but because formulation of a plan was delayed until December 1955, tentative measures had to be taken to deal with pressing problems, while the exercise to develop the long-term plan continued.

The conservative merger and the conclusion of the Japan–USSR negotiations

In the autumn of 1955 the chaotic political situation suddenly entered an entirely new phase. The two Socialist parties succeeded in increasing their Diet seats in the February 1954 election with the slogan 'a new government with the unified Socialist Party!' The parties unified themselves at a joint meeting in October and unanimously adopted a new party platform. This solid move towards the formation of a unified Socialist Party became a catalyst for the unification of the disunited conservative groups. Although serious confrontations often stalled talks, the contentious groups finally reached agreement. The most serious point of contention between the Liberal Party and the Japan Democratic Party was about who would lead the new party. This question was solved by appointing a committee for the interim. In November, one month after the unification of the Socialist Party, a joint meeting of the conservative groups was held and the new Liberal Democratic Party was created, giving the conservatives 299 of the 467

House of Representative seats and 118 of the 250 House of Councillors seats. Japan's politics then entered a period of confrontation between two major parties, conservative and reformist, with the Liberal Democratic Party holding a stable majority and remaining in power for many years.

The conservative merger did not immediately stabilize the political situation. The Hatoyama Cabinet confronted the Socialist Party concerning such major bills as the Small Electoral District Bill, the new Board of Education Bill, the National Defence Council Bill, and the Commission on the Constitution Bill. The government's hard-line attitude towards the opposition, relying on its majority position, generated continuous turmoil in the Diet, leaving the strong impression of a conservative–reformist confrontation in the public's mind. Among the bills listed above, however, all but the Small Electoral District bill were passed. The budget bill for fiscal year 1956 also passed the House of Councillors in its original form prior to 31 March, the end of the fiscal year. This was significant, because a budget bill had not passed in its original form before the beginning of the fiscal year since the 1952 budget. In other words, because the party in power controlled nearly two-thirds of the lower house seats, the dynamics of the Diet's voting patterns changed drastically. This development, as discussed later, brought about a major change in the process of economic policy formulation.

Meanwhile, the Japan–USSR negotiations—an important task for the Hatoyama Cabinet but which had been suspended from September 1954—were resumed in January 1955. They had to be suspended again, however, because of opposition within the Liberal Democratic Party and negative public reaction, both caused by the territorial issue. In the end, Prime Minister Hatoyama decided to shelve the territorial issue and bow out of the premiership on the occasion of resuming diplomatic relations. In October, Japan and the USSR signed a joint declaration, normalizing Japan's relations with the Eastern-bloc countries. Normalization had been a pending issue since the San Francisco Peace Treaty, and the joint declaration thus further advanced Japan's return to the international community. Symbolic of this return was the fact that the UN Security Council unanimously voted for Japan's UN membership on 12 December, the day the joint declaration came into effect. Japan became the eightieth member of the United Nations.

Reorganization of business organizations

With the advent of independence, various restrictions on the activities of business organizations were gradually relaxed. The question of reorganizing the organizations surfaced as hopes were pinned on renewing their activities. The question suddenly assumed concrete form when, in February 1952, President Aiichiro Fujiyama of Nissho (the Japan Chamber of Commerce and Industry) made a proposal on reorganization to President Ichiro Ishikawa of Keidanren (Japan Federation of Economic Organizations).[6]

Until then, on behalf of the business organizations active during the Occupation, Keidanren had energetically expressed the views of the business community regarding the formulation of economic policy. Besides Keidanren, there were two other major business organizations: Nikkeiren (the Japan Federation of Employers' Associations) and Keizai Doyukai (the Japan Committee for Economic Development). Nikkeiren was an organization of employers for dealing with labour and employment matters. Keizai Doyukai was not so much a business organization as a forum for expressing the views of business leaders. Keidanren came into being when the Keidanren Committee formed in August 1946 was reorganized and expanded into a federation of business organizations, including the five majors: the Council for Financial Organizations, the Japan Industrial Council, the Japan Chamber of Commerce and Industry, the Japan Foreign Trade Association, and the Japan Small and Medium Business Federation. Because of its make-up, Keidanren played a major role during the period when there were problems and objectives of national importance such as economic reconstruction. In those days, it was important that the views of the business community be coordinated and reflected in the formulation of economic policy. That way the collective will of the business community could be channelled towards resolving fundamental problems of national importance. As the economy gradually recovered, however, and the chances increased greatly of conflict among different economic interests, it became steadily more difficult for business organizations with different interests—such as the five major organizations comprising Keidanren—to work in unison towards realization of desired policy measures. As larger compromises gradually had to be forced to reach a unified position, each member organization found it increasingly difficult to keep its members satisfied. In the new era of independence, it became necessary to reorganize Keidanren so that each member organization could move in the direction it wanted.

The Japan Small and Medium Business Federation and the Japan Chamber of Commerce and Industry left Keidanren to follow their own paths during the period between July and September of 1952. Keidanren, meanwhile, absorbed the Japan Industrial Council, reorganized itself anew, and began operating as a comprehensive federation largely consisting of industrial associations mainly made up of large corporations. A new order was thus established whereby each business organization was to act to reflect the interests of its members during the process of formulating various economic policies.

Intensified political confrontation and strife

Tanzan Ishibashi, chosen as the second president of the Liberal Democratic Party in December 1956, was elected prime minister in the ordinary session of the 26th Diet called that month, succeeding former Prime Minister Hatoyama whose Cabinet had resigned. The new prime minister pledged to pursue an aggressive economic policy, one which, together with the basic direction of Finance Minister Ikeda's 1957 budget, featured expansionary economic measures under the slogan 'A tax cut of 100 billion yen, new programmes of 100 billion yen'.

Ishibashi, however, did not have an opportunity to implement this policy. He came down with an illness at the end of January 1957, and his Cabinet decided to resign, after having been in office for only nine weeks. Nobusuke Kishi was elected prime minister, and he formed his new government towards the end of February, inheriting nearly all the members of the Ishibashi Cabinet.

The Kishi Cabinet brought about far more changes than a mere transition of power within the Liberal Democratic Party. The most important of these was a diplomatic policy which placed greater emphasis on Japan–US cooperation. Japan's foreign policy had entered a new phase, as membership in the United Nations allowed Japan to rejoin the international community. Under the slogans of creating harmonious relations with the Western-bloc nations, improving relations with the Asian nations, and promotion of UN-centred foreign policy, Prime Minister Kishi reoriented Japan's diplomacy towards closer Japan–US relations. Greater emphasis on relations with the US was necessitated by the need to resolve pending issues, including revision of the US–Japan Security Treaty, restoration of the Ryukyu and Ogasawara Islands to Japanese control, and the new problem of restrictions on US imports of Japanese goods that had become pronounced in the US starting around 1956.

The Kishi Cabinet also decided on head-on confrontation with the newly reorganized Sohyo (the General Council of Trade Unions of Japan) and Nikkyoso (the Japan Teachers' Union) in the areas of labour and educational policies. Labour reacted vehemently to this stance, which changed the nature of the dynamics of Japan's domestic politics from one dominated by confrontation between the conservative parties to one of acrimonious confrontation between conservative and reformist camps. The Kishi Cabinet's hard-line position was evident in its enforcement—against vehement opposition—of an efficiency rating system for teachers, and its requirement for inclusion of moral education in school curricula. The parliamentary fight over the proposed amendment to the Law Concerning the Execution of Duties of Police Officials (Law 136, 12 July 1948) further aggravated the confrontation between the two camps. The 29th Diet was thrown into pandemonium by arguments over the Police Officials Bill and ended with a large number of unpassed bills, including the Bill to Amend the Police Officials Law, the Bill to Amend the Anti-Monopoly Law, the Bill to Amend the Public Office Election Law (Law 100, 15 April 1950; effective 1 May 1950), the Bill to Amend the Broadcasting Law, Minimum Wage Bill, the Bill to Amend the Export and Import Transaction Law, Factory Waste Regulation Bill, the Bill for Special Measures for Retail Trade, and the Bill for the Flotation of Foreign Currency Bond to Raise Funds for Loans in the Industrial Investment Special Account.[7]

In the following year (1959), the conservative–reformist confrontation intensified over the proposed revision of the US–Japan Security Treaty. While the Japanese government prepared for revision of the treaty, a move against the Treaty of Mutual Cooperation and Security between the United States and Japan (the New Security Treaty) saw the coalescence, towards the end of March 1959, of over 100 organizations. These included the Socialist Party, Sohyo (the General

Council of Trade Unions of Japan), and Gensuikyo (the Japan Council against Atomic and Hydrogen Bombs), who together formed the People's Council to Prevent the Security Treaty Revision. Involving diverse groups of scholars and men and women from the arts and literature, the movement spread to every level of society in a manner unprecedented in Japan's history, throwing the nation into utter chaos. In the midst of this confrontation, the new Security Treaty was signed in Washington on 19 January 1960, and the focus thus shifted to the treaty's ratification by the Diet. The confrontation between the conservative and the reformist camps, both inside and outside the Diet, continued to intensify until ratification was approved automatically in June.

The Diet's role of mediating among conflicting interests was often precluded by confrontations between the conservative and reformist camps or among factions within the conservative camp. As brutal political confrontations took precedence, moreover, discussions of bills relating to important government policies were often left unfinished. In attempting to prevent proposed policies from being used as political tools, the responsibility of the ministries and agencies which formulated and implemented the policies was all the heavier. They played an important role in this process, developing policies from a long-term perspective. The accumulated effect of the policies propelled the Japanese economy forward to a period of high-level growth.

NOTES

1. Concerning the political trend discussed in Sections 1 and 3 of this chapter refer, as a first step, to MITI, Committee to Edit History of International Trade and Industry Policy, *Tsusho Sangyo Seisakushi* (History of International Trade and Industry Policy), v, ch. 1, sect. 1, Tsusho Sangyo Chosakai (Research Institute of International Trade and Industry), 1989.
2. Ibid. 5, ch. 2, sect. 1, for a discussion of the details concerning reassessment of Occupation policy.
3. Ibid. vii (1991): 435–41, for a discussion of the details regarding disbanding of the Public Utilities Committee.
4. Ibid. vi (1990): 77–84, for a discussion of the details regarding disbanding of the Foreign Exchange Control Committee.
5. Ibid. v, ch. 2, sect. 1 and vi, ch. 5, sect. 6, for a discussion of details regarding the arms and aircraft industries.
6. For details concerning reorganization of business organizations, see Japan Federation of Economic Organizations (Keizai Dantai Rengokai; Keidanren), *Keizai Dantai Rengokai 10-nenshi* (Ten-Year History of Japan Federation of Economic Organizations), 1963; and *Keizai Dantai Rengokai 30-nenshi* (Thirty-Year History of Japan Federation of Economic Organizations), 1978.
7. *Tsusho Sangyo Seisakushi*, v. 13.

14

The End of Special Procurements, and the Fragile Economic Structure

14.1. Growth and Cycles in the Japanese Economy

Tasks for economic self-support

By the time Japan regained its independence in April 1952, its economy had far surpassed the targets set in the Economic Rehabilitation Plan and the Economic Self-Support Plan formulated for economic reconstruction after the war.[1] The worldwide recession that began in 1951, however, adversely affected the Japanese economy, and production, foreign trade, and price indices all remained flat in a period of extreme sluggishness. Though the post-war recovery had been fast, and economic indices for 1951—as compared with the 1934–6 base period of 100—were 131 for industrial production and 100 for agricultural production, they were 36 for exports (30 if special procurements are excluded), 49 for imports, 86 for consumption, 119 for industrial investments, and 93 for national per capita income. In other words, notwithstanding the recovery in industrial production, foreign trade remained at a very low level. Exports were particularly slow to recover, falling far short of other sectors of the economy. Special military procurements and foreign economic aid allowed Japan barely to maintain equilibrium in its international balance of payments.

A comparison of economic indices with selected Western countries (Figure 14.1) highlights the problem areas of the Japanese economy at this time. The speed of Japan's economic recovery in terms of mining and manufacturing was not much different from that of other countries, except for the US. In volume of trade, however, other countries surpassed their pre-war levels in step with their industrial production levels, and only Japan was exceptionally slow in recovering its pre-war trade levels. The publication *Nenji Keizai Hokoku* (Annual Economic Report) for fiscal year 1953 identified the following three causes of this situation. First, Japan lost all trade with its former colonies and with China, which in total had accounted for roughly 40 per cent of its pre-war exports. Second, raw silk exports, which had been Japan's largest export item to the US, decreased sharply, driven out of the market by synthetic fibres such as nylon. And third, as Asian countries became industrialized, markets for Japanese cotton goods there shrank. The Annual Economic Report then concluded that 'unless Japanese industry

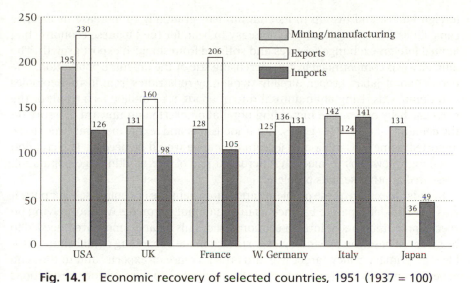

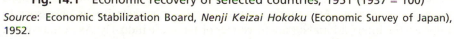

Fig. 14.1   Economic recovery of selected countries, 1951 (1937 = 100)

Source: Economic Stabilization Board, *Nenji Keizai Hokoku* (Economic Survey of Japan), 1952.

improves its structure, the recovery of its export trade over the next few years will be limited to about $1.5 or $1.6 billion, or 40 per cent of its pre-war level.'[2] This unbalanced economic recovery, particularly the sluggishness of exports, revealed more clearly than anything else the fragility of the post-independence Japanese economy.

There was also a danger that economic recovery that relied heavily on special military procurements and foreign aid could lose its momentum once the Korean War came to an end or foreign aid was suspended. In the early 1950s, production costs were generally falling in Japanese industry as the capacity-utilization rate, which declined drastically after the war when facilities were idle, gradually rose. Room for reducing costs further in this way was decreasing, however, as facilities became more fully utilized. It was obvious, therefore, that international competitiveness would have to be improved by other means, such as by introducing advanced technology from abroad and by importing low-cost natural resources and energy. Such industrial rationalization required foreign exchange, which led to strict foreign-exchange controls to prevent foreign-exchange reserves from being depleted. At the same time, exceptionally strict import restrictions could invite rising domestic prices and impede economic development; this was the nature of the dilemma faced by policymakers.

Japan also faced other economic problems after achieving independence. Following its return to the international community, Japan faced the problem of meeting the demands of countries which reserved the right to seek reparations after the Peace Treaty went into effect. Japan also had to repay US aid, service its foreign bonds, and live up to its commitment gradually to increase its defence capabilities. These burdens were not easy to bear, for the Japanese economy had limited foreign-exchange reserves and suffered from sluggish export growth. The difficulty was compounded by the increasing size of the Japanese population. The population of Japan proper, already swollen by repatriates from former colonies and China, was rising at an annual rate of about 1.25 million as a result of the post-war baby boom. The increasing population exerted an upward pressure on the demand for consumer goods. But if foodstuffs and textile materials were to be imported, some $40 million of foreign exchange would be needed. The creation of enough new jobs to meet the increased size of the working age population presented another serious problem.

In order to resolve these problems and attain genuine economic self-support, it was essential for Japan to balance its international payments without relying on special procurements or foreign economic aid. This balance, moreover, needed to be achieved based on expanding exports that made expanding equilibrium possible. The primary policy target was thus the increase of exports, and to that end export-promotion measures were needed, designed to ease various restrictions placed on exporting. As a fundamental solution, moreover, it was necessary to improve the international competitiveness of Japanese industry. As noted earlier, the international political and economic environment surrounding post-war Japan was not conducive to repeating the pre-war pattern of expanding exports with emphasis on textiles. To enhance the competitiveness of exports, therefore, Japan had to foster a set of export industries different from pre-war days. Improved competitiveness was also an important task for industries with poor export prospects because stronger domestic-oriented industries would help reduce imports as the economy became more self-sufficient. And for improving industrial competitiveness and the trade balance, higher labour productivity was crucial. At the same time, if productivity reduced employment opportunities, social unrest might result. It was necessary, therefore, simultaneously to achieve the twin goals of increasing both labour productivity and employment opportunities. The only way for that to happen was by enlarging the economy substantially. Therefore, the primary objectives of policies for attaining economic self-support became the pursuit of economic growth through export promotion and improved competitiveness to support the expansion of exports. To these ends, the government established the Industry Rationalization Council for studying industrial rationalization policy, enacted the Industry Rationalization Promotion Law, and implemented various measures, as described in Part II.

Actually, however, Japan had temporarily to postpone its efforts to balance its international balance of payments. As long as the special-procurements demand contributed to that balance, it was necessary to 'utilize the special procurements effectively for improving the qualitative and substantive dimensions of the economy', and seek to build a foundation on which to build a self-supporting and stable economy. Given the conditions of the Japanese economy in the early 1950s, trying to achieve equilibrium in the international balance of payments without the benefit of special procurements would mean limiting imports to the level of foreign currency earned from exports. Such a policy would force equilibrium on a much smaller economy. Policymakers thus sought ways to foster new export industries by utilizing special-procurement earnings. This effort was frustrated by the high price of Japanese products, the largest obstacle to export growth and a problem difficult to resolve. Thus, the reality of post-independence Japan was such that it still had a long and arduous road to travel before achieving economic self-sufficiency. It had to strengthen its international competitiveness by modernizing and rationalizing its industry, and it had to cultivate overseas markets while maintaining an orderly pattern of export expansion.

Characteristics of business cycles

For several years after independence, the Japanese economy, characterized by dependence on special procurements and low export levels, experienced repeated short cycles of growth and adjustment (booms and recessions), with patterns shaped by balance-of-payment constraints. As Table 14.1 shows, the growth of the economy in real terms consistently remained in the 5–10 per cent range, while the rate of increase in mining and manufacturing varied widely. During boom periods, when prices rose and production increased, the trade balance showed large deficits caused by rising imports of producer goods and raw materials. Limiting imports to deal with the deteriorating trade balance then led to lower economic growth. These business cycles were thus characterized by cyclical growth swings, alternating between high-growth boom periods and low-growth adjustment periods. During adjustment periods, unemployment rose and the number of bankruptcies, largely in small and medium enterprises, mushroomed, revealing the flimsy underpinnings of the Japanese economy in those days.[3]

Table 14.1 Major economic indicators, 1952–1959

	Economic growth in real terms (%)	Industrial production increase (%)	Change in wholesale prices (%)	Change in consumer prices (%)	Trade balance ($m.)
1952	11.7	7.2	2.2	5.4	−407
1953	6.3	22.1	0.7	6.3	−794
1954	5.8	8.4	−0.7	6.5	−430
1955	8.8	7.6	−1.9	−1.0	−20
1956	7.2	22.4	4.3	0.5	−61
1957	7.6	18.1	3.0	3.0	−454
1958	6.5	0.2	−6.7	−0.5	359
1959	9.2	24.2	1.4	1.0	407

Source: *Tsusho Sangyo Seisakushi* (History of International Trade and Industry Policy), xvi: 88–9.

The pattern of business cycles within the continuing growth trend that characterized this period was shaped, as described above, by the constraints imposed by the international balance of payments of foreign-exchange reserves, which frequently worked as brakes on the economy's growth rate. The long-term objective of management of the economy during this period, therefore, was raising its balance-of-payments ceiling by promoting exports. This was to be accomplished by placing highest priority on improving the international competitiveness of Japanese companies through industrial rationalization. In the short term, however, various stop-go policies were implemented to deal with either an overheated economy or a business slump, with closest attention being paid to trends in the balance of payments. Thus, the necessity to slow the pace of growth each time economic expansion hit the balance-of-payments ceiling was characteristic of the pattern of growth and cycles at least until the mid-1960s.

The business cycles during this period included the consumption boom into 1953, the recession of 1954 brought on by deflationary policies introduced to cope with a balance-of-payments crisis, the 'boom in volume' and Jimmu Boom that started in 1955, the lingering recession known as the 'pan-bottom recession' triggered by the tight-money policy of 1958, and the Iwato Boom that began in 1959. Growth was rapid during each of the upswing phases of these cycles, and sharp declines occurred during the downswing phases. The upturns were sparked by various factors, including an improvement in the global economy, an expansion in exports, a rise in domestic consumption, or brisk investment in plant and equipment—all interacting in various configurations and varying in relative importance from recovery to recovery. The cause of the slowdowns, however, was universal: a foreign-exchange crisis caused by deterioration in the international balance of payments prompted the introduction of tight-money policies which led to recession.

For instance, the serious disequilibrium in the international balance of payments in 1953 prompted the Bank of Japan to introduce a restrained credit policy in September 1953. This move was followed by a contractionary budget for fiscal year 1954. The 1954 recession caused by these contractionary monetary and fiscal measures resulted in falling prices and shrinking imports, an increased number of business failures, and 600,000 unemployed, which far exceeded the comparable unemployment statistics of 400,000 during the recession brought on by the Dodge Plan.

In 1955, however, exports expanded as the global economy continued to prosper, raising Japan's balance-of-payments surplus to $540 million, roughly equal to the special-procurements earnings of $570 million. The achievement of this long-awaited equilibrium in the balance of payments without relying on special procurements signified progress in the normalization of the economy.[4] As a result of this business upturn, known as the 'boom in volume', national per capita income in real terms and mining and manufacturing production reached their pre-war/wartime peak levels, which meant that the objective of economic recovery was more or less met in 1955.

Although the objective of restoring a self-supporting economy was thus attained in 1955 or shortly thereafter, the prosperity did not last long. With a background of high-level economic expansion, supply bottlenecks began to appear in key industries from around the summer of 1956. Once into 1957, the international balance of payments began to worsen, and in the spring of 1957 it was obvious that the worsening foreign-exchange position could no longer be ignored. The government thus imposed tight-money measures to improve the payments imbalance, and in June, as a part of overall emergency measures for improving the balance of payments, decided to defer the Fiscal Investment and Loan Programme.

The lingering recession that followed was called the 'pan-bottom recession'. From autumn 1958, however, business recovered rapidly. In December, mining and manufacturing levels exceeded the peaks attained during the Jimmu Boom, and production continued to grow sharply even in 1959. The period of prosperity that began in autumn 1958 lasted for more than three years. Meanwhile, capital investments rose in the backdrop of the National Income Doubling Plan and other growth policies announced in 1960 by the government and of the imminent liberalization of international trade that was expected following implementation of the Outline of the Liberalization Plan for Foreign Trade and Foreign Exchange. Existing industries such as metals, cars, and machinery invested heavily in automation, riding on the crest of a wave of technological innovation. Newer industries, meanwhile, such as synthetic fibres and petrochemicals, invested aggressively in new plant and equipment to build a foundation for growth. The Japanese economy thus started on a path towards an era of full-scale, high-level growth.

14.2. The Transformation of the Economic Structure

The rationalization of industry

The engine that drove the economy towards the attainment of the long-cherished goal of self-sufficiency, though with short-term fluctuations, and opened the door to a subsequent era of high growth, was provided by exports and domestic investment in plant and equipment. Although changing conditions in the global economy greatly affected the ups and downs of the Japanese economy, Japan nonetheless managed to achieve economic expansion at a rate exceeding the growth rate of world trade. There was no doubt that this expansion depended heavily on increased exports, as expressed by the concern for balance-of-payments constraints. For this reason, as examined in detail below, a primary objective of economic policy in this period was promoting exports. The principal factor that enabled Japanese exports to grow was the international competitiveness which Japanese industry acquired under the difficult conditions of competing in post-war global markets. Competitiveness, in turn, was attained through aggressive investments aimed at modernizing and rationalizing industries and enterprises. The post-independence Japanese economy had already exhausted the possibility of reducing costs by raising the operating rate, and further growth thus required cost reductions through continuous innovation. Private investment in plant and equipment for modernization and rationalization led to an expansion in domestic investment demand and contributed towards improving the balance of trade by lowering production costs. It also provided the motive power for high-level economic growth.

Increases in capital investment, which bred industrial maturation and provided a base for export expansion, were essential. In terms of the relative size of markets, this explained why economic growth during this period relied more heavily on the domestic than on the export market. According to the report *Boeki Jiyuka to Sangyo Kozo* (Trade Liberalization and Industrial Structure), prepared in 1960 by MITI's Working Group on Industrial Structure, between 1950 and 1958 export markets grew roughly in proportion to the domestic market's growth. Exports, however, 'declined from 13 per cent during 1950–4 to 5 per cent during 1954–8 in terms of their contribution to the growth of the economy measured as a percentage of the increase in GNP', and 'exports as a percentage of aggregate demand fell from 20 per cent in the 1934–6 period to the post-war level of 12 per cent.'[5] The expansion of domestic demand that replaced exports as the engine of growth was brought on by energetic domestic capital investments for rationalization. 'Investment bred further investment' as the plant and equipment needed for rationalization was supplied largely by domestic manufacturers. The circular and self-feeding expansion of the producer goods sector thus provided the motive power for growth.

This investment-led pattern of growth was formed through the government's efforts, against the background of low capital accumulation, to channel public investment and loan resources towards key industries and to direct private investment in the same direction in order to promote investment in rationalization. The government also adopted measures to restrain 'consumption beyond actual means' and to encourage household savings in order to facilitate its priority allocation of financial resources to investment. The following statements in the Economic Survey of Japan at the time of the deflationary policy of 1954 attested to the seriousness of foreign exchange constraints and the urgency of reducing consumption:

Our goal is to improve the balance of payments. The reduction of imports and suppression of domestic purchasing power are necessary means to attain that goal. . . . There is no need to recklessly reduce national income. We can draw closer to achieving our goal if everyone curtails consumption as much as possible and avoids purchasing foreign products to the extent possible. . . . For instance, if everyone reduces consumption of sugar for cooking or for coffee by one teaspoonful a day, our imports will decrease by roughly $10 million a year, which can be used to import materials for our heavy industries.[6]

Post-war economic reforms involving various democratizing measures made it easier for consumption demand to grow, as compared to pre-war years. As a result, consumption expenditures grew sharply after the war. For instance, the increase in wage income between 1951 and 1953 generated an increase in real per capita consumption of nearly 30 per cent. Objects of consumption spending spread from daily necessities to luxuries. The Korean War boom spread to the consumer market after a time lag. Having examined this consumption boom, the Economic Survey of Japan for fiscal year 1953 identified the increase in domestic purchasing power as a factor impeding the expansion of exports, which was essential for achieving economic self-support. It argued that the increase in purchasing power was reducing the nation's export capacity, and called this phenomenon the 'export-limiting effect of income'.[7] Because of the strong awareness of the balance-of-payments constraint on growth, there was little understanding in those days that an increase in personal consumption expenditures could contribute to economic growth. On the contrary, consumption was viewed negatively. In fact, the most important domestic demand, in terms of the economic reality at the time, was investment demand; the contribution of consumption demand was relatively small. The report *Boeki Jiyuka to Sangyo Kozo* (Trade Liberalization and Industrial Structure) quoted above also pointed out that the key to growth was capital investment.[8]

The economic structure that emerged during this period led to the assessment that 'in Japan, unlike in other countries, investment in plant and equipment takes precedence over the living conditions of the people in the form of private consumption or home building.'[9] The economic structure that would soon produce high growth was formed during this period, and began to reach full stride.

The shift of industrial structure towards heavy and chemical industries

The pattern of economic growth led by capital investment naturally resulted in the increased production of investment goods and the growth of the heavy and chemical industries, and gradually shaped the structure of Japanese industry into the type prevailing in the advanced industrial countries.

In terms of net domestic product by sector of origin, the proportion of agriculture, forestry, and fisheries decreased from 26.0 per cent in 1950 to 23.1 per cent in 1955, and further to 14.9 per cent in 1960, showing a particularly rapid decline in the second half of the 1950s. This decline was matched by a correspondingly sharp increase in the shares of the mining and manufacturing industries, especially manufacturing. The percentage of mining and manufacturing at 27.7 per cent in 1955 exceeded that of agriculture, forestry, and fisheries. In 1960, moreover, manufacturing alone accounted for 29.2 per cent of net domestic product. Within manufacturing, the percentage of heavy industry rose as a result of the rapid growth of the machinery industry, accompanied by relative declines in the shares of textiles, foodstuff, and others. Specifically, the proportion of the heavy and chemical industries, on an ex-factory basis, rose from just above 42 per cent in 1950 and 1955 to about 55 per cent in 1960, and that of textiles fell from 23.2 per cent in 1950 to 17.5 per cent in 1955, and further sharply down to 12.3 per cent in 1960. As a consequence of these changes, Japan's industrial structure approached those of the US and UK around 1960, as seen in Table 14.2.

These changes in Japan's industrial structure were the results of the different rates of growth of various industries during the second half of the 1950s. Unlike the parallel pattern of expansion of all industries during the reconstruction phase of the first half of the 1950s, the rate of expansion of production among various industries showed marked differences from around 1955, with the rapid expansion of heavy industry contributing to the greater sophistication of the industrial structure of the economy. The machinery industry grew particularly fast between 1955 and 1960, increasing by roughly fourfold during the five years and exceeding the overall more than 2.3-fold increase in the manufacturing industry. These changes are reflected in the figures for the increased production volume of major products shown in Table 14.3. The rapid rate of growth of the machinery

Table 14.2 Industrial structure in Japan, USA, and UK in 1958 (unit: %)

	Japan	USA	UK
Foodstuffs	8.4	11.1	9.2
Textiles	10.1	7.7	13.2
Chemicals	12.6	8.4	8.8
Metals	14.2	15.6 }	52.7
Machinery	32.2	31.7	

Source: Compiled from MITI, Working Group on Industrial Structure, *Boeki Jiyuka to Sangyo Kozo* (Trade Liberalization and Industrial Structure), Toyo Keizai Inc., 1960: 10.

Table 14.3 Output volume of major industrial products (unit: 10,000 tons)

	Coal	Pig-iron	Crude steel	Cotton yarn	Ammonium sulphate	Cement	Paper and pulp	Metal processing machinery
1952	4,336	347	699	35	186	712	105	0.50
1953	4,653	452	766	41	194	877	128	0.77
1954	4,272	461	775	46	208	1,068	136	1.05
1955	4,242	522	941	42	213	1,056	163	0.66
1956	4,656	599	1,111	51	232	1,320	183	1.16
1957	5,173	682	1,257	54	248	1,518	207	2.14
1958	4,967	739	1,212	45	264	1,498	208	2.63
1959	4,726	945	1,663	49	263	1,727	265	3.14

Sources: *Tsusho Sangyo Seisakushi* (History of International Trade and Industry Policy), xvi: 130, 142, 154, 160, and 164, *Sekitan/Kokusu Tokei Nenpo* (Annual Statistics on Coal and Cokes), fiscal year 1955.

industry, in both value and volume terms, symbolized the rapid change in the structure of Japanese industry during this period.

The changing industrial structure was characterized by more than the sharp increase in machinery production. As Figure 14.2 shows, interindustry differences in growth rates were substantial, with such established products as cotton yarn and coal coexisting with rapidly growing new products such as household electric appliances and cars. These changes in the industrial structure were realized as the centre of emphasis shifted from low-productivity to higher-productivity sectors, and from areas with a low degree of processing or low value-added to areas with a higher degree of processing or higher value-added. With these changes, the productivity of the overall Japanese economy improved and high-level growth became a reality.

This increased sophistication of the industrial structure was a result of new investments in developing innovative technology aimed at industrial modernization and rationalization. These investments triggered the development of investment-goods-producing sectors such as steel and machinery in a chain reaction of 'investment breeding further investment'. The increased industrial sophistication was also a result of a series of policy measures introduced to foster the development of new industries. These measures included programmes to promote the development of synthetic fibres (April 1953), plastics (June 1955), petrochemicals (July 1955), and synthetic rubber (July 1959), as well as the Machinery Industry Promotion Temporary Measures Law (June 1956) and the Draft Outline for Promotion of a People's Car (May 1955). The transformation process was facilitated by an ample supply of labour which enabled a smooth adjustment of employment patterns in response to the changing industrial structure. Although real wages tended to rise, these changes in the labour market did not work as a factor limiting economic growth because the modernization of heavy industry substantially raised productivity. Moreover, the increase in demand for such typical consumer durables as home electric appliances and passenger cars, backed by the increased purchasing power of households contributed markedly to the growth of new heavy industries. Towards the end of this period, a new phenomenon known as a consumption revolution began to exert a major impact on economic growth and changes in the economic structure.

The transformation of the trade structure

Exports and imports both grew rapidly, reaching levels in 1959 more than 2.1 times as high as those of 1952. The share of Japan's exports in total world exports rose from 1.5 per cent in 1953 to 3.6 per cent in 1960.

Increased exports came from heavy industry products, mainly machinery. The percentage of heavy industry goods in total exports rose from 29.5 per cent in 1953 to 43.5 per cent in 1960. In terms of individual product categories, cotton fabrics that topped the list of exports in 1955 were replaced by ships in 1958 (Table 14.4). Moreover, heavy industry exports that had consisted largely of steel

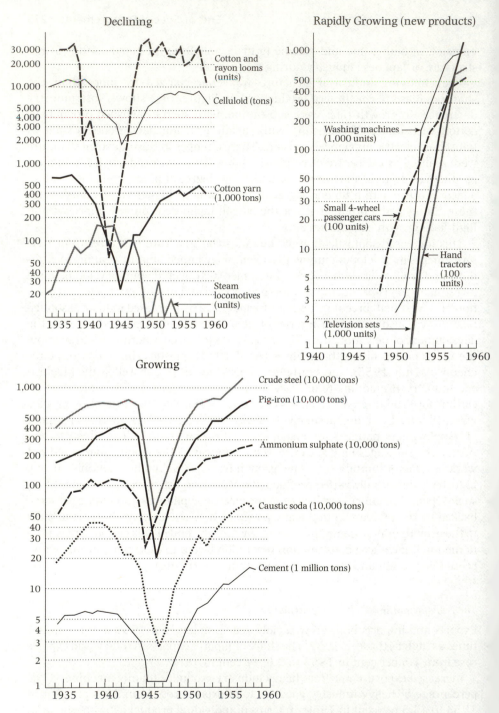

Fig. 14.2 Changing patterns of decline and growth by industry, 1935–1960

Source: Compiled from MITI, Working Group on Industrial Structure, *Boeki Jiyuka to Sangyo Kozo* (Trade Liberalization and Industrial Structure), Toyo Keizai Inc., 1960.

Table 14.4 Trends in Japan's Exports and Imports, 1952–1959

Exports (unit: $m.)

	Grand total	Foodstuffs	Iron and steel products	Machinery and equipment	Cotton fabrics	Rayon fabrics and spun-rayon fabrics
1952	1,273	98.8	263.1	110.1	180.4	65.2
1953	1,275	120.2	139.5	188.7	179.2	72.5
1954	1,629	124.3	167.2	202.3	252.3	102.7
1955	2,011	126.2	259.5	246.8	229.9	143.1
1956	2,501	179.9	223.4	483.6	266.6	210.3
1957	2,858	183.2	209.4	629.6	316.8	227.8
1958	2,877	235.8	249.9	627.4	277.0	188.3
1959	3,456	260.4	252.9	809.5	291.3	161.8

Imports (unit: $m.)

	Grand total	Foodstuffs	Raw cotton	Iron ore	Coal	Crude oil
1952	2,029	651.6	430.3	92.5	83.6	101.7
1953	2,410	624.4	396.5	61.3	89.8	120.5
1954	2,399	653.4	432.2	66.2	63.1	134.0
1955	2,471	625.1	383.2	81.5	56.2	148.6
1956	2,230	558.3	480.4	146.5	90.6	223.8
1957	4,284	574.1	448.0	205.7	174.6	323.5
1958	3,033	529.2	360.9	123.1	96.7	331.4
1959	3,599	497.1	355.3	146.2	88.6	384.8

Source: Compiled from *Tsusho Sangyo Seisakushi* (History of International Trade and Industry Policy), xvi: 238–47.

and ships in previous years became more diversified as radios, motorcycles, cars, and televisions gained relative importance. This expansion of exports was also a factor in the rapid growth of the machinery industry.

The percentage of heavy industry goods in the Japanese export trade increased in response to the changes in Japan's industrial structure. The primary reason for this increase was the marked improvement in the international competitiveness of Japanese heavy industry products. By contrast, cotton fabrics and other light industry products became less competitive because their productivity gains were small while wages moved upwards. The increased production of these goods in developing countries was another reason for the decline in their export growth rates.

Some factors continued to limit the growth of Japanese heavy industry exports. The percentage of total exports accounted for by products from the heavy and chemical industries was still lower than in the advanced Western nations, and there was still a significant difference between the relative importance of the heavy and chemical industries in Japan's industrial structure and in the make-up of its exports. In 1958, the percentage of products from the heavy and chemical industries among all Japanese exports was 39.5 per cent, considerably lower than the 51.3 per cent for the US, 75.8 per cent for West Germany, and 63.0 per cent for the UK.[10]

Among imports, the percentage of textile materials fell and that of metal ores and scrap rose in response to the increasing relative importance of the heavy and chemical industries in the domestic industrial structure. At the same time, machinery imports increased as domestic capital investment activities became vigorous. And while the percentage of foodstuffs in total imports tended downwards as domestic agricultural production expanded steadily during this period, imports of processed goods centring on consumer products tended to increase. This increase reflected the considerable strength of the latent demand for consumer goods that improved the living conditions of the people as the economy moved from the rehabilitation to the self-support phase. As noted earlier, this was in spite of the strict foreign-exchange controls, effectively preventing this latent demand from translating itself into actual demand for imports.

Geographically, the percentage of Japanese exports to industrially advanced countries increased in response to the trend towards expanding trade among these countries. As Figure 14.3 shows, Japan's exports to Asia, which accounted for 63.5 per cent of its total exports in 1934–6, declined sharply in part because trade with China, which had been the largest pre-war export market for Japan, was restricted. In its place, exports to North America rose from 17.4 per cent in 1934–6 to 36.5 per cent in 1959. Besides rapid progress in exports of light industrial products, Japanese exports to the US—which had consisted largely of raw silk before the war—also saw an expansion of heavy and chemical industry products. As a result, in 1959 Japan recorded a surplus of over $100 million in its trade with the US. The increase in the volume of trade among the industrialized countries accelerated the division of labour among them, as trade liberalization

(1)   Exports

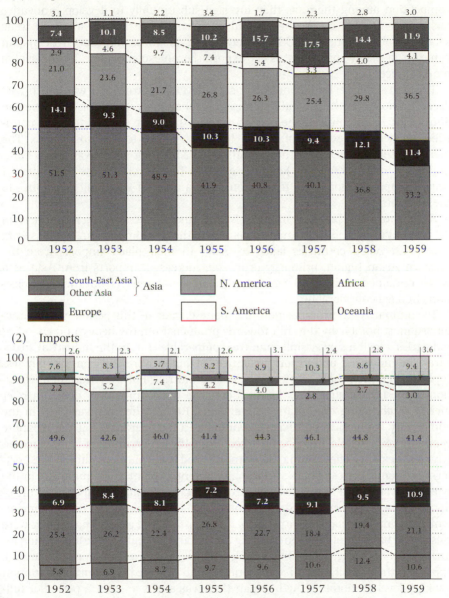

Fig. 14.3 Geographic distribution of Japan's trade, 1952–1959

Source: Prepared from *Tsusho Sangyo Seisakushi* (History of International Trade and Industry Policy).

progressed. On the other hand, the increased trade volumes also intensified the competition among them, as they invested substantially to develop innovative technology centred on the heavy and chemical industries. As a result, trade friction problems such as US restrictions on Japanese imports arose. Japan came to face new problems as its exports became competitive in the global market place.

The largest market for Japanese exports to developing countries was South-East Asia. Because of the dwindling foreign-exchange reserves of countries in South-East Asia, however, the growth rates of Japanese exports to these countries, particularly exports of heavy industry goods, tended to decline. The increased self-sufficiency of these countries in consumer goods was also a limiting factor in the growth of Japanese exports. To overcome these difficulties, it became important for Japan to promote programmes of economic assistance to these countries.

As for sources of Japanese imports, North America, accounting for more than 40 per cent of Japan's total imports, remained the most important. Imports from South-East Asian countries failed to grow. In their place, imports from the Western Asian region, primarily crude oil, increased. Imports from Asia as a whole remained at about 30 per cent of Japan's total imports, but their composition changed considerably.

To summarize, the composition of Japanese trade in this period was characterized most notably by the shift towards products from the heavy and chemical industries, albeit a slower shift than the comparable shift in the industrial structure. The industrial and export structures of Japan were still considerably less sophisticated than those in more advanced countries, but they were in a transition to the typical structures found there. The word 'transition' does not refer merely to changing quantitative dimensions. Rather, the backwardness in the commodity composition of exports worked as a factor preventing the Japanese economy as a whole from being freed from the constraints of a balance-of-payments ceiling. The limiting factor manifested itself in the repetition of short-term economic cycles, where surging investment in plant and equipment in the heavy and chemical industries was next curbed by stabilization measures introduced to correct an emerging trade imbalance. Successive boom periods, meanwhile, gradually became more prolonged, suggesting that expanding exports were raising the balance-of-payments ceiling and adding strength to the foundation for further economic growth. Expanding exports increased aggregate demand, expanded the overall scale of the economy, and provided a favourable situation for high-level economic growth. Japan thus was about to enter a period of full-scale, high-level growth.

Interfirm rivalry and formation of enterprise groups
The leading role in transforming the industrial and trade structures described above was played by fiercely competitive business firms which were strongly

growth-oriented. Influential corporations successfully resolved turbulent labour struggles under management teams which had been rejuvenated by post-war democratization measures. While responding to annual spring offensives in wage negotiations and new labour movements that were to become firmly established after 1955, these corporations energetically expanded their operations through vigorous investment activities. They constantly planned and executed new undertakings to increase production and sales.

In the context of the growing and expanding economy, standing still meant falling behind. It was thus essential to develop a plan which was a step or two ahead of the competition. The Economic Survey of Japan for fiscal year 1954 described the situation by borrowing the following words of the Queen of Hearts in Lewis Carroll's *Through the Looking-Glass*: 'it takes all the running you can do, to keep in the same place. If you want to get somewhere else, you must run at least twice as fast as that!'[11] The situation generated aggressive behaviour such as the 'mutual crushing of exclusive products' among steelmakers, where rival companies ventured into product areas that formerly were the exclusive domain of competitors.[12] And because the emergence of new industries provided many fresh opportunities, companies were eager to enter new fields and diversify their operations. The mushrooming of proposals for large-scale rationalization plans and investment-led growth where 'investment bred further investment' were the results of this type of business behaviour.

The new pattern of interfirm rivalry was an expression of the aggressive market behaviour of younger managers who had moved into leadership positions when ownership and control became separated as a result of the dissolution of the zaibatsu. These young managers responded positively to the competitive market which emerged as zaibatsu companies were broken up by the Deconcentration Law and as the new Anti-Monopoly Law came into effect. Although concentration was still high in some industries, it had declined from pre-war levels. In particular, one-firm concentration 'declined by more than 20 percentage points in the paper, steel, pulp, automobile, beer, and shipbuilding industries'[13] as a result of measures introduced to eliminate excessive concentrations of economic power. Also, competition among oligopolistic firms became keener as post-war economic reconstruction progressed. As Table 14.5 shows, three-firm and ten-firm concentrations declined during this period in all industries except food-processing and the ten-firm concentration for the metal industry. Oligopolistic rivalry intensified as new firms entered the market and smaller firms grew larger in an atmosphere of fierce competition.

As these companies raised funds for capital investment through borrowing, fierce competition had the effect of lowering net worth ratios. The excessive dependence on financing became a target of criticism. Funds were supplied under what was known as the 'main bank system'.[14] The nature of Japan's post-war financial system, characterized as keiretsu financing by former zaibatsu-affiliated banks and the Industrial Bank of Japan, was shaped by the wartime bond formed between corporations and financial institutions. In the post-war system, policy

Table 14.5 Concentration indices by industry (1950 = 100)

	Three-firm		Ten-firm	
	1953	1960	1953	1960
Food processing	101.1	112.9	102.6	115.1
Textiles, paper, and pulp	74.7	65.0	86.5	70.4
Chemicals, petrochemicals, ceramics	95.6	85.5	99.8	92.2
Metals	95.2	92.3	97.8	98.8
Machinery	85.1	80.5	93.1	87.7
Average	90.4	86.9	97.6	95.4

Source: Shuichiro Nakamura *et al.*, *Nihon Sangyo to Kasen Taisei* (Japanese Industry and its Oligopolistic Structure), Shin Hyoron Inc., 1967: 17.

financing was provided first—a form of 'seed' financing developed mainly by the Japan Development Bank in the early 1950s—and then necessary funds were supplied jointly by financial organizations with a main bank in the centre.

The development of this financing system coincided with the development of closer relationships among the companies in each of the three big former zaibatsu groups. They began to form their own 'enterprise groups' through mutual acquisition of stocks and cross-appointments of directors, and each group began to hold periodic meetings of the presidents of member firms. This new form of enterprise group was characterized as a revival of the zaibatsu, but there was an essential difference between the pre-war and post-war forms. Whereas a zaibatsu was a pyramid-shaped combine controlled by a holding company at the top, the new enterprise groupings developed under the Anti-Monopoly Law, which banned holding companies, were characterized by horizontal cross-shareholding among the member companies of each group.

These cross-shareholding relationships had their roots in the large-scale public subscription of shares made when the zaibatsu were dissolved and the large issues of new shares necessitated by the enterprise reconstruction and reorganization programmes. Increased public ownership of shares prompted corporations to seek stronger and more stable shareholders, the need for which became more urgent when, after 1950, incidents of buying up corporate shares became more numerous. These take-over attempts included those on Taisho Marine and Fire Insurance Co. in 1951 and Yowa Real Estate in 1952. The move by corporations to secure 'stable shareholders' made rapid strides in 1952 when an amendment to the Anti-Monopoly Law relaxed the restriction on corporate ownership of the shares of other companies.[15] The move to secure stable shareholders, with able assistance provided by the bank of each keiretsu or other financial institution, solidified the ties among companies in each enterprise group. Between 1951 and 1952, the cross-shareholding percentages of each of the three former zaibatsu groups increased from 1.8 to 10.8 per cent among the eighteen Mitsubishi-affiliated companies, from 0.1 to 10.5 per cent among the twelve Sumitomo-affiliated companies, and from 2.7 to 5.4 per cent among the seventeen Mitsui-affiliated companies. Moreover, the lifting of the ban on the use of zaibatsu trade names and trade marks, implemented in 1952 when Occupation policies were reconsidered, prompted the Chiyoda Bank, Osaka Bank, Teikoku Bank, and others to change their names back to the Mitsubishi Bank, Sumitomo Bank, Mitsui Bank, and so forth, further accelerating the formation of new enterprise groups. At about this time, president clubs were formed and began their activities, including the Hakusuikai (White Water Club) of the Sumitomo group and the Kin'yokai (Friday Club) of the Mitsubishi group.

Other enterprise groups, centring on the Dai-ichi Bank, Sanwa Bank, and Fuji Bank, also gradually cemented their ties. At the time, these three new groups were essentially financial affiliations centred on their respective 'main banks'. It was not until the decade after 1965, on the eve of capital liberalization, that these groups clearly acquired characteristics similar to those of the three former-zaibatsu enterprise groups.[16] Meanwhile, another type of industrial grouping emerged. Unlike the enterprise groups discussed above, in which major corporations were tied horizontally through cross-shareholding relationships, this new type of grouping was vertically organized. It was usually headed by a leading machinery manufacturer exercising control over a pyramid of subsidiaries and subcontractors serving a variety of functions, including the supply of parts, sales, and so forth. Japanese enterprises thus came to be highly organized with leading corporations serving as the nuclei of groups.

As a result of the move towards forming groups, the concentration of capital in the overall economy became greater compared to the increasing oligopolistic competition in each industry. The combined capital of the largest 100 firms as a percentage of total capital in Japan increased rapidly from 32.1 per cent in 1953 to 34.7 per cent in 1958, and then to 39.4 per cent in 1964.[17] In other words, Japan's largest corporations occupying core positions in enterprise groups consistently gained influence over the economy, solidifying the foundation of an economic system dominated by large corporations.

The formation of enterprise groups characterized the industrial and enterprise organization of post-war Japan. One aspect of this system, dubbed the 'enterprise-group one-set principle in new industries', described how each group sought to enter every new industry.[18] It argued that intergroup rivalry for viable presence was the primary reason for the fierce competition among firms representing various groups in each industry. The more important aspect of enterprise grouping, however, lay in the fact that the senior executives of each corporation, who could now rely on stable shareholders through intragroup cross-shareholding, could implement aggressive programmes for corporate growth without fear of external interference with their authority. Moreover, needed funds could be supplied in the form of keiretsu financing from the main bank of a group. Together with this formation of corporate groups, the distinctive characteristics of post-war Japanese corporations, in which the influence of shareholders was weakened, became firmly established.

The strong desire of corporations to invest in plant and equipment often produced ambitious investment projects that exceeded the limit of perennially scarce foreign-exchange reserves. One example, to be described later, was the rationalization plan for the steel industry; MITI agonized over ways to reduce the plan's overall size. Concerning the plan to commercialize the production of synthetic rubber, MITI was compelled to abandon its initial attempt to reduce the number of involved companies to only one. And in its programme for a new petrochemical industry, MITI was kept busy coordinating the large number of plans submitted. Fierce interfirm rivalry created new problems for MITI policymakers during this period in the form of the need to prevent overheating of the economy caused by excessive investment and the need to prevent excessive production capacity from developing.

Dual structure and small and medium enterprises

As economic self-support was achieved, an increasing awareness emerged of various distortions in the economic structure which might impede the economy's further growth. One example that developed from around 1956 was the problem of supply bottlenecks. The crux of this problem was Japan's weak industrial base, the inadequate accumulation of social overhead capital. Specifically, there were inadequacies in such transport facilities as railways, roads and highways, and ports, as well as insufficient supplies of industrial water, that could very well slow down economic growth. Moreover, environmental problems such as land subsidence caused by excessive pumping of industrial water, and problems related to air pollution that had become noticeable in locations where industrial activities were concentrated, came to be recognized as requiring effective countermeasures. Among these problems, one that came to receive much attention during this period was the 'dual-structure' problem. This had to do with structural problems inherent in small and medium enterprises, which had fallen behind in the wave of modernization and rationalization. The problem generated all sorts of debate, and resulted in a variety of positive countermeasures.

Even before the war, marked differences in the scale of business operations were considered characteristic of the Japanese economy. In some industries it was natural for many specialized firms of relatively small size to compete with each other. At the same time, it was considered symptomatic of the structural weakness of the Japanese economy that, compared to advanced Western countries, there were relatively more smaller firms in Japan whose productivity and technical standards were low. Towards the middle of the 1950s, sluggish exports and overproduction by large corporations caused decreases in subcontracting orders and delays in subcontracting payments. As a result, many small and medium enterprises had difficulty remaining in business. During the reconstruction period, business opportunities expanded as business conditions improved, and smaller firms had ample opportunities to develop into large enterprises. The other side of the coin, however, was the very high turnover rate of smaller firms with weak foundations, although this problem did not surface as a serious policy issue when larger corporations were struggling with their rationalization programmes and the economy as a whole was in a tenuous state of being unable to support itself. As the overall economy moved towards reconstruction, the attention of policymakers was narrowly focused on a few key issues. It was believed that all enterprises, regardless of their size, shared equal opportunities and risks.

As the machinery industry grew, however, small and medium enterprises that supplied parts to large corporations became integrated into industrial groups through their subcontracting relationships. With this development, the uncertainty of their business relationships with larger firms and the backwardness of their business operations came to be recognized as serious problems. An awareness also emerged that fostering smaller enterprises capable of supplying high-quality parts could prove to be essential to rationalization of the strategically important machinery industry.[19] Against this background, the Economic Survey of Japan for fiscal year 1957 sought to attract public attention to the problems of small and medium enterprises.[20] The White Paper raised the dual-structure issue as follows: 'In the employment structure of our country, there are, on the one hand, large modern corporations and, on the other, pre-modern small and medium enterprises and family-operated small businesses and farms. The two are poles apart, and the volume of the labour force which does not belong in either category is extremely low.' The White Paper saw a problem in the economic structure of large modern production sectors existing side by side with farming and small-business sectors characterized by labour-intensive production and low productivity and wages. It then argued: 'Full employment, the ultimate objective of the Japanese economy, does not mean simply reducing the number of unemployed workers; rather, it means eliminating the dual structure as the economy grows and becomes modernized.'

The problem was seen as having several dimensions. Full employment received attention partly because the government had listed a solution to the unemployment problem as one of the objectives of its Five-Year Plan for Economic Self-Support. Beyond that, however, it was believed that the low productivity in the small-business sector would work as fetters impeding further development of the economy. From the viewpoint of social policy, meanwhile, improvement of the poor working conditions in the small-business sector was considered essential. There was also concern that large corporations, by taking advantage of their superior economic position, might impose unfair business terms on small subcontractors. It was considered necessary, therefore, to dissolve this dual structure, improve the conditions of underemployment characterized by the low productivity and low wages of small firms, and modernize the small-business sector.

This type of thinking concurred with the conclusion in the final report of the Small and Medium Enterprise Promotion Council submitted in December 1956, which pointed out that 'many small and medium enterprises are still suffering from business stagnation, and the various differences between large enterprises and small and medium enterprises, as well as among small and medium

Table 14.6 Scale differences in selected performance criteria (units: %: 10,000 yen)

	Ratio of net profit to net sales		Rate of earnings on total capital		Capital turnover ratio		Tangible fixed assets per worker	
	Large enterprises	Small and medium enterprises	Large enterprises	Small and medium enterprises	Large enterprises	Small and medium enterprises	Large enterprises	Small and medium enterprises
1953	5.8	2.1	7.2	5.6	1.24	2.61	44	6
1955	3.9	1.2	4.4	2.8	1.13	2.24	61	12
1957	5.6	2.5	6.5	5.8	1.16	2.32	73	12
1959	5.1	2.0	5.4	3.9	1.05	1.92	89	16

Note: 'Large enterprises' are those capitalized at 10 m. yen or more.
Source: Compiled from *Tsusho Sangyo Seisakushi* (History of International Trade and Industry Policy), vii: 9 and 12.

enterprises, are still widening', and that 'the pressure of the ever-increasing number of workers seeking employment makes solution of the small-business problem difficult.'

Aside from such apprehensions, however, a structural change emerged in the labour market during this period that threatened the very existence of small and medium enterprises which relied heavily on low wage rates. High economic growth generated a brisk demand for labour, largely in manufacturing industries, generating a shortage of labour, particularly in the young age-groups. This development had a serious impact on smaller firms which relied heavily on low-cost labour. Furthermore, the rapid growth of the machinery industry from 1955 onwards raised its dependency on smaller firms for producing parts. Large companies raised the standards they demanded of their subcontractors in terms of product quality, cost, and on-time delivery. The effect of these requirements was to demand that small and medium firms shift from operations based on low wages to more modern, rationalized operations.

As Table 14.6 and Figure 14.4 show, however, the difference in net labour productivity between large and small firms consistently widened after 1955 as large enterprises pressed forward with rationalization programmes. Although the diference in wages per worker began to narrow from around 1957, the business operations of small and medium enterprises generally raised their earnings on total capital by offsetting low ratios of net profit to net sales by using high capital turnover rates. Also, the financial structure of smaller firms was yet to be improved. It was pointed out that smaller firms had the following inherent

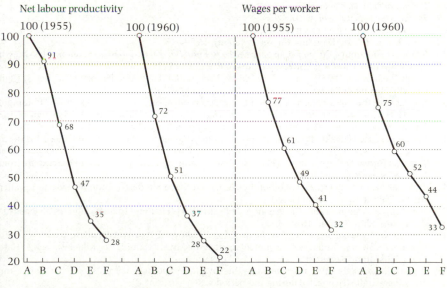

Fig. 14.4 Scale differentials in net labour productivity and wages

problems in the area of finance: their ability to procure funds was limited; their reliance on borrowing was high; their ability to obtain funds was limited due to their poor credit rating; their interest-payment burden was heavy; and their financing was highly subject to variations in money market conditions. These financial constraints worked as serious impediments to the efforts of small businesses to improve the quality of their business operations through modernization and rationalization. For that reason, a large number of very small firms were left behind without having undergone technological transformation. Parent firms in industrial groups had to guide them by instructing them how to improve their technical capabilities. This is an example of the structural problems that remained in the business sector.

NOTES

1. *Tsusho Sangyo Seisakushi*, v, ch. 1, sect. 2, for an initial discussion of economic trends during this period.
2. Ibid. v. 19.
3. Ibid. v. 20–8 and ch. 3, sect. 1.
4. The balance of payments was improved in three principal steps, from a deficit with special procurements in 1953, to equilibrium with special procurements in 1954, to equilibrium without special procurements in 1955. Economic Planning Agency, *Nenji Keizai Hokoku* (Economic Survey of Japan), 1956: 2.
5. MITI, Working Group on Industrial Structure, *Boeki Jiyuka to Sangyo Kozo* (Trade Liberalization and Industrial Structure), Toyo Keizai Inc., 1960: 4–5.
6. *Tsusho Sangyo Seisakushi*, v. 29.
7. Ibid. v. 23.
8. *Boeki Jiyuka to Sangyo Kozo*: 5.
9. *Tsusho Sangyo Seisakushi*, v. 30.
10. *Boeki Jiyuka to Sangyo Kozo*: p. 19.
11. *Nenji Keizai Hokoku* (Economic Survey of Japan), 1954: 25.
12. Takafusa Nakamura, *Nihon Keizai: Sono Seicho to Kozo, Dai 3-han* (Japanese Economy: Its Growth and Structure, 3rd edn.), University of Tokyo Press, 1993: 177.
13. Juroh Hashimoto, '1955', *Nihon Keizaishi, 8: Kodo Seicho* (Economic History of Japan, 8: High Growth), Iwanami Shoten, 1989: 89.
14. Concerning the main bank system and enterprise groups, see, as a first step, Juroh Hashimoto and Haruhito Takeda (eds.), *Nihon Keizai no Hatten to Kigyo Shudan* (The Development of the Japanese Economy and Enterprise Groups), University of Tokyo Press, 1992.
15. For details, see Hideaki Miyajima, 'Zaibatsu Kaitai' (Zaibatsu Dissolution) and Takeo Kikkawa, 'Sengo-Gata Kigyo Shudan no Keisei' (Formation of Post-War-Type Enterprise Groups) in *Nihon Keizai no Hatten to Kigyo Shudan*. The cross-shareholding percentages quoted in the text are from Kikkawa's paper, p. 264.
16. Ibid.; see also Tetsuji Okazaki, 'Shihon Jiyuka Igo no Kigyo Shudan' (Economic Enterprises after the Liberalization of Capital Flows).
17. Shuichiro Nakamura *et al.*, *Nihon Sangyo to Kasen Taisei* (Japanese Industry and Its Oligopolistic Structure), Shin Hyoron, 1966: 14.
18. Yoshikazu Miyazaki, *Sengo Nihon no Keizai Kiko* (Structure of Post-War Japanese Economy), Shin Hyoron, 1966. 53. For a cogent argument against the Miyazaki thesis, see Kikkawa, 'Sengo-Gata Kigyo Shudan no Keisei'.
19. A good illustration of this awareness was the Law on Temporary Measures for Promotion of the Machinery Industry enacted during this period.
20 For details, see *Tsusho Sangyo Seisakushi*, vii, ch. 6, sect. 1, 7–8.

15

Rationalization of Key Industries and the Nurturing of New Industries

15.1. Anti-Monopoly Law Revisions and Industrial Organization

The beginning of Anti-Monopoly Law revisions

Revision of the Anti-Monopoly Law was an important part of the review of Occupation-inspired legislation and regulation authorized by the May 1951 directive of General Ridgway.[1] The stringent provisions of the law were considered unsuitable for reconstructing the economy. A study by the Advisory Committee on Government Ordinance was initiated immediately, but the path to revision was full of twists and turns. The revision bill drafted by the commission faced a great deal of opposition because it proposed drastic relaxation of existing provisions. Although the government prepared a more moderate bill in the end, SCAP did not approve it.

When Japan was freed from the constraints imposed by SCAP after the Peace Treaty went into effect in April 1952, the clamour began again for relaxing the Anti-Monopoly Law. In particular, the end of the Korean War boom produced excess capacity in many sectors of the economy, increasing the need for companies to engage in 'collusive activities', which the existing statute prohibited unequivocally. Furthermore, it became obvious that there was a definite need to harmonize the Anti-Monopoly Law with the objectives of industrial policy, such as promoting exports and minimizing business uncertainties.

The reassessment of industrial organization policy and the issue of relaxing the Anti-Monopoly Law—controversies which were to repeat themselves often from this point on—were approached from three angles. The first, of course, was revision of the Anti-Monopoly Law itself. The second was *de facto* approval, by use of administrative guidance, of collusive activities among firms; and the third approach was legislation exempting firms from the law's provisions.

By 1952–3, immediately after the Peace Treaty became effective, all three approaches had been put into practice. First, the Export Transactions Law and the Law on Temporary Measures for the Stabilization of Designated Small and Medium Enterprises were enacted, exempting exporters and small and medium enterprises from the provisions of the Anti-Monopoly Law. Further, MITI sought to provide relief to textile manufacturers suffering from excess capacity by issuing them a kankoku sotan (advisory to curtail operations). In MITI's judgement, this inventive method did not violate the Anti-Monopoly Law because it constituted curtailment of production by administrative guidance.

At first, the Fair Trade Commission was silent on MITI-recommended production cutbacks. As prices began improving in June 1952, however, the Fair Trade Commission declared that continuation of the practice was 'undesirable in that it constituted a violation of the spirit of the Anti-Monopoly Law', advising MITI to halt the practice. This development made it necessary for the ministry to seek an alternative solution.

In this environment, from August 1952 MITI abandoned the idea of revising the Anti-Monopoly Law to exempt anti-recession cartels from its provisions, and worked instead to draft an 'Important Industry Stabilization Law' to provide relief to large oligopolistic corporations involved in excessive and destructive competition. The proposed law would authorize the responsible ministers to allow large corporations—as exemptions to the provisions of the Anti-Monopoly Law—three types of cartels for restricting production, sales, or capacity. The cartels would be assured by external authority of their power to enforce their rules. This 'stabilization bill', however, failed to find enough supporters. The Fair Trade Commission opposed it strenuously. Keidanren (Japan Federation of Economic Organizations) and the Japan Industrial Council, which had consistently argued for radical reform of the Anti-Monopoly Law, released a statement saying that 'enacting special legislation is merely a stopgap measure',[2] and demanded that MITI persist in seeking revision of the Anti-Monopoly Law. As a consequence, the idea of enacting an industrial stabilization law was abandoned.

Revision of the Anti-Monopoly Law in 1953

From the end of November 1952, the focus shifted to the question of Anti-Monopoly Law revision. The Economic Deliberation Board (formerly ESB), in its capacity as a comprehensive planning agency, announced that it planned to submit to the forthcoming Diet an Anti-Monopoly Law revision bill with a view to achieving a balance between maintaining order in the market place and achieving stability of industrial organization. Prompted by this move, MITI and Keidanren gradually clarified their support for a revision of the Anti-Monopoly Law. The revisions being contemplated at this time by the Economic Deliberation Board and MITI included proposals for (1) extensively relaxing the proscribing provisions of the existing law and limiting its scope to 'acts which substantially limit competition in a market' and 'unreasonable restraint of trade', and (2) relaxing restrictions on cartels and easing the prohibition of combines. The aim of these proposals was to change the tenet of the law from unequivocally prohibiting collusive activities to outlawing such behaviour only when it substantially restricted competition, thereby broadening the permissive range of cooperative behaviour among firms.

In contrast, Keidanren's view of revision entailed permitting, as a rule, the formation of monopolistic organizations and regulating only the harm done by such organizations when their activities ran contrary to the public interest, defined as the interest of the national economy. Keidanren from this point onwards consistently maintained this philosophy in dealing with the question of Anti-Monopoly Law revision.

Given this situation, the Fair Trade Commission subsequently took the initiative in preparing a draft bill. In February 1953 the commission published 'Guidelines for Revision of the Anti-Monopoly Law', which industrial circles and MITI took exception to, maintaining that the revisions being proposed were insufficient. MITI was also at odds with the Ministry of Foreign Affairs and the Ministry of Finance, both of which supported the Fair Trade Commission Draft bill, owing to the external circumstances and conditions for Japan's participation in the General Agreement on Tariffs and Trade (GATT) and the issue of concluding the Japan–US Treaty of Commerce and Navigation. In the end, however, the draft bill was formulated along the lines suggested in the Fair Trade Commission Draft bill. At one point, the bill was tabled as a result of the dissolution of the Diet after Prime Minister Yoshida called an opposition member a 'fool'. In the end, however, it was passed by the 16th Diet, and became effective on 1 September 1953. Thus, the revised Anti-Monopoly Law, which had been studied extensively following the May 1951 announcement of General Ridgway, finally came into being.

Implementation of the revised Anti-Monopoly Law and industrial policy

Three key points marked the 1953 revision of the Anti-Monopoly Law. First, the provisions proscribing collusive activities were deleted, and formation of cartels was permitted under certain specific conditions. Second, the provision preventing the forming of monopolies—including interlocking shareholding among competing companies—was relaxed. Third, provisions preventing monopolization by applying 'market structure criteria', such as the exclusion of unfair disparities in corporate capabilities, were deleted.

The second of these revisions helped to promote the formation of enterprise groups by encouraging intercorporate holding of stocks and debentures by business corporations and financial institutions and by relaxing the de facto restriction on interlocking multiple directorates. In contrast, the third point—deletion of preventative provisions—made corporate mergers easier, but it did not affect corporate behaviour very much until 1960, when the liberalization of trade was approaching, and afterwards when bolstering international competitiveness became an important task in every industry.

Industry was particularly interested in how cartels would be permitted through exempting legislation, but significant changes were not observed immediately in that area despite the revisions because the Fair Trade Commission continued its stringent stance on enforcing the Anti-Monopoly Law. For instance, a scrap-iron cartel which was considered a good candidate as a rationalization cartel in the Diet debate over the revision bill, and which was expected to help bring the prices of Japanese steel products closer to the world market level, did not materialize because the Fair Trade Commission refused to accept the application to form it. Also, approval was delayed for a rationalization cartel in the ball-bearing industry, cited as a case where a positive effect could be expected by forming a cartel to limit product lines.

These developments ran contrary to the expectations of MITI, which had thought that revision would bring the Anti-Monopoly Law into closer harmony with its industrial stabilization and rationalization policies, indispensable for economic self-support. They also betrayed the expectations of industry, which had hoped for relaxation of the prohibition on cartels. MITI thereupon concluded that under the 1953 revisions it would be difficult for companies to engage flexibly in collusive activities, and decided to explore further revisions. To that end, the Organization Committee of the Industrial Rationalization Council began studying new revisions to the Anti-Monopoly Law from March 1955. Around this time, MITI was emphasizing the need to reorganize industry in order to change the fundamental principle of anti-monopoly regulation to that of rejecting collusive activities only when they were harmful. The reaction of the Industrial Rationalization Council Organization Committee, however, did not support such an idea and MITI had to abandon the scheme.

When the Industrial Rationalization Council Organization Committee undertook its study in March 1955, the Fair Trade Commission announced a new policy of flexibly enforcing the Anti-Monopoly Law. The beginning of this new policy was marked by the approval of the cartel formed for joint purchases of scrap iron and scrap copper. The Fair Trade Commission declared that it would 'move positively to approve' rationalization cartels. This reversal in policy had the effect of increasing to some extent the number of rationalization cartels.

In contrast, anti-recession cartels formed much more slowly, even in the depths of the recession shaped like the 'bottom of a frying pan' that began in mid-1957. Only one such cartel had been approved by the end of 1958. One reason for this slow development was the fact that approval criteria for anti-recession cartels were very stringent. The Fair Trade Commission required applicants to submit a large volume of supporting documents, including an accounting of production costs. The long time required to gain approval meant that an applying firm could not reasonably expect to achieve its intended purposes. The other reason for the slow development of anti-recession cartels was the fact that the Fair Trade Commission, in enforcing the Anti-Monopoly Law, was lenient towards cartel-like behaviour during recessions, which mitigated the need to form an approved cartel. Specifically, after the 1953 revisions to the Anti-Monopoly Law, the Fair Trade Commission tacitly approved cartel-like behaviour during recession. It was also lenient towards the proliferation of production cutbacks by administrative guidance, action it had taken exception to before the Anti-Monopoly Law revisions. Such changes in enforcement practices were a manifestation of the changes in anti-monopoly policy that took place after the 1953 revisions. 'Advisories to curtail production' were frequently resorted to because they did not involve the complicated application procedures required under the Anti-Monopoly Law. They could also be applied swiftly and flexibly to business fluctuations because they were implemented in the form of MITI recommendations in response to an industry's appeal to the competent MITI bureau. Advisories also had a positive advantage not found in legalized cartels. That advantage was that administrative guidance by MITI was buttressed by such sanctions as reductions in foreign-exchange allocations. For these reasons, in the business downturn following the credit tightening of May 1957, MITI-recommended production cutbacks were implemented in many industries instead of allowing cartels under the Anti-Monopoly Law through its exemption provisions.

Exempting legislation included enactment of the Export Transactions Law (later, Export and Import Transactions Law) and amendment of the Small and Medium Enterprises Stabilization Law. Also, many industry-specific 'industry laws' characterized as 'temporary measures laws' with set time limits were enacted one after another, starting with the Temporary Measures Law for the Ammonium Sulphate Industry Rationalization and Export Adjustment of 1954. Attempts were also made, though ultimately unsuccessful, to legislate measures for long-term stabilization of supply and demand and coordination of capacity in the sugar-refining, steel, and chemical industries. The Steel Supply and Demand Adjustment Bill of December 1956 was one such attempt.

As exempting legislation, these 'industry laws' varied in nature, depending on their intended purposes. As discussed in detail later, the Temporary Law on Fertilizer Demand–Supply Stabilization, the Law on Extraordinary Measures for the Rationalization of the Coal-Mining Industry, and the Law on Temporary Measures for Textile Industry Equipment were enacted in order to introduce structural adjustments to mature industries, and provided for exemptions from the Anti-Monopoly Law for that purpose. In contrast, the Machinery Industry Promotion Law and the Electronics Industry Promotion Law were designed to exempt collusive activities in these industries from the provisions of the Anti-Monopoly Law, activities needed for the rationalization and healthy development of promising new industries.

Thus, after the 1953 revisions of the Anti-Monopoly Law, the scope of exemptions from its provisions expanded as existing statutes were amended and new industry-specific 'industry laws' were enacted. Although only a small number of anti-recession and rationalization cartels were approved under the Anti-Monopoly Law, the number of cartels formed under the provisions of exempting legislation increased each year.

Industrial adjustment draft bill

MITI realized that its idea of outlawing only harmful collusive activities would meet with strong opposition. Accordingly, it initiated a study of industrial organization policy by creating, separate from the Industrial Rationalization Council Organization Committee, an informal advisory group to the Minister of International Trade and Industry called the Group for Discussing Anti-Monopoly Law Issues. The work of this group led in May 1956 to a decision to draft a bill for a temporary industrial adjustment law based on ideas the group had developed from the year before. Around this same time, rising prices in basic industries had become a serious problem requiring action, as exemplified by the bottleneck problem. And even as these new problems arose, MITI was losing some of the means of enforcing its industrial policy because of trade liberalization and the general easing of the financial situation. Progress being made in import liberalization was expected to make it difficult for MITI to continue its effective implementation of production capacity (capital investment) coordination, which it had achieved by its control of foreign-exchange allocations for machinery and technology imports. Moreover, financial deregulation reduced the relative importance of Japan Development Bank loans as a policy instrument.

Consequently, MITI sought to utilize industrial adjustment legislation as a means of promoting rationalization in industries with excellent growth potential, such as cars and petrochemicals. It also wanted to utilize this legislation to promote the formation of cartels for stabilizing supply and demand in the steel industry and other basic industries, and to create cartels for regulating capital investment in structurally depressed industries. The idea bore an extremely close resemblance to the subsequent bills in 1963 for 'Temporary Promotion Laws', and thus can be considered their prototype, on three counts: (1) its objectives, which were to reduce production costs through improved organization and to increase international competitiveness, (2) applicable industries, which were steel, petrochemicals, cars, and others, and (3) nature of collusive activities, which were investment coordination, limitation of product lines, and supply and demand adjustments.

MITI's idea of an industrial adjustment bill, however, met strong opposition from all sides. Keidanren was particularly critical of MITI's plan to develop exempting legislation in the form of adjustment laws while avoiding revision of the Anti-Monopoly Law. It expressed its apprehension about the expansion of MITI's approval and validation authority possibly leading to bureaucratic control. As a result, MITI decided in the middle of January 1957 to shelve the idea of submitting an industrial adjustment bill to the Diet. That ended its attempt to legislate overall industrial organization covering all key industries for adjusting the Anti-Monopoly Law and the need to reform industrial organization.

Anti-Monopoly Law revisions in 1958

Because of the foregoing, attention shifted again to reassessing the Anti-Monopoly Law. In this connection, in early August 1957 the Enterprises Bureau conducted a survey to clarify the views of industry regarding the shortcomings of the Anti-Monopoly Law and its possible revision. Keeping MITI's views in mind, staff members of the bureau also interviewed officials of major corporations to accumulate data for supporting expansion of the permissible scope of collusive activities among them for industrial organization. In this process, Keidanren requested that the Cabinet create an advisory council to study the fundamental problems. Prompted by this request, the Cabinet in October established a temporary Anti-Monopoly Law Council attached to it, thus initiating a thorough study of the Anti-Monopoly Law revision question.

The council received, mainly from MITI, lists of problem areas in the Anti-Monopoly Law that required revision. It also solicited the opinions of industries and conducted questionnaire surveys. Opinions of various organizations were largely divided into three categories: (1) opinions submitted by industrial organizations, financial organizations, and foreign trade associations demanding extensive relaxation of the Anti-Monopoly Law, (2) views submitted by consumer organizations, small and medium enterprises, and agricultural and forestry associations opposing relaxation or demanding a stronger Anti-Monopoly Law, and (3) opinions expressed by the shipbuilding industry, commercial associations, and other organizations opposing extensive relaxation of the Anti-Monopoly Law.

Taking these views into consideration, the Anti-Monopoly Law Council in February 1958 finalized a report to the Cabinet in which it recommended maximum expansion of the scope of cartels and trusts within the limits of the Anti-Monopoly Law's 1953 revisions, which had in principle prohibited cartels and trusts. The government worked on pulling together a draft bill based on the council's report, and took steps to submit it to the Diet in October.

This revision bill, however, did not result in legislation. Various agricultural associations, consumer groups, and small and medium enterprises, which at first showed little interest in the bill, gradually intensified their opposition to it around the time it was submitted to the Diet, and launched an intense protest outside the Diet. The emergence of pro-Anti-Monopoly Law groups which may not have mounted well-articulated campaigns against the 1953 revision, suggested that the Anti-Monopoly Law had finally planted its roots deeply in Japanese soil.[3] The more serious obstacle to the passage of the bill, however, was the fact that the Diet at that time was entangled in acrimonious debate over proposed revision of the Law Concerning the Execution of Duties of Police Officials. For this reason, debate was deferred on the Anti-Monopoly Law revision bill, concerning which a confrontation with the opposition Socialist Party was believed unavoidable. In the end it was never brought before the 30th Diet for serious discussion. Thus, the revision bill was finally tabled and discarded at the beginning of December 1958—three and a half years after MITI began to study a second revision of the Anti-Monopoly Law in March 1955, and over a year since the Anti-Monopoly Law Council began its deliberations. Taking into consideration the political situation fraught with partisan warfare, the majority party decided not to submit it to the 31st Diet.

When it became clear in February 1959 that the revision bill would not be resubmitted to the Diet, MITI began exploring a new direction for its industrial policy within the existing statutory framework. It subsequently announced its intention to deal with pressing industrial adjustment problems by providing appropriately fine-tuned guidance in each industry. In its 'New Policy' developed for ministerial budget requests for the following fiscal year, MITI announced a new policy of industry-specific production-capacity (capital investment) coordination by means of administrative guidance backed by regulation of financing. In this scheme, the Finance Committee of the Industrial Rationalization Council would formulate the basic policy for production-capacity adjustment for each of the key industries. MITI would then take steps to coordinate capital investment activities by means of administrative guidance with cooperation from financial institutions. In short, MITI realized that revision of the Anti-Monopoly Law was unlikely, and it introduced the new investment adjustment scheme to utilize its power of indirect control over the financing aspects of business investment decisions.

The move to revise the Anti-Monopoly Law thus waned again, mostly because the developing political situation was expected to be hostile to such an attempt. A revision bill would have little chance of passage in the Diet because the political situation was charged with acrimonious confrontation between opposing forces over revision of the US–Japan Security Treaty. Moreover, the economy was gradually improving. After the revision bill was tabled and discarded, the Fair Trade Commission substantially relaxed its enforcement of the Anti-Monopoly Law, thereby realizing de facto, some of the objectives of the proposed revision. Particularly important was the fact that collusive activities based on administrative guidance, which had been limited before to recession periods, were now allowed even during periods of business prosperity in the form of the Open Sales System. Moreover, the system of export promotion associations—collusive activities previously limited to exporting of goods—was extended to include domestic shipments. These changes in the Fair Trade Commission's enforcement of anti-cartel provisions of the Anti-Monopoly Law, as well as the approval of large-scale merger plans developed at about the time the 1958 revision bill was submitted to the Diet, were significant additional reasons why attempts to further revise the Anti-Monopoly Law did not materialize.

15.2. Activities of the Industrial Rationalization Council

Reorganization of the Industrial Rationalization Council

As discussed in Chapter 14, industrial rationalization was an important policy objective during this period. The Industrial Rationalization Council played the key role in promoting industrial rationalization policy and undertook detailed studies for specific measures.[4]

As noted in Part II, the Industrial Rationalization Council in its first report of February 1951 defined the basic direction of industrial rationalization policy. Summarizing the results of subsequent activities of its committees and subcommittees, the Industrial Rationalization Council in July 1952 released a second report, entitled 'Methods for Rationalizing Japanese Industry', in which it suggested such measures as promoting capital accumulation by enterprises, securing funds needed by enterprises, lowering loan rates, widening the scope of machinery and equipment imports eligible for reduced import duties or exemption therefrom, and revising the Anti-Monopoly Law.

In January 1953, furthermore, the Industrial Rationalization Council redefined its operating principles in view of expected changes in the business climate following the signing of the San Francisco Peace Treaty. The Industrial Rationalization Council stressed that it would

study and discuss ways to achieve synergistic effects of rationalization which cannot be realized by such individual programmes as organizing enterprises or promoting their collusive activities, and also study an appropriate industrial structure which takes into account rationalization of the entire national economy, and particularly the relationships with exports, special procurements, new special procurements, and domestic special procurements.[5]

From these new viewpoints, the Industrial Rationalization Council's committees and subcommittees continued their activities into fiscal year 1953. In September 1953, the council published a third report, entitled 'Report on Methods for Rationalizing Japanese Industry'. It identified the following five points as the basic principles of industrial rationalization: (1) promoting rationalization of enterprise management, (2) promoting rationalization of the industrial structure, (3) promoting rationalization of industrial organization, (4) improving industry-related facilities, and (5) organizing small and medium enterprises.

Aiming for industrial rationalization which would provide a foundation for economic self-support, the Industrial Rationalization Council solicited the opinions of persons from various fields. The purpose was to study policy measures that might gain a national consensus from a variety of viewpoints. To that end, its committee structure was reassessed flexibly as policy priorities changed, and reorganized as needs arose.[6] Specifically, after it published its third report its existing system of industry-specific committees and subcommittees was abolished and a new horizontally organized structure was introduced that reflected the key issues in industrial rationalization. The following new committees were established: Coordination, Industrial Structure, Industrial Organization, Industry-Related Facilities, Market, Management, Energy, Industry-Specific, and Small and Medium Enterprises. Except for the Industrial Structure Committee, all the new committees started functioning on 1 November.

In fiscal year 1957, the Industrial Rationalization Council was further reorganized to re-examine the overall policy framework as the national goal of self-support was gradually being realized. One result of the reorganization was that no distinction was made between permanent and temporary committees. The Industrial Structure Committee, which had existed in name only from the previous reorganization onwards, was re-established for the purpose of developing an improved and more sophisticated industrial structure. Moreover, four new committees were established, including the New Metals Committee, the Chemical Industry Committee, and the Industrial Finance Committee. The Industrial Finance Committee was to ensure the availability of investment capital needed for key industries and coordinate the scale of their capital investments. The Chemical Fertilizer Committee, on the other hand, was abolished, and the Commerce Committee, which had been formed by merging the Market Committee and the old Commerce Committee, was renamed the Distribution Committee. Although the reorganized Industrial Rationalization Council was thus to start functioning with sixteen new committees, the Industrial Structure Committee did not actually start its work until fiscal year 1960. There was little specific activity in the Industrial Organization, Film Industry, Chemical Industry, and Synthetic Fibres Committees.

Activities of the Industrial Rationalization Council

Discussions held by the various committees contributed significantly to the formulation of a variety of policies, and the scope of their deliberations was far and wide. Examples of their work included developing specific rationalization measures for individual industries (one of the focuses of MITI policy during this period), and measures to 'organize' industries in relation to the Anti-Monopoly Law. As discussed in detail later, specific measures directly related to Industrial Rationalization Council committee deliberations included: subsidies, lend-lease programmes of government-owned machinery and equipment, and reduced depreciation periods for machinery and equipment use for research and development. As defined in the Industrial Rationalization Promotion Law, these 'rationalization measures' were implemented to promote technological improvements. Other measures for similar purposes included: exemptions from property taxes for machinery and equipment used for research and development, special depreciation rules for sophisticated machinery and equipment and reduction of or exemption from property taxes for modern facilities used to modernize production facilities, putting into order industry-related facilities, improvement of productivity in the use of variable inputs, and management diagnosis for small and medium enterprises.

Subcommittees engaged in highly specialized discussions. The Management Committee, for instance, divided its tasks among five subcommittees: Financial Affairs, Production, Labour, Quality Control, and Industrial Training. The Financial Affairs Subcommittee was instrumental in introducing systematic managerial accounting methods to Japan, such as budget control, standard cost accounting, and comptroller systems through its publication of the 'General Rules on Internal Control by Enterprises'. It also published 'Profit Planning for Carrying Out Management Policy' and 'Profit Management through the Business Unit System'. The Production Control Subcommittee engaged in motion study, rationalization of conveyance equipment, lubricant control, and process control, which resulted in the report 'Fostering an Increase in Machine Design Engineers'.

The Quality Control Subcommittee (renamed the Production Control Subcommittee after the reorganization of 1957) studied methods for spreading quality control to small and medium enterprises, and prepared the report 'Quality Control in Small and Medium Enterprises: Case Studies'. The Labour Management Subcommittee studied wage systems, job site management systems, job functions of foremen, employee training, and other subjects, and prepared the reports 'Employee Training', 'Basic Wage System Based on Job Evaluation', 'Job Rate System Based on Job Evaluation', 'On a System for Rationalizing Worksite Management: The Role of the Worksite Supervisor', and 'On a System for Rationalizing Worksite Management: The Role of the Worksite Staff'.

The Industrial Finance Committee, established after the 1957 reorganization, played a key role in the adjustment of plant and equipment investment and the supply and demand of funds for strategic industries. Whereas the Funds Coordination Committee of the Federation of Bankers' Associations of Japan coordinated the flow of funds from the perspective of funds suppliers, the role of the Industrial Finance Committee was to develop standards for financing by coordinating the views of the users of funds, and having those views reflected during deliberations of the Financial Institutions Funds Council of the Ministry of Finance. In the industries where funds were needed, companies submitted capital and investment plans to the industry association and made adjustments among themselves. When such autonomous coordination did not produce acceptable results, MITI intervened. The plans of the particular industry were then submitted to the Industrial Finance Committee for discussion. Important was the fact that through such coordination, it became possible to promote priority allocation of funds to strategic industries, which was essential if the industrial structure was to be upgraded. Concerning the size of the plant and equipment investment and determination of equipment standards, active discussions were held from the viewpoints of supply and demand estimates, production capacity, rate of capacity utilization, and the need for rationalization. Also, from the viewpoint of limiting excessive investments and promoting modernization investment, these discussions were effective in building a consensus for determining appropriate investments. The conclusions of the Industrial Finance Committee, which after all was not an agency for controlling allocation of funds, were, of course, not observed to the letter. Nonetheless, the work of this committee to coordinate, from an economy-wide perspective, the results of autonomous investment and fund plans in each industry, in combination with the work of the Funds Coordination Committee and the Financial Institutions Funds Council, played an important role in guiding private plant and equipment investment in appropriate directions.

Meanwhile, the Industry-Related Facilities Committee, established during the 1953 reorganization, studied the problem of ensuring a supply of water for industrial use and the issue of disposal of industrial and mining waste water. It also tackled the new policy question of improving social overhead capital. Discussions held in the Commerce Committee, on the other hand, which made a start in

September 1955, led to enactment of the Department Store Law. From the Machinery Committee emerged the idea of creating a Machinery Industry Promotion Corporation. Although the idea did not materialize, it had an important impact on the subsequent formulation of the Machinery Industry Promotion Law.

Development of the productivity-enhancement movement

In connection with the activities of the Industrial Rationalization Council, the productivity-enhancement movement contributed significantly to a subsequent improvement in the international competitiveness of Japanese industries.[7] The momentum for the post-war development of a productivity-enhancement movement in West European countries came from the inauguration, in 1948, of the US–UK Productivity Council in the UK. Subsequently, the European Productivity Centre was established in 1953 in Paris as a core organization of the pan-European movement, and the productivity-enhancement movement started its full-scale development in Europe.

MITI, which had been paying close attention to these developments, commissioned a study of the productivity council in the UK. In 1951, it proposed in a report from the Industrial Rationalization Council that a Japan Productivity Centre be established. The proposal, however, did not materialize. In December 1953, Wesley Haroldson of the US Embassy, in a talk with leaders of the Keizai Doyukai (the Japan Committee for Economic Development), announced that the US government was prepared to provide active support to establishment in Japan of a productivity organization as part of the activities of its Foreign Operations Administration. With this announcement, the movement to establish a new organization made rapid progress. Goshi Kohei, permanent secretary-general of the Japan Committee for Economic Development, and others who were acutely aware of the need for a productivity-enhancement movement, immediately appealed to other business organizations—Keidanren, Nikkeiren (the Japan Federation of Employees' Associations), and Nissho (the Japan Chamber of Commerce and Industry)—to join in the effort. As a consequence, the four major business organizations jointly created in March 1954 the Japan–US Committee for Increasing Productivity, renamed the same June to 'Japan Productivity Council'.

MITI, meanwhile, had been studying establishment of a productivity organization apart from the initiatives being made in the private sector. In August 1954, it proposed to the Japan Productivity Council the joint launching of a powerful movement to create a productivity organization to be supported by close co-operation between government and business. Subsequently, MITI held discussions with the Ministry of Foreign Affairs, the Ministry of Labour, the Japan Productivity Council, and the US Embassy. In September, these discussions resulted in a statement to the effect that 'a "Japan Productivity Centre" be established as a private organization, which, in concert with productivity-enhancement measures implemented by the government, will engage in energetic activities in the private sector and on a national scale with a view to generating a rapid improvement in the productivity of Japanese industry.'[8] With funds provided by a variety of sources, including the US government, the Japan Productivity Centre was inaugurated in March 1955. On the same day, the Japan Productivity Liaison Conference was created to coordinate the activities of the Japanese government and the Japan Productivity Centre.

In the first coordination meeting of May 1955, the so-called 'three principles of productivity' were adopted. They were as follows. (1) Although increased productivity ultimately leads to increased employment, labour redundancy may develop as a transient phenomenon. Government and business, therefore, through close cooperation and in the interest of the overall national economy, shall take appropriate measures to prevent unemployment to the maximum extent possible through such means as reassignment of workers. (2) To establish specific methods for increasing productivity, management and labour in each company shall cooperate in studying and discussing methods in a manner in keeping with the company's actual situation. (3) The fruits of increased productivity shall be fairly distributed to employers, workers, and consumers in keeping with the realities of the national economy.[9] On the basis of these principles, a call was made to labour unions to take part in the movement. The first to respond positively to this call was Sodomei (the Japan Federation of Labour). In the second meeting of its Central Committee held in June 1955, Sodomei adopted eight principles for dealing with the issue of productivity enhancement, and decided to participate in the Japan Productivity Centre on the basis of these principles.

Since its inception, the Japan Productivity Centre has engaged in a wide variety of programmes, including overseas technical exchanges (dispatching overseas study missions, sending trainees to overseas locations, inviting experts from abroad, and technical exchanges with Asian countries), managerial education (conducting wide-ranging seminars and training courses), fostering small and medium enterprises (managerial training for owners/managers of such companies, development of a unified cost-accounting system for such companies, and company consulting and guidance), study and dissemination of the labour–management consultation system, and consumer education. The most significant of these programmes was the dispatch of overseas study missions. Participants in the 306 missions dispatched during the fiscal years 1955–60 became painfully aware, at overseas locations they toured, of the disparity in the productivity levels between Japan and the advanced Western industrial nations. They were given the opportunity to consider the targets for Japanese industry, and to suggest specific measures for reaching those targets.

15.3. Rationalization of the Steel Industry and the Open Sales System

Continuation of the First Rationalization Plan

The steel industry was the most important target of the industrial rationalization programme.[10] Increased supplies and stable prices for steel products were considered essential conditions for developing the machinery industry and realizing greater sophistication in the industrial and export structures. When independence was restored, the steel industry had just recovered, owing principally to the special procurements boom and the First Rationalization Plan. Its international competitiveness, however, was still rather weak, calling for further modernization of its production facilities. Even as late as 1954, the production cost of open-hearth steel ingots was much higher in Japan than in the United States and West Germany, as seen in Table 15.1. Although the disparity was in part related to the difference in the scales of operation, a US–Japanese comparison revealed that the net cost of raw materials was much higher in Japan. In smelting, the cause of the high cost was the high prices of imported iron ore and coke on which the industry relied so heavily. In steel-making, the cause was the high price of imported scrap iron. It was therefore necessary for the iron and steel industry as a whole to further rationalize its operations.

In the mid-1950s, moreover, the demand for steel increased sharply as the economy entered the era of high growth, outstripping supply and creating serious bottlenecks. The shortage quickly translated into higher prices of steel products. These high prices, as well as high costs, symbolized the problems encountered by the industry. As a basic industry, steel was expected to provide a solid foundation for the development of other strategic industries by supplying products at stable prices. Instead, the industry during this period was plagued by wide fluctuations in prices.

The First Rationalization Plan served as a starting point for rationalizing the steel industry and was carried out over the three years 1951–3. It spent 88.8 billion yen, focusing on modernizing rolling mills. MITI, meanwhile, had been contemplating, as a solution to the problem of high steel prices, a change in policy to that of promoting integrated steel production accompanied by a shift

Table 15.1 International comparison of open-hearth steel ingots, 1954 (unit: 1,000 tons, yen per ton)

	Japan		USA				W. Germany
	Entire country	Integrated works	Non-integrated works		Integrated works		Entire country
Average scale of operations	229	440	250	1,000	500	1,000	646
Production cost:							
Net raw materials cost	18,549	18,122	13,626	13,626	12,719	12,719	
Operational expenses	6,597	5,761	6,264	5,234	4,842	4,475	
Total	25,146	23,883	19,890	18,860	17,561	17,194	18,578

Source: Compiled from MITI, Working Group on Industrial Structure, *Boeki Jiyuka to Sangyo Kozo* (Trade Liberalization and Industrial Structure), Toyo Keizai Inc., 1960: 103.

in the source of iron from scrap iron to iron ore. It was reluctant, however, to initiate this change because it was pessimistic about the outlook for business conditions once the special-procurements boom ended. It therefore adopted an alternative policy of abandoning the traditional pursuit of ever-larger production volume, emphasizing instead the modernization of equipment, cost reductions through industrial reorganization, and improvement of the international competitiveness of Japanese steel-makers. The primary concern of MITI was the excess of outdated production capacity being left behind by the wave of modernization.

This conservative policy manifested itself in MITI's response to new rationalization plans submitted in July 1953. It decided to handle the excess capacity problem by such means as regulation of financing and restriction of foreign-exchange allocation, while requesting applicant companies to scale down their plans. Meanwhile, applicant companies which initially expressed aggressive investment intentions reduced their investment plans to about 60 billion yen, roughly half the initial level, because the steel market softened in 1954. The ministry responded cautiously even to the scaled-down plans. Considering the need to tighten credit to cope with the deteriorating external payments situation, MITI decided on a policy of suggesting to companies that they should postpone starting any new construction until they were certain they could arrange funding on their own. Based on this policy, the ministry introduced specific countermeasures in continuation of the First Rationalization Plan, such as refusing to provide special consideration for financing to Kawasaki Steel for building additional blast furnaces.

Steel Industry Rationalization bills

In August 1954, MITI began studying a 'Steel Industry Rationalization Law' as part of its policy for promoting rationalization of the steel industry. The aim of the law would be to foster construction of modern facilities that would rationalize production, at the same time looking for ways to deal with the excess capacity that was likely to occur. Specifically, the bill that emerged called for establishing a reorganization committee under whose guidance rationalization programmes would be carried out. A system of licensing requirements for expansion beyond a certain size would also be introduced.

Industry, however, was critical of this bill because of its strong colouring of economic control. Accordingly, the ministry in March 1955 deleted nearly all the provisions about reorganizing industry into a concentrated system of high-efficiency production, the primary aim of the rationalization bill. It then replaced the former bill with a new one (the Steel Rationalization Promotion Bill), shifting the emphasis to 'industry stabilization' designed to make cartel formation easier. MITI, however, was still not able to secure support from industry, which wanted either repeal or substantial easing of the Anti-Monopoly Law. Like the first bill, the new bill was thus not submitted to the Diet.

As these bills designed to rationalize industry revealed, MITI during this period was concerned about the coexistence of highly productive modern facilities, installed under the First Rationalization Plan, and old facilities with lower productivity. It therefore sought to promote further rationalization by pressing ahead with industrial reorganization. To stabilize prices and the supply-and-demand situation, it sought to strengthen collusive activities among companies in the form of production agreements by product line, and by tacitly approving, when markets softened, agreements which were *de facto* anti-recession cartels. MITI regarded these measures as basic tasks of its steel policy, and attached high priority to performing them.

Steel-market measures and the scrap-iron cartel

MITI's cautious approach to rationalization programmes that included the expansion of facilities and its serious consideration of industrial reorganization is best understood by reviewing the so-called 'high steel-price problem'. Because the steel industry was not sufficiently internationally competitive at this time, high steel prices caused by steel shortages in the domestic market were seriously hurting the export of steel products and manufactured products that used steel as a material. To deal with the problem, MITI considered providing subsidies to pig-iron makers in 1953 and allowing the import of steel materials in early 1955. Responding to these moves by MITI, Yawata Steel in February 1955 announced a set of firm prices it would honour for two months. This move returned stability to the market starting in March. It was an example of the effort made by industry to provide autonomous market adjustment, in this case under the leadership of Yawata Steel.

Meanwhile, stabilizing the price of scrap iron—an important material for steel-making—was considered a more effective way to solve the 'high steel-price problem' than *ad hoc* measures that responded to temporary fluctuations in the market. This was because there was a serious imbalance between iron and steel, and companies operating open-hearth furnaces played an important role in the supply of steel materials. Formation of a scrap-iron cartel, however, which was expected as a result of the 1953 revision of the Anti-Monopoly Law, was delayed by the resistance of the Fair Trade Commission. In a March 1955 Cabinet meeting, therefore, the government adopted a resolution for 'securing the needed quantity of scrap iron' and ordered that the production volume of crude steel and the maximum amount of scrap iron imported by each steelmaker be determined according to directives from MITI. Subsequently, towards the end of March, the Fair Trade Commission finally approved the second application by eighteen companies to form a scrap-iron cartel. Approval led to the first rationalization cartel formed by steelmakers. Later, a Scrap-Iron Committee established under this cartel arrangement set purchase prices for domestic and imported scrap iron, engaged in joint purchasing activities such as the rating of scrap iron, and in general moved to stabilize supply and demand as well as prices of scrap iron, at the same time following administrative guidance provided by MITI concerning the quantity of scrap-iron imports.

Formulation of the Second Rationalization Plan and long-term prospects

Around the time the scrap-iron cartel was formed, and under improving business conditions immediately preceding the Jimmu Boom, work progressed towards formulating the Second Rationalization Plan. By February 1956, the 130-billion-yen rationalization plan had begun to take shape. In keeping with the targets of the Five-Year Plan for Economic Self-Support then being developed, the steel plan called for building new blast furnaces to increase production of pig-iron, building converters based on new technology which would conserve scrap iron, and increasing rolling capacity by building additional strip mills. As the business upswing continued and the demand for steel increased beyond expectations, actual production of steel ingots in fiscal year 1956 surpassed the target value for fiscal year 1960 as projected in the Five-Year Plan, necessitating further expansion of production capacity.

MITI, which had been cautious until then about expanding production capacity, took this opportunity to set out its plan for the future, in which it envisioned a transformation of the industry's manufacturing structure by shifting the source of iron from scrap iron to iron ore. This vision was incorporated into the Eight-Year Plan for Steel Production and the draft for the Twenty-Year Plan for Steel Supply and Demand, which MITI took the lead in preparing. These plans had the long-term effect of providing direction to plant and equipment investment in the steel industry. They also provided important guidelines for the work of the Industrial Finance Committee of the Industrial Rationalization Council in its effort to coordinate the annual procurement of funds needed for the rationalization plans each company carried out.

Implementation of the open sales system

While formulating long-term plans, the steel policymakers of MITI were hard-pressed from 1956, to cope with the problem of supply bottlenecks and rising prices. In June 1956, they implemented measures such as deferment of quoted-price increases, the emergency importation of steel products, and a large increase in the allocation of foreign exchange for importing pig-iron and scrap iron. Also, from the beginning of September 1956, MITI undertook the drafting of the Steel Supply and Demand Stabilization Bill. The core of the bill, which was developed by incorporating the views of the steel industry, was a system of reporting collusive activities by companies in the industry, against which there arose considerable objection within the government. In the end, the government decided not to submit the bill to the Diet because views regarding how to handle collusive activities differed so greatly.

In lieu of the abandoned Steel Supply and Demand Bill, MITI announced 'measures for the stabilization of supply and demand and steel prices', and strengthened the import policy that had been in effect from the previous year. MITI held discussions with seven leading companies in the steel industry about price stabilization, which led in May 1957 to an agreement to maintain low prices within a stabilized range.

This price stabilization scheme, however, lost its significance after the market softened in early June. The turn of events forced the ministry to change its earlier steel policy which focused on an easing of the supply–demand situation and holding down prices to that of dealing with rapidly falling prices. It was hard-pressed to implement various market-support measures, including the stabilization of prices by setting their minimum limits, directing firms to reduce steel ingot production by 10 per cent, and carrying out production cutbacks of steel materials by product category.

These measures, however, were not enough to prevent further deterioration of the steel market. Accordingly, once into fiscal year 1958, MITI intensified the production cutback programme it had been carrying out since the fourth quarter of the preceding fiscal year. Objections arose from within the steel industry to this policy of focusing only on production cutbacks, and a new approach became necessary for attacking the poor business situation from the price side. A joint government–business conference on steel-market measures held in June 1958 between MITI and seven steelmakers produced an agreement to implement a list-price system called the 'open sales system'. With the concurrence of thirty-two firms, including eighteen operators of open-hearth furnaces, the 'open sales system' was put into effect. Under this system, MITI, using administrative guidance, was to request production cutbacks of steel ingots, plates (including medium sheets), small bars, medium bars, medium sections, and wire rods. Steelmakers were obliged to disclose their sales volumes and selling prices.

The open sales system achieved its objectives as a recession-fighting measure in something over six months after its inception, and by the end of fiscal year 1958 the steel market showed signs of improvement. In May 1959, MITI, in consultation with the Fair Trade Commission, decided to convert the open sales system from a soft-market measure to a boom-period measure for containing sharply rising steel prices. The new system, however, had only a brief lifespan. From November 1959, the market again turned sluggish, and by January 1960 it had become necessary to find ways of dealing with the deteriorating situation. Policymakers decided that the steel open sales system should be retained by changing its character from a price-containing programme to a price-stabilizing programme on the grounds that steel is 'a basic material for the national economy, and it is therefore essential to stabilize steel prices.'[11] The open sales system thus had a new start as the 'price-stabilizing open sales system'.

Table 15.2 reveals the need for continued efforts to stabilize steel prices. For products where the degree of production concentration was high, prices were relatively stable. In product lines to which the open sales system applied, there was a large number of makers having low degrees of concentration. The attendant wide variation in their prices thus was considered a serious problem.

Table 15.2   Degree of concentration and price variations of steel materials by product (1957)

Product	Average annual % of price variation	Maximum increase (%)	Maximum decrease (%)	Degree of concentration of top 3 companies	No. of major mfrs
Steel rails	3.8	18	11	100	1
Silicon steel plates	6.8	24	4.5	100	2
Heavy rails	4.1	20	17	95	4
Tin plates	6.8	25	3	87	9
Seamless steel pipes	27.7	85	71	95	3
Large sections	50.8	75	92	85	7
Cold-rolled plates	25.5	75	49	76	9
Wire rods[a]	41.2	120	83	70	13
Medium sheets[a]	72.8	200	250	54	28
Plates[a]	94.0	202	210	52	25
Medium sections[a]	71.2	200	210	50	16
Galvanized sheets	32.8	79	82	40	27
Thin sheets	40.2	150	140	39	37
Small bars[a]	63.6	176	195	24	209

[a] Products are list-price items.

Source: Hiromi Arisawa (ed.), *Gendai Nippon Sangyo Koza* (Lecture on Modern Japanese Industry), II, Iwanami Shoten, 1959: 161.

Results of the Second Rationalization Plan

From its start, the actual results of the Second Rationalization Plan—which started in 1956, around the time the high-growth period began—surpassed its targets, which were adjusted upwards each year. The same was true with plant and equipment investment. The initial target of 178 billion yen was nearly doubled to 345.8 billion yen in a report in February 1957 by a special Steel Survey Mission. In the subsequent long-term plan formulated for the period up to 1962, the target increased further to 443.4 billion yen. Moreover, since actual construction was moved up to 1960 and additional construction was also carried out, the actual value of investments amounted to 541.6 billion yen. These immense investments were made mainly in blast furnaces built in new coastal industrial zones as a means of solving the iron-source problem, and they increased the capacity and efficiency of the iron and steel industry dramatically. The increase in productivity between 1950 and 1958 was 3.8-fold for smelting, 2.6-fold for steelmaking, and 3.1-fold for rolling ordinary (unfinished) steel materials.[12] As Table 15.3 clearly shows, new blast furnaces, and the expansion of facilities such as LD converters using new technology and strip mills, decisively contributed to rationalizing the steel industry. As a result, by the time the Second

Table 15.3 Capacity and number of units of major equipment (unit: 1,000 tons/year)

	March 1951		End of 1955		End of 1960	
	Capacity	No. of units	Capacity	No. of units	Capacity	No. of units
Smelting	2,900	146	6,344	110	12,535	138
of which blast furnaces	2,488	14	5,677	21	11,630	34
Steelmaking	9,678	736	10,110	654	28,194	821
Open-hearth furnaces	5,647	138	6,402	134	15,228	149
Converters	459	6	486	7	4,843	13
of which LD converters	—	—	—	—	4,843	13
Electric furnaces	3,572	592	3,222	513	8,123	662
Rolling	10,535	370	15,257	466	34,125	529
Hot strip mills	270	1	1,476	3	6,996	7
Cold strip mills	139	2	1,218	7	3,929	26
Strip mills	346	5	990	9	1,089	10
Plate mills	1,717	20	2,365	25	5,224	32
Wire rods mills	915	10	1,346	14	3,097	21

Source: Compiled from *Tsusho Sangyo Seisakushi* (History of International Trade and Industry Policy), vi: 475.

Rationalization was brought to a pause in 1961. If steel costs are taken as an example, the disparity between Japan on the one hand, and the United States and West Germany on the other, had virtually disappeared.[13]

The Japanese steel industry, at the end of the Second Rationalization programme, had production facilities favourably comparable with those of its counterparts in the US and Europe, and had acquired international competitiveness in terms of production costs. These accomplishments were essentially the result of vigorous investment efforts by Japanese steelmakers that helped implement the Second Rationalization Plan on a scale and at a speed that far exceeded its initial targets. Meanwhile, MITI supported the industry's efforts by means of its fine-tuned policies of equipment importation, induction of foreign capital, and development of overseas sources of iron ore. By formulating a long-term supply-and-demand plan, MITI helped the industry develop its future vision and gave a sense of direction to a large number of diverse plans that were based on the self-interest of individual corporations. Of particular importance was the fact that MITI's aggressive policy of promoting construction of blast furnaces and converters contributed greatly to the increased international competitiveness of the Japanese steel industry.

Japanese production of steel recorded an annual average rate of growth of 18.7 per cent between 1955 and 1960. In 1960, Japanese steel production ranked third in the world after the US and the USSR. Exports of steel also grew rapidly, and in 1960 steel had become Japan's largest export item.

15.4. The Rationalization of the Energy and Natural Resources Industry

'Coal first, oil second' policy

As the economy recovered, the need for more energy resources, the most noticeable effect of which was the shortage of electric power, became a serious problem needing to be addressed if a solid foundation was to be built for the rationalization of industry. Because the electric power industry in those days stood at the crossroads of the industry reorganization issue, however, it was in no position to tackle the development of new power sources. The matter was further complicated because coal and electric power, the principal sources of energy, were under the jurisdiction of two different agencies. The former was under MITI; the latter was under the Public Utilities Commission. This administrative division impeded formulation of a comprehensive energy policy.

As the Korean War boom came to an end, the high prices of coal, which reflected boom-induced inflation, came to impede industrial rationalization efforts.[14] MITI's basic policy for solving this problem was to pin its hopes on modernizing the coal mining industry. This policy was in keeping with the larger framework of the ministry's trade and industrial policy, which recognized the shortage of foreign exchange as the most serious factor preventing the restoration of economic self-support. To improve the nation's foreign-exchange position, exports had to be increased, which required that international competitiveness be enhanced. To that end, the ministry sought to promote industrial rationalization. In those days, it was believed that conserving of foreign exchange required that Japan's limited domestic resources be utilized as effectively as possible.

There was another school of thought, however, that said industrial rationalization could be achieved most efficiently if cheaper imported energy sources were utilized. Thus, there was no overall clear energy policy when Japan regained its sovereignty under the Peace Treaty in 1952. A preference for imported oil developed near the end of 1951 due to serious shortages of electric power and coal. To cope with the situation, and in response to a request from Keidanren, MITI allocated additional foreign exchange for importing crude oil. The increased use of oil proved that oil was economical and easy to manage, and demonstrated that oil improved the quality of products in metal-refining, rolling, and manufacturing of glass, cement, and ceramics. It also became clear that conversion to oil contributed significantly to cost reductions and the improved international competitiveness of Japanese industry.

Consequently, MITI began promoting conversion to oil as a means of realizing simultaneously the twin objectives of solving the coal shortage and effecting industrial rationalization. In 1952, when a lengthy coal miners' strike threatened to produce coal shortages, MITI allowed the importation of more than 1.6 times the amount of coal imported during the previous year. The coal industry and others criticized this measure as a patchwork move used to gloss over the temporary energy shortage while neglecting measures which would have a direct and positive effect on the rationalization of Japanese coal mines.

In the spring of 1953, however, the situation changed totally. The long strike ended and the supply of coal increased, lowering coal prices and causing concern over accumulating coal inventories. From 1953 and into 1954, the coal mining industry fell into a serious slump. MITI responded by reversing its oil importation policy to one of restraint, starting from the foreign-exchange budget of the second half of fiscal year 1953. It also began an earnest effort to deal with the problem of high coal prices. In other words, it abandoned the policy of applying external pressures like promoting the import of coal and encouraging conversion to oil, which were designed to stimulate modernization of the coal mining industry. Continuation of such a policy, MITI feared, would result in forcing deficits on the coal mining industry, suppressing its activities, and making continuation of its business impossible.

The problems faced by the coal mining industry were rising production costs due to low labour productivity and poor mining conditions, and a fragile financial foundation attributable to high dependence on borrowing. In order to reduce the industry's reliance on borrowed funds and to raise the net worth ratio, it was necessary for the industry to eliminate high-cost conditions and expand the demand for coal. To accomplish this, rationalization projects requiring investment of an enormous amount of funds were essential. In the short run, however, such an effort would drive coal mine operators into a vicious circle of relying ever more heavily on borrowing. It was therefore necessary for MITI to take steps to prevent business conditions from worsening, by providing low-rate financing and stabilizing the coal market, until the industry's rationalization efforts bore fruit and its competitiveness was improved.

MITI thus pressed ahead with its coal-centred energy policy by promoting rationalization of the coal mining industry while making efforts to curtail the increased use of oil, which could lead to a foreign-exchange crisis. This approach verified the 'coal first, oil second' policy, which called for effectively utilizing domestic resources.

Regulation of oil consumption and the petroleum industry

In order to solidify this 'coal first, oil second' policy, towards the end of March 1954 MITI developed what it called coal and oil adjustment measures. The essential feature of these measures was to promote the use of coal—while making efforts to lower coal prices—by encouraging energy conservation, discouraging conversion to oil, and encouraging the combined use of oil and coal in oil-burning facilities, in order to limit the increased use of oil. In keeping with this policy, the Coordination Committee for Heavy Oil Supply and Demand was established to regulate the consumption of oil. The council was to conduct surveys and publish its findings on the percentage of estimated demand which did not surface because of conservation programmes, the size of stocks of heavy oil held by petroleum refineries and heavy oil importers, and the oil conservation targets and standard purchase quantities of large oil-users in the mining and manufacturing industries. As a result, the conversion to oil was almost completely halted. MITI's administrative guidance also produced a gradual conversion to coal, particularly in the cement industry, where large-scale conversion took place. In the electric power industry, too, the reduced consumption of heavy oil was achieved by using combined coal-and-oil-burning facilities primarily for maintenance and start-up purposes, and reducing the load on oil-burning facilities to the maximum extent possible.

The legal basis for this series of measures was the Law on Temporary Measures Regarding Restrictions on Installation of Heavy Oil Boilers. Keidanren and other business organizations mounted a campaign against the proposed legislation, arguing that the bill represented a revival of the oil control of the past, and organized a Committee for Opposing Legislation Regulating Heavy Oil Consumption. The legislative outcome had the effect of merely containing increases in oil consumption because it only limited the new installation and remodelling of boilers. Nonetheless, the legislation was symbolic of the 'coal first, oil second' energy policy.

The regulation of oil consumption had a significant impact on policy measures towards the oil-refining industry and the development of oil resources.[15] The foundation of the oil-refining industry began with the reopening of refineries on the Pacific coast and entering into joint ventures with foreign companies. Even as new firms entered the industry, foreign capital and technology helped to expand existing refineries, build new ones, and generally modernize facilities. In order to secure an adequate supply of crude oil, the development of domestic resources was urgently needed. To that end, in May 1952 the Petroleum and Combustible Natural Gas Resources Development Law was promulgated, and the Five-Year Plan for Petroleum Resources Development was formulated. In 1954, furthermore, the Law for Temporary Measures for Promotion of Oil Resources Exploration was enacted. The system of developing oil resources was reinforced in December 1955 when the government-funded Japan Petroleum Exploration Co. Ltd. (JAPEX) was established.

In the meantime, however, the Japanese demand for crude oil increased dramatically. The proportion of the total supply of crude oil accounted for by domestic sources declined from 3.7 per cent in fiscal year 1955 to 1.9 per cent in fiscal year 1960. Virtually all of the increased demand was filled by crude oil imported by foreign oil companies. This situation brought about the new problem of securing stable supplies of oil, and a solution was sought in two directions. On the one hand, the newly established Arabian Oil Co. and North Sumatra Petroleum Development Cooperation Co. began exploring overseas resources. On the other hand, the oil-refining industry—which refined imported crude oil and marketed petroleum products—introduced new refining technology acquired through technical tie-ups with foreign oil companies, and undertook programmes to expand and modernize their refining capabilities and to build oil tankers.

These rationalization efforts, as those in other industries, were supported by the government with special tax incentives, such as exemptions from import duties on essential equipment and special depreciation allowances. MITI made efforts to nurture the refining industry by promoting refining in Japan through the judicious use of foreign-exchange allocations. Policy during this period, however, lacked consistency, because oil consumption was regulated through the Oil Boilers Control Law and related import duties on crude and heavy oils designed to protect the coal industry. The business climate thus remained harsh for the oil-refining industry.

The Coal Mining Industry Rationalization Temporary Measures Law

Meanwhile, measures for the delayed rationalization of the coal-mining industry were introduced in the form of the Coal Mining Industry Rationalization Temporary Measures Law. The law's objective was to 'lower the price of domestic coal to a level comparable to the prices of heavy oil and imported coal.' The law, which had a five-year limit, was a result of efforts to solidify the 'Comprehensive Energy Measures' (approved by the Cabinet) formulated in May 1955 largely under the leadership of MITI. The essential features of the law were to establish rationalization targets for the coal-mining industry, such as production volume, efficiency, and cost of production; to formulate a basic plan for rationalization (including coal-mining rationalization projects) and an implementation plan, and to secure the funds needed to carry out the rationalization projects.

After much deliberation, the newly established Coal-Mining Council adopted a basic plan for rationalizing the coal industry. The target of the plan was to raise production from approximately 43 million tons recorded in fiscal year 1954 to 51 million tons in fiscal year 1960, and to raise labour productivity (per capita monthly production) from about 13 tons to 18.4 tons during the same period, largely through increased production made possible by shaft mining. The highest priority was placed on lowering coal prices through productivity gains. Since it was government policy to curtail the consumption of oil and promote the reconversion to coal, it was essential for the basic plan to aim for a stable supply of coal at prices which were competitive with imported energy sources such as oil.

Reversal of the Coal Mining Rationalization Plan

The Coal Mining Industry Rationalization Plan, inaugurated as a five-year plan starting in fiscal year 1955, underwent several major revisions during 1955–9. From the second half of 1955, business activities became brisk and conditions in the coal market improved rapidly. The coal mining industry increased its production, and funds earmarked for rationalization programmes were used to support production increases. It was ironic that the Rationalization Law, designed to promote improvements in the essential make-up of the industry, was deprived of that role from the very beginning. Energy policy in 1956–7 was again dictated by the need to promote increased production of coal (see Table 15.4).

In 1956, the Energy Committee of the Industrial Rationalization Council began studying the long-term outlook for energy supply and demand to 1975. While judging that increased reliance on imported energy sources was inevitable, the committee nonetheless expressed in a report to MITI its hope for increased production of coal. The report of the Hartley Committee of the Organization of European Economic Cooperation (OEEC) released in May 1956 recommended that because the Suez Crisis disrupted the supply of crude oil to Europe, the European countries should secure a stable supply of energy resources through development of domestic resources, and prices should be lowered through rationalization efforts. These developments were instrumental in prompting the reversal of the Japanese government's energy policy towards increased production of coal. In response to this change of policy, the Industrial Planning Conference (Yasuzaemon Matsunaga, chairman) in November 1956 criticized the high price of coal and the restrictions placed on consumption of heavy oil. It argued that the reliance on coal was a factor impeding the progress of the Japanese economy, and stressed the need to convert the principal source of energy to economical heavy oil. Heading into 1957, therefore, opinions concerning coal and oil were sharply divided, reflecting the fact that energy policy was at a crossroads.

Table 15.4   Supply quantities and prices of coal and oil, 1951–1958

	Coal production		Ex-mine price (yen)	Crude oil	
	Large suppliers (1,000 tons)	Small and medium suppliers (1,000 tons)		Import volume (1,000 kl.)	Price of Grade A heavy oil (yen/kl.)
1951	32,333	14,157	3,866	3,304	
1952	28,989	14,759	4,598	4,825	13,352
1953	28,940	14,598	4,603	6,125	12,792
1954	29,797	13,115	4,101	7,570	13,100
1955	28,511	14,004	4,003	9,271	13,200
1956	31,988	16,293	3,940	12,514	13,183
1957	33,945	18,310	4,120	14,919	12,820
1958	31,132	17,357	4,098	16,942	11,139

Sources:
1. For coal production: *Gendai Nippon Sangyo Koza* (Lecture on Modern Japanese Industry), III, 1960: 313.
2. For ex-mine prices: *Tsusho Sangyo Seisakushi* (History of International Trade and Industry Policy), vi: 338, 360, 377.
3. For import volume of crude oil, ibid., vii: 526.
4. For price of Grade A heavy oil: *Seiji Keizai Kenkyusho, Nippon no Sekiyu Sangyo* (The Japanese Oil Industry), Toyo Keizai Inc., 1959: 82.

Against that background, MITI in March 1957 established an energy-measures study group, and began studying a long-term energy programme. In the end, Director-General Ichiro Kono of the Economic Planning Agency announced in August 1957 the 'Kono Plan' based on a 'coal first, oil second' strategy. The study of energy policy undertaken at the government level, which had begun with an exercise to develop a long-term outlook on energy supply and demand, was now shifting to a policy of aggressively promoting the increased production of coal.

This change of policy was confirmed in the New Long-Term Economic Plan which had been studied by the Economic Council. The position of the Economic Council was that 'as a means of minimizing conflicts concerning employment, and in view of the positive effect on foreign-exchange savings, it is desirable to give priority to the increased production or new development of domestic coal.'[16] This emphasis on employment and foreign-exchange conservation gave the impression that the premiss of public policy on energy had reverted to that prevailing before the enactment of the Coal-Mining Industry Rationalization Law. Thus, while admitting the inevitability of increasingly relying on imported energy sources as far as the 'direction of change in the supply and demand of energy' was concerned, the Energy Committee of the Economic Council nonetheless emphasized the importance of securing a stable supply of energy and conserving foreign exchange as far as the 'fundamental direction of energy policy' was concerned. The committee therefore concluded that, to the extent economically feasible, energy policy should be built on maximum efforts to develop domestic sources of energy. As specific measures for such efforts, the committee suggested (1) making aggressive efforts to increase production of domestic coal, (2) accelerating programmes to develop hydroelectric power generation, (3) promoting nuclear power generation, and (4) securing overseas sources of oil resources and strengthening the means of transporting them.

Energy policy thus took a sharp turn towards rationalization through increased domestic production of coal. In keeping with this change of policy, the Coal-Mining Industry Rationalization Temporary Measures Law was revised, and coal policy, the heart of energy policy, changed its direction two years after the law was enacted. The unexpectedly rapid pace of economic growth was responsible for this new policy, which pinned unreasonably high hopes on coal as the primary source for Japan's future supply of energy. This plan, however, proved unsuccessful. As discussed in detail in Part III, MITI reassessed its policy towards the coal industry in 1959 and 1960, and once again emphasized measures to rationalize its operation.

Acceleration of electric power development

As discussed in Chapter 13, MITI in August 1952 regained jurisdiction over the electric power industry when the Public Utilities Commission was disbanded. It immediately had to press ahead with electric power development and make supply-and-demand adjustments by limiting the use of electric power and adopting a system of electric power allocation.[17] The shortage of electricity was so severe for ten years from 1951 that power consumption was restricted every year except in 1958 and 1959, when demand for electric power did not increase much owing to the effects of the recession shaped like the 'bottom of a frying pan'.

Only the development of electric power sources held any promise of radically solving the energy problem. For that reason, the Electric Power Development Coordination Council, established in August 1952, formulated medium- and long-term power development plans at just about yearly intervals. From fiscal year 1956, the scale of these plans gradually became larger each time they were revised. It was noteworthy that the role of the Electric Power Development Co. in these development plans became increasingly less important, the focus of development plans shifted from hydroelectric to thermoelectric generation, and, starting with the Long-Term Electric Power Plan formulated in 1960, nuclear power generation was incorporated into development plans. These plans prompted the Electric Power Development Co. and the nine electric power companies to engage in development efforts, and also significantly affected the allocation pattern of the huge sums needed for the projects. In order to meet the need for ever-increasing project funds, the government aggressively poured funds into these projects until the second half of the 1950s, although at times it had to reduce or defer them when tight monetary conditions prevailed.

As a consequence, during the ten-year period between 1951 and 1960, the nine power companies altogether acquired new power-generating capacity of 3.5 million kW. in hydroelectric power and 6.32 million kW. in thermal power, more than doubling the total electric-power-generating capacity from 8.54 million kW. when the industry was reorganized (May 1951) to 17.81 million kW. at the end of 1960. Fiscal Investment and Loan Programme (FILP) funds supplied 38.0 per cent of the total plant and equipment investments of the electric power industry of 650.8 billion yen during fiscal years 1951–5 and 26.5 per cent of total investments of 1,425.2 billion yen during fiscal years 1956–60, or an average of 30.1 per cent during the ten-year period. As a result of these enormous investments, the chronic shortage of power was eradicated and rationalization results, such as increased heat efficiency in thermal power generation, reduced the power loss ratio, and enhanced productivity through the automation and mechanization of facilities was realized. For instance, the number of employees of the nine electric companies relative to capacity of thermal power generation fell from 3.96 per 1,000 kW. in fiscal year 1951 to 2.63 per 1,000 kW., and the rate of fuel consumption in thermal generation improved during the same period from 0.876 kg. to 0.490 kg. per kWh.[18]

Meanwhile, problems related to power development projects became increasingly serious. Particularly noteworthy was the fact that although large-dam power plants constructed successively from around 1954 onwards contributed to establishing an economical power supply, they created the problem of compensation for damages which arose from large-scale hydroelectric projects. To deal with these problems, the Cabinet approved on 14 April 1953 a 'Guidelines for Loss Compensation Related to Electric Power Development', and introduced pertinent measures, including clarification of the criteria for assessing whether property was qualified for compensation.

Another serious problem was the fact that sites for large-capacity hydroelectric power stations became increasingly difficult to find. For that reason, in the second half of the 1950s the nine electric companies focused their development efforts on thermal power generation, while the Electric Power Development Co. continued to develop hydroelectric power. This shift to thermal power moved in the opposite direction to the government's basic policy on energy, suggesting that the nine power companies should switch to an 'oil first, water second' strategy before the government did. This shift was occasioned by the 'Draft Plan for Modernizing Electric Power Facilities' (the so-called 'Matsunaga Plan') announced in March 1955 by the Central Research Institute of the Electric Power Industry. The ideas contained in the plan had been fairly widely accepted in the electric power industry. The industry, in developing a long-term outlook on the supply of energy, suggested a conversion to imported energy resources because, having considered the economics involved and the ease of handling oil, and realizing the limit to developing further hydroelectric power stations in Japan, it was concluded that a shift to heavy-oil-burning thermal stations was all but inevitable. As discussed earlier, however, this conclusion was limited by the 'just cause' of conserving foreign exchange, and did not lead to a consensus among public policymakers. The conversion to 'oil first, coal second' was not publicly espoused until 1959 and later.

Revision of electric power rates and the beginning of cross-border power interchange

In 1951 and 1952, electric power rates, which had been fixed at a low level under a system of state control, were revised upwards twice with the approval of the Public Utilities Commission. Subsequently, as the nine power companies enthusiastically pursued their programmes of electric power development, their capital costs rose sharply, necessitating rate increases to cover the increased costs. Revisions to electric power rates carried out in 1954 and 1957 were thus essentially responses to rising costs.

The 1957 rate increases, made only by Tohoku Electric Power Co. and Hokuriku Electric Power Co., created a stir in various circles since they created a geographical disparity in rates. This had been a concern of many when the industry was reorganized in 1951. The rate increases led to demand for a review of the overall system of power rates on the one hand, and a call for yet another reorganization of the industry on the other.

In that situation, MITI in December 1957 established an Advisory Committee for an Electric Power Rates System. The ministry reviewed the rate question based on a report submitted by the committee, and in January 1960 adopted the 'Guidelines for Revision of the System of Electric Power Rates'. These guidelines were intended to 'establish a rational rate system in order to effect long-term stability of power rates', and was made up of eight points, including strict adherence to historical-cost accounting, rationalization of depreciation methods, and adoption of the rate-base method for determining business returns.

The question of a second reorganization of the electric power industry prompted the start of cross-border power exchanges during the delay in enactment of the new Electric Utilities Industry Law, discussed in Chapter 13. The nine power companies sensed a crisis brewing. They realized that rate increases brought about by interdistrict differentials were spawning public criticism of the nine-company system and arguments for yet another reorganization of the industry aimed at reforming the system. In order to solve the problem of interdistrict differentials by mutual cooperation, the nine companies proposed introducing a system of large-area power interchange with participation of the Electric Power Development Co. Subsequently, after some differences in opinion between MITI and the industry concerning the method of implementing the large-area system, a cross-border power interchange system came into being in April 1958. The gist of the new system was described as follows.

The system is intended to contribute towards stabilizing the supply of electric power and power rates through the interchange of power and the joint development of power resources, while preserving the existing system of autonomous business management of the power companies. The national market is to be divided into four regions, and a system of cooperation among the companies in each region and among the regions is to be firmly established to increase power interchange, develop power resources from a supra-regional standpoint, jointly use reserve facilities, improve power-distribution linkages, rationally utilize existing facilities, reduce capital costs, conserve fuel, reduce transmission losses, and effectively utilize surplus power.[19]

Thus, the second reorganization question, triggered by the rate-increase issue, was answered for the moment.

Meanwhile, nuclear power moved into the spotlight as a new source of energy.[20] At this time, however, its peaceful use was still at the research and development phase. In December 1955, the Basic Law on Atomic Energy and the Atomic Energy Commission Establishment Law (Law 188 of 19 December 1955 which came into effect on 1 January 1956) were enacted. Research on the development of nuclear energy pressed ahead under the leadership of the Science and Technology Agency. This programme of developing nuclear power, which made a sudden start with great anticipation in the mid-1950s, was initiated on the grounds that nuclear power generation had already become commercially viable. However, the nuclear power programme, which lacked an adequate underpinning of research and development, encountered many difficulties, and failed to provide a new source of energy.

15.5. Rationalization of Mature Industries

Two fertilizer laws and rationalization of the ammonium sulphate industry

In part because of the demand for increased production of foodstuffs, the production capacity of the ammonium sulphate industry was restored in 1949 to its pre-war level ahead of all other industries. In 1950, government control of the industry was removed. Subsequent public policy towards fertilizer production was characterized by the two opposing objectives of keeping prices low from the standpoint of agricultural policy and maintaining profitable prices in order to nurture the development of the ammonium sulphate industry.[21] Among the chemical industries, because the ammonium sulphate industry was already well established—unlike emerging industries such as the petrochemical industry—it could not expect to achieve cost reductions through rapid technological advances. Moreover, the interests of the companies in the industry differed because so many of them were similar in size of operation (Table 15.5). It was therefore difficult for the government to achieve a balance between the two opposing objectives mentioned above. The supply and demand sides held sharply divided views on what constituted appropriate prices. As a result, MITI, whose objective was to rationalize the fertilizer industry, experienced many difficulties in resolving differences of opinion with the Ministry of Agriculture and Forestry, which was partial to the interest of fertilizer users, and the Economic Deliberation Board whose primary interest was price stability.

Table 15.5 Ammonium sulphate industry in Japan

Company	Total assets (Second half of fiscal year 1958) (million yen)	Production capacity (April 1958) (tons)
Toyo Koatsu Industries	31,218	836,600
Sumitomo Chemical	42,409	540,000
Mitsubishi Chemical Industries	33,127	455,000
Showa Denko	32,315	444,000
Ube Industries	31,081	400,000
Nitto Chemical Industry	18,740	330,000
Nissan Chemical Industries	15,323	295,700
Toagosei	13,239	181,400
Nippon Suiso Kogyo	6,458	179,000
Beppu Chemical	6,970	155,000
Kyowa Hakko Kogyo	17,333	152,000
Shin Nippon Chisso	18,566	150,800
and five others	54,425	586,500
Total	321,204	4,706,000

Source: *Gendai Nippon Sangyo Koza* (Lecture on Modern Japanese Industry), IV, 1959: 118.

In February 1952, the Agriculture and Forestry Committee of the House of Representatives passed a resolution concerning the stabilization of fertilizer prices, and requested that the government take measures to restrict fertilizer exports and promote increased production of fertilizers. In response to this request, the government in August announced a policy of giving priority to the domestic market and restricting long-term and large exports of fertilizers. It also showed concern for the interests of fertilizer manufacturers and agricultural organizations by setting a range of stable prices. At about the same time, however, an increase in the exports of fertilizer from Europe to the rest of the world led to a sharp decline in fertilizer prices in overseas markets, creating a disparity in Japan between export prices and domestic prices and turning the relatively high domestic prices into a political issue.

In order to deal with the problem, the government studied the issue by establishing a Fertilizer Measures Committee in the Economic Deliberation Board. In July 1953, that committee submitted two reports on measures to adjust the supply and demand of ammonium sulphate and measures to rationalize the fertilizer industry. The committee suggested that an Ammonium Sulphate Committee be established, whose functions would be to study important matters related to the price and supply-and-demand situation of ammonium sulphate and to submit reports and make recommendations to the government. The committee would be charged with developing specific measures for 'effectively stabilizing domestic prices, reducing production costs and prices through rationalization, and promoting exports by maintaining a proper balance between domestic and export demand.'

On the basis of this report, the Temporary Law on Fertilizer Demand–Supply Stabilization and the Temporary Measures Law for the Ammonium Sulphate Industry Rationalization and Export Adjustment were enacted. Under these laws, a formula for determining the selling prices of manufacturers, called the 'Method of Weighted Average within the Bulk Line' was established. Although this formula led to a decline in domestic prices, it also compelled many producers to sell their products at prices that did not cover their costs. As a result, fertilizer consumption by farmers increased, but falling prices prompted ammonium sulphate manufacturers to diversify their production to urea and other products.

As the ammonium sulphate market deteriorated further, voices were raised demanding radical revision of the two fertilizer laws, which were approaching the end of their limited terms. Within the fertilizer industry itself, however, opinions were divided between those who wanted to have production capacity regulated through legislation and those who would prefer autonomous coordination among firms in the industry. Users of fertilizers, on the other hand, strongly opposed any measures which would lead to higher prices. Since a consensus could not be easily reached, the idea of legislating capacity coordination was abandoned and the two fertilizer laws were extended for five more years in 1959 with no revisions made in the formula for determining prices. The domestic and international environments surrounding the fertilizer industry were undergoing dramatic changes, and the conflict of interests between users and producers could not be resolved. No radical changes, therefore, were made in the public policy towards supply and demand in the ammonium sulphate industry and its rationalization.

Production cutbacks by advice, and export controls in the textile industry

The textile industry, which benefited from the Korean War boom and enjoyed a rapid increase in exports, invested aggressively in plant and equipment, leading to a sharp increase in production capacity. The degree of market concentration of textile manufacturers declined, making the industry more competitive.[22] Moreover, because the production equipment installed during the boom period was more efficient than existing facilities, the competitiveness of spinners who had recently entered the market was substantial and the production capacity of the industry increased proportionally more than the increase in the number of installed spindles. This sharp increase in the production capacity of the textile industry, particularly the cotton industry, resulted in serious excess capacity as overseas demand declined from the second half of 1951 to the end of the Korean War in 1953.

In that situation, MITI resorted to an advisory to curtail operations. To ensure 'compliance' with its 'advice', it requested firms to report their production plans, amount of production, and actual consumption of electric power. The last report had to be supported by a certificate of authentication issued by a power company. Furthermore, MITI backed up its requests by endowing itself with indirect power of compulsion derived from its authority to allocate foreign exchange. The ministry announced that it intended to 'take appropriate steps in making future allocations of dollar funds for importing raw cotton, in order to secure an optimum level of capacity utilization.'

The system of foreign-exchange allocation used as a measure to supplement the advisory to curtail operations also functioned in those days as an export-promotion measure. Under the export-linkage system, foreign exchange needed for importing raw materials was allocated preferentially to successful exporters. Although this linkage system was quite effective as a measure of encouraging exports and therefore of coping with the pressing balance-of-payments problem, it also had the negative short-term side effect of encouraging spinning companies to export cotton goods at prices below cost so that they could obtain larger allocations of raw cotton imports. The practice often resulted in saturation exports of low-priced Japanese cotton goods, and produced a damaging denunciation of Japanese export practices in many parts of the world.

Towards the end of 1954, MITI revised the linkage system, and imposed voluntary export restraints, including a quantitative control over exports of cotton goods to Europe, to contend with the policy introduced by British Commonwealth countries of discriminating against imports of cotton goods from Japan. Furthermore, in order to deal with the problem encountered in exports to the US, as symbolized by the 'one-dollar blouse' issue, MITI imposed voluntary export restraints on exports of cotton goods to the US from December 1955, in response to moves in that country to legislate restrictions on imports of Japanese cotton goods.

The need to introduce measures such as recommended production cutbacks and voluntary export restraints discussed above arose from the fact that the textile industry reached maturity at about this time. It suffered an imbalance between supply and demand while the condition of excess capacity that developed during the Korean War boom was left unsolved. Manufacturers were thus driven to step up their export efforts in order to make up for weak domestic demand. To deal with this situation, MITI established in August 1955 the Council for Comprehensive Measures for the Textile Industry. Based on a report from that council, the Law on Temporary Measures for Textile Industry Equipment was drafted in February 1956. The bill addressed the problem of excess capacity, and included provisions for compulsory disposition of excess capacity and exemption of collusive activities from the provisions of the Anti-Monopoly Law. The law was promulgated in June 1956.

Immediately prior to enactment of this law, a last-minute rush on plant and equipment investment developed in anticipation of controls being applied to increases in textile production capacity. Although the increased investments at that time did not lead immediately to excess capacity because of the Jimmu Boom, it began to pose a serious problem during the recession shaped like the 'bottom of a frying pan' that ensued. To deal with the situation, MITI introduced several measures, including severe limitation on production, adjustment of inventories through purchases by agencies, and revision of the Textile Industry Equipment Law in order to accelerate a reduction in excess capacity. The textile industry, however, needed an even more extensive structural adjustment in the face of imminent liberalization of imports.

15.6. Nurturing of the Petrochemical Industry

Adoption of a policy to nurture the petrochemical industry

From around 1955, a major transformation occurred within the chemical industry. There was a shift of focus from traditional inorganic chemicals to organic chemicals, and the petrochemical industry was born.[23] The petrochemical industry was a typical emerging industry where firms vied for entry while engaging in fierce competition to adopt foreign technology. The programme of fostering the growth of this industry became one of the important pillars of MITI's policy of protecting and nurturing new industries, a principal characteristic of its industrial policy of the period. Specifically, the primary task was to develop the petrochemical industry into an internationally competitive industry by promoting the demand for new products and selecting an optimum scale and appropriate technology for the industry. This policy theme was common to all of MITI's programmes of nurturing new industries during this period, which were aimed at a greater sophistication of the economy. The economy had barely regained its self-supporting status and was starting on its way towards sustained growth.

The beginning of policies to promote Japan's petrochemical industry dates back to June 1951 when the Organic Division of MITI's International Trade Chemical Bureau prepared a report entitled 'Concerning the Oil-Based Organic Synthetic Chemical Industry'. The ministry's subsequent policy for the chemical industry, however, did not follow a path of promoting it as a basic industry supplying industrial materials. Rather, the ministry sought to nurture the synthetic fibre industry in order to ease the pressing international payments imbalance through substitution of imports by domestic products.

It was not until 1954, three years later, that MITI finally turned its attention to nurturing the petroleum cracking sector as a means of securing industrial materials. On 25 May 1954, the Lower House of the Diet passed a Resolution to Promote the Synthetic Organic Chemical Industry. Prompted by this move, MITI decided to adopt a positive policy towards promoting the development of two key industrial materials, i.e. synthetic fibres and synthetic resins (plastics), and the petrochemical industry, which would supply the raw materials for their production. The guiding principle for promoting the petrochemical industry was to establish a world-class production system from the start of commercialization with the aim of supplying at internationally competitive prices the demand projected at a certain point in the future.

The Petrochemical Consultative Group was established to study the details of the commercialization programme following the principles described above. The report prepared by the group in February 1955 recommended that the new petrochemical industry produce ethylene, its raw material, by the naphtha-cracking method. It also recommended producing 5,500 tons of ethylene annually as the minimum capacity needed for producing petrochemical products. Responding to this report, MITI prepared projections of supply and demand of chemical products through fiscal year 1959 as support for determining the most appropriate scale of the plans for proposed petrochemical projects. On the basis of these projections, MITI approved in a ministerial meeting in July 1955 the Measures for Fostering the Petrochemical Industry.

Adjustment to the first-period Petrochemical Industry Plan

These moves were suggestive of the future potential of the petrochemical industry. Starting around 1952, new petroleum refineries were constructed one after another, producing by-products which provided material for the petrochemical industry. In part prompted by this development, firms in the petroleum-refining and chemical industries began successively applying for entry into the petrochemical industry during the period 1952–5. In this first period of the Petrochemical Industry Plan, MITI from the beginning sought to promote petrochemical complexes whose scale of operation was large enough to enable the companies to be competitive in the global market. It considered it essential that project plans be such that their outcome would be adequate to meet domestic demand without creating excess capacity. It also considered it necessary, in approving importation of foreign technology requiring payment of foreign currency, to approve only those technologies which had a high probability of producing positive results. Small-scale operations that might fail in world competition would not be considered, even though various protective measures were to be made available for their nurturing. Since liberalization of trade was a worldwide trend, MITI required that the project plan of each applicant be such that the operation would remain competitive even in the environment of an open economy.

Meanwhile, MITI had nearly resolved the question of how to dispose of the former army fuel storage depots, which had become an issue related to the resumption of the petroleum-refining industry. It altered its disposition plan primarily in the direction of incorporating those refineries into the petrochemical industry projects. Meanwhile, the Foreign Capital Council approved the import of key technologies. The project plans of all the applicant companies that emerged from these developments turned out to be substantial. Fearing excess capacity, MITI made it known in February 1956 that it would consider very critically any further project plans beyond those of the six existing producers (Maruzen Oil Co. Ltd., Nippon Petrochemicals Co. Ltd., Mitsubishi Oil Co. Ltd., Sumitomo Chemical Co. Ltd., Mitsui Petrochemical Industries Ltd., and Mitsubishi Petrochemical

Co. Ltd.). Investment in the petrochemical industry, however, continued unabated. Showa Denko K.K. in July 1956 and Idemitsu Kosan Co. Ltd. in August submitted project plans at the same time that Furukawa Electric Co. Ltd. prepared a plan of its own. When MITI approved the polyethylene production plans of Showa Denko, Furukawa Chemical (subsidiary of Furukawa Electric Co. Ltd.), and Mitsubishi Petrochemical in November 1956, it attached the condition that these three companies take steps to prevent excess production and reduce their production by about 10 per cent. It also required the companies to revise their plans from the standpoints of optimum project scale and cost reduction. Thus, although the polyethylene project plan turned out to be nearly twice as large as initially planned, MITI throughout the process made the best use of overall capacity, fearing that the rush to invest might lead to excess capacity.

This sense of wariness was manifest in the repeated attempts by MITI—at about the time it was studying the first period of the Petrochemical Industry Plan—to enact an 'industry law' aimed at fostering the petrochemical industry. The Petrochemical Industry Law, as it was initially conceived, would have required that petrochemical projects be approved by the Minister of International Trade and Industry in order to avoid overcapacity, and that approval criteria be established to allow a division of labour in the production system and product categories in order to avoid market dominance by a few firms. In May 1956, moreover, a Chemical Industry Promotion Bill was formulated with greater emphasis being placed on policy measures to foster and promote the chemical industry. Both of these 'industry law' proposals would empower the government to adjust private investment plans. It is interesting that the proposals surfaced despite the fact that the government could have availed itself of administrative guidance, e.g. the authority to approve foreign-technology imports by using the Foreign Capital Law or to allocate foreign-exchange for imports of machinery and equipment. The reason these proposals failed to result in legislation was because of opposition from industries that feared intensified bureaucratic control. Still, these facts are suggestive of the intensity of MITI's awareness of the problem in trying to coordinate private plans for new petrochemical projects.

Notwithstanding MITI's misgivings, the petrochemical industry recorded rapid growth. Of course the growth reflected the effects of government-support measures. A variety of tax incentives and promotional programmes, including, for example, special allocation of foreign exchange for imports of crude oil, produced positive effects. And loans from the Japan Development Bank served as the lever for completing the first period of the Petrochemical Industry Plan by priming the pump of the lending facility of private financial institutions. As a consequence, it was estimated that domestic production of petrochemical products saved an equivalent cumulative total of $103 million worth of foreign exchange during the period 1957–9. These products also contributed much to the growth of the Japanese economy by lowering prices and improving product quality.

The rapidly growing petrochemical industry quite naturally attracted additional new entrants. The new wave of enthusiasm was precipitated by Mitsubishi

Petrochemical Co. Ltd. filing a project plan in December 1958. Other firms followed suit in rapid succession, creating once again a phenomenon called 'the petrochemical rush' during 1959 and 1960. This development compelled MITI to formulate a new set of criteria for approving project plans, as well as pressing it to deal with ever-expanding investment programmes.

Formation of the synthetic rubber industry

Of the policies to develop new industries, the synthetic rubber industry presented a somewhat unusual case. The policy to foster it was precipitated by the suggestion made in February 1952 by the International Trade General Merchandise Bureau of MITI to produce domestically styrene-butadiene rubber (SBR)—with the aim of self-sufficiency in rubber—by producing butadiene from alcohol. The bureau led the ministry's subsequent effort to continue its study on the policy of producing rubber domestically. In those days, there were two alternative approaches to the creation of a rubber industry: first, immediate formation of the industry using the alcohol method; and second, a slower approach which would use the petrochemical method. No selection had yet been made between the two approaches. While the plan to develop the petrochemical industry was yet to be formulated, it was difficult to see how the petrochemical approach to rubber manufacturing would work. In short, a foundation was lacking on which a concrete plan could be built to develop and foster a synthetic rubber industry.

In 1955, the price of natural rubber rose while the programme to develop the petrochemical industry was well under way. At this time, plans were finally submitted by Mitsubishi Chemical Industries Ltd., Sanyo Chemical Co. Ltd., and Nippon Zeon Co. Ltd. to produce synthetic rubber domestically using the petrochemical method. MITI studied these plans and concluded here again that the main problems were the uncertain future demand for synthetic rubber and the need to avoid excess capacity. MITI, however, was not able to coordinate the production plans of the three companies. Against a MITI-sponsored scheme of creating a state-policy company with the government investing about 1.5 billion yen and the Japan Development Bank providing a low-interest loan of about 7.8 billion yen, Nippon Zeon insisted on following its own plan. In the end, MITI decided to approve the Nippon Zeon plan as well as going ahead with its own scheme. Under the Law on Special Measures Concerning Synthetic Rubber Production enacted in June 1957, Nippon Synthetic Rubber Manufacturing was created. The plan for producing synthetic rubber in Japan, which started in 1952, finally became a reality.

15.7. The Promotion of the Machinery Industry

The Law on Temporary Measures for Promotion of the Machinery Industry

As was discussed in Chapter 14, the machinery industry led the transformation of the industrial structure that took place during this period. At the beginning of the period, however, the machinery industry faced many problems, including low product quality and the high cost of components arising from the backward technology in assembly and parts manufacturing, as well as the slow pace of equipment replacement and the ageing of equipment, both attributable to inadequate capital.[24] It was against this background that a subsidy on machine tool imports was introduced in fiscal year 1952 in order to help upgrade the facilities of the machine tool industry suffering from advanced obsolescence and deterioration. The aim of the programme was to facilitate imports of machine tools by providing subsidies covering 50 per cent of the import price. Further, a system of machine tool subsidies covering 50 per cent of trial production expenses was introduced in fiscal year 1953 to encourage the domestic production of machine tools.

As these measures were put into effect, it became apparent that the introduction of new machines was having remarkably favourable effects in improving quality, performance, and productivity. This realization led to a search for solutions to the problems faced by the machinery industry. As a result, a Proposal for Establishing a Machinery Industry Promotion Public Corporation was made in 1953, followed in November by the Three-Year Plan for Improvement of Machinery Industry Equipment. Two years later, November 1955 saw the introduction of the Guidelines on Measures for the Modernization of Key Machinery Industries (Five-Year Plan for Equipment Improvement), and the Plan for Establishing a Machinery Industries Promotion Agency. The second plan for creating a promotion agency was based on the idea of covering all machinery industries, including cars and electric machinery, as targets of the promotion policy, and 'selecting outstanding plants for further development of their capabilites'.[25] That plan was thus clearly based on an awareness of the same policy objective that led to the subsequent passing of the Law on Temporary Measures for Promotion of the Machinery Industry. The idea, however, did not result in legislation, partly because fiscal exigencies made government investment difficult and partly because there were 'strong objections to the proposal because there was a number of problems given the nature of the existing financial system.'[26] MITI's policy of promoting the machinery industry, therefore, changed in favour of legislating the Law on Temporary Measures for Promotion of the Machinery Industry while utilizing the 'existing financial system'.

The Law on Temporary Measures for Promotion of the Machinery Industry went into effect in June 1956. With a five-year time-limit, the law aimed at promoting the modernization of the machinery industry. A number of industries were specified for coverage, and a variety of subsidies was provided for modernization plans and modernization implementation plans that specified clear goals for improving performance, quality, or the production cost of certain types of machines. The law would also secure needed funds, promote collusive activities, and announce criteria for the improvement of manufacturing technology. It was aimed at rectifying the shortcomings of the industrial organization of the machinery industry manifest in the phenomena of 'excessive competition' and 'large-variety, small-batch production' by means of governmental efforts to secure needed funds for implementing the plans and promoting collusive activities.

Under the law's provisions, a series of specific measures were put into effect, including the work of the Machine Industry Council to select industries to be covered, to formulate the Basic Rationalization Plan, and to develop the First-Year Plan Implementing Rationalization, as well as fairly aggressive channelling of funds from the Fiscal Investment and Loan Programme budget into equipment investment projects within the limits of the tight budgetary situation. Particular emphasis was placed, in terms of the composition of FILP outlays, on machine tools, cutting-tool dies, gears, automotive parts, and sewing-machine parts.

In comparing planned equipment investments and actual investments, only five of the nineteen designated industries failed to meet the plan targets. The other fourteen exceeded their targets. Although not all of the invested funds were obtained from public sources, it was pointed out that loans from the Japan Development Bank had the effect of priming the pump of the loan facilities of private financial institutions.[27] In terms of equipment-replacement programmes, the demand for new equipment far exceeded initial projections, and newly acquired equipment far exceeded scrapped equipment, contributing noticeably to the modernization of production facilities and increased productivity. For instance, cost-reduction targets were clearly met in twelve machine categories.

Enactment of the Law on Extraordinary Measures for Promotion of the Electronics Industry

The electronics industry in Japan started with the production of radios and television receivers for household use. Television receivers were regarded as a promising product, and at the end of fiscal year 1952 there were over sixty manufacturers, including those who were planning production. New manufacturers had just started small-scale production, and the prices of their products were high—at a level nearly six times the average monthly income of a working household. The industry had a long and arduous way to go before it reached maturity.

In 1951, moreover, Post-War Measures on Industrial Property Rights of the Allied Nations were implemented, establishing patent rights in Japan for wartime inventions made in foreign countries. That made it impossible for Japanese companies to manufacture products on which foreign companies held patent rights unless they entered into licensing agreements with them. With respect to television receivers, in particular, the series of basic patents held by RCA Corporation of the US constituted a serious obstacle to domestic production. Thus, a high priority was placed on importing electronics technologies, and their aggressive importation was promoted.

In the early stages, the domestic production of electronics products was developed based on imported technologies. To that end, such measures as providing subsidies to experimental research and promoting the improvement and standardization of components were studied. For patent rights, moreover, a policy was adopted whereby 'excellent manufacturers' were selectively nurtured by approving foreign-currency payments only in cases where a particular patent was recognized as contributing positively to the development of, say, the Japanese television-manufacturing industry. The government encouraged corporations to seek the excellent manufacturer designation, and approved participation by all designated firms on the principle of equal opportunity. In line with this policy, selective allocation of foreign exchange and a large increase in research subsidies in mining and manufacturing became a reality.

Subsequently, the 'Interim Report on Measures to Promote the Electronics Industry' released in December 1956 by the Special Committee for Promoting the Electronics Industry of the Machinery Industry Council identified the electronics industry along with the nuclear energy industry as industries that would lead Japan's new industrial revolution. It expected the electronics industry to play a major role in increasing productivity and rationalizing industry. In view of this, the report recommended that a positive policy of promoting the electronics industry's development was needed if the technological gap between Japan and the advanced industrial nations of the West was to be bridged and the deficiencies in the financial and technological capabilities of Japanese companies were to be rectified. This recommendation prompted an effort to develop a systematic policy of nurturing and developing the electronics industry.

The first promotional measure considered was application of the Law on Temporary Measures for Promotion of the Machinery Industry to the electronics industry. Various problems were recognized, however, in applying that law to the electronics industry, especially since it was considerably less developed than the machinery industries. Instead, therefore, the Law on Temporary Measures for the Promotion of the Electronics Industry was promulgated in June 1957. The contents of the new law were similar to those of the Law on Temporary Measures for Promotion of the Machinery Industry. The Electronics Industry Promotion Law, however, stipulated that a Basic Plan for Promotion of the Electronics Industry would divide the targets of promotion into three categories, according to level of development—experimental research, initial production, and industrial modernization—thereby extending promotional coverage to the experimental stage.

Specifically, in the category of electronics equipment twenty-one items were designated for promotion of experimental research, eight were selected for subsidies on initial production, and two types of equipment were designated for industrial modernization. Among those designated for promotion of experimental research, digital computers were on the top of the list. Measures to be taken to promote joint development efforts already in progress included giving subsidies, providing tax incentives, securing foreign exchange for importing equipment for experimental research, securing the cooperation of national research organizations, promoting importation of needed technology, and restricting imports of competing products.

In the categories of components and materials, thirty-five items were designated, including fourteen for promotion of experimental research, five for subsidizing initial production, and sixteen for support of industrial modernization. Here, too, among those designated for promotion of experimental research, high-purity silicon and transistors, both closely related to the development of computers, received high priorities.

The target figures of the Basic Plan for Promotion of the Electronics Industry described above were rather ambitious for the period under study. Nonetheless, the actual record of achievement in 1959 exceeded the target for the year by 36.1 per cent, reaching 78.1 per cent of the ultimate targets with three years of the plan period still remaining. The rates of target achievement, however, varied markedly among products. A need thus arose in 1960 to eliminate the discrepancy between targets and actual achievements, and to revise the plan to enable it play a role of providing guidelines for the promotion policy. At this point, MITI believed that in order for the electronics industry to develop as one of Japan's key industries in the future it would have to outgrow its reliance on radios and television receivers and, as in the US, 'its development must be led by industrial electronics with a focus on computers and industrial instruments.' From this standpoint, MITI believed that policy measures and plan targets had to be established to reallocate resources towards promoting the growth of industrial electronics. Furthermore, the promotion plan needed review in response to the imminent liberalization of international trade. For these reasons, MITI decided to revise the plan, and a new plan for the period 1960–4 was formulated, giving a much higher priority than before to automation equipment, centred on computers.

Despite the high priority given to the development of computers, it was very difficult for Japan to catch up with the world leader, the US. It not only had to catch up with the use of transistors in terms of the technological innovation progressing at the time but also had to solve various problems in such areas as acquiring capability to develop peripheral equipment and related software programs, running the risk of enormous sums of development expenses, and finding ways to cultivate demand and provide the funds needed to compete with IBM's rental system. If IBM can be called a giant in the computer industry of the period, the Japanese computer industry was a dwarf preparing to pursue the giant.[28]

15.8. Stabilization and Organization of the Small-Business Sector

The Small and Medium Enterprises Stabilization Law and system of adjustment associations

As discussed in Chapter 14, against the background of the dual structure thesis the solution of problems faced by small businesses was considered crucial for developing the Japanese economy.[29] For that purpose, various measures were introduced, one of which was a policy to organize the small-business sector. This was one of the pillars of small-business policies of the 1945–54 period. Following this policy, the Small and Medium Enterprises Cooperative Association Law was enacted in 1949. Additionally, the Small and Medium Enterprises Stabilization Law and the Law Concerning the Organization of Small and Medium Enterprise Organizations were enacted during this period to improve the chronically depressed situation of the small-business sector. Also, new institutions called 'adjustment associations', a variant of anti-recession cartels, were established. The Small and Medium Enterprises Cooperative Association Law was revised six times between 1952 and 1960, during which time the legal system was being put in order and guidance and support were being energetically provided to cooperative associations. Leaders were trained and various outlines and guidelines were prepared to provide guidance for establishing and operating cooperative associations. Furthermore, various types of government aid were provided following enactment of the Law on Financing and Other Measures for Aiding Small and Medium Enterprises in 1956. These measures, however, were not sufficient to bring about substantial development in the joint activities of cooperatives.

It was anticipated that adjustment associations would replace cooperative associations because of the limited effectiveness of the latter. The Law on Temporary Measures Concerning the Stabilization of Specified Small and Medium Enterprises passed in August 1952 provided for the establishment of such associations (anti-recession cartels) outside the provisions of the Anti-Monopoly Law. These associations were to control the activities of companies with the aim of preventing overproduction and a sharp fall in prices. Their establishment was an epoch-making event in the post-war policy of organizing the small-business sector.

The need for such 'adjustment' (cartelization) activities came to be discussed because the Fair Trade Commission ruled that production cutbacks, such as those which MITI 'suggested' to textile manufacturers in 1951 and 1952 in order to overcome the business recession and export sluggishness after the Korean War ended, were in violation of the Anti-Monopoly Law. The Fair Trade Commission demanded that MITI rescind its instructions. This development led MITI to believe it might be necessary to enact a temporary law that would exempt certain anti-recession measures from the provisions of the Anti-Monopoly Law. Moreover, the textile industry's unique situation, which was the object of MITI's efforts, strengthened the inclination towards introducing new legislation. For large corporations such as those in the cotton-spinning industry, MITI could enforce its will by virtue of the authority it had of allocating the foreign exchange needed for importing raw cotton. In the textile industry, however, MITI lacked such alternative policy measures, although the presence of so many small companies made joint business activities difficult. If production were to be effectively restricted, it was necessary to form 'compulsory cartels', and to control the production activities of non-cartel members.

That was the background to the above-mentioned Law on Temporary Measures Concerning the Stabilization of Specified Small and Medium Enterprises, passed at the initiative of Diet members in August 1952 and effective until the end of March 1954. Despite provisions of the Anti-Monopoly Law to the contrary, this law allowed companies to form, under a specific set of conditions, adjustment associations (cartels) for autonomously coordinating among themselves production volumes and investment in plant and equipment. The aim was to secure the stabilization of smaller firms suffering from poor business conditions. The law would apply to industries that had a high percentage of small and medium enterprises and a severe imbalance between supply and demand of products, which might seriously threaten their survival and that of related industries.

Application of the law, however, did not adequately meet the needs of the small-business community. Of the fourteen industries designated under the law, six (woollen goods, fishing nets, hemp nets, rubber products, lacquerware, and enamelled ironware) did not form adjustment associations. In December 1952 the textile industry, which had high hopes for the coordination of activities through adjustment associations, applied through the Japan Cotton and Staple Fibre Weavers' Coordination Federation to invoke Section 29 of the law, which would force non-association members to conform to the industry's comprehensive coordination plan. MITI, however, responded only half-heartedly to this request. It could not readily take concrete steps because it found many unresolved issues in applying the law.[30]

MITI's inaction heightened the business community's dissatisfaction concerning the temporary measures law, prompting revisions in August 1953 and June 1954. These revisions changed the name of the law to the Small and Medium Enterprises Stabilization Law and made it a permanent statute. The revisions also made it easier for an industry to be designated a depressed industry by relaxing the definition of 'business slump' and changing the method of designation to a government ordinance. Furthermore, the section 29 order was changed from a two-step system of 'advice' and 'order' to an option system, and the content of orders was defined more clearly as having 'essentially the same content' as comprehensive coordination plans and adjustment rules. An order to restrict plant and equipment investment was added as subsection 2, the scope of operation of adjustment associations was expanded, and procedures related to their operation were simplified.

The law was revised again in 1955. The 1953 revision was the occasion that prompted MITI gradually to alter its stance on invoking section 29. This change came about in part because it became easier to declare the situation a recession as a tight-money policy began to take effect and in part because in November 1953 the Commerce and Industry Committee of the Lower House passed a resolution demanding the invocation of section 29. At any rate, MITI finally invoked section 29 in the spring of 1954 in response to requests in August 1953 by towel manufacturers and in September 1953 by match manufacturers.

A more important development, however, was the fact that the 1953 revision of the Small and Medium Enterprises Stabilization Law added a new dimension to adjustment activities by giving a new role to adjustment associations, whose initial role, as perceived by the original 1952 law, was that of anti-recession cartels of a temporary nature which would become superfluous once the poor business conditions affecting small businesses improved. This development was suggestive of changes in MITI's understanding of the nature of the small business problem towards: (1) viewing it as a chronic problem arising from the structural factor of excessive competition among small enterprises, and therefore (2) calling for permanent reorganization of industries in order to eliminate excessive competition.

Reports of the Small and Medium Enterprise Promotion Council and the enactment of the Small and Medium Enterprises Organization Law

As described above, efforts in the first half of the 1950s to organize small and medium enterprises made headway on two fronts: the establishment of cooperative associations, which were mutual-aid organizations engaging in joint business activities, and the establishment of adjustment associations functioning as cartels organized to restrict production. Reconciliation of these efforts was studied for the first time when the Second Committee of the Small and Medium Enterprise Promotion Council deliberated on the question of organizing small and medium enterprises.

The Small and Medium Enterprise Promotion Council, established in June 1956, studied problems affecting the small-business sector and pressing policy issues related to it. In November 1956, the council submitted one interim report on matters relating to the FILP budget and the tax system and another on matters relating to the organization of small and medium enterprises. In December, the council submitted a final report on nine topics (modernization measures, expansion of the distribution system, financing measures, bolstering organization, establishing a Small and Medium Enterprise Council, etc.), covering all aspects of small-business policy. The introduction to the final report observed that 'all sorts of disparities that exist between large and small firms, and among small and medium enterprises, have become increasingly pronounced.' The report then advocated nurturing small firms and solidifying their organization, rationalizing their management, and improving or rectifying financial and other conditions surrounding them.[31] The report recognized that small firms 'provide primary employment opportunities for the expanding labour force', and held that 'the pressure of the working-age population is expected to increase sharply and is causing difficulties in implementing small-business policy.' In arguing that problems related to small businesses will not be solved without first solving the population problem, the council's report reflected the then prevailing understanding of the nature of the small-business problem.

The council's final report had a major impact on the subsequent development of small-business policy. It bore fruit in the enactment of the Small and Medium Enterprises Organization Law, destined to become the centrepiece of the policy to organize the small-business sector: legislation of equipment modernization policies through enactment of the Law on Financial Assistance for Small and Medium Enterprise Promotion; protection of small subcontractors through enactment of the Law on the Prevention of Delay in the Payment of Subcontracting Charges and Related Matters; and securing business opportunities for small and medium retailers through enactment of the Department Store Law. The report also provided momentum for improving supplemental credit institutions by establishing the Small Business Credit Insurance Corporation, to be discussed in the following Section.

As for organizational efforts, the report argued that the healthy development and stabilization of smaller firms required a solidifying of the unity of small and medium enterprises. From this standpoint, it suggested expanding the scope of organization policy by (1) 'enacting a Small Business Organization Law (tentative name) as the basic law for organizing the small-business sector, and bolstering the cooperative associations designed to promote the modernization of small-business management'; (2) expanding the scope of industrial adjustment activities beyond designated manufacturing industries to other manufacturing industries and to the trading, mining, transportation, service, and other industries; and (3) providing adjustment associations with more effective means for controlling the behaviour of non-cartel members, and guaranteeing smaller firms the right to organize themselves and engage in collective bargaining in order to improve their economic positions. This report thus recognized the need for intensified efforts to organize the small-business sector, and urged the government to formulate appropriate policy measures in that direction.

In the business community, meanwhile, the Japan Small and Medium Enterprise Political League mounted an aggressive campaign for a small-business organization law. In the process of MITI's work to draft a Small and Medium Enterprises Organization Bill based on the final report of the Small and Medium Enterprise Promotion Council, however, many differing opinions emerged, and there were many twists and turns before the bill finally became law. For instance, the Fair Trade Commission expressed misgivings about restricting the behaviour of non-cartel members—which was suggested in the council's report—in consideration of the Anti-Monopoly Law and the possible adverse impact on consumers. Keidanren and other business organizations were also negative towards the bill. In that context, it was the positive attitude of the ruling political party that propelled the bill to successful legislation. The Socialist Party also moved positively, submitting an organization bill of its own to the Diet based on its Outline of Small and Medium Enterprise Policy. In the end, the government's Bill Concerning the Organization of Small and Medium Enterprises Organization became law in November 1957, after revisions were made jointly by the ruling and opposition parties.

Progress in small-business financing policy

Besides organization policy, small-business financing policy also became a pillar of small-business policy. The fragility of small firms in financing derived from several factors: first, they relied heavily on borrowed funds because their capital position was weak; second, they were short of funds because their credit standing was weak while their demand for funds was strong; and third, they were especially susceptible to fluctuations in financial market conditions. Steps were taken, therefore, to expand sources of funds, improve and strengthen financial institutions that would be conduits for funds for smaller firms, and build up supplemental credit institutions. In particular, measures were introduced to improve financial institutions specializing in extending credit to small firms at the same time that financial policy measures were introduced that paved the way for small-business modernization policies that materialized in the first half of the 1960s.

Establishment of the Small-Business Finance Corporation in 1953, primarily to provide long-term loans for equipment investment, brought better organization into the system of financial institutions for small and medium enterprises. The Central Cooperative Bank for Commerce and Industry (set up in 1936) provided financing to cooperatives, the People's Finance Corporation (set up in 1949) catered to the needs of the smallest firms, and private financial institutions, including mutual savings banks, credit associations, and credit cooperatives, specialized in providing largely short-term operating funds to small and medium enterprises.

Meanwhile, to improve and expand supplemental credit institutions, the Credit Guarantee Association Law was enacted in 1953, institutionalizing credit guarantee associations and building a foundation for developing a system of credit guarantees. The new problem emerged, however, of coordinating the credit guarantee system with the small-business credit insurance system. The credit guarantee system guaranteed the repayment in their entirety of borrowings by small firms from financial institutions. On the other hand, in the credit insurance system, initiated in 1950, the government paid a specified supplemental percentage of non-payments or payment in subrogation of the borrowing of small firms from financial institutions, or debts guaranteed by credit guarantee associations. Doing so distributed the risk in recovering loans, and prevented the erosion of loanable funds and credit guarantee funds.

As for the relationship between the credit guarantee system and the small-business credit insurance system, the Small and Medium Enterprise Promotion Council in an interim report pointed out that 'in managing the two systems, attention should be paid to a certain extent to coordinating their respective scopes of coverage, so that they can be managed efficiently as an integral whole.' It was ultimately decided—in line with a report from the Financial System Research Council of the Ministry of Finance—that the front-end business of supplemental credit was to be handled by credit guarantee associations, and the function of credit insurance was to be limited to providing reinsurance on credit guarantees provided by credit guarantee associations. To provide this reinsurance function, the Small-Business Credit Insurance Corporation was established in July 1958.

Evolution of small-business promotion policy

In contrast to organization policy and financing policy, small-business promotion policy was implemented to directly improve the internal and external conditions of management and production technology of smaller firms. The scope of the policy included: (1) expanding the small-business consulting system, (2) implementing measures for modernizing equipment and rationalizing management, (3) enacting the Law on Temporary Measures for the Industry-Specific Promotion of Small and Medium Enterprises and the Law Concerning the Organization, etc., of Commerce and Industry Associations, and conducting a basic, comprehensive survey of small and medium enterprises, and (4) dealing with subcontracting and labour-related problems. The core measures of this policy were systematized in the Small and Medium Enterprise Modernization Promotion Law of 1963.

First was the expanded operation of the small-business consulting system when it was given a legal foundation by the Enterprise Rationalization Promotion Law. Within it, a system of registering small-business consultants was established, group consulting was incorporated into the system, a system of travelling for on-site consulting was initiated, and the use of the loan facilities of the Small-Business Finance Corporation and the system of industry-specific integrated consulting were introduced. In fiscal year 1955, moreover, a system of using model plants was initiated, in which actual cases of modernization at model plants were introduced widely throughout the particular industry. Enterprises in the same industry were encouraged to engage in self-diagnosis, taking advantage of this system and autonomously promoting modernization of their own management. Also, in order to solve the problem of a shortage of consultants, a system of training and registering private individuals as consultants for small businesses was put into effect aggressively from 1957.

Second, in terms of measures for modernizing facilities and rationalizing management, where the problem was the disparity that existed between smaller firms and large corporations, a programme of providing subsidies for modernizing the joint facilities of smaller firms was introduced. These subsidies were aimed at promoting the construction of facilities as joint activities of associations. Regarding taxes, the special depreciation system allowed under provisions of the Enterprise Rationalization Promotion Law and the Special Tax Measures Law was also applied to small and medium enterprises. Also, application of the Law on Temporary Measures for Promotion of the Machinery Industry, designed for basic machinery and component industries—in which there were high percentages of small companies—played an important role in modernizing the equipment of small and medium enterprises.

Third, the Law on Temporary Measures for the Industry-Specific Promotion of Small and Medium Enterprises was promulgated in April 1960 as a temporary law having a time limit of five years. This law authorized the government to designate, through ordinances, industries in the small-business sector which required special support and promotion under public economic policy; to conduct studies of the actual situation in industries so designated; to determine, based on the results of those studies, the economic, technical, and business transaction aspects that needed improvement; to provide appropriate guidance to enterprises and their trade associations; and, if necessary, to issue advisories to specific small and medium enterprises and related firms. In addition, the Commerce and Industry Association Law was put into effect in response to the problems of small and very small firms. Under this law, MITI was to strengthen its policy measures for very small firms by aggressively providing subsidies to management-improvement programmes for small businesses carried out by commerce and industry associations and chambers of commerce and industry.

Fourth, as a response to the subcontracting problem, the Law on the Prevention of Delay in the Payment of Subcontracting Charges and Related Matters was enacted. In the subcontracting relationships that were becoming more common during this period, problems frequently arose because of the differences in production and technological capabilities between large corporations and small subcontractors, as well as because of the unequal market clout between large buyers and small sellers. The Small and Medium Enterprise Agency and the Fair Trade Commission viewed the problems as arising from the business relationships between the different companies, and requested their solution. Meanwhile, the keiretsu alignment of parts subcontractors was gaining headway in the motor-car and other machinery assembly industries, and parent companies were providing assistance to subcontractors by technical guidance and equipment leasing. On the other hand, however, the reality of the subcontracting relationship during this period was such that a parent company reduced the cost of its products (for example, assembled cars) by 'half forcing the subcontractors to reduce their prices when they purchased parts from them.'[32] Problems surfaced not only in pricing but in the manner in which subcontracting agreements were entered and the method of paying subcontractors. The results of studies, besides the one the above quote was taken from, revealed that payments to subcontractors often barely covered unit production costs, thereby making management of their businesses difficult for the subcontractors

Besides introducing a programme to normalize the situation and improve subcontracting relationships, legislation was introduced in the form of the Law on the Prevention of Delay in the Payment of Subcontracting Charges and Related Matters. The main measure in the programme for improving subcontracting relationships was based on a provision in the Anti-Monopoly Law, as revised in September 1953, which specified that 'trading with another party by unjustly making use of one's superior position in the transaction' was one form of 'unfair business practice'. Based on this provision, the act by a parent (purchaser) enterprise of unreasonably delaying payment to a subcontractor would be treated as abuse of a superior position in a transaction. In keeping with this policy, the Fair Trade Commission in March 1954 announced a set of criteria for defining unreasonable delays in payments to subcontractors in the machinery and tool industry and the armament manufacture and repair industry. The Fair Trade Commission conducted detailed investigations of parent companies that were delaying payments, and in cases where it found serious problems it took administrative action by issuing advisories to halt such actions.

Despite those measures, there were no substantive improvements in the actual situation concerning delayed payments, leading to demands for more effective steps. Accordingly, the Law on the Prevention of Delay in the Payment of Subcontracting Charges and Related Matters was put into effect in June 1956. The law required the parent company to prepare written subcontracting agreements and to prepare and store written documents regarding deliveries, receipt of deliveries, and payments. As items to be strictly observed, it prohibited parent companies from unreasonably refusing to accept delivery, delaying payments, unreasonably having prices reduced, and returning unsold goods. It also gave the Fair Trade Commission the authority to issue advisories to halt violations, and, if the advisories were not observed, to publish the facts. Finally, the law authorized the Fair Trade Commission, the Small and Medium Enterprise Agency, and competent ministers to require parent and subcontracting companies to submit reports to them, and authorized them to conduct on-site inspections and take other steps.

Enactment of the Department Store Law

As economic rehabilitation progressed and the living standards of Japanese citizens improved, department stores began to recover remarkably. Their subsequent growth was viewed by small and medium enterprises, whose numbers had grown by absorbing underemployed workers, as a major cause of their business stagnation.[33] The small-business community became particularly vocal in its demand for regulation of department stores during periods of business recession triggered by sluggish demand related to tight-money policies.

The campaign for a law to regulate department stores became especially vigorous from October 1955 when the League of Tokyo Retailers Preparing Department Store Countermeasures was disbanded and reorganized into the Federation of Japan Retailers Association, in which most of the trade associations of small and medium traders joined forces. Viewing this movement, MITI concluded that the problem was extremely complex and that finding an appropriate solution would be extremely difficult. It thus established a Commerce Committee in the Industrial Rationalization Council and began studying appropriate policy measures in September 1955. The problems included the question of whether regulation of department stores would violate the constitutionally guaranteed freedom of commercial pursuits, whether it would harm the best interests of consumers, and so forth.

The Commerce Committee's deliberation resulted in the conclusion that some form of regulation should be approved because 'a general *laissez-faire* policy on department stores would be inappropriate since such a policy would be damaging to a proper balance with business activities of other types of traders.' Based on this conclusion, MITI drafted the Department Store Bill, which was approved in January 1956 by all members of the Commerce Committee except those representing department stores. The bill was submitted to the Diet, became law, and was promulgated in May 1956. The objective of the new law was 'to secure ample business opportunities for small and medium traders' by 'regulating the business activities of department stores'. When the sales activities of department stores threatened to adversely affect the business activities of smaller traders, and when MITI 'finds it particularly necessary to maintain and promote the development of small traders and promote the healthy development of commerce in general', it was authorized to 'issue cease-and-desist advisories' to department-store owners.

Additionally, in order to promote retail trade more positively, in May 1957 the Bill on Special Measures for the Retail Business was submitted to the Diet on the basis of a report by the Small and Medium Enterprise Promotion Council entitled 'On Measures to Promote Retail Business'. Deliberations were drawn out, but the bill was enacted as the Law on Temporary Measures for the Adjustment of Retail Business, and was promulgated in April 1959.

15.9. Promotion of Industrial Technology and Development of an Industrial Base

Promotion of industrial technology

The promotion of technology was a key task of the policy of developing an industrial base.[34] In order to increase Japan's international competitiveness by increasing productivity, to promote the diversification of companies through the development of new fields of activity and new products, and to upgrade the industrial structure, it was essential to foster the ability of companies to develop technology which would serve as their foundation. From this standpoint, the 'Technology White Paper in 1949' ('The Present Conditions of Industrial Technology in Japan'), stressing the importance of technological development, was published in December 1949. In December 1950, its sequel, the 'Research White Paper in 1950' ('The Present Conditions of Experimental Research in Japan') was published. In this White Paper, the Industrial Technology Agency threw light on how industrial research—the source of new technology—should be conducted and how it was conducted in Japan and elsewhere, and identified pressing problems that experimental research in Japan was encountering. The White Paper particularly emphasized the importance of experimental research in industry. Although it acknowledged the contribution made by imported technology to the advance of technological standards in Japan, it nonetheless emphasized that experimental research conducted domestically made industrial applications of technology economical and made the absorption of imported technology easier. It said, therefore, that the promotion of experimental research activities held the key to overall technological improvement in Japanese industry.

These suggestions reflected an awareness of the excessive dependence on importing and absorbing foreign technology, the method used since enactment of the Foreign Capital Law in 1950 as the most effective and trouble-free way of overcoming the technical disparity between Japan and other industrially developed countries. In fact, the advance of technological innovations through the import of technology was one of the factors that brought about high growth in the Japanese economy. A study conducted in 1961 reported that the contribution made by imported technology to sales was twice as great as the contribution made by domestic technology. Companies were slow in making efforts to develop their own technologies, and the competition among them to import technologies created the problem of worsening the terms of technical licensing agreements.

Against that background, public policy of promoting technological development came to focus on private investment in research and development (R&D) while facilitating technology imports. To that end, the government found it necessary to supplement deficient R&D funds and promote the development of key research organizations. Given this situation, the 'Research White Paper in 1950' mentioned above listed four measures as specific tasks of technology policy regarding experimental research in mining and manufacturing: (1) maintaining a balance in experimental research activities, (2) providing subsidies for experimental research in mining and manufacturing technology, (3) establishing a special corporation to supply needed funds for industrial applications of technology, and (4) developing special tax measures to support private experimental research.

Of these measures, provision of subsidies for experimental research in industrial technology was of particular importance. From fiscal year 1950, three types of subsidies were provided: those for testing industrial applications of technology, those for experimental research in industrial technology, and those for research in car manufacturing. In fiscal year 1951, a programme of subsidies was created to support research for producing minicars. Such subsidy programmes acquired a legal foundation in 1952 when the Enterprise Rationalization Promotion Law went into effect. In subsequent years, high-risk research projects which private research organizations found difficult to finance were also subsidized according to their importance. From the mid-1950s, moreover, the demands of the Law on Temporary Measures for Promotion of the Machinery Industry and the Electronics Industry Promotion Law had the effect of increasing the importance among all subsidies of subsidized research in electronics equipment.

As a measure for subsidizing private-sector experimental research, the Enterprise Rationalization Promotion Law contained special tax measures related to equipment for experimental research, and other special taxation measures were adopted in 1958 for equipment related to the commercialization of new technology, thereby facilitating the acquisition of research equipment vital to experimental research.

Putting the industrial base in order

Another important policy task paralleling the promotion of industrial technology was development of the industrial base as it related to industrial water supply and industrial location.[35] Policymakers became clearly aware of issues in these two areas following enactment of the Enterprise Rationalization Promotion Law. For instance, the Industrial Rationalization Council in its 1951 report on the reduction of transportation costs pointed out the importance of improving the industrial base as follows:

In view of the present situation, where the modernization of Japanese industry is being hampered to a considerable extent by inadequate communications and transportation facilities and other infrastructural shortcomings, it is essential that these conditions be improved without delay. Above all, in order to reduce transport costs, which constitute a considerable portion of the production cost of major products, there is an urgent need promptly to expand and bolster the industrial infrastructure, including railways, roads, and port facilities.[36]

The Enterprise Rationalization Promotion Law also stipulated, as one of three particular measures the government should introduce in order to promote industrial modernization, 'the introduction of special measures to facilitate the improvement of the industrial infrastructure, such as roads and port facilities that contribute to the modernization of enterprises', thereby providing an important basis for future legislation of measures to improve the economy's industrial base.

MITI did not begin tackling industrial location policy in earnest until the mid-1950s. The industrial zone development promotion bill MITI drafted in 1953 with the cooperation of related ministries, however, did not result in legislation, suggesting that policy awareness regarding the industrial base was not yet ripe.

In 1953, the Industrial Rationalization Council was substantially reorganized and the Industry Related Facilities Committee was established inside it, marking an assertive turn of MITI's stance on the issue of improving the industrial base. In March 1955, the committee submitted a Resolution and Report on the Improvement of Conditions of Industrial Location, which cast light on the future direction of industrial location policy. The resolution stated:

For increased productivity, it is necessary to enhance not only 'direct' productivity inside enterprises but also economy-wide 'indirect' productivity by buttressing the industrial base. To that end, it is essential that the industrial infrastructure, especially the transportation, water supply, and drainage systems, be developed comprehensively, thereby positively improving the conditions of industrial location.

The resolution recommended that concrete improvement measures be formulated for each of these infrastructure systems and an all-round plan be formulated for improving conditions of industrial location in industrial zones.

Improvement of the industrial water supply

The first concrete task addressed was industrial water supply projects. The coastal industrial zones of Tokyo-Yokohama, Nagoya, Osaka-Kobe, and Kita Kyushu, where groundwater was relatively abundant, were beginning to experience problems owing to the lowering of the water table because of excessive drawing of groundwater, infiltration of sea water, and subsidence of the ground. In these four major industrial zones, moreover, sharp increases were projected in the demand for industrial water. Since industrial development was expected to be led by heavy industries that would require large quantities of industrial water, securing sufficient water was expected to become increasingly difficult.

In the middle of 1955 MITI established an Industrial Water Supply Preparation Office in its Industrial Facilities Division. In cooperation with the Geological Survey of Japan of the Agency of Industrial Science and Technology, the Preparation Office in fiscal year 1956 began a study to develop thoroughgoing policy measures. The study revealed that industrial water supply development projects initiated by a number of local governments were suffering from high capital costs. High rates had to be set for customers, therefore, because the projects received no financial support from the central government and the prospect of issuing long-term bonds to raise funds was far from certain. MITI's policy thus began to crystallize in the form of enacting an industrial water supply law, which was to regulate the pumping of groundwater, promote the construction of industrial waterworks, and, if necessary, provide government subsidies to these projects.

In terms of specific measures, government subsidies totalling 180 million yen were appropriated in the fiscal year 1956 budget for industrial waterworks projects in the Kawasaki, Yokkaichi, and Amagasaki districts. Meanwhile, the Industrial Water Law was enacted with the aim of securing a reasonable supply of industrial water while conserving underground water in specially designated areas, thereby promoting the healthy development of industry in those areas and preventing the ground from subsiding. Furthermore, in order to press ahead with its industrial water supply programme and secure supplies of abundant and low-cost water to meet the rising demand for industrial water, MITI enacted the Industrial Water Supply Business Law. Under this law, MITI accepted the responsibility of coordinating the industrial waterworks construction programmes of local government, improving the conditions of water supply, maintaining facilities, and securing the safety of water supplies.

The firm establishment of industrial location policy

In terms of industrial location policy, surveys were conducted in 1956 and early 1957 of industrial location conditions in twenty-six industrial zones throughout the country. The surveys covered existing industries and their future outlook, actual location conditions of the industrial zones and bottlenecks they faced, and policy measures for developing the zones. Also conducted were surveys of location conditions at approximately 3,000 industrial sites throughout the country, surveys of prefectures regarding the location conditions in their industrial zones, and surveys of the production outlook in each region. These surveys clearly revealed what types of locational bottlenecks existed in which regions, and what conditions required improvement most urgently. Solutions were most urgently needed for inadequate industrial infrastructure, including an insufficient supply of industrial water, a worsening of freight-train movements, and poor port facilities and roads. Bottlenecks in the industrial infrastructure were found to be particularly acute in the four major industrial areas of Tokyo-Yokohama, Osaka-Kobe, Nagoya and its environs, and Kita Kyushu, which collectively were responsible for nearly 60 per cent of Japan's total industrial production. In these areas, lagging public works investments could not keep pace with the rapid increases in private plant and equipment investment.

Based on the results of these various surveys, MITI appealed to other ministries and agencies to join with it in pressing ahead with formulation of an all-round policy for promoting the development of the industrial base with emphasis on industrial zones. As a result, in September 1956 the Mining and Manufacturing Zones Improvement Council was established in the Economic Planning Agency. Through this council, all the concerned ministries and agencies were to cooperate in studying the issue of improving the industrial infrastructure in mining and manufacturing zones, and allocate funds on a priority basis for that purpose. This arrangement made it possible for policymakers to address the issue on the basis of an all-round and prioritized plan. The results of these efforts manifested themselves in formation of the budget for fiscal year 1957. Key programmes in the four major industrial areas requiring urgent attention were studied and discussed, and budget appropriations for the programmes of improving industrial infrastructure, such as roads, port facilities, and industrial water supply, were increased sharply.

In November 1958, MITI established the Industrial Location Guidance Office in the Industrial Facilities Division. This move was in response to a report made by a study mission of industrial location specialists which the Japan Productivity Centre dispatched to industrially advanced countries to study the actual situation regarding their industrial location policy. By setting up the Industrial Location Guidance Office, which followed the examples of the UK and the US, MITI began providing guidance to companies in their industrial location decisions by providing them with information.

The progress made in nationwide surveys of the conditions of industrial location and establishment of the Industrial Location Guidance Office helped to build a foundation for a full-fledged industrial location policy. There were limits, however, to an industrial location policy based on the Guidance Office method without a statutory foundation. In 1959, therefore, the Law on Industrial Location Surveys and Related Matters was enacted. This law provided for surveys of conditions such as topography, geology, water supply, and transportation for sites deemed suited for industrial development. The results of surveys were to be made available to companies planning to build plants or other facilities on these sites, along with the provision of other materials and advice if requested. The law thus systematized the provision of information on industrial location previously carried out by the Industrial Location Guidance Office, and surveys needed for this guidance. It also established the Industrial Location Survey Council, responsible for discussing important matters related to plant location surveys.

NOTES

1. Concerning revisions to the Anti-Monopoly Law, see *Tsusho Sangyo Seisakushi*, v, ch. 2, sects. 2 and 3.
2. Ibid., v, 273–4.
3. Ibid., v. 410–11.
4. Concerning activities of the Industrial Rationalization Council, see ibid. vi, ch. 5, sect. 1.
5. Ibid. vi. 346.
6. Concerning reorganization of the Industrial Reorganization Council, see ibid. vi and v. 163–4.
7. Concerning the productivity-enhancement movement, see ibid. vi, ch. 5, sect. 1–3.
8. Ibid. vi. 385.
9. Ibid. vi. 385–6.
10. Concerning policy towards the steel industry, see ibid. vi, ch. 6, sect. 3.
11. Ibid. vi. 471.
12. Hiromi Arisawa (ed.), *Gendai Nippon Sangyo Koza* (Lectures on Modern Japanese Industry), ii, Iwanami Shoten, 1959: 77.
13. Ibid. ii. 475.
14. Concerning the rationalization of the coal mining industry, see *Tsusho Sangyo Seisakushi*, vii, ch. 8, sects. 1 and 2.
15. Concerning petroleum refining and petroleum resources development, see ibid. vii, ch. 8, sect. 5.
16. Ibid. vii. 393.
17. Concerning electric power policy, see ibid. vii, ch. 8, sect. 3.
18. These statistics are taken from Japan Development Bank, *Nihon Kaihatsu Ginko 10-nenshi* (Ten-Year History of the Japan Development Bank), 1963: 174, 180, and 186.
19. *Tsusho Sangyo Seisakushi*, vii. 471–2.
20. Concerning MITI's involvement with the development of nuclear power, see ibid. vii, ch. 8, sect. 4.
21. Concerning policy towards the fertilizer industry, see ibid. vi, ch. 5, sect. 4–4.
22. Ibid. vi, ch. 5, sect. 7, for a discussion of the textile industry; on a related topic, concerning the issue of invoking sect. 29 of the Small and Medium Enterpraises Stabilization Law, see subsection 8 of this chapter; ibid. v. 501–3, and ch. 6; concerning the allocation of foreign currency for importation of raw cotton, see ibid. ch. 4, sect. 4.
23. Concerning policy towards the chemical industry (including synthetic rubber) see ibid. vi, ch. 5, sect. 4.
24. Concerning the machinery and electronics industries, see ibid. vi, ch. 5, sect. 5.
25. Ibid. vi. 563–4.
26. Ibid. vi. 565.
27. Ibid. vi. 579.
28. Ibid. vi. 613.
29. Concerning small business policy, see ibid. vii, ch. 6, sects. 1–3.
30. Ibid. v. 502.
31. Ibid. vii. 39–40.
32. A survey conducted by the Secretariat of the Fair Trade Commission, *Jidosha Kogyo no Keizairyoku*

Shuchu no Jittai (Actual Conditions of the Concentration of Economic Power in the Automobile Industry), 1959: 43.

33. Concerning policy measures dealing with the distribution industry, including the Department Store Law, see *Tsusho Sangyo Seisakushi*, vii, ch. 6, sect. 4.
34. Concerning industrial technology promotion policy, see ibid. vii. sect. 1 and vi, ch. 5, sect. 2 for related matters.
35. Concerning development of the industrial base (industrial water supply and industrial location), see ibid. vii, ch. 7, sect. 4.
36. Ibid. vii. 303.

16

Export Promotion and the Relaxation of Trade and Exchange Controls

16.1. Return to the International Economic Community

Entry into GATT

For post-independence Japan, building stable relationships with trading partners was a prerequisite for implementing its export promotion policy.[1] Building such relationships, however, was not an easy task in the tense international situation where a multilateral currency-clearing mechanism was yet to be established, the Cold War was intensifying, and the interests of major nations such as the UK and the US were clashing. Of all the problems confronting Japan, the two considered most pressing were gaining membership in the General Agreement on Tariffs and Trade (GATT) and a solution to the reparations problem.

Joining GATT and the IMF symbolized Japan's return to the international economic community. In May 1952, Japan attained membership of the IMF with relative ease. The path to membership in GATT, in contrast, was extremely difficult with many stumbling blocks on the way. Suffering from discriminatory practices by other nations, including restrictions against its imports, Japan hoped that membership of GATT would lead to eradication of such practices. In the face of rough going in trade agreement negotiations with many countries, Japan viewed GATT membership more as a necessary step towards realizing the goal of export promotion than as the fulfilment of the admittedly important goal of being recognized as a formal member of the international economic community.

Membership negotiations with GATT were initiated during the Occupation period. Although West Germany, another country under Allied occupation, was admitted to GATT in June 1951, Japan was unsuccessful in gaining membership because of strong opposition by the UK and other nations which had a strong antipathy towards Japanese dumping of textiles in pre-war years. For this reason, membership negotiations dragged on even after the conclusion of the Peace Treaty. Japan's admission was finally approved on a temporary basis at the eighth annual meeting of GATT held in 1953.

Subsequently, from the autumn of 1954 onwards, formal admission of Japan to GATT membership was put on the agenda at GATT meetings. In the negotiations during this period, the US played a major role in championing Japan's cause. For instance, in announcing in July 1954 that it had agreed to negotiate with Japan on tariff matters, the US also declared that for any country which would effectively lower its tariff rates against Japan the US was prepared to lower tariffs of the country's choice. The intention of the US was to induce other nations to join it in tariff negotiations with Japan by giving them the incentive of lower US tariff rates.

GATT membership negotiations came to a general conclusion towards the end of May 1955, and the Protocol Concerning the Conditions of Japan's Entry into GATT came into effect in September, formally according GATT member status to Japan. Over three years had passed since Japan applied for membership.

Entry into GATT, however, did not directly lead to eradication of discriminatory practices against Japan. Invoking GATT Article 35, quite a few member nations refused to apply GATT rules to their relationships with Japan. When Japan joined GATT, fourteen nations chose to invoke this article, including the UK and France. The memories of relentless dumping of textile goods by Japan before the Second World War engendered in these countries a deep mistrust and fear of Japan. Since invoking Article 35 was tantamount to negating the benefit of Japan's membership in GATT, it became a serious task for Japan's economic diplomacy in subsequent years to negotiate with these countries to withdraw the measure. At the same time, the situation had a major impact on the nature of Japan's export promotion policy. That policy came to be focused on achieving orderly export marketing with the aim of having anti-Japanese discriminatory measures removed.

Solution of the reparations problem

Solution of the reparations problem also required efforts spanning many years. Four countries—Burma, Indonesia, the Philippines, and Vietnam—demanded reparations from Japan under the provisions of the San Francisco Peace Treaty. Japan affirmatively tackled the reparations question in negotiating with these countries, being fully aware that restoring normal trading relations through solution of the reparations issue was indispensable in order to achieve self-supporting status for the Japanese economy. MITI was especially positive towards a solution of the problem in view of the anticipated impact on its policy of promoting exports and cultivating overseas markets. It pointed out that

It is necessary to carefully examine the policies so that reparations will be effectively utilized by recipient countries for their economic development while contributing to closer economic relationships with Japan, [and stressed that] by sincerely and positively providing reparations and attendant economic assistance to these countries, Japan can expect to secure stable markets for its heavy-engineering and chemical products, develop sources of industrial raw materials, and nurture investment markets.[2]

Many of the South-East Asian countries which had had close trading relationships with Japan from pre-war years had rich reservoirs of the raw material resources needed for Japan's economic development, and could be expected as well to provide huge markets for its manufactured exports.

Reparations negotiations were settled for the interim with agreements with Burma in 1955, the Philippines in 1956, Indonesia in 1958, and Vietnam in 1960. Prior to the agreements, each of these countries had demanded huge reparations, as exemplified by the Indonesian demand for $17.2 billion. The sum of the demands from these four countries far exceeded Japan's national income of $18.9 billion in 1955.[3] The provisions of the Peace Treaty, moreover, limited Japan's reparations obligations to a sum which would 'enable Japan to maintain a viable economy'. As a result, reparations to these four countries were sharply reduced to $1.7 billion, which Japan was allowed to pay over a fairly long period. Moreover, the principal portions of reparations were to take the form of cooperation with recipient countries in their economic development and industrialization programmes through the provision of Japanese goods and services. This format helped to build a foundation in those countries for Japanese exports of capital goods.

16.2. Establishing Orderly Export Marketing

The Export Trade Transaction Law and revisions

The single most important factor that frustrated Japan's efforts to join GATT was the misgivings the member nations had about Japan's exporting methods. As mentioned, the problems many member nations had had with Japan's pre-war exports of textiles were still fresh in their memory. After Japan resumed private trading in 1949, overseas criticism of Japanese dumping and other alleged unfair trading practices became clamorous, leading to moves to restrict imports from Japan. To cope with this situation, in August 1952 Japan enacted the Export Trade Transaction Law designed to promote exports by establishing orderly export marketing. The law allowed exporters to form export associations (cartels) to eliminate excessive competition among themselves, and exempted from the provisions of the Anti-Monopoly Law, within limits, collusive activities by export associations. Export associations were permitted to conclude, with the approval of the Minister of International Trade and Industry, agreements among their members concerning price, quantity, quality, and other terms of export transactions.[4]

In the context of a tide of rising interest in revising the Anti-Monopoly Law, there was also a move in 1953 to revise the Export Trade Transaction Law. The law was subsequently revised and renamed the Export and Import Transaction Law. It contained new provisions permitting collusive activities for import trade similar to that allowed for exports. For export trade, moreover, the revised law expanded the Anti-Monopoly Law exemptions. For example, the original law allowed exporters to conclude restrictive agreements only among themselves. The revised law, however, allowed exporters to conclude agreements, in certain situations, with manufacturers or distributors as well. Also, the exemption of cartel agreements was expanded to include cases where excessive competition in a new market threatened to make it difficult to effect export transactions (preventive cartel), or where a cartel was called for to counter the effect of a cartel formed by a third party (countervailing cartel). For import trade, importers were allowed to conclude agreements among themselves and establish import associations (cartels) when competition was excessive, when it was necessary to import high-priced goods in order to meet Japan's obligations under a trade agreement, and at certain other times. Control of non-cartel members was partially permitted under certain specific conditions.

The intended effects of the 1953 revision of the Export and Import Transaction Law were not readily realized because the Fair Trade Commission stringently monitored even collusive activities the law permitted. In fact, by the end of March 1954 only four export-cartel agreements had been concluded under the law. As a result, a move developed to revise the law again. Demands for revision were heightened by the following related developments: (1) because of opposition from the FTC, the steel industry had to abandon the 'responsible exports' system it had considered as one of its export-promoting measures; (2) because of formulation of the 'New Export Plan', to be discussed later; and (3) cases of extremely low-priced exports of cotton fabrics and household sewing machines occurred because of excess competition brought about by an overstock of inventories and the mushrooming of new exporters.

The subsequent 1955 revision of the law abolished limitations on the justifications for concluding export agreements, required only notification of agreements rather than approval, and allowed agreements to be concluded among exporters, manufacturers, or distributors, as well as among exporters and manufacturers or among exporters and distributors. The law also permitted formation of an export–import association whose primary purpose was to coordinate export and import transactions within specific regions. Revisions included many important provisions, such as strengthening sanctions against exporters who conducted unfair export practices and relaxing conditions for invoking an outsider control order. Worth particular attention was legalization of cartel agreements among manufacturers, although only concerning exports. This revision was characterized as follows: 'The law essentially was turned into legislation providing a legal basis for general industrial policy.'[5]

With the 1955 revision of the Export and Import Transaction Law as a turning point, the number of agreements based on the revised law's provisions increased rapidly, reaching 200 in 1965. Among the types of cartels exempted from the Anti-Monopoly Law's provisions, those related to this law became the most numerous, second only to those based on the Small and Medium Enterprises Organization Law. Despite this remarkable increase in the number of approved cartels, however, incidents of dumping charges and calls by other countries for restrictions on imports from Japan increased. This development led to the third revision of the Export and Import Transaction Law in June 1957, later followed by several more revisions.

The New Export Plan and export conferences

Revision of the Export and Import Transaction Law was actively debated in 1953 and early 1954. Significantly impacting on the outcome of the revision controversy and leading to a substantial expansion in the scope of exemption of collusive activities from the provisions of the Anti-Monopoly Law were formulation of a New Export Plan and establishment of a system of export conferences.[6]

Prime Minister Yoshida had asked MITI to draft an export plan which was completed in September 1954. Called the New Export Plan, it had a target export value of $1.74 billion by fiscal year 1957. This target figure was arrived at by taking into close consideration for each major market and product category such factors as the actual situation in related industries, market conditions, and projected international competitiveness of Japanese products in price and quality.

The New Export Plan was characterized by: (1) selection of promising or suitable export industries; and (2) adoption of export targets. By adopting an export target system, MITI moved to extend the system of 'responsible exports'—which it had urged the steel and other industries to adopt—to all industries, and to give that system an institutional foundation rather than merely treating it as a moral corporate responsibility. To implement this policy, MITI considered reducing its allocation of foreign exchange and electric power to companies that failed to meet export targets, and conversely to provide incentives to those that exceeded the targets.

To make the export target system a reality, however, it was necessary to revise the Export and Import Transaction Law and legalize export cartels formed by manufacturers. Also, the legalization of production cartels required further extensive revision of other laws, including the Anti-Monopoly Law, as well as overcoming expected objections by the Fair Trade Commission. For those reasons, the New Export Plan announced in September 1954 did not include specific measures for adopting an export target system. All matters relating to targets, e.g. selecting products to be covered and establishing clear targets, were to be entrusted to export conferences created concurrently with the decision to adopt the New Export Plan.

In order to implement the New Export Plan, a main export conference, called the Supreme Export Conference, was established within the Cabinet, and industry-specific export conferences were established inside MITI as export promotion organizations. Because more thorough measures, such as revision of the Export and Import Industry Transaction Law, were deemed difficult in the short run, these organizations were designed to provide a forum in which government officials and industrial leaders could meet to coordinate their interests and work towards systematically achieving export targets. In short, the task of the export conferences was to give, for the interim, a practical effect to export cartels—especially those among manufacturers—which were expected to be approved by the 1955 revision of the Export and Import Transaction Law.

Within the organizational structure of the export conferences invested with these functions, the actual examination of important matters was conducted by industry-specific export conferences established in MITI and their product-specific committees. These conferences and committees set export targets for each industry and product, and studied various measures needed to achieve these targets. They moved to achieve export targets within the framework of existing legislation, and 'undertook a comprehensive study of export promotion policies, including the revision of relevant laws and regulations, and worked to create an atmosphere conducive to revision of the Export and Import Transaction Law while coordinating the interests of industry with the aims of MITI policy.'[7]

The activities of these export conferences—particularly industry-specific conferences and their product-specific committees—were vigorous until mid-1955. They stagnated for a while after revision of the Export and Import Transaction Law. For instance, the Supreme Export Conference held its first meeting in October 1955 but did not meet again for about two years. When Emergency Measures for the Improvement of the International Balance of Payments were adopted in June 1957 to deal with a foreign-exchange crisis, efforts were made to breathe new life into the export conferences as a part of export promotion policy. The export conferences subsequently acquired the role of greatly reinforcing or coordinating collusive activities widely legalized by major revision of the Export and Import Transaction Law in 1955.

16.3. Cultivating Export Markets

Establishment of JETRO

There were strict controls on travelling overseas and opening overseas branches during the Occupation period, and it was difficult to obtain the information on overseas markets needed to conduct trade. Japan was thus forced to search in the dark in its efforts to promote foreign trade.[8] In response to demands to create an organization to conduct studies of overseas markets, in February 1951 the Japan External Trade Research Organization (JETRO) was established in Osaka. From early on, however, JETRO suffered from rising administrative costs, especially because government subsidies for overseas market research were designed for specific projects. JETRO could not even dispatch resident researchers to overseas locations to support its eagerly awaited market research programme.

In the circumstances, MITI in June 1954 decided to integrate its export promotion programmes by merging the three existing organizations—the Japan External Trade Research Organization, the International Trade Fair Council, and the Japan Trade Coordination Bureau—into a new foundation, the Japan External Trade Organization (JETRO), established in August 1954. Afterwards, government subsidies to JETRO increased 1.7-fold from 112 million yen in fiscal year 1953 to 190.4 million yen in fiscal year 1954. In fiscal year 1955, the government sharply increased the endowment of JETRO to over 400 million yen from less than 200 million yen in fiscal year 1954, thereby solidifying its financial basis. Moreover, the merger of the three organizations markedly expanded the activities of JETRO to include international trade fairs and overseas exhibitions, overseas public relations activities, and trade development services, besides conventional overseas market research programmes.

Meanwhile, from mid-1956 MITI had been considering the creation of a central organization for promoting exports. It decided to turn JETRO—which still encountered financial difficulties arising from greatly expanded activities even after bolstering of its financial basis with the merger of the three organizations—into a special corporation. Under the Japan External Trade Organization Law enacted in April 1958, the new Japan External Trade Organization (JETRO) was inaugurated as a special corporation the same July.

Promotion of industrial plant exports

In November 1953, the Heavy-Engineering Machinery Counselling Office was established in the Japan Machinery Exporters' Association as part of the move to develop markets for plant exports. The purpose of the Office was to dispatch engineers to be stationed in countries such as Argentina, Brazil, Burma, India, Pakistan, and Thailand, regarded as promising markets for heavy machinery, where they would establish systems for servicing such machinery, thereby promoting heavy machinery exports from Japan. The nature of the Counselling Office was ambiguous, however, because it was attached to the Japan Machinery Exporters' Association. It could not adequately engage in its intended activities because contributions from the private sector to match government subsidies fell far short of initially anticipated amounts.

Against that background, MITI undertook a study from the second half of 1954 to expand and reorganize the Counselling Office. The study resulted in a decision to have related electric and industrial machinery industries develop a specific programme to improve the situation; specifically, eleven major corporations jointly established an incorporated association, the Japan Consulting Institute (JCI).

The objectives of the JCI were to: (1) provide technical consulting services on heavy machinery and industrial plant exports, (2) provide assistance for designing and estimating heavy-engineering machinery and industrial plant exports, (3) provide assistance on inquiries and after-sales service concerning heavy machinery and industrial plant exports, (4) provide research on industrial development, electric power development, industrialization programmes, and mechanization programmes of overseas countries, (5) collect and collate materials needed for engaging in overseas projects, and (6) introduce and promote the Japanese heavy machinery industry in other countries. The most important of these services was consulting activities. The number of inquiries for consulting activities increased from around 1958 (Table 16.1), and the involved projects began to result in successful plant exports from 1957.

Table 16.1 Inquiries received by Japan Consulting Institute, 1955–1960

	South-East Asia	Middle East	Africa	Latin America	Others	Total
1955	6					6
1956	33			13		46
1957	32	1	1	26		60
1958	103	18	10	35	5	166
1959	161	9	22	51	15	258
1960	113	14	35	61	10	233

Source: *Tsusho Sangyo Seisakushi* (History of International Trade and Industry Policy), vi: 303.

Despite the energetic consulting activities of the JCI, however, the number of orders for plants failed to grow, and tenders often failed to get accepted. The reasons for the poor showing were that Japanese bidders were slow in reacting to the aggressive government loans and attractive credit terms offered by rival bidders from other industrial nations, Japanese products were not price-competitive, and overseas buyers were not confident about Japanese technology. To respond to the situation, MITI studied the idea of converting the JCI into a special corporation funded by the State. In the end, however, it was decided that the objective of making the JCI a special corporation would be met by increasing government subsidies to the JCI and by enacting the Law on Temporary Measures to Promote Plant Exports.

Coming to grips with economic assistance

Promotion of overseas economic assistance was considered important as a measure for developing export markets. But providing economic assistance which required capital exports was not an easy task for Japan with its severe foreign-exchange limitations. Still, the importance was fully realized of aggressively pressing ahead with overseas economic assistance programmes to cultivate overseas markets and promote exports. Similar to the thinking for resolving the reparations problem, economic cooperation (assistance) was considered imperative if Japan expected to draw closer to the areas regarded as promising markets. It was becoming important for Japan to use such relationships to expand its exports and secure stable supplies of raw materials and other needed resources.

Prior to fiscal year 1956, when achieving a balance in external payments without special procurements was a primary task for public policy, Japan had to limit its overseas economic assistance programmes primarily to the export of capital goods under the deferred payment method. Overseas investment, therefore, was not positively incorporated into economic policy. In fact, the actual record of Japan's overseas investment in the decade 1945–54 was scanty at best.

From 1957, when economic policy was finally freed from the tight external-payments constraints, overseas economic assistance became a policy issue. Specifically, in terms of long-term loans, the yen loan agreement concluded with India in February 1958 was Japan's first government-to-government loan agreement. Under this agreement, Japan was to provide loans of up to 18 billion yen over a period of three years, starting in April 1958, for projects to construct railway facilities and hydroelectric and thermoelectric power plants. Besides these loans to India, yen loans were also provided around this time to South Vietnam and Paraguay. Agreements to provide credit lines for exports from Japan were also concluded with Iran, Pakistan, the United Arab Republic, and Yugoslavia. On the private level, investments were made in areas outside Asia with the aim of developing overseas sources of raw materials, including huge development projects undertaken by the Arabian Oil Co., Alaska Pulp, and Usi Minas Ironworks.

Scheme for creating an overseas investment organization and establishment of the Institute of Asian Economic Affairs

The idea of establishing an organization devoted to the task of overseas investment surfaced as progress was made in the execution of loan and investment programmes, as mentioned above. One Eric Johnston, head of a group of advisers to the US government on international development visiting Japan in February 1956, announced a scheme ('Johnston Plan') suggesting that Japan should play a leading role in the economic development of South-East Asian countries, and for that purpose should establish a quasi-governmental loan and investment corporation.

The Johnston Plan spurred the movement in Japan to establish an overseas investment organization. In March 1956, the Economic Planning Agency formulated a plan strongly supported by industrial circles represented by Keidanren to establish an overseas investment organization. MITI, too, took great interest in promoting overseas investment and developed its own proposal of creating a special overseas investment corporation. By June 1956, therefore, both the business community and the ruling Liberal Democratic Party gradually came around to support the idea of establishing an overseas investment organization apart from the existing Export-Import Bank of Japan (Ex-Im Bank).

The scheme, however, was stymied by EPA Director Takasaki's assertion that the time was not ripe for it. His opposition developed as a result of obtaining information that the Philippine government expressed objection—during the ongoing negotiations concerning reparations—to the MITI plan of creating a special corporation wholly funded by the Japanese government. It was judged that creating an investment organization funded by the State was fraught with the danger of giving recipient countries the impression that Japan had political ambitions. In the circumstances, the idea of creating an overseas investment organization was shelved for the time being. Instead, in May 1957 the Export-Import Bank of Japan Law was revised to expand the scope of the bank's overseas investment and financing business, and its technology export and financing activities. Debate on the temporarily postponed plan of creating an overseas investment organization was rekindled later by Prime Minister Kishi's proposal to create an Asia development fund. In July 1958, the Development Fund for South-East Asia was established. This was replaced in 1961 by the Overseas Economic Cooperation Fund (OECF).

As the need heightened for providing economic assistance primarily to Asian countries and expanding the intrabloc trade associated with that assistance, demands for creating a research organization for conducting an all-round study of Asia arose from both official and business circles. In response to these demands, MITI initially decided on establishing an organization totally funded by the State. The requisite fund, however, could not be secured in the 1958 budget. Consequently, MITI decided to establish it as a private organization, and sought the cooperation of Keidanren and other business organizations in a campaign to raise funds from all sectors of the business community. As a result, preparations for establishing the organization moved forward under the leadership of Keidanren, and in December 1957 the Institute of Asian Economic Affairs (Institute of Developing Economies since 1969) was inaugurated.

In 1959, MITI proposed that the Institute be converted into a special corporation partially funded by the State, which, with its scope of research activities expanded beyond Asia, would serve as an institute for an all-round study of overseas economic affairs. Based on this proposal, in April 1960 the Institute of Asian Economic Affairs was reorganized as a special corporation with a 100 million yen endowment provided by the State, and with substantially expanded functions.

16.4. Export Promotion Measures

Expansion of the export insurance system

The export insurance system was created under the provisions of the Export Credit Insurance Law promulgated in March 1950. Until fiscal year 1957, efforts were devoted primarily to creating new types of insurance, such as external investment insurance and insurance for external investment profit. Emphasis was shifted from fiscal year 1958 to the qualitative improvement of existing insurance systems, such as lowering the premiums of various types of insurance.

Export credit insurance was unpopular during these early years, and the number of export insurance policies underwritten showed a marked decrease in fiscal year 1952. In July 1953, the Export Credit Insurance Law underwent major revisions. With the revised law as a turning point, the number of export insurance policies underwritten increased sharply, as shown in Table 16.2. The system was improved qualitatively, paving the way towards export promotion. For instance, overseas investment risk could now be insured, although the number of such policies underwritten was not large.

Table 16.2 Number of export insurance policies underwritten, 1951–1959

	Month insurance programme was initiated	1951	1953	1955	1957	1959
General export insurance	June 1950	4,309	28,273	125,959	152,305	187,589
Export proceeds insurance	December 1951		15	63	49	155
Export bill insurance	August 1953		919	7,272	23,270	44,611
Export finance insurance	May 1952		1,226	4,307	1,309	498
Consignment sales export insurance	April 1954			7	3	4
Overseas advertisement insurance	April 1952		9	31	0	3
Overseas investment principal insurance	April 1956				3	6
Overseas investment profit insurance	June 1957				0	1
Total		4,309	30,442	137,639	176,939	232,867

Source: MITI International Trade Bureau, *Sengo Nippon no Boeki 20-nenshi* (20-Year History of Japanese Post-War Trade), Research Institute of International Trade and Industry, 1967: 456–7.

The export inspection system and the Export Design Law

Together with enactment of the Export Commodities Control Law in July 1948, an export inspection system was introduced to cope with dissatisfaction regarding the quality of Japanese products—one of the obstacles to export promotion at the time—and to improve their quality. The law was revised several times because criticism and complaints about Japanese exports continued unabated, and in 1957 was renamed the Export Inspection Law.

Revision of the law in 1951 opened the way to a system of compulsory inspection of exports by private organizations. On the occasion of this revision, various private inspection organizations were registered with the government. The registration system lacked adequate registration criteria, however, and revisions to the law in March 1953 addressed this inadequacy and added provisions to ensure impartial inspection of exports by objective organizations with third-party characteristics.

In subsequent years, partly because of saturation export tactics adopted by Japanese companies, moves to restrict the entry of Japanese products intensified in importing countries. Preventing the export of poor-quality goods thus became an increasingly important task. The incident of shoddy fountain pens that occurred at the Japanese product exhibition and spot sale held in Beijing in the autumn of 1956 was directly instrumental in prompting efforts to improve the quality of exports and reinforce the system of export inspection. In May 1957, the Export Inspection Law was promulgated. The essential elements of the law were: (1) compulsory export inspections to be conducted by a government agency or an inspection agency designated by the government on export goods specified in ordinances; (2) export inspections to include quality inspections, special inspections of packing conditions, inspections of materials, and manufacturing inspections; (3) inspection organizations to be designated from among applicants capable of conducting impartial inspections respecting the public nature of the business, and their activities to be supervised by the authorities; and (4) provisions for ordering law-breaking exporters to halt their export shipments and defining penalties even for attempted offences.

While progress was being made in the inspection system aimed at improving the quality of exports, a new issue arose in the form of aggravation of the design-copying problem concerning Japanese exports. In 1957, there were sixty-three cases of overseas complaints about design imitation, counting only those officially filed with the Japanese government. In response to these offences, MITI began a study of the need for appropriate legislation from mid-1958, and drafted a bill for an Export Commodities Design Protection Law.

The bill was not immediately submitted to the Diet, however, because a consensus had not yet been reached inside MITI concerning the need for legislation. Still, the International Trade Bureau was enthusiastic about this legislation, for the following reason. In the self-restraint system of this period, based on the Export and Import Transaction Law, 'outsider control' (control of non-cartel members) could not be enforced effectively because control orders could be issued only if a specific set of conditions was met. In contrast, although the design law's scope was limited to the design of exports, the law empowered the authorities to flexibly control non-cartel members by invoking the law. In that context, the Export Goods Design Law was promulgated in April 1959 with the aim of promoting the steady development of export trade by preventing design imitations. Under this law, products designated by an ordinance could not be exported until their design and trademarks were first approved by a validating organization.

Development of export financing and tax measures for export promotion

From the financing side, various export promotion measures were implemented, in which the Bank of Japan was to play a central role. The more important of these measures were related to foreign-exchange banks, the export advance bill system, the system of extending loans against negotiations of export usance bills, and export financing provided by the Export-Import Bank of Japan.

The strengthening of foreign-exchange banks had earlier been considered an important task in conjunction with the reorganization of the Foreign Exchange Control Commission.[9] With regard to this question, MITI had undertaken a study of measures to develop banks specializing in foreign-exchange transactions, and considered creating a central bank for foreign-exchange banks. The Foreign-Exchange Bank Law was finally promulgated in April 1954. Under this law, the Bank of Tokyo was established in September as a specialized foreign-exchange bank and was given responsibility to play a leading role in all of Japan's foreign-exchange transactions.

While legislation of the new foreign-exchange bank law was delayed, new measures were introduced to strengthen the functions of banks handling foreign exchange and to stimulate foreign-exchange transactions. One such measure was the foreign-exchange holding system which permitted foreign-exchange banks to open accounts in their own names in correspondent banks abroad. As a result, almost all export and import transactions came to be settled through foreign-exchange banks.

In December 1952, the MoF deposit system was introduced. Under this system, foreign-exchange funds of the Ministry of Finance (MoF) were entrusted to banks handling foreign exchange to supplement their meagre foreign-exchange holdings. The banks managed the funds under a certain set of restrictions. The system made a positive contribution in that it improved the credit standing of foreign-exchange banks, accelerated realization of their self-supporting status, and lessened the interest burden of traders through increased supplies of low-interest funds. From October 1953, however, its use as a temporary fund for purchase of export goods to Japan was restricted as part of the programme to tighten import financing. In March 1954, the MoF foreign deposit system and foreign-currency deposit system were combined into the foreign-currency deposit system.

Along with the foreign-exchange holding system for banks, a similar system was created for trading companies. This step was taken because it was considered essential, if Japan's exports were to be expanded, that trading companies be amply supplied with foreign-currency operating funds so that they could actively engage in overseas operations. Accordingly, in January 1956 the foreign-exchange holding system for trading companies was established. This was followed by establishment in April 1956 of the inter-office open and current account system whose objective was to ease the restrictions on foreign-exchange transactions between head offices and branches of trading companies, thereby promoting their business activities. This system was actively utilized as the simplest method for transferring funds for purposes other than paying for imports, and its use expanded gradually in subsequent years.

The export advance bill (export foreign trade bill) system, which played the central role in export financing, was designed to accord preferential treatment—in the form of the lowest interest rate, comparable to the rate on the discounting of bills with government bonds as collateral—to bills issued by export agents to manufacturers or assemblers to finance an export advance, or for procuring assembling funds or funds to cover expenses of transactions relating to exports. Under the system of extending loans against negotiations of export usance bills introduced in 1953, the Bank of Japan extended yen loans to Japanese foreign-exchange banks against dollar or pound export usance bills, accompanied by letters of credit, with maturity of up to three months. Both of these systems were intended to promote exports by making access to credit easier, yen loans for Japanese exporters, and letters of credit for overseas importers.

In contrast to short-term financing for trade transactions, long-term export financing such as for industrial plant exports was handled by the Export-Import Bank of Japan. The predecessor of the Ex-Im Bank was the Export Bank of Japan established in December 1950. This form was adopted because SCAP vetoed the initial idea of creating a bank which would handle both export and import financing. As the Korean War boom created a worldwide shortage of raw materials, however, making their import difficult, the Export Bank of Japan Law was revised in 1952 with the aim of ensuring long-term and stable supplies of essential raw materials. Import financing was added to the functions of the Export Bank, which was renamed the Export-Import Bank of Japan.

As a link in export promotion policy, the functions of the Ex-Im Bank were increased dramatically by revisions to the Export-Import Bank of Japan Law in August 1953 in the midst of a foreign-exchange crisis. The revisions included eliminating the five-year limit on the life of the bank, adding overseas investment and overseas project financing, expanding the scope of export financing, expanding import financing, extending loan terms, relaxing the principle of joint loans in export–import financing, and permitting the bank to engage in foreign-exchange business. As discussed earlier, in 1957 the bank's overseas investment-financing business was expanded in the context of the progress made in large-scale investment projects such as Alaska Pulp and Usi Minas Ironworks.

Special tax measures for promoting exports were developed with primary emphasis on strengthening the financial base of weakened trading companies with the expectation that they would play key roles in expanding exports. Specific measures included tax credits for export income, a reserve for losses arising from export income, and an extra depreciation allowance for the fixed assets of over-seas branches. These programmes were introduced in the tax reforms of August 1953, and were subsequently expanded further with special emphasis on tax credits for export income.

16.5. Relaxation of the Foreign Trade Control System

Normalization and simplification of foreign-exchange control

During this period, foreign-exchange transactions were strictly controlled, mainly under provisions of the Foreign-Exchange and Foreign Trade Control Law. The controls were set against the background of Japan's inadequate foreign-exchange reserves and instability in international financial markets.[10] As the convertibility of West European currencies was gradually restored and Japan's foreign-exchange reserve improved, the rigid control exercised via the foreign-exchange concentration system came to be gradually relaxed. Specifically, the open account system was successively abolished, leaving only Taiwan and South Korea under this system in April 1960. The number of designated currencies increased to include major West European currencies; between July 1954 and April 1959, the number of designated currencies rose from two—the US dollar and the British pound—to fourteen.

Foreign-exchange markets were also normalized. The single exchange rate of 360 yen to one dollar, set in April 1949, was the basic exchange rate. Decisions on the exchange rates for other designated currencies, such as the British pound and the West German mark, were made by the Minister of Finance as arbitrated cross-rates of exchange calculated on the basis of the market dollar exchange rates of these currencies—which were centred on their IMF par values—and the basic exchange rate of the Japanese yen. Among the designated currencies, the market for the US dollar, the currency which defined the basic exchange rate, was freed last, in September 1959. As for designated currencies other than the US dollar, progress was made from 1954 towards liberalization of the British pound. In fiscal year 1956, as part of the programme to normalize foreign-exchange transactions, markets for non-concentrated currencies were liberalized. Furthermore, in May 1958, the sight bill buy rate and the import bill settlement rate of foreign-exchange banks were completely liberalized for all designated currencies, including the US dollar and the British pound, and were left to market quotations by those banks. Thus, the post-independence foreign-exchange system based on the concentration system was totally revamped in response to the worldwide trend towards the liberalization of trade flows and foreign-exchange transactions.

Relaxation of the export control system

Control over trade was also relaxed gradually. After the reopening of private trade in 1949, exports were free in principle under the provisions of the Foreign-Exchange and Foreign Trade Control Law. In reality, however, the Export Trade Control Ordinance and the Export Trade Control Regulations were in effect under the provisions of the Foreign-Exchange and Foreign Trade Control Law. Control of exports based on these regulations was strengthened in response to the changing international situation and in order to stabilize the domestic economy, with an attendant increase in the complexity of export procedures. Such controls were viewed as unavoidable temporary measures during the period that Japan was promoting exports to become self-supporting.

Export controls, however, were gradually relaxed as the goal of economic self-sufficiency was achieved and in response to the trend towards trade liberalization. This relaxation was also in response to the demands by industrial leaders, who saw in freer trade an opportunity to expand Japanese exports. The first step taken was to enable exporters to obtain export licences by a simple procedure at a government office near their places of business. To that end, multiple-stage export procedures were simplified and approval authority was delegated to local governments. The second step was to streamline the list of products requiring export licences so that more items could be exported without applying for a licence. These steps helped to create favourable conditions for liberalization of trade in that they were aimed at returning to the principle of free export while paying heed to the domestic supply-and-demand situation and observing international agreements related to the export of strategic materials.

Coordination of exports

In terms of the initial objectives of limiting the export of strategic materials, easing domestic supply shortages, and maintaining stable prices, the number of products requiring export licences was gradually decreased. In contrast, new items were frequently added to the list. At the same time, because orderly export pricing and marketing were considered essential for export promotion, regulation of goods requiring orderly marketing increased, with a focus on textiles. Even as overall export trade regained normalcy, however, it was necessary to coordinate the export of specific products destined for countries where low-priced Japanese exports were being criticized by local industries. These criticisms of Japanese trading practices, as discussed earlier, were considered serious obstacles to Japan's return to the international community, to the development of healthy trade relationships, and to the promotion of exports. Falling prices caused by excessive competition for export markets no doubt sullied the reputation of Japanese products and provoked measures to restrict imports from Japan.

A representative case of disorderly Japanese export-marketing was the export of cotton textiles to the US. Once into 1955, the export of cotton textile products to the US increased sharply, recording a roughly threefold increase in cotton fabrics and a threatening tenfold increase in cotton blouses, a secondary textile product, compared with 1954. In that context, US cotton textile producers mounted a campaign to restrict imports from Japan, contending that they were causing injury to the domestic industry. In July 1955, an import restriction bill was submitted to Congress. Judging that the conditions in the Japanese cotton textile industry made it difficult for the industry to exercise self-restraint, MITI decided to impose export controls in order to achieve orderly expansion of textile exports. It thus revised the Export Trade Control Ordinance and added a number of secondary textile products, including cotton blouses, to the list of items requiring export licences. MITI also limited the quantity of cotton textile exports for 1956. After the import restriction movement was rekindled in 1957, MITI in November 1957 added all remaining secondary cotton textile products to the list of items requiring export licences, and regulated the quantity of exports of secondary cotton products to the US and Canada by product category.

As seen above, rapid increases in Japanese exports, at times criticized as saturation exporting, provoked hostile reactions from local producers in destination countries, leading to anti-dumping investigations and threats of high-tariff rates. To deal with the situation, the Japanese government imposed voluntary export restraints. The problem of trade friction, exemplified by the US–Japan textile negotiations, was to become an important issue in the subsequent formulation of MITI policy.

Relaxation of the import control system

Control on imports was more extensive and stringent than that on exports. Also, exchange controls regarding imports were exercised separately for different currency areas because the restoration of currency convertibility was delayed. When the foreign-exchange budget was finalized, importers would then conclude import agreements according to the budget figures, and applied to MITI for import licences. This system was developed in order to utilize limited foreign-exchange reserves as effectively as possible for economic development. The system was effective for ensuring imports of essential materials while preventing an influx of less important items. By exercising its authority to allocate foreign exchange and validate import applications, MITI had the power needed to provide administrative guidance to an industry to ensure its healthy development in the context of Japanese industry as a whole.

Throughout this period, however, import control measures were gradually relaxed, and import procedures were steadily simplified. Specifically, concerning settlement currencies and liquidation accounts, the previous distinction between the three currency areas was abolished. And as convertibility was restored to various currencies, the open account system was gradually abolished. The import validation system was earlier divided into the first-come system, Fund Allocation System, and Automatic Approval System. Gradually, first-come items were transferred to the Automatic Approval System list, and by 1953 or so the first-come system was virtually abolished. In the second half of 1959, the Automatic Fund Allocation System was created.

As a result of these changes, the percentage of the foreign-exchange budget devoted to the global quota was increased from 15 per cent in the second half of fiscal year 1954 to 55 per cent in the first half of fiscal year 1955, and was further increased to 91 per cent in the second half of fiscal year 1955. From the first half of fiscal year 1958, all distinctions between different settlement currencies and open accounts were abolished. In the import validation system, the coverage of the Automatic Approval System was expanded and the combined budget allocation for the Automatic Approval System and the Automatic Fund Allocation System amounted to $1.55 billion in the second half of fiscal year 1960, raising the import liberalization rate to 44 per cent.

NOTES

1. Concerning Japan's return to the international economic community, see *Tsusho Sangyo Seisakushi*, vi. ch. 4, sects. 1, 2, and 5.
2. Ibid. vi. 41–2.
3. Juroh Hashimoto: 69.
4. Concerning the Export and Import Transaction Law, see *Tsusho Sangyo Seisakushi*, vi. ch. 4, sect. 6–2 and v. ch. 2 for related matters.
5. Hitoshi Misonou, *Nippon no Dokusen Kinshi Seisaku to Sangyo Soshiki* (Anti-Monopoly Policy and Industrial Structure in Japan), Kawade Shobo Shinsha, 1987: 126–7.
6. Concerning the export plan and the export conference, see *Tsusho Sangyo Seisakushi*, vi. ch. 4, sect. 6–2.
7. Ibid. vi. 290.
8. Concerning cultivating export markets and promoting exports, see ibid. vi, ch. 4, sects. 2 and 6–3.
9. Concerning matters relating to export financing, see ibid. vi, ch. 4, sects. 3–1 and 6–3.
10. Concerning foreign trade control, see ibid. vi, ch. 4, sect. 3–2.

17

Changing Policy Keynote and Measures

17.1. Economic Planning and Industrial Policy

Economic formulae in first half of the 1950s

A variety of economic plans and schemes were developed in an attempt to answer the questions of what path Japan should follow to achieve economic self-sufficiency, and what its image of the future should be.[1] Unlike wartime or socialist economic plans, these schemes were to serve as guidelines for economic policy formulation. Of these schemes, the economic plans which the Japanese government developed during the first half of the 1950s were based on an awareness of the need to promote US–Japanese 'economic cooperation'. As such, they were based on the premiss that Japan had to wean itself from dependence on special procurements, which would necessitate promoting exports, which in turn would require rationalizing industry. Funds would have to be raised to rationalize industry, which suggested the need to promote the importation of foreign capital. Being based on US–Japanese 'economic cooperation', these plans aimed to define the nature of 'economic cooperation' that would supplant special procurements, and elucidate its essential features. The nature of these plans was evaluated as follows:

These plans emphasized an industrial structure characterized by heavy industries, and their methodology was oriented towards materials mobilization planning. Specifically, they attached much importance to increasing the production of industrial goods and improving the nation's energy base, and tackled the question of how best to develop coal-mining and other sources of energy which were restricting industrial production.[2]

It goes without saying that the nature of these plans emerged partly because the method of formulating economic plans had not been firmly established. At the same time, however, the plans emphasize heavy industries primarily because they attached much importance to US–Japanese economic cooperation. Unlike its ordinary usage, the term US–Japanese 'economic cooperation' specifically meant incorporating Japanese industrial potential into the US plan of defending East Asia and the attendant mobilization plan. In order to respond to the demands of the US in this sense and extract much-needed aid in the process, it was essential for Japan not only to expand and develop armament and munitions production but also to develop the heavy and chemical industries, which are its foundation. The policy of getting closely involved with the US defence strategy, moreover, had the effect of delaying an improvement in Japan's relations with China—which had been Japan's largest export market before the war—and minimizing the prospects for increasing markets in China. Accordingly, Japan had to rely heavily on South-East Asia if it were to expand its markets in Asia. In view of the progress towards industrialization in South-East Asian countries, chances of increasing exports to these countries would be greatest if Japan specialized in heavy industrial goods. Consequently, upgrading the structures of industry and trade towards greater emphasis on the heavy and chemical industries became an important point for consensus in policy formulation.

Developed towards these aims were 'B Materials' prepared in August 1951 by the Economic Planning Office of the Economic Deliberation Board, the 'Economic Table of fiscal year 1957' completed in February 1953, and 'On Economic Self-Support of Japan'—the so-called Okano Plan—announced in December 1953. The significance of this series of plans was threefold. First, they provided basic materials, e.g. the industry-specific foreign capital importation plans which the government announced at about the same time, needed by the Japanese government for negotiating with other countries. Second, these plans constituted the bases on which rationalization and modernization plans for the basic industries were developed. They served as guideposts for the path of development of each industry, and also served as criteria for evaluating annual implementation plans. They also provided an all-round and systematic perspective for plan formulation in an unstable political situation. Third, it is also important to note that these plans, although they responded to the demands for all-round and systematic economic policy, did not directly result in increased government control in policy implementation. In this respect, the various ministries and agencies varied in their degree of emphasis. MITI, if anything, leaned towards acknowledging the efficacy of interventionist policy and measures of direct control. Generally speaking, however, the planners refrained from imposing a choice between the extremes of planning and a free market. Rather, they emphasized minimizing the misallocation of natural resources from the standpoint of the national economy, while underlining by the criterion of economic efficiency, the responsibility of enterprises based on the principle of free competition. It was in this sense that these plans were significant as providing guidelines for economic policy formulation.

Formulating the Five-Year Plan for Economic Self-Support

The Economic Deliberation Board continued work on formulating a new long-term economic plan by incorporating aspects of the various schemes mentioned above. The resultant plan was adopted by the Hatoyama Cabinet, formed in early 1955, as the Comprehensive Six-Year Draft Plan, which became the basic policy guideline for the new government. The target year of the plan was set for 1960. The plan's objectives were: (1) to achieve equilibrium in the balance of payments through normal trade (i.e. trade without reliance on special procurements) during the plan's first three years, and (2) to achieve full employment during the second half of the period through the expansion of economic activities. Compared with the earlier economic plans, this draft plan was characterized by its emphasis on the employment problem.

Because the content of the Sixth-Year Draft Plan had not been closely scrutinized, the government in July 1955 reorganized the Economic Deliberation Board into the Economic Planning Agency, and requested the Economic Council, under the new system, to concretize the content of the draft plan. Of the two main objectives, the new draft plan placed greater emphasis on achieving full employment. Given the economic realities of those days, that emphasis was problematic in that it would require making unrealistic assumptions. Specific policy proposals that emerged from the plan, moreover, gave the impression that they were not clearly focused and seemed to have been made to please everybody.

Responding to the recommendations made by the Economic Council, MITI developed an export–import plan, an investment plan, and a materials supply-and-demand plan. While clarifying the specific measures required to give substance to these plans, MITI criticized the new draft plan. MITI's critique covered plant and equipment investment, employment, and international trade. In particular, with regard to employment, MITI maintained that in view of the past record of the income elasticity of demand for labour it would be foolish to restrain increases in labour productivity in the secondary (manufacturing) industries hoping that doing so would generate a strong demand for labour. It pointed out that there was a limit to the capacity of these industries to create jobs, because some increase in productivity was inevitable. As a means to attain the goal of full employment—the policy of the government of the Democratic Party—MITI's approach was to promote an increase in labour productivity and thereby achieve increased international competitiveness, the key to increasing exports.

Embodying the results of these discussions, the government formulated its first formal economic plan, the Five-Year Plan for Economic Self-Support. Formally approved at a Cabinet meeting in December 1955, the plan replaced the objective of full employment in the second half of the draft plan period by 'expanding the scale of the economy and increasing employment opportunities.' As primary measures for achieving its goals, the Five-Year Plan proposed reinforcing the industrial infrastructure, gradually improving the system for liberalizing imports, and improving self-sufficiency by utilizing domestic natural resources more fully and fostering new industries. Many of the plan's measures, however, were still designed to please all parties and lacked concreteness. Moreover, their key elements, i.e. reinforcing the infrastructure, promoting trade, raising self-sufficiency, etc., had been proposed in the past, albeit with greater or lesser urgency, depending on the item. At any rate, this five-year plan came to provide guidelines for the Japanese government in formulating its economic policy from then on by identifying, as the goals of economic self-support, increased employment opportunities and balance-of-payments equilibrium. The primary purposes of the plan were to define an image of the future of the Japanese economy, identify the overall framework of economic policy, and invite the various ministries and agencies to study ways and means of realizing them. MITI itself began to tackle the formulation of concrete policy measures to be incorporated into the self-support plan by approving in its ministerial meetings the proposals 'On Nurturing the Plastics Industry' in June and 'Measures for Promoting the Petrochemical Industry' in July, both in 1955, around the time the draft plan was being studied.

Formulating the long-term economic plan

Owing to the steady economic expansion in the second half of the 1950s, it became apparent that the targets of the Five-Year Plan for Economic Self-Support would be realized much sooner than initially expected, even before the midpoint of the plan period. By the second half of 1956, its significance in providing guidelines for national economic management had been lost. Moreover, the high-level economic growth produced a variety of distortions, giving rise to an acutely felt need for 'formulating new guidelines for stable economic growth'. Accordingly, the government in February 1957 formally acknowledged the need to revise the plan, and initiated a study.

The Liberal Democratic Party (LDP), which had come to power in the meantime, took a serious view of the matter and in March began to undertake a study to formulate its own draft plan by establishing a Special Committee for Economic Planning in its Political Affairs Research Committee. The special committee, acting in concert with the work being done by the Economic Council, deliberated on the matter in as many as eleven meetings, and in June 1957 presented a report entitled 'On the Long-Term Economic Plan'. After the Special Committee for Economic Planning was disbanded during a Cabinet reshuffle, the Policy Deliberation Commission directly tackled the task. When the draft plan of the Economic Council was announced in November 1957, the LDP announced its own 'Outline of a Long-Term Economic Plan'. This response by the LDP to long-term planning was quite a change from its earlier response to the Five-Year Plan for Economic Self-Support, which was described as follows: 'The formal response of the LDP was to hold one explanatory meeting of the Executive Committee at the final stage; it merely swallowed what was presented to it, so to speak.'[3]

The target of the New Long-Term Economic Plan, formally adopted in December 1957, was to achieve an average annual growth of 6.5 per cent during the fiscal years 1957–62. The pattern of economic growth envisioned by this plan was, as in earlier plans, the expansion of industrial production led by increasing exports. The novelty of the plan, however, lay in the assumption of a 38 per cent increase in per capita consumption expenditures. It predicted continued improvement in the standard of living as a result of greater diffusion and usage of consumer durables such as home electric appliances and because of a further rise in the level of employment towards the full employment level. The aim of the earlier economic plans, i.e. economic self-support in the sense of independence from special procurements, had already been achieved during the 1955–6 period of prosperity. Against this background, the new long-term plan was notable in that it shifted the target from 'economic self-support' to 'realization of a higher, more stable rate of growth'. It is also important to note that the new plan involved a shift of emphasis from the earlier position of 'curtailing consumption and expanding investment' to that of growth that would include an improvement in the national standard of living. This shift implied that the Japanese economy had definitely reached a new plateau. Consistent throughout all these plans, moreover, was the future image of the country's economic structure, which saw the development of an economy driven by export promotion, itself founded on upgrading the industrial structure by greater emphasis on the heavy and chemical industries. In line with this vision, the keynote of economic policy evolved from economic self-support immediately after independence to achieving high-level growth in the second half of the 1950s, and ultimately to upgrading the economic structure and improving the substance of the economy. This policy framework—which was later carried over to the National Income Doubling Plan, which came to symbolize the next era—defined the keynote of MITI policy in those days.

The merger of conservative forces and changing process of policy formulation

The positive and autonomous response of the ruling Liberal Democratic Party to the process of formulating the New Long-Term Economic Plan observed during the period of the Kishi Cabinet symbolized one aspect of the changed process for formulating policy after the 1955 merger of conservative forces. Before the merger, parliamentary proceedings had often been disrupted by confrontations between the two major conservative parties. As discussed in Chapter 13, budget bills were often passed well after the fiscal year actually began, and the form was that of a bill revised through negotiations between the ruling and opposition parties. Many important bills were tabled until the following Diet session or abandoned altogether. In those circumstances the business community strongly urged stabilization of the political situation.

Even in the circumstances, of course, important bills were often enacted at the initiative of the Diet, as exemplified by the laws relating to atomic energy and the Small-Business Stabilization Law. On the other hand, neither the ruling party nor the opposition parties were routinely briefed on bills before they were submitted to the Diet or presented their own views on bills. Substantiating this observation was the fact that the ruling party was formally briefed only once even on the Five-Year Plan for Economic Self-Support, a plan the Hatoyama government regarded as the nucleus of its economic policy. During the second half of the 1950s, the confrontation between the Kishi Cabinet's 'high posture' and the opposition parties led by the Socialist Party on revision of the US–Japan Security

Treaty resulted in many important bills ending up not being acted on, like many bills in the first half of the 1950s. But the successful formation of a government by the Liberal Democratic Party at the same time that it enjoyed an overwhelming majority in the Diet was highly significant in promoting the realization of many necessary policies.

Specifically, the 24th session of the Diet in fiscal year 1955, the first session after emergence of the conservative-reformist two-party system, passed the budget for fiscal year 1956 prior to the start of the fiscal year through ordinary parliamentary deliberations. From that point onwards, negotiations with the ruling Liberal Democratic Party prior to submitting a draft budget were an important factor in ensuring passage of the budget.

Similar changes occurred with respect to MITI-related bills as well. As pending bills passed the Diet with relative ease, prior coordination primarily with the LDP, as with budget bills, increased in importance. Of course the role played by the bureaucracy as a group of specialists with policy-formulating capabilities was still overwhelmingly important. Nor were there significant changes in the conventional process of policy formulation, whereby the framework of policy was determined through discussions among the concerned offices and after gathering opinions from the concerned industries. Specific bills were developed through negotiations among the involved ministries and deliberations by the relevant advisory councils. In the past, however, prior negotiations with the ruling Liberal Party or Democratic Party had not been a common practice. In contrast, the newly formed Liberal Democratic Party strictly demanded an opportunity to coordinate views on all government bills before they were submitted to the Diet. On this point, the *Tsusan Junpo* (MITI report issued every ten days) reported the following as characteristic of the 24th Diet's Ordinary Session:

Ever since it was decided that government bills were to be submitted to the Diet after obtaining the approval of the ruling party, the ministry submitted all bills to the Diet only after having the bills deliberated on and approved by, in order, the Commerce and Industry Division of the Political Affairs Research Committee, the Political Affairs Deliberation Commission, and the Executive Council, respectively, of the LDP.[4]

Thus, it became standard procedure for the government to submit bills to the Diet by way of the Commerce and Industry Division of the Political Affairs Research Committee, the Political Affairs Deliberation Commission, and the Executive Council of the LDP. In the first half of the 1950s, the normal legislation process was chronically disrupted by confrontations between parties, and between factions within parties in the conservative camp, prompting industry leaders to demand the formulation of policies based on long-term perspectives. As the political situation shifted to a confrontation between the leading conservative and reformist parties, the emergence of a standardized procedure for policy legislation gradually stabilized the system, although political confrontations as such continued unabated.

17.2. Countercyclical Policy and Measures to Fight Recession

Balance-of-payments stabilization measures

As work on formulation of the long-term economic outlook progressed, as described in Section 17.1, MITI in practice acquired the responsibility of using its various policies, and coordinating them with fiscal and monetary policies, to limit overheating of the economy and to combat recessions under constraints related to the unstable balance-of-payments situation. It implemented various stop-go policies, either to deal with an overheated economy or a business slump, paying close attention to the balance of payments.[5] It checked business overheating by limiting imports and coordinating plant and equipment investment, and provided fine-tuned support measures to financially fragile small and medium enterprises suffering during periods of bad business.

In 1953, imports increased sharply in part because of increased personal consumption expenditures. The trade deficit, which was $400 million in 1952, approached $800 million in 1953, and foreign-currency reserves fell from $1.14 billion at the end of 1952 to $600 million in mid-1954. Measures for dealing with the sharp decrease in foreign-currency reserves and improving the balance of payments included a credit squeeze, fiscal tightening, import restrictions, and export promotion. The credit squeeze included a bolstering of the penalty interest rate on Bank of Japan loans and revision of the preferential import-financing system. As well, application of the import settlement bill concerning imports of twenty-three non-essential and luxury products was suspended.

In response to the call for fiscal tightening, MITI sought to coordinate the plant and equipment investments of major corporations. Based on the plant and equipment investment survey of December 1953, MITI coordinated matters with the Japan Development Bank, the Industrial Bank of Japan, and the Long-Term Credit Bank of Japan to have loan applicants reduce or postpone new projects as much as possible while making positive efforts to supply the applicants with funds needed for modernization programmes.

In terms of measures to tighten controls over imports, the foreign-exchange budget was reduced and the number of items on the Automatic Approval (AA) list was reduced. In order to limit imports of non-essentials, import quotas on daily necessities were reduced, or allowable import limits were reduced to zero. From fiscal year 1953, import quotas on cars, mainly those on completely built-up cars, were sharply reduced. Moreover, to cope with a rush of speculative applications for foreign currencies expected because of the tightening of imports, measures such as suspension of applications for AA imports from the dollar zone and raising of the import mortgage rate on AA items were successively implemented. This was the first time the import mortgage rate was utilized as a countercyclical policy instrument.

Thus, in the foreign-exchange crisis of 1953, balance-of-payments stabilization measures that relied primarily on a credit squeeze quickly improved the payments balance—although it was inevitably accompanied by numerous business failures—in part because the government had a powerful policy measure in the form of the foreign-currency allocation system. A look at individual policy measures, however, shows that all possible measures to overcome the crisis had been introduced. Some measures contributed to export promotion, such as the export compensation linkage system and the expansion of barter trade, but there were also many harmful effects, and steps were taken fairly quickly to correct them. Through that process of trial and error, prototypes of the countercyclical measures of the subsequent period were developed.

In the foreign-exchange crisis of 1957, official foreign-exchange reserves fell from $1.45 billion in April 1956 to $460 million in September 1957, principally because of a sharp increase in imports related to brisk business conditions during the Jimmu Boom. As monetary policy measures, the Bank of Japan in May raised the official discount rate and stepped up its window guidance activities to tighten credit. In August, the Federation of Bankers' Associations of Japan decided to tighten its voluntary credit restraint programme, and agreed that in principle new loans for plant and equipment would not be granted unless they were urgent or absolutely necessary. In concert with these monetary measures, restrictive import measures were introduced, which included: strengthening the system of requiring advance deposits on imports in order to limit speculative imports, partial postponement or reduction of the foreign-exchange budget, raising the usance bill rates, limiting the issuance of import letters of credit, raising the interest on foreign currency deposits, and reducing the ceiling on local loans made by Japanese trading companies located abroad.

Furthermore, on the basis of the emergency measures for improving the balance of payments adopted by the government in June, it was decided that 15 per cent of Fiscal Investment and Loan Programme investments and loans would be deferred and private plant and equipment investments would be adjusted downwards. Concerning this second adjustment, the Financial Institution Fund Council suggested a reduction of 15 per cent or more. MITI then moved to adjust the size of plant and equipment investments in industries under its jurisdiction, and provided guidance to have those industries reduce their investments, on average by 15 per cent or more, including reductions of 15 per cent in the steel, 11 per cent in the electric power, and 10 per cent in the synthetic chemical industries.

Because of its experience with problematic export promotion measures in the previous foreign-exchange crisis, MITI formulated measures centred on preferential export financing. Specific measures that were successively implemented included removing the credit ceiling on export financing, lowering the interest rate on export advance bills, simplifying loan procedures, increasing the line of credit, lengthening loan terms, and expanding the geographical areas eligible for loans against negotiations of export usance bills. Other measures were added later, including larger tax credits for export income and lower export insurance premium rates for export promotion. Guidelines were also issued regarding the appropriate distribution of overseas branches of trading companies in order to eliminate excessive competition. As a result of these measures, the foreign currency reserves that had been falling rapidly finally bottomed out in September 1957 and moved upwards thereafter.

Thus, in order to stabilize the external payments balance during a foreign-exchange crisis, and acting in concert with the monetary and fiscal authorities to offset the effects of business cycles, MITI took advantage of its authority to control the allocation of foreign-currency funds to limit imports and promote exports. MITI also moved to stop the overheating of the economy by reducing imports through adjustments in plant and equipment investments. Some new measures were introduced, including the system of requiring advance deposits on imports—whose original purpose was to prevent a speculative rush of import applications—which acquired the character of a countercyclical tool taking effect through tightened import financing. In terms of influencing the plant and equipment investments in industries under its jurisdiction, in 1957 MITI became able to make necessary adjustments based on deliberations of the Financial Institution Fund Council and the voluntary credit restraint implemented by the Federation of Bankers' Associations of Japan. It thus gradually became possible for MITI to engage in an all-round countercyclical policy by implementing a variety of policy measures.

Development of measures for fighting business slumps

Implementing policies for stabilizing the balance of payments, however, called for dealing with frictional problems during periods of adjustment. Some problems could not be ignored—including excessive competition related to mounting inventories of unsold goods, and the fear of business bankruptcies and unemployment—particularly with respect to small and medium enterprises with fragile business foundations.

Because the recession of 1954 was relatively short and the decline in productive activities during the recession was relatively small, few recession countermeasures were needed for the overall economy, except for the textile and coal-mining industries, which were about to enter a phase of structural depression. A focus of attention in this situation was the guarded response of MITI towards the strong wish of the small-business community for MITI's invocation of Section 29 of the Small and Medium Enterprises Stabilization Law. As pointed out earlier, MITI hesitated to take specific action because it felt there were unresolved issues regarding this law. Subsequently it succeeded in having the law amended, which then allowed it from February 1955 to deal with business slumps by issuing adjustment orders to industry.

The coal mining industry, which had a large number of small mines, was hard hit in the mid-1950s by sluggishness in the market and a tight-money policy, and many mines experienced dire financial difficulties. In order to provide relief to the industry, MITI requested the Japanese National Railways and the Defence Agency to make early purchases of coal to satisfy their projected needs, and aggressively promoted the financing of reconstruction loans for the coal mining industry. Also, to deal with the increasing number of unemployed coal miners, MITI, acting in concert with other government agencies, moved to increase employment by providing re-employment services, and promoting unemployment relief work and work for restoring local environments damaged by mining pollution.

In the recession of 1957–8, MITI pushed forward with its programme of issuing 'advice to limit production' to cotton textile manufacturers in combination with a sharp reduction in foreign-exchange budget allocations for raw cotton imports. From April 1958, it carried out a programme requiring cotton-spinners to retire and seal cotton-spinning machines at a uniform rate of 30 per cent. In the steel industry, the programme of coordinating the output level of steel-makers was put into effect from January 1958 together with a move in the industry to initiate a system of autonomous coordination. Although this recession countermeasure failed to achieve the anticipated result of restoring higher prices, it provided the momentum for adopting the Open Sales System. Besides the above-mentioned products, production cutbacks were initiated under MITI's guidance for electrolytic copper and vinyl chloride from October 1957, followed by curtailments in producing superphosphate of lime as well as paper and pulp from January 1958; and of celluloid, soda, and firebricks from April of the same year. Also from April, limitations were placed on investments in new equipment for pulp production.

During the recession shaped like the 'bottom of a frying pan' that lasted from 1957 into 1958, therefore, *de facto* anti-recession cartels operated under MITI's advice and guidance in a fairly large number of industries. They engaged in systematic activities for coordinating output, capacity (investment), and prices in order to eliminate excessive competition and restore reasonable prices. MITI played a leading role in implementing these programmes while maintaining close working relationships with the industries concerned to coordinate the methods of implementation, determine the rates of adjustment, and monitor implementation.

17.3. Policy Instruments and Their Changes

The Enterprise Rationalization Promotion Law and rationalization measures

The Enterprise Rationalization Promotion Law, aimed at promoting industrial rationalization to increase the international competitiveness of Japanese industry, stipulated the following measures for achieving that aim. First, it provided for subsidies for improving technical levels, lend-lease programmes of government-owned machinery and equipment, and reduced depreciation periods and exemptions from property taxes for machinery and equipment used for experimental research. Second, it stipulated special depreciation rules and reduction of, or exemption from, property taxes for modernized machinery and equipment. It also provided for improvement of the industrial infrastructure, increased productivity in basic units, and management diagnosis for small and medium enterprises.[6]

Of the measures based on these policies, the various subsidies for experimental research on MITI-related mining and manufacturing technologies had been implemented through administrative action prior to enactment of the Enterprise Rationalization Promotion Law. These subsidies, however, were given a legal basis for the first time by enforcement of regulations related to this law. Subsidies for applied research, for testing of industrial applications of technology, and for developing prototypes of machinery and equipment were formally combined into a system of subsidies for experimental research in mining and manufacturing technology. During the fiscal years 1953 to 1960, subsidies provided under this programme amounted to about 4.6 billion yen, consisting of 1.8 billion yen (206 cases) for testing of industrial applications of technology, 1.7 billion yen (1,248 cases) for applied research, 800 million yen (149 cases) for developing prototypes of machinery and equipment, and 300 million yen (69 cases) for developing prototypes of machine tools. Total experimental research expenditures, including matching funds from the private sector, amounted to approximately 19.6 billion yen.

In terms of taxation measures, so-called priority tax reductions, a form of special taxation, became important. These measures were utilized, as recommended by the Industrial Rationalization Council in its first report, to achieve the goals of the industrial rationalization policy through incentives such as tax exemptions. They included reduction or exemption of import duties and/or property taxes on machinery and equipment for modernization, and introduction of a system of special short-term depreciation allowances on advanced machinery and equipment. Specifically, in fiscal year 1951 when the system of priority tax reductions was formally initiated, the provision of special depreciation allowances (a 50 per cent increase over three years) was introduced, followed by introduction of systems of reserves for covering price changes and exemption of import duties on important machinery and equipment. Other special taxation measures were introduced in fiscal year 1952, including the provision of an increased first-year depreciation allowance to 50 per cent of the purchase price of equipment bought for rationalization, special depreciation allowances on machinery for experimental research, and reserves for employees' retirement allowances.

Special taxation measures were expanded and reinforced until fiscal year 1955. In 1955, a Temporary Tax System Council established as an advisory council to the Cabinet filed a report in which it recommended consolidating and streamlining various special taxation measures. In response to this recommendation, MITI advocated continuation of the tax measures, arguing that the measures were important as an integral part of its industrial structure policy for fostering new industries, accumulating capital, modernizing equipment, and promoting exports. MITI defined these measures as follows: 'As the relative importance of foreign trade controls declines with the progress of trade liberalization, the importance of special taxation measures as incentives in industrial policy will increase.'[7] In fact, in terms of special depreciation allowances, the number of machinery categories eligible for 50 per cent extra depreciation over three years was increased from 431 initially (August 1951) to 1,432 in fiscal year 1960. The number of important industries to which one-half depreciation in the first year applied was increased from thirty-two initially (over 300 machinery categories) to fifty-two (467 machinery categories) in fiscal year 1960. In these industries, income tax deferments through stepped-up depreciation had a highly significant effect in providing incentives for investment. Moreover, of the successively increased number of reserves and allowances, the reduction of or exemption from corporate income tax owing to allowances for bad debt, reserves for covering price changes, and reserves for employees' retirement allowances were significant. These special taxation measures had thus become important policy instruments for inducing the modernization of industries and enterprises by promoting increased retained earnings and capital accumulation in enterprises. The general trend in taxation reform, however, was towards reducing the number of special taxation measures. In response, MITI was compelled to seek new policy measures.

As seen above, the Industrial Rationalization Council and other advisory councils played important roles in formulating specific measures for industrial rationalization. Of these councils, the Industrial Rationalization Council and the Anti-Monopoly Law Council played especially key roles in building the consensus necessary for formulating new policies. Some other advisory councils established under the provisions of the various 'industry laws' were also important. The Machine Industry Council (Machinery Industry Promotion Law), the Electronics Industry Council (Electronics Industry Promotion Law), and the Coal Mining Industry Council (Coal Mining Temporary Measures Law) deliberated on medium-term plans and annual implementation plans according to the provisions of the respective laws, thereby seeking to foster and rationalize their respective industries. These advisory councils played dynamic roles as they flexibly implemented various measures while adjusting the conflicting interests of the industries involved, including investment coordination carried out by the Industrial Finance Committee as mentioned in Chapter 15.

The Fiscal Investment and Loan Programme and activities of the Japan Development Bank

In the financial area, the Fiscal Investment and Loan Programme and the financing activities of the Japan Development Bank (JDB), which channelled Fiscal Investment and Loan Programme funds, proved useful as policy instruments. The reason was because government funds accounted for a large percentage of the source of plant and equipment investment funds in those days; the reliance on those funds was particularly pronounced in the electric power, merchant shipping, and coal-mining industries. The supply of these government funds was based on the Fiscal Investment and Loan Programme, funds from which had continually expanded from fiscal year 1951 but declined markedly during the retrenchment period of fiscal year 1954. At the same time, the primary function of the Programme changed from the conventional role of expanding production capacity and increasing effective demand to that of serving as a countercyclical instrument. Moreover, the primary objects of the Programme's funding shifted from the rationalization and modernization of key industries to housing construction and improvement of the living environment, as well as development of public-sector facilities and the industrial infrastructure, such as transport and communications, for which private financing was unsuitable.

Similar shifts in emphasis took place in the activities of the JDB. The JDB, which played a central role among government financial institutions in providing capital investment funds, reorganized its functions by shifting the responsibility of agriculture, forestry, and fishery financing, and small business financing to the Agriculture, Forestry, and Fishery Finance Corporation and the Small-Business Finance Corporation respectively, both of which were established during fiscal years 1953–4. The bank then expanded its operations by focusing its financing activities on four basic industries, with electric power and merchant shipping in the centre, and including steel and coal-mining. These financing activities not only accelerated the rationalization of key industries by providing funds on a priority basis to areas which private financial institutions found difficult to accommodate, but also primed the pump of private lending in the areas concerned. Specifically, concerning the problem of supplying funds to the four key industries, city (commercial) banks sought to coordinate their financing activities—in the Voluntary Credit Restraint Committee established in July 1951—by reference to the JDB's basic plan. Furthermore, for the Ninth Shipbuilding Plan of 1953 and subsequent plans, JDB financing was carried out through close public–private cooperation. The percentage of total financing made by the JDB was determined by joint consultation between the Ministry of Transport, Ministry of Finance, JDB, and the Federation of Bankers' Association of Japan. The terms of loans were determined largely through close consultation between the managing bank and the JDB. For electric power industry loans from the International Bank for Reconstruction and Development (IBRD; the World Bank), a new form of foreign-currency financing was introduced in fiscal year 1953 in which the JDB served as the primary borrower, lent the proceeds to power companies, and the government guaranteed the JDB obligations.

Subsequently, against a background of the 'normalization of financing' which was in progress, the need for 'shifting from quantitative to qualitative supplementing' came to be strongly urged as the proper role of JDB financing. From 1957, the percentage of JDB financing in total equipment investments declined as the demand for capital equipment funds increased sharply. With the exception of the shipping and coal-mining industries, the 'qualitative supplementing' function of JDB financing was enhanced. On the other hand, many new financing areas emerged for the JDB, including regional development, construction of small and medium steel vessels, petrochemicals, nuclear power generation, and industrial infrastructure. JDB financing was also characterized as an important tool for achieving policy goals such as fostering important industries as called for by the Law on Temporary Measures for Promotion of the Machinery Industry and the Law on Temporary Measures for Promotion of the Electronics Industry. Its financing targets diversified further as new responsibilities were added in various reports of advisory councils, basic plans for rationalization, and promotional plans.

The role played by JDB financing in the First Petrochemical Industry Plan was described as follows: 'By becoming the nucleus of huge sums of private loans and priming the pump of commercial lending, JDB funds served as the mainspring responsible for successful execution of the First Petrochemical Industry Plan.'[8] Although limited in quantity, JDB loans continued to play an important role in qualitative terms through its pump-priming function. For instance, the petrochemical industry—an industry highly dependent on external funds—was able to obtain sufficient funds from private financial institutions only with the help of such pump-priming.

Progress in the import of foreign capital

Control over the import of foreign capital and technology also served as a powerful policy instrument. The Foreign Capital Law, on the assumption of strict and total control of capital flows, defined the approval criteria for direct foreign investment in Japan as 'positive criteria' (where approval may be granted) and 'negative criteria' (where approval should not be granted). The former consisted of three criteria: foreign investment should contribute to Japan's international balance of payments, it should be conducive to the development of key industries or public utilities, and it should be necessary for the continuation or renewal of technical licensing agreements relating to key industries or public utilities. The disapproval criteria, meanwhile, related to foreign investment that was considered to have a possibly adverse effect on reconstruction of the Japanese economy.

Controls were subsequently relaxed somewhat in that foreign investment only required notification after the fact, and restrictions were eased on the acquiring of stocks by foreign investors. The primary significance of the restrictions, however, lay in deterring the advance (direct investment) of foreign capital into Japanese markets by strict control measures, thereby giving Japanese enterprises ample business opportunities. As a result of the restrictions, there was no full-scale foreign direct investment in any field but the petroleum-refining and chemical industries, where stock acquisition by foreign investors was relatively significant. Even the Screening Criteria for Stock Acquisition—which was approved at a MITI ministerial meeting in August 1960 in response to the implementation in June of measures to relax controls over the import of foreign capital—was characterized by a restrictive policy towards foreign capital. Under these criteria, approval would be granted in principle if Japanese investors held 51 per cent or more of the shares, but the application would be rejected if foreign investors acquired a majority of the equity. Protection granted Japanese industries in this form, however, eventually had to be removed as liberalization of capital flows progressed. It was a protectionist policy with a time limit, guaranteeing no long-lasting protection and compelling the protected industries to develop competitiveness during the period they were being protected.

Another important aspect of the policy regarding the import of foreign capital was the importation of high-quality capital from such organizations as the IBRD and the Export-Import Bank (Ex-Im) of the US. World Bank loans were distributed as follows: 42.9 per cent to the steel industry, 41.6 per cent to the electric power industry, 13.9 per cent to public works projects, and 1.5 per cent to machinery industries such as cars and shipbuilding, with steel and electric power accounting for more than 80 per cent of the total. In Ex-Im loans, 44.3 per cent was for electric power, 26.4 per cent for steel, 14.2 per cent for Japan Air Lines, and 13.8 per cent for cars, with the electric power, steel, and machinery industries again accounting for over 80 per cent of the total. These foreign-currency loans funded 30 to 40 per cent of the construction cost of the targeted projects, significantly priming the pumps of participation financing by domestic financial institutions, which accounted for the greater part of total loans.

On the other hand, various problems arose in relation to World Bank loans. In the steel industry, for example, Yawata Steel and Nippon Kokan were required to submit financial restructuring plans before obtaining loans in fiscal year 1955. Kawasaki Steel obtained World Bank loans in December 1956 but had to accept strict financial control by the World Bank. In the electric power industry, the World Bank strongly demanded that the power companies agree to raise their electric power rates in order to ensure an accumulation of capital and improvement of their financial position. Because the power companies had adhered to the policy of quickly developing electric power sources while deferring power rate increases to the maximum extent possible, MITI had a difficult time reconciling the conflicting positions.

Promoting selective import of technologies

The import of technology, i.e. technical licensing agreements, was approved or disapproved on the basis of the positive and negative criteria mentioned earlier, within the framework of the Foreign Capital Law. These criteria were eased in 1959 in accordance with the 'New Method of Importing Foreign Capital'. The screening procedure was speeded up and a system of 'conditional' approval was instituted. These practices continued until the Foreign Capital Council in May 1961 approved 'On the Relaxation of the Approval Policy of Technical Licensing Agreement Applications and the Simplification of the Screening Procedures'.

The actual procedures for handling applications for technical licensing agreements based on these criteria were extremely detailed. For instance, the applying company, after prior consultation with the MITI bureau having primary jurisdiction over the content of a proposed agreement, submitted an application and attached materials to the Bank of Japan. The required documents included a copy of the agreement; a detailed explanation of how the agreement was reached; summary descriptions of the overseas investor, applicant, technology involved, and content of the agreement; an operating plan; a statement of projected foreign-currency income and expenditures; and a cost statement. In some cases, after the application passed through several screening stages the applicant might be asked to alter the content of the agreement. On the basis of this request, the applicant had to enter into renegotiations with the foreign investor on the terms of the agreement. Based on instructions from the authorities, applicants frequently had to renegotiate the terms of agreements already reached. Such renegotiation, therefore, was the *de facto* primary instrument for controlling technology imports under the provisions of the Foreign Capital Law. The authorities were especially keen on recommending the reduction of prices that appeared high compared to prices paid for similar technologies, as well as the elimination of stipulation for guaranteed minimum royalty payments. Although the authorities closely considered Japan's foreign-exchange position at the time of screening, short-term fluctuations in foreign-exchange reserves did not affect their decisions much because, unlike imports of raw materials, technology imports required relatively small sums of foreign currency.

Selectively approved foreign technology imports were incorporated into the business strategy of Japanese companies as an effective way of quickly closing the technological gap which had developed between them and their American and European counterparts because of the technological vacuum of the wartime and immediate post-war years and the subsequent development of new technologies in the US and Europe. Accordingly, Japanese companies were quite eager to import foreign technology. As a consequence, a danger existed of competition among importing companies leading to a deterioration in the terms of agreements. The control over technology imports, therefore, was effective in averting such events.

Industrial organization policy and anti-monopoly regulation

MITI was able freely to exercise its control over imports of foreign capital and technology as an important policy tool that affected the activities of individual companies and aimed at wide-ranging industrial rationalization and modernization. In contrast, policies relating to industrial order and industrial organization required coordination with the various regulations of the Anti-Monopoly Law. These regulations were systematically developed and improved, causing controversy over revisions to the law in 1953 and later.[9]

MITI's views on industrial organization policy were as follows. It acknowledged that the situation of perfect competition that underlay the Anti-Monopoly Law was the guiding principle of the free enterprise system, and that the Anti-Monopoly Law was, in effect, the economy's 'constitution'. At the same time, MITI believed it would be difficult for Japan to achieve a self-supporting status for its economy and its further development by relying solely on this guiding principle. Accordingly, it argued, the aspects of the Anti-Monopoly Law that were inappropriate in the economic circumstances needed to be revised, and measures necessary for enhancing the international competitiveness of Japanese industry should be introduced.

To that end, MITI, even after the 1953 revision of the Anti-Monopoly Law, sought to have anti-recession cartels, measures to stabilize the demand for basic materials, export promotion cartels, and rationalization cartels exempted from the scope of the Anti-Monopoly Law. After the 1953 revision, attempts at further revisions which might impact seriously on the status of MITI policy were unsuccessful, as is well known. The idea of questioning the universal validity of the Anti-Monopoly Law, however, gradually took root as basic policy philosophy, and was manifested by policies implemented to foster and promote various industries. Industrial leaders, too, were sceptical about maintaining industrial order through the Anti-Monopoly Law, and sought relief from anti-monopoly regulation. What they wanted, however, was freedom to form a system of autonomous coordination by private enterprises. In other words, they wanted freedom from anti-monopoly regulation and freedom from the approval and licensing authority of the government. This second type of freedom sought by industry presented a new problem that MITI, as a policy-oriented administrative agency, had to consider carefully. Of course, demands by industry leaders for freedom from public authority did not mean advocating leaving everything to private initiative. The demands were for specific government measures fitting the industrial reality rather than of industries being regulated by a general and uniform set of policy measures. Industry leaders demanded freedom in principle on condition that they could ask for specific measures. Such demands became stronger in the second half of the 1950s as private corporations became more powerful and an oligopolistic market structure developed with enterprise groups forming its nucleus. As a result, industry-specific policy measures for industrial organization were developed, on the one hand in the form of legislation exempting them from the purview of the Anti-Monopoly Law. In those days, this was considered a highly significant development. On the other hand, Anti-Monopoly Law exempting legislation which MITI promoted sometimes was not realized because of the opposition of the business community, compelling MITI to devise more indirect measures. Such indirect measures enhanced the variety of MITI's policy instruments for different industries, enabling the ministry to engage in fine-tuned industrial and trade policy.

The foreign-exchange allocation system and industrial policy

Along with legislation that exempted industries from the provisions of the Anti-Monopoly Law, the foreign-exchange allocation system became an important tool of industrial policy. Being essentially a system which aimed at maintaining equilibrium in the balance of payments, it played an important role in stabilizing external payments and receipts which ordinarily fluctuated with business cycles.[10]

Foreign-exchange allocation, however, served another important function. Although its effect was milder than that of quantitative and price controls imposed during the post-war rehabilitation period, it became a powerful means of controlling industries, almost as powerful as quantitative controls. This was because, first, the government could give protection, in principle, to industries with weak international competitiveness by restricting imports of products related to the industries in question. Such protection, effected by means of the foreign-exchange allocation system, was far more powerful than that provided by tariffs. Second, in dealing with industries and companies whose key material imports were subject to foreign-currency allocation, the government could, by regulating the allocation, indirectly control production levels or block the entry into the market of new producers. Thus, regulating the quantities of raw material imports by means of foreign-exchange allocation had the effect of supplanting or reinforcing such measures as anti-recession cartels, thereby ensuring, through control of raw materials, the effectiveness of output coordination requested through administrative guidance.

During this period, the foreign-exchange allocation system was positively utilized in three industries which imported large quantities of raw materials: cotton-spinning, petroleum-refining, and steel. In addition, the system worked effectively in machinery industries, which were representative of industries where imports were approved, in principle, on a case-by-case basis under a protectionist policy that took into consideration their competitiveness with domestic products. Although space limitations do not allow a detailed description of it, the foreign-exchange allocation system as it was administered in these industries became the characteristic economic policy of the period, fostering potential growth industries, accomplishing output adjustments, and otherwise producing the effects intended by industrial policy. This system, however, was destined to be abolished sooner or later, because of a weakening of its principal justification, maintaining an equilibrium in the balance of payments. During the first half of the 1960s, when the liberalization of trade and capital flows made progress, the foreign-exchange allocation system gradually lost its significance as an instrument of industrial policy.

17.4. Emergence of New Policy Issues

Changing priorities in MITI policy

As seen above, in carrying out its international trade and industrial policy MITI diversified its methods and put measures into effect as necessary in response to the changing patterns of growth and development of the Japanese economy.[11]

During this period, which was characterized by fluctuations in business activities of roughly two years in duration, the most important tasks for post-independence Japan were to achieve economic self-support, place the economy on a path to stable growth, attain more widespread employment, and realize a higher standard of living. Looking ahead to these tasks, MITI gradually changed its policy priorities during this period. Roughly speaking, the priorities in the first half of the 1950s—which were to reassess the Occupation-era policies and achieve economic self-support—were upgraded to achieve a further expansion of the economy in 1955 and afterwards.

During this period, a time when moves were made to realize a self-supporting economy devoid of special procurements while Occupation-era policies were being reassessed, policy objectives were more or less achieved. Moreover, the realization of growth that far surpassed anything initially hoped for launched the Japanese economy on a path of high-level growth. Against this background, the goals of MITI policy gradually changed. To the initial goals of rationalizing basic industries and enhancing their international competitiveness were added the new goals of fostering new industries, improving the industrial infrastructure, and promoting overseas economic assistance. The scope of MITI policy was thus gradually expanded. The moves to cope with industrial pollution and consumer policy were representative of the new goals. Thus, within a short span of seven years after independence, the Japanese economy was transformed to an economy that could now aim for transition to an open economy in response to the global trend towards freer trade.

Use of indirect policy measures

Changes in policy goals brought about subtle changes in the character of MITI policy implemented during this period, albeit constrained by the changing economic conditions of the times. For instance, a new approach was introduced in the study of policy for 1955, a study undertaken after critical reflection on the deflationary policy of 1954 and later. With regard to rationalizing enterprises, one of the highest priority goals along with promotion of exports, the past practices of providing direct financing of rationalization funds and formulating specific rationalization plans were rejected. 'It is necessary for the government to make fresh efforts to improve and reinforce the business environment in ways which private companies could not accomplish by themselves in the past, and to introduce measures to further enhance the financial health and other qualitative aspects of individual companies.'[12] Emphasized here were policy measures that attached importance to indirect aid to private enterprises. Specifically, they included promoting manufacturing and mining technologies, improving and expanding industrial zones, promoting productivity-enhancement movements, improving the tax system to help increase internally generated funds of enterprises, and fostering the bond market. A similar trend was found in policy towards trade. MITI recognized that policy measures for promoting trade had to be changed, in response to the global trend towards liberalization, to indirect methods such as financing. Although the ministry was certainly paying heed to the continuity of existing programmes, it was also clearly shifting its priorities towards indirect methods in the process of formulating industrial and enterprise rationalization policy.

Perhaps because of this shift, MITI in 1955 was far more positive than previously about securing Fiscal Investment and Loan Programme funds and allocating them to priority programmes. Particularly notable was its suggestion to establish an 'investment council' in order to enhance the efficiency of investments, as well as its acceptance of a change in the use of Fiscal Investment and Loan Programme funds in response to the suggestion that those funds be transformed into 'qualitative supplementing'.

Lessons from the problem of bottlenecks

Policy such as this became a clear issue when bottlenecks arising from the overheating of the economy became serious after economic self-support—in the sense of achieving an external payments balance without reliance on special procurements—was realized. Moreover, the emergence of bottlenecks was an important lesson regarding the effects of vigorous equipment investment activities.

The basic framework of economic development up to that time was as follows. Increases in demand caused by expanding exports led to increased production and investment in equipment. At the same time, increases in imports of raw materials and producer goods caused a deterioration in the balance of payments, which worked as a brake on growth. The primary goal of economic policy, therefore, was focused on how to minimize the balance-of-payments constraints on growth and how to prolong periods of prosperity in order to achieve stable economic growth. To that end, the strategy emphasized was to enhance the international competitiveness of industries and raise the rate of self-sufficiency of the economy by expanding exports and limiting imports.

In the second half of the 1950s, even though the economy was on its way to steady expansion, Japan still had very small foreign reserves, and changes in the balance of payments alternately generated optimism and then pessimism. In this environment, however, clearly discernible changes were developing. One was the fact that investments in equipment modernization and rationalization were considerable, and were beginning to be recognized as important factors bringing about an expansion in domestic demand. A bottleneck developed, however, in the supply of producer goods needed for the investment activities. A rise in the prices of steel products led to sharp increase in the prices of machine products. The situation proved that it would be possible, by eliminating industrial bottlenecks and creating an economic environment for encouraging large private investment in plant and equipment, to promote the modernization and rationalization of equipment, thereby reducing costs and improving international competitiveness, which would contribute to the expansion of exports. Certainly the idea deserved serious consideration. In other words, attention was shifting away from pursuing a system of policies for increasing exports towards a pattern of investment-led growth in which producing an environment conducive to the realization of industrial rationalization would in the end make increased exports possible.

The two alternative approaches—the so-called export-first policy of the immediate post-war years, and the new strategy of investment-led growth—were essentially the same in that they were both rooted in the belief that in order to realize the growth of the Japanese economy under balance-of-payments constraints it was crucial to diminish those constraints. It was worth noting, however, that conditions were emerging that favoured a transition to investment-led growth, although it would be years before the concept became fully systematized. In fact, the export-first approach again dominated the thinking of economic policymakers during the 1957–8 recession. In the course of this recession, however, the policy of promoting the development of the industrial infrastructure in a broader sense, aimed at improving the investment environment, began to take root. The importance of strengthening the transport system by improving highways and port facilities, as well as improving industrial water systems and the conditions for industrial location, came to be gradually recognized. This recognition was highly suggestive of the new direction of MITI policy.

Another important development was the transformation of MITI policy into one of greater optimism. In the past, MITI was conservative in its outlook on the future of the economy and was overly concerned about a rush in capital investment generating conditions of overcapacity. This cautious attitude gave way to a newly found optimism with a more aggressive and expansionary outlook on the future of the economy and a greater willingness to welcome the growth of private companies and their ambitious investment plans. During this period, even the most optimistic economic forecasts were proved wrong by the economy's actual performance, which far outshone predictions. Nonetheless, as seen in plans such as those to rationalize the steel industry and construct new facilities in the petrochemical industry, MITI's adjustment policies worked towards validating the expansionary results while judiciously applying a brake on excessive investments.

Emergence of new policy issues

Besides improvement of the industrial infrastructure, which had become an issue in the context of a need to improve the investment environment, the fact that policy issues were being recognized from a broader perspective also indicated that this was a period of transition to an era of high-level growth. That the Economic White Paper for fiscal year 1957 initiated the discussion of the dual-structure problem was another manifestation of the broader policy perspective. As a result, the relative importance of the small-business issue in overall MITI policy was enhanced. As well as this issue, which was more or less a rearrangement of other policies of the past, there also emerged new priority policy issues which were likely to attract wide attention during the coming period of high-level growth.

For instance, in connection with the improvement in the industrial infrastructure, industrial pollution policy with a focus on the industrial waste-water problem came to be recognized as a MITI policy issue, as when it was stated in 1957 that 'in view of the fact that water pollution by industrial waste is causing a variety of problems, its rational solution must be sought.'[13] This represented the emergence of measures for dealing with the pollution problem—which reared its head as growth accelerated—as a new policy issue resulting from economic development.

The initiation of the discussion on consumer policy, along with industrial waste-water policy, signified the emergence of new policy issues. In the process of preparing new policies for fiscal year 1957, the MITI Enterprises Bureau advocated implementing measures for dealing with consumer demand as a priority policy objective for the coming year. This was symbolic of the change in MITI policy. As was discussed in Chapter 13, the view was clearly expressed in the Economic White Paper of 1953 and elsewhere that increased consumer spending brought about a rise in domestic prices, caused a deterioration in the balance of payments, and ultimately limited economic development. Although the urge to limit consumption did not fade totally during this period, MITI, while still concerned about consumption, nonetheless judged that 'dealing with its qualitative aspects is likely to lead to formulation of constructive policies.' It critically reflected on its past policy by stating that 'it cannot be denied that administrative policy has tended to strongly favour the standpoint of producers.' It then demonstrated its eagerness to tackle new policy issues in the following statement.

[Although] there were ample reasons for favouring producers during the period of economic rehabilitation, (a) today when the seller's market ('Anything made will sell') is changing into a buyer's market ('Making things that sell'), consideration for consumption or demand cannot be ignored if economic development is to continue; and, (b) moreover, raising the quality of consumption will lead to greater sophistication of the industrial structure, which in turn will bring about an increase in exports.[14]

MITI thus was intent on characterizing consumption as one of its new policy issues. Although it was still undecided as to which specific measures should be put into effect, all indications were that its attention was shifting to the rising level of personal consumption—a characteristic of post-war economic growth—which provided a foundation for the growth of consumer-durable industries.

Emerging advocacy of an inducement policy

Once into fiscal year 1959, against a background of economic prosperity, the keynote of MITI policy began to acquire colours suggesting the dawning of a new era. The transition in MITI's policy keynote was manifest in the report 'On MITI Policy from Here on' prepared by the Planning Office as it developed the new policy for that year. Being based on confidence in the prevailing situation and the future prospects of the Japanese economy, which had achieved a solid self-supporting status, this document identified an ' "inducement" policy making best use of the mechanism of capitalism' as the 'fundamental philosophy of policy implementation'.[15] Specifically, it contended that:

The task before us is how our policy can induce the economy or industry to develop in the desired direction. At present, when the tide of trade liberalization is washing our shores and domestic industrial circles are voicing their demands for autonomous coordination of business activities, our fundamental philosophy of policy implementation is crystallized in the term 'inducement' policy that makes the best use of the mechanism of capitalism.

MITI's advocacy of inducement policy can be best understood against the background of the attitude of industrial circles towards revision of the Anti-Monopoly Law and the rising tide of trade and capital liberalization. As pointed out earlier, private companies which were growing in size demanded freedom from the Anti-Monopoly Law and freedom from government intervention, and were gaining an increasingly stronger voice. For the business community, the freedom relating to industrial organization—in other words, freedom of private companies to create a system of autonomous coordination of business activities among themselves—was fundamentally alien to the 'freedom' which government was prepared to grant. The 'inducement' policy approach was in a sense a response to this critical mood of the business community.

The second, and more important, reason for MITI's increasing inclination towards the inducement approach was the liberalization of trade and capital flows. Liberalization was obviously an unavoidable trend, and it was predicted that its progress would naturally have a profound impact on the Japanese economy. How to deal with this trend loomed as a momentous policy issue. The details of this process will be examined in Part IV. What must be attended to at this point is the fact that it was believed that liberalization would render impotent the system of foreign-capital and foreign-exchange control which had occupied the central position among MITI policy tools.

As pointed out earlier, the foreign-exchange allocation system was used as an instrument of enormous effectiveness in policies dealing with business cycles, international trade, industrial structure, and energy. A policy of tighter allocation of foreign exchange reduced imports and improved the balance of payments. Moreover, selective allocation of foreign exchange was an effective instrument for overall MITI policy in that it could indicate, case by case, the direction and priorities of foreign technology imports essential for industrial rationalization. The progress of liberalization, therefore, called for a new type of MITI policy measure which could supplant the foreign-exchange allocation system. Herein lay another reason why inducement policy was advocated by MITI. Here, it must be noted that the fundamental philosophy characterized as 'inducement' laid stress on 'making the best use of the mechanism of capitalism'. This emphasis was rooted in the belief that with the transition from economic rehabilitation and self-support to the new growth phase of the economy, creating an environment that would allow totally free play for the vitality of private companies should be the principal objective of international trade and industrial policy. This belief may be regarded as an indication of the growing expectations and confidence that MITI officials had in the growth prospects of Japanese industries and enterprises. MITI's new way of thinking at this time is summarized in the following statement: 'It is incumbent on us to re-examine the question of whether or not the present system of regulation over trade and industry has degenerated into easygoing protectionism, and to seriously study at this time the prospect that deregulation will genuinely contribute to the promotion of industry from a long-term perspective.'[16] Of course this new fundamental policy philosophy, because of its very novelty, was to be partially revised through the process of coordination of views within the ministry. Nonetheless, it faithfully reflected the changing times, and was destined to become, as will be discussed in Part IV, the foundation of MITI policy in the era of high-level growth.

NOTES

1. Concerning economic planning, see *Tsusho Sangyo Seisakushi*, v, ch. 1, sect. 2.
2. Ibid. v. 44.
3. Ibid. v. 65.
4. Ibid. v. 136.
5. Concerning countercyclical policy and measures to combat recessions, see ibid. v, ch. 3.
6. Concerning industrial rationalization, FILP, and importation of foreign capital and technology, see ibid. vi, ch. 5, sects. 1 and 2.
7. Ibid. vi. 363.
8. Ibid. vi. 500–1.
9. Concerning industrial organization policy, see ibid. v, ch. 2.
10. Concerning the foreign currency allocation system, see ibid. vi, ch. 4, sect. 4.
11. Concerning the discussions in the following paragraphs, see ibid. v, ch. 1, sect. 3.
12. Ibid. v. 127–8.
13. Ibid. v. 158.
14. Ibid. v. 158–60.
15. Ibid. v. 185.
16. Ibid. v. 187.

PART IV

High-Level Growth and the Development of the Open Economy

18

The Development Process of Rapid Economic Growth

18.1. From the Iwato Boom to the Izanagi Boom

During the twelve-year period between fiscal years 1959 and 1970, the Japanese economy recorded double-digit growth every year except 1962 and 1965.[1] This was indeed an era of rapid economic growth. Those twelve years contained two periods of long-term, high-level growth, the Iwato and Izanagi boom periods, which sandwiched between them the recession of 1965. This chapter reviews the business fluctuations during this period, and concludes with a discussion on the cause of these fluctuations.

The Iwato Boom

Having emerged from the so-called recession shaped like 'the bottom of a frying pan' of fiscal years 1957–8, the economy made a V-shaped recovery. That upswing lasted for forty-two months, from June 1958 to December 1961. It was called the Iwato Boom, meaning in Japanese that in both duration and scale it exceeded the Jimmu Boom which covered the thirty-one-month period from November 1954 to June 1957. The rate of economic growth in real terms exceeded 10 per cent for three consecutive years: 11.2 per cent in 1959, 12.5 per cent in 1960, and 13.5 per cent in 1961. A sentence in the Economic Survey of Japan for fiscal year 1962 read, 'It is unprecedented in our country's history for the economy to have sustained such a high rate of growth for three consecutive years.'[2]

During the three-year period, the industrial production index rose about 1.9-fold, from 144.8 in 1958 (1955 = 100) to 179.9 in 1959, to 227.9 in 1960, and to 272.6 in 1961. Comparisons of output volumes of major products between 1958 and 1961 show the following increases: crude steel from 12.12 million tons to 28.27 million tons, electric power generation from 74.6 billion kWh to 116.8 billion kWh, passenger cars from over 50,000 to over 250,000, washing machines from over 990,000 to over 2.16 million, and refrigerators from over 420,000 to over 1.56 million. During the same period, Japan's exports increased from $2.88 billion to $4.24 billion. As could be expected, prices also rose during this same period. The national wholesale price index rose by 3.2 per cent, from 344.8 in 1958 to 355.7 in 1961 (1934–6 = 1). For the same period, the Tokyo consumer price index rose by 10.6 per cent, from 312.1 to 345.2 (1934–6 = 1).

The economy, however, did not expand at a constant rate during this long period of prosperity. Wholesale prices peaked in November 1959, and afterwards started falling slightly, notably wholesale prices of textiles and steel. Industrial production also fell during March and April 1960. These short lapses in the otherwise continuous expansion were characteristic of fiscal year 1960, although from May 1960 industrial production resumed its upward trend, followed by an upturn in prices in July. Thereafter, from the second half of 1960 and into 1961, business activities expanded even more vigorously than before.

What ended the Iwato Boom, as it did the earlier Jimmu Boom, was a deterioration in the international balance of payments. The current account fell into deficit in January 1961, and the deficit grew larger as the economy overheated. In May, the overall balance also turned negative. To deal with this situation, in July 1961 the Bank of Japan raised the official discount rate by 0.365 per cent from 6.57 to 6.935 per cent. Other measures were also implemented in September and early October to improve the balance of payments and tighten credit in general, causing the economy to enter a slowdown phase.

The recession of 1965

Although the tight-money measures slowed the economy, the balance of payments improved relatively quickly and the monetary policy was eased again in November 1962. The economic slowdown at this time was more moderate than initially expected. The primary reason for the mild downturn was the expansion of exports, which improved the balance of payments and also helped keep the level of overall demand relatively firm during the downturn. As a result, the rate of economic growth in real terms, which declined to 6.4 per cent in fiscal year 1962, again recorded a double-digit increase of 12.5 per cent in fiscal year 1963. One feature of the upswing in 1963 was vigorous investments in construction. Public works investment in particular increased sharply as construction projects were rushed to be ready for the October 1964 opening of the Tokyo Summer Olympics.

The pick-up in economic activities, however, did not last long. Yet another round of tight-money measures was introduced in December 1963 to deal with the deteriorating external balance caused by sharp increases in imports. Although the tight monetary policy was gradually relaxed from December 1964 as the payments balance stabilized, the economy failed to recover. The rate of economic growth in real terms was a very high 10.6 per cent in fiscal year 1964 and private investment in plant and equipment increased by 16.0 per cent in real terms, but there was no overall sense of prosperity as the capacity-utilization rate in production facilities dropped, business profits declined, and the stock market slumped. This paradoxical situation was referred to as the coexistence of 'a macro boom and a micro recession'.

The slump worsened in early 1965. Industrial production turned downwards after peaking in October 1964, when the Olympic Games were held. The decline in production was most pronounced in industries related to consumer durables and investment goods, but production of non-durables also declined. At the beginning of 1965, the business community was still optimistic about the economy's prospects. But the bankruptcy of Sanyo Specialty Steel Co. Ltd., in March 1965, and the problem of restructuring Yamaichi Securities Co. Ltd. that surfaced in May, convinced even the optimists that the situation was serious. The deteriorating business results of the March 1965 settlement period, which became obvious in May, emphasized further the sense of gloom. Economic activities slackened greatly, and business bankruptcies mushroomed. Some proclaimed an end to the economy's growth trend.

To counter this so-called 'recession of 1965', the Bank of Japan lowered the official discount rate three times in 1965—in January, April, and June. In July, moreover, the government announced an expansionary fiscal policy, laying stress on the issue of deficit bonds. The new phase of renewed expansion got under way starting in the second half of fiscal year 1965.

The Izanagi Boom

Once business conditions improved, they remained buoyant for a surprisingly long time. The expansion that began in October 1965 continued for fifty-seven months until July 1970, producing the longest economic boom in the post-war period. It was called the Izanagi Boom, which signified in Japanese that its length exceeded that of the Iwato Boom.[3] The rate of economic growth in real terms was over 10 per cent per year for five consecutive years, from fiscal year 1966 to fiscal year 1970. Japan's GNP surpassed that of West Germany in fiscal year 1968, becoming the second highest in the non-communist world. Japan was on the way to becoming an economic superpower.

The industrial production index for 1970, at 215.9 (1965 = 100), was more than double that for 1965. Comparisons of output volumes of major products between 1965 and 1970 show the following gains: crude steel from 41.16 million tons to 93.32 millions tons, electric power generation from 167.7 billion kWh to 307.6 billion kWh, cars from over 700,000 to over 3.18 million, black-and-white TV sets from over 4.06 million to over 6.09 million, and colour TV sets from over 100,000 to over 6.4 million. Japan's exports increased during the same period from $8.45 billion to $19.32 billion, almost reaching the $20 billion level. On the other hand, the wholesale price index, with 1965 as 100, rose to 111.3 in 1970. The consumer price index, also with 1965 as 100, showed a substantially faster increase, rising to 130.4 in 1970. Sharply rising prices became a problem.

Against that background, the Bank of Japan imposed monetary restraints in September 1969, raising the official discount rate and the required reserve ratio against deposits. Although it took considerable time for the monetary stringency to take effect, signs of a business slowdown appeared in the late spring and early summer of 1970 in the form of decreased factory shipments, rising inventories, declining orders for machinery, and eased labour supply. The rate of increase in plant and equipment investment also diminished. Thus, the curtain finally came down on the longest post-war boom, after reaching its peak in July 1970 while the World's Fair (Expo '70) was being held in Osaka.

18.2. The Structural Elements of the Iwato Boom

What were the structural elements of the Iwato Boom? The primary factor was the enormous increase in investment in plant and equipment. For example, investment in private plant and equipment more than doubled, from approximately 1.9 trillion yen in fiscal year 1957 to about 4.2 trillion yen in fiscal year 1961, while its share of gross national expenditure (GNE) rose from 16.6 to 21.3 per cent. This high rate of investment served as the motive power for the Iwato Boom.

These investments had five general characteristics. First was all-out investment in technological innovations. Equipment investment relating to new product development became especially active in new industries such as synthetic fibres, petrochemicals, and electronics. In current industries such as metals, cars, and machinery on the other hand, heavy investments were made to develop continuous and speedier manufacturing processes. The second general characteristic of this period was brisk investments by various industries to increase scales of operation. Together with the domestic market expansion and hopes of continued high-level growth, corporations became more keenly aware of the economies of scale. Third, there was brisk plant construction at new industrial locations, as exemplified by the construction of industrial complexes, generating investment as well in infrastructure such as roads, port facilities, and industrial water and sewage systems. Fourth, the promotion of trade liberalization stimulated investments to modernize production facilities to achieve greater international competitiveness. The fifth characteristic was that competition in equipment investment and the introduction of technology intensified between companies and between corporate groups.[4]

At the base of the foregoing characteristics was the important role played by what the Economic Survey of Japan for fiscal year 1961 described as the process of 'investment breeding investment'. A section of the Economic Survey reads as follows:

Equipment investment requires that investment goods be produced first. To make machinery, however, more steel must be made and more electricity generated. Increased production of machinery, steel, and electricity all require more machinery. Investment goods thus have an inherently powerful interindustry linkage effect. The condition of the Japanese economy was such that increased production of any one of these products—machinery, steel, or electricity—required plant and equipment investment. This is the mechanism of investment breeding further investment.[5]

As this passage points out, the linkage effect of investment is not very large when an economy has ample capacity to produce investment goods or key materials. The Japanese economy in the early 1960s, however, did not have an adequate supply capacity of investment goods; that was why the linkage effect was especially pronounced.

The second key element of the Iwato Boom was vigorous consumption demand, particularly a tremendous increase in demand for the new products as a result of technological innovation. During this period, the domestic consumption of goods not only increased quantitatively but also underwent a qualitative transformation. Using the term 'consumption revolution', the Economic Survey of Japan for fiscal year 1960 described the development as follows:

Over the past four years, the production of consumer durables and cars increased by about 3.7-fold. Much of this increase was accounted for by the increased production of television sets, motorcycles, and small four-wheel trucks. Recently, increased production of passenger cars has become noteworthy. Japan's per capita income in 1957 was $250 measured at the official rate of exchange, or only one-ninth of that of the US. The percentage of Japanese households owning home appliances, particularly TV sets, is very high considering the low-income level. The basic reasons for this anomaly are that income has reached a level that makes consumer durables affordable to average households, and that prices of consumer durables have declined.[6]

Thus, the first conspicuous change in consumption patterns occurred with the widespread use of consumer durables, primarily electrical appliances. The most notable was the quick spread of television sets; in 1958, 15.9 per cent of urban households and 2.6 per cent of farming households had television sets. The comparable figures were 71.9 and 28.5 per cent in 1961, and 93.5 and 81.7 per cent in 1964. Washing machines and refrigerators also spread fast (Table 18.1). The purchase of cars by households lagged somewhat behind that of electrical appliances. Small and medium enterprises also played a key role in the spread of motor vehicles. Motorization began with transformation of the most common means of transport from motor scooters to cars, and from small three-wheel trucks to four-wheel trucks.

The consumption habits of the Japanese public were also affected dramatically by the use of synthetic fibres for clothing and plastics for sundry goods, as well as by the rising popularity of instant foods. Also, the heightened interest in leisure activities such as travelling, dining out, and playing golf gave variety to the pattern of consumption behaviour and increased household consumption. The advent of this 'mass-consumption society', already noted during the Jimmu Boom, became even more evident during the Iwato Boom. It provided a solid foundation for long-term consistent demand.

The advent of a mass-consumption society and the expanding industrial linkage effect described above, combined with the government's income-doubling plan and the policy of trade and exchange liberalization discussed below, energized business activities in the private sector and engendered the great economic boom that lasted for forty-two months.

18.3. The 'Transformation Phase Thesis' and the Recession of 1965

Expanded exports during the Iwato Boom had the effect of raising the so-called 'balance-of-payments ceiling' and prolonging the life of the boom. It was also

Table 18.1 Trends in ownership of selected consumer durables by urban and farming households (unit: %)

		Sept. 1957	Sept. 1958	Aug. 1959	Aug. 1960	Aug. 1961	Aug. 1964
Television sets	(urban)	7.8	15.9	33.5	54.5	71.9	93.5
	(farming)	—	2.6	4.3	11.4	28.5	81.7
Washing machines	(urban)	20.2	29.3	36.7	45.4	55.0	75.8
	(farming)	—	5.2	6.8	8.7	14.5	47.0
Electric refrigerators	(urban)	2.8	5.5	9.7	15.7	26.6	66.2
	(farming)	—	—	—	1.3	2.5	14.5
Electric rice cookers	(urban)	—	15.6	23.5	37.5	44.7	57.3
	(farming)	—	3.8	4.7	9.1	14.2	29.3
Electric vacuum cleaners	(urban)	—	—	2.5	11.0	20.7	45.1
Transistor radios	(urban)	—	—	20.2	24.9	29.8	51.1
	(farming)	—	—	—	5.1	9.4	22.8
Cameras	(urban)	35.7	43.1	44.3	47.2	50.8	61.8
	(farming)	—	15.9	17.3	16.0	18.0	23.9
Motor scooters, motorcycles	(farming)	—	8.4	10.5	11.5	20.0	38.7

Note: Farming household surveys were in February.

Source: Economic Planning Agency, Gendai Nihon Keizai no Tenkai (Development of the Contemporary Japanese Economy: 30-Year History of the Economic Planning Agency), Economic Planning Agency, 1976: 115.

true, however, that what ended the Iwato Boom was an increase in imports caused by excessive equipment investments and an attendant deterioration in the external balance. This development led to the so-called 'transformation phase' thesis advanced by the Economic Planning Agency. The Economic Survey of Japan for fiscal year 1962 contains the following section:

The continuing increases in equipment investment have raised the percentage of GNP accounted for by private plant and equipment investment to 23 per cent, the highest in the world. The excessive equipment investment this time is greater than the last time adjustments were made. The process of curbing the present overheated economy will have to continue until an equilibrium is restored in the balance of payments. Even if production adjustments were to restore equilibrium for the interim, it is still possible that by themselves those adjustments would not complete the adjustment process.

It must also be noted that the process of restoring balanced growth is likely to produce marked changes in the key growth-inducing factors. A characteristic of this adjustment process is that there will probably be not only a pullback in rapidly expanded equipment investment but also a recovery in the relative importance of consumption, which has lagged behind the rise in equipment investment. Moreover, the percentage of government expenditures in GNP, which is already at a high level of 18 per cent, is likely to rise still higher during the adjustment period. During the 1953–5 period of low equipment investment, government expenditures were more than 19 per cent of GNP. A distinctive characteristic of an adjustment period is that changes occur in each of the growth-inducing factors, which means changing patterns in all aspects of the economy. Certainly the Japanese economy is now going through a turning point, but it may be more appropriately called a transformation phase.[7]

The Economic Survey said, in short, that the rush in private-sector equipment investment during the Iwato Boom had subsided, the economy had entered an adjustment phase, and the leading growth factor was shifting from private equipment investment to consumption and government expenditures. The EPA thus predicted a transformation in the Japanese economy's pattern of growth.[8]

The term 'transformation phase' became a catchword which described the times, and several other transformation theses emerged besides the argument presented in the Economic Survey of Japan.

The adjustment pattern of private equipment investment, however, was still moderate during the slowdown period in fiscal year 1962. As the process of 'investment breeding investment' came to an end, equipment investment in producer goods industries such as steel, heavy electric, and general machinery declined considerably. Small and medium enterprises continued to make substantial modernization efforts, however, as the labour market tightened. Exports grew markedly, moreover, and consumption demand remained strong in early 1962, even after the boom in equipment investment ended. Government expenditures also remained firm. The strong undertone of aggregate demand prevented the gap between supply and demand from widening.[9]

Once into the recession of 1965, however, the business slowdown intensified. The process of curbing business activities that followed the short-lived upswing in 1963 triggered a resumption of the downtrend in private-sector equipment investment, which had been temporarily interrupted during 1962. The more marked the increase in investment—in particular investment goods—during the Iwato Boom, the sharper were the subsequent decreases in investment and profitability. The percentage of GNE accounted for by private equipment investment fell from 21.3 per cent in fiscal year 1961 to 15.3 per cent in fiscal year 1965. These figures seemed to confirm the demise of 'investment-led growth' as argued in the transformation phase thesis described above, and from the second half of 1965 to the beginning of 1966 the structural recession thesis moved to a place of importance in the Japanese business community.[10]

The prevailing sense of a business slump in fiscal year 1965 was exacerbated by several factors. First, the downswing in equipment investment was accompanied by a downturn in consumption spending. The rapid spread during the Iwato Boom period of consumer durables to households, particularly home electric appliances such as black-and-white TV sets and washing machines, slowed further demand for these products. Second, slow growth in manufacturing employment and a reduction in working hours brought about sluggishness in consumption spending. Also, the construction industry entered a downward phase that coincided with the 1965 recession. The 'boom in construction' before the Tokyo Summer Olympics of October 1964 passed its peak in that same year. Third, the ability of corporations to weather poor business conditions was weakened, partly because a new credit squeeze had been imposed only a year or so after the thaw of the previous squeeze in 1962. Credits between corporations had expanded during the Iwato Boom, and more firms were heavily in debt. Subsequent bankruptcies and the fear of a credit crunch became psychological factors contributing to contraction in business activities.[11]

The 1965 recession, however, bottomed in October 1965, mainly because of an expansionary fiscal policy and continuing strong exports. The Japanese economy returned to its growth track. Corporations began investing in investment goods again, and fears of a 'structural recession' proved unfounded.

18.4. The Evolution of the Izanagi Boom

Plant and equipment investment was also the main reason for the longest postwar period of prosperity, lasting from October 1965 to July 1970. Private investment in plant and equipment greatly expanded each year from fiscal years 1966 to 1969, growing over 20 per cent per year. Three principal reasons accounted for the large and sustained investment. First, 'large-scale profit' was pursued energetically to attain economy of scale. Whereas equipment investment in the ten years from 1955 to 1964 was aimed primarily at modernization in response to technological innovations, investment in the ten years from 1965 to 1974 involved large-scale construction of facilities that incorporated the fruits of such technological innovations, and was aimed at expanding production capacity to meet the brisk demand. Second, equipment investment increased in order to expand exports. Against a background of rapid growth in exports from 1965 onwards, many companies increased their production capacity because they expected a further expansion of their overseas markets. Third was an increase in investment in pollution control and labour-saving equipment in response to socio-economic changes, including worsening pollution and an increasingly serious labour shortage. In the petroleum-refining, non-ferrous metal, and paper and pulp industries, approximately 10 per cent of all equipment investment was for antipollution equipment.

The second main support for the prolonged economic boom was the sustained expansion of exports. Exports, particularly from 1968 onwards, increased 20 per cent or more every year. One reason for the increase in exports was the overall growth in global trade in the context of worldwide prosperity. A distinct feature of export growth in this period was that expanding domestic demand no longer put a damper on export growth.

Besides equipment investment and exports, personal consumption and housing construction also grew rapidly. In personal consumption, in particular, a boom emerged in the consumer-durables market, fuelled by sharp increases in wages tied to the labour shortage. The so-called '3C Boom' (cars, 'coolers', i.e. air-conditioners, and colour TVs, contributed to the economy's buoyancy.

The sources of the support for the long-term, high-level economic growth were thus an increase in overall demand components, particularly private-equipment investment, exports, and personal consumption.

NOTES

1. Economic Planning Agency, 'Choki Kihon Tokeishu' (Long-Term Statistics) in *Gendai Nihon Keizai no Tenkai—Keizai Kikakucho 30-nenshi* (Development of the Contemporary Japanese Economy: Thirty-Year History of the Economic Planning Agency), 1976: 578. The base year used for these statistics is 1970.
2. Economic Planning Agency, *Keizai Hakusho* (Economic Survey of Japan), 1962, Printing Bureau, MoF: 2.
3. 'Izanagi' refers to the god Izanagi no Mikoto in Japanese mythology who is said to have given birth to the myriad of gods who make up the national land and everything else in Japan. The legend of Izanagi is even more ancient than the Iwato legend, in which the sun goddess Amaterasu Omikami hid herself in a cave.
4. *Gendai Nihon Keizai no Tenkai*: 117–18.
5. *Keizai Hakusho*, 1961: 30.
6. Ibid. 1960: 32–3.
7. Ibid. 1962: 36–7.
8. *Gendai Nihon Keizai no Tenkai*: 165.
9. Ibid. 165–6.
10. Hiromi Arisawa (ed.), *Showa Keizaishi* (Economic History of the Showa Era), Nihon Keizai Shimbun, Inc., 1976: 465–8.
11. *Gendai Nihon Keizai no Tenkai*: 166–7.

19

The Development Process
of Innovation

The word 'innovation' became widely known in Japan after it was used in the Economic Survey of Japan for fiscal year 1956. In discussing the reasons for the worldwide prosperity of the time, the Economic Survey said, 'It appears that the primary cause of the steady and robust expansion of the global economy is the increase in the sales of consumer goods due to the rising purchasing power of the public and the increases in new investment for technological innovation.' The Economic Survey further stated:

The kind of technological progress that drives these investment activities are innovations exemplified by automation and the peaceful use of nuclear energy. There are many historical precedents for technological changes bringing about long-term business booms. For example, the first Industrial Revolution was engendered by the invention of the steam engine, and the subsequent worldwide economic boom lasted from 1788 to 1815. The spread of railways produced the second long-term business upswing, one that lasted from 1843 to 1873, and the advent of aircraft, motorcars, electricity, and chemicals led to the third innovation-induced period of prosperity that spanned the period between 1897 and 1920. The contemporary era may be regarded as the fourth innovation boom, represented by nuclear energy and automation.[1]

After publication of that Economic Survey, it became common in Japan to equate 'innovation' with 'technological innovation'. It is well known that the word 'innovation' was introduced by Joseph A. Schumpeter in his *Theory of Economic Development*.[2] Schumpeter, however, did not limit the word 'innovation' to technological innovation. His idea was that entrepreneurs who combined new products, new production techniques, new markets, new production factors, and new forms of organization brought about economic development. For the Japanese economy during its periods of high-level growth, technological innovation evidently provided an engine of growth. Beyond that, however, we can see that innovations in all areas of the economy interacted with each other and accelerated the growth process. The following reviews the development process of innovation in the broader sense of the term.

19.1. 'Innovation' in Industry

Technological innovation and development in heavy industries

The steel industry. In the steel industry, the so-called Second Rationalization Plan was implemented around fiscal years 1956–60. Subsequently, starting from around fiscal year 1961, steelmakers gradually began making renewed efforts one after another to further rationalize their operations, which later came to be known as the Third Rationalization Plan. As compared to the crude-steel production of 23.16 million tons in fiscal year 1960, production in fiscal year 1965 amounted to 41.30 million tons, exceeding by 8.7 per cent the target for fiscal year 1965, which had initially been regarded as overly ambitious. Steel production continued to increase afterwards, reaching 92.41 million tons in fiscal year 1970, an astonishing figure which nearly doubled the 48-million-ton target set in the National Income Doubling Plan announced in 1960.

A distinctive feature of the steel industry's development was the increased size of investment in plant and equipment. Concerning blast furnaces, for example, the typical furnace around 1955 had an internal working volume of 1,000 cu.m. and produced about 350,000 tons of pig-iron per year. Comparable figures increased drastically from 1,500 cu.m. and 800,000 tons around 1960–1, to 2,000 cu.m. and 1.3 million tons around 1965, and further to 2,500 cu.m. and 1.8 million tons around 1970.[3] During this period, the facilities of the Japanese steel industry—not only blast furnaces but facilities in all other processes, including smelting, steelmaking, blooming, rolling, and surface treatment—were made larger and more advanced, surpassing world standards.

A driving power in the steel industry's technical progress was provided by rapidly increased use of converters in steelmaking. The LD converter was installed in Japan for the first time in 1957. In fiscal year 1968, the Japanese steel industry had 60 LD converters in operation, leading the world in the number of such units and in steel output. Comparable figures increased further by the end of 1970, reaching 83 units and 91.48 million tons. The main reasons for the zealous installation of converters were that they helped to increase the efficiency of steelmaking processes, lower equipment cost, and improve the quality of output, and they met the need of the Japanese steel industry in those days of reducing dependence on imported scrap iron.[4]

Yet another innovation that produced a significant improvement in steel production was the introduction of strip mills (continuous rolling machines) in the rolling process. Prior to the Third Rationalization Plan, the semi-continuous method had been used. From the Third Plan onwards, continuous mills were installed, and the speed of rolling operations increased markedly. The introduction of hot-rolling, and later cold-rolling, strip mills not only resulted in increased output but also in greatly improved quality. These improvements manifested themselves in the forms of domestically produced steel plate for cars and electromagnetic steel plates for electric machinery manufacturers.

These advances also led to establishment of many new modern steel mills. The more important of the mills that began operation in the 1960s and early 1970s included, in chronological order: the Mizushima Plant of Kawasaki Steel, the Fukuyama Plant of Nippon Kokan, the Kimitsu Plant of Yawata Steel, the Kakogawa Plant of Kobe Steel, the Kashima Plant of Sumitomo Metal Industries, and the Oita Plant of Fuji Steel. All these were large and modern integrated mills.

At the beginning of the 1970s, the Japanese steel industry occupied the foremost position in the world in both quantity and quality of output.

The motor car industry. The rapid growth of the car industry and the attendant transformation of Japanese economy and social life was one of the developments that symbolized the high-growth era.

The pre-war Japanese motor industry placed emphasis on producing military lorries. Production of cars, and therefore the technology for manufacturing them as well, remained underdeveloped. In the immediate post-war years, production of cars was restricted by order of the Allied Occupation authorities. The argument that Japan did not need a car industry, which was often made until around 1950, had the effect of delaying the development of car production, which occurred only from 1955 onwards. Considering that the automobile industry is a strategic industry which contributes to the development of machinery, steel, and many other industries, MITI made serious efforts to foster it. Those efforts, and the oligopolistic rivalry among car manufacturers, produced rapid growth in the industry starting in the first half of the 1960s.

In terms of automobile production, a comparison of 1959 and 1970 shows that the total volume (including cars, lorries, buses, and three-wheel vehicles) increased by 12.6-fold, from 420,000 in 1959 to 5.3 million in 1970. Noteworthy in this statistic was the sharp 40.2-fold increased volume of car production, from 79,000 in 1959 to 3,179,000 in 1970, with their percentage in total automobile production rising from 18.7 to 59.9 per cent. The phenomenon called motorization—the spread of cars to the general public—which had begun at the beginning of this period, expanded rapidly, bringing on the so-called 'My Car Era'. An international comparison of automobile production, exclusive of three-wheel vehicles, shows that Japan surpassed Italy in 1961 and attained the fifth position worldwide. Japan became the second largest car manufacturing country in the world after the US by surpassing France in 1964, the UK in 1966, and West Germany in 1967. Japanese exports of automobiles (all four-wheel vehicles combined), which had been about 10,000 in 1959, exceeded 1 million in 1970, surpassing the UK and making Japan the world's third largest exporter.

The primary driving force of the dramatic expansion of the Japanese automobile industry was vigorous investment in plant and equipment. The percentage of total private investment in plant and equipment accounted for by the industry rose from 2.2 per cent in 1956 to 11.7 per cent in 1967. The major task of the industry in the second half of the 1950s was to respond to increasing domestic demand and prepare for imminent trade liberalization by developing a system for mass production of domestic cars which could compare favourably with imports in all aspects of performance, quality, and price. Accordingly, the bulk of investment for ordinary vehicles was in machine tools. For smaller vehicles, investment was primarily in advanced equipment for specialized, high-speed, and automated production, primarily of cars, aimed at establishing a volume production system and improving performance and quality.

As early as 1955 or shortly thereafter, automobile manufacturers, including

Toyota Motor Co. and Nissan Motor Co., began setting up volume production systems by installing and operating transfer machines (automatic production and conveyance equipment). In the first half of the 1960s, they built, in close succession, plants designed exclusively for volume production of cars. First, Toyota began construction of its Motomachi Plant in Aichi Prefecture in September 1958, and began operating it as soon as the first phase of the construction was completed in September 1959. This was the first volume-production plant exclusively for cars in Japan, and for that reason the year 1959 is regarded as 'the first year of volume production' in the Japanese car industry.[5] The second phase of construction at the Motomachi Plant followed, and the plant was completed in August 1960. Production that month exceeded 15,000. Meanwhile, Nissan Motor began constructing its Oppama Plant in Yokohama in February 1961, completing it in March 1962. Elsewhere, modern volume-production plants were built one after another, including the Murayama Plant of Prince Motors, the Fujisawa Plant of Isuzu Motors, and the Hamura Plant of Hino Motors. These new plants, in combination with the expanding demand caused by rising income levels, brought about the rapid growth of the Japanese car industry.

The machinery industry. The machinery industry other than automobiles also recorded unprecedented growth during this period. First, the vigorous investment in plant and equipment that brought about high growth manifested itself as massive demand for general and electric machinery. The growth of the machinery industry was accelerated in particular by the demand from the steel, electric power, chemical, and other industries. Then, sharp rises in the export of ships and other products enhanced the international position of the Japanese machinery industry. Exports of ships increased swiftly, aided by technological progress embodied in modern welding techniques and the 'block'-building system introduced from abroad after the war. Japan became the world leader in shipbuilding in 1956, surpassing the UK, and its exports have since maintained an overwhelming share of world ship exports. Also, besides more conventional light machinery and instruments such as sewing machines and cameras, electronic products such as transistor radios and tape recorders (magnetic sound-recording and reproducing devices) became major export items. Furthermore, the boom in consumer durables symbolized by what was called in Japan 'three sacred treasures' (television receivers, electric refrigerators, and electric washing machines) fuelled the rapid growth of the electric machinery and electronics industries. Technological innovation and development in the machinery industry, focused on the electric machinery and electronics industries, are reviewed below.

TV receivers occupied a particularly prominent position among the 'three sacred treasures', impacting strongly on the living modes of the people. The diffusion of black-and-white TV sets was supported from the supply side by the importation of technology centred on transistors and printed circuits, and the establishment of mass-production technology. The demand for black-and-white

TVs, however, slowed even as their use spread widely. In 1962, the demand for black-and-white TVs nearly levelled off, and colour television receivers appeared on the market. When the Japan Broadcasting Corporation (NHK) and four commercial television networks began telecasting colour programmes in September 1960, electric machinery manufacturers who had been developing colour TV sets decided to market them right away.

Colour TVs were initially priced so high that their spread to ordinary households was very slow. The demand increased, however, as prices fell together with volume production. And when the Olympic Games were held in Tokyo in October 1964, demand took a sharp turn upward. Annual production increased explosively from 4,000 in 1962 and 1963 to over 60,000 in 1964, over 100,000 in 1965, over 1.28 million in 1967, and further to over 6.4 million in 1970. The value of output in 1970 amounted to 681.3 billion yen.

Tape-recorder production also increased sharply once into the second half of the 1960s, and their production value in 1969 surpassed that of radios.

The Japanese computer industry, meanwhile, was just beginning to develop, about ten years behind its counterpart in the US. The Agency of Industrial Science and Technology of MITI, other public research and testing institutes, and a group of electric machinery manufacturers cooperated in developing computers in Japan. Aided by technology imported from the United States and liberal promotional measures of the Japanese government, including establishment of the Japan Electronic Computer Co. in August 1961 for renting computers, each of the manufacturers, including Tokyo Shibaura Denki (later Toshiba Corp.), Hitachi Ltd., Fuji Tsushinki Seizo (later Fujitsu Ltd.), and Oki Electric Industry Co. Ltd., successfully developed their first computers by the early 1960s. In 1970, digital computers with a total value of 269.8 billion yen and analog computers with a total value of 1.8 billion yen were produced. Minicomputers appeared on the market in 1969, and expanded rapidly afterward.

Meanwhile, Japan was considerably behind the United States in manufacturing integrated circuits (ICs), which formed the foundation of the electronics industry. Volume production was finally initiated in the second half of the 1960s. Production was 292,000 in 1966 but rose sharply to 3.33 million units in 1967, and to 19.88 million in 1968. This rapid increase in IC production was in part attributed to the advent of electronic desk calculators. Electronic calculators using ICs first appeared in 1966, and the market expanded explosively afterwards.

At the end of September 1970, general-purpose computers in operation in Japan numbered 7,933 (760 mainframes, 2,714 medium-sized units, 2,795 minicomputers, and 1,664 microcomputers), with a total purchase price equivalent to 738.7 billion yen. Of these units, Japanese-made units accounted for 73.1 per cent, or 54.6 per cent in purchase price equivalent.[6]

Computer and electronic technologies found many-faceted applications in various industries. Around 1970, for instance, the machine tool industry developed numerical control machine tools and industrial robots, which in turn worked to significantly modernize other industries.[7]

Technological innovation and development in the chemical industries

The petrochemical industry began developing around 1955 in Japan and expanded rapidly throughout the high-growth era to become a nucleus of the Japanese chemical industry. It also played a key role in dramatically altering the materials used in Japanese industry. The reason for the fast growth of the petrochemical industry, which the Economic Survey of Japan of fiscal year 1957 described as 'the leading player in recent technological innovation',[8] was that a beneficial circle of larger investments, lower costs, and an enlarged market was at work. In this circle, increased investments in large-scale production facilities took advantage of the characteristics of the processing industry and drastically reduced production costs and product prices, which in turn expanded the market and induced investments in still larger facilities. The unique production system that gave substance to this beneficial circle was the petrochemical complex.

By the second half of the 1950s, four petrochemical complexes organized by Mitsui Petrochemical, Sumitomo Chemical, Japan Petrochemical, and Mitsubishi Petrochemical were already in operation. This development was the result of the first phase of the Petrochemical Industrialization Plan. The different phases were defined in terms of the period in which MITI approved the import of foreign technology. Between 1962 and 1972, eleven other complexes, including those operated by Tonen Petrochemical (in Kawasaki, 1962) and Daikyowa Petrochemical (Yokkaichi, 1963) began operation, raising the total number of complexes to fifteen.

Naphtha cracking produces ethylene and other fractions, such as propylene, butane/butylene, and cracked oil. The petrochemical industry makes integrated use of these compounds. For that reason, entire production processes from raw materials to products are organically united, and materials are transferred by means of pipelines installed at a single location. To create such a system, considerable technological, financial, and marketing capabilities are required. Because it was next to impossible for a single firm to carry out the task, petrochemical complexes were developed in Japan involving the joint efforts of affiliated companies. The Mitsui Petrochemical group was a case in point. Koa Oil Co. Ltd., supplied naphtha to Mitsui Petrochemical, which produced ethylene, propylene, butadiene/butylene, and so on. These co-products were used by Mitsui Polychemical, Daicel Chemical Industries, Mitsui Toatsu Chemicals, Japan Synthetic Rubber, Nippon Zeon, and other companies, producing a number of derivatives.

It was the competitive import of foreign technology that provided the impetus for the technical development of the petrochemical industry and industries, such as those producing synthetic fibres and plastics, which were based on the petrochemical industry. In the synthetic fibres industry, three new fibres—nylon, polyester, and acrylic fibre—had already been commercialized before the second half of the 1950s, based largely on imported technology. A new fibre, polypropylene, was regarded as 'a dream fibre' in those days. Montecatini of Italy held the patent on polypropylene and in 1959 and 1960 about ten Japanese companies negotiated for import of the technology. The event received so much media coverage that the popular expression 'pilgrimage to Monte' was coined.

The objective of MITI's policy of fostering the petrochemical industry in the first half of the 1960s was to promote establishment of a self-supporting system, anticipating forthcoming trade and exchange liberalization. Through this measure, the ministry aimed to have the industry build a solid foundation which would enable it to develop a world-class scale of operation. In October 1960, MITI published a report called 'On the Provisional Disposition of the Petrochemical Industry Plan', which aimed at coordinating the expansion plans of various companies in the industry and approved the import of technology by one company after another. The Second Petrochemical Industrialization Plan was thus initiated. The principal feature of the Second Plan was that it accelerated the conversion of raw materials of existing chemical products to petrochemical products, which induced the integrated utilization of continuous production fractions. Because early entrants received preferential approval on products that came to be domestically produced under the First Plan, new entrants tended to specialize in products for raw materials conversion.

Large volumes of various petrochemical products spread rapidly to all aspects of the lives of the general populace, including food, clothing, and housing, and they also became widely used as industrial materials. They also contributed to the development of industries such as plastics, rubber-processing, and plant-engineering.

Once into the second half of the 1960s, volumes of continuous production fractions increased as ethylene facilities became larger. The percentage of each fraction that could be utilized technically and economically became higher, and nearly all of them were used effectively. In January 1965, the Petroleum Consultative Group (consisting of representatives of MITI, the industry, and third parties) set guidelines for new naphtha facilities at '100,000 tons of ethylene production per year', and approved the building of four complexes based on these guidelines. In June 1967, on the eve of full-scale liberalization of capital flows, the Consultative Group raised the capacity standard to '300,000 tons of ethylene production per year'. The Group studied the relationship between the capacity of ethylene facilities and the unit cost of production, and compared the production costs of 200,000-ton, 300,000-ton, and 400,000-ton facilities with that of 100,000-ton facilities. The result of the study showed that the production cost of ethylene at 300,000-ton facilities was about 6 yen per kg. lower than at 100,000-ton facilities, whereas the cost at 400,000-ton facilities was only 6.60 yen lower, or not significantly lower than at 300,000-ton facilities. Because the price of ethylene in those days ranged from 35 to 40 yen per kg., the 6-yen reduction in unit cost had a decisive significance in enhancing the price competitiveness of the product. Thus, a total of nine naphtha facilities each capable of producing 300,000 tons of ethylene per year were built according to this standard, and began operation between 1969 and 1972. The scale of operation of the petro-chemical industry thus became even larger.

Development of the energy revolution

The most pronounced change in the supply of energy in the 1955–64 decade was the conversion of fuel from coal to petroleum. This was the development of the energy revolution. Being a fluid, petroleum is easier than coal to extract, trans-port, and store. At the consumption stage as well, petroleum has a technical advantage of ease in handling. Still, the decisive reason why an energy revolu-tion and the conversion to a fluid fuel took place during this period lay in the fact that imported crude oil was available at prices far lower than the prices of domes-tic coal.

After the Second World War, the Western oil majors took advantage of wartime advances in oil exploration and drilling technology and began large-scale prospecting and drilling efforts worldwide. As a consequence, confirmed oil deposits and crude oil production increased year after year, and the supply of petroleum tended to exceed demand during the 1955–64 period. To cope with this situation, some oil-producing countries in September 1960 formed the Orga-nization of Petroleum Exporting Countries (OPEC). The organization, however, could not muster enough bargaining strength vis-à-vis the oil majors. Crude oil prices, reflecting the supply-and-demand situation, remained stable at about $2 per barrel. Table 19.1 records the changes in the prices of fuels used for electric power generation during the ten years after 1955.

These market conditions resulted in a decline in the percentage accounted for by coal in the supply of primary energy. Despite legislation to support coal pro-duction and promote the use of coal, the percentages accounted for by coal and oil in primary energy production, which had stood at 49.2 per cent for coal and 20.2 per cent for oil in 1955, narrowed to 41.5 per cent for coal and 37.7 per cent for oil in 1960. And in 1962, the order was reversed, with coal account-ing for 36.0 per cent and oil for 46.1 per cent. Subsequently, the share of oil rose sharply, so that by 1970 oil at 70.8 per cent had widened its lead over coal, which accounted for only 20.7 per cent of primary energy. This change was referred to as a shift from 'coal first, oil second' to 'oil first, coal second' in energy supplies. As a result of sharp increases in imports of crude oil and oil products, the import dependency of Japan's energy supply rose from 24.0 per cent in 1955 to more than 50 per cent in 1962 (52.6 per cent), and further to 83.5 per cent in 1970.[9] The energy supply structure of Japan thus took clear form; it relied heavily on imported crude oil, most of which was coming from Middle East countries.

From the demand side, one major user of oil products was the petrochemical industry. That industry had grown rapidly on the strength of a vigorous demand from new industries such as plastics, synthetic fibres, and synthetic rubber. The rapid growth was made possible only because the petrochemical industry could

Table 19.1   Prices of fuels for power generation, fiscal years 1956–1965

	Coal		Heavy oil	
	yen/ton	yen/1,000 kcal.	yen/kl.	yen/1,000 kcal.
1956	4,426	(100) 0.847	12,160	(146) 1.233
1957	5,167	(100) 1.003	11,281	(114) 1.144
1958	4,501	(100) 0.871	8,566	(99) 0.865
1959	4,106	(100) 0.811	8,368	(104) 0.845
1960	3,887	(100) 0.777	7,480	(97) 0.755
1961	3,708	(100) 0.732	6,523	(90) 0.658
1962	3,638	(100) 0.708	6,191	(89) 0.627
1963	3,582	(100) 0.682	6,199	(92) 0.628
1964	3,546	(100) 0.686	6,048	(89) 0.611
1965	3,757	(100) 0.730	5,913	(82) 0.600

Notes:
1. Figures are average purchase prices for nine power companies.
2. Figures in parentheses are indices with coal being 100.

Source: Denki Jigyo Rengokai Tokei Iinkai (Federation of Electric Power Companies, Statistics Committee), *Denki Jigyo Binran* (Hand book of Electric Power Industry), 1966.

obtain abundant and low-cost naphtha from the oil-refining industry. Another important factor on the demand side was the advance of motorization, which markedly increased the demand for automobile fuels such as petrol, light oil, and liquefied petroleum gas (LPG). Furthermore, improvements in urban living facilities and the spread of home electric appliances such as television sets, washing machines, and refrigerators led to a rapid increase in the demand for electric power. Meanwhile, the electric power industry was making progress in its shift to a 'fire first, water second' structure, a reference to the conversion of power generation from hydroelectric to thermal methods. This shift, combined with the 'oil first, coal second' shift mentioned above, accelerated the increase in demand for oil.

Yet another feature of the energy supply situation in the high-growth era was the emergence of two new energy sources, i.e. nuclear energy and liquefied natural gas (LNG). The development of nuclear energy in Japan dated back to November 1955 when the US–Japan Nuclear Energy Agreement was signed and the Nuclear Energy Research Institute of Japan was established. In December 1955, the Basic Law on Nuclear Energy was enacted, and in November 1957 the Japan Nuclear Power Co. was established. In May 1965, the reactor at the First Tokai Plant of the Japan Nuclear Power Co. was brought to criticality. Once into the decade of 1965–74, the low cost of nuclear power generation and the difficulty of finding acceptable sites for heavy-oil-burning thermal plants arising from environmental concerns, induced power companies to build a series of nuclear power plants, including the Tsuruga Plant (maximum output 322,000 kW.) of the Japan Atomic Power Co., the First Fukushima Plant of Tokyo Electric Power (460,000 kW.) and the First Mihama Plant of Kansai Electric Power (340,000 kW.).[10]

From the beginning of the nineteenth century, natural gas was utilized in North America, Western Europe, the Soviet Union, and other regions. It was transported overland by way of pipelines. With the subsequent development of marine transportation and technology for liquefying gas, it became possible to transport large quantities of LNG overseas. LNG was first introduced to Japan in November 1969 when Tokyo Electric Power and Tokyo Gas jointly imported LNG from Alaska. In April 1970, in Minami Yokohama, Tokyo Electric began operating the world's first power plant specifically designed for burning LNG (maximum output 350,000 kW.).

Amid the ongoing energy revolution, the coal industry, which had historically played a central role in providing primary energy in Japan, came to a serious turning point. Because oil had become considerably less expensive than coal, and despite energetic efforts made by the government and industry, producers experienced cumulative deficits, and coal-mines were closed one after another. So, the number of operating mines fell sharply from 624 at the end of fiscal year 1959 to seventy-four at the end of fiscal year 1970. Domestic production of coal reached a peak of 55.41 million tons in fiscal year 1961, and by fiscal year 1970 had fallen to 38.33 million tons.

The role played by imported technology

Post-war technological innovation in Japan relied heavily on imported technology. Since the Meiji period (1868–1912), the establishment and development of industries in Japan have received sustenance by absorbing and assimilating foreign technology. During the war and immediate post-war years, in particular, the US and other Western nations made great technological advances. As Japan stagnated in this respect, a technological gap opened up. Because of the need to close this gap, Japan became even more dependent on foreign technology after the war. Specifically, Japanese companies found that importing superior foreign technology, expensive as it might be, was the safest and surest way of narrowing the technological gap with foreign companies and meeting fierce competition in the domestic market.

Table 19.2　Number of approved technology licensing agreements by type of agreement, 1950–1970

Fiscal year	1950–9 Total (A)	1960	1961	1962	1963	1964	1965
Type I	1,022	327	320	328	564	500	472
Type II	1,303	261	281	429	573	541	486
Total	2,325	588	601	757	1,137	1,041	958

Source: Science and Technology Agency, *Gaikoku Gijutsu Donyu Nenji Hokoku* (Annual Report on Foreign Technology Imports).

New technologies were thus imported after the war in virtually all fields in major industries, and they played key roles in advancing technological innovation. This trend became even more pronounced in the era of high growth, as revealed by the changing number of technology imports seen in Table 19.2. Foreign technology was introduced to Japan through technology-licensing agreements entered into with foreign investors. As described in Part III, these agreements were divided into Type I and Type II. Type I agreements required approval under the Law Concerning Foreign Capital, whereas Type II agreements required approval under the Foreign Exchange and Foreign Trade Control Law. Table 19.2 shows the number of the two types of licensing agreements approved. According to this table, a comparison between the ten-year period fiscal years 1950 to 1959 and the eleven-year period fiscal years 1960 to 1970 shows that Type I approvals increased by about 7.1-fold while Type II approvals increased by roughly 4.1-fold. The number of approvals, moreover, became greater from 1966. These increases were accounted for by the fact that, facing import liberalization in the first half and capital liberalization in the second half of the 1960s, Japanese companies made strenuous efforts to improve their international competitiveness, and sought imported technology as a means to achieve that goal. This trend was further accelerated from fiscal year 1968, when measures were taken to liberalize technology licensing.

The content of licensed technology, however, varied from period to period. In the second half of the 1950s, technology imports were most numerous in the fields of revolutionary technology and new industries. Many of them were related to manufacturing processes and most were directed to the heavy and chemical industries. In the first half of the 1960s, in order to improve the international competitiveness of Japanese companies in the face of imminent trade liberalization, efforts were made to import new technology and adopt new production machinery, and investments were made to increase the scale of operations. At the same time, however, technology relating to new manufacturing methods, new products, and new materials was imported enthusiastically. In the second half of the 1960s, in contrast, licensing of investment-goods-related technology and large-scale, revolutionary technology decreased, and imports of technology

1966	1967	1968	1969	1970	1960–70 Total (B)	B/A
601	638	1,061	1,154	1,330	7,295	7.1
552	657	683	475	438	5,376	4.1
1,153	1,295	1,744	1,629	1,768	12,671	5.4

related to consumer goods, secondary and tertiary processing, and sales and distribution increased. These changes indicated that the import of technology for the heavy and chemical industries had reached a satisfactory level, and the focus of technology-licensing efforts had shifted to light industries, distribution, and small and medium enterprises.

An examination of the technology imported during the high-growth era by different industries reveals that nearly all the technological innovation that took place in major industries as described above was realized by relying on foreign technology. In the steel industry, both Type I and Type II technology were imported for all aspects of manufacturing, including LD converters for steelmaking and strip mills for rolling operations. In the car industry, between 1952 and 1953 licensing agreements were entered into between Nissan Motor and Austin Motor of the UK, between Hino Diesel Motor (later Hino Motors) and Renault of France, and between Isuzu Motors and Rootes Motors of the UK. The Japanese companies developed domestic models using licensed technology, which prompted Toyota, a company which had no licensing agreements, to develop its own domestic model. Also, the development of domestically produced auto parts for foreign cars using imported technology significantly elevated the technical standards of the car parts industry in Japan. Other industries that played central roles in technological innovation during this period—machinery, electronics, petrochemicals, etc.—also imported technology in many of their manufacturing processes.

Thus, technological innovation in Japan made progress through the process of shortening the research-and-experiment phase by using advanced technology imported from Western countries, thereby realizing its industrial application in a short period. In this process, many Japanese companies did not simply apply the imported technology to a manufacturing process, but rather made efforts to improve the technology and incorporate it into their own production system.[11]

Towards the end of the 1960s, technological innovation spread to many new areas—for more advanced processing of raw materials, from manufacturing to packaging and distribution processes, and further to equipment for leisure-time amusement, furniture, and sundry goods, which were directly related to consumption activities. As a result, these new technologies stimulated plant and equipment investment and quickened the rate of economic growth.

19.2. 'Innovation' in Economy and Business

Development of interfirm competition

One of the forces that prompted technological innovation in Japanese industries after the war and brought on high growth was vigorous interfirm competition. There is no established theory on the relationship between technological advance and competition or monopoly, but Joseph A. Schumpeter, the originator of the 'innovation' theory of economic development, believed that innovation by business firms and investment based on it would be furthered, rather than impeded, by monopoly. His famous statement, 'It is exactly because automobiles have brakes that they run faster than when they don't have them', succinctly expressed his belief.[12] In general, when considering the relationship between competition and technological progress, both facilitating and impeding effects must be considered. In post-war Japan, it appears that competition had more a facilitating than an impeding effect.

Why did interfirm competition become so vigorous in post-war Japan? The reason was primarily implementation of the zaibatsu dissolution programme by the Allied Occupation authorities. The Allied Powers, particularly the US, which played the leading role in the Occupation, regarded the zaibatsu, which significantly influenced the pre-war Japanese economy, as the economic mainstay of Japanese militarism. They believed, therefore, that the democratization of Japan would not be possible without dissolving the zaibatsu. Accordingly, the zaibatsu holding companies, including those of the Big Four—Mitsui, Mitsubishi, Sumitomo, and Yasuda—were dissolved. Also, large companies such as Nippon Steel, Mitsubishi Heavy Industries, and Oji Paper, which were considered to be 'excessive concentrations of economic power', were broken up into smaller firms. As a result, when Japanese companies resumed full-scale production activities after the war, the advantage of the former zaibatsu-related companies had been lost, and the entry of new firms became easier.

When the former zaibatsu groups began reorganizing in the post-war reconstruction process, they clustered around, not holding companies as before, but large banks, because the banks escaped dissolution. As the banks reunited the former zaibatsu-affiliated companies, which existed in virtually all major industries, enterprise groups centred on banks—the Mitsubishi, Mitsui, Sumitomo, Fuji (former Yasuda), and other groups—were formed. Companies belonging to each of these groups cemented unity within the group and engaged in fierce competition with firms in the same industry belonging to other groups.

The government, moreover, in approving import licences for foreign technology which had a major impact on technological innovation, was generally guided by the principle of equal opportunity to all companies. As a result, companies vied in importing new technology, and many companies entered new markets on the strength of the imported technology.

Yet another factor contributing to the vigour of interfirm competition in post-war Japan was the fact that many top managers of large companies active during the Second World War left their positions as a result of purges from public service carried out immediately after the war. Consequently, the average age of top corporate leaders was lowered, and those young managers engaged in innovative corporate management.

All the factors mentioned above interacted with each other to make interfirm competition generally vigorous after the war, often enabling entry of new firms into industries which would normally be considered difficult to break into because of the substantial 'economies of scale' required.

For instance, initially there were only three integrated steel manufacturers, companies that constituted the core of the steel industry. They included Yawata Steel and Fuji Steel, which had been established when the old Nippon Steel was broken up, and Nippon Kokan (later NKK). Subsequently, however, Kawasaki Steel, Sumitomo Metal Industries, Kobe Steel, and other companies became integrated steelmakers.

In car manufacturing, new companies such as Isuzu Motors, Hino Diesel Motor Co. (later Hino Motor Co.), Fuji Seimitsu Kogyo (later Prince Motors), Fuji Heavy Industries, New Mitsubishi Heavy Industries, Toyo Kogyo (later Mazda Motor Corp.), Suzuki Motor Corp., Honda Motor Co., and Daihatsu Motor Co. entered the industry in close succession, joining the ranks of the two existing manufacturers, Toyota Motor Corp. and Nissan Motor Co.[13]

In the electric machinery industry, Hitachi, Tokyo Shibaura Denki, Matsushita Electric Industrial, Mitsubishi Electric, Fuji Electric, NEC, Sanyo Electric, Hayakawa Electric Industry Co., Sony, Oki Electric Industry Co., and others engaged in fierce competition.

In the oligopolistic market structure thus formed, major corporations were able to utilize their accumulated profits for increased research expenditures, which in turn led to further technological innovation. Oligopolistic competition not only promoted technical innovation but also brought about major changes in such aspects of national economic life as international trade, distribution, and the daily living situation of the general populace, and contributed to the realization of high growth. On the other hand, however, the intensified competition among these firms in production, sales, and investment lowered their profitability, threatening to deter an expansion in the scale of their business operations. In the face of imminent trade and capital liberalization in the 1960s, this fear made MITI and industry focus on strengthening Japan's international competitiveness, giving particularly serious consideration to the task of improving the overall industrial structure of the country and reorganizing each industry.

Innovation in business management

Technological innovation also had a significant impact on business management. The development of new products, reform of manufacturing methods, and the utilization of new materials made modernization of business management inevitable. Demands for cost reduction, quality improvements, and the shortening of delivery periods arising from fierce interfirm rivalry gave impetus to the urge to modernize.

Management innovation, as in technological innovation, began by adopting methods developed abroad, particularly in the United States. During the Occupation, Japanese companies had studied, under the guidance of SCAP, a variety of modern management methods such as quality control (QC) and personnel management.[14] The establishment of the Japan Productivity Centre in 1955 provided an opportunity to systematically introduce these methods to Japan. As discussed in Part III, the Centre engaged in such activities as dispatching overseas study missions, sending long-term trainees to overseas locations, and holding seminars. Particularly noteworthy was the dispatch of study missions. Leaders of business, government, academia, and labour were grouped into small teams and sent to the United States and Europe. During the ten-year period between fiscal years 1955 and 1964, 5,679 persons in 532 teams were sent overseas.[15] The shock which these leaders experienced in seeing first-hand the scientific management practised in the advanced countries, especially in the United States, produced a boom among Japanese business leaders of American-style business administration and management methods.

Representative of the management methods introduced in the second half of the 1950s were industrial engineering (IE) and marketing. Placing the management of a company on firm basis by urging top executives to establish solid management methods became an important task during this period. The Management Committee of the Industrial Rationalization Council attached to MITI conducted a detailed study of these methods and made recommendations.

Around 1960, more new methods were introduced, including systems engineering (SE), operations research (OR), the behavioural sciences, Programme Evaluation and Review Technique (PERT), and Critical Path Method (CPM). Industrial engineering found a wide following during this period. Against the background of a consumption revolution, marketing techniques became highly refined and thoroughly developed. It was also a characteristic of this period that an increasing number of companies engaged in long-term business planning.

From 1965, companies facing the 'recession of 1965' saw a greater need to rationalize their management, and the activities of their QC, IE, SE, and OR staffs became even more energetic. Their cost-reduction efforts, too, gradually developed from case-specific ones into multifaceted, complex programmes. A Zero Defects (ZD) movement also spread throughout the country, practised primarily in the electric machinery industry.[16]

Of particular importance in this modernization trend in management was the introduction and rapid spread of computers. In the mid-1950s, the mainstream of the automation of office work was found in the punchcard system (PCS, a data-processing system using a punchcard machine) and single-function office machines. In 1957, there were only three computers in operation in Japan. The number increased to forty-six in 1959, 102 in 1960, and 1,790 in 1965, making Japan the third in the world after the US and West Germany in terms of number of computers installed.[17]

As data-processing methods advanced from PCS to EDPS (electronic data-processing system), the types of work to which computers were put to use spread from the earlier ones of general office work (accounting, general affairs, sales, and so forth) to analysis, research, and application, and further to production management. This development was called a transformation from 'office work automation' to 'business automation'. Furthermore, during this period, on-line real-time processing was introduced and put to practise in some business firms, such as financial institutions. In this system, essential data were input into a mainframe computer at a central location. A large number of terminals located at remote locations could then access the central computer and either input or output information, thereby performing real-time processing of a large volume of information.

The remarkably successful management innovation of this period thus consisted of pursuing the target of modern management methods, largely American, and absorbing those methods as quickly as possible. On the other hand, the aspects of 'Japanese-style management',[18] such as the concept of the 'company as a family' and the system of seniority-based wages and promotion were severely criticized as aspects to be rejected in most cases. These characteristics of Japanese management, however, remained intact during the high-growth era with minor modifications, and gradually became blended with American management techniques. The so-called 'QC circles' and the 'kanban system' of production management at Toyota Motor Co. were cases in point. It was in the 1970s that these modern management methods rooted in Japan received international recognition.

Innovation in distribution

Innovation spread from manufacturing to distribution. In the distribution sector, however, it lagged considerably behind innovation in manufacturing. The primary reasons for the delay were the economic controls of the wartime and post-war reconstruction years, particularly rationing and price controls. As the controls were lifted, production resumed and consumption activities became robust, and the importance of distribution—linking production and consumption—came to be appreciated. The realization of distribution's important role led to the advent of mass selling, which corresponded to mass production and mass consumption.

In the traditional Japanese distribution system prevalent in those days, there existed between manufacturers and consumers several layers of wholesalers and a large number of retailers, most of whom were very small businesses. Moreover, the relationships among the wholesalers and retailers were complex and varied from industry to industry. As a result, even if manufacturers modernized themselves and reduced costs substantially, the end prices which consumers paid did not necessarily fall. The supermarket emerged as a new type of distribution business that broke down this mechanism and brought about low-price selling through volume purchasing and use of the self-service method.

The supermarket first appeared in Japan as a promoter of innovation in distribution in 1956. The world's first supermarket is said to have been the King Kullen store, which Michael Cullin opened in New York City in 1930. Cullin adopted a system of selling a large variety of food items at low prices and with a narrow margin in a large store using the self-service system. This format became the archetype of the supermarket.[19] In December 1953, the Kinokuniya food store (floor space of approximately 130 sq.m.) in the Aoyama part of Tokyo adopted the self-service system. This is said to have been the first self-service store in Japan. (The store, however, did not use the low-price sales system.)[20] It took considerable time, however, before Japanese shoppers—who had been accustomed to face-to-face contact between buyer and seller—fully accepted the self-service system.[21] Japan's first supermarket is said to have been the Maruwa Food Centre (floor space of approximately 400 sq.m.) in Kokura in northern Kyushu, which in March 1956 began low-price sales using the self-service system.[22]

Once into the second half of the 1950s, the number of supermarkets increased explosively. In 1957, 'Daiei for Housewives' (later The Daiei, Inc.) and Toko Store (later Tokyu Store Chain) were opened. The number of supermarkets (defined as self-service stores with floor space of 300 sq.m. or more) increased to 1,297 in 1964 and further to 2,632 in 1968, many of which formed chains. In view of this development, in 1962 some scholars and researchers began championing a 'distribution revolution' thesis.[23] The thesis predicted that the emergence of mass-sales stores would have a major impact on the nature of traditional retail stores and wholesalers, producing a revolutionary change in the Japanese distribution system.

In this debate, some advanced an argument that 'wholesalers were becoming useless'. Although this prediction did not materialize, the distribution system continued to change. The share of supermarkets in total retail sales reached 3 per cent in 1964, and annual sales of some of the leading supermarket operators exceeded 10 billion yen. Although the 1965 recession led to bankruptcies of some stores as a result of overinvestment and price-war sales, the number of super-markets had risen to 5,274 by 1972 and their combined sales approached those of department stores. By this time, the retail format known as the supermarket was firmly established. MITI took a positive view of this development as furthering the modernization of the distribution system. On the other hand, it found it necessary to pay attention to the effects of the expansion of supermarkets on existing small- and medium-sized retailers.

In this period, department stores also developed in both number and quality. Between 1960 and 1971, department stores increased by 85 per cent in terms of number of firms, 54 per cent in number of stores, and 154 per cent in floor space. This increase was relatively slow because the Department Store Law, put into effect in June 1956, required approval for establishing a new business, opening new stores, or expanding existing stores.[24] Because supermarkets were exempted from this requirement, small and medium enterprises began in 1961 or so to call for their regulation. MITI initially responded to such requests negatively, maintaining that regulation was not needed. As supermarkets became larger and more numerous from 1965, however, MITI requested the Distribution Committee of the Industrial Structure Council to study regulation as a 'quasi-department-store question'. Consequently, the Law Concerning the Adjustment of Retail Business in Large-Scale Retail Stores came into effect in March 1974, and large-scale retail stores other than department stores also became objects of public regulation.

Meanwhile, manufacturers also began taking steps to reform the distribution system. They found it essential that mass production be linked with mass consumption. In 1957, Matsushita Electric Industrial Co. set out to form a vertical keiretsu grouping of wholesalers, and initiated the exclusive franchise system and the monthly instalment payment system.[25] 'Marketing' was the method adopted as a means of realizing innovation in distribution. Marketing was introduced to Japan in part during the Occupation, but its systematic application occurred only after the above-mentioned establishment of the Japan Productivity Centre. In this case, innovation in distribution was set in motion as an aspect of innovation in management. One characteristic of marketing efforts by manufacturers was that the stimulation of demand through advertising and the systematization of distribution channels were pursued jointly. On the other hand, the domination of distribution by manufacturers came to provoke negative reactions from volume retailers such as supermarket operators.

During this period, other areas of distribution such as transport, cargo-handling, storage, and packaging made great strides. As roads and highways were improved, conveying goods by lorry became more widely used and the packaging revolution proceeded. From the mid-1960s onwards, the term 'materials handling' came to be widely used.

Towards the end of the 1960s, shopping centres appeared mainly in the outskirts of cities, giving further impetus to innovations in distribution.[26]

The advent of the mass consumption age

As discussed in the preceding chapter, the Economic Survey of Japan for fiscal year 1960 used the term 'consumption revolution' to describe how rapidly such consumer durables as electric appliances and cars spread among the Japanese populace. The Economic Survey pointed out that technological innovation was generating 'revolutionary' changes not only in manufacturing but also in the consumption patterns of the people.

The primary reasons why these changes in consumption patterns spread throughout the country were an increase in income levels and the equalization of income. Between 1955 and 1964, incomes of both urban workers and farmers nearly doubled. The annual rate of increase in wages for all industries rose from the 1955–60 average of 5.6 per cent to the 1960–5 average of 10.4 per cent. As a shortage of labour, primarily of younger workers, began to develop around 1959–60, wage rate differentials between large and small companies and between age groups began to diminish. Also, the percentage of farming household income compared to urban working household income was reversed from 90 in fiscal year 1961 to 103 in fiscal year 1966. This trend continued until about 1970.

Signs of changing consumption patterns were apparent as early as 1953. In February 1953, NHK Tokyo Television started regular programming. In August, Sanyo Electric marketed Japan's first jet-stream electric washing machine for 28,500 yen. Electric appliance manufacturers also sold electric refrigerators for 80,000 to 120,000 yen. Also, observing that bread was becoming a popular food, Tokyo Shibaura Denki introduced a pop-up toaster. Because of these and other developments, 1953 came to be called the 'first year of the electrification of Japanese consumption patterns'.[27] In 1954, television sets, electric washing machines, and electric refrigerators were dubbed the 'three sacred treasures'.

In 1955, when it was said that 'Japan is no longer in the post-war era', the black-market prices of rice became lower than official distribution prices, partly because of a favourable rice crop, marking a turning point in the post-war era of chronic rice shortages. As though by coincidence, automatic rice-cookers were marketed in the same year. Toshiba, which developed the product, tentatively put 500 on the market, but by the next year the monthly volume of production reached 100,000. Other manufacturers produced similar products, and as of January 1964 half of all Japanese households were using electric rice-cookers. Other products which enjoyed rising popularity at this time were vacuum cleaners, desk fans, and electric kotatsu foot-warmers.[28] Consumer durables other than home electric appliances, such as cameras and sewing machines, also sold well. Once into the 1960s, as noted earlier, ordinary families began buying cars as motorization spread.

Generally speaking, greater production of items such as consumer durables can lead to lower costs. Falling costs lead to lower prices, which increase consumption. This process in turn leads to even greater production and further reductions in cost. These 'scale economies' were especially large for new products, such as television receivers. The price of a black-and-white 14-inch table model, which was 175,000 yen in February 1953 when NHK TV began regular broadcasting, fell to 90,000 yen in October 1955, to 76,000 yen in 1956, to 68,000 yen in 1957, and further to the 50,000–60,000 yen range in 1962. Reflecting this downward trend in prices, production volumes increased sharply from 13,367 units in 1953 to 137,000 in 1955, 613,000 in 1957, and eventually to 4.86 million in 1962.

These new products, developed one after the other out of technological innovations, stimulated the buying interest of 20 million households through such advertising media as newspapers, radio, and television, which in itself was a revolutionary new product. Japan thus entered the age of mass consumption. In the first half of the 1960s, a new '3C boom' began, which involved cars, colour TVs, and coolers (air conditioners). The process of the rapid spread of consumer durables lasted into the early 1970s.

Consumer durables, however, were not the only driving force behind changing consumption patterns. Sizeable changes were also occurring in such consumer non-durables as clothing and personal effects. Japanese consumers, finally freed from the poor-quality textile products of the wartime and immediate post-war years, became increasingly fashion conscious. Cotton goods were resin finished (for non-wrinkling and non-shrinking), and woollen products became more sophisticated. The development of synthetic fibres led to supplies of products made of nylon, acrylic fibre, polyester, and polypropylene. The demand for plastics increased markedly for personal-use items as well, and plastic materials came to be widely used in kitchen utensils, bags, sandals, and home electric appliances. Dietary habits also changed, and Japanese consumption of animal protein in the form of meat, milk and eggs increased. Once into the second half of the 1950s, instant foods such as instant noodles (from 1958) and instant coffee (from 1960) experienced explosive sales growth.

People also became more interested in leisure-time activities such as travelling, eating out, golfing, fishing, hiking, baseball, mountain climbing, and skiing. In 1960, expenditures for broadly defined leisure-time activities exceeded 10 per cent of total household consumption expenditures.[29] The reduced housekeeping work load made possible by the use of various household electrical appliances accelerated the trend towards increased leisure time. For the Japanese who had endured wartime and post-war hardships, these changes in their lifestyle were indeed 'revolutionary'.

19.3. Growth of Exports and the Move Towards an Open Economy

The changing structure of trade

As innovations blossomed, the international competitiveness of Japanese companies increased markedly, leading to a remarkable expansion of exports. In 1970, the value of exports on a customs-clearance basis was $19,317.69 million, or within striking distance of $20 billion. This figure represented a sharp 5.6-fold increase over the 1959 figure of $3,456.49 million. Needless to say, the increased competitiveness of Japanese companies was not the only reason for this export expansion. It also owed much to the expanding global economy in the 1960s and to the government's export-promotion policy.

Looking at the world economy, it is seen that advanced countries led by the United States recorded sustained growth at a high level, most notably in the first half of the 1960s, producing a similarly healthy rate of growth in world trade. Between 1960 and 1965, the twenty or twenty-one member nations of the Organization for Economic Cooperation and Development (OECD) grew at an annual rate of 4.9 per cent, which far surpassed the average rate of 3.5 per cent for the 1955–60 period. During the same period, world exports increased at an annual rate of 6.3 per cent, as compared to 5.6 per cent in the 1955–60 period. This expansion in exports was primarily due to the liberalization of trade and exchange carried out among the advanced industrial nations. In contrast, once into the second half of the 1960s, each country found that, internally, the high growth of the past created problems related to full employment and upward pressures on prices. Externally, the instability of the dollar and the pound brought about confusion in the international monetary system. The value of world trade, however, showed a growth rate of 10 per cent or higher from 1968 partly because of worldwide inflation.

As for the export-promotion policy of the Japanese government during this period, at the beginning of the 1960s Japan was still suffering from the balance-of-payments ceiling that worked as a major constraint on economic growth. It was believed that the promotion of exports was crucial in order to remedy the situation. With the exception of 1950, Japan's trade balance had consistently been in deficit from immediately after the war to 1957. Reflecting on these facts, the 1958 Economic Survey on International Trade stated, at the end of its overview, that 'The phrase "developing the country on the basis of international trade" has never been more poignantly significant than it is today. Although we can anticipate many hardships ahead, we must be united and make further efforts to promote international trade for a better future.'[30] To that end, the government in 1954 established the Export Conference, chaired by the Prime Minister, and implemented and expanded various export-promotion measures. The measures dealing with finance, tax, and export insurance directly strengthened the international competitiveness of Japanese companies. A number of products that resulted from these efforts were widely exported, aided by public policy measures on market research and advertising.

Japanese exports in the 1960s thus increased rapidly through the strenuous efforts of government and industry, aided by the expanding trend of global trade. The value of exports surpassed $4 billion in 1961, $5 billion in 1963, $10 billion in 1967, and $20 billion in 1971. The trade balance turned to a surplus of $360 million in 1958. It increased gradually afterwards, and in 1971 reached $7.8 billion.

Besides the change in volume, the structure of trade also changed markedly. The most significant change was found in the increased share of heavy and chemical industry products in exports. As Table 19.3 shows, the share of heavy and chemical industry goods (metals and metal products, machinery and equipment, and chemicals) increased from 41.0 per cent in 1960 to 72.4 per cent in 1970. Particularly pronounced was the increased share of machinery and equipment, which rose from 22.9 per cent in 1960 to 46.3 per cent in 1970, thus approaching nearly one-half of total exports (machinery and equipment exceeded 50 per cent of total exports in 1972). The percentage of metals and metal products in total exports also increased during this period, from 13.9 to 19.7 per cent. The percentage of heavy industry and chemical industry products in Japanese exports surpassed those of the US and the UK in 1968, coming close to the West German level. If this rise in the percentage of heavy and chemical industry product exports is characterized as 'a process of the rising sophistication of the export structure' and a process of transformation of the export structure to that of an industrially advanced country, it can be concluded that the age of high growth was indeed a period in which this maturation process manifested itself most dramatically.

Similar changes were also apparent among heavy and chemical industry products. Ships, which had earlier accounted for a large share of exports, recorded a relatively stable share at 7.1 per cent in 1960 and 7.3 per cent in 1970. In contrast, the percentage accounted for by steel rose from 9.6 to 14.7 per cent, and that of cars increased from 1.9 to 6.9 per cent. Equally remarkable were the increases in the shares of electronic and optical products such as radios, television receivers, and tape recorders. On the other hand, problems remained in that the percentage of chemicals did not rise much (4.2 per cent in 1960 to 6.4 per cent in 1970) and that, among machinery and equipment exports, the percentage of capital goods was relatively low.[31]

In contrast, the percentage of textiles, which had accounted for nearly one-half of total exports during the post-war reconstruction period, declined to 30.2 per cent in 1960, and further to 12.5 per cent in 1970. It can be seen, however, that while exports of cotton yarn, cotton fabrics, and silk and rayon fabrics decreased in absolute terms, the share of synthetic yarns and fabrics increased, reflecting the successful results of technological innovation in the textile industry.

Meanwhile, imports increased from $4,491.13 million in 1960 to $18,881.17 million in 1970. In terms of the change in the structure of imports, the most conspicuous change was the increased share of mineral fuels—from 16.5 per cent in 1960 to 20.7 per cent in 1970—owing to the steady advance of the energy revolution. This change was attributed largely to increased imports of crude oil, but also in part to the sharp increase in imports of coal used as raw materials, as domestic production of coal declined. Imports of machinery and equipment also increased, reflecting the rising import of foreign technology. On the other hand, the import percentages of textile materials such as raw cotton and wool fell sharply, from 17.6 to 5.1 per cent (Table 19.4).

These changes in the structure of trade, particularly the increased share of total exports accounted for by heavy and chemical industry products, reflected

Table 19.3   Values of exports by principal commodity, 1960–1970 (units: $1,000; %)

	Total	% of total	Foodstuffs	% of total	Textiles	% of total	Chemicals	% of total	Non-metallic mineral manufactures	% of total	Metals & metal products	% of total	Machinery & equipment	% of total	Others	% of total
1960	4,054,537	100.0	267,585	6.6	1,223,352	30.2	169,225	4.2	145,178	3.6	561,464	13.9	928,261	22.9	759,472	18.7
1961	4,235,596	100.0	251,517	5.9	1,155,519	27.3	202,283	4.8	169,482	4.0	566,612	13.4	1,107,382	26.1	782,801	18.5
1962	4,916,159	100.0	339,522	6.9	1,256,612	25.6	260,981	5.3	188,127	3.8	742,485	15.1	1,232,643	25.1	895,789	18.2
1963	5,452,116	100.0	289,324	5.3	1,246,864	22.9	314,955	5.8	212,342	3.9	944,321	17.3	1,473,540	27.0	970,770	17.8
1964	6,673,191	100.0	323,054	4.8	1,426,482	21.4	383,525	5.8	241,943	3.6	1,202,853	18.0	1,967,811	29.5	1,137,473	17.1
1965	8,451,742	100.0	343,843	4.1	1,581,746	18.7	546,911	6.5	265,108	3.1	1,718,164	20.3	2,642,693	31.3	1,353,277	16.0
1966	9,776,391	100.0	382,625	3.9	1,762,412	18.0	669,429	6.8	284,689	2.9	1,778,244	18.2	3,756,959	38.4	1,142,033	11.7
1967	10,441,572	100.0	372,412	3.6	1,703,651	16.3	684,314	6.6	296,977	2.8	1,781,429	17.1	4,394,916	42.0	1,207,874	11.6
1968	12,971,662	100.0	431,774	3.3	1,977,269	15.2	805,222	6.2	329,208	2.5	2,346,901	18.1	5,655,831	43.6	1,425,457	11.0
1969	15,990,014	100.0	571,612	3.6	2,270,601	14.2	1,015,927	6.4	388,825	2.4	2,935,206	18.4	7,122,688	44.5	1,685,153	10.5
1970	19,317,687	100.0	647,744	3.4	2,407,524	12.5	1,234,462	6.4	372,376	1.9	3,805,336	19.7	8,941,266	46.3	1,908,978	9.9

Sources: Ministry of Finance, *Gaikoku Boeki Gaikyo* (Summary Report on Trade of Japan); *Tsusho Sangyo Seisakushi* (History of International Trade and Industry Policy), xvi: 238–9.

Table 19.4 Values of imports by principal commodity, 1960–1970 (units: $1,000; %)

	Total	% of total	Foodstuffs	% of total	Textile materials	% of total	Metal ores & scrap	% of total	Raw materials	% of total	Mineral fuels	% of total	Chemicals	% of total	Machinery & equipment	% of total	Others	% of total
1960	4,491,132	100.0	547,196	12.2	789,620	17.6	673,230	15.0	…	…	741,595	16.5	265,202	5.9	402,715	9.0	1,071,574	23.9
1961	5,810,432	100.0	669,230	11.5	951,456	16.4	955,966	16.5	880,017	15.2	931,979	16.0	335,982	5.8	599,212	10.3	486,590	8.4
1962	5,636,524	100.0	740,466	13.1	741,202	13.2	712,717	12.6	939,232	16.7	1,041,308	18.5	300,352	5.3	767,251	13.6	393,996	7.0
1963	6,736,337	100.0	1,087,936	16.2	883,767	13.1	766,887	11.4	1,137,129	16.9	1,210,809	18.0	368,959	5.5	799,643	11.9	481,207	7.1
1964	7,937,543	100.0	1,386,497	17.5	873,575	11.0	971,551	12.2	1,252,658	15.8	1,407,410	17.7	458,088	5.8	824,595	10.4	763,169	9.6
1965	8,169,019	100.0	1,470,030	18.0	847,405	10.4	1,019,182	12.5	1,354,302	16.6	1,626,043	19.9	408,151	5.0	711,273	8.7	732,633	9.0
1966	9,522,702	100.0	1,676,294	17.6	923,460	9.7	1,207,534	12.7	1,742,195	18.3	1,803,694	18.9	497,039	5.2	820,071	8.6	852,415	9.0
1967	11,663,083	100.0	1,804,680	15.5	897,662	7.7	1,600,368	13.7	1,995,007	17.1	2,239,481	19.2	610,596	5.2	1,053,372	9.0	1,461,921	12.5
1968	12,987,243	100.0	1,878,690	14.5	951,539	7.3	1,648,958	12.7	2,265,041	17.4	2,674,984	22.6	689,803	5.3	1,326,855	10.2	1,551,373	11.9
1969	15,023,536	100.0	2,141,232	14.3	926,912	6.2	1,971,522	13.1	2,502,403	16.7	3,043,939	20.2	782,557	5.2	1,634,685	10.8	1,020,283	13.5
1970	18,881,168	100.0	2,574,111	13.6	962,712	5.1	2,696,290	14.3	3,017,688	16.0	3,905,469	20.7	1,000,483	5.3	2,297,686	12.2	2,426,729	12.9

Sources: Ministry of Finance, *Gaikoku Boeki Gaikyo* (Summary Report on Trade of Japan); *Tsusho Sangyo Seisakushi* (History of International Trade and Industry Policy), xvi: 240–1.

the rising relative importance of the heavy and chemical industries in the industrial structure. A time lag existed, however, between changes in the industrial structure and those in the export structure. The percentage of total manufacturing accounted for by heavy and chemical industry products increased from 46.2 per cent in 1955 to 62.4 per cent in 1960, and remained thereafter at the 60 per cent level.[32] In contrast, the percentage of total exports accounted for by heavy and chemical industry products, which was 33.7 per cent in 1955, about one-third of the total, rose to 41.0 per cent in 1960, 58.1 per cent in 1965, and further to 72.4 per cent in 1970.[33] On this point, the 1970 Economic Survey on International Trade (Overview) stated:

The relative stability of the industrial structure compared to the sizeable change in the export structure can be attributed to the differences in the rates of increase between home and export demand in each industry. . . . The export structure of our country adapted well to world demand in the 1960s, not so much because of a change in the domestic industrial structure as because of a rising increase in exports aided by increased competitiveness, primarily exports of heavy and chemical industry products, for which world demand was expanding rapidly.[34]

Balance-of-payments surplus

'The deficit in the international balance of payments was the Achilles' heel of the post-war Japanese economy.'[35] During the period from 1945 to 1954, Japan had trade balance deficits every year except 1950, the year the Korean War broke out. It managed to stay in surplus in its overall balance because the trade deficit was offset by a surplus in transfers in the second half of the 1940s and by a surplus in services in the first half of the 1950s. Once into the second half of the 1950s, the trade balance frequently moved into surplus as exports increased. The protracted prosperity, however, led to sharply increased imports of raw materials, machinery, and equipment, and the trade balance—and consequently the current-accounts balance—went into deficit (the services account remained in deficit from 1959 onwards because of large ocean-freight payments), often producing a deficit in the overall balance as well. Such a situation invariably prompted tightening policies aimed at eradicating the external deficits. The frequently repeated sequence of events had the following pattern: business upswing → increased production → increased equipment investment → increased imports → worsening external balances → tightening of money and credit → business downswing → decreased imports → improving external balances. The periods of credit squeeze in 1957–8 and 1961–2 were typical examples of this pattern. In order to avoid a recession, it was essential that exports be expanded, foreign-exchange reserves be increased, and the payments-balance 'ceiling' be raised. This was why government and industry made concerted efforts to promote exports.

Once into the second half of the 1960s, the situation began to change. Although a tight-money policy was invoked towards the end of 1963 in response to deteriorating external balances, the external balances improved in 1965 not so much because of falling imports as expanding exports. The Thirty-Year History of the Economic Planning Agency said that 'the balance of payments has made a remarkable export-led recovery.'[36] In fact, exports in 1964 amounted to $6.7 billion, an increase of $1.31 billion or 24.4 per cent over 1963, as against imports of $6.33 billion, an increase of $770 million or 13.8 per cent over 1963, despite the restrictive credit policy. Further, exports in 1965 reached $8.33 billion, an increase of 24.3 per cent over 1964, providing one of the factors that led the economy out of the 1965 recession. The improved international competitiveness of Japanese manufacturers began to show impressive results, turning the underlying tone of the trade balance to a surplus.

This emergence of a perennial trade surplus that began in 1964 brought about a major improvement in the overall international balance of payments. The balance of payments, of course, records the totality of the current-account balance which consists of trade, services, and transfer balances, and the long- and short-term capital balances. Table 19.5 shows the changes in the balance of payments between 1960 and 1970. As mentioned earlier, the services account consistently showed deficits, which increased year after year. The capital-account balance, too, was in deficit from 1965 because of the sharp increases in capital outflow in the form of foreign direct investment, trade credits, and loans. For the overall balance to be in surplus, therefore, the surplus in the trade balance had to be sufficiently large to offset the deficits in the services and capital accounts. In fact, the overall balance was negative in 1967 because the trade-balance surplus fell to almost one-half of the 1966 surplus. The slowdown in exports in 1967 was caused by a combination of a declining export capacity of domestic manufacturers because of a boom in domestic business and business stagnation in overseas markets. On the import side, increases were caused by increased imports of raw materials and capital goods resulting from expanded domestic demand.[37] (Consequently, the interim stabilization policy introduced at this time had only a minor effect on business conditions.)

In these ways, the surplus in the trade balance was firmly established by 1967 or thereabouts. Although some uncertainties remained concerning the overall balance, rapid increases in exports from 1968 caused a sharp increase in the trade surplus, thus gradually improving the surplus of the overall balance as well. Consequently, foreign-exchange reserves increased sharply from over $1 billion up to 1964 to over $2 billion in 1965, over $3 billion in 1969, and over $4 billion in 1970. According to a trial calculation made by MITI in November 1969, the reserves would approach $11.5 billion five years later, at the end of fiscal year 1973, if the upward trend continued with no specific policy steps taken to moderate it.[38] On the significance of this perennial surplus of international payments, the 1970 International Trade Economic Survey stated:

In the past, external balances were regarded as the single most important constraint on economic growth. This constraining effect, however, has diminished significantly. Instead,

Table 19.5 Balance of payments, 1960–1970 (unit: $1 m.)

	Current balance	Trade balance	Exports	Imports	Services	Unrequited transfers	Long-term capital	Basic balance	Short-term capital	Errors and omissions	Overall balance	Foreign exchange reserves
1960	143	268	3,979	3,711	−100	−25	−55	88	−16	33	105	1,824
1961	−982	−558	4,149	4,707	−383	−41	−11	−993	21	20	−952	1,486
1962	−48	401	4,861	4,460	−420	−29	172	124	107	6	237	1,841
1963	−780	−166	5,391	5,557	−569	−45	467	−313	107	45	−161	1,878
1964	−480	377	6,704	6,327	−784	−73	107	−373	234	10	−129	1,999
1965	932	1,901	8,332	6,431	−884	−85	−415	517	−61	−51	405	2,107
1966	1,254	2,275	9,641	7,366	−886	−135	−808	446	−64	−45	337	2,074
1967	−190	1,160	10,231	9,071	−1,172	−178	−812	−1,002	506	−75	−571	2,005
1968	1,048	2,529	12,751	10,222	−1,306	−175	−239	809	209	84	1,102	2,891
1969	2,119	3,699	15,679	11,980	−1,399	−185	−155	1,964	178	141	2,283	3,496
1970	1,970	3,963	18,969	15,006	−1,785	−208	−1,591	379	724	271	1,374	4,399

Sources: Bank of Japan, *Kokusai Shushi Tokei Geppo* (Balance of Payments Monthly); *Keizai Tokei Nenpo* (Economic Statistics Annual); and *Tsusho Sangyo Seisakushi* (History of International Trade and Industry Policy), xvi: 260–1.

the high rate of economic growth has become an important factor in improving external balances as it helps increase supply capacity, raise productivity, and enhance international competitiveness.[39]

In other words, the Economic Survey indicated that external balances were barriers to economic growth in the past, but that now growth helped to improve them. By the end of the 1960s, therefore, the deficits in the balance of payments, which had been called the 'Achilles' heel of the Japanese economy', were eliminated.[40] On the other hand, the increases in the balance-of-payments surplus and the attendant accumulation of huge foreign-exchange reserves generated a variety of repercussions from abroad. As Japan entered the 1970s, it was compelled to adopt policy responses that were different from those used earlier. In May 1971, the Industrial Structure Council submitted an interim report entitled 'International Trade and Industry Policy in the 1970s', in which it emphasized the need to formulate a new external economic policy by stating that it was necessary

to transform a trade policy centred on exports and imports into an external economic policy or developmental policy that addresses trade, technology, capital flows, and overseas economic assistance in a comprehensive manner, and to implement such a policy autonomously while fundamentally keeping in mind the importance of international cooperation.

The so-called 'dollar shock' occurred three months later, in August 1971.

Intensified international economic friction

After the Second World War, Japan successfully reconstructed its economy amid great social and economic disruptions, achieved economic self-support without relying on foreign aid, and achieved high-level economic growth unprecedented in world history. As observed thus far, one of the primary reasons for these achievements was the expansion of Japanese exports. The first International Trade Economic Survey which MITI issued in 1949 contained the following words: ' "Export or Die" is no longer a slogan applicable to the British people alone. It is also why we endeavor to frankly tell all ranks of our people about the realities of our country's trade.'[41]

The ideology of developing Japan primarily by promoting exports was in the background of the creation of MITI, and it remained intact with slight modifications until the end of the 1960s. Urged by this ideology expressed as public policy, and stimulated by fierce interfirm rivalry, Japanese corporations made strenuous efforts to increase their exports as a means to increase market share. As a consequence, their competitiveness in world markets was enhanced remarkably, and the total value of Japanese exports increased from $470 million in 1949 to $19.32 billion in 1970, nearly fortyfold in approximately twenty years. In a sense, the policy objective of promoting exports, which MITI held since its inception, produced much greater results than originally anticipated.

The rapid growth of Japanese exports, however, caused frequent economic friction with other nations. As a result, Japan's export policy became two-pronged: it did its utmost to promote exports on the one hand, and made the adjustments needed to develop orderly exports on the other.

Needless to say, export problems do not occur with all products or in all areas but with specific products in specific areas. In terms of product categories, problems arose early on in light industry products such as textiles, sundry goods, and foods. Many of these goods were manufactured by small firms, and competition among them and among trading companies often produced sharp increases in exports to specific overseas markets, accompanied by incomplete quality control and excessive price cutting.[42]

In terms of the geographic distribution of exports, the largest number of problems were encountered in the US. Although trade friction occurred in other areas, such as with Canada, the countries of Western Europe, and developing countries, it was not as pronounced as with the US because in the 1950s West European countries had not restored the convertibility of their currencies, and because many of the developing countries found it necessary to restrict imports in order to promote domestic industry. In contrast, the US, which was still enjoying favourable external balances, was one of the very few countries without trade and exchange controls.

As a result, exports of light industrial goods to the US constituted the hub of the external economic friction in the 1950s. Specifically, problems arose with respect to frozen tuna, canned tuna, cotton goods, silk products, woollen fabrics, metal tableware, umbrellas, footwear, pottery, plywood, sewing machines, and so forth. Numerous problems began to develop from the first half of the 1950s with exports of fish and fish preparations, and from around 1955 with respect to other products, including textiles. The percentage of the value of exports whose quantities were restricted in total Japanese exports to the US increased from about 10 per cent in 1955 to over 30 per cent in 1959.[43]

The most important issue in the 1950 was US–Japanese negotiations on cotton goods that started in 1955. In those days, over 80 per cent of the Japanese companies producing cotton fabrics were small and medium enterprises. Thus, the industry inclined to generate cutthroat competition and to concentrate its exports to specific overseas markets. In 1955, exports to the US increased sharply over 1954, by 2.9-fold for cotton fabrics, 4.6-fold for cotton goods, and as high as about twenty fold for cotton blouses. These large-volume and low-price exports of Japanese cotton goods to the US became a major issue in the US, referred to as the 'one-dollar blouse issue' (the International Ladies' Garment Workers' Union mounted an anti-dumping campaign against Japanese blouses selling in the US for about a dollar each). The issue came to symbolize the movement calling for restrictions of cotton goods imports.

In response to this movement, the Japanese government decided to impose voluntary restraints on cotton fabrics and blouse exports to the US for one year beginning in January 1956. But the campaign in the US calling for import restrictions intensified. This development led to negotiations between the US and Japanese governments, which resulted in an agreement that Japan would impose voluntary restraints on exports of all cotton goods to the US for five years beginning in January 1957, and that the limits of the restraints would be negotiated annually. The system of comprehensive restraints (the overall volume of exports is determined, and then case-by-case restrictions are imposed on individual products) introduced at this time could prove restrictive to the exporting country depending on how it was applied. The cotton goods case set a precedent for comprehensive restraints adopted in subsequent US–Japanese textile negotiations (for woollen and synthetic fabrics).[44]

Even after voluntary restraints were adopted by mutual agreement between the US and Japanese governments, the import restriction campaign in the US did not wane, and the issue was not resolved until the 1960s. Although the share of Japanese goods in total US imports of cotton fabrics fell from 72 per cent in 1958 to 20 per cent in 1960, the shares of products of developing countries such as Hong Kong, India, and Pakistan increased sharply. For that reason, the US requested that an international conference on cotton textiles be held in Geneva in 1961 under the sponsorship of the General Agreement on Tariffs and Trade (GATT). This conference, in which twelve importing countries and five exporting countries (including Japan) and Hong Kong and others participated, produced, in July, the Short-Term Arrangement on Cotton Textiles (STA).

The STA was in effect for one year starting in October 1961. Its main provisions included: (1) countries which had import restrictions would relax them substantially, (2) when an import market was disrupted, exporting countries would impose export restraints; if export restraints were not possible, the importing country could impose the same level of restrictions, and (3) a long-term solution would be considered for cotton textile trade after expiration of the STA.

Long-term solutions were subsequently discussed. After many twists and turns, the Long-Term Arrangement Regarding International Trade in Cotton Textiles (LTA) was agreed in February 1962, and was put into effect for five years starting from October 1962. The LTA was extended in 1967 and 1970, each time for three additional years. In 1973, moreover, it was extended for three more months to coincide with the date (January 1974) when the Multifibre Arrangement (MFA) would come into effect. The LTA expired at the end of December 1973.

Thus, the LTA worked to regulate international trade in cotton textiles for eleven years and three months including the STA year, and was later succeeded by the MFA into the 1970s. During this period, the Japanese government, while maintaining that the LTA was an exceptional and provisional measure for regulating trade flows which in principle should be unrestricted, cooperated with other parties in formulating and implementing it in the interest of international cooperation. The negotiations on cotton textiles, however, exerted a variety of effects on later US–Japanese textile negotiations (on woollen and synthetic fabrics).

The foregoing discussion relates to friction in the textile trade. Once into the 1960s, as a result of the increased sophistication of Japan's export structure, heavy and chemical industry products such as steel, television sets, chemicals, as well as light industry products, became involved in trade friction. Geographically, in contrast to the friction in the 1950s which was largely with advanced industrial countries, Japan began to experience trade friction in the 1960s with developing countries. The problem lay in the fact that while Japanese exports to developing countries increased appreciably, its imports from them did not increase much. Against the background of worldwide trade liberalization and economic unification in the 1960s, the international climate for ever-expanding Japanese exports became harsher.

Demands for an open economy

The International Monetary Fund (IMF) and GATT were international economic institutions that played major roles in the post-war world economy. Japan's entry into the IMF and GATT marked the important first step in its return to the international community of nations. The IMF is an organization designed for promoting international cooperation in monetary matters, expanding and liberalizing trade, stabilizing exchange rates, establishing a multilateral payment system, and eliminating foreign-exchange controls. GATT, on the other hand, is an agreement designed for realizing free trade by eliminating tariffs and other barriers to trade, and by abolishing discriminatory measures in trade matters. Japan's participation in the IMF and GATT, therefore, meant that sooner or later Japan would have to liberalize its exchange and trade transactions.

The IMF, however, allowed its member nations to impose foreign-exchange controls only during transitional periods of post-war reconstruction. GATT, too, had provisions allowing temporary import restrictions and discriminatory measures against imports. As discussed earlier, Japan for many years had maintained import restrictions on the grounds of the vulnerability of its external payments. In other words, its expansionist economic policy tended to lead to sharp increases in imports, generating large deficits in the balance of payments. At the same time, however, it cannot be denied that import restrictions were utilized as a policy measure for protecting and nurturing domestic industries.

In the second half of the 1950s, major changes emerged in the international economy. First, the external payments of the US deteriorated, resulting in an increased outflow of dollars. The world economy after the Second World War was supported by the 'strong dollar'. But in the second half of the 1950s, a decline in the relative economic position of the US became increasingly obvious, and a dollar drain became particularly noticeable from 1958. The outflow of US dollars created a condition directly conducive to economic liberalization on a global scale, and the demands by the US for freer trade and capital flows swiftly intensified.[45]

The second change in the international economy was related to the return to currency convertibility of the West European countries. This development took place between the end of 1958 and early 1959, and marked an important first step by the world economy towards a free trading system. In January 1959, the European Common Market was created, and the liberalization percentage (the percentage of imports free of restrictions) of the intra-bloc trade in Western Europe increased from 83 per cent in January 1958 to 89 per cent in January 1959, and further to 92 per cent in January 1960. Moreover, the liberalization of imports paid for in US dollars, which had lagged behind intra-bloc trade, also made progress, with the liberalization percentage increasing from 64 per cent in January 1958 to 73 per cent in January 1959, and further to 86 per cent in January 1960.

It was inevitable that the changes in the international economy taking place principally in the advanced Western countries would have a major impact on Japan, which continued to practise stringent restrictions on exchange and trade. The trade liberalization percentage (the percentage of the foreign-exchange budget for importable goods set aside for automatic approval) of Japan in the first half (April–September) of fiscal year 1959 was only 33.3 per cent. Moreover, Japan in the second half of the 1950s, which began with the Jimmu Boom and ended with the Iwato Boom, was in the midst of a period of major economic expansion. Japanese exports increased from $2.01 billion in 1955 to $3.45 billion in 1959, and its balance of payments recorded a surplus in both 1958 and 1959.

The annual meeting of the IMF in September 1959 passed a resolution urging Japan to liberalize its trade and exchange flows, stating that: 'The Japanese economy has recovered considerably, approaching the level of the European countries. Nonetheless, Japan still imposes import restrictions to achieve equilibrium in its balance of payments, restrictions that have been utilized for industrial policy. This practice clearly violates the spirit of the IMF. Its use of the foreign-exchange budget system is also doubtful.'[46] Japan was also strongly urged to liberalize trade at the general meeting of GATT held in Tokyo in October 1959.

After the autumn of 1959, therefore, Japan faced a very serious policy issue in the form of trade and foreign-exchange liberalization. On 26 December 1959, the Economic Ministers' Meeting announced that imports of raw cotton and wool would be liberalized starting in April 1961. On 5 January 1960, the Cabinet decided to establish the Ministerial Meeting for the Promotion of Trade and Foreign Exchange Liberalization, and on 12 January the ministerial meeting announced a basic policy on trade and exchange liberalization. Throughout the 1960s, Japan responded positively to a series of demands to open its economy, from trade liberalization to liberalization of capital flows.

NOTES

1. *Keizai Hakusho*, 1956, Shiseido: 34–5.
2. Joseph A. Schumpeter, *The Theory of Economic Development*, trans. as *Keizai Hatten no Riron* by Yuichi Shionoya *et al.*, Iwanami Shoten, 1970: 151–2.

3. MITI, Committee to Edit History of International Trade and Industry Policy, *Tsusho Sangyo Seisakushi* (History of International Trade and Industry Policy), x, Tsusho Sangyo Chosakai (Research Institute of International Trade and Industry), 1990: p. 137.
4. Leonard H. Lin, *Inobeishon no Honshitsu: Tekko Gijutsu Donyu Purosesu no Nichibei Hikaku* (Essence of Innovation: US–Japanese Comparison of the Process of Importing Steelmaking Technology), trans. by Yushi Enta, Toyo Keizai Inc., 1986: 35.
5. Japan Car Manufacturers Association, Inc., *Nihon Jidosha Sangyoshi* (History of the Japanese Car Industry), 1988: 155.
6. Japan Computer Usage Development Institute, *Konpyuta Hakusho 1971* (Computer White Paper 1971), Computer Age Sha, 1971: 123–5.
7. Hisao Kanamori, Economic Research Centre of Japan, *Inobeishon to Sangyo Kozo* (Innovation and the Industrial Structure), Nihon Keizai Shimbun, Inc., 1987: 114.
8. *Keizai Hakusho*, 1957: 96.
9. *Tsusho Sangyo Seisakushi*, x. 429–30.
10. The Institute of Energy Economics, Japan, *Sengo Enerugi Sangyoshi* (Post-war History of Japanese Energy Industry), Toyo Keizai Inc., 1986: 258.
11. Hisao Kanamori (ed.), *Inobeishon to Sangyo Kozo*: 114.
12. Joseph A. Schumpeter, *Capitalism, Socialism and Democracy*, trans. as *Shihonshugi, Shakaishugi, Minshushugi* by Ichiro Nakayama and Seiichi Tohata, Toyo Keizai Inc., 1962: 159.
13. Hiromi Arisawa (ed.), *Nihon Sangyo 100-nenshi* (100-Year History of Japanese Industry), final volume, Nihon Keizai Shimbun, Inc., 1967: 133–5.
14. Kazuo Noda (ed.), *Sengo Keieishi* (Post-War Business History), Japan Productivity Centre, 1965: 409 and 441.
15. Japan Productivity Centre, *Showa 30–39 nendo Jigyo Hokokusho* (Operating Report for Fiscal Years 1955–1964).
16. Post-War Japan Business Research Group, *Sengo Nihon no Kigyo Keiei* (Business Management in Post-War Japan), Bunshindo, 1991: 252.
17. Japan Computer Usage Development Institute, *Konpyuta Hakusho 1967* (Computer White Paper 1967), 1967: 23.
18. James C. Abegglen is credited with being the first to point out these characteristics of Japanese management (James C. Abegglen, *The Japanese Factory: Aspects of Its Social Organization*, 1958, trans. as *Nihon no Keiei* (Japanese Management) by Tomi Urabe, Diamond Inc., 1958). See also Kosai Iki, *Shogen: Sengo Nihon no Keiei Kakushin* (Testimony: Managerial Innovation in Post-War Japan), Nihon Keizai Shimbun, Inc., 1981: 160–72.
19. *Ryutsu Yogo Jiten* (Glossary of Distribution Terms), Nihon Keizai Shimbun, Inc., 1970: 82.
20. Masamichi Okuzumi, *Shogen: Sengo Shogyoshi* (Testimony: Post-War Commercial History), Nihon Keizai Shimbun, Inc., 1983: 53–8.
21. Kosai Iki, *Shogen: Sengo Nihon no Keiei Kakushin*: 122–6.
22. *Tsusho Sangyo Seisakushi*, xi (1993): 421. If supermarkets are said to have begun with introduction of the self-service method, the first supermarket in Japan was the Kinokuniya food store in Aoyama, Tokyo, which first used the method in 1953. See Nikkei Ryutsu Shimbun, *Ryutsu Gendaishi* (Contemporary History of Distribution), Nihon Keizai Shimbun, Inc., 1993: 7 and 20.
23. The representative works in this category were Yoshihiro Tajima, *Nihon no Ryutsu Kakumei* (Distribution Revolution in Japan), Japan Management Association, 1962, and Shuji Hayashi, *Ryutsu Kakumei* (Distribution Revolution), Chuo Koronsha-sha, 1962.
24. Hiromi Arisawa (ed.), *Showa Keizaishi*: 420.
25. Hisao Kanamori (ed.), *Inobeison to Sangyo Kozo*: 108.
26. *Ryutsu Gendaishi*: 25.
27. Household Overall Research Group, *Showa Kateishi Nenpyo* (Chronological Table of the Household History of the Showa Era), Kawade Shobo Shinsha, 1990: 259.
28. Kageharu Iwasaki (ed.), *Nihon Denki Kogyoshi* (History of Japanese Electrical Manufacturing Industry), ii, The Japan Electrical Manufacturers' Association, 1970: 283.
29. *Gendai Nihon Keizai no Tenkai*: 116.
30. MITI (ed.), *Tsusho Hakusho* (White Paper on International Trade), 1958 edn., General Survey Volume: 101.
31. *Tsusho Hakusho*, 1970 edn., General Survey Volume: 146.
32. Industrial Structure Research Committee, *Nihon no Sangyo Kazo* (Industrial Structure of Japan), i, Tsusho Sangyo Kenkyusha (International Trade and Research Co. Ltd.), 1964: 38.

33. Ministry of Finance, *Gaikoku Boeki Gaikyo* (The Summary Report on Trade of Japan).
34. *Tsusho Hakusho*, 1970 edn., General Survey Volume: 148–51.
35. Hiromi Arisawa, *Showa Keizaishi*: 492.
36. *Gendai Nihon Keizai no Tendai*: 156.
37. Ibid. 191.
38. *Nihon Keizai Shimbun*, 6 Nov. 1969.
39. *Tsusho Hakusho*, 1970 edn., General Survey Volume: 128.
40. The deficit in the overall balance of payments was to reappear after the oil crisis of 1973.
41. *Tsusho Hakusho*, 1949 edn.: 5.
42. *Tsusho Sangyo Seisakushi*, ix (1989): 282.
43. *Tsusho Hakusho*, 1960 edn. Detailed Discussion Volume: 375.
44. *Tsusho Sangyo Seisakushi*, ix. 314.
45. Hiromi Arisawa (ed.), *Showa Keizaishi*: 440.
46. *Tsusho Sangyo Seisakushi*, viii (1991): 179.

20

Economic Planning and International Trade and Industry Policy

20.1. The National Income-Doubling Plan and Social Stability

At the beginning of the 1960s, there was an economic policy issue in Japan known as the National Income-Doubling Plan. This plan was comparable in importance to the liberalization of trade and exchange. In 1960, the Japanese economy was at the height of the Iwato Boom (1958–61). The US economy was also enjoying prosperity in 1959 and into 1960, a time that has been called the 'threshold of the Golden Sixties'. Despite the brisk economic conditions, the Japanese political scene in 1960 was in turmoil over controversy created by the revision of the US–Japan Security Treaty.

In 1958, the Japanese prime minister, Nobusuke Kishi, initiated negotiations with the US government for a revision of the US–Japan Security Treaty (which had been signed concurrently with the San Francisco Peace Treaty in September 1951). The focus of the revision would be to emphasize the principles of autonomy, equality, and reciprocity. In January 1960, the two governments agreed on the revised treaty. Japanese public opinion, however, was sharply divided on the nature of the revisions, particularly on the issues of mutual defence, prior consultation, geographical areas to which the treaty would apply, and Japan's obligation to assume increasing responsibility for its own defence. From April to June 1960, a stormy movement continued against the new security treaty, and the National Diet building was surrounded every day by thousands of citizens demonstrating against the treaty's ratification. On 19 May, the government and the ruling Liberal Democratic Party forced approval through the Diet, and ratification became automatically effective on 19 June. As a result of the ensuing turmoil, the government asked US President Eisenhower to cancel his scheduled visit in June, and the entire Kishi Cabinet resigned on 15 July.

The Cabinet of Prime Minister Hayato Ikeda, formed on 19 July 1960, realized it was necessary to implement a new economic programme to re-establish social peace and harmony in Japan, which had become disrupted by the security treaty controversy. It was out of this concern that the National Income-Doubling Plan was born.

The nature of Prime Minister Ikeda's idea was his assessment of the high growth potential of the Japanese economy. In order to double the GNP in ten years, the economy would have to grow at an annually compounded rate of 7.2 per cent. The Economic Council had, in fact, already been studying an income-doubling plan based on this growth premiss when Ikeda formed his Cabinet. Ikeda and his personal brains trust, however, were even more ambitious. Deciding that the economy had very high growth potential based on progress in technological innovations, they believed a growth rate of 9 per cent per year or higher was possible.

On 27 December 1960, the Cabinet formally approved the Income-Doubling Plan. Reflecting the debate concerning the country's growth potential, economic planners aimed to 'double the scale of the national economy in real terms in a period of about ten years', and they expected to achieve an 'annual average growth rate of 9 per cent for the first three years of the plan period.' The plan's target year was set for fiscal year 1970.

The Income-Doubling Plan became the third long-term plan, the first and second of which were the Five-Year Plan for Economic Self-Support of 1955 and the New Long-Term Economic Plan of 1957. The distinguishing characteristic of the Income-Doubling Plan, as mentioned above, was its formulation at a time of changed thinking regarding the Japanese economy. In fact, the economic growth rate at the time the plan was formulated was already into double digits: 12.5 per cent in fiscal year 1960 and 13.5 per cent in fiscal year 1961, which far exceeded the 9 per cent level. It was in this period that the expression 'high-level economic growth' came into popular use. The political era characterized by the security treaty controversy came to an end, and was followed by an era of 'high growth' during which Japanese society regained its stability. In that sense, this plan was the most effective economic policy scheme of the post-war era of high-level economic growth.

The Income-Doubling Plan was closely related to international trade and industrial policy. A unique characteristic of the plan, comparable to its premiss of a high rate of economic growth, was the fact that it made efforts to state clearly the essential elements of economic policy underlying the plan. The result was a highly operational plan, and in that sense, it was more of an income-doubling 'policy' than an income-doubling 'plan'.[1] The ultimate goal was 'progress towards marked improvement in the national living standard and attainment of full employment.' To this end, the five key elements which the plan called for were: (1) increasing social overhead capital, (2) upgrading of industrial structure, (3) promoting trade and international economic cooperation, (4) improving the capabilities of human resources and promoting science and technology, and (5) moderating the dual structure of the economy and securing social stability.[2] Because of their significant bearing on international trade and industrial policy, these five key elements deserve further comment.

Increasing social overhead capital

Roads, port facilities, land for development, water works, and other social overhead capital was relatively underdeveloped compared to the private productive capital and therefore constituted an obstacle to growth. The plan called for quantitative and qualitative improvements. Since industrial production was expected to increase about 3.3-fold during the plan period, the rational geographical disposition of industry became correspondingly important. The plan emphasized the following policy measures. New medium-scale industrial zones were to be built at midway points on the industrial belt linking the four established large industrial areas (Tokyo and Yokohama, Nagoya, Osaka and Kobe, and northern Kyushu). Special policy measures were to be adopted to correct the income disparity of economically backward regions (southern Kyushu, western Kyushu, the San'in area, southern Shikoku, etc.). The formulation of this plan marked the start of a full-scale industrial location policy in Japan.

Upgrading the industrial structure

It was considered essential to promote the increased sophistication of the industrial structure in both production and demand. 'Upgrading of the industrial structure' was defined as promoting the further reorganization of the industrial structure, centred on the heavy and chemical industries as has been done thus far in the post-war period, while promoting the diversification of production and the expansion of scale through the healthy development of industry.'[3] To this end, the plan projected an increase in the percentage of the value added to manufacturing by the heavy and chemical industries from 61.2 per cent in fiscal year 1959 to 73.1 per cent in the target year. The noteworthy fact of this plan was that it emphasized the 'formation of a new industrial order' as a prerequisite for increased sophistication and modernization of industry. It also announced a switch in the projection of energy supply and demand from the strategy of 'coal first, oil second' to 'oil first, coal second'.

Promoting trade and international economic cooperation

Although it was considered likely that the constraints (so-called 'ceiling') imposed by the balance of trade would become less restrictive as Japan's exports became increasingly more competitive, imports were also expected to increase as trade was liberalized. The balance of payments, therefore, or, more specifically, the growth of exports, was the key to success for the entire plan. The plan projected that, during the plan period, the volume of Japanese exports would increase 3.5-fold and imports 3.2-fold, while the volume of world trade was expected to increase at an average annual rate of 4.5 per cent. In order to attain this export goal, it was considered essential that a powerful export-promotion policy be pursued, including pressing ahead with economic diplomacy, expanding export markets, and improving the international trading system. Moreover, the Income-Doubling Plan postulated that international economic cooperation would become increasingly important in the years ahead. Accordingly, it planned to increase the scale of the assistance programmes by more than twenty fold, including invest-ment in overseas projects, loans, and deferred payment exports, during the plan period.

Improving the capabilities of human resources and promoting science and technology

The Income-Doubling Plan attached special importance to 'improving the capa-bilities of human resources'. Although labour-force problems had not affected economic growth up to that time in the post-war period, a slowdown was predicted over the long run in the rate of increase in the labour force. Moreover, qualitative improvements in the labour force were demanded to keep up with advances in science and technology and the increased sophistication of the indus-trial structure. It was therefore considered essential to improve the capabilities of human resources as part of economic policy in response to the rapid advance of science and technology. In the past, much of Japan's technological progress had been accomplished by the importation of foreign technology. But it was consid-ered that development of domestic technology would be important in the years to come, so the plan explored measures for dealing with a shortage of scientists and engineers. It also emphasized the promotion of science and technology, including the advocation of research and development and an acceleration of industrialization.

Moderating the dual structure of the economy and securing social stability

The Income-Doubling Plan addressed the long-standing question of the Japanese economy's dual structure. It stated that although there were signs that the economy's high-level growth might moderate this dual structure, the structure would not dissolve naturally. Therefore, the plan argued for a need to improve the social mobility of the populace and also to promote labour-force mobility among industries. Specifically, the 'dual structure' referred to the problem of the relative backwardness of agriculture, forestry, and fishery compared to other industries, and also of the tardiness and the need for modernization of small and medium enterprises compared to larger companies. From the standpoint of international trade and industrial policy, the problem of small and medium enterprises was the primary concern. To modernize these small and medium enterprises, the plan called for moderation of the extreme disparity in firm size, and strove to have those companies achieve an appropriate scale of business operations. It called for mod-ernization of facilities, raising the percentage of owned capital, improvement of the business environment, and modernization of working conditions.

   As described above, the Income-Doubling Plan involved almost every area of international trade and industrial policy, including policies dealing with indus-trial structure, industrial order, industrial location, natural resources and energy, international trade, economic cooperation, small and medium enterprises, and industrial technology. Along with the issue of liberalizing trade and exchange, it thus defined the direction of MITI policy at the beginning of the 1960s. The effects of this plan, however, were not limited to these individual policies. More than anything else, the belief in high growth (the underlying principle of the plan) provided government and industrial leaders with a bullish outlook on the Japanese economy. As is stated in the '30-Year History of the Economic Planning Agency': 'From a long-term perspective, the historic significance of this plan was that it sought to ride the wave of technological innovation in Japan and bring out the latent growth potential of the Japanese economy.'[4]

20.2. From a Medium-Term Economic Plan, an Economic and Social Development Plan, to a New Economic and Social Development Plan

The Income-Doubling Plan made a dramatic debut, but it was not without problems in its implementation process. First, the imbalance in the economy between the private and public sectors intensified. The plan expected the government to provide necessary information and guidance to the private business sector—which had no means of its own to execute the plan's objectives—and to fine-tune the implementation by indirect measures such as financial and fiscal policy. However, because the pace of expansion in the private sector, which was driven by plant and equipment investment, became far greater than the plan had projected, aggressive public investment in accordance with the plan's targets failed to rectify the relative inadequacy of social capital.

Another problem was related to rising consumer prices. The Income-Doubling Plan did not account for the rise in prices during the plan period. In reality, however, consumer prices rose persistently. After rising at an annual average rate of 6.5 per cent during the 1961–3 period, the inflation rate slowed down somewhat to 3.9 per cent in 1964, only to rise sharply again by 6.7 per cent in 1965, despite the fact that it was a recession year. The immediate cause of these increases in consumer prices was a tightening of labour-market conditions against the background of high-level growth, which resulted in rising prices for the output of small and medium enterprises and agricultural sectors, where labour productivity was relatively low. Higher consumer-goods prices adversely affected living standards, and became a source of widespread criticism of the plan itself.[5]

A third problem was the worsening of industrial pollution. Although the Income-Doubling Plan anticipated acceleration of various types of pollution and pointed out the need for prevention measures, anti-pollution measures were not given much weight in the plan, especially since such measures had just begun to take shape in those days. As the economy grew rapidly, however, air and water pollution grew much worse than anticipated, and became a serious social issue.

In short, the Income-Doubling Plan was plagued by what could be called the 'strains of high-level economic growth'. The plan was subsequently revised prior to its target fiscal year 1970, by the following three plans.

The Medium-Term Economic Plan

The Economic Council submitted a report on 17 November 1964, in the midst of the 'recession of 1965', for a Medium-Term Economic Plan. It was approved at the 22 January 1965 meeting of the first Cabinet of Prime Minister Eisaku Sato. This interim plan covered the fiscal years 1964 to 1968. The report was based on a predicted annual rate of growth in real terms of 8.1 per cent, which in turn was based on the assumption that the balance-of-payments current account would be in equilibrium by fiscal year 1968 and that the average rate of increase in consumer prices during the plan period could be held down to 2.5 per cent per year.

The plan set the goals of correcting distortions caused by high growth and aiming at the realization of a 'welfare society' by focusing the policy of economic reform on five points: (1) promoting trade and upgrading the industrial structure; (2) improving the capabilities of human resources and promoting science and technology; (3) modernizing sectors with low productivity; (4) promoting labour-force mobility, and utilizing the labour force effectively; and (5) improving the quality of national life. The plan also attracted attention for being the first national economic plan developed by using a large-scale econometric model.

The Medium-Term plan as approved by the Cabinet in January 1965, however, did not set specific figures for growth rates. It merely stated that the targets of the Income-Doubling Plan would be exceeded somewhat, and that the annual average growth rate for the plan period would be considerably lower than the actual rate of 10.7 per cent over the three-year period immediately preceding the plan period. This conservative estimate was no doubt influenced by the fact that the plan was formulated during the recession of 1965.

This interim plan was rescinded by a Cabinet decision on 27 January 1966, exactly one year after it was put into effect. Two principal reasons explain the short life of this plan. First, the rise in consumer prices averaged 6.1 per cent over fiscal years 1964–5, far exceeding the 2.5 per cent postulated in the plan. Second, as a means to combat the 1965 recession, the government issued deficit bonds in November of 1965 for the first time since the war (despite the fact that the Medium-Term Economic Plan had said that 'It is not appropriate to issue national bonds during this plan period').[6] These events necessitated the formulation of a new plan for addressing consumer prices and to deal with an economy encumbered with deficit bonds.

The Economic and Social Development Plan

The Economic and Social Development Plan, unlike the Medium-Term Economic Plan, was developed at the height of an economic boom—the Izanagi Boom (1965–70). It was based on a report from the Economic Council submitted on 27 February 1967, and was formally adopted at the 13 March Cabinet meeting of the second Sato government. The plan covered the five-year period from fiscal years 1967 to 1971. The plan was subtitled 'Challenging the 1965–74 Decade'.

This subtitle meant that Japan had to find ways to develop its economy under a set of three harsh conditions of the 1965–74 period, which were: (1) the internationalization brought about by liberalization of overseas capital transactions and other deregulation that was about to expose the economy to fierce competition with other countries, (2) labour shortage would become increasingly serious, and (3) urbanization, i.e. concentration of population in larger cities, would escalate.[7]

As measures for improving the quality of life, the plan called for emphasizing: (1) improvement of economic efficiency as a basic policy, (2) stabilization of prices, and (3) promotion of social development. Furthermore, in order to maintain an equilibrium in the balance of payments, ease the labour shortage, and stabilize prices, the plan set a conservative target of 8.2 per cent for real growth, and aimed at bringing the rate of increase of consumer prices down to 3 per cent or so per year.

The plan had three distinctive characteristics. First, it aimed to attain the twin goals of economic growth and price stability. To that end, it kept the projected real growth rate at about 8 per cent, as mentioned above. It also planned to gradually reduce the increase in consumer prices in the first half of the plan period by increasing the supply of perishable foods and making effective use of imports. For the second half, the plan called for creating more permanent conditions for price stability by stabilizing food prices and enhancing productivity in the overall economy. By the end of the plan period, the increase in consumer prices was projected to come down to about 3 per cent per year.

The second distinctive characteristic of this plan was its emphasis on improving the efficiency of the economic system through an optimum allocation of resources. Improved economic efficiency was necessary for price stability, but the plan emphasized that it was also essential to reorganize industry more efficiently because liberalization of capital flows was approaching. In this respect, the plan had significant bearing on international trade and industrial policy. Aiming to develop 'a system in which companies could achieve an international scale and engage in effective competition', the plan called for efforts to promote judicious application of the Anti-Monopoly Law to provide a favourable environment for corporate mergers and joint investment projects.

The third characteristic of the plan was that it was the first long-term plan in Japan to contain the word 'social' in its title and to include social development as one of its primary policy objectives. For social development, it listed the building of affluent regional communities, providing housing with ample amenities, eliminating pollution, and so forth.

Those were the main features of the Economic Social Development Plan. During the Izanagi Boom, however, the scale of economic activities expanded at a much faster rate than the plan projected. The average growth rate for the fiscal years 1967–70 exceeded 10 per cent in real terms, and the rate of increase in consumer prices exceeded 6 per cent during the same period. The balance of payments produced large surpluses and the backwardness of social capital became acute. Yet another plan became necessary.

The New Economic and Social Development Plan

The New Economic and Social Development Plan supplanted the Economic and Social Development Plan with revisions made in response to various changes in the environment. The report submitted by the Economic Council on 9 April 1970 was approved by the third Sato Cabinet on 1 May. This plan covered the six-year period, fiscal years 1970–5. As suggested by the subtitle— 'Towards Building an Economic System Rich in Human Qualities'—the new plan stressed two principal aims: rigorous promotion of internationalization of both the economy and society in keeping with the enhanced international status of the nation, and the attachment of greater importance to the quality of life, particularly in terms of the social infrastructure.[8]

Reflecting critically on the previous plan, the new plan gave a degree of latitude to the figures it contained. It stressed the importance of understanding its contents by dividing them into three major categories: (1) matters pertaining to macroeconomic development and policy implementation, including the rate of economic growth, the balance of payments, prices, etc.; (2) matters pertaining to public policy measures, such as public investment, social security, etc.; and (3) matters pertaining largely to private-sector activities, including private equipment and machinery investment and personal consumption.[9]

The new plan emphasized (1) the increasing international interchange and enhanced international status of the nation, (2) the increased sophistication and intensity of the social economy, and (3) the changing labour-market situation and attendant changes in social conditions. Taking these perspectives into consideration, the plan listed four goals: (1) greater economic efficiency from an international viewpoint, (2) price stability, (3) promotion of social development, and (4) maintenance of optimum economic growth and cultivation of a suitable development base.

The new plan was formulated at the peak of the Izanagi Boom, the longest period of economic prosperity in the post-war era. In the light of the previous sustained growth rate exceeding 10 per cent per year, the plan set a growth goal of 10.6 per cent, the first double-digit growth target in the annals of post-war long-term economic plans. Not long after the new plan was announced, however, the economy began to slow down. With President Nixon's removal of the US dollar from the gold standard (the 'Nixon shock') one year later (August 1971) as a turning point, the high-growth era suddenly came to an end. It is ironic that the economy has never recorded double-digit growth since then.

20.3. Government and Business in the Plan-Formulation Process

The government was responsible for formulating and executing economic planning, which is at the heart of public economic policy. In the planning-formulation process, however, opinions of persons outside the government were taken into account. Let us examine this process as it was applied to the Income-Doubling Plan.

The formal work for formulating the plan began on 26 November 1959 when Prime Minister Nobusuke Kishi asked Ichiro Ishikawa, chairman of the Economic Council (an advisory body to the prime minister on economic policy) to have his council prepare a report on 'what the nature and contents of a long-term economic plan aimed at doubling national income should be.' The council's work was completed when Chairman Ishikawa submitted a report on 1 November 1960 to Prime Minister Hayato Ikeda, successor to Nobusuke Kishi. The Economic Council proceeded with deliberations after having created, besides the existing Policy Planning Committee, three additional committees—the Government and Public Sector, Private Sector, and Econometrics Committees. The Planning Bureau of the Economic Planning Agency served as the council's secretariat. The Policy Planning Committee was made up of twenty members, including Professor Ichiro Nakayama of Hitotsubashi University as chairman. The membership included five academics, five industrialists, three persons representing financial circles, six officers of business organizations, and one journalist. The chairpersons of the other three committees were: Hidezo Inaba, chief director of the Kokumin Keizai Kenkyu Kyokai (Institute of Research on National Economy) (Government and Public Sector Committee); Kamekichi Takahashi, president of the Keizai Kenkyusho (Private Sector Committee); and Yuzo Yamada, professor of Hitotsubashi University (Econometrics Committee).

The Government and Public Sector Committee had ten subcommittees: Investment Allocation, Industrial Location, Transport Systems, Housing and Living Environment, Forestry and River Conservation, Energy, Science and Technology, Education and Training, Social Security, and Fiscal and Finance. The Private Sector Committee had seven subcommittees: General Affairs of Private Sector, Industrial Upgrading, International Trade, Agricultural Modernization, Small and Medium Enterprises, Wages and Employment, and Living Standards. The council had thirty regular members, eighteen temporary members, and 191 specialist members.

As mentioned above, these members included academics, managers of private companies, business organization officers, journalists, and representatives of labour unions and consumer organizations. Related ministries and agencies also supplied specialist members. MITI was represented by the directors-general of the Minister's Secretariat and the Enterprise, Mine, Coal, Public Utilities, and International Trade Bureaux, as well as the director-general of the Coordination Department of the Agency of Industrial Science and Technology and the director-general of the Promotion Department of the Small and Medium Enterprise Agency.

The composition of these committees meant that the work to formulate the Income-Doubling Plan was conducted through the cooperative efforts of persons in government and business. The plan's annual target growth rate of 7.2 per cent could be attained only if the policy measures on demand factors, supply capacity, and the balance of payments envisioned by each committee were realized. Accordingly, each committee carefully prepared a ten-year projection for the sector of the economy it was concerned with, and studied policy measures needed to realize its projection. In formulating this plan, economic activities were divided into public-sector and private-sector categories. For the public sector, where the government had direct measures for implementation, efforts were made to develop a plan which was as specific and feasible as possible. For the private sector, where the quality of activities basically hinged on the creativity and devices of private corporations, 'planning' did not go much beyond forecasting. The guiding policy philosophy was to direct private activities, as much as was possible, in a desirable direction.[10]

Concerning the role played by private corporations in the private-sector portion of the plan, Part 3 entitled 'Projection on Private Sector Activities and Policy to Guide Them', opened with the following statement:

This plan respects the initiatives of private business entities in pursuing their objectives while exercising their own creativity, relying on their own devices, and pursuing economic rationality through free private enterprise and the market mechanism. Accordingly, the nature of this plan *vis-à-vis* the private sector is essentially that of providing a future outlook. It is expected that private companies will develop their own long-term economic plans on the basis of the expected future direction of the national economy and the variety of information provided in this plan, and that they will establish a system of self-responsibility ridding themselves of excessive dependency on public policy measures.[11]

The role of the government, in contrast, was defined in the plan as one of providing an environment conducive to the free play of business initiatives, creating a basic condition in which free activities through the market mechanism will produce economic rationality, as well as removing stumbling blocks and relieving bottlenecks. It was also stated that the government should simultaneously stimulate, support, and guide private activities in a supplementary role as needs arose.

As stated earlier, the Private Sector Committee had seven subcommittees. Its Industrial Upgrading Subcommittee was involved in the following activities. It proposed that industrial production in the plan target fiscal year 1970 had to be 2.8 times that of fiscal year 1960 if the doubling of national income was to be achieved. The subcommittee estimated that, when the above goal was attained, the industrial structure would have been reorganized with a focus on the heavy and chemical industries. The rates of increases in output would be 2.6-fold for the steel industry, 3.5-fold for the machinery industry, and 3.1-fold for the chemical industry. The machinery industry, in particular, was 'expected to play a leading role in the attainment of the plan's targets.'[12] Of special importance was the projected increase in the production of cars from 145,000 in fiscal year 1960 to 1.04 million in fiscal year 1970, a sharp 7.2-fold increase.

The industrial upgrading subcommittee listed seven measures for promoting this increase in industrial production and industrial upgrading: (1) enhancing international competitiveness through modernization of equipment and firm establishment of the volume-production system, (2) securing funds for fixed-equipment investment and accumulating owned capital, (3) securing a stable supply of important basic materials, (4) developing and improving industrial locations, (5) promoting science and technology and fostering new industries, and (6) modernizing small and medium enterprises. As a prerequisite for realizing these objectives, the plan also stressed (7) the need to develop a new industrial order.

As seen, therefore, the role of the Income-Doubling Plan for the private sector was 'characterized as one-half forecasting and one-half guidance'.[13] The plan served as a guideline with a long-term perspective for companies as they engaged in their activities. This relationship between government and business was followed in essentially the same form in subsequent economic plans. In this sense, the nature of economic planning in Japan was far from that practised in socialist countries.

It was still true, however, that the positive stance of the plan regarding the potential of the Japanese economy had a significant effect on the initiatives of business firms, inducing vigorous plant and equipment investment and other aggressive business activities. In that sense, the Income-Doubling Plan not only 'forecast' high growth but also 'amplified' it.

20.4. Specific Methods of Guidance

As seen in the foregoing, the Income-Doubling Plan postulated that in order to achieve the goals of the plan, the government should stimulate, support, and guide the activities of business corporations while respecting their autonomy. There were two dimensions to the emphasis placed on guidance policy in the plan. One was that of avoiding as much as possible the exercise of direct control over individual business activities, which was done extensively during the postwar period of economic rehabilitation and still remained to some extent. It was believed that this policy was influenced by the issue of liberalization of trade and exchange, which was considered an urgent task of the times. The other dimension was the admission that certain aspects of the economy required a degree of public intervention in the form of measures to complement the workings of the market mechanism. Even then, however, the plan called for pursuing economic rationality to the maximum extent. As an illustration of such intervention, the plan stated that, although cartels which might be harmful to the interests of consumers should in principle be eliminated, it was also important to bear in mind the need to develop a new industrial order which would foster the international competitiveness of industry and upgrade the industrial structure in response to the challenges posed by trade liberalization.[14]

An examination of the specific formulation process of the guidance policy, with a focus on international trade and industrial policy, will help to explain how the Japanese government formulated and implemented it.

The role of councils

As with the Economic Council, other councils also played important roles in the process of formulating international trade and industrial policy as organizations for obtaining a consensus of the government and the private sector. From a legal standpoint, councils are attached to administrative agencies of the State. They are deliberative bodies which, in response to questions posed by the head of an agency, study and deliberate specific issues.[15] Although a council is a type of 'attached organ' belonging to an administrative agency, it is nonetheless characterized as 'a more or less independent organ'[16] in relation to top-level administrative agencies inasmuch as it is a deliberative body. The following are some of the reasons why many such councils came into existence in post-war Japan: (1) democratization of public administration (direct participation of citizens in administration), (2) introduction of specialized knowledge, (3) ensuring fairness, (4) harmonization of special interests, and (5) overall coordination of public policy and so forth.[17] In keeping with the principle that public administration should be based on the will of the people, many private-sector individuals with specialized knowledge were commissioned to serve on these councils. The report of a council submitted to the head of an administrative agency is usually based on a draft proposal prepared by secretariat officials who sound out and coordinate the opinions of concerned parties. The council members discuss the draft, which is then revised to reflect their views. In some cases the draft is accepted by a council with few changes, and at other times major revisions are made or decisions are reserved and the draft is returned to the secretariat. In any event, concurrence of the private sector is considered to have been secured through the process of deliberating on the implementation of a specific policy measure. An alternative form of administration thus became possible that was different from the one-sided imposition of policy common during the period of a controlled economy.

Large-scale councils that covered much of MITI's sphere of jurisdiction were formed three times in the past. The first was the Industrial Rationalization Council formed in 1949, the second was the Industrial Structure Advisory Committee created in 1961, and the third was the Industrial Structure Council established in 1964. There was essentially little difference between the last two, although the second was not called a 'council'. The difference was a matter of emphasis. Whereas with the 'committee' the emphasis was on the investigation of long-term, fundamental policy direction, with the 'council' the emphasis was more or less on deliberations concerning specific, important policy measures.

When the Income-Doubling Plan was being developed, MITI was assisted in its policy deliberations by the Industrial Rationalization Council's seventeen committees, many of which had earlier submitted numerous reports. These committees were: Coordination, Industrial Structure, Industrial Finance, Automation, Management, Industrial Organization, Energy, Industrial Location, Distribution, Small and Medium Enterprises, Statistics, Film Industry, Chemical Industry, Special Steel, Synthetic Fibres, New Metals, and Nuclear Energy Industry committees. (Of these committees, the Industrial Structure Committee had not been formally established, and the Industrial Organization, Film Industry, Chemical Industry, and Synthetic Fibre Industries committees had no substantive activities.)

The Industrial Rationalization Committee, however, was mainly concerned with the question of rationalization of each industry and the individual companies in it. It was not a forum for undertaking a comparative study of industries from an economy-wide perspective, or for deliberating on the question of the desirable industrial structure of the country. MITI therefore established, in April 1961, a new council—the Industrial Structure Advisory Committee—in order to 'study and deliberate on basic questions relating to industrial structure.' The committee was created for a limited term of three years. Twelve committees were established in the Industrial Structure Advisory Committee; they were: Coordination, Small and Medium Enterprises, International Trade, Industrial Finance, Industrial Labour, Industrial Technology, Industrial Order, Heavy Industry, Chemical Industry, Textiles and Miscellaneous Goods, Mining and Non-Ferrous Metal Industries, and Energy committees. At the first meeting of the Coordination Committee held in November 1961, it was confirmed that the meaning of the term 'industrial structure', which was the object of deliberations by the Industrial Rationalization Council committees, was to include not only the quantitative aspects of the relationships among industries, but also their environment or institutions they operated in, the internal structure of each industry, and the internal structure of companies. Subsequently, deliberations were held in each committee. Regular and specialist committee members selected from industrial and financial circles, academia, mass media, and government agencies numbered 331 persons, supported by a working staff of nearly 500 persons.

In the Industrial Order Committee, in particular, heated debates took place between the academic and industrial members over the nature and substance of the 'new industrial order' and the 'kanmin kyocho' (government—business cooperation) system, both submitted to the committee by MITI. In the end, the deliberations resulted in a report submitted by Chairman Arakazu Ojima of the Industrial Structure Advisory Committee (president of Yawata Steel) to the Minister of International Trade and Industry on 29 November 1963, entitled 'The Direction and Problems of Industrial Structure Policy'.

The report identified the basic direction of the upgrading of the nation's industrial structure, and specified the means to achieve that end in order to better adapt to the international economic community in the approaching age of trade liberalization. Because the deliberations were completed in essentially a little over two years, many serious problems including those relating to distribution, prices, consumer issues, industrial location, and industrial pollution were left unexamined. Also, of the issues that were fully discussed, many required reexamination in view of the realities of Japanese industry during the period of tumultuous changes.

For that reason, the question was raised within MITI as to whether or not the Industrial Structure Advisory Committee should be continued. The conclusion reached was to combine the functions of the Industrial Structure Advisory Committee with those of the Industrial Rationalization Council—a permanent organization that had existed for some years—and create a new council, the Industrial Structure Council. In this case, the new council would have twin sets of functions: deliberations for making important policy decisions, as in the Industrial Rationalization Council, and the study and deliberation of long-term basic policy directions, as in the Industrial Structure Advisory Committee. Accordingly, in the new council, the committees that inherited the nature of the Industrial Rationalization Council would continue their work as before, and the committees that inherited the assignments of the Industrial Structure Advisory Committee would place emphasis in their work on following-up Industrial Structure Advisory Committee reports and deliberations on the 'yet-to-be-examined issues' mentioned above.

Thus, on 31 March 1964, the Industrial Rationalization Council and the Industrial Structure Advisory Committee were abolished, and on the following day the Industrial Structure Council was established. The membership of the Industrial Structure Council was limited to 130 persons. Arakazu Ojima, chairman of Yawata Steel, was elected chairman. Although the objective of the Industrial Structure Council, like the Industrial Structure Advisory Committee, was to 'study and deliberate on basic questions relating to industrial structure', the Industrial Structure Council differed from the Industrial Structure Advisory Committee in that the new council was a permanent deliberative body with no time limit. At its inception, the Industrial Structure Council had eighteen committees, including the Coordination, Distribution, Industrial Pollution, Investment Finance, Management, Film Industry, Nuclear Energy Industry, Energy, International Economy, Consumer Economy, Heavy Industry, Chemical Industry, Miscellaneous Goods and Construction Materials, Textiles, Industrial Finance, Industrial Labour, Industrial Location, and Industrial Technology committees. Two of these committees, the Energy Committee and the Nuclear Energy Industry Committee, had their organizations and functions moved to the Advisory Committee for Energy when it was established in 1965. Meanwhile, the Steel Committee was created in fiscal year 1966, followed by the Information Industry Committee formed in fiscal year 1967, and the Housing Industry Committee and the Marine Development Committee were established in fiscal year 1969.

As we have seen above, by the end of fiscal year 1970, there were twenty committees of the Industrial Structure Council. These committees, along with twenty-four subcommittees and two special committees, deliberated a wide range of diverse questions on industrial structure in a dynamic and flexible manner. The membership of the Industrial Structure Council, including temporary and specialist members, numbered 770, making it by far the largest of all the advisory councils attached to MITI. It is safe to say that the essential part of industrial policy, developed from fiscal year 1964, emerged from deliberations of this council.

Administrative guidance

In the post-war years from the rehabilitation period to the period of re-establishing self-support, much of international trade and industrial policy was implemented by orders and regulations based on statutes. During the rehabilitation period, control was imposed on the production, distribution, and prices of basic materials, and violators were punished according to penal regulations. Without these measures, it was impossible to give priority to the production of goods necessary for economic reconstruction, or to distribute goods fairly to the people according to their needs. As the level of production recovered, direct controls were gradually withdrawn. For those industries which were behind in modernizing their facilities and those whose recovery was crucially important, new industry-specific 'rationalization laws' and 'promotion laws' were enacted. Examples of these laws were: the Law on Special Measures for the Ammonium Sulphate Industry Rationalization and Export Adjustment (1954), the Law on Extraordinary Measures for Rationalization of the Coal-Mining Industry (1955), the Law on Temporary Measures for Textile Industry Equipment (1956), the Law on Temporary Measures for Promotion of the Machinery Industry (1956), the Law on Temporary Measures for Promotion of the Electronics Industry (1957), and the Aircraft Industry Promotion Law (1958). Furthermore, many laws were enacted to promote international trade and small and medium enterprises. Because many of these laws contained provisions for exempting industries from the provisions of the Anti-Monopoly Law, they were often referred to as 'Anti-Monopoly Law exemption legislation'.

Once into the 1960s, however, and as demands for economic liberalization intensified, the conduct of economic policy through legislation began to show signs of change. From a legal standpoint, liberalization of trade and exchange meant the discontinuation or relaxation of trade and foreign-exchange regulations based on the Foreign-Exchange and Foreign Trade Control Law. Many of the rationalization and promotion laws enacted during the period of re-establishing self-support had continued in force with some revisions. The use of legislation, however, shifted—with the exception of the mining and small and medium enterprises that required special support from the State—to such new policy fields as industrial location, industrial pollution, and consumer protection. Gaining importance was the non-authoritarian administrative method known as 'administrative guidance'.

There is no generally accepted definition of administrative guidance. The Cabinet Legislation Bureau at a hearing of the Committee on Commerce and Industry of the House of Councillors in March 1974 presented a statement tentatively defining it as follows:

Administrative guidance has no legal force limiting the rights of citizens or imposing obligations on them. It refers to a method used by an administrative agency, in carrying out a policy within the realm of its competence as defined by the establishing statute, to persuade and induce parties who are objects of the policy to take or refrain from certain actions.[18]

Also, one expert on public administration defined it as follows:

Administrative guidance may be defined as a series of actions which an administrative agency takes, in matters pertaining to its realm of competence, in order to induce specific individuals, organizations, or public or private corporations to work towards formation of a specific order which the agency believes is desirable. Actions of this nature may or may not be based on specific statutory authority or legalistic procedures.[19]

Administrative guidance in this sense was actually practised in every field of public administration, and was seen in MITI since the early post-war period. The changes in the objective circumstances that brought about the shift from direct control to inductive measures (which was pointed out in the Income-Doubling Plan) served to enhance the relative importance of administrative guidance.

The first post-war case of administrative guidance conducted in the area of international trade and industrial policy which attracted public attention was related to curtailments of production in the cotton-spinning industry. In February 1952, MITI advised cotton-spinning companies to curtail production to help them recover from the severe business slump that developed after the Korean War boom ended. This was the beginning of the so-called 'kankoku sotan' ('advisory for curtailing production'). A notice sent to major cotton-spinners dated 25 February 1952 and issued in the name of the director-general of MITI's International Trade Textiles Bureau was entitled 'On the Proper Level of Capacity Utilization in the Cotton-Spinning Industry'. The notice 'recommended' a production curtailment of 40 per cent, but it was not based on statutory provisions and therefore lacked legal force. MITI maintained that subsequent production curtailments were not a violation of the Anti-Monopoly Law because they were not the result of joint action among firms based on a voluntary agreement. MITI informed the cotton-spinners, however, that appropriate measures would be taken regarding subsequent allocations of raw cotton imports in cases where production exceeded the 'proper' level of capacity utilization. In other words, the MITI-recommended production curtailment was buttressed by a judicious use of the foreign-exchange allocation system.[20] In this sense, this policy method can be said to be backed up by the coercive force of public authority.

In June 1952, the Fair Trade Commission made a presentation to MITI with regard to the 'Case of Production Curtailment by Advice in the Cotton-Spinning Industry', arguing that the 'advice' produced a result similar to that of a joint action by firms to limit their production.[21] This policy method of recommending production curtailment was used subsequently in many industries during recession periods to positive effect, but it also generated frequent clashes of opinion between MITI and the Fair Trade Commission on the legal status of the practice.

The list-price system ('Open Sales System') implemented from June 1958 was a type of administrative guidance used to deal with business slumps. Under this system, manufacturers reported the prices and expected production volume of their products to an appropriate agency, and sold the products simultaneously under its guidance, thereby achieving price stability. When the steel market deteriorated in 1958, for example, MITI recommended production curtailment from March 1958 of thin steel plate, medium-size shaped steel, and bar steel. As the market for those products continued to decline, the list-price system was invoked as a means to achieve effective implementation of production curtailments and long-term stability of steel prices. Concerning this practice, the Fair Trade Commission expressed the opinion that, although it did not violate the Anti-Monopoly Law, it could very well induce a cartel among steel suppliers. It acquiesced in this practice on the assumption that MITI would provide careful surveillance.[22] The system was converted to a 'boom-period list-price system' as business conditions improved in 1959 and steel prices rose sharply. It changed character again in 1960 to that of a 'price-stabilizing list-price system'.

Since administrative guidance did not have the legal force of compulsion, there was no assurance that companies subjected to it would always observe the guidance provided. The classic examples of large Japanese corporations temporarily not abiding by administrative guidance were the Idemitsu Petroleum case of 1963–4 and the Sumitomo Metal Industries case of 1965. Both cases involved conflicts of viewpoints with regard to MITI-sponsored counter-recession measures.

After the Petroleum Industry Law was enforced in July 1962, MITI, on the basis of Article 3 of the law, published the Petroleum Supply Plan for fiscal years 1962–6. Responding to this plan, the petroleum refiners submitted production plans for petroleum products to the Minister of International Trade and Industry. The petroleum industry in those days, however, was in the midst of fierce competition in anticipation of the imminent liberalization (October 1962) of crude oil imports, and the earnings of the refiners during that time were reduced. For that reason, the total quantity of crude oil estimated to be refined by all the refiners in the second half of fiscal year 1962 exceeded the supply plan on the basis of a processing account by about 29 per cent. To deal with this situation, MITI used administrative guidance to set a quota for crude oil to be refined by each firm, which was calculated largely on the basis of three criteria: past production results, sales capacity or sales results, and equipment capacity. These criteria, however, tended to fix market shares at existing levels, and thus were sources of bitter complaint by firms trying to expand their market share. Idemitsu Petroleum objected to the programme of adjusting production volumes for the second half of fiscal year 1963, arguing that the refining capacity of newly installed facilities was relatively underrated. It withdrew from the Petroleum Association of Japan in November 1963, and increased production beyond the MITI quota. In January 1964 MITI, in consultation with the Petroleum Council, developed a new formula for output coordination which assessed the capacity of newly installed facilities at a higher level than the old formula did. Idemitsu Petroleum then declared its willingness to abide by the quota, and the issue was settled for the interim. (Idemitsu Petroleum rejoined the Petroleum Association when the production curtailment programme was discontinued in October 1966.)[23]

Meanwhile, the slump in the steel industry worsened in early 1965. In July 1965, MITI exercised administrative guidance and instructed steel makers to reduce their crude-steel production. Specifically, the production volume for the second quarter of fiscal year 1965 was to be reduced to 90 per cent of the average for the last two quarters of fiscal year 1964. Although MITI's guideline for this quarter was observed by all steel manufacturers, Sumitomo Metal Industries demanded that MITI make a thorough re-evaluation of the method before it would continue with the programme of production curtailments, and objected to extension of the programme into the third quarter. The contention of the company was summarized in three points: (1) exports should be excluded from the guidance, (2) rules for operating new facilities should be clearly established, and (3) the reference period for calculating production quotas should be the one closest to the period being regulated. MITI in November suggested a revised plan incorporating the demands made by Sumitomo. The company rejected it, and resumed production according to its own plans. Thereupon MITI declared that if Sumitomo continued production above the suggested levels, it would have no alternative but to adjust downward the allocation of coke imports for Sumitomo to a level commensurate with the suggested production level. Subsequently at a meeting held in December between Takeo Miki, Minister of International Trade and Industry, and Hosai Hyuga, president of Sumitomo Metal Industries, an agreement was reached to the effect that (1) Sumitomo would observe the production limit suggested by MITI for the third quarter, and (2) the handling of the first quarter of fiscal year 1966 and subsequent quarters would be considered later. Thus, the issue was finally settled.[24]

An expert on public administration classifies administrative guidance into advisory, regulatory, and adjustive types, and states:

Since administrative guidance is essentially 'guidance', its observance is, in theory, left to the party receiving the guidance. How significant this theoretical voluntariness is in reality depends on whether a given act of guidance is advisory or regulatory/adjustive. Observance of 'advisory' administrative guidance is totally voluntary both in name and reality. In contrast, the recipient of 'regulatory' or 'adjustive' administrative guidance does not necessarily have a similar option.[25]

From this suggested categorization of administrative guidance, it might be concluded that the cases of administrative guidance discussed above belong to the regulatory or adjustive categories. Indeed, MITI has effectively practised this type of administrative guidance in implementing its international trade and industrial policy. However, it must also be noted that the ministry has always made use of advisory administrative guidance. In fact, it has conducted its policy by judiciously combining the three types of administrative guidance.

Thus, administrative guidance as practised by MITI played an important role in the ministry's successful pursuit of its policy objectives. On the other hand, criticisms were voiced by some academics and journalists denouncing the 'adhesive' relationship between the government bureaucracy and the leadership of industrial circles nurtured through the practice of administrative guidance. As the high-growth rate of the Japanese economy became a focus of worldwide interest, this relationship began to attract attention from abroad.

Japan, Inc. published by the US Commerce Department in 1972 argued that

'"Administrative guidance" is the most representative term used to express the variety of persuasive methods which MITI uses to induce Japanese industry to carry out important measures for the national economy.'[26] It pointed out that Japanese enterprises accept the 'carrot and stick' of administrative guidance in the spirit of close cooperation between business and government.

Elsewhere, Professor Chalmers Johnson of the University of California, Berkeley, argued, in his book *MITI and the Japanese Miracle*, that MITI's administrative guidance gained in relative importance in the 1960s. He stated:

During the 1950s, administrative guidance was rarely mentioned in connection with MITI's actions because most of its orders, permissions, and licences were then firmly based on explicit control laws. Administrative guidance came to be openly practised and discussed during the 1960s, and then only because MITI lost most of its explicit control powers as a result of liberalization and the failure to enact the Special Measures Law.[27]

Although this view of Professor Johnson underestimates the role of administrative guidance in the 1950s, it nonetheless laid a finger on the process, as stated earlier, of transition of the focus of administrative practices from explicit legislation to non-authoritarian, inductive methods.

With regard to this same issue, an administrative vice-minister of MITI, in a speech in June 1970 to the Industries Committee of the Organization for Economic Cooperation and Development (OECD), remarked as follows:

In the steel, automobile, petrochemicals, computer, and other industries, administrative guidance was practised between MITI and the industries in the form of exchanges of views, MITI's advice or recommendations to the industries, or approvals based on statutory provisions in pursuit of intensive investments and economies of scale. . . . MITI's administrative guidance is not authoritarian. The role the government has played in the past 100 years in protecting and nurturing industries, and particularly the contributions which MITI's policies have made towards the recovery and development of industries in the postwar period, as well as the appreciation by the industries of these contributions, and the relationship of trust between industry and MITI, all combine to form a solid foundation for MITI's administrative guidance.[28]

NOTES

1. Saburo Okita, *Shotoku Baizo Keikaku no Kaisetsu* (The Income-Doubling Plan Explained), Nihon Keizai Shimbun, Inc., 1960: 21–2.
2. National Income-Doubling Plan, pt. 1, ch. 2, sect. 1.
3. Ibid., pt. 3, ch. 3-1, 'Kogyo no Kodoka to Kokusai Kyosoryoku no Kyoka' (Industrial Upgrading and Enhancement of International Competitiveness).
4. *Gendai Nihon Keizai no Tenkai*: 136.
5. Ibid. 138–9.
6. Economic Planning Agency, Planning Bureau, *Zusetsu: Keizai Shakai Hatten Keikaku* (Economic and Social Development Plan Illustrated), Shiseido, 1967: 11–12.
7. Ibid. 1.
8. *Gendai Nihon Keizai no Tendai*: 202.

9. *Tsusho Sangyo Seisakushi*, viii. 86.
10. National Income-Doubling Plan, pt. 1, ch. 1, sect. 2.
11. Ibid., pt. 3, ch. 1, sect. 2.
12. Ibid. 175–86.
13. Saburo Okita, *Shotuko Baizo Keikaku no Kaisetu*: 18.
14. National Income-Doubling Plan, pt. 3, ch. 1, sect. 2.
15. Shuzo Hayashi *et al.* (eds), *Horei Yogo Jiten* (Glossary of Legal Terms), Gakuyo Shobo, 1986: 405.
16. Isao Sato, 'Shingikai' (Advisory Council), *Gyoseiho Koza* (Lectures on Administrative Law), iv, Yuhikaku Publishing Co. Ltd., 1965: 98–9.
17. Ibid. 108.
18. From the reply of Reijiro Tsunoda, Director of First Department, Cabinet Legislation Bureau, to the interpellation of the Commerce and Industry Committee of the House of Councilors, 26 Mar. 1974.
19. Yoriaki Narita, 'Gyosei Shido' (Administrative Guidance) in *Gendai Ho* (Contemporary Law), iv, Iwanami Shoten, 1966: 132.
20. *Tsusho Sangyo Seisakushi*, vi (1990): 664.
21. Fair Trade Commission, Secretariat, *Dokusen Kinshi Seisaku 30-nenshi* (Thirty-Year History of Anti-Monopoly Policy), Printing Bureau, MoF, 1977: 96.
22. Ibid. 99.
23. Petroleum Association of Japan, *Sengo Sekiyu Sangyoshi* (Post-War History of the Petroleum Industry), 1985: 174–5.
24. The Japan Iron and Steel Federation, *Tekko 10-nenshi: Showa 32–42 nen* (History of the Japanese Steel Industry: 1958–67), 1969: 101.
25. Kazuo Yamauchi, *Komuin no Tame no Gyosei Shidoron* (Theory of Administrative Guidance for Public Employees), Printing Bureau, MoF, 1986: 1.
26. US Dept. of Commerce, *Japan: The Government–Business Relationship*, trans. as *Kabushikigaisha Nippon* by Susumu Ohara and Toyoaki Yoshida, Simul Press, Inc., 1972: 55. For details of this document, see chapter 23.
27. Chalmers Johnson, *MITI and the Japanese Miracle*, Stanford University Press, 1982, trans. as *Tsusansho to Nippon no Kiseki* under the supervision of Toshihiko Yano, TBS Britannica, 1982: 292.
28. Speech made by Yoshihisa Ohjimi, Administrative Vice-Minister of MITI, entitled 'Basic Philosophy and Objectives of Japanese Industrial Policy' (at a meeting of the OECD's Industrial Committee), June 1970, quoted in 'MITI Materials': 11–12.

21

Trade and Capital Liberalization and International Trade Policy

21.1. Adoption of Liberalization Plan for International Trade and Foreign Exchange

One more important characteristic of the growth-centred Japanese economy in the 1960s was the progress made in the liberalization of trade, foreign-exchange transactions, and external capital transactions. Liberalization of trade and foreign exchange, which had been an important task in Japan's international trade policy, made rapid progress in the first half of the 1960s. In April 1964, Japan accepted the obligations of IMF Article 8, which prohibits restrictions on current transactions for balance-of-payments reasons. Once into the second half of the 1960s, however, Japan faced yet another problem—movements to liberalize capital. Capital liberalization began with the first liberalization programme of 1967 and ended with the fifth programme implemented in 1973.

As discussed earlier, major West European nations had restored the convertibility of their currencies by the end of the 1950s. Meanwhile, the rapid growth of Japanese exports generated trade friction between Japan and Western countries, especially the US, leading to intensified US demands for removal of Japanese restrictions on imports. At the autumn 1959 meetings of the International Monetary Fund (IMF) and General Agreements on Tariffs and Trade (GATT), Japan was exposed to strong demands for removal of trade and exchange restrictions for balance-of-payments reasons. Thus, external pressure on Japan for import and foreign-exchange liberalization increased markedly.

The 'White Paper on International Trade for 1960' described the reasons for the delay in Japan's trade and foreign-exchange liberalization as follows:

1. Uncertainty concerning the balance of payments. For Japan, which relied on foreign sources for large proportions of its supplies of key raw materials, maintaining adequate foreign-exchange reserves was of utmost importance.
2. To protect small-scale agriculture and underground-resource industries which relied on relatively scanty natural resources.
3. To protect new industries relying on backward industrial technology.
4. To prevent excessive competition, especially to maintain appropriate order in the small and medium enterprise sector.
5. To promote exports to developing countries, it was necessary to import relatively expensive materials from them. The system of allocating funds for imports was utilized for this purpose.[1]

Intensifying external pressure compelled Japan gradually to alter its stance on liberalization. Beyond the question of external pressure, it was also necessary for Japan to respond positively to foreign demands for liberalization in order to establish its credibility in the international economic community and to eradicate mistrust and misgivings towards Japan that were deeply rooted, especially in advanced nations. Furthermore, liberalization was expected to produce positive benefits to the Japanese economy, including: (1) more advantageous purchases of raw materials and products from overseas, (2) increased benefits to consumers, (3) acceleration of industrial rationalization resulting from removal of import restrictions, (4) contribution to increased exports, and (5) progress, throughout the whole of Japanese industry, in harmonizing industrial structure and price structures with those of the outside world.[2]

MITI had begun a study on measures to deal with trade liberalization from about the beginning of 1959. The exercise made rapid progress subsequent to the IMF and GATT annual meetings mentioned above. It was believed that the positive stance of the then MITI minister Hayato Ikeda on the liberalization issue had a favourable effect on this progress.

On 26 December 1959, the government announced it would apply the Automatic Approval (AA) system to imports of raw cotton and raw wool as from April 1961, thereby taking a first important step towards import liberalization. On 12 January 1960, the Cabinet adopted a basic policy towards liberalization entitled 'On the Promotion of Trade and Foreign Exchange Liberalization'. This basic policy set forth transfer of scrap iron, soya beans, and others among restricted imports payable in US dollars to the AA list, and an increase in the number of items on the AA and the Automatic Fund Allocation System (AFA) lists. (Under the AFA system, created in November 1959, import licences were as a rule granted automatically upon application.) The policy called for formulating a concrete liberalization programme by the end of May.

Many business leaders expressed misgivings about the development of the liberalization plan because it was more extensive than anticipated. Many also took the 'agreement in general, objection in particular' position—that is, they supported the idea of liberalization in principle, but wanted the liberalization in the industry to which their companies belonged to be delayed as much as possible. Also, not a small number of MITI officials were cool towards a programme of rapid liberalization. The general consensus, however, was that liberalization basically had to be accepted as a worldwide trend, but serious efforts should be made at this time to develop measures to strengthen those industries which were vulnerable to international competition. The Diet held hearings to find the views of witnesses invited from academic and industrial circles on the liberalization issue, but here again opinions were sharply divided between support for and opposition to liberalization.

On 1 March 1960, MITI's International Trade Bureau announced a report entitled 'On Trade and Foreign Exchange Liberalization', reaffirming the importance of liberalization and defining the timetable and accompanying measures of the liberalization programme. On 8 March following the Cabinet's decision of January, MITI decided on the 'Basic Guidelines for Trade and Foreign Exchange Liberalization'. On 12 March, it announced the specific import-liberalization measures.

Amidst the whirlwind of pros and cons, the government adopted the Cabinet resolution 'Outline of the Liberalization Plan for International Trade and Foreign Exchange' on 24 June 1960, a little less than a month behind schedule. This resolution, subsequently revised a few times, was highly significant as a plan that defined the basic direction of Japan's trade and foreign-exchange liberalization programme. The resolution consisted of four parts: (1) the fundamental principles of liberalization, (2) the basic direction of economic policies attendant on liberalization and measures for achieving liberalization, (3) liberalization programmes by product category, and (4) foreign exchange liberalization. Part 1 of the resolution declared that liberalization was a fundamental trend that would stimulate economic interchange among nations and contribute to worldwide economic development. The resolution maintained that the Japanese economy, having recently attained high growth with stable prices and balanced external payments, was building a solid foundation for liberalization programmes. Moreover, the report identified the benefits of liberalization as promoting the overall interests of the country through its effects on achieving economic rationality of the national economic system as well as demanding that enterprises make efforts to rationalize themselves. On the other hand, the resolution argued, the particular characteristics of the Japanese economy should be taken into due consideration in carrying out liberalization programmes, and the programme should be implemented in a flexible manner in response to changes in both internal and external circumstances.

Embodying these basic principles, Part 2 of the resolution identified the nature of the immediate liberalization measures as specifically as possible, while indicating the basic directions of the economic policies dealing with economic growth and industrial structure. Of greatest interest was Part 3—liberalization programmes by product category. Imports were divided into four categories: (1) those to be liberalized presently (within a year), (2) those to be liberalized in the near future (within two or three years), (3) those to be liberalized in due course, and (4) those whose liberalization would be difficult for a considerable length of time. The report then declared the target of raising the liberalization percentage (the percentage, by value, of 1959 imports on a customs-clearance basis, exclusive of government imports), which stood at 40 per cent in April 1960, to 80 per cent (90 per cent if coal and petroleum were liberalized) by April 1963, three years later. With regard to liberalization of foreign exchange, the resolution stated that current transactions would be liberalized in principle within two years, and capital transactions would be gradually deregulated.

21.2. Staged Liberalization of International Trade

Nevertheless, as international demands for liberalization intensified, it became increasingly difficult for Japan to adhere to its liberalization programmes spelled out in the 'Outline of the Liberalization Plan for International Trade and Foreign Exchange'. In February 1961, ten countries, including West Germany, the UK and France, announced that they would accept the obligations of IMF Article 8, leaving Japan as the only industrial country, and the only country with large foreign-exchange reserves (exceeding $1.8 billion in 1960), that still enjoyed the protection of IMF Article 14, which exempted a member from the obligations of Article 8. US demands for liberalization arising from its 'defence of the dollar' considerations also became increasingly intense.

Because a sharp increase in imports caused by high-level economic growth led to a deterioration of the balance of payments in 1961, Japan requested of the IMF in the annual consultation held in June 1961 that its advice on Japan's acceptance of the Article 8 obligations be postponed for one year. In exchange for agreeing to this request, the IMF demanded that Japan implement a liberalization programme aimed at raising the liberalization percentage to over 90 per cent by September 1962, to which Japan had no alternative but to agree. This commitment was embodied in the resolution 'Trade and Foreign Exchange Liberalization Promotion Programme' adopted by the Cabinet on 26 September 1961.

The promotion programme revised the liberalization target from '80 per cent by April 1963' pronounced in the resolution to '90 per cent by 1 October 1962'. Since the target date was moved up by half a year, the promotion programme was essentially a liberalization plan for the one-year period starting in September 1961. Partly because of the vigorous delaying campaigns mounted by affected industries, the results of the programme fell short of the target and produced only 88 per cent liberalization. Approximately 260 products remained on the 'negative list' (the list of non-liberalized imports) as of October 1962. Mining and manufacturing products on this list included coal, lead, zinc, heavy oil, mercury, soda ash, ammonium sulphate, gunpowder, colour film, large thermal electric generators, cars, automotive engines, digital computers, colour television sets, woollen fabrics, synthetic fibre yarn, and cowhide.

On 6 February 1963, the Executive Board of the IMF adopted a resolution to advise Japan to accept Article 8 obligations. On 20 February, Japan notified the GATT Council of its decision to accept the provisions of GATT Article 11, which prohibits restrictions on current transactions for balance-of-payments reasons, and declared that it would observe the procedures stipulated in GATT as to the handling of the residual import restrictions. Subsequently, by the Cabinet decision in November, Japan came under IMF Article 8 as of 1 April 1964. At this time, Japan abolished the foreign-exchange budget. Also in that month (April 1964), Japan was formally admitted to the Organization for Economic Cooperation and Development (OECD), the organization to which Japan had expressed a desire to join since 1961. Thus, Japan's transformation into a genuinely open economy became closer to reality.

Paralleling these developments, the import liberalization percentage rose from 89 per cent in April 1963 to nearly 93 per cent at the end of 1964, approaching, at the time, the West European level. At this stage, however, the non-liberalized items on the 'negative list' numbered 162 in terms of four-digit headings in the

Brussels Tariff Nomenclature (BTN), or 123 'residual import restrictions' (of which forty-five items were under MITI's jurisdiction) after thirty-nine items were subtracted which were exempted from liberalization obligations under GATT Articles 20 and 21. During the decade 1965–74, therefore, liberalization efforts were devoted to surmounting these difficult remaining problems. In October 1965, long-pending liberalization of the import of fully assembled cars was put into effect. In 1973, programmes to free imports of computers and integrated circuits were decided on. Thus, as of April 1976, only twenty-seven items, largely agricultural and fishery products, remained as cases of residual import restrictions. The import liberalization programme entered its final stage.

21.3. Driving Capital Liberalization Forward

From around 1964, when the trade liberalization issue just about passed its critical stage, Japan faced yet another serious policy issue—liberalization of international capital transactions. Although capital transactions, broadly defined, would include internal portfolio investment and overseas investments by residents, the capital liberalization issue was particularly focused on deregulation of internal direct investment by foreign investors in the form of establishing subsidiaries in Japan or acquiring stocks in existing Japanese companies with management participation. In view of the level of development of the Japanese economy in those days, many in industrial circles feared that liberalization of internal direct investment would result in foreign companies with superior financial and technological resources making inroads into Japan and dominating many industries there. As a result, vocal opposition sprang up likening capital liberalization to 'the second coming of the black ships'. On the other hand, it was understood that capital liberalization was a worldwide trend, and that Japan could not help but do its best to deregulate capital transactions—following liberalization of trade and foreign exchange, which it had strictly controlled until then—if it wanted to deepen its relationships with the international economic community. For these reasons, heated debates similar to those at the time of trade liberalization developed in business, political, administrative, academic, and journalistic circles over the pros and cons, scope, timing, methods, and countermeasures with regard to capital liberalization.

The government had already made public its policy of 'gradually relaxing control, being mindful of not adversely affecting the healthy development of the economy' with regard to capital transactions in the 'Outline of the Liberalization Plan for International Trade and Foreign Exchange', decided on by the Cabinet in June 1960. Subsequently, control of internal direct investment based on the Foreign Capital Law was gradually being relaxed. Particularly noteworthy was the fact that the policy on the liberalization of invisible current transactions and capital transactions approved in the March 1963 Cabinet meeting set forth the following: (1) the period of deferment on 'principal withdrawn' for stocks which foreign investors acquired with an approval under the Foreign Capital Law would be abolished from April, and (2) repatriation of principal and dividends for stocks which non-residents acquired using a foreign currency would be allowed without restrictions. This trend was given a decisive impetus on 28 April 1964 when Japan was admitted to the OECD, which obligated Japan to press ahead with its programme to free capital transactions.

OECD is an international economic organization established in September 1961 by twenty countries including the member nations of the Organization for European Economic Cooperation (OEEC) and its two associate members, the US and Canada. Its objectives were (1) to attain a high rate of growth, full employment, and rising living standards in the member countries, (2) to contribute to the economic expansion of developing countries, and (3) to contribute to multilateral and non-discriminatory expansion of world trade. Japan had made efforts from about the middle of 1961 to join the OECD, judging that the membership would be helpful to its efforts to gather information on trends in advanced nations and to promote better mutual understanding through exchanges of information and opinions. Japan also hoped that its membership of the OECD would give it a stronger voice in the international economic community. Whether or not Japan could be admitted to the membership, however, depended crucially on how far Japan could abide by OECD's codes of liberalization of invisible current transactions and capital transactions. Japan in those days was far behind the West European nations in these regards.

The two OECD codes of liberalization covered a total of eighty-two specific transactions or transfers, of which fifty-four were covered by the 'Code of Liberalization of Invisible Current Transactions' and twenty-eight fell under the 'Code of Liberalization of Capital Transactions'. After lengthy negotiations, an agreement was reached to allow Japan to lodge two full and seven partial reservations to the Invisible Transactions Code, and one full and seven partial reservations to the Capital Transactions Code, a total of seventeen reservations. With this agreement, Japan was admitted to the membership of the OECD in April 1964. Soon after Japan joined the organization, however, negotiations were reopened inasmuch as the 'Code of Liberalization of Capital Transactions' was thoroughly revised in July of that year. The revision essentially involved reclassifying specific transactions which members were obligated to liberalize into two categories—List A items, on which reservation rights of members were limited, and List B items, on which reservation rights were broader. On List A, Japan made full reservations to internal direct investment and overseas direct investment, and lodged partial reservations to the remaining seven items. On List B, Japan made seven full reservations and two partial reservations. The OECD Convention required an examination of all reservations maintained by a member at intervals of not more than eighteen months by its Committee for Invisible Transactions. Thus, it became an important question in Japan as to how it should deal with these examinations.

In addition to these liberalization demands by the OECD, from 1965 the US repeatedly made its own demands for liberalization of capital transactions through such channels of diplomatic negotiation as the meetings of the Joint US–Japan Committee on Trade and Economic Affairs. The primary ground for the US demands was its contention that Japan's regulation of capital movements violated Article 7 of the US–Japan Friendship, Commerce and Navigation Treaty which stipulated that 'nationals and companies of either Party shall be accorded national treatment with respect to engaging in all types of . . . business activities.' Specifically, the US expressed its strong dissatisfaction at Japan's stringent regulation of internal direct investment, and especially at the fact that Japan made it next to impossible—by limiting equity investment percentages—for foreign investors to acquire more than 50 per cent of the stocks of new or existing companies. Indeed, the record of foreign direct investment for the period 1950—when the Foreign Capital Law was enacted—to 1966 showed that 'claimable assets of loans' amounted to $3.464 billion, or 68 per cent, in contrast to acquisition of stocks (direct investment) of $935 million, or 18 per cent.[3]

MITI began a thorough study of liberalization of capital movements with a focus on internal direct investment in the middle of 1966 or thereabouts. The report entitled 'Views on the Liberalization of Capital Transactions' expressed Japan's response to demands by other countries for the liberalization of capital transactions as follows:

In liberalizing capital flows—unlike relaxing controls over goods—it is necessary to develop policy measures by carefully taking into account the fact that the financial strength of Japanese companies is still much less than that of companies in more advanced countries. However, inasmuch as liberalization is unavoidable now that Japan has rejoined the international economic community, and because it appears certain that Japan will not be able to achieve genuine development in the world economy unless its economy be made strong enough to withstand liberalization, our intention is to tackle the liberalization programme with increased vigour in the months ahead. Specially, we: (1) will make the utmost efforts to avoid excessive domination of our industries by foreign capital, and (2) will carry out liberalization programmes gradually and systematically in keeping with the progress being made in the programmes of our industries to improve and reinforce their internal structure, but (3) will from now on promote liberalization by setting target years— based on the premiss that liberalization is inevitable and on the realities of each industry— and positively moving forward to consolidate the industrial system and improve its make-up.[4]

On 23 January 1967, MITI posed the question 'How should we proceed with liberalization of capital transactions, and what should be our basic policy measures for it?' to the Coordination Committee of the Industrial Structure Council. In order to have this question studied, MITI created, within the committee, the Special Committee on Measures for Liberalization of Capital Transactions. In February of that year, MITI proposed, as a set of operating criteria for liberalizing internal direct investment, the system of dividing industrial/business activities into three groups for the purpose of evaluating applications by foreign companies for establishing new companies. In Group A, all foreign investment applications for validations of up to 100 per cent of the total shares of a new company would be approved in principle. In Group B, applications of up to 50 per cent of total shares would be approved in principle. In Group C, applications would be subject to case-by-case screening. This three-group classification was later changed to a two-way classification involving Category I (applications of up to 50 per cent approved in principle) and Category II (case-by-case screening). Work to classify industry categories continued, and in June 1967 MITI obtained the agreement of the Coordinating Committee of the Industrial Structure Council on the result of the work as well as the immediate liberalization measures.

Having heard the views of the concerned government agencies and of various associations representing industrial circles, the Foreign Capital Council in June 1967 submitted its report on measures for liberalizing internal direct investment to the Minister of Finance. The essential elements of the report were as follows: (1) Japan should autonomously tackle liberalizing capital transactions in order to promote long-term development of its economy; (2) the aim should be to put liberalization into practice in a substantial number of industries by the end of fiscal year 1971; (3) liberalization efforts to the end of fiscal year 1971 should be focused on increasing the number of industries in which applications for 50–50 joint ventures—which are based on the principle of substantive equality and co-prosperity—be automatically approved; (4) although corporate and industrial leaders should positively tackle the liberalization issue, the government—in order to induce and supplement private initiatives—should make efforts to provide an environment that makes it easier for businesses to deal with liberalization; and (5) after an appropriate span of time of one to two years, the liberalization measures should be reassessed and the scope of liberalization should be expanded.

Furthermore, the Foreign Capital Council, as immediate measures for liberalization, divided industrial/business activities—for applications involving establishment of new companies—into liberalized and non-liberalized groups, and further divided the liberalized group into Category I, in which applications for approval of acquisition up to 50 per cent of total shares of a new company would be automatically approved, and Category II, in which applications involving acquisition of up to 100 per cent of total shares would be automatically approved. The 'liberalized industrial/business activities' announced at this time are listed below with a focus on those which were under the jurisdiction of MITI.

Category I: A total of thirty-three industrial/business activities (of which twenty were under MITI jurisdiction), including pharmaceuticals, consumer electronic machinery and equipment, radio and television receivers, cameras, clocks and watches, plate glass, synthetic fibres, and others

Category II: A total of seventeen industrial/business activities (of which ten were under MITI jurisdiction), including beer, ordinary steel, forged steel, motorcycles, cement, cotton and rayon spinning, synthetic fibre spinning, pianos, shipbuilding, and others

The government, in its 6 June 1967 meeting of the Cabinet, adopted this report as a programme of liberalization of capital transactions, and put it into effect as of 1 July. Paralleling this move, MITI decided to give priority to implementing the following four measures: (1) strengthening technological development capabilities, (2) lowering interest rates and improving net worth, (3) promoting improvement of industrial structure, and (4) modernizing small and medium enterprises and distribution sectors. Although foreign governments and international organizations such as the OECD generally responded favourably to these liberalization measures, some business leaders and the press in the US and other Western nations expressed severe criticism of them, suggesting that Japan had no alternative but to launch out into yet another round of liberalization sooner or later.

Subsequently, on 10 May 1968, the Cabinet approved a programme of liberalizing technology imports and enforced it from 1 June. In this programme, (1) technological assistance agreements—with the exception of those involving the 'non-liberalized technologies' including aircraft, arms and weapons, atomic energy, computers, etc.—would be routinely approved by the Bank of Japan on behalf of the minister concerned unless the minister notified the Bank otherwise within one month of the application, and (2) all technological assistance contracts involving a fixed payment of less than $50,000 or its equivalent would be automatically validated by the Bank of Japan regardless of the nature of the technology involved.

Subsequently, over the period 1969–73, the second to fifth rounds of capital liberalization were carried out. The particulars of these rounds may be summarized as follows. In the second round of liberalization decided on in the Cabinet meeting of February 1969, 135 activities were added to Category I, twenty items were added to Category II, and nine items were moved from Category I to Category II. Further, in October of that year, the Cabinet approved the liberalization of the automobile industry (as a Category I item) and enforced it from October 1971. (At the same time, the liberalization of the importation of automotive engines, to be put into effect in October 1971, was also decided on.) Furthermore, the Cabinet approved the third round of liberalization in August 1970, the fourth round in August 1971, and the fifth round in April 1973. With the completion of the fifth round, direct investment in all Japanese industries except agriculture, forestry, fishing, mining, oil refining and sales, leather and leather products, and retailing was liberalized (except that grace periods were established for the 100 per cent liberalization of seventeen items, including integrated circuits, computers, and data processing).

21.4. Export Promotion and Overseas Economic Cooperation

Export promotion policy

As discussed in Chapter 19, the balance-of-payments ceiling worked as a major constraint on economic growth in Japan in the early 1960s. To remedy the situation, promotion of exports was considered crucial. Moreover, upgrading the commodity composition of exports was just as important as expanding the volume of exports if the high rate of growth envisaged by the National Income-Doubling Plan was to be realized. Furthermore, increased imports expected as a result of the progress in trade liberalization required ever-increasing exports. Meanwhile, the trend towards formation of regional economic blocs as epitomized by the establishment of the European Economic Community (EEC) in January 1958 and the European Free Trade Association in July 1960 made the environment for Japanese exports less hospitable. For these reasons, a variety of export promotion measures were set in motion in the 1960s as in the 1950s.

The Export Conference which was established in 1954 had been playing a central role as a forum for debating export promotion measures. In the Export Conference of fiscal year 1961, 'heightening export mindedness' was promoted as a slogan, and the importance of industrial and trading circles striving for export expansion was stressed. Paralleling the establishment of the Export Conference, there were rising sentiments in the business community for promoting export expansion as a national movement. In November 1958, the first National Conference for the promotion of Foreign Trade was held with the support of MITI, where the 'Japan Foreign Trade Charter' was adopted. A Foreign Trade Promotion Headquarters established at the conference started functioning in November 1959. This headquarters was organized jointly by the Japan Chamber of Commerce and Industry, Japan Foreign Trade Council, Inc., and Japan External Trade Organization (JETRO). Subsequently it took the initiative in mounting a mass-education drive for promoting international trade.

Thus, both official and business circles made serious efforts during the 1960s to promote exports. A few of the more important of the export promotion measures implemented during this period will be discussed below.

(a) *System for recognizing outstanding exporters*   Under this system, approved by the Cabinet in March 1964, corporations that contributed substantially to exports were recognized by the Minister of International Trade and Industry. They were selected from two categories of firms—trading houses (including suppliers) and manufacturers (including processors)—on the basis of the total number of points earned in the three criteria of export value, export ratio, and export growth rate or number of years of exporting experience.

Initially, there were no economic benefits in being selected as outstanding exporters. Subsequently, however, provisions were made under the 1968 revision of the Special Taxation Measures Law to accord special tax benefits to recognized companies.

(b) *Improvement in export financing*   Improving export financing was carried over from the 1950s as an important task for export promotion. Besides being divided into short- and medium/long-term financing, export financing was also broken down into pre-loading financing (export advance financing) and post-loading financing. A representative type of the former (pre-loading) was the Export Trade

Bill System of the Bank of Japan, and an example of the latter (post-loading) was the Foreign Exchange Fund Loan System of the Bank of Japan (revised from the Foreign Exchange Reserve Loan System in September 1961). During the period of high-level growth, the government sought to improve these systems, including export financing by the Export-Import Bank of Japan, by expanding their applicable limits and expanding covered loans. In 1962, the Plant and Equipment Rationalization Loans System for manufacturers of exports was established in the Japan Finance Corporation for Small Business. In 1964, the Consignment Sales Export Financing System was created in the Export-Import Bank of Japan. The loan approval amount of the Export-Import Bank of Japan increased sharply from 92.5 billion yen in fiscal year 1960 to 205.8 billion yen in fiscal year 1965, and further to 535.6 billion yen in fiscal year 1970.

(c) Preferential tax treatment for exports   The export income deduction system which was established in 1953 played an important role in promoting exports as it accorded preferential tax treatment to firms engaged in exporting. It was abolished, however, at the end of March 1964 inasmuch as it was considered in conflict with the revised GATT rules. In April 1964, deliberations at the Export Council produced the following new set of preferential tax treatments:

 (i) Accelerated depreciation allowances for businesses trading internationally.
 (ii) Reserve for opening up overseas markets.
(iii) Reserve for opening up overseas markets for small and medium enterprises.
(iv) Reserve for losses arising from overseas investment.
 (v) Special deduction for income arising from technological exports.
(vi) Special tax measures on entertainment expenses related to exporting.

These measures, with the exception of (v) and (vi), however, were merely treating reserves as expenses, thereby deferring tax liabilities to future periods. Their preferential effects, therefore, were indirect at best.[5] Inasmuch as major trading nations of the West in those days were making positive efforts to develop preferential tax treatment to promote export expansion, the response of Japanese trading circles to these new tax measures was not necessarily enthusiastic.[6]

(d) Improvement of the export insurance system   In 1950, the Export Insurance Law was promulgated for the purpose of 'firmly establishing a system for insuring risk which cannot be covered by ordinary insurance' for export trade and other external transactions. The law was revised several times thereafter. In November 1962, the coverage of insurance, which had until then been limited to plant exports, was expanded to coincide with the expansion of coverage of Export-Import Bank of Japan loans. With this change, it was now possible to insure deferred-payment exports of consumer durables, chemical fertilizers, and other goods, in addition to industrial plants. Insurance premium rates were successively lowered, until they fell to a level somewhat higher than one-half of the previous level.[7]

(e) Revision of Export and Import Transaction Law   In order to achieve export promotion in the long term, a proper order had to be established in the export trading
business. Arranging a proper exporting order required not only cooperation
among exporting firms but also an improvement in the entire domestic trading
system. In April 1962, the Export and Import Transaction Law was revised, and
new provisions were added setting forth tighter control of non-cartel members,
conclusion of agreements on adjustment in exporting and importing, and establishment of trading cooperatives. Under the revised Export and Import Transaction Law, new agreements were concluded on numerous products.

(f) Trading with communist-bloc countries   It is also worth noting that during this
period trading with communist countries was actively promoted, although it
had little to do with an overall export promotion policy. Against a background of
the worldwide trend of expanding East–West trade, demands for opportunities to
trade with communist-bloc countries were rising in Japan in those days. The
interest was especially strong in trade with China, which had been suspended
for more than two years since it was disrupted in May 1958 by the 'Nagasaki
Flag Incident'. (A Japanese youth hauled down the national flag of China at a
Chinese postage-stamp fair in Nagasaki.) With the proclamation of the 'Three
Principles of Trade with Japan' by Chinese Premier Zhou Enlai in August 1960,
'friendship trade' was reopened from December between China and Japanese
companies regarded by China as 'friendly firms'. In November 1962, 'LT trade'[8]
was initiated upon signing of the Japan–China Trade Memorandum (with a five-
year term) between Tatsunosuke Takasaki, chairman of a Japanese economic
mission to China, and Liao Chengzhi, chairman of China's International Trade
Committee.

Overseas economic cooperation policy

The foregoing surveyed the export promotion policy in the 1960s. This was also
the time when economic cooperation with developing countries began on a full
scale. At the December 1959 summit meeting of the US, the UK, West Germany,
and France, and at the Atlantic Economic Conference held in January 1960,
problems of developing countries were discussed, leading to a decision to create
an organization in which eight industrialized countries, including the four
listed above and the EEC Commission, were to discuss ways of cooperating among
themselves on the question of economic assistance. Based on this decision, in
March of that year the Development Assistance Group (DAG) of the OEEC
was organized, which was later renamed the Development Assistance
Committee (DAC) of the OECD. Japan participated in this organization from the
beginning.

Against the background of the rising awareness of the importance of cooperating with developing countries on an economic level, Japan found it necessary
to consolidate its own internal organization for dealing with it. Until then, the

Export and Import Bank of Japan had served as a primary organization for providing assistance loans to developing countries. In March 1961, the Overseas Economic Cooperation Fund (OECF) was established as an organization dedicated to overseas economic cooperation. In June 1962, the Overseas Technical Cooperation Agency was founded to carry out technical cooperation programmes in a comprehensive and efficient manner.

In the early 1960s, however, securing funds necessary for economic cooperation was not an easy task for Japan, which faced balance-of-payments constraints and had inadequate accumulation of capital. The pursuit of economic cooperation policy, therefore, had to meet the twin objectives of: (1) contributing to the economic development of developing countries, and (2) promoting exports of plants and machinery as well as developing sources of imports of industrial raw material and fuel resources.

In the second half of the 1960s, however, so-called North–South problems became a serious issue, and developing countries began demanding increased economic cooperation in both quantity and quality terms in such arenas as the United Nations Conference on Trade and Development (UNCTAD). This development exerted pressure on Japan to alter the nature of its cooperation programmes, which in the past had leaned towards export promotion. Also, the rising economic strength of the country, the result of years of high growth, made such a change possible. It thus became necessary for Japan to alter the nature of its economic cooperation programmes to genuinely contribute to the economic development of recipient countries. Specific tasks that became important in economic cooperation policy included attaining the goal of providing assistance equal to 1 per cent of Japan's GNP, increasing the percentage of official development assistance (ODA), carrying out more untied assistance, and catching up in the various fields where the provision of preferential duties on imports from developing countries had fallen behind.

In terms of the statistics of economic cooperation, net disbursements reached an all-time record level of $381.4 million in 1961, but remained below $300 million per year during the period 1962–4. This decline was largely attributable to the balance-of-payments constraints. As the surplus tone of the balance of payments firmed up in the second half of the 1960s, the size of aid began to increase sharply beginning around 1965. Specifically, it rose from $485.9 million in 1965 to $1,049.3 million—topping the $1 billion mark—and further to $1,824 million in 1970. The aid given in 1970 was about a 4.8-fold increase over the level in 1961, making Japan the second largest aid giver next to the US among the DAC member nations. As for the content of the aid, however, it still had high proportions of private economic cooperation, such as export credits and direct investment. Official development assistance was 25.1 per cent of the total aid value, and constituted only 0.23 per cent of GNP as against the target proportion of 0.7 per cent. This relatively low level of ODA as compared to the records of other advanced countries remained a problem to be addressed.

21.5. US–Japan Textile Negotiations

As discussed in Chapter 19, economic friction developed frequently between Japan and its trading partner as Japan's exports increased. Although in the 1950s the key problem areas were in light industry exports, once into the 1960s heavy- and chemical-industry products such as steel, TV sets, chemical products, and so forth also became objects of friction. The issue that produced the most serious friction in the 1960s and into the early 1970s was the problem of Japanese exports of woollen and chemical/synthetic textiles to the US known generally as the 'Japan–America textile dispute'.

As mentioned earlier, US–Japan friction related to textiles started with the 'one-dollar blouse' problem of 1955, which resulted in the Short-Term Arrangement Regarding International Trade in Cotton Textiles (STA) of 1961 and the Long-Term Arrangement Regarding International Trade in Cotton Textiles (LTA) of 1962. The 1960s, however, was also a period in which the focus of worldwide production and trade in textiles shifted from natural to synthetic fibres. The expansion in the production of synthetic fibres was particularly remarkable in Japan. In Japan's export of fabrics to the US, synthetic fabrics in 1969 became, for the first time, the leading product category, surpassing cotton and woollen fabrics. Paralleling this growth, Japan's exports of woollen and chemical/synthetic (rayon and acetate) goods also became large. The scope of the controversy over Japanese textile exports to the US thus expanded from cotton goods in the 1950s to encompass all types of fibres, including woollen and chemical/synthetic fibres.

In the US, a movement to have the long-term cotton agreement extended to other fibres started under the influence of the textile industry at about the time the LTA was concluded. When Richard Nixon ran as a Republican candidate in the 1968 presidential election, however, the tension between the US and Japan over the textile issue suddenly became heightened. In August of that year, Nixon, in order to obtain votes in the Southern states where textile plants were concentrated, made a campaign promise that he would, if elected, extend the LTA to cover all fibres. With Nixon's victory in November, import restrictions on textiles became a pressing issue.

In May 1969, US Secretary of Commerce Maurice Stans visited Japan to initiate the USA–Japan textile negotiations which were to last for thirty-three months until January 1972. Stans requested that Japan, South Korea, Taiwan, and Hong Kong voluntarily restrain their exports of woollen and chemical/synthetic textiles to the US, and suggested that an international conference on textiles be held in GATT. Meanwhile, in Japan, the textile industry and textile-related labour unions had been mounting a vehement anti-regulation campaign after the inauguration of President Nixon in February of that year. The Diet and government agencies spearheaded by MITI were united in supporting the anti-regulation campaign. As expected, therefore, the Japanese government rejected Stans' proposals, leading to a breakdown in negotiations. Subsequently, intense offensive and defensive battles were repeated between the US and Japan on the issue. The fundamental positions of the two countries in this dispute were as follows.

The US stressed low wages being paid in Japan and other textile-exporting countries, and argued that the sharp increases in textile imports from these countries would bring about a decline in the US textile industry and destabilize US society. For these reasons, the US advocated concluding long-term, all-round bilateral agreements on textiles. Against this position, the Japanese side repeatedly stressed the following 'four principles':[9]

1. Inasmuch as there is no economic justification for all-round regulation, restraints, if imposed, must be on specific products for which injury arising from increased imports can be demonstrated (the 'selective' principle).
2. Inasmuch as Japan is not the only exporter of woollen and man-made textiles to the US, restraints, if imposed, must encompass all the major exporting nations (the 'multiple' principle).
3. All these measures must be implemented within the GATT framework observing GATT rules (the 'GATT' principle).
4. Inasmuch as a proper solution should be achieved by invoking GATT Article 19 (emergency measures against specific imports), restraints, if imposed, must be a stopgap measure until the situation in the US becomes conducive to invoking Article 19 (the stopgap principle).

Because of the wide disparity that existed between the positions of the two countries, the series of negotiations at all meetings—the first preliminary US–Japan meeting held in November 1969, the second preliminary meeting of December of the same year, and the Washington meeting attended by MITI Minister Kiichi Miyazawa, Foreign Minister Kiichi Aichi, Secretary of Commerce Maurice Stans, and Secretary of State William Rogers—produced no satisfactory results. In March 1971, the Japanese textile industry, at the request of MITI, took a bold step of unilaterally announcing all-around voluntary export restraints. This proposal, however, was rejected by President Nixon. On 20 September of the same year, the US government notified Japan and other textile exporting countries that unless they agreed to voluntarily restrain their exports to the US, or agreed to participate in government-to-government negotiations premised on achieving such an agreement by 1 October, the US would impose unilateral import restrictions from 15 October. Prime Minister Eisaku Sato and MITI Minister Kakuei Tanaka, therefore, sought the cooperation of the textile industry towards concluding a governmental agreement, but the industry refused to honour this request. The government thereupon initialled, on 15 October, a memorandum of understanding regarding restraints of woollen and manmade textile exports to the US, without further efforts to persuade the industry.

The memorandum of understanding essentially stated that Japan would impose, using the actual record of exports to the US during fiscal year 1970 (April 1970 to March 1971) as the base period, all-around restrictions on exports of textiles except for woollen and manmade staple and monofilament; and group and case-by-case restrictions on eighteen specified items. On non-specified items, the trigger-point mechanism[10] would be used. The agreement allowed an annual increase of 5 per cent for total exports and 1 per cent for woollen textile exports.

Although there were some concessions on the part of the US as compared to the initial US demands, the content of this memorandum of understanding was essentially along the basic US position, including all-round restrictions, case-by-case restrictions on specified items, and the use of the trigger-point mechanism on non-specified items. The Japanese textile industry, therefore, objected to its formal signing, and expressed the hard-line position of being prepared to take the case to a court of administrative litigation. In response to this stance, the government decided on a policy of taking every possible step to provide relief to the industry from injury caused by restraints of exports to the US. On 4 January 1972, the US–Japan Agreement on Woollen and Man-Made Textiles, having essentially the same content as the memorandum of understanding mentioned above, was formally signed in Washington.

Thus, the entangled US–Japan textile negotiations, which produced a rumour of a 'secret understanding' between US and Japanese leaders,[11] came to a conclusion for the time being. The US subsequently concluded agreements on roughly the same lines with South Korea, Taiwan, and Hong Kong. The transformation of international trade in textile products into managed trade, however, by no means ended with these agreements. The main arena of international negotiations subsequently moved to GATT. In June 1972, a working party was created in GATT to study the textile trade issue. The GATT Council in January 1974 formally adopted the Multifibre Arrangement (MFA), in which Japan participated. MFA was an agreement which expanded the LTA to cover all major textile products.

The fact that the US–Japan textile negotiations—notwithstanding the nearly three years it took from the beginning to the signing of an agreement—were ultimately settled in the form which was close to the initial US demands reflected the relative power positions of the two countries at the time. It also suggested, however, the likelihood that more extensive and serious economic friction covering wider areas would develop between the two countries as Japan's economic strength gradually increased.

NOTES

1. *Tsusho Hakusho*, 1960 edn., General Survey Volume: 97–8.
2. Ibid. 103–4.
3. *Tsusho Sangyo Seisakushi*, viii. 376.
4. Ibid. viii. 384.
5. Takashi Shiraishi, *Sengo Nippon Tsusho Seisakushi* (International Trade and Industrial Policy of Post-War Japan), Zeimu Keiri Kyokai, 1983: 235.

6. Editorial Committee of the Thirty-Year History of the Japan Foreign Trade Council, *Nihon Boekikai 30-nenshi* (Thirty-Year History of the Japan Foreign Trade Council, Inc.), Japan Foreign Trade Council, Inc., 1980: 284–5.
7. Ibid. 284.
8. LT stands for Liao-Takasaki.
9. *Tsusho Sangyo Seisakushi*, ix. 505–6.
10. Under this system, a maximum import limit (trigger point) is established for each item. When the actual import quantity reaches this point, the exporting country automatically stops exporting and enters into negotiations with the importing country, the results of which will be used to limit or regulate further exporting. See *Tsusho Sangyo Seisakushi*, ix. 507.
11. It is rumoured that at the summit conference in Washington in Nov. 1969 between Prime Minister Sato and President Nixon there was a secret understanding between them to the effect that Japan would resolve the textile issue essentially along the line advocated by the US in return for which the US would return Okinawa to Japan 'without nuclear weapons, as on the mainland'. There has been much controversy on the veracity of this rumour, and many studies have been published on the subject. See e.g. I. M. Destler, Haruhiro Fukui, and Hideo Sato, *Nichibei Sen'i Funso—Mitsuyaku wa Atta no ka* (The US–Japanese Textile Wrangle: Was There a Secret Agreement?), Nihon Keizai Shimbun, Inc., 1980.

22

The Evolution of Industrial Structure Policy

22.1. From Industrial Rationalization Policy to Industrial Structure Policy

MITI's Enterprise Bureau released in 1957 a White Paper on Industrial Rationalization to which the Bureau had 'devoted all its energies'.[1] The report defined 'rationalization' as consisting of the rationalization of: (1) the internal management of enterprises, (2) the condition of enterprises, (3) the organization of industries, and (4) the overall industrial structure. The objective of 'rationalizing the industrial structure' was to 'remedy the backwardness of the industrial structure of the capitalist economic system of the national economy in order to meet international competitive standards.'[2] The industrial rationalization policy initiated in 1949 on the occasion of the Dodge Line began as a programme for rationalizing enterprise management. It was later extended to encompass the external conditions of enterprises (conditions of industrial location) and the organization of individual industries. In part owing to the success of this policy, Japanese industry continued its growth throughout the 1950s, with the so-called 'heavy and chemical' (chemicals, metals, and machinery) industries achieving especially remarkable growth. The percentage share of the heavy and chemical industries in total manufacturing output increased from 49.4 per cent in 1955 to 65.9 per cent in 1961. In terms of percentage figures, therefore, Japanese industry could have been regarded as having met world standards.[3] In other words, if the industrial structure of economics were measured by the commodity composition of their output, it could be concluded that the objective of 'rationalizing the industrial structure' of Japan mentioned above had been largely achieved by the beginning of the 1960s.

'Industrial structure', however, meant much more than that. It was necessary to define it as a broader concept encompassing the internal structure of enterprises and industries, as well as the external environment affecting enterprises and industries, including the financial and distribution systems, labour markets, and international trade.[4] In those terms, it was clear that the Japanese industrial structure still had many problems requiring improvement. The policy aimed at creating a desirable industrial structure, or the optimum industrial structure, was called 'industrial structure policy'. Once into the 1960s, the emphasis of Japan's public economic policy shifted gradually from industrial rationalization to industrial structure policy. More precisely, the latter came to subsume the former.

There were two principal reasons why industrial structure policy was of particular importance during this period. Trade liberalization was one. Japanese industries which had enjoyed a comfortable existence under strict government control of foreign exchange would soon face a totally new situation in an open-economy environment. In order to compete with companies in the US and other Western nations in this new environment they had to improve their international competitiveness dramatically. Moreover, 'international competitiveness' in this case transcended the competitiveness of individual products and entailed all aspects of industry. The policy direction of upgrading the industrial structure was to answer this mandate.

The second reason for the importance of industrial structure policy during this period had to do with adoption of the high-level growth policy exemplified by the National Income-Doubling Plan. The report on this plan published by the Economic Council listed 'inducing an upgrading of the industrial structure' as one of its key objectives. In other words, the report argued that upgrading the industrial structure on both the production and demand sides was considered necessary if the productivity of the entire national economy were to be raised. Specifically, it found the key to realization of the income-doubling plan in the upgrading of the industrial sector—the sector which served as the engine of economic growth—with emphasis on the heavy and chemical industries.

At the threshold of the period of high-level growth, the Japanese economy was faced with rapid structural changes in all sectors. Against this background, MITI was urged to attain two objectives simultaneously in its policy: liberalizing trade, and sustaining rapid growth. As a prerequisite for formulating such policy, it became absolutely necessary to undertake two types of work that had not been considered much in the past: (1) to systematically analyse the actual situation in industry, and (2) using the knowledge thus gained to design the desirable industrial structure.

Given this requirement, the Industrial Structure Research Committee, discussed in Chapter 20, was established in April 1961 as an organ attached to MITI. In a report dated November 1963, the Industrial Structure Research Committee listed an 'income elasticity criterion' and a 'productivity increase criterion' as the two standards for mapping out industrial structure policy, i.e. the policy for realizing the desirable industrial structure. The report concluded that on the demand side industries enjoying a high income elasticity of demand should be promoted, and that on the supply side the expansion of industries showing a rapid increase in productivity, or having a high potential of technological growth, should be promoted. The report was also noteworthy in that it pointed out the logical distinction between 'heavy and chemical industrialization' and 'upgrading of the industrial structure', which previously had been considered roughly synonymous. From the standpoint of the upgrading of the industrial structure, 'heavy and chemical industrialization' theoretically referred not to 'the heavy and chemical industries' as a whole but symbolically to that portion of such industries which met the 'income elasticity criterion' and the 'productivity increase criterion'.[5]

As discussed in Chapter 20, after functioning effectively for three years, the Industrial Structure Research Committee was dissolved and reorganized in April 1964 into the Industrial Structure Council. Through its deliberations the Industrial Structure Council subsequently contributed greatly to the evolution of industrial structure policy.

22.2. Further Efforts to Accelerate Industrial Upgrading of the Heavy and Chemical Industries

Throughout the 1960s, MITI moved to accelerate the process of upgrading the heavy and chemical industries along the lines discussed above. The following examines the efforts undertaken in the steel, machinery, electronics, and chemical industries.

The steel industry

The so-called Third Rationalization Plan that was initiated over a long period from around fiscal year 1961 was, as were the first two plans, a sum total of the in-house rationalization programmes of each company. As a result of the accomplishments in the Second Rationalization Plan, the Japanese steel industry had reached a level of maturity that no longer required extensive policy intervention by MITI. On the basis of the company rationalization plans, large-scale investments created new and powerful steel mills throughout the country, as described in Chapter 19. Gradually, then, the focus of policy introduced in the 1950s regarding the steel industry shifted from financial aid and tax incentives to the question of how to coordinate the stiff competition among the integrated steel manufacturers (Yawata Steel, Fuji Steel, Nippon Kokan, Sumitomo Metal Industries, Kawasaki Steel, Kobe Steel and others).

The first focus of coordination policy was to strengthen output coordination. The list-price system, which began in 1958 as a recession-fighting programme, continued its existence while its character was transformed into a 'boom-period list-price system' in 1959 and into a 'price-stabilizing list-price system' in 1960. In the recessions of 1962 and 1965, however, the new list-price system could no longer function effectively. In 1962–3 and again in 1965–6, therefore, a programme of curtailing crude steel output was put into effect under MITI's guidance. Also, from December 1962, recession cartels permitted by the provisions of the Anti-Monopoly Law were formed for medium-size shaped steel, alloyed structural steel, and other steel products.

Investment coordination thus constituted the second part of the coordination policy. Investment in plant and equipment was the primary factor in modernizing steel mills and increasing their size. Because the scale of investment was huge, however, intensified competition in investment often brought about a deterioration in business results. For this reason, investment coordination was put into effect from 1959 under MITI's guidance. Specific measures taken included scaling down investment plans or deferring construction by major category of productive facilities—smelting, steelmaking, and rolling. Because plant investment projects were vital undertakings which could critically affect the future of an enterprise, however, companies frequently disagreed among themselves as to the nature of coordination programmes, and MITI sometimes faced difficulties in its coordination efforts. This problem, as discussed later, became a factor in bringing the steel industry reorganization issue to the surface in the second half of the 1960s.

The machinery and electronics industries

Policy measures to promote the machinery and electronics industries were put into effect largely on the basis of the Law on Temporary Measures for Promotion of the Machinery Industry of 1956 and the Law on Temporary Measures for Promotion of the Electronics Industry of 1957. The machinery industry in Japan was dual-structured in a pyramid shape. The assembly machinery industry sector, mostly large corporations, comprised the top half of the pyramid. Those corporations were supported by a large base of small and medium enterprises supplying them with materials and parts. The goal of the Law on Temporary Measures for Promotion of the Machinery Industry was to modernize the structure of the industry by rectifying the dual structure. The main elements of the law were as follows: (1) MITI would map out basic rationalization plans and related implementation plans for specific industries designated by the MITI minister, also following advice provided by the Machine Industry Council; (2) the government would secure the funds necessary for carrying out the plans; and (3) the MITI minister could direct the carrying out of joint action among companies when such action was deemed necessary for achieving the rationalization targets in the plans.

A major feature of the law was its focus on the basic machinery sectors and parts sectors of the machinery industry, where small and medium enterprises predominated. Most of the 'machines designated' under this law shortly after its enforcement belonged to those sectors. In all, seventeen product categories were thus designated, including high-tension castings, screws, gears, metalworking machines, bearings, and automotive parts. Japan Development Bank loans were made available for industries producing specified machines.

Originally effective for five years, the Law on Temporary Measures for Promotion of the Machinery Industry was extended another five years when it was amended in 1961. As with the original legislation, the amended law (Second Law on Temporary Measures for Promotion of the Machinery Industry) emphasized the modernization of facilities. But in order to cope with trade liberalization, it was also given new dimensions, such as strengthening international competitiveness, promoting specialization in product types, establishing mass-volume production, and, in order to attain these objectives, reinforcing rationalization cartels. The Basic Rationalization Plan in the original law was renamed the Basic Plan for Industrial Promotion in the revised law, and the number of designated product categories was increased to forty. When the revised law was ready to expire in 1966, it was extended yet another five years. The newly revised law placed special emphasis on strengthening the export competitiveness of machinery industries. In it, the number of designated product categories was reduced to thirty-six, with deletion of some categories (industrial vehicles, analysis machinery, etc.) and addition of others (rolling stock, industrial sewing machines, etc.).

Thus, the Law on Temporary Measures for Promotion of the Machinery Industry functioned flexibly, with removal of categories of products for which targets were more or less met and addition of categories of products requiring support for rationalization and other promotional assistance. In this manner, the law helped the machinery industry to correct its structural deficiencies, thereby contributing much to the growth and modernization of Japanese industry in general.

The Law on Temporary Measures for Promotion of the Electronics Industry enacted in 1957 was structured much like the law for the machinery industry. Rather than five years, however, its initial time limit was seven years, because the Japanese electronics industry in those days was in a position to become a key industry for the future but lagged very much behind the US and other Western nations. In 1964, the law was extended for another seven years. Throughout the years it was in effect, the law played an important role in nurturing and improving the manufacture of 'electronic machinery and equipment, etc.' including computers. It thus played a key role in modernizing the facilities and technologies of Japanese industry in general. In 1971, when both laws expired concurrently, MITI, upon consultation with the Industrial Structure Council, decided to combine the two laws. In March of that year, the Law on Temporary Measures for the Promotion of the Specified Electronics Industries and Specified Machinery Industries was promulgated, with a time limit of seven years.

Meanwhile, support for assembly machinery industry sectors, such as automobiles, heavy electric machinery, communications equipment industries, etc., was provided by economic means such as special financing and tax reductions rather than by legal and regulatory means. The induction of foreign technology also played an extremely important role in all industries, including those covered by the Law on Temporary Measures for Promotion of the Machinery Industry and the Law on Temporary Measures for Promotion of the Electronics Industry. Concerning the automobile industry, when trade liberalization became imminent in 1961 MITI planned the '3-group concept' for consolidating car manufacturers into three producer groups. Although the concept did not become reality at the time, the idea of consolidating car manufacturers resurfaced in the controversy over the Draft Law on Temporary Measures for Promotion of the Specified Manufacturing Industries, which will be discussed below, as well as in the 1966 merger of Nissan Motor and Prince Motors. Concerning the electronics industry, and especially the computer industry, it is worth noting that in 1961 seven domestic computer makers jointly established the Japan Electronic Computer Company, a computer-leasing organization, partly as a way to compete with heavily capitalized IBM Corporation of the US.

The chemical industry

Up to this period, in order to nurture and bolster the raw-material chemical industries, with the petrochemical industry at the centre, MITI had studied and drafted a number of different kinds of industry laws, including a chemical industry promotion bill. But none had become law. Accordingly, there was no legislation that dealt directly with only the chemical industry, although there was legislation that dealt with some parts of the industry. MITI thus sought to foster development of the industry by combining a number of policy measures.

As noted earlier, a major event in the Japanese chemical industry from the second half of the 1950s into the 1960s was the successive construction of petro-chemical industrial complexes. What decisively shaped the pattern of formation of these complexes was the authority the government had to approve the import of foreign technology. Because the Japanese petrochemical industry was a latecomer, developed in post-war years by relying almost exclusively on imported technology, the securing of government approval under the provisions of the Foreign Capital Law for obtaining foreign technology licences was a prerequisite for building new facilities or expanding existing ones, and for commercializing new products. Commercialization of products using domestic technology did not fall within the purview of the Foreign Capital Law; in such cases, support measures such as the indigenous technology promotion finance system were utilized.[6]

MITI's promotion policy towards the petrochemical industry was generally limited to indirect intervention, including financial and tax incentive measures. There were, however, exceptions, such as the establishment of Japan Synthetic Rubber Co. Ltd. Although rubber was a basic material, Japan in the 1950s depended on imports for all its rubber needs. Domestic production of synthetic rubber, therefore, was imperative. Still, the minimum optimum scale (MOS) of rubber production domestically was substantial, at about 50,000 tons per year. Construction of world-class, large-scale production facilities would be likely to be followed by financial deficits lasting for many years. In June 1957, therefore, the Law on Special Measures Concerning Synthetic Rubber Production was promulgated. Japan Synthetic Rubber was established under the provisions of the law, with capital supplied by the Japan Development Bank. In 1958, this investment was taken over for the government by the Industrial Investment Special Account of the Ministry of Finance. As the business results of Japan Synthetic Rubber—which started as a 'state policy company'—improved, the government began disposing of its stockholdings in the company, turning it into a wholly privately owned firm in 1969.

Concerning the chemical fertilizer industry, meanwhile, the so-called 'two fertilizer laws' were enacted in 1954, to be in effect for ten years. When these laws expired in 1964, the Law Concerning Temporary Measures for Stabilization of Fertilizer Prices, Etc. was promulgated with the aim of promoting the development of agriculture and the chemical fertilizer industry.

22.3. Draft Law on Temporary Measures for the Promotion of Specified Manufacturing Industries and Improvement of Industrial System

Facing difficult problems related to the imminent liberalization of trade and foreign exchange, a new policy issue concerning improvement of the industrial system emerged in Japanese official and business circles. Although it was recognized that transition to a free and open economic system was unavoidable if Japan were to regain full membership in the international economic community, the liberalization of trade—which progressed much faster than initially anticipated—generated a sense of crisis among many companies and industries which admittedly lagged far behind their counterparts in the advanced industrial countries in terms of international competitiveness. The 'new industrial order' argument, in the development of which MITI assumed a leading role in the first half of the 1960s, and its statutory manifestation—the Draft Law on Temporary Measures for Promotion of Specified Manufacturing Industries—were novel concepts in industrial policy designed to achieve the task of crossing the hurdle of trade liberalization while maintaining high-level economic growth.

The National Income-Doubling Plan formally approved by the Cabinet towards the end of 1960 stressed, in its section on 'inducing an upgrading of the industrial structure'—which it defined as one of its central objectives—the necessity for 'developing a new industrial order'. This question was studied in greater detail, however, by the Industrial System Committee, established in April 1961 within the Industrial Structure Research Committee. MITI provided the May 1962 meeting of the new committee with a document entitled 'On Formation of a New Industrial Order'. This proposed, as a means of overcoming insufficient scale and excessive competition, a system of 'kyodo chosei' ('cooperative coordination') in which government and business would jointly set up targets and cooperate in efforts to realize them. A concrete embodiment of this concept was enlarging the scale of operation of companies through mergers and in other ways so that they could become internationally competitive. It was thought that MITI could not avoid becoming actively involved in this process. MITI's scheme generated a great deal of controversy. In August, MITI submitted a document entitled 'On the Cooperative Coordination System' to the Industrial System Committee of the Industrial Structure Research Committee, which subsequently approved it. In that document, 'cooperative coordination' referred to the method of having representatives of industry, finance, a third party, and the government participate, on equal footing, in discussions concerning a specific industry whose order was in need of tightening, with a view towards shaping the direction of the industry's future development. This method was suggested as an alternative to the systems of voluntary coordination by private companies or direct government control.

The Specified Industries Bill was formulated against the background of the cooperative coordination controversy. Sometime around the autumn of 1962, MITI began an internal study of the Bill, which was formally approved by the Cabinet in March 1963. After a few major changes, the essential elements of the Bill after Cabinet approval were as follows:

1. The term 'specified industries' as used in this law referred to the ferro-alloy, special steel, automobile, automotive tyre, petrochemical, and other industries whose trade associations requested designation by the Cabinet.
2. Representatives of the industry in question, representatives of financial circles, the competent minister, and the Minister of Finance shall jointly deliberate on 'promotion standards' for developing industrial standards, production specialization, appropriateness of plant and equipment investment, joint business operations, and promotion of mergers. The promotion standards were to be established by joint agreement of industry representatives and the competent minister.
3. In honouring loan requests from designated industries, banks were to attend to the spirit of this law.
4. The government was to secure the funds needed to carry out the promotion standards.
5. Special tax measures were to be provided for mergers and the establishment of joint ventures which meet the promotion standards.
6. Formation of rationalization cartels was to be permitted for limiting types of product or production methods, limiting or disposing of production capacity, and agreeing on how to procure parts, and so forth, provided they meet the promotion standards.

The Bill, submitted to the ordinary session of the 43rd Diet (December 1962 to July 1963), was tabled and withdrawn. Subsequently, it was submitted to the extraordinary session of the 44th Diet (October 1963) and to the ordinary session of the 46th Diet (December 1963 to June 1964), but was tabled again and finally abandoned without coming to a vote. Thus, MITI's hope of creating a new industrial system by means of a Specified Industries Law was not realized. As reasons why the Bill was not accepted, mention could be made of the fact that the Fair Trade Commission, related ministries—including the Ministry of Finance—and financial circles, all remained cool towards it from beginning to end, despite MITI's efforts to remove from it all traces of bureaucratic control. With few exceptions, even industrial leaders did not enthusiastically support the passage of the Bill. In the background of developments, moreover, was arguably the fact that major Japanese industries had reached a level of maturity that no longer required improvement of the industrial system by means of laws and regulations.

The failure of the Specified Industries Bill to become law, however, did not mean that the concept of government–business cooperation was not realized. From fiscal year 1963, for example, a specific amount was set aside in the Japan Development Bank loan programme for 'structural finance'. Also, from fiscal year 1964, consultative groups were established for the chemical fibre, petrochemical, and ferro-alloy industries, although these groups worked somewhat differently from the government–business cooperation scheme envisaged by the Specified Industries Bill.[7] In any event, after the bill was dropped MITI's policy of improving the industrial system was to be developed by relying primarily on administrative guidance rather than on statutory means.

Subsequently, in the second half of the 1960s, the Japanese economy faced problems related to capital liberalization, which followed on the heels of trade liberalization. It became necessary to develop 'internationally competitive enterprises and industries'.[8] Against this background, the importance of industrial reorganization, and particularly of enhancing the international competitiveness of Japanese companies through enlarged scale of enterprise and facilities, came to be stressed anew. The most noteworthy development in this trend was the many mergers of large corporations, the so-called large-scale mergers.

Large-scale mergers in industries over which MITI had jurisdiction included the revival of Mitsubishi Heavy Industries (1964) through the merger of three Mitsubishi heavy-engineering companies (Shin Mitsubishi Heavy Industries, Mitsubishi Nippon Heavy Industries, and Mitsubishi Shipbuilding & Engineering), Kobe Steel and Amagasaki Iron & Steel Manufacturing (1965), Toyobo and Kureha Spinning (1966), Nissan Motor and Prince Motors (1966), Fuji Steel and Tokai Steel (1967), Nichibo and Nippon Rayon (1969), and Yawata Steel and Fuji Steel (1970). Among these mergers, the formation in 1970 of Nippon Steel Corporation through the merger of Yawata Steel and Fuji Steel created a sensation because it was the largest post-war merger—between the first and second largest companies in Japan's foremost industry—and from the standpoint of possible conflicts between industrial reorganization and anti-monopoly policy.

The Industrial Structure Council in August 1966 released an interim report entitled 'On Promoting Reform of the Structure of Industry', in which it argued that MITI should aggressively pursue industrial reorganization by promoting mergers, joint investment, and disposal of excessive production capacity. Implementing the report's recommendations, MITI frequently provided indirect aid to proposed large-scale mergers. The provisions of the Anti-Monopoly Law, meanwhile, included restrictions on mergers, joint investment, and disposal of excessive capacity. At times, therefore, a sharp division of opinion on these practices developed between MITI which sought to promote improvement of the industrial system and improvement of the structure of industry, and the Fair Trade Commission which sought to preserve a competitive environment. This conflict said much for the difficulties MITI faced at the time in implementing industrial policy that would guide industry in general towards an open economic system.

22.4. Comprehensive Energy Policy

The 1960s witnessed a revolution in the energy field. The primary source of energy rapidly shifted from coal to oil and new energy sources, such as natural gas and nuclear power, made their debuts. A comprehensive energy policy examining various energy sources in an all-embracing manner was also formulated during this period. Although efforts had been made in the 1950s to examine fuel policy and energy policy comprehensively, they were by no means adequate. As the July 1961 report of the Study Mission of the European Energy Policy (headed by Kiyoshi Tsuchiya, member of the Coal Mining Council) pointed out,[9] the energy policy of Japan until that time had been essentially for specific energy industries, and thus basically lacked a comprehensive quality.

In September 1961, the government adopted the International Trade and Foreign Exchange Liberalization Promotion Programme, and moved up the timing for liberalization of petroleum imports—initially scheduled for April 1963 or later—to October 1962. Because liberalization of petroleum imports would not only affect the petroleum industry but would also impact greatly on other energy industries, such as coal, electric power, and gas, measures for dealing with such liberalization thus had to be developed together with overall energy policy. Given this requirement, MITI began anew the study of comprehensive energy policy by establishing, in August 1961, the Energy Consultative Group (chaired by Professor Hiromi Arisawa, president of Hosei University). Its members were experienced persons from academic circles.

The coal mining industry, which had occupied an important position among Japanese mining and manufacturing industries in the post-war period, lost markets to petroleum because of the relatively high price of coal, and was suffering from a structural depression. The December 1959 report of the Coal Mining Council announced the basic policy of rationalizing the coal mining industry, including a reduction of the price of coal for fiscal year 1963 by 1,200 yen per ton versus the price for fiscal year 1958. The price of crude oil, however, continued to fall afterwards. Liberalizing petroleum imports at this point, therefore, would have inevitably dealt an even heavier blow to the coal mining industry. Against this background, the Energy Consultative Group from the end of 1961 into 1962 successively released interim reports on coal, petroleum, and electric power.

The Petroleum Industry Law was enacted in May 1962 on the basis of the 'Interim Report on Petroleum Policy' prepared by the Energy Consultative Group. The law placed a portion of the domestic petroleum market under the influence of the government in order to secure stable and low-price supplies of petroleum. The essential elements of the law were: (1) formulating a petroleum supply plan, (2) requiring government approval for engaging in the petroleum refining industry, (3) requiring government approval for new construction or expansion of certain types of facilities, and (4) setting standard selling prices according to the need. Some members of the Energy Consultative Group, however, held the minority view that a sufficient share of the domestic market was already securely under the influence of the government and therefore no legal measures to regulate it were called for. Opinions were similarly divided in the petroleum and related industries, leading to continued debate on the pros and cons of the need for the law. When the law was enacted, both houses of the Diet passed a supplementary resolution calling for 'swift formulation of a comprehensive energy policy'. Responding to this resolution, MITI in May 1962 established the Energy Committee (chaired by Hiromi Arisawa) in the Industrial Structure Research Committee. In a report in December 1963, the Energy Committee set forth three principles—low price, stability, and independence (from the international oil majors)—for a comprehensive energy policy centred on petroleum.

Meanwhile, the predominance of petroleum and the relative decline of domestic coal in Japan's energy supply progressed rapidly. This trend was tragically symbolized by the defeat of the coal-miners' union in the dispute at the Miike Coal Mines that took place from 1959 to 1960. The Ikeda Cabinet, formed after the confrontation over revision of the US–Japan Security Treaty, established a Ministerial Meeting on Coal Measures in October 1961, chaired by the prime minister. Also announced was a set of emergency measures, including those for unemployed miners and special financing for small and medium mine-owners. In November, the Law on Extraordinary Measures for the Development of Coal Mining Areas was enacted. The report (First Report) of the Coal Mining Study Group (chaired by Hiromi Arisawa) released in October 1962 concluded that even if the reduction of the coal price by 1,200 yen per ton decided on in 1959 were to be realized, 'It is now certain that coal can no longer compete with heavy oil.' The report then enunciated a change in the direction of coal mining policy. The new policy called for securing demand for coal by such policy means as asking for cooperation from key industries and dealing with the unemployment problem and other problems of coal mining areas. In November, the Cabinet adopted the Outline of Coal Mining Measures based on the report of the Coal Mining Study Group, and announced that the government would amend or enact eleven coal-related laws, including the Law on Extraordinary Measures for the Rationalization of the Coal Mining Industry.

Subsequently, in December 1964 the Coal Mining Study Group released its second report, and in July 1966 the Coal Mining Council announced its third report. By this time, business conditions in the coal mining industry had deteriorated further, prompting the Coal Mining Council to recommend, in its third report, the 'unprecedented' measure of using public funds to shoulder the heavy financial burden of the industry. As a legal basis for this measure, the Law on Extraordinary Measures for the Reconstruction and Organization of the Coal Mining Industry was enacted in July 1967. The fourth report of the Coal Mining Council submitted in December 1968, however, said there was a limit to fiscal aid. The report said that if reconstruction of the industry were difficult even with government subsidies, the industry 'should make a courageous decision on an appropriate course of action.' It thus made clear its position that reconstruction on a self-support basis had become quite difficult.

Earlier, a report in February 1967 by the Advisory Committee for Energy—which had evolved from the Energy Committee of the Industrial Structure Research Committee mentioned earlier—concluded that although the future supply of energy would rely primarily on petroleum and nuclear power, it was still necessary to maintain production of about 50 million tons of coal annually as the most important domestic source of energy. The fourth report of the Coal Mining Council mentioned above, however, gave no figures on annual coal production. In its fifth report released in June 1972, the figure for annual coal production was drastically reduced to 20 million tons, and the decline of the coal mining industry was further accelerated. As comprehensive energy policy was formulated and developed, only the coal mining industry policy encountered numerous difficulties.

During this same period, the electric power industry expanded rapidly, responding to the sharp increase in demand for power primarily by large industrial users and residential users. Electric power development changed from the initial pattern of 'water first, fire second' to that of 'fire first, water second' by the mid-1960s, and thermoelectric power plants became larger and technologically more sophisticated. Moreover, fuels used for thermoelectric power generation changed from coal to petroleum, establishing a pattern of 'oil first, coal second'. As these changes took place, MITI abolished the Law Concerning Temporary Measures Related to Electricity and Gas (December 1952) enacted immediately after termination of the Allied Occupation, and in July 1964 enacted a new law, the Electricity Utilities Industry Law. The objectives of the new law were protection of electricity users, healthy development of electric power companies, and maintenance of electricity facilities. It differed from the preceding legislation in that the new law had provisions for large-area power interchange among electric companies.

The development of nuclear power generation got under way during this period. In May 1965 the reactor at the First Tokai Plant—the first nuclear power plant in Japan—of the Japan Atomic Power Company was brought to criticality. The plant began commercial operation in July 1966. The Atomic Energy Committee (chaired by Soichi Matsune, vice-chairman of the Japan Atomic Energy Industry Forum, Inc.) of the Advisory Committee for Energy in its first report released in February 1967 stressed the importance of early domestic manufacture of nuclear power generation equipment, securing supplies of uranium resources, and domestic development of new types of power reactors. In October 1967, the Nuclear Fuel Corporation was dissolved into a new organization, the Power Reactor and Nuclear Fuel Development Corporation. By the end of 1970, the corporation had started construction projects with total power-generating capacity of 3.74 million kW. The first report mentioned above set the targets of nuclear power development at 6 million kW for fiscal year 1975 and 30–40 million kW for fiscal year 1985. In July 1970, the target for fiscal year 1985 was raised to 60 million kW.

22.5. Policies Promoting Industrial Technology

Technological innovation played a crucial role in realizing the high-level growth of the Japanese economy. Industrial technology policy of this period helped the development of technology, particularly indigenous technology, in various ways.

In February 1961, the Agency of Industrial Science and Technology of MITI established the Committee for Promotion of Industrial Technology where study then began of the research system, research organization, research environment, and the relationships between technology administration and experimental research against the background of trade liberalization policy, the National Income-Doubling Plan, and the policy of upgrading the industrial structure. In this study, particular attention was paid to the roles played by the experimental research institutions under the jurisdiction of the Agency of Industrial Science and Technology with a view to firmly establishing an appropriate organization for the research institutions and ways to improve their research environment.

A report in November 1963 by the Industrial Technology Committee of the Industrial Structure Research Committee enunciated what had to be done in technology areas in order to strengthen international competitiveness in the environment of an open economy. It said it was necessary to transform the economy from one that relied on imported technology to one driven by domestically developed technology, a pattern that prevailed in all industrially advanced countries. The report pointed out that this transformation could most effectively be accomplished by selecting core technologies—those that would play key roles in upgrading the industrial structure and increasing international competitiveness—and giving high priority to them in technology development programmes.

Based on that report, MITI initiated in fiscal year 1964 a programme of research and development in mining and industrial technology. The programme system was aimed at improving Japan's R&D capabilities, which were markedly underdeveloped as compared to other industrially advanced nations. Of the basic research in important mining and industry technology and large-scale experimental research which would require huge research expenditures, the support programmes covered research difficult for the government to be engaged in directly. The government would bear the research expenses in order to promote efficient operation of the programmes, and would commission research and development to private sector researchers in order to fully utilize their capabilities.

In October 1965, the Industrial Technology Committee of the Industrial Structure Council released a report in which it proposed that a system of cooperative research by industry, government, and academe be created. In this system, the government would select from among epoch-making and leading-edge technologies expected to have an important impact on the development of Japanese industry those large-scale projects it felt were urgently needed for nurturing Japanese industry and strengthening its international competitiveness. The government would bear the risk involved in developing the projects. In response to this proposal, in fiscal year 1966 the system of research and development of mining and industrial technology mentioned earlier was dissolved into the system of large-scale industrial technology research and development, so-called large-scale projects.

In fiscal year 1966, three subjects were selected for these large-scale projects: (1) magnetohydrodynamic power generation, (2) super high-performance computers, and (3) desulphurization of flue gas from thermoelectric power plants. The combined budget appropriations for these projects were 1.03 billion yen. In fiscal year 1967, research on a new manufacturing process for olefin, etc., was added, and desulphurization of flue gas from thermoelectric power plants was combined with direct desulphurization of heavy oil for general research on desulphurization technology. Two subjects added in fiscal year 1969 were the desalination of sea water and utilization of by-products, and remote-control offshore deep-sea oil-drilling rigs. Total budget appropriations for these six projects in fiscal year 1970 were raised to 5.05 billion yen. This system of large-scale projects was epoch-making in that the research was conducted in comprehensive projects that were much larger, longer, and riskier than those previously supported under various other systems for promoting the development of industrial technology.

Other programmes to aid the development of technology in the private sector during this period included: (1) subsidies for R&D expenditures for important technology, (2) tax incentives for R&D and facilities required for commercializing new technology, (3) indigenous technology promotion financing (Japan Development Bank loans), and (4) mining and manufacturing technology research associations. Of these programmes, item (4) was a system created on the basis of the Research Association for Mining and Manufacturing Technology Law enacted in May 1961. That law made it possible for several companies to jointly engage in experimental research. By the end of fiscal year 1970, thirteen research associations were approved.

As a result of these technology policies of the government and the efforts made by private companies, research expenditures in Japan increased from 184 billion yen in fiscal year 1960 to 1.195 trillion yen in fiscal year 1970, or from 1.15 per cent to 1.63 per cent of GNP.[10] Consequently, the technological gap between Japan and the advanced nations in the West gradually narrowed.

In terms of patents applied for, publicly announced, or granted in Japan— involving both Japanese and foreign applicants—it is seen that technology related to the basic-oxygen furnace converter in steelmaking, the small personal video cassette recorder in electronics, and polyvinyl chloride resin and acrylonitrile in petrochemicals were judged technologically more advanced than their counterparts in the advanced Western nations. Also, microwave technology in electronic communications and plant engineering in petrochemicals were considered roughly at the same level in Japan as in the advanced Western countries. A technological disparity remained between Japan and other industrial nations in the steel, transistor, petrochemical, and synthetic fibre industries, but the gap was gradually narrowing.[11]

About Japan's patent system, laws on industrial property rights, including the Patent Law, were completely revised in 1959 after a decade of deliberations. The new Patent Law, Utility Model Law, Design Law, and Trademark Law went into effect on 1 April 1960. Afterwards, however, applications for patents and utility models continued to increase, resulting in a large backlog of pending cases. In May 1970, the Patent Law and the Utility Model Law were amended in order to improve examination procedures by adopting the examination-on-demand, early-disclosure, and pre-examination systems. The pre-examination system refers to the examination of new or revised materials related to patent applications that have been turned down but for which the applicant has requested adjudication. It is called pre-examination because it is conducted prior to the adjudication. The amended laws went into effect in January 1971.

22.6. Industrial Location Policy

MITI began tackling industrial location policy in earnest in the second half of the 1950s, in the context of high-level growth having enhanced the importance of such policy. As a result of a rapid increase in the volume of industrial production, industrial activities became concentrated in four major industrial areas, including the Keihin (Tokyo-Yokohama) area and the Hanshin (Osaka-Kobe) area. The underdevelopment of conditions of industrial locations such as industrial sites, industrial water systems, highways, and ports threatened to become serious bottlenecks to continued rapid growth. Also, regional inequality widened between the industrially advanced and backward areas, leading to demands by those in underdeveloped areas for corrective measures. The National Income-Doubling Plan developed in 1960 identified 'increasing social overhead capital' as the first of its five central objectives, stressing the importance of improving the conditions of industrial locations. The report of the Industrial Location Subcommittee submitted to the Coordination Committee of the Economic Council had envisaged the Pacific coast belt—the industrial belt along the Pacific coast containing the four major industrial areas—as forming the core of the industrial location programme of the National Income-Doubling Plan. This concept, however, was not included in the final report on the National Income-Doubling Plan submitted by the Economic Council because of objections raised by regions outside the Pacific coast belt.

Taking into due consideration the trend to attach importance to balanced development of regions, MITI in June 1961 set forth the 'Concept for Optimum Industrial Location', in which it proclaimed a new policy of eliminating regional inequality by preventing excessive concentration of industrial activities in the existing industrial zones, and attracting new industries to other regions without violating the principle of business rationality in making siting decisions. Considering the benefits of industrial concentration and its effects on regional economic development, MITI adopted the 'point development system' as a strategy for inducing companies to site industrial plants in the provinces.

As MITI expanded its regional development programme focused on industrial development, from improvement in industrial infrastructure to the expansion of industrial water supply business and then further to providing guidance on industrial location, other ministries and agencies began to develop similar schemes of their own. These schemes were coordinated and combined into a coherent whole by seven ministries and agencies under the leadership of the Economic Planning Agency, and were enacted into law in May 1962 as the New Industrial City Construction Promotion Law.

At about the same time, work to formulate the Comprehensive National Development Plan was underway, also under the leadership of the Economic Planning Agency. The plan was based on the Comprehensive National Land Development Law enacted in 1950; the law found its concrete embodiment after an elapse of over ten years following its enactment. The plan was formally adopted by the Cabinet in October 1962. With regard to industrial problems, the plan adopted the point development system which MITI had developed earlier, and aimed at the twin objectives of solving the problem of overcrowding in the existing large industrial zones and achieving balanced growth among other regions. The aim of the New Industrial City Construction Promotion Law was to nurture the development of industrial complexes—which were mushrooming at that time—from a nationwide perspective, using the point development system embodied in the Comprehensive National Development Plan.

The situation became confused, however, as every region in Japan began campaigning to seek the 'new industrial city' designation for their major cities. This was because the designation would bring benefits in the form of public project expenditures and funding by the Fiscal Investment and Loan Programme, as well as government subsidies for nurturing the development of invited enterprises. In the end, thirteen areas were selected from among the forty-four areas in thirty-nine prefectures which applied for designation, and the list was approved at a Cabinet meeting in July 1963. Of the thirteen areas, twelve were coastal industrial zones because the new industrial complexes, largely petroleum and steel, required coastal locations to facilitate the transportation of raw materials and shipment of products. Because other regions continued to lobby for designation, six more were designated as 'special regions for industrial development'. (Subsequently, to provide a legal basis for this new designation, the Law on the Promotion of the Development of Special Regions for Industrial Development was enacted in July 1964 at the initiative of the Diet.)

Although the new industrial cities attracted nationwide attention as large-scale development focal points in the Comprehensive National Development Plan, some people criticized the programme, saying that promotional measures promised for medium- and small-scale development focal points were not adequately implemented. To deal with this criticism, the Law on the Promotion of Industrial Development in Underdeveloped Regions was promulgated in November 1961 with the aim of narrowing regional inequalities through industrial development.

During the 1955–64 period, therefore, various regional development laws and policies were introduced to disperse industry throughout Japan in order to achieve balanced regional development. Despite these efforts, however, concentration of industrial activities in large urban areas and along the Pacific coast belt continued unabated, mainly because industrial siting was essentially the prerogative of private companies in a capitalist economic system. Consequently, urban and industrial pollution, which had existed from 1955 to 1964, came to be felt still more keenly in the mid-1960s.

In order to deal with the situation, MITI in December 1968 announced the Concept for Developing Industrial Areas. This was a concept for nationwide industrial location which the ministry mapped out after the passage of seven years since it announced the Concept for Optimum Industrial Location in 1961. The principles embodied in this plan were as follows. In developing industrial areas, the government would adhere to the existing focal-point development system even as it: (1) adjusted the pattern of land utilization to achieve harmony with the living environment of local residents from the standpoint of preventing pollution, and (2) promoted the dispersion of plants to outlying regions to prevent overcrowding in large urban areas. According to this plan, regional inequality would gradually be reduced by 1975 at first and further by 1985 as industrial activities became dispersed from overcrowded areas to the provinces, and balanced growth among all regions would progress.

Subsequently, in May 1969 the Cabinet approved the New Comprehensive National Development Plan. The new plan approached the problem of land development from the new perspectives of urbanization, information, and high-speed transportation. The basic objective of this new land development plan was to create an amenable environment for residents by harmonizing the four objectives of (1) permanent protection and preservation of nature, (2) improvement of the infrastructure supporting development and a balanced dispersion of developmental potential to all parts of the country, (3) reorganization and greater efficiency of land use programmes to fit the unique characteristics of each region, and (4) improvement and preservation of environmental conditions in both urban and rural areas. The new plan also suggested a new method of development while recognizing the achievements of the conventional focal-point development system. The key ingredient of the suggested development programme was creating networks for systematically linking concentrated central-control functions with the distribution system. Related to these networks, autonomous and efficient large-scale development projects making the most of the strengths of each region would be planned, through which the benefits of development would be dispersed throughout the country. This plan, formulated on the threshold of the 1970s, had to be revised drastically with eruption of the first oil crisis in October 1973.

22.7. Small and Medium Enterprise Policy

Japanese government policy towards small and medium enterprises in the 1960s centred on enactment of the Small and Medium Enterprises Basic Law of 1963. Towards the end of the 1950s, the focus of that policy gradually shifted from primarily protective individualized measures, such as traditional anti-recession measures, stabilization measures, and export-promotion measures, towards improving the low productivity and low income of small and medium enterprises, regarded as the manifestation of the so-called 'dual-structure' problem, and taking steps to modernize them. As factors that brought on this shift from a protective to a modernizing policy, it can be seen, first of all, that under conditions of rapid economic growth it became necessary to improve the technological and managerial capabilities of small and medium enterprises, which served as the manufacturing base of large corporations. Moreover, the shortage of young workers became pronounced, especially in larger urban areas, forcing a gradual change in the pattern of the competitive advantage of small and medium enterprises which had relied on surplus labour.

The National Income-Doubling Plan announced in 1960 listed as one of its key objectives the 'elimination of the dual structure'. It said that although the continuing high-level growth of the economy was likely to moderate the dual structure, that structure would not be eliminated as a natural consequence of high growth. The plan then urged introduction of a set of modernization programmes, such as moderating the extreme disparity in the size of firms, achieving the optimal scale of business operation, and modernizing production facilities.

As mentioned in Chapter 20, dual structure in this case referred to problems to do with the relative backwardness of the agriculture, forestry, and fisheries industries. And within the same industry, it referred to the relative backwardness of small and medium enterprises, and especially to the marked disparity in productivity between large enterprises and small and medium enterprises. It became an important task, therefore, from the standpoint of economic growth policy, to clarify the future prospect of agriculture and small and medium enterprises, and establish an effective policy agenda for these two sectors of the economy. With enactment of the Basic Agriculture Law in 1961, there developed a sudden surge in public demand for a similar basic law for the small and medium enterprise sector.

The move to enact a basic law for small and medium enterprises dates back to the mid-1950s. The nature of the basic law discussed at that time, however, was generally for strengthening and expanding protective measures for small and medium enterprises. In contrast, the basic law for small and medium enterprises discussed in the early 1960s had less content related to protective and social policy matters. It differed from the earlier proposal in that it moved to characterize small and medium enterprise policy as an integral part of industrial modernization policy.

At any rate, in July 1963 the Small and Medium Enterprises Basic Law was enacted and put into effect. The distinctive characteristic of this law, designed for the small and medium enterprise sector and destined to play an important role in the Japanese economy,[12] was suggested by a statement in its preamble: 'This law is established to define the new direction of the development of small and medium enterprises, and to identify the objectives of public policy towards them.' Unlike other laws which provided legislative content to individual policy measures, the Small and Medium Enterprises Basic Law was designed to define the fundamental direction of small and medium enterprise policy over the long term. The policy objectives, which were subsumed under the slogan 'Upgrading the structure of small and medium enterprise'—which meant modernizing facilities, improving technology, rationalizing business management, optimizing company size, and converting to different lines of business—were elucidated for the first time in this law, and were to take root in subsequent small and medium enterprise policy.

Along with the bill for the Small and Medium Enterprises Basic Law, ten other related bills were submitted to the 43rd session of the Diet and became law. Four representative new laws were the following:

1. Small and Medium Enterprise Modernization Promotion Law
   This law designated business categories in accordance with the Small and Medium Enterprises Basic Law with the aim of promoting their modernization.
2. Partial Revision of the Law on Financial and Other Measures for Aiding Small and Medium Enterprises
   A Fund for the Upgrading of Small and Medium Enterprises was set up, and the method of public assistance through the fund was changed from subsidies to loans. Also, the name of the new law was changed to the Law on Financial and Other Assistance for Small-Business Modernization.
3. Small and Medium Enterprise Guidance Law
   The purpose of this law was to promote the small enterprise guidance business systematically and efficiently in accordance with Article 10 (upgrading technology) and Article 11 (rationalizing business management) of the Small and Medium Enterprises Basic Law.
4. Small-Business Investment Co. Ltd. Law
   This law established the Small-Business Investment Co. Ltd. as an organization for assisting incorporated small and medium enterprises in their efforts to improve their net worth ratio.

In February 1964, a 'Report on the Trends of Small and Medium Enterprises and Government Policy Measures Taken for Them' (so-called 'White Paper on Small and Medium Enterprises in Japan') was submitted to the Diet as required by the Small and Medium Enterprises Basic Law. A similar report was to be published every year thereafter. The White Paper summarized the state of small and medium enterprises and their problems for the preceding year, measures the government introduced for them, and measures planned for the future.

The rapid growth of the economy in the second half of the 1960s brought about sustained prosperity to the small and medium enterprise sector and an increase in the size of operations for some companies. On the other hand, the business climate of small and medium enterprises was not necessarily optimistic. A shortage of labour developed, the emergence of technology-intensive industries transformed the industrial structure, and pollution problems worsened. In international trade, meanwhile, developing nations such as South Korea, Taiwan, and Hong Kong caught up with Japan, bringing heavy pressure to bear on small and medium enterprises in textile-related industries. Against this background, it became necessary to explore a new direction for small and medium enterprise policy in order to formulate policies for eliminating the dual structure as required by the Small and Medium Enterprises Basic Law, as well as for responding effectively to the pressing problems faced by small and medium enterprises. This new direction was concretized under the designation of 'small and medium enterprise structural improvement', and came to characterize small and medium enterprise policy in the second half of the 1960s.

'Structural improvement' measures made their debut in the area of small and medium enterprise policy in the form of a special tax measure called a 'Reserve for Structural Improvement of Small and Medium Enterprises' introduced in fiscal year 1964 by revising the Law on Financial and Other Assistance for Small Business Modernization mentioned above. The concept embodied in structural improvement policy was to go beyond the limitation of modernization efforts by individual enterprises and to improve the structure of entire industries through cooperation from enterprises in each industry. This concept gradually developed into the idea of establishing an organization devoted to that purpose. With establishment in August 1967 of the Small Business Promotion Corporation, the upgrading of the industrial structure of the small and medium enterprise sector came to be systematically pursued with a focus on cooperative and joint business operation.

Revision of the Small and Medium Enterprise Modernization Promotion Law in May 1969 opened the way for designating the business categories which especially required structural improvement as 'designated business categories', and assisting their structural improvement efforts with special financial and taxation measures.

Thus, the 'dual-structure nature' of the small and medium enterprise sector gradually changed, and the sector came to be appreciated for the vital role it played in Japanese industry.

NOTES

1. MITI, *Tsusho Sangyo-sho Nenpo* (MITI Annual Report), 1957: 100.
2. MITI, *Sangyo Gorika Hakusho* (White Paper on Industrial Rationalization), Nikkan Kogyo Shimbunsha, 1957: 4.

3. *Nihon no Sangyo Kozo*, i. 15. According to this source, the 'heavy and chemical' industrialization percentages in 1961 were 74.6% in France, 63.8% in West Germany, 62.5% in the US, and 60.8% in Italy.
4. Ibid. 1.
5. Ibid. 34.
6. *Tsusho Sangyo Seisakushi*, x. 338.
7. Ibid. x. 84–5.
8. Japan Economic Research Institute, *Nippon no Sangyo Saihensei* (Industrial Restructuring in Japan), Shiseido, 1967: 20.
9. *Tsusho Sangyo Seisakushi*, x. 425.
10. Ibid. x. 497.
11. Patent Office, *Asu wo Hiraku Tokkyo—Gijutsu no Yakushin no Tame ni* (Patents Open Doors to Tomorrow: For Rapid Advance in Technology), Research International Trade and Industry, 1968: 22–66.
12. The relative importance of small and medium enterprises in nonprimary industries was 99.6% in terms of the number of business establishments, 78.7% in terms of number of employees, and 48.9% in terms of manufacturing shipments. Small and Medium Enterprise Agency, *Chusho Kigyo Hakusho* (White Paper on Small and Medium Enterprises), 1966, Fuzoku Tokeihyo (Attached Statistical Tables), Printing Bureau, MoF.

23

The Fruits of Rapid Growth and the Response to Diversified Policy Issues

23.1. Diversified Policy Issues

Expansion of areas that cannot be left to workings of market mechanism, and the necessity for government intervention

As discussed in the foregoing, in the 1960s the Japanese economy realized an overall unprecedented rate of high-level growth while experiencing occasional recessions. During this period, MITI worked with the industries under its jurisdiction employing a combination of legal, administrative, and/or economic (financial or fiscal) policy measures in an effort to contribute to their development. As a consequence, Japanese industry developed both qualitatively and quantitatively, and a large number of global-scale enterprises emerged. Meanwhile, Japan's total exports, which stood at less than $500 million in 1949 when MITI was established, approached $20 billion in 1970. In May 1971, the Coordination Committee of the Industrial Structure Council filed an interim report entitled 'What Should Be the Basic Direction of International Trade and Industry Policy in the 1970s?' In its opening sentences, the report stated that 'In twenty-odd years, Japanese have created a "Super-GNP nation", which they themselves find hard to believe, out of the scorched land filled with hunger, like Japan was during the Tenmei Famine and the Onin War.' (Several hundred thousand people died during the Tenmei Famine of 1782–87; Kyoto was devastated during the Onin War of 1467–77.) The report concluded with a sense of pride that 'Japan's industry and industrial policy have contributed to this success in a very stormy age, a period of a great leap forward for the entire nation.'[1] The report then suggested that the guiding principle of economic management in the new era—that is, the 1970s—should be transformed from one of 'pursuing growth' to one of 'energetically utilizing the benefits of growth'.

In managing the economy while utilizing the benefits of growth, industrial policy was to be based on maximum use of the market mechanism. The report described this point as follows:

In the areas in which we can expect the market mechanism to produce optimum allocation of resources, efficient use of resources, and technological innovation, we should respect the autonomy of private companies and depend on their display of creativity and vitality through competition. Excessive government intervention and overprotection of industries merely as a continuation of past practices should be avoided at all cost, and necessary steps should be taken to ensure a smoother functioning of the market mechanism.[2]

While denouncing 'excessive government intervention and overprotection of industries merely as a continuation of past practices' in the industrial policy of the new decade of the 1970s, the report also recognized that many new areas were emerging in which markets could not produce the desired effects because the industrial environment had changed considerably and achievements expected of industries had become quite diversified. Specifically, the market mechanism could not be relied on in (1) areas in which non-economic—that is, social—outcomes were expected, such as overcrowding, environmental disruption, safety, and quality of working life; and (2) areas in which positive outcomes in international relations were expected, such as avoidance of trade friction and cooperation with the international economic community.[3]

The report then suggested that in these areas it was necessary for the government to expand its active roles in improving, supplementing, or substituting for the market mechanism.

The report further pointed out that problems were increasing in the 1970s that made it difficult to expect a solution to the dichotomy of whether to have free enterprise that relies on the market mechanism or to have government intervention. It placed these problems in what it called 'the grey zone'—and maintained that continued emergence of problems in this zone and the failure to solve them were responsible for the mutual distrust and friction between producers and consumers, local residents, and others. The report then concluded that 'it is necessary to create an optimum mix of private and public initiatives by making the best use of their relative strengths, and to effectively address the grey zone problem.'[4]

As seen above, the report of the Industrial Structure Council prepared at the outset of the 1970s took the view that government intervention in the market was necessary in some areas and in some circumstances, while basically stressing the importance of maximally utilizing the market mechanism. The following is an examination of MITI's industrial pollution policy and its policy towards consumers and the distribution system as illustrations of cases where such intervention was necessary.

Industrial pollution countermeasures

The problem of 'industrial pollution' became a social issue in Japan in the second half of the 1950s and early 1960s when companies increased their production activities and coastal industrial zones were created and developed in many parts of the country. Here, 'pollution' means a large unspecified number of residents in a given locality suffering damage in terms of life, health, or quality of living.[5] Smog began to appear in Tokyo from around 1955, for instance, and air pollution became a serious problem in the industrial zones in Kawasaki, Chiba, and other cities. In May 1956, the director of a hospital affiliated to the Minamata Plant of Shin Nippon Chisso Hiryo Corporation (later, Chisso Corporation) reported to the local health centre the hospitalization of a patient with a strange disease of the central nervous system of unknown cause. This disease came to be known as Minamata disease. Subsequently, in June 1958, fishermen in Urayasu in Chiba Prefecture staged a sit-down demonstration in front of the Edogawa Plant of Honshu Paper Co. complaining about the damage being done to fishing in the area by plant effluents. With this case as a starting point, in December 1958 Japan's first pollution countermeasures laws—the Law Concerning the Preservation of Public-Use Water Quality and the Law Concerning Regulations on Industrial Waste Water, Etc.—(the so-called 'two water-quality laws') were promulgated.

The pollution problem, however, did not shake Japan's politics and administration to any significant extent until the second half of the 1950s. Even in the National Income-Doubling Plan of 1960, the pollution problem was merely mentioned briefly in the section on 'Improvement of Housing and Living Environment' in 'Part 2: Government and Public Sector Planning'.

Once into the first half of the 1960s, however, the worsening state of the pollution problem became evident to everyone, giving rise to demands for full-scale pollution countermeasures. Once into the second half of the 1960s, major incidents of industrial pollution—the Yokkaichi air pollution (asthma) case in Yokkaiichi in Mie Prefecture, the Minamata disease in Kumamoto Prefecture, the mercury poisoning case along the Agano River in Niigata Prefecture, and 'itai-itai' disease along the Jintsu River in Toyama Prefecture—broke out in succession, creating serious social and political issues. In all four of the above-mentioned cases, the victims sued for damages, and all cases were decided in favour of the plaintiffs. These four important pollution-related court cases provided the momentum for informing the entire nation of the seriousness of the pollution problem, and made political, administrative, and industrial circles aware of the respective responsibility of all the parties involved in pollution, as well as the importance of taking effective countermeasures.

Regarding air pollution, starting from around the summer of 1961 the Ministry of Health and Welfare formulated the Air Pollution Control Bill, and MITI developed the Bill for the Control of Factory Smoke. The two bills were subsequently combined into one, and in June 1962 the Law Concerning the Control of Emissions of Soot and Smoke was enacted. But MITI's pollution countermeasures up to that time had been less than adequate. In April 1963, the Industrial Pollution Division was established in its Enterprises Bureau, providing MITI for the first time with an organization specializing in the administration of industrial pollution matters. Subsequently, in June 1965, the Law Concerning an Environmental Pollution Control Service Corporation was enacted. In October 1965 the Environmental Pollution Control Service Corporation was established with the aim of preventing industrial pollution in areas where industrial plants and business offices were concentrated. Furthermore, the experience of applying pollution countermeasures in the industrial zones of Yokkaichi, Kawasaki, and elsewhere revealed that preventing pollution was not an easy task once plants were constructed and operating. This realization led from 1965 to the comprehensive investigation beforehand of industrial pollution in the new industrial areas created in new industrial cities and the special regions for industrial development mentioned above.

In the second half of the 1960s, the problems of air, water, and noise pollution became more serious. In October 1966, the Industrial Pollution Committee of the Industrial Structure Council filed an interim report entitled 'On the Desired Status of Industrial Pollution Countermeasures'. It studied pollution problems and made recommendations from a new perspective, discussing the concept of pollution, areas of responsibility in pollution, the question of who bears the cost of fighting pollution, environmental quality standards, industrial siting regulations, improving the administrative system, and providing relief to pollution victims. At about the same time, the ministries and agencies concerned set forth their own pollution countermeasures. In August 1967, the Basic Law for Environmental Pollution Control that reflected these measures passed the Diet and went into effect.

The objective of this law was to 'promote comprehensive pollution countermeasures, thereby protecting the health of the people and preserving their living environment.' Article 1 of the law stated that 'in preserving the living environment, efforts shall be made to maintain harmony with the wholesome development of the national economy.' This was a basic law with a clear significance, and specific measures were expected to be carried out separately in keeping with the law's intent. The law limited its application to six representative types of pollution, including air, water, and noise pollution, vibration hazards, land subsidence, and offensive odours.

Subsequent legislation expanded the list of anti-pollution laws with enactment of the Air Pollution Control Law and the Noise Control Law in 1968, the Law 01 Concerning Special Measures for Compensation for Health Problems relating to Environmental Pollution in 1969, and the Law for Settling Environmental Pollution Disputes in 1970. Meanwhile, however, the types of pollution became even more diverse and complex, raising serious social issues. Successive outbreaks of new types of pollution included photochemical smog, lead poisoning caused by automotive emission, cadmium poisoning, harmful industrial wastes, and noise pollution generated by aircraft and high-speed (Shinkansen) trains. Thus, in the extraordinary session of the 64th Diet held in November and December of 1970, fourteen bills relating to pollution and environmental matters, including a bill to amend the Basic Law for Environmental Pollution Control, were submitted to the Diet. The Diet enacted all of these bills into law, and thus came to be known as the 'anti-pollution Diet'.

The essential elements of the December 1970 amendment to the Basic Law for Environmental Pollution Control were as follows: (1) in the statement of the objectives of the law in Article 1, the phrase 'harmony with the wholesome development of the national economy' was deleted, elucidating the philosophy that there was no growth without welfare; (2) in the definition of pollution in Article 2, 'soil pollution' was added; and (3) the responsibility of private enterprises in industrial waste management was clarified. Additionally, in the same month, a sweeping set of legislative measures resulted in enactment of the Law Concerning Punishment of Environmental Pollution Crimes relating to Human Health, the Law concerning Allocation of the Burden of Anti-Pollution Expenses, the Water Pollution Control Law, the Waste Disposal and Public Cleaning Law, and others.

This 'anti-pollution Diet' was in session towards the end of 1970—the final year of the National Income-Doubling Plan—and it enacted a large number of anti-pollution laws. This development revealed the dark side of Japan's economic 'miracle'. Pollution and environmental problems were to become extremely serious issues for MITI policy in the 1970s.

Consumer and distribution policies

Consumer policy was another area which rapidly became important in the 1960s. The economy grew much faster than expected, and sharp rises in prices, particularly consumer prices, became serious social and political problems. In fact, the problem of rising prices constituted one of the factors that caused frequent revisions of the National Income-Doubling Plan prior to its final target of fiscal year 1970.

Furthermore, with the progress of mass production, mass sales, and mass consumption, new consumer problems—quite different in nature from the traditional problem of 'getting rid of inferior articles'—arose one after another. Starting from around 1960, in response to this development, consumer organizations and labour unions became increasingly vocal in campaigns opposing increased prices, particularly proposed increases in public utilities charges. Opposition and protest movements also intensified against pollution, drug hazards, misleading labelling, and unfair sales methods (e.g. door-to-door sales).

Against these moves, the government in September 1960 took steps to control prices by approving 'On Measures for Stabilizing Consumer Prices' at a Cabinet meeting, and establishing a Consumer Price Policy Coordination Council within the Economic Planning Agency. Subsequently, the Cabinet frequently approved proposed changes in public utilities charges. Towards the end of 1965, the Ad-Hoc Ministerial Council for Price Stabilization Measures was established, followed in February 1967 by establishment of the Price Stabilization Promotion Council as an advisory council reporting to the prime minister. These price measures thus approved at the Cabinet level were implemented primarily by the Economic Planning Agency. MITI, too, implemented several price measures, including the improvement of competitive conditions in industries under its jurisdiction, checking increases in electric and gas rates, and modernizing the distribution system, which will be discussed below.

Meanwhile, consumer protection policy made great strides during this period. First, in July 1961, the Instalment Sales Law was enacted. With respect to 'instalment sales',[6] a system which spread rapidly from the second half of the 1950s, this law was aimed at protecting consumers who entered into instalment agreements. For sellers, the law provided for protection against the risk of bad debts. On the one hand, instalment sales were highly significant in that they enabled consumers to satisfy their desire to raise consumption standards. On the other hand, however, they gave rise to frequent problems concerning down payments, instalment periods, and the right of consumers to cancel sales agreements. Although the law had an aspect of consumer protection policy, it also had a dimension of helping traders and distributors. MITI, however, emphasized the consumer protection aspect of the Instalment Sales Law.[7] The Japan Consumers' Association, established in 1961 as an organization under MITI's jurisdiction, published the results of product tests it conducted, and engaged in activities to help consumers make the right decision in choosing products to buy. In November 1961, the Electrical Appliance and Material Control Law was enacted 'with the aim of preventing danger and injury caused by electrical appliances of inferior quality', followed in May 1962 by promulgation of the Household Goods Quality Labelling Law 'aimed at improving the quality of labelling of household goods and protecting the interest of the consuming public.'

After the establishment in April 1964 of the Consumer Economy Division in the Enterprises Bureau as a division having exclusive jurisdiction over consumer policy, MITI's consumer policy was promoted with increasing vigour. As consumer policy was bolstered in other ministries and agencies as well, and consumer protection policy was expanded in other countries, numerous demands were raised for the legislation of a 'basic consumer law' which would articulate the basic principle of consumer protection in Japan. As a consequence, the Basic Law for Consumer Protection was enacted at the initiative of the Diet, and promulgated and put into effect in May 1968.

Because of its very nature, the Basic Law for Consumer Protection was primarily directive. It established the respective responsibilities of the State, local governments, and private companies in protecting the interest of consumers, while urging consumers to 'behave independently and rationally'. It also had provisions that enabled necessary legislation and fiscal measures. Also, at about the time the Basic Law was enacted, a number of consumer-related laws were enacted or amended. Those relating to MITI included the enactment in December 1967 of the Law Concerning the Securing of Safety and the Optimization of Transactions of Liquefied Petroleum Gas, and the amendment, in May 1968, of the Electrical Appliance and Material Control Law and the Instalment Sales Law. With the wider diffusion and increased consumption of liquefied petroleum gas (LPG), the number of accidents involving consumers had risen. The Law concerning the Securing of Safety and the Optimization of Transactions of Liquefied Petroleum Gas was aimed at preventing accidents by regulating the sale of LPG and making certain that LPG transactions were conducted fairly.

Another characteristic of this period was the increasingly conspicuous lag in the development of the distribution sector as compared to that of the production sector, as a result of the high-level growth of the economy. Because the complexity and low efficiency of the distribution system were believed to be causes of rising consumer prices, distribution policy centred on modernizing the distribution system came to be regarded as an extremely important policy objective not only for the benefit of business enterprises but also in the interest of consumers as well. Concrete measures proposed for modernizing the distribution system included promoting the system of voluntary chains of retailers, systematically locating distribution centres, systematizing distribution, and ensuring the 'fairness' of business transactions. Voluntary chains were formed by independent retailers joining together to enjoy the economies of scale in planned cooperative buying, advertising, management guidance, and product development.[8] The voluntary chain system emerged in Japan around the mid-1950s, but had developed unevenly.

As was touched on in Chapter 19, supermarkets showed a remarkable pattern of growth in Japan. Although their growth was desirable from the standpoint of consumers, retailers saw in that growth a serious threat because supermarkets were not regulated under the Department Store Law. Accordingly, MITI treated it as a 'quasi department-store problem' from around 1968, and studied how to handle the matter. This study resulted in enactment of the Law Concerning the Adjustment of Retail Business in Large-scale Retail Stores, as discussed in Chapter 19.

23.2. Benefits of High-Level Growth and 'Growth-Utilizing' Economic Management

Level of economic development in 1970

In December 1960, the Cabinet formally approved the National Income-Doubling Plan and designated fiscal year 1970 as its target year. During the 1960s, the Japanese economy grew at a very high rate that exceeded the ambitious target of the Income-Doubling Plan. By a curious coincidence, the period of double-digit growth ended in fiscal year 1970, the target year of the plan. The following examines the level of development of the Japanese economy in 1970 compared with that in 1960 (Table 23.1).

Gross national product in 1970 (calendar year, unless otherwise noted) in nominal terms reached 73,188.4 billion yen, or 4.6 times that of 1960. During the decade, however, wholesale prices rose by 14 per cent and consumer prices increased by 74 per cent. Accordingly, the increase in real GNP during the ten-year period was 2.6-fold, more than double in 1970 what it was in 1960. Meanwhile, industrial production increased 3.6-fold, exports rose 4.8-fold, and imports increased 4.2-fold. The change in the industrial structure during the decade is expressed in statistics on national income by sector of origin. In fiscal year 1960,

Table 23.1 Main economic indicators, 1960 and 1970

	Unit	1960 (A)	1970 (B)	B/A	Source/Remarks
Population	10,000 persons	9,342	10,467	1.12	Management and Coordination Agency, *Kokusei Chosa* (Population Census)
Labour force	10,000 persons	4,511	5,153	1.14	Management and Coordination Agency, *Rodoryoku Chosa* (Labour Force Survey)
Gross national product (calendar year)	100 m. yen	159,980	731,884	4.57	Economic Planning Agency, *Kokumin Keizai Keisan Hokoku* (Report on National Accounts)
Real GNP (calendar year)	100 m. yen (1985 = 100)	654,454	1,712,926	2.63	ditto
Gross national product (fiscal year)	100 m. yen	166,620	751,520	4.51	ditto
Real GNP (fiscal year)	100 m. yen (1985 = 100)	667,688	1,730,287	2.59	ditto
Industrial production index	1985 = 100	15.8	56.4	3.57	MITI, *Kokogyo Shisu Soran* (Long-Term Data Book of Standard Indices of Industrial Production)
Wholesale price index, all commodities	1985 = 100. Linked index numbers	42.8	48.6	1.14	Bank of Japan, *Bukka Shisu Nenpo* (Price Index Annual)
Consumer price index, all Japan	1985 = 100. Linked index numbers	21.2	36.9	1.74	Management and Coordination. Agency, *Shohisha Bukka Shisu*

Table 23.1 *Continued*

	Unit	1960 (A)	1970 (B)	B/A	Source/Remarks
					Nempo (Annual Report on the Consumer Price Index)
Value of exports (customs clearance basis)	$1 m.	4.055	19.318	4.76	Ministry of Finance, *Gaikoku Boeki Gaikyo* (Summary Report on Trade of Japan)
Value of imports (customs clearance basis)	$1 m.	4.491	18.881	4.20	Ministry of Finance, *Gaikoku Boeki Gaikyo* (Summary Report on Trade of Japan)
National income by sector of origin (fiscal year)	100 m. yen				Economic Planning Agency, *Kokumin Keizai Keisan Hokoku* (Report on National Accounts) (exclusive of net income from abroad)
Primary industries		18,014 (15.2%)	44.515 (7.5%)		
Secondary industries		45,237 (38.0%)	224.416 (38.0%)		
Tertiary industries		56,336 (47.3%)	323.046 (54.7%)		
Value added by industry	1 bn. yen	4,837 (100.0%)	24.572 (100.0%)		MITI, *Kogyo Tokeihyo* (Census of Manufactures)
Heavy industries		2,903 (60.0%)	15.248 (62.1%)		
Light industries		1,934 (40.0%)	9,324 (37.9%)		
No. of business establishments by scale (non-primary industries)		3,561,695	(1969) 4,649,880	1.31	Management and Coordination Agency, *Jigyosho Tokei Chosa* (Establishment Census)
Large establishments		36,168	32,299	0.89	
Small and medium establishments		3,525,527	4,617,581	1.31	

the shares of the primary, secondary, and tertiary industries in national income were 15.2 per cent, 38.0 per cent, and 47.3 per cent, respectively. In fiscal year 1970, comparable figures were 7.5 per cent, 38.0 per cent, and 54.7 per cent, respectively. The relative decline of the primary industries and the expansion of the tertiary industries are worthy of note. During the decade, the percentage share of the heavy and chemical industries (minerals, chemicals, and machines) in total value added in manufacturing increased slightly, from 60.0 per cent to 62.1 per cent. The number of business establishments in non-primary industries increased by about 30 per cent, from 3.56 million in 1960 to 4.65 million in 1969. This increase was attributed to the increased number of small and medium establishments.

Table 23.2 shows changes in the volume of production of major commodities. Increases in production during the decade were 4.2-fold for crude steel, 3.2-fold for metal processing machines, 19.3-fold for cars, 6.5-fold for synthetic fabrics, 6.3-fold for fuel oil, and 3.1-fold for electric power generation. By contrast, the production indexes fell to 78 for coal and 81 for cotton fabrics (base year = 1960), revealing a changing pattern of industry.

What kind of changes did these rising levels produce in the relative international position of the Japanese economy? First, Japan's nominal GNP of $42.5 billion in 1960, which placed Japan fifth among the capitalist nations, increased

Table 23.2 Production of principal commodities, 1960 and 1970

	Unit	1960(A)	1970(B)	B/A
Pig-iron	1,000 tons	11,896	68,048	5.72
Crude steel	1,000 tons	22,138	93,322	4.22
Passenger cars	units	165,094	3,178,708	19.25
Electric washing machines	1,000 units	1,529	4,349	2.84
Electric refrigerators	1,000 units	904	2,631	2.91
Television receivers (black and white)	1,000 units	3,578	6,089	1.70
Television receivers (colour)	1,000 units	—	6,399	—
Metal-processing machines	units	80,143	256,694	3.20
Cotton fabrics	1 m. sq. m.	3,222	2,616	0.81
Woollen fabrics	1 m. sq. m.	316	426	1.35
Synthetic fabrics	1 m. sq. m.	424	2,746	6.48
Western-style paper	1,000 tons	2,868	7,135	2.49
Cement	1,000 tons	22,537	57,189	2.54
Fuel oil	1,000 kl.	28,303	178,651	6.31
Coal	1,000 tons	51,067	39,694	0.78
Electric power	1 m. kWh.	115,497	359,539	3.11

Source: Compiled from *Tsusho Sangyo Seisakushi* (History of International Trade and Industry Policy), xvi.

to $197.2 billion in 1970, raising Japan's level to second in the world next to the United Sates (Table 23.3). This change was concomitant with the fact that the annual rate of increase in Japan's real GNP during the 1960s was much higher than those of other countries. Japan, however, was still far behind the United States, the world leader. During the same period, Japan's per capita national income rose from $378 to $1,515. Japan's per capita national income in 1970 was only 35 per cent of the US level of $4,352, highest in the world, and Japan ranked only nineteenth among the capitalist nations.[9] Meanwhile, in terms of the value of exports, Japan's relative position rose from sixth in 1960 to fourth in 1970, following the US, West Germany, and the UK. As for the volume of production of principal commodities, Japanese levels rose from fourth among the capitalist nations in 1960 to second in 1970 in terms of crude steel production, from seventh to third in car production, and from fourth to second in electric power generation. In 1968, Japan's GNP exceeded that of West Germany. After this, the country's economy would be the second largest in the world.

Industrial Structure Council Interim Report: 'Vision of MITI Policies in the 1970s'

As mentioned earlier, in February 1972 the US Commerce Department published a document entitled 'Japan: The Government–Business Relationship—A Guide for the American Businessman'.[10] This document attributed the remarkable economic growth of post-war Japan in part to the unique relationship between government and business in Japan, and analysed the actual situation. Having used the term 'Japan, Inc.' to describe the close working relationship between the Japanese government and the business community, the document moved to clarify the characteristics of the relationship by conducting case studies of the Japanese computer, automobile, and steel industries. Arguments similar to those contained in this document had appeared earlier in the British magazine *The Economist* as well as the American magazine *Time*. The US Commerce Department document is worthy of note because it was an 'official' characterization of the Japanese system as a corporation.

In its introduction section, the Commerce Department document stated the following:

In recent years, the American business community has come to view Japan with decidedly mixed feelings compounded of admiration and growing uneasiness. The admiration stems from the manner in which Japan has recovered from the setbacks caused by World War II, and has emerged as one of the world's foremost economies. The uneasiness stems not just from the impact which Japanese economic growth has had on the American economy, but from the feeling that Japan may be playing the economic game under a different set of rules than obtain in this country.[11]

The document then found the key to the analysis of this 'different set of rules' in the 'interaction' between government and business, and described the Japanese economic system as being run by a consensus which is formed through

Table 23.3   International comparison of economic levels

(1) Gross national product (nominal)
($100 m.)

	1960	1970
Japan	425	1,972
USA	5,037	9,771
UK	718	1,221
W. Germany	742	1,874
France	600	1,457
Italy	337	932
Canada	336	818

Source: *IMF Monthly Report.*

(2) Annual rate of real economic
growth (%)

	1950–60	1960–70
Japan	9.1	11.3
USA	3.2	4.2
UK	2.8	2.7
W. Germany	7.9	4.7
France	4.5	5.6
Italy	5.6	5.7

Source: OECD.

(3) Value of exports (FOB) ($1 m.)

	1960	1970
Japan	4,055	19,318
USA	20,526	43,224
UK	10,352	19,352
W. Germany	11,418	34,188
France	6,864	17,935
Italy	3,650	13,186
Canada	5,826	16,863

Source: Economic Planning Agency, *Sekai Keizai Hakusho* (White Paper on the World Economy).

(4) Production of crude steel
(1,000 tons)

	1960	1970
Japan	22,138	93,322
USA	90,067	119,308
UK	24,695	28,316
W. Germany	34,100	45,041
France	17,281	23,774
Italy	8,229	17,277
Canada	5,252	11,200

Source: *Kokuren Tokei Nenkan* (United Nations, Statistical Yearbook).

(5) Production of cars (1,000 units)

	1960	1970
Japan	165	3,179
USA	6,674	6,552
UK	1,352	1,640
W. Germany	1,674	3,528
France	1,184	2,458
Italy	596	1,720
Canada	326	937

Source: *Kokuren Tokei Nenkan* (United Nations, Statistical Yearbook).

(6) Electric power generation
(including private generation)
(1 m. kWh)

	1960	1970
Japan	115,497	359,539
USA	840,946	1,638,010
UK	136,666	248,588
W. Germany	116,418	237,209
France	72,118	140,708
Italy	56,240	117,423
Canada	114,000	203,702

Source: *Kokuren Tokei Nenkan* (United Nations, Statistical Yearbook).

'energetic consultations' between official and business circles and through a complex organization of interaction, such as deliberation councils. 'The government' here, of course, did not refer to MITI alone, but it was apparent that the primary object of the analysis contained in the document was MITI policy, and particularly its policy in the 1960s.

As stated at the beginning of this chapter, in May 1971 the Industrial Structure Council published an interim report entitled 'What Should Be the Basic Direction of International Trade and Industry Policy in the 1970s?' If the report of the US Commerce Department looked at Japan's economic growth with 'admiration and uneasiness', then this Industrial Structure Council report could be said to have looked back at the same growth record with 'pride and self-reflection'. Here, there no longer was the fervent advocacy of enhancing international competitiveness through industrial upgrading towards the heavy and chemical industries, which was characteristic of the earlier report published in November 1963. The report stated: 'Until now, we have climbed a narrow path without glancing aside, aiming at the faraway "cloud above the mountaintop". Our efforts bore fruit and the Japanese economy now stands on a ridge commanding a distant view of the entire world.' It went on to say that now 'the wants of the Japanese people are spreading out in all directions', and therefore 'industry should rid itself of the simplistic thought and behaviour mode of condoning simultaneous production of both "things" and pollutants, and meet the diversified wants by drawing on all its resources.'

From such a perspective, the report identified the following three as the principal tasks for the nation in the 1970s: (1) securing a life for each citizen which is genuinely rich in humanity, (2) positively contributing to the peace and development of the international community, and (3) preserving and enhancing the creativity and vitality of the people to make (1) and (2) possible. Then, as the tasks required of industry as means for accomplishing these national tasks, the report listed the following five: (1) strengthening the comprehensive development capacity of industries and nurturing their development base, (2) qualitatively improving the living conditions of the people, (3) securing healthy social and natural environments and building an attractive country, (4) expanding opportunities for work that makes life worth living and securing safe and pleasant work environments, and (5) promoting development in cooperation with the international economic community.

Bearing these tasks in mind, the report suggested that the guiding principle of macroeconomic management in the 1970s be transformed from one of single-mindedly pursuing growth for the sake of quantitative expansion of the economy to that of actively utilizing the benefits of growth as the means for achieving the tasks required of the industrial economy—that is, a shift from a 'growth-pursuing' to a 'growth-utilizing' pattern of economic management. Accordingly, the report emphasized, specific roles to be played by industrial policy should be studied on the premiss of maximum utilization of the market mechanism.

The report discussed specific policies in four parts—industrial structure, industrial organization, industrial internationalization, and industrial technology. Of these discussions, it was particularly worth noting that the report made the following statement with regard to industrial structure policy. In generating a desired image of the future industrial structure, four standards were to be used. Two new standards—the overcrowding and environment standard and the quality of working-life standard—were to be added to the conventional criteria for promoting industrial upgrading, i.e. the standard of a high income elasticity of demand and the standard of a rapid rate of increase in productivity. The report recognized that these four standards might at times be in conflict with each other with trade-offs among them. It maintained that in such a case an optimum 'image of the future' should be chosen, taking into due consideration the conditions that surround the Japanese economy and the changing patterns of the needs and wants of the people. Summing up these discussions, the report concluded that the industrial structure policy in the 1970s should be focused on creating what it called the knowledge-intensive industrial structure. The core of this structure was to consist of industries which were intensive in the use of intellectual activities (knowledge-intensive industries), and policy measures for the basic and other industries which support the core industries should aim at raising their knowledge intensity as much as possible.

As can be seen from the foregoing, this Interim Report, announced in the final stage of the period of high-level growth, recommended a transformation of the policy of managing Japan, Inc., as characterized by the US Commerce Department document. In short, the report recommended the restructuring of Japan, Inc. itself.[12] However, on 15 August 1971, roughly three months after this report was announced, President Nixon announced his new economic policy, jolting Japan sharply. With this day as a turning point, the Japanese economy and MITI policy entered a new era.

NOTES

1. From the introductory chapter of the interim report of the Industrial Structure Council, Coordination Committee, *70-nendai no Tsusho Sangyo Seisaku no Kihon Hoko wa Ika ni Arubeki ka* (What Should be the Basic Direction of International Trade and Industry Policy in the 1970s?).
2. Ibid., ch. 3.
3. Ibid.
4. Ibid.
5. *Tsusho Sangyo Seisakushi*, xi. 73.
6. Art. 2 of the Instalment Sales Law defines an 'instalment sale' as 'selling a specific piece of merchandise where the seller receives from the buyer payments extending over two or more months in three or more instalments.'
7. *Tsusho Sangyo Seisakushi*, vii (1991): 179–80.
8. Ibid. vii and xi. 410.
9. *Gendai Nihon Keizai no Tenkai*: 205.
10. Two translated versions of the document are available. One is by Susumu Ohara and Toyoaki Yoshida, trans., *Kabushikigaisha Nippon* (Japan: The Government–Business Relationship), Simul

Press, Inc., and the other is by Mitsuaki Nakao, trans., *Nippon Kabushikigaisha* (Japan, Inc.), Mainichi Newspapers Co. Ltd. Both versions were published in 1972.
11. Susumu Ohara and Toyoaki Yoshida, trans., Preface: 9.
12. This US Dept. of Commerce document did not mention the 1971 Interim Report of the Industrial Structure Council.

PART V

Changes in the International Economy and Knowledge-Intensive Industry

24

The Transition to a Floating Exchange Rate System and the Oil Crises

24.1. The Nixon 'Shock' and Changes in International Monetary System

President Nixon announced new economic policies on 15 August 1971. The policies included 'a temporary suspension of the conversion of US dollars held by foreign governments against gold or other foreign exchange reserves held by the US.'[1]

Under the post-war IMF system, if the government office in charge of currency in an IMF member country requested permission, it could convert US dollars into gold at the rate of 35 dollars per ounce of gold, an exchange rate established in 1934. The assurance that US dollars could be converted at a fixed rate to gold, which historically was considered to fluctuate relatively very little in value, was evidence of the dollar's stable value. And because the dollar could be exchanged at a fixed rate, this meant a mechanism was in effect whereby the currencies of the IMF member countries, tied to the dollar, were indirectly guaranteed to have stable values. But Nixon's declaration removed the US dollar from its role as the core currency supporting the IMF system. In other words, the announcement meant nothing other than the disassembly at its very foundation of the international monetary system that was tied to a fixed dollar rate.

The US dollar can be said to have been the world's strongest currency at the end of the Second World War. Endorsing the dollar's strength were factors such as rich gold reserves and foreign accounts receivable, domestic industries free from the destruction of war, and new, high-capacity production facilities built in wartime. The countries that suffered from the war could not restore themselves without US aid. Influenced also by the outbreak of the Cold War, the US distributed goods and funds to the nations of the free world in the form of aid under the Marshall Plan, EROA, GARIOA, and so forth. At the time, most countries, including the advanced European nations, had deficit trade balances with the US, and 'the shortage of dollars' was a major issue. At any rate, in the period following inauguration of the IMF system, no country expressed apprehension about the US dollar.

US gold and foreign-exchange reserves peaked in 1949. In June of the following year, the Korean War broke out, beginning a pattern of US intervention in localized conflicts. Related to such conflicts, the US dollar became increasingly diffused in the form of military expenses, foreign aid, and so forth. In the 1950s, however, the US trade balance was still in surplus, as was the private-sector balance, including services. Despite the huge diffusion of dollars by the government sector, the current balance seldom went into deficit. Because of a rapid increase in foreign direct investments from the second half of the 1950s, however, a tendency towards deficit in the basic balance started to take firm hold. IMF member countries holding US dollars gradually began requesting conversion of their holdings into gold.

In 1958, all European currencies recovered their exchangeability, and the international monetary market became vigorously active. Coupled with the widespread diffusion of US dollars, this development triggered a dollar crisis in the 1960s. In October 1960, the price of gold rose in the London Gold Market to 40 dollars per ounce, precipitating a rapid increase in the demand for converting dollars into gold. The crisis was temporarily resolved when President Kennedy promised in February 1961 to maintain the gold–dollar exchange rate. This was the first US action taken to defend the dollar; afterwards, the US had to take other measures to defend the dollar.

Various other events in the 1960s induced huge outflows of dollars. These included US entrance into the Vietnam War, intensified missile-development competition between the US and the USSR, increased US aid to developing countries, and expanded foreign investments by multinational corporations. The countries of Western Europe, meanwhile, completed their reconstruction and as export surplus countries began obtaining and holding large amounts of US dollars. The dollar thus shifted from 'shortage' to 'excess'. In the second half of the 1960s, in these changing circumstances, the market demand for exchange rate adjustments strengthened. Because of its accumulation of foreign reserves, pressure increased especially on West Germany to revaluate the Deutschmark upward. Conversely, pressure increased on the UK to depreciate the English pound, against the backdrop of the UK bid for entry to the EEC being rejected and the Labour Party coming into power. The British pound was eventually devalued in November 1967. In France, a general strike took place in 1968, and the franc was devalued in August 1969. Two months later, in October 1969, the Deutschmark was finally revalued upward.

In the second half of the 1960s, therefore, through successive speculative shifts of money, US dollars that accumulated in the European short-term funds market served to shake the foundation of the IMF system, formerly protected by fixed exchange rates and the guarantee of dollar conversion into gold at the rate of 35 dollars per ounce. Despite such developments, President Nixon, elected in 1969, allowed a further increase in the US fiscal deficit, higher commodity prices, and aggravation of the US trade balance. Most of the US trade deficit came from trade with Canada, West Germany, and Japan. Pressures therefore mounted for appreciation of the Deutschmark and Japanese yen. A major factor contributing to the previous upward revaluation of the Deutschmark in 1969 was the US trade deficit. Around that same time, Japan's trade surplus was increasing steadily, and it was normal for the foreign exchange rate (the interbank closing yen–dollar exchange rate for immediate delivery, final spot) to be quoted at 357 yen to the dollar.

Starting from 1971, funds shifted rapidly from the US to Europe, and speculative purchase of the Deutschmark became especially pronounced. This signalled a loss in the credibility of the US dollar, and West Germany finally decided in May to abandon the system of fixed exchange rates and to move to a system of floating exchange rates in order to defend the Deutschmark. The Netherlands followed soon afterwards. On the other hand, the Swiss franc and Austrian schilling were revalued upward. Meanwhile, gold was gradually moving out of the US, and US gold reserves approached the critical level.

The US dollar weakened so badly that it was no longer possible to adjust the IMF system by modifying foreign exchange rates (devaluation of weaker currencies, or revaluation upward of stronger currencies). The conversion of dollars at the rate of 35 dollars per ounce of gold was at its survival limits. During the twenty-five years since the end of the Second World War, the balance of international competitiveness among the free nations had completely changed. The US, one of the world's so-called superpowers, experienced an increase in military spending as a result of the Vietnam War and expanded foreign investments by multinational corporations whose activities had become more vigorous. The real value of the US dollar fell, and the accumulation of gold reserves in the US continuously dwindled. With its options becoming gradually limited, the US was finally obliged to solve the problem by suspending the dollar's conversion with gold. Assistance to the Nixon administration in the form of currency upward or downward revaluations by the countries of Western Europe had virtually ended in early 1971, and President Nixon's new economic policies thus served as shock therapy. The historically unprecedented international monetary system based on the US dollar's fixed exchange rate with gold thus collapsed, and a system of floating exchange rates gradually replaced it.

24.2. Shift of the Yen to the Floating Exchange Rate System, and Background

In April 1964, Japan became an Article 8 nation of the IMF. Until then, Japan was seldom asked to join deliberations among the advanced countries about the international monetary system. Japan was not invited to join the Gold Pool established in November 1961, for example, and could not participate in discussions about par value changes of the British pound and the Deutschmark. After joining the IMF, although Japan was called upon to participate in the comprehensive credit grant to the UK to rescue the British pound in November 1964, the credit grant requested from Japan—perhaps because the grant was assembled mainly by European countries—was less than 2 per cent of the total, a smaller amount than the grants requested from Belgium and the Netherlands.

For many years, therefore, Japan had been kept outside of deliberations on the international monetary system. From 1968 and early 1969, however, pressures increased for the upward revaluation of not only strong currencies like the Deutschmark and Canadian dollar, but also the yen. Even when the Deutschmark was revalued upward, however, no one in the US government approached the officers of the New York Federal Reserve Bank to have them persuade the Japanese government of the importance of revaluing the yen upward. According to recollections by the financial officer of the Ministry of Finance at the time, neither the Japanese government nor the Bank of Japan received advance official notice that President Nixon would announce a devaluation of the US dollar and suspension of the dollar's conversion to gold, and it was thus difficult for the Japanese authorities to understand the true intent of the announcement. Because of the lack of communication, the Japanese authorities had firmly believed the US would forcefully support the exchange rate of 35 dollars per ounce of gold. They could not imagine the fixed exchange rate system under the IMF collapsing.[2]

Two reasons help to explain why Japan believed the fixed exchange rate system under the IMF was perpetual. First, Japan's high-level economic growth had been achieved under the fixed exchange rate system, and, second, unlike the countries of Europe, Japan's currency had remained fixed at an exchange rate of 360 yen to the dollar for twenty-two years. Patterns of behaviour were established in Japan's export industries which meant that efforts toward rationalized processes and increased productivity were constantly made so that low-productivity industrial products could be exported at 360 yen to the dollar. And when exports at that exchange rate became difficult because of domestic commodity price increases, new rationalization efforts were introduced. In a sense, the fixed exchange rate of 360 yen was a yardstick Japanese industry used to adjust its products to international price levels. The fixed rate of 360 yen to the dollar can thus be applauded as having provided criteria for Japanese industry in establishing rationalization goals. It also worked as a safety device, preventing Japan's commodity prices from rising sharply apart from international price trends.

The authorities in charge of currency in Japan had witnessed the damage wreaked by the catastrophic inflation that prevailed in Europe after the First World War, and made efforts to maintain the yen's value in ways other than adjusting the exchange rate when the nation's international balance of payments worsened. When the balance fell into deficit, for instance, credit was tightened, domestic demand was suppressed, and exports were increased by forcing the price of products down. Those actions brought the balance back to surplus. The exchange rate of 360 yen to the dollar thus functioned effectively as a frame within which the balance of payments could be controlled.

The productivity of labour in Japan, meanwhile, improved greatly from 1964 to 1973, achieving average annual growth of 15 per cent. With 1963 as 100, 1964 was 110.9, 1965 was 115.2, 1966 was 130.4, 1967 was 152.2, 1968 was 173.9, 1969 was 197.8, 1970 was 217.4, 1971 was 226.1, 1972 was 252.2, and 1973 was 302.2. The equivalent figures in the US showed average annual growth of 3.4 per cent. With 1963 as 100, the figures were 104.7 in 1964, 110.6 in 1965, 111.8 in 1966, 110.6 in 1967, 116.5 in 1968, 118.8 in 1969, 117.6 in 1970, 125.9 in 1971, 134.1 in 1972, and 141.2 in 1973. As seen in these figures, productivity growth in Japan surpassed that in the US throughout the ten years prior to the first oil crisis. Notice, too, that while Japan's productivity rose every year during this period, the growth of productivity in the US was not smooth, showing declines in 1967 and 1970 compared with previous years. The average annual growth rate of productivity in the US was also lower. In other advanced industrialized countries, the average annual growth rate of productivity was 3.8 per cent for the UK, 5.8 per cent for West Germany, 6.9 per cent for France, 5.7 per cent for Italy, and 4.0 per cent for Canada.[3] When disparities in productivity occurred under the fixed exchange rate system, it became easier for a country with a higher rate of increase, such as Japan, to increase its exports. At such times, the fixed exchange rate of 360 yen to the dollar had the effect of 'devaluing' the yen.

Supported by the 'low-yen' effect of the 360 yen to the dollar exchange rate, Japan's trade surplus expanded and its foreign-exchange reserves increased in the second half of the 1960s. In the eyes of other countries, Japan seemed to be conducting unfair competition with dumping built into the foreign exchange rate.[4] In 1969, West Germany, with a large trade surplus, revalued its currency upward, and Canada opted for a floating exchange rate system. Those countries took such action because they were both geographically close to international monetary markets such as London and New York, and tended to be influenced by flows of speculative funds. There was a delay in Japan being recognized as a full-fledged participant in the international monetary market, however, and Tokyo was still an immature monetary market. It was not inevitable, therefore, for the yen to have to be revalued upward because of pressures from a dramatic inflow of hot money.

Pressure for upward revaluation of the yen was not especially strong until around 1968. Criticism of the yen–dollar exchange rate began strengthening after exports from Japan of sophisticated heavy industrial products such as steel, television sets, cars, and so forth increased to levels that contributed to accumulation of a trade surplus and an increase in foreign-exchange reserves. Some American businessmen became sceptical about whether the dollar's fixed exchange rate with the yen could be maintained in the context of the strong competition from Japan, and even if the system of a fixed exchange rate were desirable. In 1969, Japan's trade surplus reached $3,699 million, and Japan's foreign-exchange reserves exceeded the $3-billion level for the first time, reaching $3,496 million. In 1970, the trade surplus reached $3,963 million and foreign-exchange reserves reached $4,399 million. The huge surplus was supported by a rapid increase in exports to the United States. In the spring of 1971, currency speculation became brisk in Europe. On 5 May, $1 billion flowed in to purchase Deutschmarks during the first four hours of trading. On 9 May, the

Deutschmark was shifted to a system of floating exchange rates. From around this same time, pressures on the yen increased, and yen buying turned aggressive. For instance, foreign parties who had ordered ships to be built in Japan moved desperately to secure yen in order to cover themselves with advance payment for ships under construction. During the first half of 1971, Japan's foreign-currency reserves increased by $3 billion.

In view of the upward revaluation of some European currencies (Austria and Switzerland), the shift to a floating exchange rate system by others (West Germany and the Netherlands), and brisk yen buying, the Japanese government and the Bank of Japan began seriously considering countermeasures. The Bank of Japan reduced the official discount rate four times in less than one year: in October 1970, January 1971, May 1971, and July 1971. In June 1971, the government announced yen countermeasures comprising eight items.[5] The countermeasures were aimed primarily at reducing the trade surplus. The salient points were: (1) the promotion of imports by liberalizing imports, granting preferential duties to developing countries, reducing import duties, and removing non-tariff barriers; (2) the promotion of overseas investment through capital liberalization and an increase in Official Development Assistance (ODA); and (3) the promotion of export controls by a re-examination of preferential tax treatment and by orderly marketing activities. These policies aimed at preventing flood-like exports to specific destinations through the use of 'orderly marketing', such as increasing imports as part of liberalization policies, and enforcing control over exports by bilateral agreements or having industries practise self-restraint, rather than trying to rectify the trade imbalance through currency adjustments, such as upward revaluation of the yen from the rate of 360 yen to the dollar. Of course, these measures had been formulated without any expectation that the US would introduce economic measures drastic enough to overturn the IMF system itself. There was a variance between Japan and the US as to the crisis feeling about the IMF system, and the structuring of currency policies.[6]

The Nixon declaration of 15 August 1971 was far beyond anything the Japanese government and currency authorities could have expected. At first, they were rather more concerned about the levying of the 10 per cent import surcharge included in the announcement, and never considered the possibility of closing the Tokyo foreign-exchange market or revaluating the yen upward. They responded, therefore, by selling dollars and buying yen to support the 360 yen exchange rate. It was not until 28 August, almost two weeks after Nixon's declaration, that Japan abandoned the system of a fixed exchange rate.

24.3. Influence of the Floating Exchange Rate System on the Japanese Economy

When President Nixon made his announcement, it was already 10.00 a.m. on 16 August 1971, in Japan. The Tokyo foreign-exchange market was open and transactions were being completed as usual at the 360 yen rate. Even after hearing

Nixon's declaration, the Ministry of Finance and the Bank of Japan did not close the market, principally because they were concerned that doing so would invite further speculation and appreciation of the yen. But because the market was not closed, there was an onrush of orders to buy yen that afternoon. The Bank of Japan ended up having to purchase 598 million dollars on that day.

Three principal reasons have been offered to explain why the Tokyo foreign-exchange market was not closed on 16 August 1971, like the markets in other countries. First, the authorities thought that if the market were closed it could not be reopened unless the yen were revalued upward or Japan shifted to a floating exchange rate system. Second, it was thought that closing the market would affect the large flows of goods and capital between Japan and the US. Third, it was thought to be possible to restrict the inflow of speculative money even if the market remained open, because Japan controlled foreign exchange strictly. There were also strong objections against closing the foreign-exchange market because of the belief that the 360 yen exchange rate was sacred and had to be protected at all costs.[7] Behind this theory of the 360 yen rate being sacred was the reality that the exchange rate had been fixed for twenty-two years, and that exports and imports had always been conducted on the basis of this exchange rate. The management plans of Japanese corporations were also based on the 360 yen exchange rate. It was considered that most export-oriented companies would suffer losses and possible managerial difficulties if the exchange rate were adjusted upward.[8]

Among the after-effects of the new economic policies, the import surcharge and the yen's upward revaluation were discussed, mainly concerning Japanese products that relied heavily on export to the US. By industry category, it was expected that the damage to labour-intensive, small and medium enterprises in industries such as textiles, toys, Western tableware, sundry goods, and so forth would be serious, and that industries producing household electric appliances such as televisions, which faced competition from developing countries, and cars, which faced generally strong competition, would be placed in disadvantageous positions. It was expected that even the steel industry, which was price-competitive, would find it difficult to increase prices to reflect the import surcharge and cost increases accompanying a higher yen rate.[9] The Ministry of International Trade and Industry conducted a survey of Japanese industry on the influence of the 10 per cent US surcharge. The survey's results revealed that the products of small and medium enterprises, such as textiles, sundry goods, light machinery, wire products, copper rolled-mill products, and so forth were expected to sustain tremendous damage, while stereo systems, bicycles, bearings, tyre tubes, and other products, for which there were few competitors in the US or in third countries, were expected to experience little negative influence. The steel industry, too, was competitive in both price and quality and was not expected to face problems. On the other hand, dumping duties had been levied on television sets, and companies producing them would face some problems because of the difficulty in introducing price increases.[10]

The opinions of people in industry and the results of the MITI survey suggested that labour-intensive export industries, which depended on inexpensive labour, would experience difficulties in coping with a higher exchange rate. At the time, most of Japan's export industries were in the labour-intensive category, and even capital-intensive industries such as electric machinery and cars were supported by parts manufacturers that depended on inexpensive labour. The yen's upward revaluation thus raised a new issue, because there were limits felt as to how far these supporting companies could raise their productivity.

During the period that the Tokyo foreign-exchange market was kept open and the exchange rate remained fixed at 360 yen, dollar sales and yen purchases were hectic every day, reaching a total of $4.28 billion. The nation's foreign-exchange reserves thus came to exceed $12.3 billion, the second largest holdings in the world after West Germany, even surpassing the US. Behind the Bank of Japan's purchase of such a huge amount of dollars were factors such as the conversion into yen by trading companies of advance receipts for exports, and conversion into yen of the dollar credits of Japan's city banks. But dollar buying eventually reached its limit, and the fixed exchange rate of 360 yen to the dollar terminated its historical role on 27 August 1971.

The yen had been the only currency that remained fixed under the IMF system, and its shift to a floating exchange rate was welcomed widely by the governments and the financial authorities of the US and the countries of Europe. It was followed by multilateral currency adjustments. And in December 1971, the Smithsonian Agreement was finalized, specifying fixed exchange rates moving within temporary ranges. The yen was revalued upward by 16.88 per cent to 308 yen as a standard rate. But as early as June 1972, the UK violated the terms of the Smithsonian Agreement by shifting the British pound to a floating exchange rate system. And in February 1973, following severe currency speculation, the dollar was further devalued by 10 per cent. The yen was then also shifted to a floating exchange rate system. Even then the turmoil did not stop. Currency speculation ignited again in March, and all currencies, including European currencies, shifted to the floating exchange rate system. Efforts to return them to a fixed rate system were suspended.[11]

From Nixon's declaration to that point, the yen had appreciated by about 35 per cent, from 360 yen to around 260 yen to the dollar. Despite that high rate of appreciation compared to the average of about 20 per cent appreciation of other currencies, the influence on Japanese exports was relatively limited. The major products whose exports decreased during 1971 were only processing machines for non-ferrous metals and other metals destined for the US, radio receivers destined for markets in South-East Asia, and machinery for non-ferrous metals and textiles destined for the countries of Western Europe. In 1972, the list of products most severely affected by the yen's appreciation included only textile products and radio receivers for the US, foodstuffs, raw materials and fuels, agricultural machinery, textile machinery, and radio receivers for South-East Asia, and raw materials and fuels for Western Europe.[12] Overall, however, exports to the countries of Western Europe increased due to an economic boom there, and Japan's trade surplus in Europe increased. Exports to the US slowed in 1973, with light industrial products, textiles, chemicals, iron and steel, television receivers, and other products recording negative increases compared with the previous year. The slowdown in exports was due to the dollar-based price increase of Japanese products, market shifts, official controls on exports, and other factors. The year 1973 also saw substantial increases in imports mainly of raw materials and foodstuffs from the US. As a result, trade between Japan and the US almost reached a balance.[13]

In October 1973, the fourth Middle East War broke out, followed by the first oil crisis. Japan was affected enormously by the substantial crude-oil price increases and supply restrictions imposed by OAPEC. Commodity prices skyrocketed, the current balance fell into deficit, foreign-exchange reserves decreased, and overall economic growth slowed. The oil crisis revealed clearly that the principal weakness of the Japanese economy was owing to the lack of natural resources. In the new circumstances, the yen–dollar exchange rate reversed itself, and the yen rapidly depreciated. As explained later, however, the oil crisis became an opportunity for Japanese corporations to adopt energy- and resource-conservation strategies and to adopt policies for reducing the burden on management. One result was a strengthening of their international competitiveness.

As the impact of the first oil crisis wore off, the yen strengthened again, following a path of steady appreciation after hitting a low of 305.15 yen to the dollar in December 1975. Once into 1977, the tempo of the yen's appreciation accelerated, and the exchange rate finally reached 176.05 yen in October 1978. In the background were factors such as a growth in exports, an increased trade surplus, and a rapid increase in Japan's foreign-exchange reserves. Exports that increased during this period were cars, ships, scientific optical equipment, tape recorders, and others, accounting for about 60 per cent of total exports of machinery and equipment. From 1965 into 1975, Japan steadily increased its share of total world exports of high-growth industrial products such as medical equipment, iron and steel construction materials, ships, office equipment, cars, radios, and television sets. During the same period, the share of those exports by US, UK, and West German companies decreased.[14] As this export trend shows, Japanese companies adjusted the composition of their export products in the same direction as world trade growth. Against the background of the yen's appreciation and the oil crisis, Japanese corporations shifted their export emphasis to knowledge-intensive products. It can be said that the yen's appreciation accelerated the conversion of Japan's industrial structure. At the same time, the composition of imported products did not change much, and raw materials and fuels accounted for 64 per cent of total imports. Machinery and equipment imports increased only slightly, while imports of finished products such as direct consumer goods and non-durable consumer goods increased more noticeably. It can be said that import increases were limited to low-value-added products.

On 1 November 1978, when the dollar had fallen to about its lowest level, the US announced new dollar-defence measures. They consisted of joint intervention by West Germany, Switzerland, and Japan in the foreign-exchange market by providing for the swapping of funds totalling $30 billion in order to restore the dollar's value, and introduction by the US of a tight-money policy by increasing the official rate and reserve requirement ratio. Immediately after announcement of these measures, the money market shifted towards a higher-dollar, lower-yen trend. During November, the yen's value dropped by about 10 per cent, to reach 197 yen to the dollar. The Iranian Revolution in early 1979 and the subsequent second oil crisis accelerated the yen's depreciation. As a result, the exchange rate dropped to 224.5 yen on 2 May 1979. And on 27 November 1979, after a series of small increases in the US official rate and oil price increases by OPEC, the yen–dollar exchange rate fell to 251.5 yen to the dollar.[15]

Through the above process, it can be seen that fluctuations in the yen's exchange rate after the shift to a floating exchange rate system came to be greatly influenced by US economic policies and oil prices, as well as by the nation's trade balance (more specifically, by the overall balance of payments). In this respect, it can be said that the floating exchange rate made it easier for the market mechanism to function and made product price and quality more directly reflected in the market in terms of their international competitiveness. This fact meant that corporations were required to constantly rationalize their production costs and strengthen differentiation of their products. Companies thus came constantly to pursue product kaizen (improvement), the conservation of energy and natural resources, and curtailment of the labour force.

To cope with the yen's rapid appreciation and the oil crisis, the Ministry of International Trade and Industry (MITI) introduced relief measures as needed for depressed industries, small and medium enterprises, and consumers. At the same time, MITI moved to dispel uncertainties about energy supplies and to ease the impact on costs from price increases in raw materials and fuels by promoting long-range measures for conserving energy and natural resources. MITI also promoted the planned withdrawal and conversion to other industries of companies in structurally depressed industries and those clearly unable to maintain their international competitiveness in the future because of the yen's appreciation and oil price increases. Among the alternatives considered were the transfer overseas of production sites and business conversion to the import of intermediate and finished products. MITI also provided assistance for R&D related to advanced technology in fields where high growth was expected in the future. These measures also promoted foreign investments by Japanese companies, and contributed to improving Japan's trade structure and wise utilization of its accumulated foreign-exchange reserves.

Concerning the measures introduced to cope with the yen's appreciation, even though there were temporary shifts to a weaker yen, companies did not respond by immediately suspending or changing the measures because although the price of imported raw materials and fuels might increase due to the weaker yen, the measures enabled the companies to conserve energy and resources, which reduced their unit cost prices considerably and allowed them to minimize the impact of the higher prices on costs. In assembly-type machine industries such as cars, electronic equipment, business equipment, and others, cost reductions by subcontractor parts makers was made possible through increases in productivity and by enforcing thorough quality control and inventory control methods. It is thought that the so-called 'dual structure' of Japanese industry made it possible for companies to absorb the negative impact of the yen's appreciation little by little at various stages and thus overcome the overall impact. Thanks to the function of this cost-absorption mechanism, combined with lower prices for imported raw materials and fuels, the competitiveness of Japanese products was not affected very negatively by the more expensive yen. On the contrary, the yen's appreciation became an opportunity to strengthen the competitiveness of Japanese corporations. Also, rather than price competitiveness, emphasis was placed on product differentiation through high product quality, superior design, and other factors, and the range of exported products tended to be less restrictive than the yen's exchange rate fluctuations.

24.4. Changes in the International Oil Situation and Oil Crises

Increased dependence on oil, and the first oil crisis

The twenty years from 1950 to 1970 saw marked changes in the composition of energy consumed by the world's advanced industrial nations. The first marked change was that the dependence on coal decreased dramatically, as is clearly seen in statistics showing the percentage of total energy consumption accounted for by coal. In 1950, the coal percentage was 71.3 per cent for the UK, 70.7 per cent for West Germany, 61.8 per cent for Japan, 59.3 per cent for the Netherlands, 58.1 per cent for France, 34.0 per cent for Italy, and 27.7 per cent for the US. By 1970, however, the percentage had changed to 22.2 per cent for the UK, 17.8 per cent for West Germany, 14.2 per cent for France, 10.2 per cent for Japan, 5.5 per cent for the Netherlands, 4.9 per cent for Italy, and 4.8 per cent for the US. Of these countries, four—the UK, West Germany, Japan, and the Netherlands—showed tremendous declines of about 50 per cent. In contrast, the second marked change was an increased dependence on oil. In 1950, the oil percentage of total energy consumption was 33.8 per cent for the US, 23.0 per cent for Italy, 16.9 per cent for the Netherlands, 16.1 per cent for France, 9.0 per cent for the UK, 5.3 per cent for Japan, and 2.9 per cent for West Germany. Of these seven countries, only the US depended on oil for as much as one-third of its energy consumption, and it was also producing oil of its own. The dependence on oil of the UK, West Germany, and Japan was under 10 per cent. In 1970, however, the oil percentage of total energy consumption changed to 54.1 per cent for Italy, 50.2 per cent for France, 47.9 per cent for Japan, 43.0 per cent for West Germany, 41.0 per cent for the Netherlands, 36.0 per cent for the US, and 34.4 per cent for the

UK. Not a few countries came to depend on oil for about half or more of their total energy consumption.[16]

Countries producing little oil domestically—such as West Germany, Italy, and Japan—were forced to rely on overseas sources for supplies. In 1970, in fact, all the advanced industrial nations except the US depended on overseas sources for over 90 per cent of their oil. The figures were 99.9 per cent in the UK, 99.7 per cent in Japan, 98.4 per cent in France, 97.3 per cent in Italy, and 94.8 per cent in West Germany. For the US, the figure was 29.7 per cent. This dependence increased the percentage of their total energy consumption accounted for by foreign sources. In 1970, that percentage was 83.5 per cent for Japan, 81.7 per cent for Italy, 69.3 per cent for France, 45.4 per cent for the UK, and 45.0 per cent for West Germany.[17] The third marked change, therefore, was an increase in the dependence on foreign sources for energy resources, leading to problems of national security.

The share of the world's total production of crude oil accounted for by the oil-producing countries in the Middle East increased gradually from 24.9 per cent in 1962 to 29.7 per cent in 1970 and 36.9 per cent in 1973. The share of the world's total exports of crude oil accounted for by countries in the Middle East, which was 53.2 per cent in 1968, changed to 51.9 per cent in 1970, 61.0 per cent in 1973, 64.1 per cent in 1974, and 62.6 per cent in 1976. The share was thus over 60 per cent during the years following the first oil crisis of 1973.[18] The fourth marked change, therefore, was an increase in the share of the world's production and export of crude oil by countries in the Middle East. After the Second World War, the Middle East had continued to be politically unstable, as seen in such events as the conflict between Israel and the Arab nations, the rise of nationalism, the establishment of revolutionary governments, and so forth. The world's supply of and demand for crude oil came to depend greatly on political developments in the Middle East.

Two major events in the 1960s that affected the oil trade were establishment of the Organization of Petroleum Exporting Countries (OPEC) in September 1960, as proposed by Saudi Arabia and Venezuela, and establishment of the Organization of Arab Petroleum Exporting Countries (OAPEC) in 1968, as proposed by Saudi Arabian Petroleum Minister Ahmad Zaki Yamani. OPEC insisted on phased increases in crude oil prices, participation by the OPEC nations in the oil business, and increases in profits allotted to the oil-producing countries. As well, it made strong demands from a nationalistic viewpoint on the advanced nations, who were also importers of crude oil. OPEC made decisions on prices and production volumes of crude oil, thus diminishing the influence of the international majors that previously controlled the oil trade.

As these changes were occurring the advanced industrial nations increased their dependence on oil imports, particularly on crude oil from the Middle East. A growing sense of crisis emerged even in the US, an oil-producing country. In April 1973, President Nixon announced an 'Energy Message' that proposed lifting regulations on and subsidizing overall energy development (including natural gas, coal, and nuclear power), promoting energy-conservation programmes, and reforming the administrative organization regarding energy. It was around that time that OAPEC began to warn countries friendly with Israel of the possibility of crude oil being used as a 'weapon' against them.

In Japan, MITI closely watched changes in the international situation regarding crude oil. To respond to the situation after the Teheran Agreement in 1971, MITI expanded the special account for coal to cover both coal and petroleum for the fiscal year 1972 budget. It also decided to promote the exploration and development of oil, stockpiling, and improvements in the distribution system. In addition, national oil reserves would be increased from forty-five days to sixty days in a three-year plan to begin in fiscal year 1972. From late April to early May 1973, Minister of International Trade and Industry Yasuhiro Nakasone visited Iran, Kuwait, Saudi Arabia, and the United Arab Emirates to discuss petroleum-related issues and economic cooperation with Gulf States in the Middle East. Next, in July 1973, MITI implemented major organizational reforms. Actually, the plan for reforms was first discussed around 1970. One of its priority items was the establishment of the Agency of Natural Resources and Energy within MITI. By integrating the divisions relating to petroleum and coal under the Mine and Coal Bureau with the Public Utilities Bureau controlling electric power and gas, MITI planned to create a system capable of promoting administrative matters related to natural resources and energy from a unified, comprehensive viewpoint. On 25 September, two months after its founding, the Agency of Natural Resources and Energy published a report entitled 'Japan's Energy Problems'. The report warned the government about a tightening between supply and demand of crude oil and a possible price hike. It also emphasized the need to develop new energy sources and related technology and to promote energy conservation.

On 6 October, only ten days after the above report, the fourth Middle East War broke out. The OAPEC member countries immediately put into effect their strategy of using oil as a weapon by introducing a ban on the export of crude oil to pro-Israeli nations, announcing major crude-oil price hikes, and reducing their supply of crude oil. These moves triggered the first oil crisis of 1973. Unlike the position in the 1960s and earlier, it was suddenly no longer possible to enjoy using large volumes of inexpensive crude oil. The various moves were followed by entirely unexpected events. OAPEC's reduced oil supplies caused the international oil majors to announce their own tough measures to reduce oil supplies. After that happened, Japanese consumers concerned about supply shortages rushed to hoard petroleum-related products, resulting in runaway inflation. As a consequence, the Japanese government implemented emergency measures, including the enactment of two special laws relating to petroleum (the Petroleum Supply and Demand Optimization Law and the Law on Emergency Measures for National Life Stabilization). Although the fourth Middle East War lasted only fifteen days, soaring crude oil prices and the fear of short supplies were prolonged.

The second oil crisis and diversification of energy resources

The first oil crisis pushed up the price of crude oil per barrel 3.9-fold—from $3.0 to $11.6—in eleven months. From 1975, however, crude oil prices remained rather stable, although nominally showing a steady rising trend. Still, the effects of the crisis caused commodity prices to begin rising rapidly in countries that relied heavily on overseas sources for their oil supplies. Higher commodity prices, in turn, raised the prices of industrial products the oil-producing countries were purchasing. For this reason, the oil producers believed that the increase in their import of industrial products would not match the increase in crude oil prices. This belief caused OPEC to devise a long-term strategy to assist oil-consuming countries in maintaining or increasing their ability to purchase crude oil. The strategy called for adjusting crude oil prices according to economic indicators in the advanced countries, including the export price index, consumer price index, a currency basket index related to the exchange rate versus the US dollar, and the rate of economic growth in real terms. The price adjustments were probably intended to absorb the effects of inflation and any decrease in the dollar's value in order to have the OPEC member nations achieve higher economic growth than that of the advanced countries. At any rate, based on those indicators, OPEC voted to revise crude oil prices quarterly. And by setting upper limits on oil production, the member nations also wanted to regulate the supply–demand relationship and thus support the pricing system.[19]

At a general assembly held in December 1978, OPEC decided to introduce small-step increases in crude oil prices on a quarterly basis, eventually amounting to 14.5 per cent per year.[20] In the background of these price increases were inflation and a decrease in the value of the dollar. In addition, increased opposition to the regime of Shah Pahlavi in Iran caused a reduction in crude oil production and strain in the supply–demand relationship. What was worse, on 26 December 1978, Iran placed a total ban on crude oil exports. The Shah left Iran on 16 January 1979, and at that stage in the revolution it became impossible to resume crude oil exports. This event triggered soaring spot prices for crude oil and caused the international oil majors to announce oil supply reductions. A second oil crisis thus began. During its June 1979 general assembly, OPEC raised the benchmark crude oil price to $18. And during an extraordinary general assembly held in September 1980, OPEC implemented another increase in the benchmark crude oil price to $30. Also in September, Iraqi troops invaded Iran, and war broke out between those two countries. Before long, the weighted average of crude oil prices rose to $32.30 per barrel. This meant that in less than two years, from December 1978, when the weighted average was $12.29 per barrel, crude oil prices had risen 2.5-fold.[21]

During the second oil crisis, there were several noteworthy events relating to energy: first, in March 1979, there was a reactor accident at a nuclear power plant at Three Mile Island in Pennsylvania; second, a petrol panic erupted in the US, also in March; and third, the age of '$20 crude oil' arrived in June 1979, the same month that the Tokyo Summit was held. The leak of radioactive material at the Three Mile Island nuclear power plant drew renewed attention to the safety of using nuclear power generation as a powerful source of energy for replacing oil. The petrol panic in the US, meanwhile, a country blessed with far more natural resources than Japan and depending on overseas sources for only 20–30 per cent of its oil supplies, served as a warning that too tight a relationship between the supply of and demand for oil could develop into a social problem. At any rate, after the petrol panic the interest of American consumers turned towards small cars with high fuel economy. In June 1979, '$20 crude oil' appeared on the market. In fact, radicals within OPEC, such as Algeria, Libya, and Nigeria, raised market prices higher than that level, and Iraq and Kuwait followed them. This demonstrated the arrival of a seller's market for crude oil and caused the nations at the Tokyo Summit to adopt a declaration on the conservation of energy.

The Iran–Iraq war that broke out in September 1980 was between two oil-producing countries in the Middle East. Because the two countries attacked each other's oilfields and oil-loading facilities, it was expected that the production and export of the crude oil of both countries would be reduced, which accelerated the soaring trend of crude oil prices. At its extraordinary general assembly in September 1980, OPEC voted to raise the benchmark price of crude oil to $30 per barrel, and Saudi Arabia implemented the new price retroactive to August purchases. At one point in late November spot prices rose to $42 per barrel. At its December 1980 general assembly, OPEC voted to raise the benchmark crude oil price once again, to $32. And once again Saudi Arabia implemented the price increase retroactively, this time to November purchases. These high prices for crude oil invited soaring commodity prices in oil-importing countries. Inflation thus occurred during a time of economic stagnation, and the advanced industrialized nations became afflicted by stagflation.

The impact of soaring crude oil prices was less significant during the second than during the first oil crisis, for four principal reasons. First, non-OAPEC countries took the first oil crisis as an opportunity to develop oil resources of their own. In particular, countries in Western Europe, the Far East, and Eastern Europe (including the USSR) increased their production of domestic oil. That action, and successful efforts by the UK to develop oilfields in the North Sea, and those by Mexico, Indonesia, and China to produce more crude oil, combined to slow the impetus of the OPEC nations.

Second, many countries had increased their reserves of oil to sufficient levels. The International Energy Agency (IEA), established by the Organization for Economic Cooperation and Development (OECD) in November 1974, became an international venue for discussing matters such as an international petroleum accommodation scheme designed for oil-consuming countries in an emergency. In one of its early studies, the IEA concluded it was necessary for the oil-consuming countries to raise the level of their imported oil reserves. This was followed by the International Energy Programme (IEP) Agreement, which called for countermeasures in stockpiling, suppression of demand, and mutual accommodation. The agreement required member countries to increase their oil reserves to seventy days by 1 January 1976, and to ninety days by the year 1980. In Japan, the government formulated a plan for increasing the nation's oil reserves to ninety days. The purpose of the plan, which was to start in fiscal year 1975, was to increase crude oil reserves by five days each year until they reached ninety days at the end of fiscal year 1979. The plan was based on the July 1974 interim report of the Petroleum Subcommittee under MITI's Advisory Committee for Energy. Because of that plan, Japan had about eighty-five days of private-sector reserves and seven days of government reserves when the second oil crisis broke out in 1979. The system in Japan for responding to temporary supply reductions, therefore, was quite formidable compared to the roughly sixty days of oil reserves available when the first oil crisis erupted in 1973.

Third, during that same period many countries made increasing efforts to bolster their non-petroleum resources. As a result, the growth rates in the supply of coal, natural gas, hydropower, and nuclear power exceeded that of crude oil. In fact, it can be said that except for the countries in the Middle East, every country in the world was making efforts to increase the production of energy resources to replace oil. Among the different alternatives, nuclear power was the most promising candidate, and the advanced industrial nations aggressively built new nuclear power plants and expanded existing ones. From 1972 to 1978, the amount of electricity generated by nuclear power multiplied thirteenfold in Sweden, sevenfold in the USSR, nearly fivefold in the US, fourfold in Canada, nearly fourfold in West Germany, and threefold in Japan.

Fourth, the advanced industrial nations took the first oil crisis as an opportunity to promote energy-conservation policies, and their efforts showed substantial results. Taking the amount of energy consumption per gross domestic product (GDP) unit as an average of 100 in the advanced countries in 1973, the figure was about 90 in 1979. Similarly, the amount of oil consumption per GDP unit was down to around 80 in 1979.[22] Such energy-conservation efforts helped to weaken the impact of soaring crude-oil prices significantly. Among the advanced countries, however, the US lagged noticeably in its efforts to conserve oil. Its oil consumption per GDP unit index was about 97 in 1978; it was no wonder that a petrol panic erupted there in March 1979.

A spot price for crude oil of $42 per barrel, even though only transitory, would have been unthinkable in the 1960s. But crude oil prices at high levels in the 1970s led to strong efforts by the advanced industrial nations to practise greater control over their oil consumption. The success of their efforts resulted in the reverse problem of an excess of crude oil supplies. At the end of 1981, Iran began discounting the price of its oil to earn revenues to support its war against Iraq. Urged by Iran's action, Mexico and Venezuela also reduced their prices, and the price of crude oil from the North Sea also dropped. As a result the crude-oil market underwent an overall change. Oil consumption was decreasing in the advanced countries, and the crude-oil market turned into a buyer's market, forcing OPEC to reduce its oil production. The crises related to oil had passed for the moment.

24.5. Two Oil Crises, and Emergency Measures

The degree to which the advanced industrial nations depended on Middle East oil differed widely by country. In 1973, the year in which the first oil crisis broke out, the percentages of crude oil purchased from Iran, Iraq, Kuwait, Saudi Arabia, and other countries in the Middle East were: the US 20 per cent, Canada 37.2 per cent, West Germany 49.1 per cent, Italy 68.1 per cent, France 70.1 per cent, the UK 74.8 per cent, the Netherlands 77.1 per cent, and Japan 78.6 per cent.[23] Because of Japan's heavy dependence on oil from the Middle East, it was natural for it to be one of the countries most seriously affected by the first oil crisis.

Also, the share of Japan's total imports of crude oil accounted for by crude oil from oilfields developed by Japanese companies on their own, such as Arabian Oil Co. Ltd., had declined from the 1965 level of 13–15 per cent to 9 per cent in 1971. So there was no expansion in the imports of crude oil from Japanese-developed oilfields.[24] Figures for 1971 show that a large 70.7 per cent of Japan's total imports of crude oil was imported by international oil majors. Of this figure, 55.4 per cent and 15.3 per cent, respectively, were imported by American and British majors. Eighteen of the thirty-three oil companies operating in Japan in 1972 were foreign affiliates, accounting for 52.6 per cent of total domestic sales; eight were so-called all-Japanese-capital oil companies, accounting for 31.7 per cent; and seven others were affiliated with the Kyodo Oil group, accounting for 14.1 per cent. In other words, Japan was largely dependent on the international oil majors for everything from exploitation to importation and domestic sales.

These characteristics of the oil supply situation in Japan contributed to magnifying the impact on Japan of the first oil crisis. OAPEC regarded countries that supported Israel as enemies and halted oil supplies to them. Included among those countries were the US and the Netherlands, where most of the international oil majors were based. Japan, therefore, which was importing crude oil through the majors, was forced to accept supply reductions and stiff price increases. The size of the supply reductions was larger than the reductions made by the Arab countries themselves, causing much confusion among Japanese oil companies. In particular, the US majors cut off all supplies to the all-Japanese-capital oil companies in Japan, with whom they had no capital ties, and to the Kyodo Oil group of companies, placing both groups in extremely tight supply situations. On the other hand, some US majors were affiliated with Aramco Oil, and the Japanese oil companies that had ties with these majors were able to obtain relatively inexpensive crude oil because of Saudi Arabia's pricing policy. In contrast, only relatively expensive crude oil was available to the all-Japanese-capital oil companies and to the Japanese oil companies linked to the British majors that had ties with Iran; both groups were forced to struggle in their management.[25]

The reasons Japan was hit hard by the two oil crises, therefore, related to the peculiarities of its oil supply structure, and a need to correct this structural weakness had long been pointed out. For example, Japan's Energy Problems (the first White Paper on Energy), published just prior to the first oil crisis, recommended the adoption of policies such as cooperating more closely with the oil-producing nations and the international oil majors, developing Japan's own oil supply sources, and diversifying the areas from which oil was being procured.[26] War erupted in the Middle East before these recommendations could be acted on.

The Japanese government implemented a three-phase policy for coping with the first oil crisis.[27] The first phase involved emergency measures. On 16 November, the government established the Headquarters for Promotion of Emergency Petroleum Measures, headed by the Prime Minister, and the Cabinet adopted 'Guidelines for Emergency Petroleum Measures'. The key points in that outline were reductions in oil and electricity consumption. On the same day, the Cabinet also adopted 'Measures to Conserve Oil and Electric Power at Government Offices'. Next, on 19 November, the administrative vice-ministers of the various ministries agreed on 'administrative guidance for reducing oil and electricity consumption in the private sector', and the next day began implementing powerful administrative guidance for reducing oil and electricity consumption. In order to reduce oil and electricity consumption by industry, moreover, individual guidance was given to large-scale users in eleven industries, including the steel and automotive industries, two consumers of large amounts of oil. Efforts were simultaneously made to secure the necessary minimum oil allocations for public transport, hospitals, small and medium enterprises, and homes. Various ministries were assigned responsibility for implementing these measures. Administrative guidance for large-scale users was assigned to MITI.

The second phase of government activity for coping with the first oil crisis related to emergency oil legislation and associated regulatory measures. During its first meeting on 20 November, the Promotion Headquarters for Emergency Petroleum Countermeasures Policy decided to have MITI assume the leading role in designing a bill for the Petroleum Supply and Demand Optimization Law and to have the Economic Planning Agency assume the leading role in designing a bill for the Law on Emergency Measures for National Life Stabilization. In the course of drawing up the two bills, their relationship to the Anti-Monopoly Law became an issue and they were revised after repeated negotiations between MITI and the Fair Trade Commission. The bills were introduced to the National Diet for deliberation, and after some additional revisions they became law on 22 December 1973. Associated regulatory measures were then implemented.[28] In June 1974, however, after OAPEC eased its restrictions on the supply of crude oil to Japan, supply conditions improved and the government lifted the legal restrictions and instead depended on administrative guidance. Finally on 31 August 1974, the 'Emergency Declaration' was cancelled. In other words, the government took a flexible approach, and cancelled the legal restrictions after conditions improved.

In the third phase, the government promoted a policy of reducing the Japanese economy's heavy dependence on foreign oil, through energy conservation and the development and wide application of technology for alternative sources of energy. As early as May 1971, the Industrial Structure Council had issued a report called 'Vision of MITI Policies in the 1970s' that stressed a need to transform the Japanese industrial structure into one that would conserve natural resources and energy. The first oil crisis became an opportunity to implement recommendations in that report as actual policy. For developing alternative energy sources to replace oil, in December 1973 the Industrial Technology Council issued a report entitled 'On Promoting the Development of New Energy Technology'. Based on this report, in March 1974 MITI's Departmental Council issued an 'Outline for Implementing the Sunshine Project'. The Sunshine Project was thus initiated in 1974, promoting research and development of solar power generation, geothermal energy, coal liquefaction and gasification, and hydrogen energy. In April 1974, moreover, a separate MITI committee issued the 'Interim Report on Promoting Policies for Conserving Natural Resources and Energy', which emphasized a special need to promote the development of technology for more efficient and rational use of energy in the industrial sector and recommended a policy of building systems for conserving energy. The recommendations took systematic form as the 'Moonlight Project' in 1978, the Law Concerning the Rational Use of Energy in June 1979, and the Law Concerning Promotion of the Development and Introduction of Alternative Energy in May 1980.

As seen in the foregoing, Japan decreased its dependence on oil in stages and on multiple fronts. Noticeable improvements were realized by the time the second oil crisis ended.

24.6. Effects of the Oil Crises on the Japanese Economy and Industry

The two oil crises had profound effects on Japanese industry and the economy. First, the oil crises severely slowed the growth of the economy, ending its previous phenomenal growth rate. For example, GNP growth in real terms turned negative in 1974 for the first time since the end of the war, and subsequent growth never exceeded 6 per cent. Despite the slowdown, however, Japan's economy still grew faster than that of countries as advanced as the US, UK, West Germany, and France. While the US, UK, and West Germany showed negative growth even in the first half of the 1980s, Japan showed positive growth during the same period. Still, Japan's growth pattern was clearly different from that of newly industrializing economies such as Korea, Taiwan, Hong Kong, and Thailand. Japan entered a period of low, stable growth, while those countries experienced annual economic growth of over 7 per cent in the 1980s (see Table 24.1).

Second, the oil crises significantly changed the composition of Japan's industries, particularly the mining and manufacturing industries. A comparison of the

Table 24.1   GNP growth rate at constant prices: 1970–1984 (unit: %)

	1970	1971	1972	1973	1974	1975	1976	1977	1978	1979	1980	1981	1982	1983	1984
Japan	10.9	7.3	8.7	10.2	-1.3	2.4	6.5	5.4	5.1	5.6	4.3	3.7	3.1	3.2	5.1
USA	0.5	3.2	6.2	5.9	-1.7	-1.8	5.7	4.9	4.8	3.2	-0.2	1.9	-2.5	3.5	6.5
UK	1.8	2.4	3.1	6.0	-0.6	-2.1	3.8	0.6	3.9	1.1	-2.9	-0.8	1.3	4.1	2.1
W. Germany	5.6	4.5	3.4	5.3	0.5	-3.2	5.1	2.6	3.6	4.5	1.5	—	-1.0	1.5	2.7
France	—	5.3	5.7	6.0	3.8	-1.0	4.6	3.1	3.7	3.5	1.0	0.5	1.8	0.7	1.5
Thailand	8.0	5.8	3.1	8.3	4.7	5.8	7.8	6.4	11.7	6.7	5.8	6.3	4.1	5.8	6.0
Malaysia	—	8.9	7.1	9.7	6.3	—	11.1	7.6	7.6	8.5	7.9	6.9	5.6	6.3	7.6
Philippines	6.3	5.6	4.4	9.0	4.9	5.4	7.5	6.1	7.6	6.0	5.2	3.9	2.9	1.1	-4.6
Korea	8.6	9.8	7.3	16.9	8.8	8.8	13.0	10.3	11.3	7.4	-3.0	6.9	5.5	9.5	7.9
Taiwan											7.3	6.1	2.8	7.7	9.6
Hong Kong											11.0	9.4	2.9	6.5	9.4
OECD											1.1	1.9	-0.5	3.4	3.4

Sources: Compiled based on Toyo Keizai Inc., *Keizai Tokei Nenkan* (Annual Economic Statistics), 1975: 364; and annual editions of *Nihon Keizai wo Chushin to Suru Kokusai Hikaku Tokei* (Comparative Economic and Financial Statistics, Japan and Other Major Countries), published by Statistics Bureau, Bank of Japan.

composition of shipments of manufacturing industry products in 1970 and in 1980 shows that the shares held by the textile, steel, non-ferrous metal manufacturing, and metal product manufacturing industries were smaller in 1980. While the decline in the share held by the textile industry was mainly due to competition from developing countries where wages were lower, the decline in the steel, non-ferrous metal manufacturing, and metal product manufacturing industries were mainly due to higher energy costs stemming from the oil crises and the resulting 'structural recession'. In contrast, shares increased for the following: the transportation machinery and equipment manufacturing industry, which includes cars; for the electronic machinery and instruments manufacturing industry, which includes computers and components; and for the precision machinery and instruments manufacturing industry, which includes cameras. The reason for the increases was that those industries produced technology-intensive products. A popular phrase of the time was 'lighter, thinner, shorter, and smaller'. That phrase expressed the fact that industries that were energy-efficient, relied heavily on technology, and produced lighter, thinner, shorter, or smaller products were achieving higher growth rates than other industries, leading to the change in Japan's industrial structure (see Table 24.2).

Third, the two oil crises were accompanied by rapid and substantial price increases (as measured by wholesale and consumer price indexes), which, in effect, kept increases in real wages and consumption low. Behind those developments were rampant consumer prices accompanying the first oil crisis, which led to speculative behaviour by some companies and panic-buying by consumers.

Fourth, the oil crises altered Japan's energy supply and demand structure, particularly the composition of its primary energy supply. As mentioned earlier, Japan's dependence on oil declined and nuclear power and other alternative energy sources increased in importance. The composition of the nations supplying oil to Japan also became more diverse, resulting in less dependence on countries in the Middle East. Also, the introduction of energy conservation measures in many sectors, as will be discussed later, led to steady decreases in unit energy costs.

The fifth effect of the oil crises resulted indirectly while measures were being taken to cope with rising oil prices and tightening oil supplies. In fact, it was more a result of the yen's appreciation under the system of floating exchange rates. As the yen rose in value, companies were forced to reduce costs and improve their product quality, leading to the strengthened international competitiveness of Japan's manufacturing industries, particularly those producing high-technology products, such as cars, electronic components, and precision machinery. As a result, although Japan's exports declined for a short while after the two oil crises, they expanded afterwards at a pace generally not experienced in any other advanced country, and eventually became the cause of international trade friction. Japan set new records every year in its trade balance surplus, and despite

Table 24.2   Trends in Japan's industrial output, 1970–1980 (units: billion yen, %, multiple)

Industry	1970	% of total	1975	% of total	1980	% of total	1980 vs. 1970
Food manufacturing	7,150	9.7	15,130	11.9	22,512	10.5	3.15
Manufacture of textile mill products, except apparel and other finished products made from fabrics materials	4,389	6.4	6,457	5.1	8,105	3.8	1.85
Manufacture of apparel and other finished products made from fabrics and similar materials	956	1.4	2,180	1.7	3,026	1.4	3.17
Manufacture of lumber and wood products, except furniture	2,231	3.2	3,618	2.8	5,454	2.5	2.44
Manufacture of furniture and fixtures	1,009	1.5	1,974	1.5	3,036	1.4	3.01
Manufacture of pulp, paper, and paper products	2,269	3.3	4,210	3.3	6,799	3.2	3.00
Publishing, printing, and allied industries	1,999	2.9	4,162	3.3	6,979	3.3	3.49
Manufacture of chemical and allied products	5,540	8.0	10,438	8.2	17,978	8.4	3.25
Manufacture of petroleum and coal products	1,971	2.6	7,572	5.9	15,197	7.1	7.71
Manufacture of rubber products	766	1.1	1,427	1.1	2,488	1.2	3.25
Leather tanning and manufacture of leather products and fur skins	342	0.5	647	0.5	1,015	0.5	2.97
Manufacture of ceramic, stone, and clay products	2,469	3.6	4,801	3.8	8,394	3.9	3.40
Iron and steel industry	6,564	9.5	11,306	8.9	17,895	8.3	2.73
Manufacture of non-ferrous metals and products	3,054	5.1	3,908	3.1	8,118	3.8	2.66
Manufacture of fabricated metal products	3,727	5.4	6,573	5.2	10,646	5.0	2.86
Manufacture of general machinery (including ordnance)	6,806	9.9	10,621	8.3	17,617	8.2	2.59
Manufacture of electrical machinery equipment and supplies	7,330	10.6	10,821	8.5	22,234	10.4	3.03
Manufacture of transportation equipment	7,275	10.5	14,793	11.6	24,953	11.6	3.43
Manufacture of precision instrument and machinery	891	1.3	1,729	1.4	3,457	1.6	3.98
Miscellaneous manufacturing industries	2,465	3.6	5,060	4.0	8,787	4.1	3.56
Total	69,034	100.0	127,432	100.0	214,699	100.0	3.11

Source: Compiled from *Tsusho Sangyo Seisakushi* (History of International Trade and Industry Policy), xvi: 171–2; percentages and multiples have been rounded.

sizeable increases in Japanese overseas investments and temporary declines after the two oil crises, its foreign-currency reserves also continued to increase.

In these ways, emergency measures averted catastrophes that could have been caused by the two oil crises, occurring as they did under a system of floating exchange rates. Subsequent long-term, structural measures made possible the transformation of Japanese industry and the economy. While this transformation was taking place, Japan also moved to correct problems that emerged relating to its period of high economic growth and to ease international economic friction.

NOTES

1. For background to this section, see: Charles A. Coombs, *Inside Story of International Currency Diplomacy*, trans. by Nobuyoshi Araki, *Kokusai Tsuka no Uchimaku*, Nihon Keizai Shimbun, Inc., 1977; Kazuhiro Tatebe, *Amerika no Kokusai Tsuka Seisaku* (US International Monetary Policy), Ochanomizu Shobo Publishers, 1987; Makoto Utsumi (ed.), *Atarashii IMF* (The New IMF), Foreign Exchange Trade and Research Association, 1976; Paul Volker and Toyoo Gyoten, *Tomi no Kobo—En to Doru no Rekishi* (Changing Fortunes: History of the Yen and Dollar), Toyo Keizai Inc., 1992; Ministry of Finance (ed.), *Showa Zaiseishi; Showa 27–48 nendo* (The Financial History of Japan in the Showa Period: 1952–73), Toyo Keizai Inc., ix (1991) and xii (1992).
2. Charles A. Coombs, *Inside Story of International Currency Diplomacy*: 240; and Paul Volker and Toyoo Gyoten, *Tomi no Kobo*: 139.
3. The Bank of Japan, Research and Statistics Dept., *Nihon Keizai wo Chushin to suru Kokusai Hikakutokei* (Comparative Economic and Financial Statistics, Japan and Major Countries), 1975: 9–10.
4. Masaru Hayami, *Kaizu naki Kokai—Hendo Sobasei 10–nen* (Voyage without Nautical Charts—Ten Years of the Floating Exchange Rate System), Toyo Keizai Inc., 1982: 16. According to Hayami, the attack against Japan started in London, where it was said that 'Japan was using the fixed rate market to support a weak yen in order to expand its exports and accumulate foreign exchange reserves.'
5. For discussion of yen countermeasures taken by the Japanese government, including MITI, before and after the Nixon Shock, see: MITI, Committee to Edit History of International Trade and Industry Policy (ed.), *Tsusho Sangyo Seisakushi* (History of International Trade and Industry Policy), Tsusho Sangyo Chosakai (Research Institute of International Trade and Industry), xii (1993), ch. 2, sect. 1.
6. Paul Volker and Toyoo Gyoten, *Tomi no Kobo*: 120–1.
7. Opinion of Yusuke Kashiwagi, then Special Adviser to the MoF. See Ushio Shioda, *Kasumigaseki ga Furueta Hi* (The Days that Shook Kasumigaseki—Twelve Days of Monetary War), Simul Press, Inc., 1983: 95–6, 103–6.
8. *Nihon Keizai Shimbun*, 28 Aug. 1971.
9. Refer to newspaper reports of the time, such as articles appearing in the 17 and 28 Aug. 1971, editions of the *Nihon Keizai Shimbun*, *Asahi Shimbun*, and *Mainichi Shimbun*.
10. *Nihon Keizai Shimbun*, 23 Aug. 1971.
11. For events occurring over the period between the Nixon Shock up to the Smithsonian Conference, see *Tsusho Sangyo Seisakushi*, xii, ch. 1, sect. 1.
12. *Tsusho Hakusho*, 1973 edn., General Survey Volume, table 15 in pt. 1, ch. 2: 99.
13. *Tsusho Hakusho*, 1974 edn., General Survey Volume: 104–8.
14. *Tsusho Hakusho*, 1978 edn., General Survey Volume, table 6 in pt. 2, ch. 1: 126–7 and table 11 in pt. 2, ch. 1: 142–3.
15. For discussion of yen rate from the first oil crisis to the end of 1981, see Tsuyoshi Muramoto, *En Soba 10-nen no Dainamizumu* (Dynamism of Yen Exchange Market for Ten Years), Yuhikaku Publishing Co. Ltd., 1984, chs. IV, V, and VI.

16. Isao Kamata and Setsuo Takagaki, *Nihon no Enerugi Kiki—Tenkanki no Sekiyu Senryaku* (Japan's Energy Crisis—Turning Point for Oil Strategy), Nihon Keizai Shimbun Inc., 1973: 156 (table 29).

17. MITI (ed.), *Nihon no Enerugi Mondai* (Japan's Energy Problems), Research Institute of International Trade and Industry, 1973, Reference Materials nos. 1–8: 99.

18. General Coordination Division, Director-General's Secretariat, Agency of Natural Resources and Energy (ed.), *Sogo Enerugi Tokei* (Energy Balances in Japan), editions for each year, see ch. 7 on overseas energy.

19. The Institute of Energy Economics, Japan (ed.), *Sengo Enerugi Sangyoshi* (Post-War History of Japanese Energy Industry), Toyo Keizai Inc., 1986: 25–6.

20. *Nihon Keizai Shimbun*, 18 Dec. 1978.

21. For discussion of Middle East crude oil price fluctuations at the time of the second oil crisis, see the Institute of Energy Economics, Japan (ed.), *Oiru Ripoto—Sekiyu Shijo de Nani ga Okite Iru ka* (Oil Report), Nihon Keizai Shimbun Inc., 1980, ch. 2.

22. *Tsusho Hakusho*, 1981 edn., General Survey Volume, Fig. 10 in pt. 1, ch. 3: 94.

23. *Sogo Enerugi Tokei*, 1977 edn., calculated from 364–9.

24. Isao Kamata and Setsuo Takagaki: 193 (table 38) and 117 (table 24).

25. Energy Journalist Group (ed.), *Sekiyu to Tatakatta Nihon Keizai—Enerugi Kiki 10-nen no Shogen* (The Japanese Economy's Oil Battles—Comments on Ten Years of Oil Crisis), Denryoku Shimposha, 1983: 129–3.

26. *Nihon no Enerugi Mondai*; *Tsusho Sangyo Seisakushi*, xiii (1991): 48–9.

27. For a discussion of the emergency measures taken at the time of the first oil crisis, see *Tsusho Sangyo Seisakushi*, xiii, ch. 4; MITI (ed.), *Tsusho Sangyo-sho Nenpo* (MITI Annual Report), 1973; Agency of Natural Resources and Energy (ed.), *Enerugi Seisaku no Ayumi to Tenbo* (Energy Policies, Past, Present, and Future), Research Institute of International Trade and Industry, 1993; Yasuhiro Nakasone, *Kaizu no nai Kokai—Sekiyu Kiki to Tsusansho* (Uncharted Waters—Oil Crisis and MITI), Nihon Keizai Shimbun Inc., 1975; and Energy Journalist Group (ed.), 1983.

28. For the process of legislating the two oil-industry laws, see *Tsusho Sangyo Seisakushi*, xiii. 54–63.

25

Energy Measures and Structurally Depressed Industries

25.1. Promoting Conversion to Non-Petroleum Energy

Problems in structure for supplying primary energy

The first oil crisis clearly revealed the Achilles' heel of the structure for supplying primary energy in Japan, which had become highly dependent on imported oil from the Middle East to satisfy its rapidly expanding energy requirements. A change in the primary energy supply structure emerged in the course of high-level economic growth from around 1965, influenced by what was then called an energy revolution. The percentage of primary energy produced domestically before then had by no means been small.

The percentage of the total volume of primary energy accounted for by domestically produced energy declined rapidly from 76.9 per cent in 1953 to 73.6 per cent in 1956, 52.1 per cent in 1961, 31.3 per cent in 1966, and 15.1 per cent in 1971. Amidst this dramatic change, the percentage of domestic coal as a source of energy declined even more remarkably, from 46.8 per cent in 1953 to 6.3 per cent in 1971. The supply of hydropower, meanwhile, which was relatively inexpensive and pollution-free, increased almost double during the same period, but because there were major restrictions on the rapid increase of hydroelectric power generation plants, the percentage of the total supply of primary energy accounted for by hydropower fell during the same period from 19.7 per cent to 6.7 per cent. In contrast, the percentage of imported oil (total of crude oil, oil products, and LPG) showed rapid growth during the same period from 17.1 per cent to 73.3 per cent. During the course of high-level economic growth, the transition from coal to less expensive, easier-to-handle oil progressed, and as total energy consumption increased tremendously, the percentage of domestically supplied energy dropped dramatically. In short, high-level growth was a principal reason for the severe impact on Japan of the first oil crisis.

High-level economic growth also brought about a structural change in the private consumption of energy through urbanization, home electrification, and motorization. In 1955, the structure of energy consumption was as follows: firewood accounted for 26.8 per cent, electricity for 20.3 per cent, coal for 17.9 per cent, charcoal for 13.1 per cent, briquettes and oval briquettes for 7.3 per cent, oil for 6.5 per cent, and city gas for 6.4 per cent. As these figures show, there was no heavy dependence on a particular source of energy. Traditional fuels such as charcoal and firewood, which have wood acquired from thinnings and from miscellaneous trees as their raw materials, accounted for about 40 per cent of the total, and briquettes and oval briquettes, made from coal and coal residue, accounted for about 25 per cent of the total. Cooking stoves, portable clay cooking stoves, hibachi heaters (charcoal braziers), hearths, and so forth, which were not so different in form from the same items used in the early Meiji period, were still being widely used for cooking, heating of bathwater, and home heating. In 1955, such household appliances as washing machines, vacuum cleaners, refrigerators, TVs, air-conditioners, and so forth still had a diffusion rate close to zero. Even the production of wholly Japanese-made cars had barely begun by that time.

Urbanization (including construction of high- and mid-rise apartments), greater use of home electric appliances, and motorization accompanied high-level economic growth, all of which brought about drastic changes in the private energy consumption structure. In 1971, just before the first oil crisis, energy consumption in the domestic sector consisted of oil (including paraffin and LPG) 49.4 per cent, electricity 36.3 per cent, city gas 8.4 per cent, firewood 2.4 per cent, coal 2.1 per cent, briquettes and oval briquettes 1.4 per cent, and charcoal 0.2 per cent. Oil and electricity together thus accounted for over 85 per cent of total energy consumption. And because almost 70 per cent of all electric power was generated by thermal generators burning heavy oil, it is no exaggeration to say that three-quarters of private-sector energy depended on oil. Actually, for about fifteen years 'modernization' of the Japanese life style had been gradually taking place in both urban and rural areas, such as switching from cooking stoves and portable clay cooking stoves to electric rice cookers, city gas and LPG, from charcoal braziers and coal stoves to electric footwarmers and paraffin stoves, from hand fans and electric fans to air-conditioners, from neighbourhood public baths to home baths and showers provided with hot water from boilers, and from wooden clogs and bicycles to private cars. Traditional sources of energy, such as coal, briquettes, oval briquettes, charcoal, and firewood were forced from use in the daily lives of the Japanese people. These lifestyle changes were additional reasons for the severe impact on Japan of the first oil crisis.

The supply structure for primary energy in Japan differed considerably from that of the advanced Western nations (except Italy). The degree that selected countries depended on oil in 1970 was 77.3 per cent for Italy, 70.8 per cent for Japan (fiscal year 1970), 65.0 per cent for France, 56.0 per cent for West Germany, 49.5 per cent for the UK, and 44.6 per cent for the US. The dependence on coal in 1970 for the same countries was 43.9 per cent for the UK, 38.0 per cent for West Germany, 25.4 per cent for France, 21.0 per cent for the US, 20.7 per cent for Japan (only 8.1 per cent was domestic coal), and 9.9 per cent for Italy. As these figures show, only Italy and Japan depended especially heavily on oil, while countries like the UK, France, and West Germany continued depending largely on coal as their primary source of energy. The dependence on natural gas in the same year was 32.8 per cent for the US, 8.8 per cent for Italy, 6.2 per cent for France, 5.3 per cent for the UK, 5.1 per cent for West Germany, and 0.9 per cent for Japan. Compared with the advanced Western nations, therefore, Japan lagged considerably in its use of natural gas. Nuclear energy, meanwhile, was still not in great use even in the advanced Western nations. The figures for 1970 were 1.1 per cent for the UK, 0.4 per cent for France, Italy, and Japan, 0.3 per cent for West Germany, and 0.2 per cent for the US. As seen, although the overall percentages were low, Japan compared favourably with all the advanced nations except the UK.[1]

Direction of energy resources diversification

After passing through the first oil crisis, much attention came to be focused on Japan's structural problems related to energy. It was essential, of course, for Japan to secure stable supplies of energy to maintain and expand its economy, and for that purpose it was necessary to establish a long-range energy plan covering both supply and demand which would emphasize the securing of sufficient quantities of energy at stable prices, the effective use of energy by implementing energy-conservation policies, and the control of overly rapid increases in energy consumption.

On 15 August 1975, the Advisory Committee for Energy (Chairman Kogoro Uemura) submitted an interim report entitled 'Concerning Energy Stabilization Policy for 1975–1984' in response to a request from the Minister of International Trade and Industry for recommendations on what Japan's overall energy policy should be. The interim report said that based on the experience of the oil crisis the first objective should be to assure a stable supply of energy sources. The report reviewed the situation regarding each supply source and presented a long-term energy supply and demand plan, starting with actual 1973 figures, and estimating demand for 1980 and 1985. Its salient points were as follows:[2]

1. Among domestic energy resources, hydropower is expensive to develop and cannot be expected to grow by any more than an annual average of about 3.4 per cent. Its share of total energy will decline slightly in fiscal year 1985.
2. Geothermal energy should be actively developed. If developed at an average annual growth rate of 39.7 per cent, its share in fiscal year 1985 will be 0.5 per cent.
3. Domestic coal is another important source of energy, but several factors influence its development. For example, the condition of the reserves (depth, ease of access, etc.), the securing of sufficient labour for mining, and improvement of the business structure. Because of these difficulties, little growth in coal supplies can be expected. Coal's share of total energy supplies in fiscal year 1985 will be 0.8 per cent, down from the 3.8 per cent in fiscal year 1973.
4. Nuclear power, which can be considered pseudo-domestic energy, is most promising as an alternative to oil. If siting problems are resolved and the safety of facilities is assured, nuclear power can be developed at an annual average growth rate of 32.3 per cent and its share of total energy in fiscal year 1985 will be 9.6 per cent.

5. LNG is an imported source of non-petroleum energy. Because it is a clean source of energy and has no production bias towards particular regions, and since by its nature there is little possibility that production restrictions will be introduced, it can be expected to grow at an average annual rate of 27.1 per cent. Its share of total energy in fiscal year 1985 will be 7.9 per cent.
6. Imported coal, another non-petroleum imported energy, is the most abundant fossil fuel in the world. It also exists in areas other than the oil-producing countries. It will be developed at an average annual growth rate of 4.8 per cent and in fiscal year 1985 will account for 11.2 per cent of total energy in Japan.
7. Although about 500 million kl. of imported oil are expected to be supplied in fiscal year 1985, the balance between supply of and demand for oil is predicted to be stable structurally for a long time. Steps should be taken to assure stable supplies by promoting worldwide exploration and development in order to diversify supply sources and supply systems. The 77.4 per cent share held by oil in fiscal year 1973 will be lowered to 63.3 per cent in fiscal 1985.

As seen in the above forecasts by type of energy resource, the long-term supply and demand energy plan aimed to resolve the problems that existed in Japan's energy supply structure before the first oil crisis. The basic direction of the plan is seen in four areas: (1) lowering Japan's dependence on oil and diversifying the types of non-petroleum-based energy; (2) securing stable supplies of oil; (3) promoting energy conservation; and (4) research and development of new types of energy. At this point, therefore, the previous policy of depending on oil for ample, inexpensive, and stable energy supplies was discarded and MITI moved to promote a comprehensive energy policy as outlined in the interim report, with emphasis on multiple sources of energy.

25.2. Promoting Construction and Maintaining Safety of Nuclear Power Plants

The first oil crisis clarified the risk of depending heavily on imported oil from the Middle East. Electric power being generated in Japan in 1973 came from the following types of power plants: thermal 71.5 per cent, hydro 24.3 per cent, and nuclear 4.2 per cent. The share of thermal power generation was overwhelmingly large, and most plants depended on oil for fuel. In fact, oil accounted for 61.2 per cent of total power-generation resources, far more than coal's 5.5 per cent or LNG's 2.8 per cent. Electric power generation in Japan thus depended heavily on oil as a source of energy, and if another oil crisis occurred it was possible that an electric power crisis would immediately result. Nuclear energy was considered most promising as an alternative energy source for reducing Japan's dependence on oil, responding to increased demands for electric power, and providing stable supplies of power.

Construction of Japan's first nuclear power plant began in March 1961 for the Tokai Generation Station of the Japan Nuclear Energy Power Generation Corporation. The years 1967 to 1972 saw the first boom in construction of nuclear power plants, and when the first oil crisis occurred Japan had five nuclear power generators (total output of 1.82 million kW) at four power stations: the Tokai and Tsuruga Stations of the Japan Nuclear Energy Power Generation Corporation, the Fukushima No. 1 Station of Tokyo Electric Power Co., and the Mihama Station of Kansai Electric Power Co., while seventeen other nuclear power generators (total output of 13.653 million kW) were under construction for electric power companies throughout Japan, including those in the Chugoku, Tohoku, Chubu, Shikoku, and Kyushu areas. The wave of nuclear power plant construction met opposition from citizen groups living in the communities around proposed plant sites, not only because of concern for safety and environmental pollution but also because nuclear power plants created few new job opportunities and returned few benefits to the local community. The siting of new nuclear power plants thus became gradually more difficult.

The controversies concerning siting focused on assurances concerning safety and protection of the environment. In May 1971, it was reported that in experiments conducted with an emergency core cooling system (ECCS) at the Idaho Federal Nuclear Reactor Laboratories of the Atomic Energy Commission in the US to prepare for possible empty ignition of a nuclear reactor, efforts to inject cooling water had failed. This suggested the possibility that ECCS cannot prevent a reactor core meltdown. Since the model which most nuclear power plants planned for introduction into Japan was the boiling-water reactor (BWR) type, the same model as in the experiments, residents at the proposed sites became anxious, and opposition to construction intensified. In Japan at the time, it was widely believed that the light-water reactor was fully tested and approved, and therefore there had been no all-out study in Japan of its safety. Until then, the direction of policies concerning nuclear energy was focused on developing the industry, and MITI's priority measures were securing uranium resources, subsidizing nuclear energy power generation, fostering and bolstering the nuclear energy equipment industry, and promoting the development of technology for wider use of nuclear energy.[3]

In that situation, and in order to eliminate the uneasiness regarding the safety of, and environmental pollution from, power plants, the Japanese government decided to legislate to enhance the social welfare system in regions where there were power generation stations, including not only nuclear power plants but also thermal and hydroelectric plants. In June 1974, three laws, the Law on the Development of Areas Adjacent to Electric Power Generating Facilities, the Electric Power Development Promotion Law, and the Law on Special Accounts for Electric Power Development Acceleration Measures (the so-called three power resources laws), were promulgated. The salient points of the three laws were: (1) to levy an electric power development promotion tax on power companies; (2) to include that tax income in special accounts for electric power development acceleration measures; and (3) to utilize the taxes as a source of revenue to provide public welfare facilities around the sites of power generation facilities, to promote the welfare of local residents, and to obtain their understanding and cooperation so that the development of power resource sites might be advanced. The designation of sites under the Electric Power Site Development Plan started in October 1974, and a total of 126 sites were designated in fifteen phases up to March 1979. The breakdown was nineteen sites for nuclear energy generation, thirty-two sites for thermal generation, and seventy-five sites for hydropower generation.[4]

Among the priorities of international trade and industry policies in fiscal year 1975, the subject of tests to evaluate and reconfirm the safety of new types of reactors was rediscussed, and expenses for investigating the reliability of light-water reactors were scheduled for inclusion in the special accounts for measures accelerating electric power development. In 1976, a further step forward was taken to incorporate in priority policies the thinking that it was necessary to drastically reinforce safety measures in order to promote the utilization of nuclear energy. For that purpose, the priority policies stated that such measures will be energetically pursued in order to restore the confidence of the general public in the safety of nuclear power generation, to expand experiments to confirm the safety of light-water reactors so that the selection of nuclear power generation sites may be made smoothly, to establish a Nuclear Power Engineering Experiment Centre (temporary name), to promote improvement and standardization of equipment and reactor types, to enhance safety, to reinforce public relations activities in order to promote an understanding among local residents of the safety of nuclear energy, and so forth. A budget totaling 3,839 million yen was appropriated as expenses for commissioning safety and other measures for nuclear power generation, subsidies for nuclear power generation safety and other measures, and expenses necessary for public relations activities related to nuclear power generation.[5] Afterwards, measures to assure nuclear power generation safety and conduct tests to confirm the reliability of facilities were always incorporated in priority policies and the budget for them continued increasing.

On 4 October 1978, the Atomic Energy Commission was reorganized and the Nuclear Power Safety Commission was newly established to handle safety issues. Safety regulations related to nuclear energy reactors for practical power generation were placed under the jurisdiction of the Minister of International Trade and Industry, who exercised integrated control over nuclear energy reactors for practical power generation under the Law Concerning the Regulation of Nuclear Source Material, Nuclear Fuel Material, and Reactors and the Electricity Utilities Law. In January 1979, the Nuclear Power Safety Examination Division and the Nuclear Power Safety Administration Division of the Agency of Natural Resources and Energy were made independent from the previous Nuclear Power Division, thus making the safety control system more firmly established. On 28 March 1979, meanwhile, a serious accident occurred at the Three Mile Island nuclear power station in the US when a part of the reactor core was damaged at the No. 2 reactor (TMI-2). The Nuclear Power Safety Commission of Japan dispatched an investigation team and subsequently reviewed Japan's nuclear power plant safety measures. In January 1980, MITI established the Quality Guarantee Investigation Committee for Nuclear Power Stations to consider a system of quality guarantees based on an analysis of accidents, breakdowns, and abnormalities.

Other issues for promoting the use of nuclear energy included securing safety at plant sites, ensuring a stable supply of nuclear fuel, developing technology for enriching uranium, recycling of nuclear fuel, managing of waste material, research and development of new types of reactors, and so forth. These issues were discussed at the Nuclear Energy Subcommittee of the Advisory Committee for Energy and elsewhere and were later made into policies. As a result, nuclear energy, which accounted for only 0.4 per cent of primary energy supplies in fiscal year 1970, came to account for 5.1 per cent in 1980. The percentage of nuclear power generation among total power generation increased from 1.27 per cent in fiscal year 1970 to 14.3 per cent in 1980. The percentage in 1980 approached that of hydropower, which was 15.9 per cent.[6]

25.3. Coal, Natural Gas, and Other Forms of Non-Petroleum Energy

Coal, natural gas, and other forms of non-petroleum energy

Influenced by the first oil crisis, many countries turned new attention to coal as an energy resource because of its relative abundance. The US and USSR, for example, the two major producers of coal, increased their production, and the countries of Europe tended to maintain production at existing levels. Coal production in Japan had been reduced to 31.73 million tons in fiscal year 1971, mainly because domestic coal had become relatively more expensive compared to imported energy resources when the yen appreciated after the Nixon 'shock'. Also, sales of coal declined due to depressed conditions in the iron and steel industry, and electric power companies became less enthusiastic about using coal because of environmental problems. Companies in the coal mining industry thus fell on hard times. Although emergency measures were introduced to help those companies, the measures treated only the symptoms, not the ailment. They included an easing of repayment conditions for modernization financing, cooperation in obtaining new financing for year-end and new-year funds, improved availability of funds for subsidizing the construction of structural supports inside mines, and an increase in the unit price for general coal among the subsidies earmarked for stabilizing the coal mining industry. In that situation, and in order to demonstrate the industry's future prospects to coal producers, a need emerged to formulate a supply–demand plan and to clarify new policies related to the coal industry. It was at that point that the Coal Mining Council began to study the fifth-phase coal policy.

In the fifth-phase coal policy, based on the supposition that the demand for coal in fiscal year 1975 would not fall below 20 million tons, the government agreed to absorb industry loans worth 70 billion yen, increased the percentages of various subsidies and loans, requested large-scale users to purchase domestic coal, established a rule for annual adjustments to coal prices based on price trends of competitive energies, established a Management Committee inside the Coal Mining Industry Rationalization Corporation, and extended until fiscal year 1976 the duration of the Special Accounts for Coal and Petroleum Countermeasures.

With the outbreak of the first oil crisis, domestic coal was re-evaluated as an important non-petroleum source of energy. On 16 July 1975, the Coal Mining Council submitted 'Recommendations Concerning Coal under the New Comprehensive Energy Policy'. That report became the basis for the sixth-phase coal policy. It set three principal goals, premised on the possibility of coal being utilized in the future as an all-out, long-range energy resource: (1) supporting the production of domestic coal, (2) facilitating the development and import of overseas coal, and (3) promoting research of coal utilization technology. Specific measures cited were developing and importing overseas coal, promoting international cooperation, promoting the development of technology for liquefying and gasifying coal, and so forth. Other measures included the securing of funds from special accounts and the extension of related laws and regulations, such as the Law on Extraordinary Measures for Rationalization of the Coal Mining Industry.[7]

Despite the post-oil crisis review made of the coal industry, the conditions inside the coal mines and the financial condition of coal mining companies continued worsening. Coal mining divisions were turned into subsidiaries, management was made separate, and mines were closed. At one point during the second oil crisis, the prices of heavy oil and coal were temporarily reversed, and some companies experimented with converting from heavy oil to coal for their fuel source. Also, because the price of imported coal increased, the price disparity between imported and domestic coal decreased, leading to a slight revival in the consumption of domestic coal. In those circumstances, domestic coal production was maintained at the level of 17.7–18.6 million tons a year. Still, because of the generally large price disparity between imported and domestic coal, not only for raw material coal but also for general coal, imports of general coal continued to increase gradually with the second oil crisis as the turning point. The percentage of primary energy supply dependent on domestic coal was only 8.1 per cent in fiscal year 1970, and that percentage did not increase despite the two oil crises. In fiscal year 1980, in fact, the figure became 3.1 per cent. The closing of coal mines one after the other affected mine workers tremendously and caused disruptions in local communities. MITI reviewed its coal policy about every five years, reducing production coal targets each time. Substantial fiscal spending was aimed at rationalizing operations and absorbing loans, but no decisive remedy was found to maintain the domestic coal mining industry as an energy industry, and it went defunct.

Liquefied natural gas and city gas

In the past, Japan had never used much natural gas or liquefied natural gas (LNG), although both were regarded as clean types of non-petroleum energy. Just prior to the first oil crisis, they combined to account for only about 1 per cent of total primary energy consumption. The low level of consumption was due partly to the fact that supplies of natural gas had not grown, and for the interim even existing demand could not be met, although it was possible that supplies might grow following the exploration and development of gas fields on the continental shelf. In that situation, Japan was forced to depend on imported LNG.

To secure a stable supply of LNG, it was necessary to enthusiastically promote Japan-led development projects overseas, to construct liquefaction plants in host countries, to arrange for exclusive-use tankers for transportation, and to establish receiving stations at home. Large investments were thus needed, as well as the building of long-term, stable relationships regarding both supply and demand. It was recognized, therefore, that the expansion of LNG demand should be promoted as a project that tied together production, transportation, and consumption. This same point was emphasized in 'Energy in 1975–1984', a report from the Advisory Committee for Energy in August 1975. The report also proposed organizing the latent demand for general industrial and other uses of energy, as well as putting into order the network of pipelines to tie in with the demand from large-scale users of electric power and city gas.[8]

In the past, MITI had provided budgets from special accounts for the survey and development of continental shelf oil resources. In new policies established in fiscal year 1974, a budget for developing natural gas was provided from the special account. And in policies for fiscal year 1975, subsidies for exploring natural gas resources became an independent budget item. When the new policies for fiscal year 1976 were finalized, a budget was provided for treasury investments and loans to promote LNG imports by businesses supplying LNG in the Tohoku district, based on the report of the Advisory Committee for Energy.[9] Budgetary measures were continuously provided afterwards that fitted the various stages of development of the LNG supply system.

LNG was first imported in fiscal year 1969, amounting to 182,000 tons. Imports reached 5 million tons in fiscal year 1975, and exceeded 16 million tons in fiscal year 1980, of which about 12 million tons were used for power generation, about 3 million tons for producing city gas, and the remaining roughly 500,000 tons for industrial fuel. LNG was imported from Brunei, Indonesia, the United Arab Emirates, the US and other countries.[10] Compared with the Western countries, the use of LNG in Japan was still low, but some growth was seen in using it as a clean form of energy and a substitute for oil.

The city gas industry took the initiative in developing overseas LNG for import into Japan. The demand for city gas as a fuel for the needs of daily life increased as the Japanese population became more concentrated in urban areas and as more mid- and high-rise buildings were constructed in the cities. It can be said that the period of high-level economic growth was also a period of high-level growth in the consumption of city gas. City gas supplies were 17,100 billion kcal. in fiscal year 1961, and increased 2.87-fold to 49,400 billion kcal. in fiscal year 1971.[11] The demand for LNG as a non-polluting, clean form of energy increased as it was consumed not only in homes but also by business and industry. Supplies continued increasing even after the oil crisis.

In view of these trends, the Gas Utility Industry Law was substantially revised in April 1970. Included among the revisions were a bolstering of security, the introduction of regulations concerning gas utensils, the regulation of community gas undertakings, and a responsibility by city gas companies to submit supply plans.[12]

The first oil crisis brought about cost increases in gas obtained from petroleum, as well as wage increases because of inflation. Those increases, plus the burden of the capital expenditures required to raise the calories in gas, placed gas companies in difficult managerial circumstances. They were forced to raise gas prices several times.

The first task the city gas companies tackled in the oil crisis was shifting the emphasis in the raw materials they used. In fiscal year 1970, the raw materials the three largest gas companies (Tokyo Gas, Osaka Gas, and Toho Gas) depended on were coal 43.4 per cent, naphtha and other hydrocarbon mixtures 41.8 per cent, LNG 7.7 per cent, domestic natural gas 4.1 per cent, LPG 2.8 per cent, and others 0.1 per cent. Raw materials obtained from petroleum, such as naphtha and LPG, accounted for 44.6 per cent of the total. In fiscal year 1980, during the second oil crisis, the make-up of raw materials was changed to LNG 59.7 per cent, naphtha and other hydrocarbon mixtures 17.1 per cent, coal 16.4 per cent, LPG 5.3 per cent, domestic natural gas 1.4 per cent, and others 0.1 per cent. The percentages accounted for by coal and raw materials obtained from petroleum thus declined.[13] By shifting the weight of the raw materials they used, the city gas companies obtained better heating value and were able to introduce more efficient production and supply facilities. It also became possible to utilize more effectively the effluent heat of LNG, including its use for heating and cooling. A contract system was introduced in fiscal year 1979 to promote the industrial use of LNG. Conversion to LNG required considerable investment in plant and equipment as well as expenses for conversion operations, however, and provincial gas companies that did not have the funds to respond quickly continued depending heavily on LPG. Survey expenses for introducing LNG were budgeted in new MITI policies for fiscal year 1980.[14] The use of LNG as a source of energy to replace oil was pursued as policy during the second oil crisis.

Hydropower, geothermal energy, etc.

Because of the first oil crisis, a need came to be keenly felt to secure stable sources of energy supplies and to formulate a long-term supply–demand plan for energy. And because they were not influenced by international instability, attention was also drawn to the effective utilization of domestic non-oil energy resources. The interim report of the Advisory Committee for Energy, 'Concerning Energy Stabilization Policy for 1975–84', which proposed establishment of a comprehensive energy policy, listed not only oil, natural gas, and coal as domestic sources of energy but also hydropower and geothermal energy, and emphasized a need to include development of those sources as well in the long-term supply–demand plan for energy.[15]

The development of geothermal energy as a new form of energy was designated a principal goal in the large-scale technological development project called the 'Sunshine Project', which also included the development of solar energy, coal energy, and hydrogen energy.[16] Because Japan is a volcanic country, there are high expectations of developing an abundant supply of geothermal energy. It was also expected that developing geothermal energy resources would contribute to the economic development of local areas, and the possibilities were energetically pursued while also considering the local environment, including the despoiling of local scenic beauty. However, because only about 10 per cent of the radiated heat can be used, quantitative limitations were felt concerning exploitation of the potential of geothermal energy. The needs were pointed out for more thorough basic surveys, the effective use of hot water, and reduced costs for developing steam wells.[17]

Because the development of geothermal energy was included in the Sunshine Project and because some small-scale geothermal energy power plants were already operating in the mid-1960s, six electric power plants using geothermal energy were already operating when the second oil crisis occurred. In November 1979, following a proposal to accelerate promotion of the Sunshine Project, the development of deep, large-scale geothermal energy projects became a target.[18]

The interim report of the Advisory Committee for Energy in August 1975 contained recommendations on hydropower by dividing it into two categories. For general hydropower, it recommended government support such as for financing, because the scale of power generation is generally small and in some areas there are problems regarding the economic return on operating such plants. On the other hand, for pumped storage hydraulic power generation, the report recommended development of facilities sufficient to satisfy about 20 per cent of the expected increase in demand, because peak demand could be adjusted and the overall economics of supplying electric power can be improved.[19]

MITI, based on the recommendations of the Advisory Committee for Energy, decided to apply the Law on the Development of Areas Adjacent to Electric Power Generating Facilities, one of the three power resource laws, to geothermal and hydropower plants generating 10,000 or more kW per unit and to return profits to the local communities, thus making site selections easier. As a result, seventy-five sites were approved under the Electric Power Resource Site Consolidation Plan for hydropower stations from fiscal year 1974 to fiscal year 1979.

25.4. Development of New Energy-Related Technology and Technology related to Alternative Energy

High-level economic growth led to an increase in the demand for both industrial- and private-use electric power. But the increase in new and expanded power plants was not sufficient to meet the increase in demand, principally because of siting difficulties. This was evidenced by critical shortages of electric power almost every summer. It was around this same time that the possible exhaustion of worldwide oil resources came to be discussed widely, and problems related to environmental pollution began to make people realize that a limitless increase in the use of oil was difficult. In the circumstances, the development of substitute forms of energy to replace fossil fuels became an urgent issue.

On 18 August 1972, the Minister of International Trade and Industry requested the Industrial Technology Council to prepare recommendations on how to develop and promote new energy-related technology. The minister also outlined the Sunshine Project, a project in which the Agency of Industrial Science and Technology played the lead role in devising a plan to develop new energy-related technology, with the year 2000 as a target date.

Three principal points were mentioned in the Sunshine Project in order to have energy respond to the needs of Japan in the twenty-first century: first, energy should be secured in abundant quantities; second, new forms of energy should not be more expensive than traditional forms; and third, they should be pollution-free. The development of new forms of energy would require long-term development and huge investments. Such a development plan, therefore, should be promoted as a national project, in which the government, national research institutes, universities, and private enterprises would participate.

Separate from the fast breeder reactor which the Power Reactor and Nuclear Fuel Development Corporation was developing and the Basic Plan for Nuclear Fusion Research and Development which the Atomic Energy Commission had decided on and was promoting, MITI thus began supporting the development of technology for solar energy, geothermal energy, synthetic natural gas, and hydrogen energy.[20] Among the technology, the projects for developing solar energy included solar houses, photovoltaic power generation, and solar thermal power generation; the projects for developing geothermal energy included large-scale, deep geothermal power generation, power generation using hot water, deep-layer hot water supply, and power generation from volcanoes and high-temperature rocks; the projects for developing coal-related energy included liquefaction, low-calorie gasification power generation, and high-calorie gasification; the projects for developing hydrogen-related energy included research into the electrolysis and thermal chemical methods; and the projects for developing ocean- and wind-related energy included studies of ocean thermal energy conversion and wind power generation.[21]

The second oil crisis prompted a quickening of the pace to develop alternative forms of energy to replace oil. In the summer of 1979, MITI clarified its thinking that the targets of technological development and the supply of alternative energy should be clearly defined by law, that an organization called the New Energy Development Organization be established for that purpose, that the Coal-Mining Industry Rationalization Corporation be dismantled, and that New Energy Development Organization be supported by treasury investments and loans, and subsidies. The resultant Law Concerning Promotion of the Development and Introduction of Alternative Energy was promulgated and enforced on 30 May 1980. The law contained an article stipulating that the government would introduce the financial, lending, and tax measures needed to promote the development and introduction of alternative energy. Pursuant to this article, systems for treasury investments and loans, financing, and specially recognized depreciation were instituted for the New Energy Development Organization as a new type of special corporation. The name 'organization' was used for the first time, as it was expected to expand in scale in the future.[22] Later it also acquired R&D projects such as the alcohol project, large-scale industrial technology, and projects to develop basic technology for next-generation industries.

25.5. The Outbreak of Structural Recession

Overall demand control measures were introduced to restrain the rapid increase of commodity prices that occurred after the first oil crisis. Those measures brought about major economic changes, and the economy moved into recession. The rapid increase of imported oil prices aggravated Japan's international balance of payments, and the yen dropped in value, reaching 290 yen to the dollar in early 1976. On the other hand, costs increased because of the drastic hike in oil prices, and some industries lost their international competitiveness. Because Japanese industry depends so heavily on overseas supplies of raw materials and fuels, the lower-valued yen made overseas raw materials and fuel costs more expensive, which led to export stagnation. In particular, energy-intensive industries lost their competitiveness *vis-à-vis* imported products. The textile industry suffered the greatest. Most textile companies, including major corporations, introduced restructuring measures, including voluntary retirements, plant closures, business ties with other companies related to natural fibres, and assistance from trading companies. There was also a succession of bankruptcies. In the heavy and chemical industries, major electric appliance manufacturers reduced the salaries of managers, leading steelmakers halted operation of blast furnaces, aluminium and special steel manufacturers reorganized their industries, and a major machinery manufacturer went bankrupt. The financial situation in a wide range of companies worsened, including trading companies, companies in mass communications, and printing companies.

After bottoming out in the spring of 1975, the economy turned towards recovery. Investments in plant and equipment mainly for rationalizing operations and labour saving showed signs of improvement. As observed in housing investments, however, capital investments were not as strong as before the oil crisis. The unemployed workforce totalled over one million, and the multiple for number of jobs available compared to number of job seekers fell under 1.0 for the first time since the oil crisis. The overall size of the workforce continued to show negative growth compared with the previous year. Although the government introduced four different sets of economic-stimulation measures, and the Bank of Japan lowered the official discount rate five times, these steps were not effective in bringing about economic recovery. Exports grew only slowly in fiscal year 1975, and only in fiscal year 1976 finally started to improve noticeably, followed by a high level of growth in fiscal year 1977. This export growth, however, was calculated on the basis of value in US dollars; because of the yen's appreciation, exports did not grow quantitatively. In other words, growth was due to the increase in dollar prices, and on a yen basis export amounts decreased for some items. Overall, the recovery of exports was slow.

The yen appreciated further in 1977 and 1978, against a background of increases in exports and foreign-currency reserves. In October 1978, the exchange rate went as high as 175 yen to the dollar. Compared to the lowest yen level reached after the first oil crisis, which was 307 yen to the dollar in December 1975, the yen had thus appreciated by 43 per cent. Although some felt that the yen should be allowed to appreciate as a reflection of favourable fundamentals in Japan, the mass media called for countermeasures to cope with the yen's appreciation, by increasing domestic demand through income tax cuts and practising self-restraint in export activities. It was around this time that, as a result of a lowering of the yen cost of imported fuels, consumers strongly demanded that electric power and gas utility companies refund the excess profits they were realizing because of the yen's appreciation.

Just as the yen's appreciation was thought to have reached its peak, the Iranian revolution broke out. As already discussed, the second oil crisis occurred and oil prices increased sharply again. Japanese exports declined, imports increased, the international balance of payments moved into deficit, and the yen's value dropped.

After the Nixon Shock, the yen's exchange rate and the prices of raw materials and fuels vital for industrial activities began fluctuating widely because of the system of floating exchange rates and the oil strategy of the Arab oil-producing countries. Some Japanese industries fell into a structural recession. Those industries can be classified as follows.[23]

Group A: Industries that had invested aggressively in plant and equipment around the time of the first oil crisis, and which, as a result of a decline in demand, came to suffer from excessive capacity. These included open-hearth and electric furnaces, aluminium smelting, corrugated cardboard manufacturing, and others.

Group B: Industries that suffered from a supply–demand imbalance because of a substantial reduction in domestic and overseas demand. These included chemical fertilizers, polyvinyl chloride, and others.

Group C: Industries whose international competitiveness declined because of increases in the cost of raw materials. Their exports declined and imports increased. They included spinning, synthetic fibres, steel alloys, and others.

A considerable percentage of the production of these industries became excessive after the Nixon Shock and the first oil crisis. Companies were forced to reduce their operating rates and to lower their prices below production costs, and many suffered financial deficits and excessive debt. Some companies went bankrupt. Representatives of the affected industries discussed countermeasures with MITI officials, such as having a production control cartel in the corrugated cardboard manufacturing industry, freezing production facilities by 30 per cent under a recession cartel in the spinning industry, and introducing production decreases under administrative guidance in the synthetic fibres industry. The steel alloy industry, among others, took the initiative in reducing the number of workers, closing some facilities, and halting operations at others.

The rationalization efforts of individual companies alone, however, were not sufficiently effective, and temporary industry cartels and curtailed production under administrative guidance also had only limited positive effects. In order to implement improvements and stabilize industries that had to cope with drastic changes that followed the shift to a system of floating exchange rates and the new energy situation after the oil crisis, it was necessary to enforce appropriate measures through legislation.

25.6. Establishment of Countermeasures for Structurally Depressed Industries, and the Law on Temporary Measures for Stabilizing Specific Depressed Industries

In order to cope with the serious recession caused by the first oil crisis and the yen's subsequent appreciation, on 3 September 1977, it was decided at a Meeting of Ministers in Charge of Economic Affairs to introduce a set of comprehensive economic measures. The measures included the following: (1) fiscal and financial measures for promoting public investment, housing construction, and lower interest rates; (2) measures to stimulate private demand, such as promoting private investment in plant and equipment, promoting large-scale overseas investments, and improving conditions for providing credit to consumers; (3) measures aimed at structurally depressed industries, such as carrying out adjustments in production and pricing, measures for dealing with excess capacity, and measures to assist in converting to other businesses; (4) measures aimed at small and medium enterprises, such as establishing an emergency loan system to help those companies cope with exchange rate fluctuations, lengthening the existing emergency loan system to help prevent those companies from bankrupting, utilizing the designation of depressed industries according to the Small and Medium Enterprise Credit Insurance Law, efficiently using the prefectural loan system for preventing bankruptcy, and supporting those companies through loans from the

Small-Business Credit Insurance Corporation; (5) employment measures, such as efficient use of the fund system for providing stable employment, use of the system for providing subsidies to workers laid off from designated industries, the development of jobs, and the construction of housing projects for promoting employment; (6) commodity price measures; and (7) economic measures directed overseas.

As these measures show, the comprehensive economic stimulation measures were extremely broad, a reflection of the wide scope and serious nature of the recession. Also, the countermeasures proposed for structurally depressed industries were more extensive than similar measures ever introduced before. This was also the first time for tailored measures to be directed at structurally depressed industries.

MITI announced its new policies for fiscal year 1978 on 29 August 1977, before the Meeting of Ministers in Charge of Economic Affairs introduced its set of comprehensive economic measures. The opening chapter of the publication introducing MITI's new policies was entitled, 'Promoting Business and Developing New Industrial Policies'. MITI gave top priority in its policies to promote countermeasures for structurally depressed industries. The following explained this aim.

In line with the Anti-Monopoly Law and the Law Concerning the Organization of Small and Medium Enterprise Organizations, production and price adjustments will be made, depending on the industry, for the open-hearth and electric furnaces industries, the textile industry, and other structurally depressed industries which have long been burdened with excessive production capacities because of external changes related to slower economic growth after the oil crisis, changes in the supply situation concerning raw materials and fuels, and increased competition from developing countries. At the same time, the disposal or freezing of excessive plant and equipment, the conversion of companies to new types of business, employment measures, and other measures will be promoted. Employment measures, in particular, will be promoted through close cooperation with concerned ministries and agencies in order to prevent unemployment and to create new job opportunities.

Special tax measures will be taken concerning funds contributed by corporations for disposing of open-hearth and electric furnace facilities. Also, concerning the textile industry, measures will be introduced that include the use of loans of the Small-Business Promotion Corporation (interest free for sixteen years) for joint disposal of facilities, application of the tax system for subsidizing the pulling out of business or conversion to new types of business, and the bolstering of vertical integration mainly of companies in the apparel industry aiming to make themselves more knowledge-intensive.

Based on these aims, a total budget of 165 million yen and financial investment plans of over 40 billion yen were appropriated for the following four categories of items: (1) expenses to survey the demand structure of basic industries; (2) expenses for measures to internationalize the principal basic materials industries; (3) expenses to promote projects for improving the structure of the textile industry; and (4) expenses for measures to prevent bankruptcies among leading middle-size corporations.[24]

Based on a decision by MITI's Departmental Council, MITI established a Head-quarters for Structural Recession Countermeasures on 7 September 1977, and on 20 September announced recession countermeasures based on the revised budget. These steps made it clear that MITI would introduce financial measures aimed at the textile and open-hearth and electric furnace industries and would promote disposal of their excess plant and equipment.

On 30 September 1977, moreover, the Headquarters for Structural Recession Countermeasures published a report entitled, 'On Measures for Structurally Depressed Industries'. The report presented detailed and systematically formu-lated countermeasures for structurally depressed industries, such as spinning, polyvinyl chloride, corrugated cardboard, small rods, synthetic fibres, open-hearth and electric furnaces, aluminium smelting, aluminium rolling, chemical fertilizers, and others. Included in the report was a section entitled, 'Promoting the preparation of plans for structural improvement'. It was decided to promote the early formulation of the specific supply–demand outlook and structural inno-vation plans by industry-related organizations. For the open-hearth and electric furnaces, aluminium smelting, and corrugated cardboard industries, it would be the Industrial Structure Council; for the synthetic fibres industry, it would be the Chemical Fibres Consultative Group; for the polyvinyl chloride industry, it would be the Group for Studying Basic Problems Related to Polyvinyl Chloride Pipe; and for chemical fertilizers, it would be the industry's Basic Problems Research Group. These councils and groups would indicate the direction towards which counter-measures appropriate for each industry would best be implemented, based on existing laws.

On 28 November 1977, the second Fukuda Cabinet was inaugurated, and dis-cussion about new legislation concerning structurally depressed industries sub-sequently came to the forefront. MITI officials conferred with those concerned in the Ministry of Finance and in business organizations and obtained favourable reactions regarding the proposed legislation. MITI thus started drafting the new law. In mid-January 1978, a bill was almost drafted, but because it contained articles that would exempt application of the Anti-Monopoly Law to designated cartels, discussions had to be held with the Fair Trade Commission. The Com-mission expressed objections concerning those exemptions, designated cartels, outsider control, the merger of structurally depressed enterprises and transfer of their business, and the designation by government ordinance of target industries. In view of the Commission's opposition, and taking into account opinions expressed by outside experts, including academics, MITI removed from the draft bill the exemption of applying the Anti-Monopoly Law to outsider control, mergers, and so forth. Also, an article was added to the draft stating that the Fair Trade Commission agreement was required in order to exempt designated cartels from the Anti-Monopoly Law. Adjustments were thus successfully made among the concerned ministries and agencies, and the draft bill was submitted to the Diet for deliberation after obtaining Cabinet approval.

Diet deliberation of the proposed Law on Temporary Measures for Stabilizing

Specified Depressed Industries began in March 1978. The bill was partly modified by the Commerce and Industry Committee of the House of Representatives, and then was passed and made into law in April. It was published and enforced in May. The Industry Stabilization Law had three basic points:

1. The minister in charge shall formulate basic stabilization plans for specified depressed industries, and clarify the standards to be used by those industries mainly for disposing of excessive plant and equipment.
2. The minister in charge may direct joint action to be taken if implementation of the basic stabilization plans does not move forward by the spontaneous efforts of industry.
3. A trust fund for specified depressed industries will be established to serve as the institution for guaranteeing loans required for disposing of excessive plant and equipment under the basic stabilization plans.

The Law on Temporary Measures for Stabilizing Specified Depressed Industries designated as target industries those that had excessive plant and equipment and expected their excess capacity situation to continue for some time. In addition, there had to be general agreement that disposing of such plant and equipment was necessary for the healthy development of the national economy. The basic stabilization plans were to be finalized after obtaining the opinions of related councils, and after implementation of measures concerning excessive plant and equipment (scrapping or long-term storage, or transfer based on the premiss of suspension of use or scrapping). The Law on Temporary Measures for Stabilizing Specified Depressed Industries stipulated the securing of funds, stabilization of employment, guaranteeing repayment of loans, designation by the minister in charge of the joint action, and so forth as ways to implement the smooth carrying out of the measures.

The Law on Temporary Measures for Stabilizing Specified Depressed Industries designated four industries as targets: open-hearth and electric furnaces, aluminium smelting, synthetic fibres, and shipbuilding. Basic stabilization plans were decided for these industries under procedures stipulated by the law, and disposal of the excess facilities moved forward. In July 1978, a government ordinance designated another four industries: ammonia manufacture, urea manufacture, wet-process phosphoric acid manufacture, and the spinning industry. Additional designations were made for steel alloy manufacture in August 1978, and cardboard manufacture in March 1979. As a result, ten industries (in detail, fourteen industries) were designated as structurally depressed industries under the Law on Temporary Measures for Stabilizing Specified Depressed Industries by the end of March 1979. Among them, only the shipbuilding industry was under the jurisdiction of a ministry other than MITI. The basic stabilization plan of each industry was more or less implemented as scheduled, including the disposal of excess facilities (average ratio of disposal achieved: 95 per cent).

The measures for providing relief to structurally depressed industries were important from both the economic and social viewpoints. As part of MITI's policies, therefore, efforts were made to reduce as much as possible the negative effect on workers in the depressed industries, on related industries, and on the communities where depressed industries were located.

NOTES

1. *Nihon no Enerugi Mondai*, Reference Materials 1–1, 'Trends in the Supply of Japan's Primary Energy': 83–9. Also, for a discussion of the resources and energy policy at the time of the oil crisis, see *Tsusho Sangyo Seisakushi*, xiii, ch. 4, and 'Tsusho Sangyo Seisaku no Juten' (Highlights of International Trade and Industry Policies), *Tsusansho Koho* (MITI Official Bulletin), Research Institute of International Trade and Industry, for each year.
2. MITI (ed.), *Showa 50-nendai no Enerugi—Antei Kyokyu no Tame no Sentaku* (Choices for Securing Stable Energy Supplies in 1975–84), Research Institute of International Trade and Industry, 1975: 22–3. For details by category of energy, see pp. 35–40 of same publication. The following section about the outlook for the make-up of energy and the situation regarding the construction and operation of nuclear power plants is also based on this publication.
3. Nuclear Power Journalist Group (ed.), *Jyanarisuto no Shogen—Genshiryoku 25-nen no Kiseki* (From the Eyes of Journalists in Nuclear Power Field—The Loci of Nuclear Power for the Past 25 Years), Denryoku Shinposha, 1981: 80–7, and 'Tsusho Sangyo Seisaku no Juten', fiscal year 1972, *Tsusansho Koho*, 25 Aug. 1971: 6.
4. For details regarding the process of legislating the three electric power laws, their content, and the situation in carrying them out, see *Tsusho Sangyo-sho Nenpo*, fiscal 1974: 276–81, and *Tsusho Sangyo Seisakushi*, xiii. 238–42.
5. See 'Tsusho Sangyo Seisaku no Juten', fiscal 1975, *Tsusansho Koho*, 27 Aug. 1974: 4, except that the budget was undecided at the time of this publication. Also see 'Tsusho Sangyo Seisaku no Juten', 1976, 23 Aug. 1975: 5.
6. *Sogo Enerugi Tokei*, 1984 edn.: 267 and 274; *Tsusho Sangyo Seisakushi*, xiv (1992): from 207; for reference, nuclear generated power surpassed hydroelectric power in fiscal year 1982, when the former accounted for 17.6% and the latter for 14.5% of total electric power generated.
7. *Enerugi Seisaku no Ayumi to Tenbo*: 344–5.
8. *Nihon no Enerugi Mondai*: 61–2; *Showa 50-nendai no Enerugi*: 87; for discussion of LNG project in fiscal year 1977, see 141 of Agency of Natural Resources and Energy (ed.), *Waga Kuni Enerugi Mondai no Choki Tenbo, Choki Enerugi Bijion Kenkyukai Hokoku* (Long-Term Outlook for Japan's Energy Problems in Japan, Report by Long-Term Energy Vision Research Group), Research Institute of International Trade and Industry, 1977.
9. See 'Tsusho Sangyo Seisaku no Juten', fiscal year 1974, *Tsusansho Koho*, 12 Sept. 1973: 5, and same reports for fiscal year 1975, 27 Aug. 1974: 4; for fiscal year 1976, 23 Aug. 1975: 5.
10. *Sengo Enerugi Sangyoshi*: 348.
11. *Tsusho Sangyo Seisakushi*: xiv. 209.
12. Ibid. xiii. 285.
13. *Enerugi Seisaku no Ayumi to Tenbo*: 369.
14. See 'Tsusho Sangyo Seisaku no Juten', fiscal year 1980, *Tsusansho Koho*, 27 Aug. 1979: 3.
15. *Showa 50-nendai no Enerugi*: 36.
16. For discussion of the Sunshine Project, see *Tsusho Sangyo Seisakushi*, xiii. 184–97; also, *Tsusho Sangyo-sho Nenpo*, fiscal year 1974: 219–22, discusses the aims of the project when initiated and the research situation; also, *Showa 50-nendai no Enerugi*: 53, touches on the development of geothermal energy.
17. *Waga Kuni Enerugi Mondai no Choki Tenbo*: 188–9.
18. Industrial Technology Council, New Energy Technology Development Committee (interim report), *Sanshaiin Keikaku no Kasokuteki Suishin Senryaku* (Strategy for Accelerating Promotion of Sunshine Project), Nov. 1979; and MITI (ed.), *Sekiyu Daitai Enerugi Ho no Kaisetsu* (Interpretation of Law Concerning Promotion of the Development and Introduction of Alternative Energy), Research Institute of International Trade and Industry, 1980: 274–9.

550 Knowledge-Intensive Industry

19. *Showa 50-nendai no Enerugi*: 36.
20. Ibid. 53; also see materials in n. 16.
21. See chart on progress of Sunshine Project in *Tsusho Sangyo Seisakushi*, xiii. 194–5.
22. See *Sekiyu Daitai Enerugi Ho no Kaisetsu*; also see *Enerugi Seisaku no Ayumi to Tenbo*: 183.
23. For discussion of outbreak of structural recession and process of legislating the Law on Temporary Measures for Stabilizing Specified Depressed Industries, the law's content, and how it was promulgated, see *Tsusho Sangyo Seisakushi*, xiv (1993), ch. 6.
24. See 'Tsusho Sangyo Seisaku no Juten', fiscal year 1978, *Tsusansho Koho*, 29 Aug. 1977: 1–13.

The Implementation of Measures to Cope with Rising Commodity Prices, and Consumer Protection Policy

26.1. Inflation from Economic Measures, and Rampant Prices

Even after the announcement on 15 August 1971, by President Nixon of new economic policies, the Japanese government kept the Tokyo foreign-exchange market open and supported the exchange rate of 360 yen to the dollar. As a consequence of eleven days of continuous purchase of dollars, $3.9 billion entered Japan, corresponding to the issuance of new yen notes worth about 1.5 trillion yen. From that time until the Smithsonian Agreement of December 1971, Japan's foreign-exchange holdings increased by $2.7 billion. This action sowed the seeds for excess liquidity in the Japanese economy. There was strong concern that the yen's appreciation would lead to a recession, however, and the Japanese government continued to promote fiscal and financial policies that would minimize the range of the yen's appreciation.

As a first step, the government increased treasury investments and loans, and prepared a large-scale budget to buoy the economy and ease the negative impact of the yen's appreciation. Public investment was earmarked for projects such as construction of the New Tohoku and Joetsu lines (Shinkansen), and extension of the New Sanyo line. Government and public demand was thus used as a lever to overcome the recession, and government construction bonds were issued to raise funds.

Other steps were introduction of a relaxed monetary policy and lowering of the official discount rate. Even before Nixon's announcement, the official discount rate had been lowered as a part of economy-boosting measures. It was reduced again in December 1971 and then in June 1972, eventually reaching its lowest post-war level.

The move to stimulate demand through fiscal and financial measures brought about an increase in wholesale prices, including the prices of construction materials needed for public works projects. Those increases subsequently led to a rise in consumer prices. Despite the increased prices, however, the trend towards a surplus in the international balance of payments did not change. Pressure to appreciate the yen mounted under the influence of currency fluctuations in

Europe in February 1973 and the resulting devaluation of the US dollar. In March 1973, Japan halted trading on the Tokyo foreign-exchange market, and the yen was finally shifted to a floating exchange rate system. The majority opinion among economists at the time gradually moved towards believing that the role of fiscal and financial policies for preventing the yen's appreciation had ended, and it would now be best to approve the flotation of the yen in view of the advance of inflation.

Even after the shift to the floating exchange rate system, the yen continued to appreciate and commodity prices continued to increase. As a result, the view gained ground that the situation was an inflationary one, and countermeasures against inflation were required from the viewpoint of the daily life and welfare of the populace. From April 1973, wholesale prices increased 10 per cent or more every month compared with the same month of the previous year. Consumer prices increased at about the same rates. In September, the month before the first oil crisis occurred, consumer and wholesale prices both showed their highest increases compared with the previous year since the Korean War (early 1950s): 118.7 for wholesale prices, and 114.8 for consumer prices.

The events accompanying the first oil crisis accelerated the upward trend of wholesale and consumer prices in Japan. Wholesale prices versus the previous month rose abnormally from October 1973 to February 1974, up 2.1 per cent in October 1973, 3.2 per cent in November, 7.0 per cent in December, 5.5 per cent in January 1974, 3.8 per cent in February, and 0.7 per cent in March. Consumer prices, on the other hand, were up 0.4 per cent in October 1973, 0.8 per cent in November, 3.3 per cent in December, 4.2 per cent in January 1974, 3.3 per cent in February, and 0.6 per cent in March. The increases from December 1973 to the end of February 1974 were so large that inflation was described as 'rampant'.[1] Although the prices of certain items, such as non-food agricultural and forestry products, lumber, wood, and textiles, had risen between 1972 and March 1973, prices rose across the board from April to September 1973 because of the rapid expansion of overall demand. And from October prices rose abnormally because of the oil crisis.[2] The skyrocketing price increases had begun originally because of excess fluidity, but they reached levels at which it was no longer possible to leave them unattended.

26.2. Measures for Stabilizing Prices and Everyday Life

Measures for controlling the overheated economy and rapidly rising consumer price increases were not necessarily neglected during the course of time it took to reach the level of 'rampant' price increases. For example, the official discount rate was first raised on 2 April 1973. On 13 April, the Ministerial Committee for Commodity Price Stabilization decided on new commodity price stabilization measures. The following month saw implementation of measures such as deferment of public works projects to the second half of the fiscal year, expansion of import quotas for items that were still restricted, and a more flexible application of preferential tariff ceiling allocations. These measures were not entirely effective, however, and consumer prices continued to rise. The official discount rate was raised three times more, on 30 May, 2 July, and 20 August, 1973, and the reserve deposit requirement ratio was increased four times, on 16 January, 16 March, 16 June, and 1 September' 1973. Using these financial measures alone for curtailing excessive liquidity, however, was not enough for sustainable control.

In July 1973, the Law Concerning Emergency Measures Against Engrossing and Withholding the Sale of Materials Vital to National Life (Law to Prevent Engrossing and Withholding) was promulgated and enforced. Soya beans, logs, lumber, cotton, gauze for medical-use, wool, silk, and seven other items were designated as items covered by the law. The law did not halt the sharp upswing in prices, and on 31 August the Ministerial Committee for Commodity Price Stabilization decided on a set of five emergency measures concerning price stabilization. Included was postponement until the following year of fiscal spending amounting to 1.0428 trillion yen. Also, administrative guidance was introduced as a step to suppress overall demand. Six industries in the private sector, including the electric power and steel industries, were asked to reduce their capital investments plans for fiscal year 1973 by 3.8 per cent. It was also decided to recommend postponement or a reduction in the scale of construction of non-essential building of 5,000 sq.m. or more in size. The standard conditions for the sales of cars by instalment were also revised.[3] Paraffin, meanwhile, an item closely tied to the daily lives of the populace, was added in September to the items designated in the Law to Prevent Engrossing and Withholding.

The first oil crisis quickly magnified the feeling of a shortage of consumer goods, and encouraged hoarding and price increases. For example, large-scale hoarding of toilet paper began in the Kansai region towards the end of October 1973. MITI's Osaka Bureau reported an incident of injuries among persons rushing to buy toilet paper at a store in the Amagasaki part of Osaka on 2 November. MITI immediately issued an emergency vice-minister's notice and introduced measures such as urging self-restraint in hoarding, urgent production increases, a freezing of ex-factory prices, emergency shipments to the Kansai region, and the adding of toilet paper to the list of items under the Law to Prevent Engrossing and Withholding. After toilet paper came the hoarding of synthetic detergents, which also began in the Kansai region on 6 November, and gradually expanded to other parts of the country. In December, hoarding included miso, shoyu, edible oils, toothbrushes, toothpaste, canned food, sugar, petrol, paraffin, and salt. In that situation, the government requested producers to increase production and release inventories, and trading companies to make emergency deliveries of the items being hoarded. At the same time, the government gradually added the same items to the list of designated items under the Law to Prevent Engrossing and Withholding. As of 1 February 1974, the list had twenty-four items. Fourteen were under the jurisdiction of MITI, including cotton yarn, cotton fabrics, wool, paraffin, toilet paper, printing paper, petrol, LPG, and synthetic detergents.[4]

Consumers began hoarding a wider variety of items, and the hoarding trend spread nationwide, stimulated partly by panic reports in the mass media. A need arose for a new law to stabilize the situation. Accordingly, a bill for the Law on Emergency Measures for National Life Stabilization was accepted at a Cabinet meeting on 7 December 1973. It was submitted to the 72nd Ordinary Diet session on the same day, together with a bill for the Petroleum Supply and Demand Optimization Law. The emergency measure bill was deliberated at an unusually high speed, and although some revisions were made in the House of Representatives, it passed the House of Councillors on 21 December as amended.

The Law on Emergency Measures for National Life Stabilization covered three principal areas: (1) price changes for items closely related to the lives of citizens or important to the national economy, (2) emergency measures for supply and demand adjustments, and (3) allowing the government to prepare ordinances for allocating and distributing consumer goods. To accomplish the aims of the law, a 'standard price system' and 'specific standard prices' were established for making price adjustments. Items designated under the standard price system related closely to the daily lives of citizens and either already showed or were apt to show sharp price increases. Standard prices were fixed and announced for those items at all stages from production to retail sale. The relevant minister would publish the names of offenders who sold designated items at higher than standard prices. When it became obviously difficult to stabilize the prices of some items even under this standard price system, they were designated as items whose prices should especially be stabilized (specified items). The prices established for such items were called 'specific standard prices'. Anyone who sold such items at prices exceeding the specific standard prices were obliged to pay surcharges to the government. Also, as a measure to adjust the balance between supply and demand, the Law on Emergency Measures for National Life Stabilization also specified items whose production should be increased. Producers of such specified items were requested to prepare production schedules and submit them to the relevant minister. As felt necessary, the minister could publish the names of violators. The law also contained stipulations for restraining capital investments and for allowing the government to order the allocation and distribution of specified items. Four items were thus specified: paraffin, liquid petroleum gas (LPG), toilet paper, and tissue paper. The first two products were designated in January 1974; the other two were designated in February 1974. In May 1974, toilet paper and tissue paper were removed from the list. Paraffin was removed the following month, and the LPG designation was revised one time and then LPG was removed from the list in May 1976.

In March 1974, MITI approved aggregated price increases for petroleum products to an average of 8,946 yen per kl. and began providing administrative guidance to maintain that price level. The practice of self-restraint in price increases and the system of preliminary price-increase approval was applied principally to petroleum products but also covered basic materials and materials related to the daily lives of citizens. These measures were decided by the Headquarters for Emergency Measures for National Life Stabilization, but required Cabinet approval. The preliminary approval system covered fifty-nine items, forty-five of them under MITI jurisdiction. This system was abolished in September 1974.[5]

In this way, laws to prevent hoarding and to stabilize the daily lives of citizens were urgently enacted to prevent sharp rises in the prices of foodstuffs and other items. The system of preliminary approval for increase in the price of certain items, meanwhile, was established to halt the rampant increase in commodity prices. In parallel, measures to control overall demand were promoted to suppress price increases tied to speculative, temporary demand.

26.3. Progress of the Consumer Protective Policy

MITI set the protection of consumers as a core goal of its administration policies, and concentrated its efforts on commodity prices. It did this through administrative guidance regarding increases in the cost of public utilities under its jurisdiction, and by enacting and promoting laws in its area of responsibility, such as the Instalment Sales Law, Electrical Appliance and Material Control Law, Household Goods Quality Labelling Law, and Law Concerning the Securing of Safety and the Optimization of Transactions of Liquefied Petroleum Gas. In April 1964, in particular, the Consumer Affairs Division was established in the Enterprises Bureau and assumed exclusive charge of consumer administrative matters. Various measures were taken from that point to protect and promote the best interests of consumers. After enactment of the Basic Law for Consumer Protection, measures were introduced to enforce the law and protect consumers from unfair transactions and to assure the quality and safety of products. Even after the Nixon Shock, MITI continued its stance of emphasizing consumer protection.

Ensuring the safety of products used in daily life

In July 1971, the MITI minister requested the Industrial Structure Council to prepare recommendations regarding ways to ensure the safety of consumer products. The Council responded in a December 1972 report entitled 'Concerning the Assurance and Improvement of the Safety of Consumer Products'. Based on this report, a draft of the Law for Consumer Product Safety was prepared. The Cabinet approved the draft in February 1973 and it was submitted to the Diet. In May 1973, the bill passed the Diet as drafted by the government and it was promulgated in June. The main points of the law were as follows:

1. Consumer products requiring special safety considerations will be designated as 'specified products'; the government will determine safety standards for them and prohibit the sale of products which do not meet the standards.
2. The Consumer Product Safety Association will be established with the approval of the MITI minister. It will be a private organization for conducting activities to assure the safety of consumer products. The Consumer Product Safety Association will be in charge of inspecting the 'specified products',

designating the safety of products, and establishing a system for assisting consumers who suffer harm from products.
3. It may be necessary to take action regarding consumer products other than 'specified products', including the emergency recall of dangerous products.[6]

Five products were designated as 'specified products' when the law was enforced in March 1974, including pressure cookers and pressurized rice cookers. The Consumer Product Safety Association was established in October 1973 and became responsible for conducting tests and issuing qualifications. One of its first tasks was testing crash helmets. Under this system, products that passed safety-standard examinations were marked with an SG seal. If an SG-marked product were later proved to have caused harm to the life or body of a consumer, a private non-life insurance company would pay damages to that person. The Consumer Product Safety Association performed its qualification duties based on the Consumer Product Safety Law. In 1974, the Association certified ten products including baby strollers, walkers, swings, slides, can openers, and horizontal exercise bars for children. Specified products and certified products of the Consumer Product Safety Association were later added to the list.

Revision and operation of instalment sales law

During the high-growth period of 1955–70, the percentage of total annual retail sales accounted for by credit sales increased steadily, reaching 44 per cent in 1970.[7] That 44 per cent included credit sales and others (28.5 per cent), instalment sales (13.8 per cent), and ticket purchases (1.7 per cent). The percentage of credit sales was high, but it is worth noting that instalment sales exceeded 10 per cent in 1970. The equivalent figure in 1958 was only 4.9 per cent.

The percentage of total retail sales accounted for by instalments in 1970 was about 60 per cent for cars, 50 per cent for household machines and tools, 35 per cent for household electric appliances, 33 per cent for men's clothes (non-manufacture and retail), and 31 per cent for bicycles (Figure 26.1). Instalment sales for these five products exceeded 30 per cent of total retail sales. It should be noted, too, that the percentage of instalment sales was high for consumer goods whose prices were relatively high, such as men's clothes (manufacture and retail), musical instruments, bedding, agricultural cultivating tools, and others. Motorization, home electrification, and the Westernization and diversification of lifestyles provided the background for these trends. It became convenient for consumers to purchase expensive products on credit, backed by their future income, and then to pay the debt in a prescribed manner. Some adverse effects accompanied this trend, however, including high-pressure sales tactics by salesmen who convinced consumers to purchase expensive products they did not especially need. Between 1965 and 1975, moreover, a wider diversity of products became available for purchase by instalments, and the number of cases increased where consumers did not clearly understand what they were buying when they signed a purchase agreement and where there was doubt about whether the seller

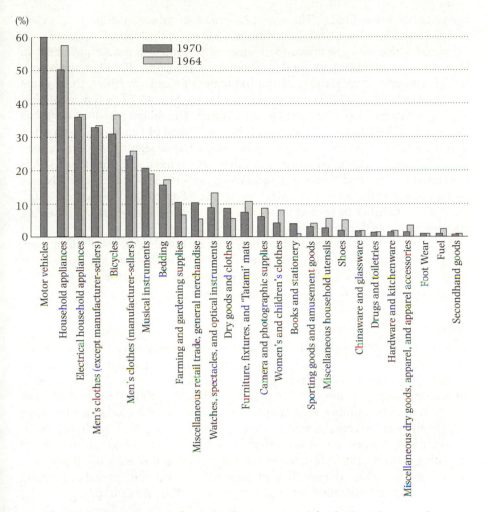

Fig. 26.1   Percentage of retail sales accounted for by instalment sales

Source: Compiled by Research and Statistics Department, Minister's Secretariat, *Wagakuni no Shogyo* (Commerce in Japan), MITI, 1973.

would abide by the sales agreement. As instalment sales expanded and the awareness of consumers increased, a need emerged to normalize instalment-sales methods for the healthy development of the industry.

In August 1971, the MITI minister requested the Credit Sales Council to prepare recommendations on measures for coping with the diversification of consumer credit in Japan, for establishing a system to assure fairness in transactions, and for promoting the interests of consumers. In January 1972, the Council presented a report entitled 'Concerning the Protection and Promotion of Consumer

Interests Related to Credit'. The report covered four principal subjects: (1) clear indication of instalment sales conditions, and normalization of contracts, (2) expanded scope of application, (3) measures to protect advance payments in instalment payment systems, and (4) provisional measures. Based on the report, MITI prepared a draft revision of the Instalment Sales Law, which the Cabinet approved in March 1972. The bill passed the Diet in May 1972, was promulgated in June, and went into effect the following March. The salient revisions were that the format of instalment sales contracts be established by ministerial ordinance, that a cooling-off period of four days be allowed after signing a contract, and that the law be expanded to protect advance payments by including sellers who provide loans and Tomonokai (friendship associations) that receive advance money. Based on the revised law, MITI prepared and distributed a standard instalment sales contract to related industries with a ministerial circular providing administrative guidance.

As more products were offered for purchase by instalment, MITI added them to the overall list as required, approved and registered merchants and others offering products for sale on instalment, and performed on-the-spot inspection of their offices. These actions were taken to protect consumers.

Establishment of PO Box 1

In April 1973, MITI opened PO Box 1 in the Tokyo Central Post Office for receiving complaints, opinions, and requests from consumers throughout Japan. The content of letters would be attended to and if pertinent would be reflected in administrative procedures. PO Box 1 received about 7,000 letters in fiscal year 1973. The large number was mainly due to the excessive commodity prices and the shortage of consumer goods that occurred as a result of the first oil crisis. In fact, nearly 75 per cent of the letters were related to these issues. In terms of preparing administrative procedures, the letters proved there was strong consumer concern about the shortage of goods. They also contributed to opening channels of communication between the public and the government.

Holding of meetings of the Consultative Group for Discussing Consumer Price Issues

Among the 'Priority Objectives of International Trade and Industry Policies for Fiscal Year 1971', the protection and promotion of consumer interests was listed second. Four ways were outlined for accomplishing the objectives of protecting consumer interests and taking effective and appropriate measures to stabilize commodity prices: holding discussions about consumer prices by product category; monitoring consumer prices; reinforcing the network for testing consumer goods; and furthering consumer education. Efforts would also be made through chambers of commerce to promote fairness in advertising. It was around this time that funds were first budgeted to support activities related to consumer price monitoring and the promotion of fairness in advertising.[8] By clearly listing the above concerns as important policies, it was hoped that consumers would be encouraged to express their opinions for consideration in administrative proce-dures. In order to promote a dialogue with consumers regarding problems they face and price issues, and to incorporate their views into business behaviour and administrative policy, a series of meetings of the Consultative Group for Dis-cussing Consumer Price Issues was established in fiscal year 1971. Three types of meetings were held: a general discussion with consumers was held once a year (with the MITI minister attending), discussions by product category were held occasionally, and regional discussions were held annually. In fiscal year 1972, a general discussion with consumers was held in September, with the MITI minis-ter attending. The focus was on product safety assurances, but there were also lively discussions about price and environmental pollution issues. Product cate-gory discussions were held concerning the safety of products such as sheet glass, stationery goods, and bicycles. In addition, regional bureaux of MITI held regional meetings. In fiscal year 1973, another general discussion with con-sumers was held in October with the MITI minister in attendance, and product category discussions were also held that focused on vending machines, product quality labelling, plastics, and replacement parts for electric home appliances. Meeting directly and regularly with consumers in these ways became an impor-tant source of information for MITI, which had tended until then to emphasize the production side rather than that of the consumers.

Establishment of the Law Concerning Door-to-Door Sales, Etc.

In November 1973, the Distribution Committee of the Industrial Structure Council established a Special Sales Subcommittee to study measures regarding special sales practices, including door-to-door sales, mail order sales, pyramid sales, and so forth. The subcommittee presented an interim report in December 1974 entitled 'Direction of Regulations concerning Pyramid Sales, Mail Order Sales, Door-to-Door Sales, Etc.'. The report said that for the rational and fair pro-tection of consumers, it was necessary to devise appropriate rules regarding the diversified sales methods that were emerging, and that it was necessary to take strong action against pyramid sales, as well as introducing preventive measures and measures for providing relief to consumers harmed by pyramid sales. MITI recognized the need for new administrative measures because these newly and rapidly growing sales methods were the source of many problems affecting con-sumers. Effective measures were difficult to introduce, however, because the actual situation concerning special sales methods was unclear. While waiting for the interim report of the subcommittee, therefore, MITI implemented a survey to clarify the actual situation. Based on that survey, a draft bill of the Law Con-cerning Door-to-Door Sales, Etc. was submitted to the Diet in April 1976. The bill passed the Diet in May and was promulgated in June. The law covered door-to-door sales, mail order sales, chain sales, and negative options. It was an epoch-making law for consumer protection because it adopted a system of designating products, required the registration of sales personnel, set a cooling-off period, and set maximum limits on indemnification.

26.4. A Vision for the Distribution Industry in the 1970s, and the Large-Scale Retail Stores Law

A feature of Japan's distribution industry was the extremely large number of very small companies doing business, and a multilayer structure that included several stages for products to pass through from producer to consumer. The result of this system was generally high distribution costs due to the low productivity of the small companies, operating mainly as family enterprises. From a statistical point of view, 85 per cent or more of these companies had 1–2 or 3–4 employees. Although the number dropped slightly during the period of high economic growth, these small companies still accounted for as much as 86 per cent (1,328,867 companies) of all companies in the distribution industry in 1974, the year after the first oil crisis. Thus, little structural change was seen in the industry. In contrast, the number of retailers with fifty or more employees accounted for only 0.3 per cent of the total in 1974, and this group thus also did not show any remarkable increase (Table 26.1).

On the other hand, the percentage of annual sales per employee for companies in the distribution industry changed considerably during the period of high growth. Companies with one to four employees accounted for 50 per cent or more of sales in 1958 but fell to account for around 34 per cent of sales in 1976. Companies with 100 or more employees, meanwhile, increased their percentage of sales during the same period from 10.7 per cent to 14.7 per cent (Table 26.2). In sales amount, the share of large retailers increased steadily, which meant that a shift of share to more productive companies took place in the distribution industry as well.

Among large retailers, the most conspicuous growth during the ten years from 1965 to 1974 was seen in supermarket chains operating with self-service

Table 26.1 Trends in size of companies in retail industry (unit: %)

No. of employees	1958	1964	1970	1974
1–2	70.0	70.3	64.0	63.1
3–4	21.4	19.2	22.5	22.9
5–9	6.8	7.5	9.6	10.1
10–19	1.3	2.0	2.6	2.7
20–29	0.3	0.5	0.6	0.6
30–49	0.1	0.3	0.4	0.4
50–99	0.1	0.1	0.2	0.2
100 or more	0.0	0.1	0.1	0.1

Source: Compiled by Research and Statistics Department, Minister's Secretariat, *Wagakuni no Shogyo* (Commerce in Japan), MITI, 1971: 4; 1973: 24; and 1975: 4.

systems. The number of such chains reached sixty-two in 1969, and the actual number of store locations exceeded 1,000. The share of total annual retail sales nationwide accounted for by these self-service stores moved closer to the share accounted for by department stores.[9] Thus, modernization and structural changes to the distribution industry progressed steadily. But the changes also created social problems, because of the negative effects of these changes on small companies. Policy related to the distribution industry in the 1970s, therefore, inevitably came to have dual aspects: promotion of modernization and protection of small companies.

The so-called 'distribution revolution' began and evolved rapidly in the 1960s. The development of large retail chains discounting their prices by cutting costs through self-service systems gradually affected traditional family-owned retail stores and department stores that relied on consumer services and a high-class image to retain their customers. The multilayer wholesale distribution system was shaken at its foundations as moves grew to eliminate some layers in the distribution process and to shorten the time from production to retail delivery. In the early 1970s, economic growth brought about tremendous increases in the volume of goods being distributed at the same time that a shortage of labour emerged. The situation thus called for greater streamlining of the distribution industry. In contrast, the difficulties faced by family-run retail stores and other small and medium stores became regional and social problems. It became necessary to search for solutions to contradictions produced by modernizing and streamlining the distribution system.

In May 1964, the MITI minister requested the Distribution Committee of the Industrial Structure Council to prepare a report on measures required to modernize distribution systems. In July 1971, the committee submitted its ninth interim report entitled 'Distribution in the 1970s' to Minister Kakuei Tanaka.

Table 26.2 Trends in percentage of annual sales by number of permanent employees (unit: %)

No. of employees	1958	1964	1970	1976
1–2	24.9	21.8	15.5	14.8
3–4	26.7	20.7	18.9	19.3
5–9	22.3	20.3	21.2	21.5
10–19	9.2	11.5	12.9	12.5
20–29	2.9	4.5	5.5	5.7
30–49	2.2	4.2	5.7	5.7
50–99	1.7	3.7	6.2	5.8
100 or more	10.7	13.3	14.2	14.7

Source: Compiled by Research and Statistics Department, Minister's Secretariat, *Wagakuni no Shogyo* (Commerce in Japan), MITI, 1973: 14; 1975: 14; and 1981: 17.

The interim report emphasized the importance of formulating a vision for modernizing the distribution industry, and for distribution industry policy, it specifically mentioned a need for greater sophistication of the market structure, maintenance and promotion of effective competition, promotion of consumer benefits, more rationalized distribution, development of human resources, and ordering of the distribution environment. The report also contained recommendations regarding current issues, such as ways to promote the modernization of small and medium enterprises, what legislation should be prepared for large retailers, the matter of producer-aligned distribution channels and the fixed price system, how to move forward with capital liberalization, harmony with regional interests, and so forth. These recommendations were later reflected in legislation.

The most important among the recommendations were those related to the control of large retail stores (pseudo-department stores), which fell outside the scope of the Department Store Law. Starting around 1968, quite a large number of applications were filed and approved, including those in regional cities, for entering the department store business, adding new stores, expanding the floor space in existing stores, and so forth, to deal with the increased diversification and sophistication of consumption. A problem emerged regarding pseudo-department stores, which were similar to department stores in scale and diversity of goods handled but were permitted to do business not as a single retailer but as chains of affiliated and group stores. Because expansion of these stores did not violate any law, their numbers increased more quickly than did those of department stores. They also spread to small and medium provincial cities, creating problems in regional communities. In August 1972, the Distribution Committee submitted its tenth interim report, this one entitled, 'Retailing Industry in the Distribution Revolution—Direction of Revisions in the Department Store Law'. The main point of this report was that the policy to support small and medium retail stores should be enforced by placing legal restrictions on the pseudo-department stores and making the opening of new stores and the expansion of existing stores subject to prior reporting of such plans. Doing so would cope with some of the problems arising from the rapid expansion of these stores, and would offset some of the differences between large and small retailers. After receiving this interim report, MITI strengthened its administrative guidance on pseudo-department stores by issuing circulars to them. It also began preparing a draft bill of the Law Concerning the Adjustment of Retail Business Operations in Large-Scale Retail Stores (Large-Scale Retail Stores Law). A bill was submitted to the 71st Diet in March 1973. Although some revisions were made to the bill, it passed the Diet and became law in September 1973. It was promulgated and enforced in March 1974.

The principal points of the Large-Scale Retail Stores Law, promulgated at the same time that the Department Store Law was abolished, were: (1) to add 'protection of consumer interests' to the objectives of the law, (2) to designate as 'large-scale retail stores' those stores with total floor space of over 500 sq.m. in one building, including large shopping centres, and to regulate them, (3) to abolish the system of approval under the Department Store Law and introduce instead a system of application, examination, recommendation, and order, and (4) to have the Minister of International Trade and Industry recommend or order a reduction in store size or length of business hours, etc., after reviewing an application. Reviews were made in the context of population trends and the prospects for modernizing small and medium retail stores in the area and after listening to the opinion of the Large-Scale Retail Stores Council, especially when it was recognized that opening a new store would have a considerable negative effect on nearby small and medium retail stores.[10]

The number of applications for constructing new buildings under the Large-Scale Retail Stores Law was 398 in fiscal year 1974 (including March 1974), 280 in fiscal year 1975, 265 in fiscal year 1976, 318 in fiscal year 1977, and 243 in fiscal year 1978. The total number of applications received during these five years amounted to 1,507. Since there was a total of only about 1,700 large retail stores operating before promulgation of the law, those increases were remarkable. The features of the newly opened stores were their large size and their location either in suburban areas outside large cities or in small and medium provincial cities. In some instances there were sharp confrontations between small and medium local retailers and the new stores. In that situation, MITI established a Consultative Group for Discussing Retail Issues. This group, comprising knowledgeable persons, served as a private consultative body for the Director-General of the Industrial Policy Bureau and the Director-General of the Small and Medium Enterprise Agency. The group began studying retail problems in July 1977, and presented its first report in February 1978.

Based on that report, a joint meeting of the Retailer and Commercial Policy Subcommittee of the Small and Medium Enterprise Policy-Making Council and the Distribution Committee of the Industrial Structure Council was held that same month to discuss revision of the Large-Scale Retail Stores Law. Both councils accepted the recommendations of their subcommittees and submitted their opinions to the Minister of International Trade and Industry in April 1978. The recommendations included: (1) combining into one law the Large-Scale Retail Stores Law and the Law on Special Measures for the Adjustment of Retail Business, (2) studying a system for settling disputes concerning stores not covered by either law, (3) investigating traditional retail markets, agricultural cooperatives, cooperative societies, and so forth, from the viewpoint of protecting small retailers, and (4) implementing improvement measures concerning the Commercial Activities Coordination Committee to enable it to make a wider range of adjustments. MITI accepted the recommendations and began full-scale work for revising the laws. Although drafts of revisions of both laws were submitted to the Diet in June 1978, they did not pass because of drawn-out deliberations. Study of the revised laws began again in the 85th Diet, and the drafts were finally passed after partial amendment and became law. The laws were enforced in May 1979. The main amended points were that the floor area subject to adjustment was reduced to 500 sq.m., participation of prefectural governors in coordination was strengthened, severe enforcement of adjustment measures was implemented, and the coordination period was extended to a maximum of six months. In parallel with these, the Adjustment of Retail Business Law was also revised. The Large-Scale Retail Stores Law and the Law on Special Measures for the Adjustment of Retail Business subsequently made it difficult for large retail stores such as department stores, supermarkets, shopping centres, and so forth to open new stores or expand existing stores without coordinating with small and medium retailers, retailer associations, and local governments. The laws also required large retail stores to reduce their sales area and to provide space for public facilities. Despite these new laws, adjustments between modernizing the distribution system and protecting small and medium retailers remained an issue.

26.5. Promoting Systematization and Modernization of Distribution

The ninth interim report of the Industrial Structure Council was entitled 'Distribution in the 1970s'. In chapter 4, 'Direction of Distribution Policy', the first of the current issues discussed was 'Sophistication of Market Structure'. The policy for making Japan's market structure more sophisticated emphasized four points: (1) pursuit of economies of scale, (2) establishment of a rationalized division of labour and a supplementary system, (3) promotion of systematization, and (4) promotion of modernization of small and medium enterprises. For economies of scale, the expansion of business operations by building larger stores and by having multiple stores or cooperative stores was emphasized. The report focused on the latter, especially cooperative organizations such as chain stores and voluntary chains of multiple stores, wholesaler industrial parks, and integrated wholesale centres that aimed at bringing wholesale businesses together.[11]

Chain stores achieved remarkable growth using a strategy of mass sales with low profit margins and turnover. This led to legislation such as the Large-Scale Retail Stores Law, as seen above. Measures to promote the development of voluntary chains opened the way for participation by small and medium enterprises, while still providing economies of scale similar to chain stores without requiring large capital investment or the acquisition of land. A voluntary chain is defined as an 'organization in which many retail stores in various locations (sometimes including wholesalers) establish permanent "chain" relations and cooperate with each other while remaining independent.'[12] Some problems voluntary chains faced included a lack of funds and human resources at their headquarters, an insufficient selection of merchandise, and a lack of managerial experience. With that background, the member stores did not increase their dependence on the chain organization. Also, to become a member of a voluntary chain, member stores were required initially to invest a certain amount of capital. Quite a few retail stores could not take on the burden of raising the needed funds. These various factors delayed the development and growth of voluntary chains. MITI backed loans from the Japan Development Bank for improving the facilities in the headquarters of voluntary chains and provided loans from the Trust Fund

Bureau for leasing equipment for use at the headquarters and member stores (via the Industrial Bank of Japan and the Long-Term Credit Bank of Japan).

In the 1970s, convenience stores of the franchise chain type grew rapidly in the overall retail chain system. A convenience store is defined as a 'retail store providing conveniences to consumers'. Located close to residential areas, convenience stores are generally open twenty-four hours a day, and have a wide assortment of daily necessities.[13] Social factors such as the increased employment of women, increased night population in cities, and increased one-person households created the need for convenience stores. The number of retail stores wanting to join franchise chains increased as it became more difficult to operate small retail stores. In a franchise chain, a relationship is developed in which a franchiser grants a franchisee the right and licence to operate a business using the trade name and trademark of the franchise, at the same time assisting the franchisee in merchandising and management, in organizing the business, and in training employees.[14] Convenience stores spread rapidly in Japan because they provided services traditional retail stores did not provide. As part of its plan to make small and medium retail operations more sophisticated, the Small and Medium Enterprise Agency conducted an awareness survey concerning chain and voluntary chain store operations, and surveyed the available details of such operations, including the rules determining membership in franchise chains, the systems, and actual performance.

MITI, meanwhile, recommended that wholesalers group together to build wholesale industrial parks and integrated wholesale distribution centres. In order to deal with over-concentration of various functions in urban centres and a general worsening of the distribution situation, it was necessary to rationalize the distribution system and support the system of distribution centres. The Japan Development Bank provided finance for building integrated wholesale centres in Tokyo and Osaka.

Concerning establishment of a rationalized division of labour and a supplementary system, strong efforts were made to promote joint projects by utilizing the converter function of wholesalers, the convenience store function of retailers, the functional specialization of wholesalers, the transformation of retailers into speciality shops, and the form of shopping centres.

As for systematization of distribution activities, the Distribution Committee of the Industrial Structure Council published its seventh interim report in July 1969 entitled 'Regarding the Systemization of Distribution Activities'. Based on that report, a 'Committee to Promote Systemization of Distribution' was established in September 1970. That committee discussed basic policies for systematizing distribution by issue and by region and included its recommendations in a report. The committee's discussions were held in parallel with the Distribution Committee of the Industrial Structure Council preparing its 'Distribution in the 1970s' report, and the two reports were published at about the same time. The report included a distribution forecast for fiscal year 1975. It emphasized that the distribution system would have to be systematized in order to efficiently handle sales volumes expected to reach triple actual fiscal year 1968 volumes, distribution volumes about double those of fiscal year 1968, and fivefold the volume of information. The report stated that in order to increase productivity and have distribution function in more sophisticated ways, it was important to approach the issue at the national level by promoting and realizing 'the systematization of distribution' through combined government and private-sector efforts. Several basic surveys were conducted after 1971 based on this policy, including a survey of representative domestic examples, a survey of the distribution structure by product category, and a survey of distribution information services. As a result of these surveys, the concept of modernizing distribution by industry was formulated, simulation models were developed, manuals were prepared for systematizing distribution, transaction vouchers were integrated, conditions for transactions were normalized, and integrated transaction codes were prepared.

For developing the distribution system, pallet pooling was promoted and POS (point of sales) data-management systems and the system of physical distribution were developed. Also, measures to assist pioneering projects from the financial and tax sides were introduced. Among these different approaches, POS systems grew very rapidly. A basic survey was made in fiscal year 1974 of trends in Europe and the US regarding POS systems and how they were applied in actual situations. Standard POS specifications were developed in fiscal year 1975, followed by a detailed design of POS systems for department stores and chain stores in fiscal year 1976 and the development of methods for assessing POS systems. Experiments for reading source markings were carried out in fiscal year 1977; JIS standards for bar-code symbols to be used with products having common elements were established; common product codes were initially registered; and a user's manual for POS systems was prepared in fiscal year 1978. In fiscal year 1979 the study of using price tags that can be read by OCR (optical character reader) was completed.

The preparatory and experimental stages were thus completed, and 1980 saw the start of the introductory and propagation stages. By the end of fiscal year 1980, a POS system for foodstuffs and sundry products had been introduced at eighty-six stores of seventeen companies. By October 1983 the number had increased to 2,500 stores with 18,000 POS terminals. The introduction of POS systems contributed to greater accuracy, quicker service, and labour saving at check-out counters in stores, and also contributed to quicker computer processing, order receipt and delivery, and more reliable inventory control, as well as more rationalized shipment and delivery operations.

MITI also carried out various surveys in order to keep up with changes occurring in the retail and distribution industries. Surveys of the actual situation in stores located in large residential complexes, the actual situation concerning chain stores and stores located in high-rise buildings, and the activities of trading companies were a few of MITI's survey activities. The information from these surveys contributed towards determining what distribution activities were considered best.[15]

From fiscal year 1969, MITI was also concerned with making transaction conditions fair by product category, and each fiscal year published guidelines for about fifteen products. MITI also prepared a manual for the advertising industry to improve advertising activities, and commissioned research and studies to check the content of advertisements, and to study the economic effects of advertising. Administrative guidance was given to companies preparing improper advertising in order to rectify the situation. Also carried out were inspections and surveys of commodities exchanges and the lease industry to ensure that proper transactions were being made in those areas as well. MITI thus promoted the modernization and systematization of the distribution industry by expanding its administration of distribution to deal with the increase in the relative importance of the distribution industry in the national economy and the appearance of new types of businesses, technical innovations in distribution, and the progress of information systems.

NOTES

1. Based on economic indicators in Katsunobu Takeuchi, *Nenpyo de Miru Nihon Keizai no Ashidori* (Japan's Economy Viewed Chronologically), Zaisei Shohosha, 1988: 226–8; also, discussions in this chapter concerning economic trends depend on other parts of this book.
2. *Tsusho Hakusho*, 1974 edn., General Survey Volume: 76.
3. Ibid. 86–7; for discussion of the content and the process of legislating the Law Concerning Emergency Measures Against Engrossing and Withholding the Sale of Materials Vital to National Life, see *Tsusho Sangyo Seisakushi*, xiii. 408–12.
4. Yasuhiro Nakasone: 56–61, and *Tsusho Sangyo Seisakushi*, xiii. 412, table 1 in pt. 5, ch. 1.
5. For discussion of content, legislation process, and promulgation of the Law on Emergency Measures for National Life Stabilization, see ibid. xiii. 416–28.
6. *Tsusho Sangyo-sho Nenpo*, fiscal year 1972: 98 and fiscal year 1973: 104; unless specified otherwise, for all later mention of consumer protection and distribution industry policy refer to related years in *Tsusho Sangyo-sho Nenpo*; also see *Tsusho Sangyo Seisakushi*, xiii. 448–51.
7. MITI Minister's Secretariat, Research and Statistics Department (ed.), *Wagakuni no Shogyo 1973* (Commerce in Japan, 1973), Research Institute of International Trade and Industry, 1974, table 1 in pt. 8: 25.
8. *Tsusansho Koho*, 27 Aug. 1970: 3–4.
9. MITI, Enterprise Bureau (ed.), *70-nendai ni Okeru Ryutsu* (Distribution in the 1970s), Printing Bureau, MoF, 1971: 111; for most other discussions of distribution industry policy see *Tsusho Sangyo Seisakushi*, xiii, ch. 5, sect. 4.
10. See MITI, Industrial Policy Bureau, Coordination Officer for Large-Scale Retail Stores (ed.), *Shin Daikibo Kouritenpo Ho no Kaisetsu* (Interpretation of New Large-Scale Retail Stores Law), Research Institute of International Trade and Industry, 1980.
11. *70-nendai ni Okeru Ryutsu*: 62–5. Many other parts in this Part are also based on that report. But also see MITI, Enterprise Bureau (ed.), *Ryutsu Shisutemuka Kihon Hoshin* (Basic Plan for Distribution Systematization), Printing Bureau, MoF, 1971; *Tsusho Sangyo Seisakushi*, xiii, ch. 5, sect. 1, subsect. 4; and Shuji Ogawa, *Zu de Miru 80-nendai no Ryutsu Bijion* (Vision of Distribution in the 1980s Viewed by Graph), Distribution Systems Research Institute, 1984: 174–9.
12. Small and Medium Enterprise Agency, *Konbiniensu Sutoa Manyuaru* (The Manual of Convenience Store), 1972: 17.
13. Ibid. 11–12.
14. Ibid. 17.
15. *Tsusho Sangyo-sho Nenpo*, various years.

27

Problems of the Post-High-Level Growth Period

27.1. Emergence of Problems Related to the Expanded Scale of Economy

High-level economic growth during the 1960s gave Japan the world's second largest gross national product and promoted it to 'economic power' status. A shift to emphasis on the heavy and chemical industries was realized, trade surpluses took fairly firm root, and the living standard of the Japanese people improved. On the other hand, however, high-level growth also brought with it certain problems related to areas where improvements were relatively delayed and those where high-level growth had produced serious distortions. Examples of problem areas on the negative side of high-level growth included those related to small and medium enterprises, industrial pollution, overpopulation, depopulation, and so forth. These problem areas became part of the issues that could not be neglected in trade and industry policy during the 1970s, the decade following the period of high-level growth.

Small and medium enterprises account for an extremely high percentage of the total number of companies in Japan. Statistics show that in 1969 the percentage of the total number of places of businesses accounted for by small and medium enterprises with less than 300 employees was 98.8 per cent in mining, 99.8 per cent in construction, 99.4 per cent in manufacturing, 99.4 per cent in finance and insurance, 100 per cent in real estate, 99.3 per cent in transportation and telecommunications, and 98.6 per cent in electricity, gas, and water. In the same year, small and medium enterprises accounted for 99.6 per cent of the total number of places of business in wholesaling and retailing, and 98.9 per cent in the service industry, although establishments with under 100 employees were designated as 'small and medium enterprises' in wholesaling and those with under fifty were so designated in retailing and the service industry.

The percentage of employees accounted for by small and medium enterprises compared to the total number of employees in non-primary industries was 77.2 per cent.[1] As this high percentages shows, small and medium enterprises were underprivileged for many years. In 1960, when the period of Japan's high-level economic growth started, the index numbers of these companies relative to that of large enterprises (=100) in terms of per capita wages, capital equipment ratio, and productivity of added value were only 46, 18, and 36, respectively (see Table 27.1). Though these figures improved considerably, in 1970 the indices in terms

Table 27.1 Changes in disparity by scale (all industries), 1960–1970

	Fiscal year 1960	Difference in fiscal year 1960	Fiscal year 1970	Difference in fiscal year 1970
Per capita wages				
Small and medium enterprises	161	46	769	65
Large enterprises	351	100	1,192	100
Capital equipment ratio				
Small and medium enterprises	295	18	953	26
Large enterprises	1,631	100	3,612	100
Productivity of capital				
Small and medium enterprises	1.36	239	1.19	183
Large enterprises	0.57	100	0.65	100
Productivity of added value				
Small and medium enterprises	306	36	1,138	49
Large enterprises	855	100	2,338	100

Notes: Small and medium enterprises are capitalized at less than 100m. yen; large enterprises are capitalized at 100m. yen or more; unit for per capita wages, capital equipment ratio, and productivity of added value is 1,000 yen; productivity of capital is expressed in multiples; differences are expressed as indices, with large enterprises as 100.

Sources: Compiled by Small and Medium Enterprise Agency, 1969, *White Paper on Small and Medium Enterprises in Japan*, Ministry of Finance Printing Bureau, Annexed Statistics: 19, and 1972 edn.: 19; original materials are from *Hojin Kigyo Tokei Nenpo* (Statistical Survey of Corporations, Annual), the Ministry of Finance.

Table 27.2   Value of imports classified by product
(unit: $1m.)

	1970	1975	1980
Foodstuffs	2,574	8,814	14,666
Textile materials	962	1,524	2,393
Metal materials	2,696	4,416	8,429
Other materials	3,017	5,718	12,937
Mineral fuels	3,905	25,640	69,991
Chemicals	1,000	2,057	6,202
Machinery and equipment	2,297	4,285	9,843
Others	2,426	5,404	16,064
Total	18,881	57,863	140,527

Source: *Tsusho Sangyo Seisakushi* (History of International Trade and Industry Policy), xvi: 240–1, table 11-2-2, Value of imports classified by product.

of per capita wages, capital equipment ratio, and productivity of added value were still 65, 26, and 49, respectively. In the course of high-level growth, small and medium enterprises grew compared to what they were previously. But when compared with large enterprises, their accomplishments were relatively small. They needed to be modernized and made more sophisticated.

Another problem of the post-high-level growth period was industrial pollution. Economic expansion was naturally accompanied by increases in production and consumption, which resulted in the import and consumption of huge amounts of raw materials. As shown in the changes in the dollar amount of imported goods and materials during the 1970–80 period (see Table 27.2), the amount of imported foodstuffs increased 5.7-fold, textile materials 2.5-fold, metal materials 3.1-fold, and other materials 4.3-fold. The amount of imported mineral fuel grew an amazing 17.9-fold, chemical products 6.2-fold, machinery and equipment 4.3-fold, and others 6.6-fold. The total value of imports increased 7.4 times compared with ten years earlier. These figures show that the major reason for the increased imports was an increase in the amount of imported mineral fuel, i.e. crude oil and coal. Enormous amounts of imported mineral fuel were consumed at factories, power plants, and at homes, as well as in the transportation sector. Such consumption, usually taking place in densely populated areas, resulted in emissions of SO_2 and NO_2, generated in the combustion process. Air pollution problems were related to these chemical substances. From when the period of high-level growth began, air pollution had become a common problem in industrial complexes concentrated along the Tokaido seaboard from Tokyo to Osaka. During the 1970s, however, motorization progressed and even residential areas located far from industrial districts suffered from photochemical smog. Moreover, the network of roads and motorways being developed spread air pollution widely throughout the country, even decimating mountain forests.

Furthermore, development giving priority to economic efficiency caused land prices to rise to unreasonably high levels, destroyed entire ecological systems, and resulted in water pollution and the ruin of invaluable fauna and flora.

From the second half of the 1960s, there was already an awareness of the distortions accompanying high-level economic growth. The Basic Law for Environmental Pollution Control, for instance, was enacted in August 1967. That law aimed at regulating the discharge of harmful pollutants by establishing environmental standards according to region, and companies were required to eliminate or reduce the concentration of harmful substances in emissions and waste water.

In May 1971, the Industrial Structure Council submitted an interim report entitled 'Vision of MITI Policies in the 1970s' to the Minister of International Trade and Industry. In the section of the report that referred to policies on industrial organization and industrial technology, the Council recommended the promotion of measures to combat industrial pollution. Based on that report, MITI announced 'the improvement of systems to prevent industrial pollution' as one of its priority policies for fiscal year 1972 and asked for budget appropriations. Also included in the priority policies and budget requests were plans for conducting training courses and national examinations to qualify persons as pollution-control managers, the establishment of industry-specific conferences to discuss anti-pollution measures, special depreciation measures for pollution-control facilities, and the bolstering and expansion of financial support. The policies also included establishment of a system for approval of anti-pollution equipment and devices, promotion of R&D related to technology for preventing industrial pollution, and others.[2]

A third category of problems that can be mentioned as post-high-growth period problems is depopulation and overpopulation tied to the types of pollution noted above. Except for mining areas, the main areas where environmental damage was serious were those where industrial plants were concentrated. Industry in Japan generally developed in areas along the Tokaido seaboard, and by the early twentieth century four major industrial districts emerged: the Keihin (Tokyo-Yokohama), Tokai, Hanshin (Osaka-Kobe), and Kita-Kyushu districts. In the mid-1930s—especially with munitions plants being relocated to provincial areas—industry began spreading along the Tokaido seaboard in areas between the four major industrial districts. In the context of post-war economic growth, the heavy and chemical industries in particular came to be concentrated along coastal industrial districts. In the 1970s, the locating of new production plants in existing industrial districts brought about problems of overconcentration. As shown in Table 27.3, shipments of industrial products from the Kanto Coastal, Tokai, and Kinki Coastal industrial districts accounted for 65.3 per cent of total nationwide shipments of industrial products in value terms, and the total area of

Table 27.3 Industrial location and environmental pollution (1970)

Region	Value of industrial shipments (100 m. yen)	Land area of sites (sq. km.)	Amount of water used (1,000 cu.m./day)	Projected amount of NO$_2$ discharged (No. cu.m./hr.)
Hokkaido	15,111	76	5,129	7,000
Tohoku	31,747	113	7,214	7,200
Kanto (inland)	47,327	124	4,660	8,800
Kanto (coastal)	204,497	234	16,424	35,200
Tokai	114,791	230	18,007	17,300
Hokuriku	16,657	47	3,447	1,900
Kinki (inland)	25,245	51	2,011	1,300
Kinki (coastal)	131,612	167	13,320	24,500
San'in	3,391	10	553	400
Sanyo	47,555	115	11,009	22,200
Shikoku	17,622	49	4,596	3,100
Kyushu	34,791	91	8,403	15,500
Nationwide	690,347	1,301	94,773	144,400

Source: Compiled by MITI, 1975 edn., *Sangyo Kozo no Choki Vision* (Japan's Industrial Structure: A Long-Range Vision), Research Institute of International Trade and Industry: 281–2, 293.

land for industrial facilities located in these districts accounted for 48.5 per cent of all industrial-use land area in Japan.

This concentration of industry in certain areas led to similar concentrations of waste water and emissions from plants. One way to estimate the amount of waste water discharged from plants is to review figures on the amount of water they use. The three industrial districts just mentioned, for instance, accounted in 1970 for 50.4 per cent of the nation's total amount of industrial water. Naturally, the amount of water used in plants is not directly proportionate to the amount of pollutants found in waste water, because the level of pollution in industrial waste water varies from one industry to another and from one water-treatment facility to another. Still, there was no denying that the quality of water had to be improved in these three districts more than elsewhere. Air pollution caused by smoke emissions also became a problem in these highly industrialized districts. Although the amount of NO$_2$ discharged in a particular area calculated on the basis of the amount of fuel consumed is not always proportional to the value of industrial products shipped from that area, the Kanto Coastal, Tokai, and Kinki Coastal districts accounted for 53.3 per cent of all NO$_2$ discharged in Japan in 1970. In terms of the value of industrial shipments, total land area of plant sites, amount of water used, and projected amount of NO$_2$ discharged, the industrial districts along the Tokaido seaboard, combined with the Sanyo and Kyushu districts, accounted for, respectively, 77.2 per cent, 64.3 per cent, 70.9 per cent, and 79.4 per cent in 1970, all high percentages. The concentration of industry in specific areas was considered the principal cause of environmental pollution, and it was essential to realize that promoting industrial relocation and promoting anti-pollution measures were inseparable issues.

Companies pursuing economies of scale and scope in their business activities inevitably build new plants in or near existing industrial areas. Such siting follows the principle of benefiting from integration. But it also brought about various problems related to overconcentration, and it can be said that the negative effects on society owing to high-level economic growth, such as environmental destruction, income disparities, soaring land prices, and inadequate social overhead capital, surfaced in the form of overpopulation in some areas and depopulation in others. As it progresses, local industrial concentration may bring beneficial effects from integration up to a certain point, but it can become disadvantageous if it results in overconcentration that increases negative effects such as environmental destruction, soaring land prices, traffic paralysis, increased housing costs, and so forth. The negative effects of integration became an issue in the 1970s and required urgent solution. It can be said that policies on industrial location, ports and harbours, roads, and industrial water use, adopted to promote high-level economic growth, were mainly designed to facilitate the salutary effects of integration and alleviate any bottlenecks to the intended benefits of integration. The times had changed, however, and new policies were needed. A clear shift to knowledge-intensive industries making use of advanced technology was taking place, a shift destined to lead to resource and energy savings in industry and to the relocation and dispersion of industry.

27.2. The Appreciation of the Yen, Oil Crises, and Promoting Modernization of Small and Medium Enterprises

In the 1970s, small and medium enterprises in Japan were forced to cope with economic fluctuations occurring on an international scale. The collapse of the fixed exchange rate system triggered by an announcement on 15 August 1971 by US President Nixon that removed the dollar from convertibility with gold, and the subsequent appreciation of the yen, brought a sense of crisis to Japanese small and medium enterprises highly dependent on exports and concerned about losing their markets. Almost at the same time, the Japanese government granted preferential tariffs to developing countries. This move dealt another severe blow to small and medium enterprises in labour-intensive industries that competed with manufacturers in developing countries. These companies were forced, therefore, to choose between relocating their operations in developing countries or converting to different industries or different products. The first oil crisis in October 1973 and the second in January 1979 made it increasingly difficult for these companies to import materials and fuel and pushed up their prices, thereby reducing profits. In the meantime, the liberalization of trade and the lowering of tariffs that had reached their final stage of implementation in Japan removed the remaining barriers aimed at protecting industries in

Japan, thus forcing small and medium enterprises to compete directly with overseas products and capital.

The foregoing economic fluctuations also seriously affected large corporations in Japan and led them to search for opportunities to enter any part of the domestic market that was potentially profitable. This move intensified the competition between large corporations and small and medium enterprises. Large corporations that were exporting, moreover, moved to reduce their production costs by urging small and medium enterprises to substantially lower the price of products they manufactured as subcontractors. This move also reduced the profits of small companies. Some large corporations chose to reduce production, convert to different products, or move production facilities overseas, thus jeopardizing the very existence of affiliated subcontractors.

As described earlier, Japan has a great number of small and medium enterprises that account for an overwhelmingly high percentage of the total number of companies and employees in Japan. For those reasons, importance has long been attached to policy related to these enterprises. That policy has a long history and has held a unique position among other trade and industry policies. In view of the importance placed on policies dealing with them, the Small and Medium Enterprise Policy-Making Council was requested to study the direction of such policy for the 1970s. In December 1969, the Council submitted a report entitled 'What Small and Medium Enterprise Policy Should Be in the Future'. In its report, the Council mainly recommended that small and medium enterprises modernize themselves from an economic viewpoint, make efforts to be self-reliant, and raise their processing capabilities. The report also urged them to convert to business fields marked by high productivity and high wages, as found among small and medium enterprises in other of the advanced countries. In May 1971, the Industrial Structure Council submitted an interim report titled 'Vision of MITI Policies in the 1970s'. In that report, the Council envisioned a knowledge-intensive structure as Japan's industrial structure for the 1970s and considered it necessary to change it in order to respond to a shortage of labour, rising commodity prices, issues related to developing countries, and the need to raise the domestic standard of living. The Council also suggested that small and medium enterprises currently marked by low productivity and low wages could find a way out of their difficulties by becoming increasingly knowledge-intensive, and that outstanding companies in particular might realize more advantages in fields characterized by production of small quantities, such as producer goods very close to end products, capital goods, precision machinery, machine tools, parts processing, fine chemicals, high-grade clothes, and high-grade sundry goods.

President Nixon announced the removal of the US dollar from gold convertibility not long after the Industrial Structure Council submitted its interim report, and as a result it became necessary to review the direction for small and medium enterprises. The Small and Medium Enterprise Policy-Making Council subsequently compiled its opinions into a report entitled 'The Form of Small and Medium Enterprises in the 1970s and the Direction of Small and Medium Enterprise Policy' (released in August 1972). Keywords used in that report to describe the future vision of small and medium enterprises were 'knowledge-intensive', 'diversified', and 'highly motivated'.[3]

Behind the emphasis on the need for small and medium enterprises to make stronger efforts to become self-reliant and highly motivated was the idea that the formation of policy should be based on the classification of these enterprises into two types: outstanding companies that can adapt themselves to a conversion to knowledge-intensive businesses, and small enterprises being operated primarily to earn a living for their owners. The opinion offered in the August 1972 report was that the definition of small and medium enterprises should be changed by enlarging the scale of these companies in terms of their capitalization and number of employees so that more companies could be included in the category, and that separate measures should be considered for small enterprises. These proposals were incorporated in the revised Small and Medium Enterprises Basic Law of October 1973. The new upper limits for capitalization and the number of employees were 100 million yen and 300 persons, respectively, for manufacturing, mining, and transportation, and the upper limits were also raised for the retail, service, and wholesale industries. Also, manufacturers with twenty or fewer full-time employees, and service and retail companies with five or fewer employees, were defined as 'small enterprises'. From this time on, when policy affected 'small companies' it had to clearly state it. This change in the definition of small and medium enterprises reflected their ongoing bipolarization. Upper-level small and medium enterprises equipped with highly automated machinery and computers were competitive and fully supplied with capital, but they were small in terms of business size when compared with large corporations and still smaller in terms of equity capital. Even companies capitalized at 100 million yen could not be excluded when implementing policy on small and medium enterprises. Lower-level small companies, meanwhile, with limited managerial resources and operated by their owners to earn a living, tended to remain at the bottom of the scale and were unable to respond to policies aimed at modernizing and developing small and medium enterprises. It was necessary, therefore, to formulate policy from a viewpoint different from that of small and medium enterprises in general. The change in definition resulted, in a sense, from the bipolarization of small and medium enterprises caused by high-level economic growth.

Even as the direction of policy regarding small and medium enterprises, as specified in the keywords 'knowledge-intensive', 'diversified', and 'highly motivated', was announced, emergency countermeasures were being required in response to a situation where rapid and massive changes were occurring in the international economic environment. During the 1970s, amidst hectic economic fluctuations, even as it made adjustments in its policy for promoting the modernization of small and medium enterprises, which was in effect from the period of high-level growth, MITI was obliged to introduce emergency measures to alleviate damage caused by liberalization, the appreciated yen, and the two oil crises, and to improve the conditions for enabling small and medium enterprises to meet the needs of the emerging market situation.

In August 1971, following the countries of the European Community and ahead of the US, Japan introduced a system of preferential tariffs in which import barriers to products from developing countries were lowered. The preferential tariffs granted by Japan, however, were carefully designed to protect processed agricultural products and products manufactured by small and medium Japanese enterprises. For example, a ceiling was set on all import items for which basically no tariffs were levied, and the benefits of the system of preferential tariffs ceased to be granted when the volume of imports reached 50 per cent of the ceiling volume. Also, tariffs were reduced only by 50 per cent for fifty-seven specially designated items, no preferential tariffs were granted to seven items considered less competitive in international markets, and safeguards were established concerning fifty-nine processed agricultural items, as specified in an escape clause. Earlier, in April 1971, the Law on Temporary Measures for Preferential Treatment of Small and Medium Enterprises was enacted with the aim of lessening the damage which might be caused to small and medium enterprises by the implementation of preferential tariffs and helping such enterprises find a way to deal with the current difficulties. One of the two main purposes of the law was to modernize and rationalize small and medium enterprises, and to promote their structural change, etc., with financial support from the Small-Business Promotion Corporation and other organizations. The other main purpose was to assist these enterprises in converting to other businesses through measures related to financing, taxation, and labour.

In September 1971, the government decided at a Cabinet meeting to introduce measures to offset the import surcharges imposed on Japanese companies by the US government in August 1971, through financing, the supplementing of credit, measures to stabilize foreign exchange, taxation, and steps to facilitate the conversion to new businesses. In December, furthermore, the government promulgated the Law on Temporary Measures for Small and Medium Enterprises in relation to Adjustment Measures taken with respect to the International Economy (International Economy Adjustment Measures Law) in preparation for the new exchange system under the Smithsonian Agreement. This law aimed at stabilizing the management of small and medium enterprises deemed as having been hurt by the yen's appreciation, helping them convert to other businesses, and finding job opportunities for the unemployed.

In February 1973, when the yen was shifted to a floating exchange rate system, the government introduced emergency measures related to financing, deferment of repayments, and new ceilings on credit insurance, as well as measures such as those for facilitating the smooth conversion to different businesses. The government also revised the International Economy Adjustment Measures Law so that it would be effective for another two years, until 1976, thereby contributing further to stabilization of the management of small and medium enterprises exporting their products. And through the 'Outline of Emergency Financing

System for Export-Related Small and Medium Enterprises', in which 114 industries and eighty-two production areas were designated as recipients of financing, the government provided relief to small and medium enterprises included in the designations.

Later, during times when the yen repeatedly appreciated very suddenly, the government took similar measures regarding financing, credit insurance, taxation, the conversion to different industries, and employment. It also introduced measures on a priority basis for industries and production areas designated as having been seriously affected. The Law on Temporary Measures for Assisting Small and Medium Enterprises to Cope with Yen Appreciation, promulgated in February 1978, was designed for similar purposes.

Successful conversion to different businesses had been included in the measures taken to deal with the appreciated yen. The opinion was expressed, however, that instead of taking measures to evade emergency situations, the government should encourage small and medium enterprises to voluntarily and actively convert to different or new business fields. This opinion appeared in a December 1974 report, 'On the Future Direction of Measures to Modernize Small and Medium Enterprises'. The report led to the promulgation and enforcement in November 1976 of the Law on Temporary Measures for Business Conversion by Small and Medium Enterprises. The distinctive feature of this law, effective only for ten years, was that it aimed at implementing comprehensive countermeasures for companies voluntarily converting to different businesses.

From early in the 1970s, more and more large corporations developed new technology and entered fields dominated by small and medium enterprises, thereby threatening those enterprises. The large corporations affected the business operations of the small enterprises by entering traditional and labour-intensive industries with mass production systems and powerful sales networks. The types of industries affected included bean curd, bean sprouts, light printing, laundry, spectacles, boiled fish paste, Japanese cakes, and others. In that context, the Law on Securing Business Opportunities for Small and Medium Enterprises by Adjusting the Business Activities of Large Enterprises was enforced in September 1977.

Partially revised several times, the Small and Medium Enterprises Modernization Law promulgated in 1963 continued to function even as the yen appreciated in value. In particular, revisions to the law in 1969 provided for establishment of a system to plan the structural improvement of small and medium enterprises, a system that was effective in times of rapid change. Structural improvement plans were classified by industry, region, and purpose, and were applied extremely flexibly to additionally designated industries as well as to those specified from time to time. For example, the plans were carried out in elaborate combination with measures to offset the effects of the yen's appreciation, measures to encourage conversion to knowledge-intensive industries, and those to promote specified industries.

So-called 'upgrading projects' had been widely promoted since 1967. They aimed at rationalization and greater efficiency by encouraging small and medium enterprises to share and integrate facilities. Examples included the joint use of factories, joint anti-pollution efforts, joint use of specified stores, joint establishment of special shopping areas, and joint execution of measures related to structural improvement (specified) and special wide areas (specified). The sharing of anti-pollution facilities was particularly effective for the times.

The Law on Temporary Measures for Small and Medium Enterprises in Specified Depressed Regions enforced in November 1978 and the Law on Temporary Measures for Small and Medium Enterprises in Producing Regions enforced in July 1979 addressed serious economic fluctuations even when they were limited to specific areas. In addition, other projects and measures were also continuously carried out or introduced. Examples included guidance to and diagnosis of small and medium enterprises, policy financing, measures for small enterprises, measures for subcontractors, measures to prevent delays in payment for subcontracted work, and providing opportunities for small and medium enterprises to obtain government and public agency contracts. These projects and measures reflected the fact that changes in the external environment were forcing small and medium enterprises to face new challenges before they resolved old problems.

As described above, small and medium enterprises faced various external environmental changes, such as the shift to a floating exchange rate system, the yen's appreciation, two oil crises and subsequent increases in costs, and the emergence of strong competitors in developing countries. Even faced with such severe circumstances, however, small and medium enterprises increased their productivity quite a bit during the 1970s. Value-added productivity increased 2.87-fold from 1,125,000 to 3,234,000 yen, per capita personnel expenses increased 3.15-fold from 782,000 to 2,464,000 yen, the capital equipment ratio increased 2.64-fold from 1,021,000 to 2,696,000 yen, and productivity of capital increased 1.08-fold from 1.102 to 1.2. Investments in up-to-date equipment raised the capital equipment ratio and more effective use of equipment improved the productivity of capital, thereby increasing the productivity of value-added level and enabling small and medium enterprises to pay higher wages (see Table 27.4). Despite these gains, however, the disparity between small and medium enterprises and large enterprises expanded slightly, except for the capital/equipment ratio. This trend was in contrast to the 1960s when the disparity narrowed. The reasons for the increased disparity was that large enterprises, facing the same difficult environment as small and medium enterprises, also made efforts to increase their productivity and raise wages while streamlining their operations.

27.3. Industrial Relocation and Environmental Policy

During the period of high-level economic growth, heavy and chemical industry zones were developed in the two major centres of the Tokyo Capital Region and Kinki district and along the Tokaido seaboard connecting them. It was also

Table 27.4 Comparison of selected indices (all industries), 1970–1980

	Fiscal year 1970	Difference in fiscal year 1970	Fiscal year 1980	Difference in fiscal year 1980
Per capita wages				
Small and medium enterprises	782	62	2,464	61
Large enterprises	1,256	100	4,054	100
Capital equipment ratio				
Small and medium enterprises	1,021	26	2,695	28
Large enterprises	3,942	100	9,711	100
Productivity of capital				
Small and medium enterprises	1.102	187	1.200	166
Large enterprises	0.590	100	0.722	100
Productivity of value added				
Small and medium enterprises	1,125	48	3,234	46
Large enterprises	2.327	100	7.015	100

Notes: Small and medium enterprises are capitalized at less than 100 m. yen; large enterprises are capitalized at 100 m. yen or more. Units of per capita wages, capital equipment ratio, and value-added productivity are 1,000 yen. Unit of productivity of capital is multiples. The difference is indicated by an index with large enterprises as 100.

Sources: *White Paper on Small and Medium Enterprise in Japan*, compiled by Small and Medium Enterprise Agency, Printing Bureau, Ministry of Finance, 1979 edn., table 21, p. 25; *White Paper on Small and Medium Enterprises in Japan*, 1982 edn., table 22, p. 24. Data originally from Ministry of Finance's *Hojin Kigyo Tokei Nenpo* (Statistical Survey of Corporations, Annual).

natural from the viewpoint of operational efficiency that industries dependent on imported materials and fuel would locate themselves in prime areas near ports and harbours facing the Pacific. Such siting brought about population increases in already densely populated areas, aggravating problems such as housing shortages, traffic congestion, land shortages, environmental pollution, and so forth. On the other hand, areas located far from the Tokaido seaboard saw no high-level economic growth. There were thus no job opportunities created there, which urged young persons to seek employment elsewhere, leading to the depopulation of these remote areas. In extreme cases, the infrastructure, including public transport, could not be maintained, which accelerated the depopulation trend.

It became apparent that the imbalance of industrial location had to be corrected so that stable growth could be maintained and a comfortable life guaranteed for the people. In the early 1970s, various proposals were put forward for building new industrial zones at locations distant from existing zones.

In May 1971, the Industrial Structure Council submitted an interim report entitled 'Vision of MITI Policies in the 1970s'. In the report, under the heading of 'Response to Overpopulation/Environmental Problems and Improvement of Social Overhead Capital', the Council mentioned five points: (1) promoting the development of large industrial bases; (2) more appropriate siting of inland-type industries, including the introduction of industry into agricultural areas; (3) forming international networks for industrial siting; (4) innovation of social overhead capital; and (5) developing industries related to social overhead capital and the prevention of pollution. The report also stated:

It is necessary to develop new large-scale industrial areas located far from the existing developed areas. The new industrial areas should be based on carefully planned, wide-scale use of land and water resources and should be fully equipped not only with industry-related facilities but with urban functions and living environment facilities as well.

In July, immediately after the interim report was submitted, Kakuei Tanaka assumed office as Minister of International Trade and Industry. He insisted on forcing plants to move from urban centres for dispersal to local areas. In response to Minister Tanaka's idea, MITI formulated measures for promoting the relocation of plants. He also introduced his 'Nihon Retto Kaizoron' (Plan for Rebuilding the Japanese Archipelago) at a press conference held on 11 June 1972. This plan designated the Tohoku, Hokuriku, San'in, Shikoku, and Kyushu areas, as well as Hokkaido, Okinawa, and several other prefectures, as locations with depopulated areas where production facilities could be relocated from built-up areas such as the Tokyo Capital Region and the Kinki district. This plan took form in the Industrial Relocation Promotion Law promulgated in June and enforced in October 1972. At the same time that the law was enacted, the Coal Mining Areas Development Corporation Law was revised and renamed the Industrial Relocation and Coal Mining Areas Development Corporation Law so that the corporation could also conduct business related to industrial relocation. Kakuei Tanaka also requested legislation that would establish environmental standards for the inside of plants and make it possible to instruct plants failing to comply with those standards to make improvements. This request led to promulgation of the Factory Location Law in October 1973.[4]

In 1977, plans to promote industrial relocation based on the Industrial Relocation Promotion Law were announced. The Third Comprehensive National Development Plan was also announced in the same year. In 1978, moreover, Hokkaido, Okinawa, and ten other prefectures—located in northern Tohoku, San'in, southern Shikoku, and southern Kyushu—were designated as special areas for relocating production facilities. Areas dependent on structurally depressed industries were also designated the same way.

The Industrial Relocation Promotion Law contained unique schemes for resolving the problems of overpopulation and depopulation, but the two oil crises and the appreciation of the yen prevented plants from moving out of built-up urban centres on a large scale. Certainly, some plants that had been located in urban centres were relocated or shut down, but there were few instances of sizeable industrial areas being built in areas designated as attractive investment locations. In fact, in order to realize the benefits of integration, companies continued to construct new plants along the Tokaido seaboard and in areas neighbouring the Tokyo Capital Region and Kinki district.

In December 1978, Masayoshi Ohira was elected prime minister. From around 1971, well before he became prime minister, Ohira embraced a concept he called a 'plan for pastoral cities'. In it, Ohira proposed building a number of cities throughout Japan that would have limited populations of about 300,000. The cities would feature a mixture of urban and agricultural functions. Once Ohira became prime minister, his 'pastoral city' concept came to the forefront. A special committee was established in the Policy Committee of the Liberal Democratic Party to study the concept's feasibility.

The Industrial Location and Environmental Protection Bureau of MITI also began a separate study of Ohira's concept. From the Bureau's study a plan emerged to build 'technopolis' cities containing both residential and industrial functions—mainly of high-technology industries. This plan was made public in the MITI report entitled 'Vision of MITI Policies in the 1980s'. Eventually, the plan was included in the Law for Accelerating Regional Development based upon High-Technology Industrial Complexes, promulgated in May 1983.

It was expected that knowledge-intensive industries would be central to the industrial structure and that innovative technology would play an increasingly important role in industry and the economy in the future. Particularly strong expectations were held regarding regional technopolises and there was much enthusiasm towards preparing related legislation. This is a noteworthy example where a MITI plan perked the interest of regional policymakers.

In the mid-1960s, a period marked by continued high-level economic growth, environmental pollution emerged as a social problem in all parts of Japan. In April 1963, however, MITI had already established an Industrial Pollution Division to study anti-pollution measures. In August 1967, the Basic Law for Environmental Pollution Control was promulgated and in 1971 the Environment Agency was established. In the meantime, MITI moved to improve and expand measures related to financing and taxation in order to encourage companies to install anti-pollution equipment. In that year, moreover, MITI inaugurated a system for conducting training courses and national examinations to qualify persons as pollution-control managers. In other action, MITI created the new position of senior research coordinator for the prevention of industrial pollution in the Agency of Industrial Science and Technology in 1965, began tackling the study of desulphurization technology—one of the research subjects included in the system for large-scale industrial technology development—expanded the scope of special pollution-related studies conducted by its affiliated research institutes, and promoted private-sector studies by granting subsidies to important technology research and development projects. In July 1970, the MITI-affiliated Resources Technology Laboratory was reorganized as the National Research Institute for Pollution and Resources. After the first oil crisis, the ministry promoted measures to reduce harmful engine emissions from cars and other motorized transport, to increase the use of unleaded petrol, to combat NO_2 emissions, to dispose of and recycle waste matter, and to conduct environmental assessments. In particular, based on a decision made at MITI's Departmental Council, in June 1979 the ministry institutionalized the assessment of power generation stations.[5]

The joint efforts made by the government, academic, and private sectors to develop and commercialize anti-pollution technologies and systems bore much fruit. In particular, the activities of the Association for Control of Industrial Pollution promptly resulted in the emergence of an anti-pollution technology and systems industry, a new industry for Japan.

NOTES

1. Small and Medium Enterprise Agency (ed.), *Chusho Kigyo Hakusho* (White Paper on Small and Medium Enterprises in Japan), 1972 edn., Printing Bureau, MoF, attached tables of statistics: 2 (table 2) and 3 (table 3).
2. 'Tsusho Sangyo Seisaku no Juten', fiscal 1972, 25 Aug. 1971: 4–5.
3. For discussion of small and medium enterprise policy see *Tsusho Sangyo Seisakushi*, xv (1991): ch. 8.
4. Ibid. xv. ch. 9 for discussion of industrial relocation.
5. Ibid. xv, ch. 10 for discussion of anti-pollution and environmental policy.

28

The Roles of Trade and Economic Cooperation in the Evolution into a Major Economic Power

28.1. Expansion in the Scale of the Economy and Revision of the Industrial Structure

The high-level economic growth during the 1960s greatly expanded the scale of Japan's economy, taking its gross national product (GNP) into the number-two position among capitalist nations. In 1971, the year President Nixon removed the dollar from convertibility with gold, Japan's GNP was the equivalent of $230 billion, only about 20 per cent of the US GNP that year of $1,077 billion. Nevertheless, Japan moved ahead of West Germany with its $215 billion GNP, Great Britain with its $140 billion GNP, and France with its $158 billion GNP to assume second place position behind the US (based on the Bank of Japan's 'International Comparative Statistics').

It was assumed that the collapse of the IMF-based international currency system and the two oil crises would inflict considerable damage on Japan's economy. This was because high-level growth had transformed Japan's economic structure into a form whereby Japan acquired its foreign currency via its exports, and then used that foreign currency to purchase the great majority of the raw materials, fuel, and foodstuffs needed to maintain Japanese industrial production and the Japanese lifestyle. The appreciated yen under the floating exchange rate system made it difficult for Japan to acquire foreign currency through exports, and, highly dependent as it was on Middle East oil, the oil crises suddenly increased energy costs, factors expected to substantially reduce the international competitiveness of Japanese products.

As expected, a number of industries lost their international competitiveness in a short time. These were labour-intensive industries that were unable to enhance productivity by means of labour cutbacks and whose production expenses were accounted for largely by energy costs, so that they found it difficult to lower costs to any extent by energy conservation measures. Industries such as the export-oriented textile industry, aluminium-refining industry, and other 'structurally depressed' industries were dealt a blow from which they were unable to recover. However, the positions occupied by these types of industries within Japan's industrial structure were such that their collapse did not have a serious, long-term impact on the overall Japanese economy.

In fact, the economy adapted to the oil crises and rising yen rate, and Japanese industry enhanced its productivity, compressed its energy costs, and improved and strengthened its international competitiveness. This held especially true in knowledge-intensive advanced technology industries, where vigorous R&D and large-scale investment in state-of-the-art equipment raised labour productivity, and resource and energy conservation measures achieved remarkable reductions in energy consumption while still producing high-quality and extremely reliable products. The R&D and pre-emptive investments implemented in this process paid off handsomely for certain advanced technology industries, enabling them to achieve stable export competitiveness and to take the lead in production technology over the same industries in other countries.

Countries that took the easy route to domestic equilibrium, relying on the weakened exchange rate of their currencies, lagged in reducing costs and improving quality and thus lost at an accelerating pace their ability to compete on international markets. Of course, the weakening of a country's currency against those of other countries as a result of the floating exchange rate reduces that country's imports and makes its exports more attractive. But these beneficial effects are only temporary in nature. The benefits of protective trade measures are also limited.

In 1981, the year that rising crude oil prices associated with the second oil crisis reached their peak and the effects of the crisis began mellowing, Japan's GNP reached $1,139 billion at nominal prices, 4.95-times what it was when Nixon announced his new economic policy in 1971. The US GNP in 1981 was less than three times what it was in 1971. The same figures for selected European nations show that France's GNP had grown 3.62 times, the UK's 3.6 times, Italy's 3.18 times, and West Germany's 3.17 times. None of these countries had seen their GNP grow at the same high rate as Japan's. Thus, in terms of GNP, Japan remained in second place behind the US. It was, moreover, closing the gap between itself and the US, and had lengthened its lead over the nations of Europe. It should be noted that the GNP for countries in the group of newly industrializing economies (NIES), comprising South Korea, Taiwan, and Hong Kong, grew at a much higher rate than that of Japan during the oil crises, mainly because of the abundant supply of inexpensive labour in those countries that filled the void left by the 'hollowing out' of industries in the advanced nations.

Thus, although Japan, as an advanced nation, managed to achieve relatively high economic growth in the midst of the two oil crises and a greatly appreciated yen, when viewed in terms of individual industries and product items, this growth was not altogether even.

A look at the Bank of Japan's 'International Comparative Statistics' shows how the percentage of products produced worldwide accounted for by Japanese products changed during the 1970–80 period.

The percentage of the global output of agricultural and forestry products, such as grain, pulse, and lumber, accounted for by Japanese products dropped during this period. In particular, rice output decreased in absolute terms as a result of Japan's acreage reduction programme.

Japan's percentage of global output of minerals also declined across the board for gold, iron ore, copper, zinc, lead, coal, and crude oil, with the Japanese mining industry clearly entering a withdrawal phase after Nixon introduced his new economics in 1971.

The slight drop in Japan's share of the global output of cotton yarn and cotton fabrics was due to the appearance in this market of China with a 20 per cent or so share. The normalization of Sino-American diplomatic relations was reflected in the 1970s by the entry of Chinese products, especially light industrial products, onto the world market. In the face of the low exchange rates of the currencies of the developing nations and their abundant sources of inexpensive, diligent labour, Japan's textile industry was doomed to decline under the greatly appreciated yen. The sudden drop in Japan's share of the synthetic textile fabrics market was the result of a rapid increase in South Korean and Belgian products. Here, too, the increasing presence of the developing nations can be seen.

The same held true in the field of nitrogenous fertilizers. As the US and Japanese shares of this market declined, China and the Soviet Union increased their output significantly, expanding their shares. In addition, the Soviet Union and China also concentrated on domestic economic construction by greatly increasing their production of pulp, synthetic rubber, cement, and other basic materials.

In the area of electronic equipment, Japan's share of the market for relatively easy-to-assemble radios dropped sharply. This was the result of rapid increases in radio production by Hong Kong, China, and Singapore. Japan's radio manufacturing industry was the worldwide leader in 1970, but due to the shift of production bases to South-East Asia, within ten years Japan's production output by value had declined 50 per cent and its world ranking dropped from first to fourth place. Japan is still the number-one producer of television sets, but South Korea, Brazil, and China are close behind it in this area as well.

The areas where Japan's share of worldwide production rose markedly during the 1970–80 period were cars and commercial vehicles. In particular, car output doubled during the 1970s, with Japan overtaking second-place West Germany in 1970 and subsequently going on to capture the number-one world production standing from the US. Japan already led the world in commercial vehicle output in 1970, and by 1980 had increased its share of this market, solidifying its hold on top position. By establishing itself as a leading producer of television sets and cars, whose manufacturing processes require the assembly of large numbers of parts, Japan raised the overall level of its industrial capabilities. Qualitative structural changes thus took place in the form of a shift in emphasis to knowledge-intensive industries on top of the existing foundation for quantitative GNP growth.

One such knowledge-intensive industry is electronic equipment. A review of 'Industrial Statistics Monthly' dealing with output levels of electronic equipment shows that during the 1970–80 period production increased 42.4-fold for electronic desk calculators, 7.3-fold for copying machines, 5.7-fold for cash registers, 4.2-fold for vending machines, 4.5-fold for microwave ovens, 1.7-fold for colour television sets, and 3.9-fold for digital computers. The value of shipments of manufactured goods in this category during the 1970–80 period (industrial statistics; all business offices) rose from 69 trillion yen in 1970 to 214 trillion yen in 1980, a roughly 3.1-fold increase, indicating that except for colour televisions the growth rate for electronic equipment was higher than the average for all manufactured products. Naturally, this kind of growth inclined the industrial structure towards knowledge-intensive industries.

28.2. Trade Trends under Rising Yen Conditions

Throughout the high-growth period of the 1960s, Japanese imports and exports increased considerably each year. Exports rose from $4.0 billion in 1960 to $19.3 billion in 1970, a 4.8-fold increase, and imports increased 4.2-fold during the same period, rising from $4.5 billion in 1960 to $18.8 billion in 1970.[1] The types of products exported also underwent rather drastic changes. Whereas textiles and related products accounted for 30.2 per cent of overall exports in 1960, by 1970 this percentage had dropped to 12.5 per cent; during the same period, the percentage of exports accounted for by machinery and equipment rose significantly from 22.9 per cent to 46.3 per cent. Exports of metals and related products also increased during this period, rising from 13.9 per cent to 19.7 per cent. This increase signified a structural change in Japanese exports from a composition headed by textiles and related products to one in which nearly half of all exports were accounted for by machinery and equipment. This structural change in the composition of Japan's exports resulted in direct competition with key industries in the US and Europe, giving rise to trade friction.

Trade trends during the 1970s—a decade which saw a shift to a system of floating exchange rates, a progressively appreciating yen, and two oil crises—can be considered a continuation of those of the 1960s, although the 1970s trends were based on a move towards knowledge-intensive industries, as discussed in the previous chapter. Exports of textiles and related products declined yet further from the 12.5 per cent recorded in 1970 to 4.9 per cent in 1980, leaving hardly a trace of the Japanese spinning industry's export capacity of the 1930s, which at the time caused difficulties for the Manchester region of Great Britain. Instead of textiles, exports of machinery and equipment increased from 46.3 per cent of all exports in 1970 to 62.8 per cent in 1980, placing Japan clearly in the position of a high-technology, heavy industrial nation engaged in the export of high-quality equipment. The percentage of total exports accounted for by metals and related products dropped slightly from 19.7 per cent in 1970 to 16.4 per cent in 1980, signifying that Japan had already evolved beyond an industrial structure centred around heavy industries supplying basic materials.

A breakdown of machinery and equipment exports in 1980, which accounted for roughly 63 per cent of Japan's overall exports for that year, shows that cars accounted for the highest amount of exports by value at $23,273 million, giving them a commanding lead over the other products in this category. Shipping came in second place with $4,681 million worth of exports; third place went to optical instruments with $4,526 million; fourth place went to tape recorders with $3,305 million; and fifth place went to radios with $3,008 million. These were followed by exports of motorcycles, office equipment, and electronic tubes, in that order. These figures show how the percentages of overall exports accounted for by the main products in the machinery and equipment category in the 1960s, i.e. shipping, radios, and optical instruments, had all dropped, while those for video tape recorders (VTRs), which did not even exist in the 1960s, and for office equipment, tape recorders, and electronic tubes, whose export value had been low during the 1960s, increased rapidly. During the 1970s, even exports of machinery and equipment focused on high-value-added products utilizing advanced technology.

This change in the composition of Japan's exports generated subtle changes in the breakdown of exports by destination (Table 28.1). The first noticeable change was a drop in exports to North America from the beginning of the 1970s. Japan had increased the percentage of its exports to North America during the 1960s, but the decrease early in the 1970s implied the US–Japan trade had not necessarily progressed smoothly, a consequence of 'trade friction'. The second change worth noting relates to exports within Asia. These exports, which accounted for a high percentage of total exports in the early 1960s, steadily dropped during the mid- to late 1960s and then rose again upon entering the 1970s. This phenomenon had its roots in the economic growth of the NIES and changes in the types of products exported to them. The third change to note is that the percentage of Japanese exports destined for Europe had increased slowly but steadily, reflecting the spread of Japanese cars, electronic equipment, and other knowledge-intensive products in European markets. The percentage of exports to Oceania and South America remained at a low level throughout the 1960s and 1970s, and exports to Africa, although the percentage fluctuated, remained relatively low as well. The value of trade between Japan and these regions rose greatly over

Table 28.1 Japanese exports by region (unit: %)

	1960	1965	1970	1975	1980
Asia	36.0	32.5	31.2	36.7	38.0
Europe	13.3	15.4	17.4	18.6	19.4
North America	33.2	33.2	36.7	26.4	29.3
South America	4.4	2.9	3.1	4.2	3.7
Africa	8.7	9.7	7.4	10.0	6.2
Oceania	4.5	4.8	4.2	4.1	3.4
Total ($m.)	4,054	8,451	19,317	55,752	129,807

Source: Compiled from Tsusho Sangyo Seisakushi (History of International Trade and Industry Policy), xvi: 250–1.

the twenty-year period from 1960 to 1980, increasing 24.7-fold with Oceania, 26.5-fold with South America, and 22.8-fold with Africa. However, because Japan's overall exports during this same period rose 32-fold, the increase in the value of exports to those regions did not result in an increase in their percentage of overall Japanese exports.

The reverse side of the coin regarding these changes in the composition of Japan's exports was the changes in its imports. Raw materials for textiles accounted for the largest percentage of imports to Japan during the early 1960s, reaching 17.6 per cent of the total. Later, however, this percentage rapidly declined and in 1980 accounted for only 1.7 per cent of total imports. Dramatic changes such as this were the result of the rise of the developing countries and NIES and changes in the labour supply and demand situation in Japan, and also reflected the decline of the Japanese textile industry. The percentage of imported metal raw materials also tended towards decline, signifying that steel and non-ferrous metals had reached a saturation level. Products whose import percentages rose significantly were crude oil, liquefied natural gas (LNG), coal, and other mineral fuels. A particularly sharp rise in these imports was noted after entering the 1970s. This reflected not only the increased energy consumption associated with high-level growth but also an 'energy revolution' that eventually resulted in the closing of domestic coal-mines. Also, a slight decline in the percentage of machinery and equipment imported into Japan during the 1970s signified that the quantitative and qualitative development of the Japanese machinery and equipment industries had offset much of the need for imports of completely built-up machinery and equipment. This shift gradually became another cause of trade friction. The 'others' category in imports includes imported products other than foodstuffs, chemical products, and machinery and equipment. But the import percentages for these products did not exhibit the gains that the progress made in liberalizing Japan's imports during the 1970s should have produced. Import gains recorded after the first oil crisis, slight as they may have been, were product import increases linked to the appreciated yen, trade friction, or other such causes.

The 1970s were ten years of quite high growth of product imports. Total imports of processed products during the ten years rose 5.34-fold, from $5,725 million in 1970 to $30,568 million in 1980 (Table 28.2). This growth rate did not keep pace with the 7.44-fold growth recorded for imports overall, but certain items exhibited high growth. The 1970s witnessed a 16.8-fold increase in clothing imports, particularly of high-priced European *haute couture* and inexpensive clothing produced in Asia. Following clothing was an 11.2-fold increase in imports of optical equipment and precision instruments. And imports of chemical elements and compounds showed an 8.1-fold gain. Imports of other products, however, fell below the growth rate for imports overall, with those of general machinery, electric machinery, transport equipment, and other machinery growing only 4.1 fold. This can probably be attributed to the fact that 1980 marked the midpoint in the recession resulting from the second oil crisis.

Table 28.2   Trends in Japanese imports of finished products, 1970–1980 (units: $m.; %)

Product name	1970	1975	1980	1980: % of total	1980/1970
Chemical industry products	1,000	2,057	6,202	20.3	620.2
Chemical elements/Compounds	349	742	2,834	9.3	812.0
Medical/Pharmaceutical products	216	440	1,074	3.5	497.2
Raw material products	1,869	3,643	10,578	34.6	566.0
Steel	276	189	894	2.9	323.9
Non-ferrous metals	945	1,284	4,480	14.7	474.1
Thread/Textile products	224	772	1,650	5.4	736.6
Machinery/Transport equipment	2,132	3,831	8,756	28.6	410.7
General machinery	1,262	2,058	3,789	12.4	307.4
Electric machinery	464	1,004	2,722	8.9	586.6
Transport equipment	406	768	2,246	7.3	553.2
Miscellaneous products	632	1,989	5,030	16.5	795.9
Clothing	91	538	1,530	5.0	1,681.3
Optical/Precision instruments	115	303	1,286	4.2	1,118.3
Total processed products	5,725	11,747	30,568	100.0	533.9

Source: Prepared using data from p. 70 of appendices to a general outline of the 1979 edn. and p. 458 of the 1982 edn. of the 'White Paper on International Trade, Japan'.

Consequently, although imports of machinery grew considerably, that growth was not altogether commensurate with the efforts made to promote imports.

28.3. Trade Balance Trends and the Shift to a Constant Surplus

Viewed in terms of business cycles, Japanese trade trends followed a fairly clear pattern after the end of the Second World War. This pattern showed growth in domestic consumption and various investments during periods of good business, leading to increased imports, and moves to sell more products overseas when domestic business was sluggish, leading to increased exports. The shift to a floating exchange rate and the two oil crises that occurred during the 1970s altered this pattern slightly.

President Nixon's removal of the US dollar from convertibility with gold in August 1971 raised the spectre of recession brought on by the yen's appreciation. Despite these events, however, exports increased. Exports even rose amidst adjustments made for inflation and the political storm that surrounded the 'Plan for Remodelling the Japanese Archipelago'. But exports stagnated temporarily after the first oil crisis that broke out in October 1973 sharply increased energy costs. Exports declined once again in 1982 following the second oil crisis of 1979. It should be noted that export trends between 1976 and 1978, the period when business perked up following the first oil crisis, exhibited characteristics not seen during the period of high-level economic growth. That is, exports on a value basis, when calculated in terms of US dollars, exhibited a fairly high growth rate, but when calculated in terms of yen they showed either stagnation or decline. The appreciating yen was responsible for a statistical aberration. Viewed from the Japanese perspective, despite the fact that dollar calculations indicated exports had risen somewhat, yen-based net receipts had dropped, nullifying export growth in real terms. But from the perspective of the US, which had been paying in dollars all along, Japanese exports seemed to be growing as rapidly as ever. To ameliorate the international balance-of-payments problems caused by this situation, Japan based its export policy on previous-year export volume levels, or figures under those levels, and achieved export policy objectives in terms of volume.[2] But because the price of export goods rose in dollar terms, Japan's trade balance rose sharply into surplus, and in the end its efforts to deal with exports on a volume basis did nothing to ameliorate its international balance-of-payments problems.

The progress of global inflation, especially inflation in countries whose exchange rates had dropped, served to offset any feelings of Japanese products being expensive because of the greatly appreciated yen. As a result, there was no immediate drop seen in the outflow of Japanese products proportional to the increase in the yen rate.

On the other hand, the import pattern for the period of high-level growth changed, and imports of raw materials for production no longer increased simply because domestic business was good. The change occurred because after the first oil crisis Japan promoted energy and natural resource conservation measures that lowered various consumption rates, especially for energy. Raw fuel imports stagnated on a volume basis, and the sharp rise in the value of imports was not due to increased volumes but rather to the high prices levied on crude oil by the Organization of Arab Petroleum Exporting Countries (OAPEC). A process evolved in which increases in the value of yen-based imports were initially brought about by sharp rises in the international price of crude oil, which in turn triggered lower yen rates. Then the increased costs of imported goods resulting from the lower yen rates were reflected in import values. This process created a perception gap between the US and Japan, whereby from US eyes the dollar-based value of Japanese imports did not seem to rise while from Japanese eyes it did not seem that yen-based exports had risen to the extent the US claimed they had.

Thus, the system of floating exchange rates created a situation whereby trade balance trends were affected not only by changes in the volume of trade related to business fluctuations but also by fluctuating commodity prices and exchange rates.

Still, exports in dollar terms exceeded imports every year throughout the 1970s, and despite the two oil crises Japan's trade balance continuously recorded a surplus. As a result, the invisible trade and transfer balances continued to be in deficit through the period of high-level growth and during the 1970s but the current account balance remained in surplus except for a few years related to the two oil crises. Thus, although the oil crises caused Japan's foreign reserves to dip temporarily, the resultant trend was foreign capital accumulation. The yen weakened temporarily during both oil crises, but looking at the 1970s overall the yen's position against the dollar remained strong. While the trade balance fluctuated, Japan continued to record trade surpluses with the US throughout the 1970s, and by the end of 1980 its foreign reserves had reached $25,232 million. These foreign reserves, although small compared to those of the US and Europe at the time, were high for Japan.[3]

Japan's persistent trade surplus caused various countries concern over their trade deficits with Japan, and nettled the US in particular. The only year during the 1970s that the US recorded a trade surplus with Japan was 1975; the trade balance favoured Japan in every other year. Also, except for the oil crises years this deficit tended to expand, and the US trade deficit with Japan became structurally rooted. In fact, this phenomenon was not limited to the US; the number of advanced nations experiencing trade deficits with Japan increased during the 1970s. Even West Germany and France, which both maintained trade surpluses with Japan during the 1960s, began showing signs of more imports from than exports to Japan following the first oil crisis, and their trade deficits increased by the year. Exceptions to this rule were Italy, whose trade balance with Japan shifted irregularly between surplus and deficit, and Canada, which, because of Japanese imports of resources, maintained a trade surplus throughout the 1970s (Table 28.3). Many Asian countries (or regions) also fell into trade deficits with Japan during the 1970s; these trade deficits continued for South Korea, China, Taiwan, Hong Kong, and Thailand. The Japan–Philippines trade balance see-sawed between surplus and deficit, and that of Indonesia, which exports crude oil to Japan, remained in surplus.[4]

Table 28.3 Trade balance between Japan and selected countries (unit: $m.)

	USA	UK	W. Germany	France	Italy	Canada
1970	380	84	−66	−59	57	−365
1971	2,517	157	51	−7	54	−128
1972	2,996	478	249	−17	64	−44
1973	179	596	154	−176	13	−1,015
1974	117	652	43	143	−45	−1,088
1975	−459	662	521	198	−31	−1,348
1976	3,880	556	1,014	428	134	−1,163
1977	7,320	990	1,285	445	−22	−1,173
1978	10,124	962	1,657	348	−166	−1,395
1979	5,971	1,415	1,412	317	−311	−2,366
1980	6,959	1,827	3,205	725	16	−2,287

Source: Prepared using data from Tsusho Sangyo Seisakushi (History of International Trade and Industry Policy), xvi: 250–1. Figures reflect Japan's trade surpluses (negative figures represent trade deficits) with its trading partners.

28.4. Trade Friction and Review of Trade Policy

As the number of countries experiencing persistent trade deficits with Japan increased, and the extent of those deficits grew larger, trade friction erupted at the individual product level and raised issues concerning the activities of Japanese corporations, the 'closed' nature of the Japanese market, and about Japan's industrial policy.[5] In the US, whose trade deficit with Japan was particularly large and seemed structural in nature, friction developed in the 1969–72 period around textile products, with a settlement of sorts being reached in the 1972 US–Japan Textile Agreement. At about that same time, Japan implemented long-term, self-restraint on exports of steel destined for the US. Around 1970, the US Department of the Treasury began investigating a number of Japanese products suspected of violating US anti-dumping laws, and by the time the first oil crisis occurred had halted customs inspections of television sets, condensers, plate glass, microwave ovens, reinforced glass, woollen goods, wool and polyester blended fabrics, television tubes, stainless steel, and cadmium, and levied countervailing duties on Japanese imports it determined were being dumped on the US market. Thus, the US government's initial approach to dealing with its trade deficit with Japan involved import restrictions on individual products.

The US government continued to enforce dumping regulations on one Japanese product after another even after the first oil crisis. In August 1975, for example, the US Department of State opened dumping investigations on cars imported from Japan and seven other countries; in February 1977, the US steel manufacturer, Gilmore Steel, appealed to the Department of the Treasury to investigate possible dumping by five Japanese steelmakers; in June 1977, Harley Davidson Co. alleged that Japanese-made motorcycles were being dumped in the US; in January 1978, the Treasury determined that Japanese steel plate was being dumped; in March 1978, the Treasury notified Japan of its intent to assess dumping duties on Japanese-made colour television sets (a settlement was reached between the US Treasury and Japanese vendors in April 1980, and import restrictions were lifted in May); and in August 1980, customs duties on small Japanese trucks were raised sixfold. It was possible to see a pattern where a US vendor lodged a dumping complaint, the Treasury opened an investigation, dumping was verified, customs duties were raised, the Japanese vendor(s) introduced self-restraint, and the matter was settled amicably.

Next, the US and Japan opened import regulation talks on a product-by-product basis, and cases where Japan introduced self-restraint in exporting increased. In June 1976, for example, the US and Japan reached a compromise agreement concerning restrictions on speciality steel exports to the US; in May 1977, the US and Japan signed and exchanged formal documents concerning self-restraint on the Japanese colour television set exports (agreement for maintaining orderly marketing); and in December 1977, at the US–Japan steel negotiations, the two countries agreed to introduce a trigger price system.

This enforcement of import regulations against Japanese-made products by the

US government influenced the nations of the European Community (EC), some of which imposed similar dumping tariffs and demanded self-restraint in exporting. The pattern that emerged in Europe closely resembled that in the US, with matters being settled by Japan imposing self-restraint on its exports. In April 1973, for example, the EC placed emergency restrictions on exports of Japanese tape recorders to Italy; in December 1975, Japan–EC textile negotiations reached a compromise settlement; in May 1976, agreement was reached in government-level deliberations between Japan and the EC regarding cars; in July 1976, Japan and the EC signed an agreement lifting import restrictions on Japanese textiles; in February 1977, the EC levied provisional dumping tariffs on Japanese-made ball bearings; in May 1977, Italy announced its intent to enforce import restrictions against five Japanese-made products, including motorcycles; in July 1977, the UK Department of Trade notified Japan it intended to levy dumping tariffs on Japanese-made small-sized shaped steel; in January 1978, the EC Committee levied dumping tariffs on Japanese hot-rolled sheet steel and other products; and in March 1978, at the Japan–EC steel talks, the two sides agreed that Japan would impose self-restraint on its exports.

In response to these demands from various countries for Japan to rectify its trade imbalances, MITI moved to negotiate frameworks for self-restraint by product and country. As necessary, the ministry also took it upon itself to provide guidance on export restraints, deciding policy for preparing 'orderly export' guidelines combined with measures to counter the appreciating yen (June 1972); applying the Export Trade Control Order, aimed at reducing exports, to major items whose exports had increased rapidly (January 1973); deciding policy for rectifying Japan's trade imbalance with the EC (November 1976); providing guidelines for restricting exports of five major items, including cars, to previous year levels (April 1978); and sponsoring talks between the government and the private sector on the export of cars to the US (June 1980).

Meanwhile, amid rapidly increasing trade surpluses under the Smithsonian system and the yen's tendency to appreciate against foreign currencies, and in order to increase imports, the government, i.e. MITI, switched from the export promotion policies of the high-level growth period to an approach that promoted the liberalization of imports, lowered customs duties, and stressed product imports. Measures taken in May 1972 to counter the appreciating yen were also Japan's first steps towards the system of interdependence.

As import promotion measures, this second round of yen countermeasures called for expanding import quota limits, improving the quota method, and enhancing the import distribution mechanism.[6] In fiscal year 1972, the government decided to expand import quota limits of consumer-related quota goods in particular, and, in principle, set about expanding these limits 30 per cent or more over previous year's figures. Products that had not achieved 7 per cent of domestic consumption were increased to the 7 per cent level. Improvements to the quota method included the implementation of streamlined, simplified import procedures, the liberalization in February 1972 of all eleven automatic import quotas

(AIQs), and abolition of the AIQ. With regard to improving the distribution of imports, parallel imports of genuine products were approved commencing October 1972. In addition, increased import financing was also pushed forward.[7]

Considerable importance was attached to import expansion in Japan's third set of yen countermeasures in November 1972. These countermeasures pinpointed six issues: liberalized imports, uniformly lower customs tariffs, an improved system of preferential duties, expanded import quota limits, increased import financing, and simplified import procedures.

Around this same time Japan decided to further promote the measures incorporated into the above-cited yen countermeasures,[8] summarizing the fundamental prospects of its new import policies in the following four points: (1) make good use of imports to enhance the lifestyle of Japanese citizens and to stabilize commodity prices; (2) increase imports to expand and balance Japanese trade; (3) import to achieve stable supplies of resources; and (4) import to contribute to establishing a worldwide free-trade system. Contributing to establishment of a worldwide system of free trade was a new position for Japan. The Cold War was still very much a reality at the time, and Japan had reduced its trade friction with the US and EC through efforts to increase imports, and it intended to contribute towards establishing and bolstering a free-trade system.

28.5. Promotion of Trade Liberalization

Having taken this position, Japan redoubled its efforts following Nixon's announcement of his new economics to promote trade liberalization in accordance with the 'General Rules for Liberalizing the Exchange Rate and Trade' of 1960. Most of the items that fell under MITI's jurisdiction were liberalized.[9]

1. June 1971: Pyrites, amorphous graphite, tungsten, soda ash, leather wear, leather footwear parts, and car engines.
2. October 1971: Coal for making coke, brown coal, turbines, digital-to-analog converters, electronic telephone exchanges, and system switching control devices.
3. February 1972: Electronic computer peripheral devices (except terminal equipment and storage devices), radar equipment for use in airplanes, light aircraft, and light aircraft parts.
4. April 1972: Sulphur, and gas and fuel oil.
5. April 1973: High-grade calculators and electronic accounting machines, and integrated circuits (under 200 devices).
6. December 1974: Integrated circuits (over 200 devices).
7. December 1975: Electronic computers and peripheral equipment (limited to terminal equipment and storage devices), and parts for electronic computers and peripheral equipment.
8. April 1978: Seasonings containing sodium glutamate as their main ingredient, and smokeless coal.

9. January 1980: Ores of radioactive elements, gold ore, gold dross, shavings and other scrap from machined gold and gold alloys, airplane engines, balloons and airships (dirigibles), gliders, airplane parts, parachutes and their parts, and catapults.

Points worth noting about these lists of MITI-related liberalized items are: (1) that since 1972 they have included electronic computers and peripheral equipment, integrated circuits, and other information-related equipment; (2) that they include airplanes and related products; and (3) that they also include uranium and other minerals used in nuclear fuels, as well as gold ore and gold. It is widely known that Japan finally began liberalizing high-tech items upon entering the 1970s, but this move also reflected the fact that Japan's domestic computer manufacturers had achieved substantial international competitiveness by that time. With these additions, practically all import items under MITI's jurisdiction had been liberalized; residual import restrictions applied to five items, including coal and four types of leather goods.

Liberalization thus reached its final stages. But issues related to Japan's persistent trade surpluses had not been resolved, and numerous problems related to solving the trade friction issue remained for the 1980s. These included distribution practices that served as non-tariff barriers and the 'keiretsu' issue, Japan's industrial policy, the administration of licensing and approval procedures, and import programmes stipulating numerical objectives.

28.6. Progress towards the Final Stages of Capital Liberalization and its Completion

Enforcement of the fourth stage of capital liberalization

The government decided in June 1967 on a policy of capital liberalization, and set a goal of implementing liberalization measures in most sectors of the economy by the end of fiscal year 1971. The centrepiece of the policy was a gradual and considered expansion of industry categories eligible for automatic approval of 50:50 joint ventures. In accordance with this new policy, the government launched its capital liberalization programme in four stages. The first stage began in July 1967, the second in March 1969, and the third in September 1970. From April 1971, liberalization of the automotive industry was carried out.

Calls for Japan to liberalize its economy increased in both number and urgency as Japan grew in economic power. Consequently, policymarkers felt it necessary to implement the entire capital liberalization programme even before the original target date of the end of fiscal year 1971. Accordingly, the decision was made to go ahead with the fourth-stage capital liberalization programme in August 1971, some eight months earlier than planned.

Policymakers decided to abandon the positive list method previously used and instead shift to a negative list method for defining so-called Step 1 industry categories (over 50 per cent capital participation) under the fourth stage of the capital liberalization programme. This method resulted in liberalization of all industries already well established, leaving categories for separate review in only seven product categories. The liberalization rate for Step 1 was 94 per cent overall and 97 per cent for manufacturing enterprises. Step 2 liberalization (100 per cent) substantially increased the industry categories covered, from seventy-seven industry categories under the third stage of liberalization to 228 industry categories under the fourth stage.[10]

In addition, previous regulations had limited automatic approval of the shares of existing corporations to 7 per cent or less per foreign investor, but this limit was raised to less than 10 per cent under the fourth stage of liberalization. However, the previous limit of less than 25 per cent for total foreign stockholdings was left in place, because a rapid increase in stock purchases would tend to increase foreign-currency reserves.

Implementation of the fourth stage liberalized capital holdings in a number of primary industries, such as film, ethylene centres, non-ferrous metals (which had experienced monopoly problems concerning basic materials such as copper, nickel, and antimony), leasing, NC machine tools and other sophisticated machinery, construction equipment, chemical plant and other industrial equipment, electrical machinery, and several important consumer goods industries. Other industry categories subject to 100 per cent liberalization included advertising agencies, air-conditioners, electric audio equipment, paper pulp, prefabricated housing accessories, and bowling alleys. The liberalization programme proved highly attractive to foreign investors.

Only five industry categories remained subject to separate review by MITI after the fourth stage of liberalization was carried out: oil refining and retailing, leather and leather goods manufacturing, manufacturing, sales, and leasing of electronic computers (including attached devices and parts) or electronic computer-based automatic control equipment, information processing (including items related to software production), and retail businesses with more than eleven retail outlets. Some categories remained subject to review by other government ministries or industrial organizations, including those from the agriculture and real estate industries.

In May 1973 the fifth stage of capital liberalization was put into effect, which in principle resulted in 100 per cent capital liberalization. Only five industry categories were excluded from the programme: agriculture, forestry and fisheries; mining; petroleum products; leather and leather goods manufacturing; and retail businesses with more than eleven outlets. Four industry categories, including mining and retail businesses with fewer than eleven outlets, were only 50 per cent liberalized. They remained subject to separate review. Seventeen other industry categories were 'semi-liberalized' with fixed conditions, including integrated circuit manufacturing, meat product manufacturing, processed tomato product manufacturing, feed grain manufacturing, food service industry prepared food manufacturing, garment manufacturing and wholesaling, pharmaceuticals and agricultural pesticides manufacturing, ferro-alloy manufacturing, hydraulic equipment manufacturing, wrapping and packing equipment manufacturing, electronic precision instrument manufacturing, gramophone record manufacturing, real estate, manufacturing, sale and leasing of computer equipment, information processing, fruit juice and fruit beverage manufacturing, and photosensitive material manufacturing.

The decision was made to gradually liberalize these industries as well, and within three more years all were 100 per cent liberalized.[11] In August 1974 the electronic computer industry and related industries were moved into the 50 per cent liberalized category, and were 100 per cent liberalized as of December 1975. The information-processing industry was 50 per cent liberalized in December 1974 and 100 per cent liberalized as of April 1976. Integrated circuit manufacturing was 100 per cent liberalized in December 1974, and twelve other industry categories, including meat product manufacturing, were 100 per cent liberalized as of May 1975. Fruit juice and fruit beverage manufacturing and photosensitive material manufacturing were 100 per cent liberalized as of May 1976.

From that time onwards foreign capital inflows, stock purchases, and the establishment of subsidiaries increased steadily, subject only to the effects of changing economic and international currency conditions. After the electronic computer and information-processing industries were granted 50 per cent capital liberalization in 1975, there was an increase in the acquisition of stock to participate in management, and from 1977 almost all requests for stock acquisitions for this purpose were automatically approved.

Second stage liberalization of technology acquisition

For many years after the Second World War, contracts for technology acquisition from foreign enterprises were mostly linked to capital investment, and initial payments and royalty payments had to be made in foreign currencies. Provisions of the Law Concerning Foreign Capital required that such contracts be reviewed and approved. With foreign-currency and trade transactions being progressively liberalized, however, foreign-technology acquisition contracts were also liberalized after implementing the first stage of the capital liberalization programme. Except for a small number of industry categories that remained subject to review and approval requirement, technology acquisition contracts were completely liberalized as of June 1968. This was the first stage liberalization of technology acquisition.[12]

This liberalization was achieved through one of the following two methods for industry categories other than those that remained subject to separate review:

1. Partial Bank of Japan (BOJ) Delegation Method (Partial Liberalization)
   Contracts for acquisition of technologies not covered by separate review requirements are automatically approved by the BOJ unless there are contrary instructions within one month of application from the minister whose ministry is responsible for the industry. Said minister may issue an order to void

the contract only if there is a danger of significant negative impact on the Japanese economy (consequently, the government does not oversee the cost or the term of the contract, leaving those issues to the voluntary judgement of the enterprise).

2. Full BOJ Delegation Method (Full Liberalization)

The BOJ automatically approves all contracts based on a fixed price equivalent to $50,000 or less, regardless of the type of technology involved. Such contracts are not subject to separate review or to the partial BOJ delegation method requirements described above.

However, cross-licensing contracts and technology acquisition contracts between a parent company and a subsidiary in which it held 50 per cent or greater equity remained subject to either separate review or partial BOJ delegation method requirements, depending on the type of technology involved, even for contracts of $50,000 or less.[13]

Seven types of technology remained subject to separate review: (1) aircraft technology, (2) military weapons technology, (3) gunpowder technology, (4) nuclear power technology, (5) aerospace technology, (6) electronic computer technology, and (7) petrochemical technology. The decision was made to retain pre-existing separate review requirements on these technologies because of their sophistication and their relationship to national security.

After technology acquisition contracts were liberalized in conjunction with the fourth stage of capital liberalization, the second stage of technology acquisition contract liberalization was put into effect in July 1972. This programme removed the seven types of technology still subject to separate review requirements, although these requirements were not removed until January 1973 on petrochemical derivatives and until July 1974 on electronic computer technology.

The government retained the right to take steps deemed necessary to maintain Japan's commitments to the OECD, to protect public health and safety, and to maintain national security. This included the right to review contracts on the technology areas reserved under the first stage of liberalization (aircraft, military weapons, gunpowder, nuclear power, and aerospace) even after routine review requirements had been eliminated. Consequently, the decision was made to conduct a separate review on these technologies if problems emerged.[14]

In December 1973 the government expanded the range of technology assistance contracts subject to BOJ approval by lowering the limit on automatic approval from the equivalent of $50,000 or less to the equivalent of $300,000 or less. The government also expanded the scope of BOJ processing of contract modifications and contract renewals, as well as simplifying portions of the approval application process.[15]

Technology acquisition contracts were liberalized in the field of electronic computer technology in July 1974. This completed the process of technology acquisition contract liberalization and eliminated the practice of routine separate review of such contracts.[16]

28.7. Full-Scale Expansion of Foreign Direct Investment

Liberalization of foreign investment

Capital liberalization was carried out not only for the inflow of foreign capital to Japan but also for the investment of Japanese capital overseas. After the Second World War, Japanese capital was not permitted to be invested overseas until 1951, and because Japan had only meagre foreign reserves it was a long time thereafter before it was possible to receive approval from the government for any but a few limited types of investment. Nevertheless, the liberalization of capital transactions gradually progressed as Japan's foreign reserves increased after it achieved a high-level rate of economic growth and as a result of Japan becoming a member of the Organization for Economic Cooperation and Development (OECD). In order to sustain the high-level rate of economic growth, not only did it become increasingly necessary for Japan to procure raw materials used by heavy industries and to secure fuel resources such as crude oil, but it also became increasingly necessary to establish production bases overseas in order to respond to changes in the Japanese labour market and to import restrictions set by some countries. These factors also contributed to the liberalization of capital transactions.

A general review of the steps leading to the liberalization of foreign investment shows the following. First, the partial BOJ delegation method was adopted in January 1964 whereby the BOJ was in principle given authority to approve foreign investment and loans for participation in management provided the amount was $50,000 or less. Under this method, the BOJ would receive an investment application and would approve the investment within a certain period of time after consultation with the Ministry of International Trade and Industry and the Ministry of Finance, provided those ministries expressed no reservations.

The first liberalization measure took effect as of 1 October 1969 when the partial BOJ delegation method was applied to prospective investments of $300,000 or less. Prospective investments of over $300,000, and investments that were not targeted by liberalization measures, still required approval under a separate review process.

The second liberalization measure took effect in September 1970 when the limit for automatic approval from the BOJ was raised to $1,000,000.[17]

The third liberalization measure took effect in July 1971 when regulations on foreign investment were relaxed across the board and the $1,000,000 limit for receiving automatic approval from the BOJ was lifted.

The fourth liberalization measure took effect in June 1972. Prior to then, automatic approval had been granted only when foreign direct investment was to be made to provide actual support for a foreign corporation the investor had actual control of. Thereafter, however, automatic approval would be granted in principle only by the BOJ for all foreign direct investment. At the same time, restrictions that limited the acquisition of foreign real estate to instances based on actual necessity such as personal use were also removed. In May 1972, furthermore, restrictions on the acquisition of foreign securities were also relaxed. As a result of these measures, the BOJ was permitted to grant automatic approval for all foreign transactions except those that were recognized as possibly exerting a seriously negative influence on the Japanese economy. As a result of this liberalization, the amount of money approved for foreign direct investment increased dramatically from a total of $2.6 billion between 1966 and 1970 (annual average over $500 million) to a total of $858 million in 1971, $2.338 billion in 1972, and $3.497 billion in 1973.[18]

The rapid increase in these types of foreign direct investment created the foundation which made possible the dramatic inflow of US dollars and the increase in foreign-currency reserves after President Nixon removed the dollar from its convertibility with gold in August 1971. In order to encourage such foreign direct investment, various policies were introduced, such as making financing available through government funds from institutions such as the Export-Import Bank of Japan and the Overseas Economic Cooperation Fund. Due to liberalization and these promotion policies, foreign direct investment and loans increased after 1972.[19] Behind the increase in foreign direct investment were conditions that promoted the investment: requests for technology transfers from developing countries; the vital importance of developing resources; and establishing distribution and financial bases to exploit overseas markets. The types of investment that would not have expanded so quickly without the liberalization of foreign investment included: investment for the development and import of oil, coal, and metal ores, investment to move labour-intensive industries to developing countries in Asia where there was an abundant supply of inexpensive labour, investment for the local production of items such as televisions and cars, and investment made by small and medium enterprises that followed large corporations to new production facilities overseas.

Investments to secure a stable supply of resources

Liberalization of foreign direct investment was completed in all but a few exceptional areas and the amount permitted to be invested reached an unprecedented level in 1974, before the trauma of the first oil crisis had subsided. In September 1974, the Industrial Structure Council submitted a key report to MITI entitled, 'The Direction of Japan's Industrial Structure'. The following passage is taken from Chapter V of that report, 'International Development of Japan's Industries'.

The late 1960s and early 1970s constituted a new age which opened foreign investment to Japanese industries. During the 1970s and 1980s, however, new international developments centred around foreign investment are likely to take off. These international developments refer to the qualitative improvement and quantitative expansion of foreign investment by Japanese industry. They will exert an enormous influence on Japan's industrial structure and could also provide an opportunity to promote a rational international division of labour.[20]

A review by industry category of foreign direct investment as of the end of 1973, just after the first oil crisis erupted, shows that of the total of $10.27 billion, 29.8 per cent went to mining, 12 per cent to commerce, 8.9 per cent to finance and insurance, 7.2 per cent to textiles, 5.2 per cent to chemicals, and 14.6 per cent to 'other' categories. By region, 24 per cent of the investment went to North America, 23.3 per cent to Asia, and 19.4 per cent to Europe. Reviewed in further detail, it is seen that large investments were made in the commercial, financial, insurance, mining, and wood and pulp industries in North America. In Central and South America, large investments were made in the chemical, financial, and insurance industries. In Asia, the largest percentage of investment went to the textile and mining industries. In the Middle East it was mining, in Europe it was mining and finance, and in Oceania it was mining that saw the largest investment. In other words, investment in the industrialized countries in North America and Europe went to tertiary industries such as commerce, finance, and insurance while investment in Asia went to the textile and electronics industries in search of inexpensive labour and to mining industries in search of raw fuels. Investment was also directed towards the mining industry in search of natural fuels in the Middle East, Africa, and Oceania. The percentage of investments in securing resources was extremely high.

The report of the Industrial Structure Council mentioned above listed four primary reasons to encourage foreign investment under the heading 'The Future Outlook of Japan's Foreign Investments': (1) to plan for stability in the domestic supply and demand of goods; (2) to respond to stability in the international supply and demand of goods; (3) to provide economic cooperation to developing countries; and (4) to strengthen the base and maintain the vitality of major industries. Steel, petrochemicals, paper, pulp, and aluminium were designated as industries to be included under the first two reasons. Industries that could become vital to the economic development of foreign countries were included under the third reason, although this included a diverse array of developments which depended on the domestic circumstances of the host country. The fourth reason pointed to the most appropriate locations in the world for bolstering the base and maintaining the vitality of major industries. It predicted energetic developments in the fields of electronics, cars, textiles, and commerce. At that time, immediately after the oil crisis, the effects of the unstable balance in the supply and demand for resources and weakening yen were felt. This was when the idea of directing Japan's foreign investment towards developing countries was conceived. At the time, conditions were such that investment activities carried out by the industrialized countries in developing countries, and especially the activities of large corporations, including Japanese corporations, came to be watched closely by the developing countries. In 1973, the Japan Federation of Economic Organizations (Keidanren) announced its 'Aims of Investment Activities in Developing Countries'. In July 1976 the OECD announced its 'Declaration Regarding Multi-National Corporate Activities' and adopted 'guide-lines' related thereto.[21]

Since Japan does not have sufficient natural fuel resources of its own, its reliance on imports is extremely high. Historically, Japan has often sought overseas supplies of natural resources. After the Second World War, as early as the 1950s, Japan began mining iron ore and minerals in India and Malaysia and importing them into Japan. By the 1960s foreign direct investment had been made to secure resources on a large scale, such as pulp from Alaska and oil from Saudi Arabia and North Sumatra. After the mid-1960s, mining investments were made around the world to develop and import resources. The first oil crisis exposed the fragile nature of Japan's resource supply and led to increased investments for securing resources. A typical example of this was the establishment of joint ventures for investing in aluminium smelting operations in countries where inexpensive electric resources could be used, such as NZAS (New Zealand Aluminum Smelters Ltd.) in New Zealand, Venalum in Venezuela, Alpac in Canada, Asahan in Indonesia, and the Amazon project in Brazil.[22]

Siting production bases overseas

Japan's high-level rate of economic growth brought about a labour shortage and a concomitant increase in wages. Due to these developments, during the late 1960s and early 1970s a move developed in the labour-intensive textile and assembly industries to seek production bases in developing countries where there was an abundant supply of inexpensive labour. This shift focused primarily on Asian countries.

After the liberalization of foreign investment began from around 1965, however, investment turned brisk in industries other than those merely seeking inexpensive labour resources. For example, one after another Japanese electronics, car, metal, and machinery manufacturers established joint ventures in South Korea. Most were based on technological ties that eventually contributed to the development of the heavy and chemical industries in South Korea.[23]

After the first oil crisis, foreign investment to establish overseas production bases in industrialized countries began to stand out. One example of this trend was the establishment of plants in the US by colour television manufacturers. By 1972, Sony Corporation had built a plant in San Diego, California, and was producing and selling colour television sets. Following Sony, Matsushita Electric Industrial Co. purchased Motorola Inc.'s television operations in 1974, and Sanyo Electric Co. acquired Whirlpool Corp.'s television operations in 1977, both companies thereby making bold starts to produce colour television sets. Afterward, Mitsubishi Electric, Toshiba, Sharp, and Hitachi built US plants and began domestic US production. There were some other developments in the background of this investment. Japanese exports of colour television sets to the US had increased dramatically. In 1968, the US television manufacturing industry filed a dumping suit against the Japanese manufacturers. In 1970, the US Department of the Treasury levied countervailing duties against imported Japanese colour television sets. From that point on, accusations of unfair competition were made against Japanese manufacturers and every available administrative means was used to criticize Japan. An agreement was reached in negotiations between the US and Japanese governments in June 1977 whereby Japanese manufacturers would voluntarily restrict colour television exports to the US to 1.75 million units. The Japanese manufacturers recognized that their exports to the US would decline because of the voluntary export restrictions and thus decided to invest in local plants.[24]

Another example of such an investment pattern can be seen in the car industry. Like the television manufacturers, Japan's car manufacturers were obliged to establish voluntary restraints on exports as a result of being sued for dumping and subsequent intergovernment negotiations. Due to US demands, Japanese car manufacturers began local production either through joint ventures with American companies or on their own.[25]

28.8. Expansion and Diversification of Economic Cooperation

Expansion of economic cooperation

The 1970s ushered in a new stage in the development of Japan's economic cooperation. Japan had achieved a high-level rate of economic growth that produced the world's second largest GNP. Accordingly, Japan received more requests from developing countries for a greater level of assistance in both quantitative and qualitative terms. From Japan's perspective as well, unless the developing countries developed economically and realized the political and social stability that such development could bring, it would grow increasingly difficult for Japan to secure a stable supply of natural resources from overseas and to realize smooth growth in trade.

In other words, without the raw materials and fuels and the domestic markets of the developing countries, Japan's high-level economic growth could not be sustained. For their part, the developing countries felt that Japan's economic growth was leading to an increasing disparity between the size of their respective economies and they requested Japan to expand its economic assistance to them in order to reduce that disparity. From Japan's perspective, on the other hand, the expanded size of its economy increased its dependence on foreign countries and, as was witnessed during the first oil crisis, just the slightest anxiety regarding the supply of even a marginal quantity of raw materials and fuels could entirely disrupt the overall economic activities. Also, the 'full employment' that resulted from high economic growth brought about a labour shortage in labour-intensive industries, and concomitant wage increases cut into corporate profits. Moreover, the increased international competitiveness of Japanese companies brought about almost continual trade surpluses. In the end, Japan was pressured to effectively use the foreign reserves it had accumulated.

On an international level, the 1970s were also a time when the issue of correcting the discrepancy between industrialized and developing countries, i.e. the 'north–south problem', was brought to the attention of the United Nations and other international organizations as a unanimous demand from developing countries. Most of the demands of developing countries, which constituted majorities in these international organizations, were incorporated into formal resolutions. Many of the developing countries did not benefit from technological innovations and simply remained as 'monoculture' suppliers of raw materials and fuels. Other of the developing countries did not effectively use assistance and investment from industrialized countries as production capital and ended up merely accumulating debt. In short, both the quantity and quality of assistance and investment for developing countries had been insufficient and had done little more than confirm and intensify the so-called 'north–south problem'. As a result, the industrialized countries were requested to respond in new ways.

In 1970, the UN General Assembly passed a resolution known as the 'International Development Strategy for the Second UN Development Decade'. The resolution established a target whereby an amount equal to 0.7 per cent of the GNP of industrialized countries was to be earmarked for official development assistance. As a member of the Development Assistance Committee (DAC), Japan expanded its economic cooperation towards this target. This was not an easy target to achieve, and there was no choice but to adjust the target because of the state of Japan's foreign reserves, affected as they were by economic recession and the oil crisis. Looking at the level of official development assistance as a percentage of GNP in 1973, the allocation from Japan stood at a mere 0.21 per cent while that from France was 0.67 per cent, that from the Netherlands was 0.67 per cent, that from the UK was 0.39 per cent, that from West Germany was 0.31 per cent, and that from the US was 0.29 per cent. Half or more of Japan's economic cooperation at that time took the form of private-sector assistance in exchange for which compensation was received (Table 28.4). As opposed to the make-up of Japan's economic cooperation, the new economic cooperation proposed by the UN included a plan to increase the weight of official assistance and to make loan aid with limiting conditions 'generally untied', which meant that contract procurements would be open to international competition, rather than 'partial untied' assistance which was limited to Japanese and developing country bidders. Because it was not uncommon to receive compensation in exchange for assistance provided to developing countries, assistance was often conditional upon the purchase of products. This system was modified, however, to accommodate the demands of the developing countries. During the 1970s, Japan also adopted a new approach and switched to official development assistance. In August 1974 Japan established the Japan International Cooperation Agency under which all government-based technology cooperation institutions were unified. In June 1975, the Overseas Economic Cooperation Fund was clearly positioned as a specialist organization for providing assistance to governments.

During the late 1970s, the level of Japan's economic cooperation *vis-à-vis* developing countries was by no means substantial, whether viewed in terms of total amount contributed or percentage of grants made. Even if the level of assistance

Table 28.4 Total net flow of financial resources from major DAC countries to developing countries and multilateral agencies (1973) (unit: $m.; %)

	Total official and private (net)	Official development assistance and other official flows			Private flows, at market terms (net)
		Total (net)	Official development assistance	Percentage of GNP	
Australia	354	287	285	0.59	44
Belgium	506	238	234	0.55	253
Canada	1,104	591	514	0.47	435
France	2,800	1,565	1,488	0.67	1,244
W. Germany	1,790	1,331	1,102	0.31	301
Italy	645	535	192	0.09	88
Japan	5,844	2,189	1,011	0.21	3,647
The Netherlands	612	336	322	0.67	260
Norway	93	84	84	0.43	1
Portugal	236	194	61	1.79	41
Sweden	359	275	275	0.48	54
Britain	1,322	643	603	0.39	624
USA	7,520	3,445	2,968	0.29	3,182
DAC Totals	23,877	11,992	9,405	0.34	10,552

Note: Amounts less than $1m. were not calculated.

Source: Toyo Keizai Inc. (ed.), *Keizai Tokei Nenkan* (Annual Economic Statistics), 1975: 360. This manuscript was taken from MITI's 'Japan's Economic Cooperation'.

is calculated as a percentage of GNP, it was only in the range of 0.9 per cent, including private-sector assistance, according to the Bank of Japan's 'International Comparative Statistics'. At that time, because Japan's international balance of payments came out of deficit during the first oil crisis and began to accumulate a surplus again, and because the yen appreciated, the DAC requested quantitative expansion and qualitative improvement in Japan's official development assistance. The Japanese government announced in May 1977 at the Ministers' Conference of OECD that it would double its official development assistance over the next five years. This plan was incorporated in the following year's budget, which was subsequently increased by a large percentage every year until fiscal year 1980 when the goal of doubling the official development assistance was achieved. This assistance took the form of assistance pursuant to bilateral treaties with the recipient countries and as funds invested in international organizations. Moreover, the percentage of grants and quasi-grants was also increased. Although Japan narrowed the gap between the level of assistance provided by it and the industrialized Western countries as it became an 'economic superpower', that level of assistance still remained low.

A look at the regions to which assistance was sent clearly shows that Japanese assistance was concentrated on countries in Asia. There are historical and geographical reasons for this phenomenon. In fact, much European and US assistance to countries in Africa and Central and South America can be said to have been be due largely to the relationships the industrialized countries had with former suzerain states and colonies. In that sense, Japan's concentration on assisting Asian countries was not an unusual phenomenon.

A review of the form that economic cooperation took shows that there were more government-financed loans and other forms of financial assistance than grants. Japan provided more large-size loans and financial assistance than the UK, West Germany, France, and Italy. Loans and investments from the private sector in Japan grew rapidly during the 1970s, to such an extent that, if they were included in the totals, by the 1980s Japan's total assistance would rank with that of the European countries.

Diversification of economic cooperation

Japan is heavily dependent on trade. Therefore, establishing stable economic relationships based on interdependence with foreign countries, including developing countries, was of paramount importance from the perspective of economic security. For this reason, Japan increasingly considered the Asian region to be important and promoted diversified economic cooperation.

Although various government-related institutions had been established in the past for promoting economic cooperation, the Japan International Cooperation Agency was created under legislation of the same name passed in May 1974. Economic cooperation, which previously had been distributed among and performed by government organizations such as the Overseas Agricultural Development Fund, the Japan Overseas Development Corporation, the Overseas Technology Cooperation Agency, and the Overseas Emigration Agency, were unified and centralized under the Japan International Cooperation Agency. The Ministers of the Ministry of Foreign Affairs, Ministry of Finance, Ministry of Agriculture, Forestry, and Fisheries, and the Ministry of International Trade and Industry had joint jurisdiction over the Japan International Cooperation Agency. With regard to development of the mining and manufacturing industries and the maintenance of the industrial base, it was decided that the Minister of International Trade and Industry would share responsibility with the Minister of Foreign Affairs, who was the competent minister.

MITI promoted various economic cooperation undertakings through institutions other than the Japan International Cooperation Agency, including the Japan External Trade Organization (JETRO), the Japan Overseas Development Corporation, the Association for Overseas Technical Scholarship, the Engineering Consulting Firms Association of Japan, the Japan Consulting Institute, the Japan Chamber of Commerce and Industry, and the Institute of Developing Economies.

Economic cooperation was promoted from the three perspectives of finance, technology, and trade.

Direct bilateral yen loans played a leading role in government-based financial cooperation. Initially, such loans were handled by the Export-Import Bank of Japan. However, due to an administrative reorganization that took place in 1975, that responsibility was delegated to the Overseas Economic Cooperation Fund. Project loans formed the principal axis of yen loans, a trend that continued throughout the 1970s. By the end of 1979, project loans accounted for approximately 74 per cent of all loans. The remaining loans took the form of product assistance, although the quantity of such assistance was less than that provided by project loans throughout the 1970s.

Private-sector financial cooperation is provided by direct loans from the Export-Import Bank of Japan and export financing by either the Export-Import Bank of Japan or private banks. After the first oil crisis, large-scale projects funded by private-sector financial cooperation increased. The major, large-scale projects such as Brazil's Paper and Pulp Resource Project, Indonesia's Asahan Aluminum Project, and Iran's Petrochemical Project were promoted as national projects by MITI.

Most technical cooperation was conducted on a bilateral basis through the Japan International Cooperation Agency. Compared with other industrialized countries, Japan was slow to provide technical cooperation, and obtaining the human resources needed to support technical guidance became an issue. As a result, the government promoted the training of foreign technicians in Japan by budgeting funds to subsidize the costs of research operations, the costs of dispatching private-sector specialists, and the costs of providing technical cooperation to small and medium enterprises in other countries. General development project studies are an example of how government-based technical cooperation is extended. During the 1970s, MITI subcontracted and conducted feasibility studies for industrial development in countries in South-East Asia, the Middle East, Thailand, and Mexico.

A preferential duty system is one way of providing economic cooperation through trade policy. Beginning in 1971, Japan and the EC were the first to enforce a general preferential duty system, thereby cooperating to promote exports from developing countries. The number of countries that received preferential treatment steadily increased and the scope of preferential treatment was expanded to include economic regions and territories in addition to countries. A 'ceiling system', which limited the quantity of imports that would benefit from preferential duties, was adopted with respect to mining and manufacturing goods, which fell under MITI's jurisdiction. The government established the 'one-half ceiling clause' which would halt preferential tariffs on particular imports from any one country when such imports from that country reached one-half of the ceiling. This prepared Japan for a flood of imports from developing countries. Furthermore, considering the negative influence that could be exerted on Japanese producers, processors, and distributors by greatly increased imports, in the beginning a prior allotment system was set up.

Besides the above, the Japanese government promoted the sale of products from developing countries, assisted in experiments for developing forests in the South

Pacific, and promoted trade and the development and import of products from developing countries. Japan thus promoted economic cooperation related to the development of trade with developing countries in various ways.

In conclusion, after the first oil crisis Japan sought to enhance and strengthen existing programmes such as the Overseas Investment Loss Reserve Fund System in order to secure a stable supply of resources. The 1970s saw the advent of the 'International Development Strategy for the Second United Nations Development Decade', mentioned earlier, and expansion in the scale of Japan's economy due to its high-level growth rate. As described in the foregoing, with its advanced technology Japan has extended diverse forms of economic cooperation to assist the growth of developing countries.[26]

NOTES

1. *Tsusho Sangyo Seisakushi*, xvi, statistics table 11 on trade and foreign exchange: 237–59, for discussion related to quantity.
2. *Tsusho Hakusho*, 1979 edn., General Survey Volume: 181.
3. At the time of both oil crises, the overall trade balance and the current balance fell into deficit but the trade balance only had its surplus reduced, it did not fall into deficit. The trade balance in 1974, the year after the first oil crisis, showed a surplus of $1.436 billion, the current balance showed a deficit of $4.693 billion, and the overall balance showed a deficit of $6.839 billion. In 1979, the year of the second oil crisis, the trade balance showed a surplus of $1.845 billion, the current balance showed a deficit of $8.754 billion, and the overall balance showed a large deficit of $16.620 billion. Three years during the 1970s showed a decrease in foreign currency reserves versus the previous year: 1973 was $6.119 billion, 1975 was $730 million, and 1979 was $12.692 billion; these figures are from *Tsusho Sangyo Seisakushi*, xvi. 260–1.
4. Ibid. xvi. 254–5.
5. Ibid., taken from Chronology; also see *Tsusho Hakusho*, 1981 edn., General Survey Volume: 259–60 (table 1 in pt. 3, ch. 1).
6. For discussion of second-stage and third-stage yen measures, see *Tsusho Sangyo Seisakushi*, xii, ch. 2, sect. 1.
7. *Tsusho Hakusho*, 1973 edn., General Survey Volume: 117–19.
8. *Tsusho Sangyo-sho Nenpo*, fiscal year 1973: 40.
9. Ibid., fiscal year 1980: 59–60.
10. For discussion of fourth-stage of capital liberalization, see ibid., fiscal year 1971: 70–3.
11. *Tsusho Hakusho*, 1973 edn., General Survey Volume: 120–3.
12. Ibid. 71, for discussion on first stage of liberalizing technology imports.
13. *Tsusho Sangyo-sho Nenpo*, fiscal year 1972: 86.
14. Ibid. 86–7 for discussion on second stage of liberalizing technology imports.
15. Ibid., fiscal year 1973: 89.
16. Ibid., fiscal year 1976: 108; during the years before liberalization, about thirty separate applications a year were investigated for introducing computer-related technology; for a discussion of how separate investigations of such applications dropped remarkably after liberalization, see ibid., fiscal year 1974: 81.
17. For a discussion of liberalization measures for first-stage and second-stage overseas investment and financing, see *Tsusho Sangyo Seisakushi*, xii, ch. 2, sect. 3-2.
18. For a discussion of liberalization measures for third-stage and fourth-stage overseas investment and financing, see *Tsusho Sangyo-sho Nenpo*, fiscal year 1973: 91.
19. MITI (ed.), *Sangyo Kozo no Choki Bijion* (Japan's Industrial Structure; A Long-Range Vision Report by Industrial Structure Council), 1976 edn., Research Institute of International Trade and Industry: 182–3.

20. Ibid., fiscal year 1974: p. 179; other discussions depend on this same report.
21. In developing countries, the over-presence of Japanese companies became a problem; investments increased rapidly, there was a lack of understanding of local practices and legal system, and friction with Japanese management in host countries led to criticisms of Japan; see *Sangyo Kozo no Choki Bijion*, 1976: 176–7.
22. *Sangyo Kozo no Choki Bijion*, 1978: 330.
23. See Yoshikazu Miyazaki, *Nihon Keizai no Kozo to Kodo* (Structure and Behaviour of Japanese Economy), Chikumashobo Publishing Co., 1985: 117–78.
24. Industrial Bank of Japan Ltd., Industrial Research Department (ed.), *Nihon Sangyo no Shintenkai* (New Development of Japanese Industry), Nihon Keizai Shimbun Inc., 1982: 322–33.
25. For discussion of US–Japan automotive negotiations see *Tsusho Sangyo Seisakushi*, xii, ch. 3, sect. 2; other references include I. M. Destler and Hideo Sato (ed.), *Nichibei Keizai Funso no Kaimei* (Coping with US–Japanese Economic Conflicts), ch. 3, Nihon Keizai Shimbun Inc., 1982; and Keiichi Ohshima and P. McCracken (eds.), *Nichibei Jidosha Masatsu* (US–Japan Friction Regarding Cars), Nihon Keizai Shimbun Inc., 1984.
26. For discussion of overseas investment and economic cooperation, see *Tsusho Sangyo Seisakushi*, xii, ch. 2, sects. 3 and 4.

29

The Nurturing of Advanced Technology Industries, and Policy Vision

29.1. Development of Knowledge-Intensive Industries

In May 1971, the Industrial Structure Council submitted a report to the Minister of International Trade and Industry entitled 'Vision of MITI Policies in the 1970s'. The report said in part that Japan should aim for an industrial structure in the 1970s based on knowledge-intensive industries, and it recommended that a technology policy be promoted for that purpose. It had become gradually clear during the recession of 1965 that the industrial policy of the high-level growth period that centred on developing the heavy and chemical industries, which are basic materials industries, had reached a turning point. The growth of the computer industry and the spread of factory automation (FA) in the US seemed to point at the future image of the industrially advanced countries. The developing countries of Asia, meanwhile, had risen above their monocultural level and were moving to establish an industrial structure that make them self-supporting. Instead of only labour-intensive industries they were beginning to develop their heavy and chemical industries. Therefore, if Japan continued to depend on the heavy and chemical industries with their relatively low proportion of value added, then sooner or later Japanese industry would be forced to compete with those countries at the same level. It was thought possible that at that time the developing countries with their lower labour and other costs would gain an advantageous position. As well, in order to raise per capita national income and ensure an acceptable level of living comfort for the Japanese people, it was important to develop high added-value knowledge-intensive industries.

MITI early on recognized the strategic importance of knowledge-intensive industries. Even before the start of the period of high-level economic growth it had promoted legislation such as the Law on Temporary Measures for Promotion of the Machinery Industry and the Law on Temporary Measures for Promotion of the Electronics Industry, the former enforced in June 1956 and the latter in June 1957. During the period of high-level economic growth from the mid-1950s to the late 1960s, large numbers of products based on new technology were introduced mainly for use as capital equipment in the machinery industries and as electric household goods. The appearance of various machine tools, such as lathes and numerical control (NC) machines, industrial robots, and transfer machines that systematized NC machines, contributed to increasing the productivity of Japan's assembly industries tremendously. The next stage of Japan's electronics industry began with the fitting of transistors in radios and moved to solid-state audio equipment and television sets, and the development of magnetic memory media and reproduction technology for tape recorders and VTRs for the private sector. Mass production of such items raised the international competitiveness of electronic products and their components.

In the early 1970s, colour television sets, transformers, loudspeakers, tuners, and so forth were exported in huge quantities. It was around that time that the US began levying dumping charges on these products and the first trade friction problems arose.[1] A look at the composition of Japan–US trade in electronic products at that time shows Japan exporting more home-use electronic products to the US than the US exported to Japan, and importing more industrial-use products and components from the US than the US imported from Japan. Among the imports to Japan, products such as wireless application devices, computers and related devices, and semiconductor elements were particularly notable.[2] This imbalance in trade of electronic products demonstrated the weak international competitiveness of Japan's electronics industry. For computer-related products, meanwhile, there was increasing pressure for Japan to liberalize its market, which had been postponed a number of times, and calls were being made for a new industry promotion law.

In 1970, there were 6,718 sets of computers installed in Japan. In comparison, the US was the leader with 47,997 sets followed by West Germany with a little over 6,670, the UK with 5,350, France with 5,190, the Soviet Union with 4,000, Italy with 2,780, and Canada with 1,920 sets. Japan was thus second in the world in terms of computer installations. What was notable at the time was the large share of worldwide computer installations accounted for by IBM machines. In the UK, IBM machines accounted for 30.4 per cent of the total, in France for 65.7 per cent, in West Germany for 57.1 per cent, in Italy for 68.8 per cent, and in the Benelux countries for 51.8 per cent. In value terms, IBM computers accounted for 57.9 per cent of the world's markets, not including the US market.

Meanwhile, as of the end of March 1971, domestic-made computers accounted for 55.3 per cent of the total value of all computers in operation in Japan, broken into 41.5 per cent of the mainframe market, 71.0 per cent of the medium-size computer market, and 72.4 per cent of the small-size computer market. The total for the medium- and small-size computer markets was over 70 per cent, but the share was not even 50 per cent for the mainframe market. IBM's share of the mainframe market, on the other hand, was large. As seen in the situation in the computer market, domestic-made computers had reached a certain level but to achieve a higher level it was essential that computers and peripheral equipment be improved and supported in both qualitative and quantitative terms.

The Law on Temporary Measures for Promotion of the Electronics Industry was promulgated in 1957 with development of the domestic computer industry in mind. The law had a time limit of seven years, however, and in 1964 it was extended another seven years, to run until March 1971. As the law's second time limit approached, it was decided to merge it with the Law on Temporary Measures for Promotion of the Machinery Industry in new legislation.

The new law was called the Law on Temporary Measures for Promotion of Specified Electronics Industries and Specified Machinery Industries. This law was aimed at promoting improved production technology and rationalization of specified electronics and machinery industries, thereby contributing to their development. For enterprises stipulated by Cabinet Order, the Minister of International Trade and Industry would have 'advanced plans' prepared. Based on those plans, funds would be secured, instructions would be given for joint undertakings, restrictions would be set on standards, the Anti-Monopoly Law (AML) would not be applied, notice would be given of participation in joint undertakings, and special tax measures would be provided.[3] MITI would issue notifications based on the law that outlined 'advanced plans' with equipment identified by name, the content of experimental research, target years, needed funds, and other important items, and would provide research subsidies and arrange for financing.

In fiscal year 1971, the first year of the Law on Temporary Measures for Promotion of Specified Electronics Industries and Specified Machinery Industries, MITI provided total subsidies of 620 million yen for experimental research on twelve types of machinery scheduled for promotion according to the law, and arranged through the Development Bank for fourteen cases of special financing worth 1.45 billion yen related to six types of machinery scheduled for promotion of commercialization and mass production and seven out of fourteen types of machinery scheduled for promotion of production rationalization, including semiconductor ICs (integrated circuits), chemical compound semiconductor elements, materials for same, colour VTRs, digital computers, electronic desktop calculators, and accounting machines.[4] The time limit on the Law on Temporary Measures for Promotion of Specified Electronics Industries and Specified Machinery Industries was 31 March 1978, but each fiscal year before that saw slight additions and changes to the types of experimental research and other aspects of the 'advanced plans' and related subsidies and financing arrangements, thereby contributing to R&D, mass production, and production rationalization of the targeted items.

29.2. Liberalization and Promoting Development of the Computer Industry

The Law on Temporary Measures for Promotion of Specified Electronics Industries and Specified Machinery Industries went into effect in April 1971. Not long afterwards, the liberalization of computers, peripheral equipment, integrated circuits, and so forth, a matter which had been postponed several times, emerged as a serious issue. At one point it had almost been firmly established that the computer industry would not be liberalized, but in July 1971, as part of a general review of yen countermeasures, a clear schedule was set for liberalizing computers. On 22 July, the Minister of International Trade and Industry announced a general policy that included the following: (1) capital would be liberalized for ICs, except for sophisticated LSIs; (2) for the interim, computers, peripheral equipment, and parts would not be liberalized but capital in those areas would be liberalized in three years, when the fourth stage of capital liberalization was carried out; (3) software would not be liberalized; and (4) imports would be liberalized from the end of March 1972 for peripheral equipment, except for memory devices and terminals. In order to offset the effects of liberalization, the minister announced the following measures: (1) establishment of a special budget account for the computer industry with funds directed for R&D of advanced computers, the development of peripheral and terminal equipment, and the purchase of computers by government offices; (2) an expanded limit of Japan Development Bank financing to 50 billion yen for the Japan Electronic Computer Co.; (3) a shortening from 5.2 to 4.2 years depreciating computers; and (4) raising by 5 per cent the reserve for losses related to buy-out of leased computers, thereby making it 20 per cent. The minister also requested that the computer industry consolidate and reorganize itself.[5]

In this way, a clear schedule was set for liberalizing the computer industry. The special budget account the MITI minister announced was established in fiscal year 1972, and four types of subsidies were paid from it mainly to manufacturers that promoted consolidation and reorganization of the computer industry. The subsidies were paid for promoting the development of new computer models, peripheral equipment, ICs, and the information-processing industry. The Japan Development Bank, meanwhile, provided financing for production equipment and equipment to be used for experimental research on general-purpose digital computer systems by domestic computer manufacturers that were putting their organizations into order through business ties.

Among the four subsidies, those for promoting the development of new computer models were provided in the autumn of 1971 to three groups that completed business ties: Fujitsu and Hitachi; Oki Electric and Mitsubishi Electric; and NEC and Toshiba. The three groups set up research associations according to the Research Association for Mining and Manufacturing Technology Law, and the subsidies were paid to these associations. In fiscal year 1976, subsidies were added to promote the development of LSIs for use with next-generation computers. Total subsidies paid in all categories between fiscal years 1973 and 1976 reached 71,622 million yen (see Table 29.1).

Japan was not the only country that provided subsidies and promoted the reorganization of its computer industry to enable its domestic companies to compete on an equal level with giant corporations.[6] In October 1968, for example, when the ICT and EEC groups merged to form ICL in the UK, the British government provided £3.5 million in equity and secured 10.5 per cent of the shares of ICL. In addition, £7.5 million were loaned to ICL as development funds and during the

Table 29.1   Subsidies to computer industry, 1972–1976 (unit: million yen)

	Promoting development of new computer models	Promoting development of peripheral equipment	Promoting development of ICs	Promoting development of information-processing industry	Promoting development of LSIs for use with next-generation computers
1972	4,510	700			
1973	14,026	936	1,700	600	
1974	15,250	1,400	1,800	1,200	
1975	12,475	900		1,200	
1976	10,825	600			3,500

Source: Japan Electronic Computer Company, *JECC Computer Notes*, 1977: 87.

four years from ICL's establishment to 1971 a total of £13.5 million was provided as R&D subsidies. Besides those expenditures, from 1964 the British government also bore 50 per cent of the development expenses related to a plan it devised for developing advanced computer technology. This policy of supporting the computer industry was carried out while the Labour Party was in power. After the Conservative government came into power it did away with policies devised to protect industry. But not long afterwards there was a new recognition of the strategic importance of the computer industry and development subsidies were provided to ICL. In France as well a plan was formulated in 1966 for developing the computer industry. The government urged four manufacturers in related industries to merge, which they did to form CII. Over the next five years the government provided CII with subsidies worth 600 million francs. The government's plan to develop the French computer industry, called the 'Plan Calcul', was formulated under the leadership of President De Gaulle. Despite the strong support, however, IBM's share of the computer market was so great that CII's development was not completely smooth. As a result, a second-stage 'Plan Calcul', was formulated to run from 1971 for five years. Subsidies and financing worth 2.1 billion francs were provided to the computer industry, including software projects.

In West Germany, a five-year plan for advanced data processing was formulated in 1967 and a public corporation called GMDV was established. For this purpose, the government provided DM 300 million. Without waiting for the first stage of the plan to end, a second-stage plan was introduced in September 1971 with DM 3.3 billion in support from the government.

In Japan, the groups receiving subsidies introduced three new series of computers in May 1974. The NEC-Toshiba group introduced the ACOS series, the Mitsubishi Electric Oki Electric group introduced the COSMO series, and the Fujitsu-Hitachi group introduced the M series. These three series of machines compared favourably with the products of IBM and other US makers at the time.

New computers were thus developed in Japan. Around that time, however, it was learned in the midst of an IBM *vs*. Telex Corporation anti-monopoly dispute that IBM was developing a Future System (FS) that utilized VLSI (very large-scale integration). In that situation, MITI developed the idea of building a computer industry structure that would allow Japanese companies to compete with IBM's FS. It suggested forming two groups of companies, with Fujitsu, Hitachi, and Mitsubishi Electric in one group and NEC and Toshiba in the other, to develop two types of machines for competing with IBM's FS. One would be IBM-compatible and the other would be non-IBM-compatible. That idea resulted in the Japanese computer industry shifting to a new structure.

The second principal area receiving government subsidies in Japan was promoting development of peripheral equipment. Peripheral equipment, terminal equipment, and related devices accounted for 70 per cent of the cost of computer systems at the time. The subsidies in this area were to cover 50 per cent of the costs of developing and commercializing the most expensive of the products mentioned, especially those for which there were not many product choices and whose commercialization had fallen behind. A wide variety of products and companies were targeted for these subsidies.

The third principal area receiving government subsidies in Japan was promoting development of ICs. The subsidies in this area were to cover 50 per cent of the costs of developing and commercializing advanced ICs able to compete with US-made products. The subsidies were provided to semiconductor makers with sophisticated R&D capabilities and outstanding sales organizations.

The fourth principal area receiving government subsidies in Japan was promoting development of the information-processing industry. To raise the production efficiency of software development and cultivate the technological capabilities needed for responding to large-scale software development projects, subsidies would cover 75 per cent of the costs for software module R&D performed by groups of companies in the data-processing industry working in one of five fields: clerical processing, business management, design calculations, OR calculations, or automated control. Subsidies were provided to five groups formed in early 1974.

In the above context, an overall computer industry structure with competitive capabilities was put roughly into order by the time limit set in the fifth stage of the capital liberalization programme for liberalizing the computer and related industries.

29.3. New Stage for Developing Machinery and Information Industries

Preparations for responding to approaching liberalization of the computer and related industries moved forward in the context of the hectic situation following the first oil crisis. At the time, several of the government's advisory councils were preparing reports on the future prospects of the machinery and information industries.

The Information Industry Committee of the Industrial Structure Council, for example, was studying a question posed to it in October 1973: 'What Should the Future Information Industry be Like and What Policies Should be Prepared for Dealing with It?' In September 1974, the Industrial Structure Council presented an interim report on 'The Information-Oriented Society and the Information Industry'. The report especially noted that besides being knowledge-intensive the information industry conserved energy and natural resources and would play a major role in making Japanese industry more sophisticated. The information industry should be viewed closely for its contribution in making industry and society more information-oriented. In particular, the report presented the Industrial Structure Council's opinions in detail in three areas: putting information systems into order, encouraging the foundation for introducing information systems, and the future direction of the information industry. For putting information systems into order, the report discussed development of advanced model projects by the government, providing guidance to the private sector in systems development, promoting the development of advanced technology, and promoting standardization. For supporting the foundation for introducing information systems, the report discussed matters such as building databanks, developing information distribution networks, promoting data-processing education, and responding to the internationalization of information. Concerning the future direction of the information industry, the report recommended reinforcing protection of the industry, including providing funds for strengthening the system of cooperation among the existing three groups of companies. The report also recommended that the government energetically promote areas such as the development of pattern recognition, which was a difficult area for the private sector to tackle.[7]

Another interim report, entitled 'Vision of the Machinery Industry for 1975–84', was presented in December 1974 by the Machinery Industry Committee of the Industrial Structure Council.[8] This report mentioned five problems faced by Japan's machinery industry in the post-oil crisis period, and warned that the past growth pattern of the industry was vanishing. The problems were: (1) sluggishness in expansion of investment in plant and equipment; (2) spread of the usual type of consumer durables had come a full turn; (3) concern about worsening in price competitiveness; (4) uneasiness about the supply of basic materials; and (5) difficulty of introducing technology. The report outlined five directions for future growth patterns: (1) energetic response to satisfy needs; (2) energetic development of overseas operations; (3) promoting development of technology; (4) reinforcing of the infrastructure, promoting greater efficiency; and (5) emphasizing corporate social responsibility. For promoting the development of technology, the report emphasized a need for powerful development of unexplored innovative technology particularly in the electronics industry. Other essential tasks the report pointed out were the development of high-technology products related to computers, ICs, aircraft, and nuclear power equipment.

In the course of the Machinery Industry Committee of the Industrial Structure Council pulling together the above report, its Industrial Electronics and Electrical Machinery Industries Subcommittee reported to it on industrial-use electronic equipment. The subcommittee emphasized the need to firmly establish the computer and IC industries as domestic industries. For that purpose, it said that development assistance was needed in the areas of next-generation computers, software, and VLSIs. In particular, it said that 'ICs are the most representative products of technological innovation in the electronics industry' and therefore measures must be introduced to provide special assistance to cover R&D expenses, to handle worn-out production facilities, and to counter the sale of unfairly inexpensive foreign-made ICs. The report thus positioned 'industrial-use electronic equipment', including ICs and software, as the industrial area that would determine the future of Japanese industry, and it emphasized the need for providing assistance. When MITI presented its budget requirements for fiscal year 1976, it took this report into consideration and added a new budget item of expenses for developing VLSIs for next-generation computers.

In October 1977, the Machinery Industry Committee and Information Industry Committee of the Industrial Structure Council jointly presented an interim report entitled 'The Future Direction the Machinery and Information Industries should Move in, and Policies for that Purpose'. In pulling together the report, the committees conducted joint deliberations, particularly regarding the matter of integrating policies concerning hardware and software, for which demands had recently become vociferous. Detailed discussions were left to a planning subcommittee set up for that purpose. The report recommended a selective improvement in government assistance in seven industries expected to support the nation's future economic growth. The industries specifically mentioned were the aircraft, nuclear power equipment, ocean-development-related equipment, computers, information services, consulting, and engineering. The report cited the need to improve government assistance in these industries in the form of R&D subsidies, arranged financing, tax benefits, and credit guarantees. In the area of developing technology, the report said it is most important for Japanese companies to develop original technology but it is also important to participate in joint international research and to promote the transfer of technology resulting from research. The report thus emphasized the need for an international perspective to government assistance. Regarding improvement of the coordination function, the report emphasized not only industry-level action such as forming cartels or groups and conducting joint activities but a need for guidance in the areas of safety, pollution control, and the conservation of energy and natural resources, as well as considering the best interests of consumers and avoiding trade friction.

The Law on Temporary Measures for Promotion of Specified Electronics Industries and Specified Machinery Industries had a time limit of March 1978, and the joint report from the Machinery Industry Committee and Information Industry Committee of the Industrial Structure Council proposed that new legislation be enacted after the law expired. MITI acted on that proposal and began drafting a bill. It took form as a draft for the Law on Temporary Measures for Promotion of Specified Machinery and Information Industries. The Cabinet approved the draft in March 1978 and it subsequently passed the House of Representatives in May and the House of Councillors in June and was promulgated and enforced in July.[9]

One principal difference between the Law on Temporary Measures for Promotion of Specified Electronics Industries and Specified Machinery Industries and the Law on Temporary Measures for Promotion of Specified Machinery and Information Industries was that for the first time the software industry became a target of legislation. Other features of the law were its emphasis on the mutual interdependence of the electronics, machinery, and software industries, and as criteria for providing assistance it added the degree of contribution in conserving energy and natural resources to the earlier criteria of combining machines and using them in systems. It also abolished stipulated cartels related to purchasing basic and raw materials and outlined procedures for conducting discussions with the Fair Trade Commission (FTC). As well, the law stipulated tax measures for spreading and promoting the use of machines and equipment used in combination. The machinery and equipment targeted for promotion included, for electronic equipment, promoting experimental research of 15 items, promoting industrialization of 8 items, and promoting rationalization of 9 items; for machinery, it included promoting experimental research for 20 items, promoting industrialization of 4 items, and promoting rationalization of 32 items—a total of 88 items. Compared to the 98 items covered in the Law on Temporary Measures for Promotion of Specified Electronics Industries and Specified Machinery Industries, the targeted equipment was thus selected more carefully and emphasis was placed on promoting experimental research related to electronic equipment and promoting rationalization related to machinery. Equipment and machinery to be made more sophisticated according to the law included for electronic equipment 1 item in experimental research, 8 items in industrialization, and 9 items in rationalization; for machinery, it included 2 items in experimental research, 4 items in industrialization, and 37 items in rationalization. One item was also included from the software industry, for a total of 62 items. This number, too, was less than the 89 items covered in the Law on Temporary Measures for Promotion of Specified Electronics Industries and Specified Machinery Industries. The Law on Temporary Measures for Promotion of Specified Machinery and Information Industries had a time limit of seven years. Targets were set by item to be accomplished within that time frame, and financing of funds for plant and equipment and tax measures were put in place. Included among the equipment targeted for promotion of experimental research were electronic application electric measuring equipment, electronic application equipment for medical use, high-performance digital-type computers, ICs, high-performance facsimile storage and exchange devices, NC machine tools for metals, and industrial robots.

The Law on Temporary Measures for Promotion of Specified Machinery and Information Industries added the software industry as an area needing greater sophistication. As early as 1969, MITI had begun formulating a 'Plan for More Sophisticated Information Processing'. To realize that plan, the Law Concerning the Information-Technology Promotion Agency and Related Matters was enforced in July 1970.[10] This Agency was established in October 1970 to promote the use of computers, to promote the development of software programs, to expedite the distribution of software programs, and to nurture the information-processing services industry. The government provided part of the equity, and the Agency commissioned the development of advanced, general-purpose programs, the purchase and dissemination of programs developed in the private sector, credit guarantees for funds borrowed by companies in the information-processing services industry for modernizing their operations, and credit guarantees for computer users who borrow funds to support the development of computer programs. MITI provided funds to support the Agency's operations each year from fiscal year 1970, and as the Agency expanded its operations the government's capital participation gradually increased. As of the end of fiscal year 1980, the Agency was promoting the dissemination of 106 software programs. From fiscal year 1976, moreover, the government commissioned the Agency to develop technology for basic improvement of methods of producing computer programs. Based on the Law Concerning the Information-Technology Promotion Agency and Related Matters, MITI prepared a plan for more sophisticated use of computers, a list of available software programs (commissioned the Agency to prepare), and conducted examinations for information-processing engineers. In addition, from fiscal year 1971 financial measures were introduced to promote the information-processing industry. The Trust Fund Bureau used the funds realized from issuing bank debentures to have the Industrial Bank of Japan, the Long-Term Credit Bank of Japan, and the Real Estate Bank of Japan (later, the Nippon Credit Bank) provide software program development financing to computer users, on condition that the Information-Technology Promotion Agency provided credit guarantees. In line with the content of the Law on Temporary Measures for Promotion of Specified Machinery and Information Industries, the promotion of joint development efforts and formulation of the plan for raising the sophistication of the software industry tied directly to the assistance mentioned earlier for developing and disseminating software programs. In that sense, the law aimed at establishing an industrial structure that was appropriate for the software industry, reflecting the fact that most companies in the industry were small and medium enterprises or outstanding companies.[11]

Besides development through the Law on Temporary Measures for Promotion of Specified Machinery and Information Industries, MITI's measures for nurturing advanced industries included promotion of R&D for next-generation computers. One such project was a VLSI R&D project running from fiscal year 1976 for four years. The expenses for developing VLSIs were huge and it was difficult for Japanese computer companies with their still weak financial bases to conduct such R&D on their own. The R&D was thus integrated into the single VLSI Technology Research Association to which initial subsidies of 30 billion yen were provided. This became a national project, bringing together the total R&D resources of the nation. R&D related to operating systems (OS) and peripheral equipment was also promoted by establishing a single research association, the Association for Research and Development of Basic Technology for Electronic Computers, and providing it with a total of 47 billion yen in R&D assistance (including 23.5 billion yen in subsidies) in a five-year plan that began in fiscal year 1979.

The nurturing of advanced industries achieved a modicum of success, especially in the context of external events such as the shift to a floating exchange rate, two oil crises, achievement of liberalization, and increased trade friction. The increased production during the 1970s of industrial-use robots, NC machine tools, digital computers and peripheral equipment, semiconductor elements, and ICs was remarkable. Production was 30-fold for computer terminal devices, 26-fold for external memory devices, 20-fold for NC lathes, 20-fold for semiconductor ICs, and 15-fold for machining centres. Exports from Japan up to then tended to be electronic products for home use, such as colour television sets, VTRs, and stereo sets, but from around 1979 exports of products such as communications equipment, desktop calculators and other industrial-use electronic equipment, and components such as ICs, picked up rapidly.

29.4. Nurture of the Aircraft, Space, and Nuclear Power Equipment Industries

The aircraft industry

The aircraft industry is a comprehensive assembly machinery industry in which up-to-date technology is essential for engines, bodies, electronic equipment, and metals and other materials. An extremely large number of parts are used in aircraft, and a broad base of other industries supports the industry. In addition, the up-to-date technology, parts, and materials used in the industry are applicable to many other areas, from home-use equipment to military aircraft. With that background, many countries have established and nurtured aircraft industries based on domestic-developed technology.

Japan's post-war aircraft industry began with development of the YS-11 turboprop commercial airliner. Developed using domestic technology, the YS-11 carried sixty passengers. In the background of the YS-11's development was the expectation that technological fall-out from the project could be used in other areas. As of the end of May 1970, 167 units of the YS-11 had been produced and delivered. Seventy were for domestic commercial flights, twenty-seven were for use by government ministries and agencies, and seventy were exported. The YS-11 had a fine reputation as a highly economical plane that could be used for flying safely in and out of even small airfields. But production was not profitable, and the manufacturer—Japan Aircraft Manufacturing Co. Ltd. (JAMC)—suffered very heavy losses. In January 1971, the Aircraft Industry Council of MITI established an expert committee for studying ways to improve its management. The Council studied measures for that purpose and submitted a report in April 1971 recommending ways to distribute the company's losses. In August 1971, however, President Nixon announced new economic policies that caused the dollar to drop sharply against the yen, and the debt burden of JAMC expanded because of dollar-denominated deferred payment credits it had. At the same time, sales of the YS-11 turned sluggish because of the aircraft industry's unexpectedly rapid shift towards jet aircraft, as well as their increasing passenger capacity. In fiscal year 1973, after having produced 182 units, production of the YS-11 was halted. The debt burden for production of the YS-11 as of fiscal year 1982, including after-sales servicing, was estimated to be 36 billion yen. The government eventually covered 24.577 billion yen of that debt.[12]

In this way, although the YS-11 was a technically outstanding aircraft, changes in the aircraft market prevented it from reaching the mass-production stage and the project ended in failure. From about 1967, meanwhile, a concept emerged of developing a new-generation commercial airliner (the YX) by making use of technology developed for the YS-11. In the YX concept, Boeing of the US would cooperate with Japanese manufacturers to develop a mid-size, relatively noise-free, pollution-free, short-haul jet aircraft. For this purpose, an incorporated foundation called the Association for Development of Commercial Aircraft was founded, and research and surveys were begun with wide-ranging government support. The first oil crisis occurred in October 1973, however, and the level of economy of the YX became a topic of discussion. Boeing proposed that Air Alitalia of Italy be invited to participate in a three-way joint development project, but the Japanese side did not respond to the proposal in fiscal year 1974. In the end, the opinions of the two sides remained sharply divided, with the Japanese side emphasizing the use and improvement of domestic technology, and in September 1976 the negotiations with Boeing were halted. In July 1977, Boeing asked that the negotiations be reopened, and the two parties eventually reached an agreement in which the Japanese side would participate in the Boeing development organization, thus making it a joint development project. The Japanese side would work mainly on the aircraft body and would assume the burden for about 15 per cent of the overall development costs. On 22 September 1978, an agreement was signed and work began on producing a prototype of the Boeing 767. In August 1981, orders were received for 311 units of the Boeing 767, which was looked forward to as the aircraft of the 1980s. The YX development plan ended with several unanswered questions. The Japanese side participated only in designing the forward, middle, and aft body sections, and the fairing and ribs of the main wings, as well as market surveys and product support. Development costs borne by the Japanese side amounted to about 30.7 billion yen, of which about half was government subsidies. These funds were disbursed from the treasury as payment to Commercial Aircraft Inc. The first Boeing 767 was flown in September 1981, and it was first used for commercial flights from September 1982.

Besides the YX plan, another large-scale project was R&D related to aircraft engines, starting in fiscal year 1971. The first stage of this project, dubbed the FJR710 Plan, set its development target at catching up with the world-level for aircraft engines by developing a prototype engine with five tons of thrust. The first-stage plan, put into effect by the Aerospace Technology Research Centre, requested cooperation from Ishikawajima-Harima Heavy Industries, Kawasaki Heavy Industries, and Mitsubishi Heavy Industries. The project moved forward and achieved its initial aim in fiscal year 1975 and then began its second stage. Development investments for the first five years (1971–5) were about 6.7 billion yen. The second stage ran from 1976 to 1982. As one step in the second stage, the XJB Project began in fiscal year 1980, aiming to develop a commercial-use jet engine. This project benefited from the results of the previous FJR Project. The three participating companies established a research association, and the project moved forward by having complete business ties with Rolls Royce of the UK. From fiscal years 1976 to 1981, a six-year period, total investments in this project were 13.9 billion yen. All research and experiments ended when the goals of the project were achieved in December 1982. The FJR710/600 prototype engine produced in the second stage of this project was mounted in a STOL experimental plane, the *Asuka*.

Nurturing the space industry

The space industry is becoming increasingly important industrially as satellites are used for communications, broadcasting, weather observations, and the exploration of the Earth's natural resources. It is expected in the future that there will be space plants and satellites for solar power generation. As of fiscal year 1980, Japan had successfully launched twenty satellites into space, including four stationary satellites. Space development activities in Japan are centred on the National Space Development Agency of Japan (NASDA), established in October 1969. Major roles are also played by two research organizations: the National Aerospace Technology Laboratory in the Science and Technology Agency and the Aerospace Laboratory of the University of Tokyo (since fiscal year 1982, the Institute of Space and Astronautical Science of the Ministry of Education). Most development funds budgeted in the space area go to NASDA. Outside companies then contract with NASDA. Concerning the H-2 rocket for launching large satellites, Mitsubishi Heavy Industries was in overall charge of development, Mitsubishi Heavy Industries and Ishikawajima-Harima Heavy Industries were in charge of the first stage and second stage of the rocket, Nissan Motor Co. was in charge of the solid-state rocket booster, Kawasaki Heavy Industries was in charge of the satellite fairing, and Japan Aviation Electronics was in charge of the guidance system.[13] Total sales in the Japanese space industry for fiscal year 1979 were 103.2 billion yen, a figure equivalent to about one-tenth of the US space industry. The principal technology in the industry also depends on American technology, so Japan lags behind the US and other of the advanced Western countries in this field.

A look at the percentage of overseas and domestic technology making up the satellites Japan has launched thus far reveals the following facts. The stationary satellite Kiku 2 launched in 1977 was built by Mitsubishi Electric working with Ford Aerospace Communications; the technology was 41 per cent Japanese. The stationary satellite Himawari launched in the same year was built by NEC working with Hughes Aircraft; the technology was 11 per cent Japanese. Also, the broadcasting satellite Yuri launched in 1978 by NASA for Japan was built by Toshiba working with General Electric; the technology was 15 per cent Japanese.[14] The low percentages of Japanese content say much for the situation in Japan's space development industries. The development of domestic technology and nurturing of the industry are major tasks to be faced.

Because MITI is the ministry overlooking the industries manufacturing machinery and equipment for space development, it recognized from early on a need to develop advanced technology and the major technological effect that space technology has on other industries. It began promoting R&D of related equipment in three research facilities under the Agency of Industrial Science and Technology: the Mechanical Engineering Laboratory, the Electrotechnical Laboratory, and the Osaka National Industrial Technology Experimental Center. From fiscal years 1968 to 1976, research was conducted in the Mechanical Engineering Laboratory on spectroscopic devices for rocket launchings, and a sun follower was developed that is both a high-precision spectrometer and ultra-precise servo-mechanism. R&D was begun in fiscal year 1977 at the same laboratory for precision-tracking technology for use in space observations. Research was made into control technology and equipment for a large-calibre, ultra-high precision-tracking telescope for mounting aboard balloons. At the Electrotechnical Laboratory, the idea emerged of replacing rockets using chemicals for propulsion with electric propulsion systems in order to raise the performance of satellites and prolong their life, and from fiscal year 1968 research was begun on electronic-bombardment-type (Kaufman-type) ion engines. Research was begun at the same laboratory in 1971 on pulse-type plasma engines using teflon fuel for posture control of satellites. From fiscal year 1973, other research was begun at that laboratory into small, light, highly efficient thermoionic power generation for possible use as a power source for satellites. Research was conducted at the Electrotechnical Laboratory regarding the wearing out of electronic equipment aboard satellites. From fiscal years 1967 to 1976, for instance, research was conducted on the wear on silicon solar batteries caused by radiation in space and it was established that at low temperatures of minus 100 °C. the wear accelerated sharply. At the Government Industrial Research Institute in Osaka research was conducted from fiscal years 1969 to 1973 on the design, grinding, and measurement of non-spherical lenses used with super Schmidt cameras mounted aboard geodetic survey satellites. In the process, an NC-type non-spherical lens grinding machine was developed.[15]

In order to develop and nurture space-related industries, MITI in 1979 established a Space Industry Office inside its Machinery and Information Industries Bureau. This office was placed in charge of all administrative matters related to the development and use of machinery and equipment used for space development and research. Its first project was related to remote sensing, the exploration of natural resources from space, and from fiscal year 1980 it began promoting development of an earth exploratory satellite with a launching target of fiscal year 1987.[16] MITI also established the incorporated foundation Earth Resources Analysis Centre in September 1981 for analysing, processing, and providing information services concerning data transmitted from satellites, thus promoting the development of data analysis technology.

MITI's budget for space development at first remained at an average of about 100 million yen each year. Funds were expended as subsidies to the Agency of Industrial Science and Technology for R&D of important technology related to space development and for expenses related to commissioned research, and to the various Government Industrial Research Institutes for experimental research (special research) related to space technology.[17]

The nuclear power equipment industry

The first oil crisis brought about a new recognition in Japan of the need to diversify the country's sources of energy. In particular, the importance of nuclear power as a source of non-petroleum energy became an issue. In overall energy policy, the promotion of nuclear power generation was given particular emphasis. Not much time had yet passed since nuclear power generation had been commercialized, however, and local communities felt serious concern regarding the safety of nuclear reactors and about the possibility of radiation leaking from a nuclear power plant. In that context, three power generation laws were enforced in June 1974 that took local communities into close consideration in order to smooth the development of electric power generation. The three laws also reinforced measures related to the safety of nuclear power plants. MITI moved at that time to conduct well-planned experiments for proving the reliability of nuclear power generation facilities, and sponsored a number of projects between fiscal years 1975 and 1978. Two projects in fiscal year 1975 were experiments to prove the reliability of evaporation generation equipment and experiments to prove the reliability of nuclear power generators in earthquakes. Two projects in the following year were experiments to prove the reliability of valves, and experiments to prove the reliability of fuel aggregate. Two projects in fiscal year 1977 were experiments to prove the reliability of welded spots and spots affected by heat, and experiments to prove the reliability of pumps. Two projects in fiscal year 1978 were experiments to prove the reliability of maximum heat load, and experiments to prove the reliability of the facilities during public use.[18]

In September 1974, after passage of the three laws related to power generation, radiation leaked from the *Mutsu*, a nuclear-powered ship. This accident brought about changes in administrative policy related to nuclear power safety. In 1979, the Nuclear Safety Commission was set up inside the Cabinet and a system was put into order for investigating the safety of nuclear power reactors. Several laws, including the Law Concerning the Regulation of Nuclear Source Material, Nuclear Fuel Material, and Reactors, and the Electric Utilities Industry Law, gave the Minister of International Trade and Industry the authority to enforce strict safety regulations for nuclear power plants from the initial siting authorization stage, to accepting the construction plan, inspection before use, inspection of fuel materials, inspection of welding, and regular inspections after beginning of operations, as well as operations management. Thus, the minister assumed full responsibility for the safety of nuclear power plants, from the basic design stage to operations management.[19] MITI's authority was thus bolstered regarding the nuclear power equipment industry, and administrative guidance subsequently turned brisk regarding quality control and quality assurance activities for equipment related to nuclear power. MITI also carried out various experiments for proving the reliability of the various parts of nuclear power generation facilities by commissioning them to two incorporated foundations, the Japan Nuclear Power Testing Centre and the Association of Thermal Engines for Power Generation.

Later, MITI promoted the domestic production of nuclear power equipment and its standardization. Japan's nuclear power equipment manufacturing industry got its start by production commissioned from overseas companies. Through technical tie-ups, the domestic production of nuclear reactors for commercial use was promoted. The technology for boiling-water reactors (BWR) was developed in the US, and Toshiba and Hitachi imported that technology from General Electric. Ishikawajima and Babcock-Hitachi teamed together to be in charge of boiler-related equipment. By the mid-1970s, nuclear power plants were constructed by Tokyo Electric Power in Fukushima, Chubu Electric Power in Hamaoka, Chugoku Electric Power in Shimane, and Tohoku Electric Power in Onagawa. Technology for another type of light water reactor developed in the US around this same time, called a pressurized water reactor (PWR), was introduced from Westinghouse by Mitsubishi Electric. Working jointly with Mitsubishi Heavy Industries, nuclear power plants using PWR technology were built by Kansai Electric Power in Mihama, Takahama, and Oi, by Kyushu Electric Power in Genkai, and by Shikoku Electric Power in Ikata. A construction boom in nuclear power plants thus took place at the hands of these electric power companies in the early 1970s. The domestic content of the equipment used in these plants increased greatly to between 70 and 92 per cent.[20] In 1979, when the second oil crisis occurred, the capacity of Japan's nuclear power plants was about 12.67 million kW, making Japan the world's second largest nuclear power generation country after the US (Table 29.2).

In the background of the development of Japan's nuclear power generation

Table 29.2   Nuclear power generation capacity in selected countries in 1980

	Total electric power supplied (A)	Electricity supplied from nuclear power plants (B)	B/A
USA	2,354,384	251,115	10.67
Canada	377,518	38,499	10.20
Japan	577,521	82,591	14.30
India	119,150	3,001	2.52
France	246,415	57,946	23.52
W. Germany	368,770	43,700	11.85
UK	284,937	37,023	12.99
Sweden	96,695	26,488	27.39
East Germany	98,808	11,889	12.03
USSR	1,293,878	60,000	4.64
World	8,227,989	681,205	8.28

Note: Unit is million kWh; totals include public and private use; ratio is %.

Source: General Coordination Division, Director-General's Secretariat, Agency of Natural Resources and Energy, *Sogo Enerugi Tokei* (Energy Balances in Japan), 1984. *Tsusho Sangyo Kenkyusha*, 1984: 438–42.

facilities was a system of deferred payment for equipment purchased to use with nuclear power facilities. The system was introduced as a support measure for promoting the industry's development. In that system, financing was provided for 50 per cent of the funds required for the purchase of the principal equipment used for nuclear power generation. Financing was provided based on each year's construction plans for nuclear power plants. The system was introduced in fiscal year 1966. In it, the nine electric power companies in Japan were provided low-interest financing from the Japan Development Bank for the purchase of domestic-made equipment used in nuclear power plants. Through this system MITI contributed to bolstering the technical and managerial foundations of the domestic manufacturers of equipment for nuclear power plants. From fiscal year 1976, nuclear fuel aggregate was added to the list of products eligible for financing, but the ceiling for those products was reduced to 40 per cent. Financing provided through this system amounted to 37.1 billion yen in fiscal year 1976, 58.1 billion yen in fiscal year 1977, 70.3 billion yen in fiscal year 1978, 95 billion yen in fiscal year 1979, and 160 billion yen in fiscal year 1980.

In order to raise the safety level and the efficiency of nuclear power plants, MITI promoted the introduction of improvement criteria for light water reactors from February 1975. Inside the Machinery and Information Industries Bureau it established a committee for investigating standardization of equipment for use in nuclear power plants. The committee's work was divided into two stages. Work in the first stage was carried out from fiscal year 1976, and based on the results the second stage work for standardization was carried out from fiscal year 1978.

Based on the results achieved in those two stages, experiments to prove the reliability of light water reactors were begun in fiscal year 1981.

Although domestic content accounted for a high percentage of the equipment used in Japan's nuclear power plants, equipment such as recirculating pumps and the main evaporator separation (isolation) valves were still not being made in Japan as of 1975. And as indicated by the fact that the main contractors for constructing Japan's first nuclear power plant were US companies, the nuclear power technology of foreign companies remained superior and Japanese companies had little experience with constructing commercial-use reactors. In that situation, the Machinery Industry Committee of the Industrial Structure Council presented an interim report entitled 'Vision of the Machinery Industry for 1975–84'. The report recommended raising the domestic content of equipment used in nuclear power plants and said that because of the expected difficulty in obtaining uranium, it was important not to depend just on light water reactors but to put into place an efficient R&D system regarding new types of reactors such as advanced thermal reactors (ATR), fast breeder reactors (FBR), and high-temperature gas-cooled reactors (HTGR). It also recommended promoting experiments for proving the safety and reliability of nuclear power plants, as well as standardizing equipment in order make the Japanese nuclear power equipment industry self-supporting. The report also recommended support for securing necessary human and other managerial resources for the nuclear power industry, measures for supplying funds needed for advance investments, government–business cooperation to establish related industries, and establishment of a nuclear fuel cycle.[21]

MITI also planned a large-scale research project entitled 'Direct steel manufacture through use of high-temperature reduction gas' (called 'Nuclear-power steel manufacture') in the Agency of Industrial Science and Technology. The project was for studying ways to utilize nuclear power and it lasted from 1973 for a period of eight years.[22]

29.5. New Policy Vision and Organizational Reform

'Vision of MITI Policies in the 1970s' and organizational reform

In May 1971, the Industrial Structure Council presented an interim report entitled 'Vision of MITI Policies in the 1970s'. The report predicted that as a result of the high-level economic growth up to then the 1970s would be a period of diversified value standards and needs for the Japanese people. Five tasks for industrial policy were mentioned: cultivation of a foundation to support industrial development, qualitative improvement in the standard of living, securing a healthy natural environment, securing a pleasant working environment, and cooperative growth with the international community. The report said that in order to realize these it was necessary to shift the nation's industrial structure to one emphasizing knowledge-intensive industries. It then made detailed recommendations for industrial structure policy, industrial organization policy, industrial internationalization policy, and industrial technology policy.[23]

The report from the Industrial Structure Council viewed the 1970s as a 'period of opportunity', and said that 'To make the most of the opportunity, it is hoped that the wisdom and creativity of the Japanese people will make a new leap forward. To do so, it will be necessary to discard old and worn-out concepts, structures, and interests, and take new ideals and concepts to heart.'[24]

The report also presumed that people would make increasing administrative-related demands to the government in the 1970s and said:

There are many problematic points concerning the existing administrative structure as far as its response to people's demands. The administrative structure not only of the Ministry of International Trade and Industry but of the entire government needs reform. It is most important to establish a system for responding appropriately to the needs of the times through policy. Consideration of such reform is a major task remaining to be faced in the future.[25]

In short, the report called for new industrial policy and establishment of a system suitable for that purpose, and pointed out a need to reform MITI's administrative structure.

MITI's administrative structure at the time consisted of the minister's Secretariat, four bureaux in charge of handling problems that touched horizontally across all industries, and five bureaux in charge of specific industries vertically. The first four bureaux were: International Trade Bureau, Trade and Development Bureau, Enterprise Bureau, and Mine Safety Bureau; the second five bureaux were: the Heavy Industry Bureau, Chemical Industry Bureau, Textile and General Merchandise Bureau, Mine and Coal Bureau, and Public Utilities Bureau. Attached organizations included the Agency of Industrial Science and Technology and regional bureaux and departments. In addition, there was the Patent Office and the Small and Medium Enterprise Agency. Although some changes had been introduced to this organization, it had remained basically unchanged since MITI was established in May 1949. The 'Vision for the 1970s' report recommended that the MITI structure that had continued for over twenty years be reformed.

Moves began for structural reform inside the Ministry immediately following presentation of the report. The General Coordination Division of the minister's Secretariat began studying a reform plan. A ministry-wide committee was established to study structural problems that would lead to a new structure in effect from January 1972 that would be able to handle mid- and long-term administrative demands on it for at least the succeeding five years. By the autumn of 1972, a reform plan emerged that mainly proposed five bureaux to handle problems running horizontally across all industries and four bureaux in charge of specific industries vertically. In addition, the plan proposed establishing a new agency to be called the Agency of Natural Resources and Energy. The three main features of the reform plan were a strengthening of the bureaux handling problems stretching horizontally across all industries, which was in response to administrative needs related to international cooperation, consumer administration, and pollution control measures; a reorganization of the bureaux in charge of specific industries vertically for smoother response to policy tasks; and establishment of a specialist agency to handle problems related to natural resources and energy, two areas that had increased in importance. This plan was accepted by MITI's Departmental Council on 6 November 1972.[26]

Items in the structural reform plan that became problems in negotiations with the Ministry of Finance and the Administrative Management Agency related to an increase in the number of divisions, an increase in the number of deputy director-general posts, what was considered essentially an increase in the number of bureaux, and other items that tied to an overall more expansive structure than previously. The Ministry of Finance and the Administrative Management Agency stressed a policy of simplified administrative structure and suppressing the number of budgeted personnel, and requested MITI to introduce modifications to the reform plan by merging a proposed new bureau called the Distribution and Consumption Bureau into the Industrial Policy Bureau. MITI responded by agreeing to give up the new bureau in return for establishing the new post of Vice-Minister for International Affairs, equivalent to director-general of a bureau. The reform plan was subsequently accepted. The Cabinet accepted the reform plan in February 1973 and in June of the same year the revised Ministry of International Trade and Industry Establishment Law passed the Diet and was promulgated on 25 July 1973. MITI began carrying out its reforms on the same day.

The new organization was comprised of the minister's Secretariat, seven bureaux, attached organizations, and regional bureaux and departments. The seven bureaux were the International Trade Policy Bureau, International Trade Administration Bureau, Industrial Policy Bureau, Industrial Location and Environmental Protection Bureau, Basic Industries Bureau, Machinery and Information Industries Bureau, and Consumer Goods Industries Bureau. The Agency of Natural Resources and Energy was established as an external bureau, at the same level as the Patent Office and the Small and Medium Enterprise Agency. The following were the main features of the reformed organization.[27]

1. Establishment of the Agency of Natural Resources and Energy: In the situation where energy-related problems were expected to become more strained internationally, the bureaux and departments related to natural resources and energy were integrated and a consolidated, powerful structure for energy administration was established that would maintain close relations with related bureaux and departments under the general coordination of the minister's Secretariat. An International Affairs Division was established in the director-general's Secretariat for handling matters related to the development of overseas resources and associated economic cooperation, surveys, and the dissemination of information.

2. Reorganization of the international Trade Bureau and Trade and

Development Bureau into the International Trade Policy Bureau and the International Trade Administration Bureau: To promote cooperation and smooth economic relations with other countries, the International Trade Policy Bureau was put in charge of preparing overall economic policy plans covering all matters related to exports, imports, and economic cooperation. The International Trade Administration Bureau was put in charge of all administrative matters related to trade, such as export and import management and insurance.

3. Establishment of Industrial Policy Bureau: This bureau has greater functions than the Enterprise Bureau it replaced. It views industrial policy in an integrated way in order to promote overall and systematic policies related to industrial structure, industrial organization, and industrial coordination. Several new divisions were set up, including: the Industrial Structure Division, for formulating and implementing plans and policies related to industrial structure; the Business Behaviour Division in overall charge of administrative matters related to appropriate corporate behaviour as well as improvements in, and increased efficiency of, business management; the International Business Affairs Division in charge of administrative matters related to overseas business activities, the introduction of foreign technology, the acquisition of shares by foreign investors, and the introduction of foreign capital; and the Price Policy Division in charge of price policy and the prevention of cornering of markets and holding back of goods from the market.

4. Establishment of the Environmental Protection and Industrial Location Bureau: This bureau was established to maintain close coordination between industrial location policy for relocation of industry and environmental protection policy.

5. Reorganization of vertically structured bureaux: For bureaux operating vertically, reorganization was carried out in terms of the similarity of the problems faced by each industry and the position of particular industries in the industrial structure. The three bureaux were: the Basic Industries Bureau for handling common problems related to siting and energy; the Machinery and Information Industries Bureau in charge of advanced industries with a high level of technology concentration; and the Consumer Goods Industries Bureau in charge of industrial areas closely related to people's daily living.

MITI's structural reform was evaluated as 'A move to completely reform the former structure to fit the recent changes occurring inside and outside Japan related to natural resources, energy problems, the environment, pollution problems, consumer problems and the promotion of international cooperation.'[28] Another commentator said 'It is aimed at changing the direction of trade and industrial policy so that it emphasizes "industrial development, harmony with society, and close coordination with the international economy".'[29]

Even after this major reform of MITI's structure, partial changes were made to the structure as needed when new demands were made towards government administration. Related to the Agency of Natural Resources and Energy for responding to the oil crises, for example, the Extraordinary Office for Petroleum Supply and Demand Countermeasures and the Extraordinary Office for Petroleum Price Countermeasures were set up in the Petroleum Department in fiscal year 1974; the Nuclear Energy Industry Division and the Energy Conservation Policy Planning Office were set up in the Director-General's Secretariat in fiscal year 1975; the Refining and Distribution Division of the Petroleum Department was divided into the Refining Division and the Distribution Division in the same year; the Nuclear Power Safety Division was established in the Public Utilities Department in fiscal year 1977; the Petroleum Reserve Division was established in the Petroleum Department in fiscal year 1979; and the Alternative Energy Policy Division was established in the director-general's Secretariat in fiscal year 1980. The overall organization was thus expanded and improved as necessary.

Trade and industry policy for the 1980s

In March 1980 the Industrial Structure Council presented a report entitled 'Vision of MITI Policies in the 1980s'. For preparing the report, the Industrial Structure Council established a Special Subcommittee for Policy in the 1980s in the Coordination Committee. The subcommittee was comprised of thirty-eight academics and knowledgeable persons selected from wide areas. The subcommittee met nine times to formulate a draft plan.

The report pointed out that Japan's economy had come to account for 10 per cent of the world economy and there was now a need to form national objectives fitting for its economic position. The report emphasized the need to carry out trade and industrial policies tied to those objectives.[30]

Three objectives were outlined: (1) international contributions fit for an economic power; (2) overcoming the restrictions of being a country with poor natural resources; and (3) being a vigorous people living amenable lives.

1. Concerning international contributions fit for an economic power, four proposals were made: (a) maintaining international peace, and avoiding international friction; (b) maintaining the system of free trade; (c) cooperation with developing countries; and (d) tackling problems related to the development of technology common throughout the world, particularly related to energy.

2. Concerning overcoming the restrictions of being a country with poor natural resources, specific mention was made of the lessons learned during the two oil crises in the 1970s. For a country such as Japan, with almost no natural resources, there is a strong need to obtain 'economic guarantees'. To realize them, the report said, four matters had to be promoted: (a) strengthening the mutual interdependence of the advanced and developing countries; (b) dispersing and diversifying the sources of energy supply, and developing alternative forms of energy; (c) promoting the development of creative and home-grown technology, and nurturing the development of advanced technology industries; and (d) bolstering cultural and human exchanges to deepen the mutual understanding

between Japan and other countries. Related to these items, the report also emphasized establishing a 'crisis management system'.

3. Being a vigorous people is important for international contributions and for overcoming the restrictions of being a country with poor natural resources. Without vigour, the Japanese people will not be able to resolve problems related to those two areas. As the Japanese population ages, however, people want to live more amenable lives. At the individual level, however, the living of amenable lives tends to reduce the level of vigour. The pursuit of amenable living readily leads to the so-called 'advanced nation sickness', and there is thus a need to realize both vigour and amenable living.

The report listed six ways for maintaining vigour. First, to constantly review social restrictions such as administrative practices and the systems of licences and approvals in order to secure venues for free activities. Second, to rid the education system of uniformity and its closed nature and search for a system that will enable full expression of individual characteristics. Third, to enable the principle of competition to function fully by developing energetic competition policies even while maintaining an appropriate balance between industrial policy and the Anti-Monopoly Law. Fourth, to maintain the vigour of organizations, prepare environments that allow human resources to develop their capabilities to the maximum extent and to heighten their creative abilities. Fifth, to expand the system of sharing risk between the public and private sectors for R&D that involves heavy risk. And sixth, to take steps to deepen the understanding of consumer needs by improving communications with consumers.

For amenable living, the following items were discussed in the report. First, to have Japanese appreciate their individual characteristics and to establish lifestyles of their own, thereby maintaining psychological leeway. Second, to emphasize more room in terms of space and time, rather than just the income side, which requires escaping from densely populated situations, reducing working hours, increasing free time, and improving recreation facilities. Third, to make the overall economy more amenable, it is hoped that corporations will behave without over concern about risk and that the government will encourage measures for promoting such behaviour.

Based on achievement of the foregoing, the report emphasized a number of areas needing attention, including mutual interdependence with other countries, guarantees for acquiring energy sources and de-emphasizing the use of petroleum, development of domestic technology, improved standard of living, promoting the development of outlying regions, building an industrial structure that is richly creative, vitality in small and medium enterprises, and searching for new frontiers in Japan's main areas of industry. If all this can be realized, the 1980s will become an 'age for putting knowledge to use'. Worded another way, 'the 1980s will become an age in which Japanese become discerning and are able to utilize their knowledge creatively.'

In the 'Vision of MITI Policies in the 1980s' report the recommendation was made to switch to a knowledge-intensive industrial structure. This new report took that a step further and recommended 'creative knowledge intensity'. It said that creativity and the development of software require emphasis.

Putting the 'Vision of MITI Policies in the 1980s' report into action

MITI moved quickly to formulate specific policies and obtain the budget for putting into action the March 1980 'Vision of MITI Policies in the 1980s' report of the Industrial Structure Council. It is usual for MITI to begin in late August to outline its budget needs and a plan for special tax measures for the next fiscal year and to make them both public just before presenting them to the Ministry of Finance. The following discusses MITI policies, fiscal measures, and general budget requests as they related to the 'Vision of MITI Policies in the 1980s' report.

On 28 August 1980, MITI announced its new trade and industrial policies for fiscal year 1981.[31] The new policies had as a subtitle, 'Aiming for economic security and a society full of vitality'. The six main elements in that announcement were: (1) establishing securities for energy supplies and preparing for moving away from the use of petroleum; (2) moving towards development of technological independence; (3) foreign policy emphasizing interdependence; (4) developing industrial policies that make use of creativity; (5) developing policies for small and medium enterprises that emphasize making use of their vigour and knowledge; and (6) raising the people's standard of living and forming attractive regional societies. Among new policies were the following seven: (1) establishing a new university, tentatively called the Oil Development University; (2) establishing a system for providing funds for siting electric power plants; (3) establishing a tax system for promoting overall investments in the energy field; (4) establishing a system for conducting R&D in technology for supporting next-generation industries; (5) establishing a centre for promoting local industries; (6) establishing a tax system for promoting the relocation of industries to the provinces; and (7) formulating new legislation for optimal use of industrial water.

The above policies were all related to items mentioned in the 'Vision of MITI Policies in the 1980s' report. The second oil crisis had occurred in 1979, the year before the report was put together, and it was therefore not strange that the first item mentioned in MITI's announcement was establishing securities for energy supplies and preparing for moving away from the use of petroleum. A budget of 517,586 million yen was requested for this item, to cover obtaining of stable supplies of oil, promoting electric power generation not dependent on petroleum and ideal location of power generation facilities, promoting the development of alternative sources of energy and their stable supply, promoting energy transition, promoting energy conservation, promoting investments in energy-related facilities, and obtaining a stable supply of energy communication resources. That request accounted for 56.9 per cent of MITI's total budget request of 909,043 million yen. The government earmarked 339,340 million yen in its general account for these energy countermeasures.

The policy of moving towards development of technological independence included items such as promoting the development of basic technology for establishing the next generation of industry, promoting the development of energy-related technology, promoting the system of large-scale projects, supporting the development of technology, promoting the development of technology and a social system for improving citizens' welfare, promoting international research cooperation, and improving the administrative system related to industrial property rights. A budget of 91,959 million yen was requested (10.1 per cent of total requests). Included in promoting the development of energy-related technology were the 'Sunshine Project' and the 'Moonlight Project'. The government allotted 85,726 million yen in its general account for this overall category.

The policy of emphasizing interdependence in foreign policy included items such as foreign policy related to energy, promoting comprehensive economic cooperation, and cooperating with and contributing to international society. MITI's budget request was for 27,694 million yen (2.9 per cent of total requests); the government earmarked 25,516 million yen in its general account.

For developing industrial policies that make use of creativity, which included supporting the economic base by improving the supply conditions, nurturing advanced technology industries promoting the basic and raw materials countermeasures of basic industries, promoting consumer goods industries that respond to consumer needs, and promoting the recycling of natural resources, MITI's budget request was for 19,396 million yen (2.1 per cent of total requests). The nurturing of advanced technology industries included the information, aircraft, space, and nuclear power equipment industries. The budget request was for 18,100 million yen. The government earmarked 17,750 million yen in its general account for this category.

Developing policies for small and medium enterprises that emphasize making use of their vigour and knowledge included responding energetically to the response of small and medium enterprises to environmental concerns, nurturing small and medium enterprises as well as the areas where they are located, strengthening the managerial foundation of small and medium enterprises, improving measures related to very small businesses, and improving measures for promoting small and medium trading and service companies. MITI's budget request was for 196,149 million yen (21.6 per cent of total requests). In response, the government earmarked 177,127 million yen in its general account for this category. Included among the items in responding energetically to the response of small and medium enterprise to environmental concerns were improving the software side of managerial resources and promoting smoother overseas investments by small and medium enterprises and their energy policies. These considerations reflected the increased emphasis on information, internationalization, and energy conservation.

Besides its announcement of policies and budget requests, MITI also provides the government each year with a report containing its opinions on the tax system. This report, as with budget requests, must first be accepted by the Coordination

Committee of the Industrial Structure Council and the Commerce and Industry Committee of the Liberal Democratic Party before being announced. For fiscal year 1981, final approval was given to the report on 28 August 1980 and it was announced on 3 September. Mentioned in the report for promoting the creative knowledge intensity of the industrial structure were extension of the system of reserves for losses related to buy-out of leased computers, extension of the period of application for the system of reserves for software programs, and extension of the period of application of the special depreciation system for machining centres and other important machinery.

The 'Vision of MITI Policies in the 1980s' report was given strong support through budgetary and tax measures and items recommended in the report were expressed in specific policies. The country's industrial structure was subsequently changed to better fit the contemporary age.

NOTES

1. For a discussion from the US side of the US–Japan colour television dispute, see J. Baranson (Noboru Makino trans.), *Nihon no Kyosoryoku—Amerika no Gyakushu wo Fusegeru ka* (The Japanese Challenge to US Industry), Diamond Inc., 1982; problems remain because the book is based on the Japan Inc. theory.
2. Statistics related to the electronics industry in 1970 are based on *Denshi Kogyo Nenkan* (Electronics Industry Almanac), 1971–2 edn., Dempa Publications, Inc., 1971.
3. For discussion of content, legislation process, and promulgation of the Law on Temporary Measures for Promotion of Specified Electronics Industries and Specified Machinery, see *Tsusho Sangyo Seisakushi*, xiv, ch. 7, sect. 2.
4. *Tsusho Sangyo-sho Nenpo*, fiscal year 1971: 137.
5. For discussion of liberalization of computers and reorganization of the computer industry, see *Tsusho Sangyo Seisakushi*, xiv, ch. 7, sect. 2; and *Denshi Kogyo Nenkan* for each year.
6. For discussion of policies in Europe for promoting development of the computer industry see *Denshi Kogyo Nenkan*, 1974.
7. For an outline of this interim report, see *Tsusho Sangyo Seisakushi*, xiv. 355–9.
8. This interim report was published by MITI, Machinery and Information Industries Bureau (ed.), *Showa 50-nendai no Kikai Sangyo* (The Machinery Industry in 1975–84), Research Institute of International Trade and Industry, 1975.
9. For a discussion of the Law on Temporary Measures for Promotion of Specified Machinery and Information Industries, see MITI, Machinery and Information Industries Bureau (ed.), *Kijoho no Kaisetsu* (Interpretation of the Law on Temporary Measures for Promotion of Specified Machinery and Information Industries), Research Institute of International Trade and Industry, 1979.
10. Regarding the Law Concerning the Information-Technology Promotion Agency and Related Matters, see *Tsusho Sangyo-sho Nenpo*, 1971: 141–3; and *Denshi Kogyo Nenkan*, 1971–2 edn.: 204–8 and 1099–104.
11. From Foreword and section entitled 'Gijutsu Sentan Sangyo no Ikusei' (On Nurturing Advanced Technology Industries) in each year of *Tsusho Sangyo-sho Nenpo*; also *Kijoho no Kaisetsu*: 73–7.
12. For discussion of YS-11 and YX policies, see section on aircraft industry in each year's *Tsusho Sangyo-sho Nenpo*; and the Society of Japanese Aerospace Co. Inc., *Nihon no Koku Uchu Sangyo* (Aerospace Industry in Japan), 1993 edn.
13. Ibid. 131.
14. Industrial Materials Research Association, *80-nendai ni Okeru Uchu Kaihatsu, Shakai Kaihatsu no Arikata ni Kansuru Kenkyu, 1. Waga Kuni ni Okeru Uchu Sangyo no Genjo to Tenkai no Hoko* (Space Development in the 1980s, Research into What Development of Space and Society Should be

Like; Present Situation and Future Direction of Japan's Space Industry), Economic Research Institute, Japan Society for the Promotion of Machine Industry, 1980: 41.

15. Editorial Committee of History of Japan's Space Development (ed.), *Wagakuni no Uchu Kaihatsu no Ayumi* (History of Japan's Space Development), Space Activities Commission, 1978: 109–11.

16. International Trade Policy Research Association (ed.), *Tsusansho Sono Yakuwari to Seisaku* (MITI, Role and Policies), 1988: 178; and *Tsusho Sangyo-sho Nenpo*, 1980: 213.

17. Science and Technology Agency, Research and Coordination Bureau (ed.), *Uchu Kaihatsu Handobukku 1973, 1974* (Handbook of Space Development, 1973, 1974), Japan Federation of Economic Organizations, Space Activities Promotion Council, 1974: 138–9.

18. Japan Atomic Industrial Forum, Inc., *Genshiryoku Nenkan '79* (Nuclear Almanac '79), 1979: 84.

19. Agency of Natural Resources and Energy, Director-General's Secretariat, Nuclear Energy Industry Division (ed.), *Nihon no Genshiryoku Sangyo* (Nuclear Energy Industry in Japan), *Denki Times*, 1982: 70–2.

20. For policies to nurture the nuclear power equipment industry, see section on nuclear power technology in each year's *Tsusho Sangyo-sho Nenpo*.

21. *Showa 50-nendai no Kikai Sangyo*: 312–18.

22. Agency of Industrial Science and Technology, Office for Development Programme (ed.), *Ogata Purojekuto 20-nen no Ayumi* (Twenty-Year History of National R&D Programme (Large-Scale Project), Research Institute of International Trade and Industry, 1987: sect. 3, ch. 9.

23. See pt. iv, ch. 23, subsect. 23.2 in this book, interim report of Industrial Structure Council entitled *70-nendai no Tsusho Sangyo Seisaku no Kihon Hoko* (Trade and Industry Policy for the 1970s), (commonly called 'Vision for the 1970s').

24. Industrial Structure Council (ed.), 'Vision for the 1970s', Printing Bureau, MoF, 1971: 10.

25. Ibid. 21.

26. For other discussion of reforms conducted in 1973, see *Tsusho Sangyo Seisakushi*, xv, ch. 11, sect. 4.

27. Tsusho Sangyo Gyosei Kenkyukai (ed.), *Tsusho Sangyo (1)* (Trade and Industry (1)), Gyosei Publishing, 1983: 38–40.

28. *Mainichi Shimbun*, 30 June 1973.

29. *Nihon Keizai Shimbun* (evening edn.), 25 July 1973.

30. Unless indicated otherwise, discussion based on MITI, Industrial Structure Council (ed.), *80-nendai no Tsusan Seisaku Bijion* (The Vision of MITI Policies in the 1980s), Research Institute of International Trade and Industry, 1980; also see Katsuhisa Yamada, *Tsubasa no Aru Sozo* (Imagination with Wings), Research Institute of International Trade and Industry, 1988; and Seisaku Jihosha (ed.), *Ikinuku Tame no Bijion—Wakate Tsusan Kanryo ga Kataru 80-nendai* (A Vision for Making it through Difficult Times—Young MITI Bureaucrats Talk about the 1980s), 1980; also, *Tsusho Sangyo Seisakushi*, xv, ch. 11, sect. 5 has a somewhat detailed discussion.

31. *Tsusansho Koho*, 1 and 3 Sept. 1980; also 28 Jan. 1981, for discussion of MITI-related budget for fiscal year 1981.

Index